apparitions

MYSTIC PHENOMENA
AND WHAT THEY MEAN

Kevin Orlin Johnson, Ph.D.

IMPRIMATUR

✠

MOST REVEREND CHARLES GRAHMANN, D.D.
BISHOP OF DALLAS
MCM XC VIII

also by Kevin Orlin Johnson

Why Do Catholics Do That?

Rosary:
Mysteries, Meditations,
and the Telling of the Beads

Nihil Obstat
Rev. Robert A. Coerver
Censor Librorum

Imprimatur
✠ Most Reverend Charles Grahmann, D.D.
Bishop of Dallas

The *Nihil Obstat* and *Imprimatur* are official declarations
that a book or pamphlet is free of doctrinal error.
No implication is contained therein
that those who have granted the *Nihil Obstat* and *Imprimatur*
agree with the contents, opinions, or statements expressed.
The decree of the Congregation for the Propagation of the Faith,
A.A.S. 58, 1186 (approved by Pope Paul VI on 14 October 1966),
states that the *Nihil Obstat* and *Imprimatur* are no longer required
on publications that deal with private revelations,
provided that they contain nothing contrary to faith and morals.
And in conformity with the decrees of Urban VIII, the author declares
that when writing of intuitions, prophecies, miracles, visions,
and other facts of the supernatural order
he is only following the received practice of the Faithful
and has no intention of anticipating the judgement of the Church.
If he should misunderstand or be mistaken on some point,
whether deduced from Scripture or not,
his intention is not to deviate from the true meaning of Sacred Scripture
or from the doctrine of the Church.
If this should happen, he submits entirely to the Church,
or even to anyone who judges more competently about the matter than he.

Quotations from the Bible follow the *New American Catholic Edition of the Holy Bible*,
Confraternity version, Benziger Brothers, New York, 1961.

Library of Congress Catalog Card Number 96-92395

ISBN 0-9653660-0-6

First Edition May 13, 1998

Design by David Lloyd Beck, Dallas
Cover art: *Holy Family with Sts. Anne and Catherine of Alexandria* by Jusepe de Ribera, 1648.
Photo copyright © The Metropolitan Museum of Art, New York. Used by permission.
Illustration of the Sacred Heart by Richard Baratz, American Banknote Company, Philadelphia,
Pennsylvania, copyright © 1998 by Pangæus Press. All rights reserved.

Manufactured in the United States of America
Printed by Padgett Printing, Dallas, Texas

to Jesus

through

Mary

for

J. D. and F. K.

I thank thee ... and be sure
I count myself in nothing else so happy
As in a soul remembering my good friends.

— *Richard II*, Act II scene 3

thanks

to all of the people who helped in the preparation of this book, particularly Jeffrey Barnard, M.D., Chief Medical Examiner, Dallas County; Mr. Charles Bransom, Mango, Florida; Mr. R. W. Carstens, Ohio Dominican College, Columbus; Rev. Roger Charest, S.M.M., Montfort Publications, Bay Shore, New York; Rev. Robert M. Coerver, Holy Trinity Seminary, Dallas; Dr. David L. Cowen, Professor Emeritus, Rutgers University; Mr. Henry Dunow, New York; Rev. Glenn Gardner, Vicar General, Diocese of Dallas; Mr. Michael Gillett, Dallas; Rev. Michael Gorman, Diocese of La Crosse, Wisconsin; Rev. Claude Heithaus, Milwaukee, Wisconsin; Mr. Peter Heneghan, Press and Information Office, Archdiocese of Liverpool; Mr. and Mrs. Lamar Hunt, Jr., Dallas; Rev. Niel Jarreau, S.J., St. Rita's Catholic Community, Dallas; Mr. Dennis Kalter, Dallas; Mr. Carl Keating, Catholic Answers; Ms. Bonnie Langhaar, Urbana, Illinois; Prof. Dr. François Ledermann, President, Swiss Society of the History of Pharmacy; Mr. and Mrs. George Lilja, Hudson, Ohio; Prof. Mark Lowery, Department of Theology, University of Dallas; Rev. Michael Martens, Diocese of La Crosse, Wisconsin; Mr. Warren K. Miller, Silver Spring, Maryland; Mr. Michael Nikonchuk, Cottage City, Maryland; Rev. John O'Connor, S.C.J., Sacred Heart School of Theology, Hales Corners, Wisconsin; The Passionist Monastery, Chicago, Illinois; Joseph B. Quatman, Esq., Lima, Ohio; Mark Schwartz, Esq., Houston; Alison Thomas, McKinney, Texas; Jonathon D. Warner, Esq., New York; and Professor Ladislav Zgusta, Director Emeritus, Center for Advanced Study, University of Illinois, Urbana.

contents

part one

the substance
of things unseen

He who has my commandments and keeps them
he it is who loves me. But he who loves me
will be loved by my father;
and I will love him
and I will manifest myself to him.

John 14:21

one

so inflamed with love

Wherever you go in the Catholic world, you're probably near a church dedicated to the Sacred Heart of Jesus. In fact, inside just about any church you enter, you'll see a statue or a painting of Christ pointing to his Heart, visible on his chest—a Heart pierced by an encircling Crown of Thorns, topped by a little Cross, and shooting flames from its top, and sometimes with more flames coming from the wound of the lance in its side.

You'll see images of the Sacred Heart itself everywhere, carved into the stonework of churches, glowing in stained glass, stamped on medallions, and printed in books and on holy cards. This image may even be so familiar that people within the Church—by which is meant the Catholic Church, headquarterd in Rome—probably take it for granted. To those outside the Church it might be really rather disconcerting, a disembodied heart bursting into flame. Where did that image come from?

Like many other devotions in the Church's culture—like the Miraculous Medal and the scapulars[1] in all their variety—devotions centered on the image of the Sacred Heart came from an apparition. But it didn't just happen in a flash. It's not as if someone reported that Christ appeared and revealed this image, his Heart wounded and inflamed with love, and the Universal Church dropped everything and started teaching the story as an article of faith.

In fact, the reported apparition of Christ that sparked all of the devotions that are centered on the Sacred Heart didn't add anything to the Church's teachings, and it didn't change anything that the Church had taught since the beginning. It isn't even taught as a fact—apart from his *post-mortem* appearances recorded in the Bible, the

1. A scapular is a sacramental consisting of two pieces of cloth about the size of large postage stamps, with embroidered or printed pictures on them; they're joined by strings so that they can be worn around the neck, one cloth in front and the other in the back. They're the vestiges of the part of a religious habit that goes by the same name, derived from the Latin *scapula*, shoulder. Religion has its own vocabulary, and, particularly in the study of apparitions, even some familiar words are used in specialized senses. The terms of mystic theology are italicized here at first reference, or at the place in the text where they're defined. Check the index and the glossary.

Church never officially says that on such a date Christ appeared to such-and-such a person and said this and that. So it's worth knowing something about how the Church investigated this report and exactly what kind of approval she finally gave it. In fact, the story of how this previously rare image became one of Christianity's most familiar symbols can serve as a kind of pattern, showing exactly how visits from the next world fit into this world, and how apparitions and other mystic phenomena fit into the general context of organized religion.

The present form of the Church's devotion to the Sacred Heart of Jesus got its start in the 1670s, when Sister Margaret Mary Alacoque, a nun of the Visitation Order in France, had an extraordinary experience. She was praying before the Blessed Sacrament, the consecrated bread of the Eucharist that is, in the Church's teaching, truly and substantially the living Body of Christ. She tells in her autobiography what happened next:

> I felt myself utterly penetrated with that Divine Presence, but to such a degree that I lost all thought of myself and of the place where I was and abandoned myself to this Divine Spirit, yielding up my heart to the power of his love. He made me rest for a long time on his sacred breast, where he disclosed to me the marvels of his love and the inexplicable secrets of his Sacred Heart that until then he had concealed from me. It was then that, for the first time, he opened to me his divine Heart in a manner so real and sensible as to be beyond all doubt, by reason of the effects that this favor produced in me, fearful, as I always am, of deceiving myself in anything that I say about what passes in me.
>
> It seems to me that this is what took place: "My divine Heart," he said, "is so inflamed with love for mankind, and for you in particular, that, being unable to contain within itself any longer the flames of its burning charity, it must spread them abroad by your means, and manifest itself to enrich mankind with the precious treasures that I show to you, which contain the graces of sanctification and salvation that are needed to withdraw them from the abyss of perdition. I have chosen you as an abyss of unworthiness and ignorance for the accomplishment of this great design, so that everything may be done by me."

But that wasn't all. She recorded that he showed her his Sacred Heart again, on the first Friday of the month, again while she was praying before the Sacrament. He presented himself to her as the Risen Christ, resplendent with glory, his Five Wounds shining like suns. Flames issued from every part of his figure, she said, especially from his bosom, which looked to her like an open furnace containing his Heart, the living source of the flames. As he opened his Heart, one flame engulfed her, she said, a flame so ardent that she thought her soul would be burned to ashes. On the first Friday of the next month, she saw him in this way again; and then again and again, always on the first Fridays.

She lost all consciousness again at the first of these Friday phenomena, no longer knowing where she was. Her sisters came to rouse her, but she could neither reply to them nor even stand up; shaking and feverish, she was taken to the Mother Superior, who spoke to her sharply about the apparition business but saw that she got the medical attention that she needed for her physical collapse.

Now, all of the Church's orders operate on strict rules, and each has its own sort of personality, its "spirit". The spirit of the Visitation Nuns was defined by their foundress, St. Jeanne Françoise de Chantal (1572-1641). She was herself a mystic of some advancement, but she established them as the female branch of the Visitation order for men established by St. François de Sales (1567-1622): that is, as an order of contemplatives. Their rule of life and their activities are designed to accommodate contemplative prayer. Their discipline and their seclusion let them live a life of mortification and atonement for sin as a way of attaining a close union with God—a hard and silent path to tread. The Nuns of the Visitation don't expect their nuns to have such vivid experiences as this. No order does. No order even welcomes a report of any extraordinary spiritual activity. The whole point of the organized religious life is to keep things on an even keel, spiritually.

Nor was this the first sign of extraordinary things from Sister Margaret Mary. She had been reporting visions of Christ since the time she was a novice—a beginner in the order—years before. She had never bragged about these apparitions, but, under the rules, she had been obliged to report her spiritual state to the Mistress of Novices, Sister Anne-Françoise Thouvant. Even back then, Sister Anne-Françoise had told Sister Margaret Mary that the spirit of their order permitted nothing extraordinary. Such things, she said flatly, were "not suitable" for a nun of the Visitation, not even if they were genuine—not even if Christ were actually appearing to her and speaking to her— and if Margaret Mary didn't renounce it all, she could not be received into the order.

Margaret Mary knew full well that her apparitions, beautiful and spiritually exhilarating though they were, may have come from her own imagination or a devil. In obedience to her superiors, she fought them off as best she could, but her attempts to stay strictly within the bounds of her order's spiritual exercises were to no avail. She could accomplish those exercises, all right, but on her own time she was called irresistibly to mental prayer, usually before the Blessed Sacrament, and, she said, Christ came to her again and again.

She asked him to stop. "Why, my Sovereign Master, why not leave me in the ordinary way of the daughters of Saint Mary?" she asked. "I beg you, give these extraordinary graces to those chosen souls that will correspond better with them and glorify you more than I do, for I only resist you... All I want is to become a good nun, which is all I desire." Yet, she said, the only answer that she got was reassurance and the promise of further struggle.

She worked on through her noviciate toward her solemn and irrevocable entrance into the order. But as the date for her profession drew near, her superiors told her again that she was incapable of receiving the spirit of the order, "which feared all such ways as are open to deception and illusion." But yet another apparition of Christ told her to obey her superiors in everything: "I shall know well how to find means for the accomplishment of my designs," the apparition told her, "even though your superiors may appear to be opposed and contrary to them."

She obeyed her superiors—religiously, you might say—and kept resisting the apparitions. Having reported extraordinary phenomena, she was subjected to extraordinary scrutiny; they didn't let her get away with anything, not even the little freedoms and recreations that would have been allowed to an ordinary novice. Still, they took note of her heroic efforts to resist the apparitions; they saw that the struggle was hard for her, and they recognized her impressive progress in humility and sanctity as well as her absolute obedience. On that basis, she was allowed to make her solemn profession in November, 1672. Yet the apparitions continued.

After that most impressive experience of the Sacred Heart, the regular apparitions persisted, on the first Friday of the month. Then, she wrote, in June of 1675, Christ appeared to her and asked for a special feast day to be kept in the Universal Church. It would be observed every year on the first Friday after the Feast of Corpus Christi, the feast honoring the Body of Christ in the Eucharist; it would be a Feast of the Sacred Heart of Jesus at which people might receive the Eucharist in reparation for their sins that particularly wound his Heart. "This Heart," she quoted him as saying, "that has loved mankind so much that it has spared nothing, even to exhausting and consuming itself, to testify to them its love; and in return I receive from the greater number of them nothing but ingratitude ... irreverence and sacrileges ... coldness and contempt... I promise you that my Heart shall expand itself to shed the influence of its divine love in abundance on those who shall thus honor it and cause it to be honored."

At this report, the Mother Superior, Marie-Françoise de Saumaise, stepped up the disciplines and mortifications. This was, and is, standard procedure, imposed not so much to punish Sister Margaret Mary as to strengthen her spirit so that she could resist these events more effectively. Margaret Mary herself fought heroically to bring herself back to the spiritual norms of her order, cheerfully accepting whatever discipline her superiors prescribed and asking again and again for permission to take on still more austerities. Yet the more mortifications Margaret Mary undertook, the more she submitted her own will to the will of her superiors, the more vivid and the more reassuring the apparitions became.

During all of this time her health kept getting worse; high fevers and all kinds of other illnesses kept her under a doctor's constant care. Frail as she was, her superiors never let up on her. Yet she stuck to her story through any amount of humiliation, persecution, and even harassment. She never pressed the matter, and she was never disobedient, but she never changed her story. And the apparitions intensified still more, including not only Christ but all three persons of the Trinity, Father, Son, and Holy Spirit.

Finally, Mère de Saumaise ordered the visionary nun to ask for health as proof of the divine origin of her apparitions. Ask for five months of good health, she said, during which time you will not have to take any medication whatsoever. Margaret Mary asked as she had been ordered, but only under obedience, she said, because she would have preferred to continue embracing her bad health as a penance, just as she was glad to have the humiliations as mortification.

But she asked as ordered. As ordered, too, she dragged herself out of the infirmary into the oratory for Mass. She presented her request to God and, at the elevation of the Blessed Sacrament during that Mass, she said, "all of my infirmities were withdrawn, as though a garment had been taken off of me…" In good health, she said, "I spent the time desired, at the expiration of which I relapsed into my former state."

When the Mother Superior informed him, the local bishop began a canonical inquiry into the matter. The commission started with Margaret Mary's written record of everything that she claimed happened, which her confessor, the Jesuit François Rolin, had made her write down under obedience, and with interviews of everybody involved. But the investigation seemed to take forever, as it always does. The Church is in no hurry to institute new feast days, nor even to approve new devotions. Still less does she rush to judgement on any report of an apparition from Heaven.[2]

The Church, of course, doesn't require belief in any apparitions except those in the Bible; obviously, even credit-worthy apparitions aren't necessary for salvation, so Christians are free to take apparitions or let them alone. Their value is that they can focus our attention on some specific aspect of the Faith; that they can prompt spiritual action on our part, not giving us something new to believe in but refreshing our belief in something that Christ has already taught us. So the report had to be picked apart microscopically, to make sure that it contained nothing whatever that was contrary to any tenet of the Faith; all of its implications had to be subjected to the same intense scrutiny. If any particle of it contradicted any of Christ's teachings, the whole episode would be laid to rest, on the principle that Christ's teachings are free from internal contradictions and that they're perfect as he left them, needing no extraordinary correction later.

In Margaret Mary's case, the local bishop and his adjutants had already been thinking that the time was right for a special observance to revive faith and devotions in the diocese. A feast focussed on the Heart of Jesus, on his humanity, might be just what was needed; after all, the Church had a long and spiritually fruitful history of meditations and devotions centered on Christ's humanity. And not only that: it might be a good way to get people thinking again about God's overreaching love for all mankind, which they'd started to forget about, what with the growing influence of heresies like Calvin's ideas about predestination.[3]

2. For example, when the people of Viluena in Spain reported in 1601 that the silver pyx containing the Eucharist was found intact when their church burned down, standing atop a mound of glowing embers twenty feet from its locked tabernacle, its linen veil still unscorched, the Hosts inside still perfect, the bishop, living in nearby Tarazona, agreed to investigate the reported miracle, but he didn't get around to it for seven years.

3. "Heresy" might seem to be too strong a word, but it's the only correct term, technically. We've been

But the local bishop and his adjutants didn't just turn to Sister Margaret Mary and ask her what she wanted. They sort of abstracted the general idea from what she had written. Then they had to determine specifically whether the idea of such a feast contained anything contrary to the Faith, and whether it would work to the propagation of the Faith and the increase of devotion, regardless of whether the idea came from Margaret Mary herself or from Heaven. And they had to dig around to find whatever roots, if any, the idea had in Christian theology up to that point in time.

In fact, there are specific references to the Heart of the Messiah in Scripture: Psalms 15:9; 21:15; and 68:21, for instance, the Psalms about the Passion, as well as the Gospels. Christ promised his Heart as "a fountain of living waters" (Jn 7:38), recalling a good many Old-Testament prophecies in the matter,[4] as well as predicting the wound made by the centurion at the Crucifixion (Jn 19:33). It was the touch of St. Thomas, the encounter with Christ's wounded humanity by means of that wound to the Heart, that made him declare, "My Lord and my God!", changing him from a skeptic to a believer (Jn 20:24-29). So the seeds of the devotion were already lying dormant in the Bible.

When they reviewed the Church's record on devotion to the Heart of Jesus, the bishop, his adjutants, and the scholars they consulted didn't just find that these verses *could* be interpreted that way but that these verses *always had been* interpreted that way. And they found that the idea of devotion centered on the Sacred Heart of Jesus had a fairly steady, continuous development from the very earliest days of Christianity. The blood and water that issued from Christ's Heart at the Crucifixion, for example, were already objects of meditative prayer, departure points for contemplation of his suffering humanity.[5]

taught to define the term as an arbitrary condemnation of any opinion other than our own, but the word comes from the Greek meaning *to pick and choose*. The word simply names the process of picking through the interlocked elements of Christianity, throwing away the difficult parts and keeping only those parts that you happen to like. It's a description of an intellectual process; Sir William Blackstone, in his *Commentaries on the Laws of England*, defined it as "not a total denial of Christianity, but of some of its essential doctrines, publicly and obstinately avowed". Or, as Hilaire Belloc put it, "heresy is the dislocation of some complete and self-supporting scheme by the introduction of a novel denial of some essential part therein." Belloc's books, notably *The Great Heresies* (1938) and *How the Reformation Happened* (1928) are particularly good, clear outlines of these matters. But the word always has to be understood clinically, as it were, to denote the willful refusal of some of Christ's teachings; people who truly seek Christ but—without intending to reject any of his teachings—accept any of the variant and partial creeds professed by separated sects aren't called heretics but "separated brethren".

4. Is 12:3; Ex 47:1-12; Zc 13:1; Jer 30:21-24; also Ps 39:7-9.

5. See for example Jl 2:28; Is 44:3; Ac 2:17. Of course, the phrase "Sacred Heart of Jesus" is used, by metonymy, as a title for Christ himself. That's why you'll hear images of Christ with his Heart visible on his chest referred to as a picture of the Sacred Heart, just as other kinds of image are called Christ the King, the Good Shepherd, etc. All are simply ways to focus on one or another aspect of Jesus and his relationship to humanity. As Pius XII Pacelli wrote in his encyclical letter in 1956 on the centenary of the universal institution of the Feast, "When we adore the Most Sacred Heart of Jesus Christ, we adore in it and through it both the uncreated love of the Divine Word and his human love and all his other affections and virtues... The veneration ... paid to ... the picture of the pierced Heart of Christ ... is paid to the very person of the Incarnate Word as its final object." Information about devotions to the Sacred Heart can be had from the National Enthronement Center, Box 111, Fairhaven MA 02719-0111.

Among the Fathers of the Church, Apollinaris of Hierapolis, Hippolytus, Irenæus, Justin, and Tertullian all discourse on the Heart of Jesus, specifically on the living water streaming from it, the saving water that dispenses the Spirit. They even developed the metaphor, from this, of the Church as the new Eve, born from the side of the new Adam—an image that ran steadily through the Church's literature from before St. Cyprian of Jerusalem (d. 387) used it in the fourth century, and long after St. Bonaventure (1217-1274) referred to it in the thirteenth.

By about the year 1000, though—nearly seven hundred years before Margaret Mary's apparitions—the wound in the side was universally seen as symbolizing the wound of love, the wound in the Heart. After all, the heart is the prime symbol of human love; and whenever you offend anyone who loves you—a sister or brother, a child, a parent, a spouse, a friend—whenever you offend anyone who loves you, the offense is as a knife to the heart.

The symbolism of the sins of humanity as wounding Jesus to the Heart is certainly the best way to convey the idea that sin is a personal offense to Jesus, who has given humanity nothing but love, love even to death. No other symbol could possibly make the cruelty of sin more immediately clear to people. No other symbol could possibly carry the sting of sorrow to one's own heart more forcefully, or make Christ's surpassing love more embraceable or more reassuring.

St. Albert the Great, St. Anselm, St. Bernard, and the Benedictines had all, within the next few centuries, focussed on the Heart as the object of intense personal devotion. In the thirteenth century, a lot of thought and imagery about the Sacred Heart came out of the Benedictine abbey of Helfta in Saxony, a great center of mystic activity. St. Mechtilde von Hackenborn-Wippra (1248-1298), the choirmistress there, began in about 1290 to confide the secrets of her extraordinary graces, her apparitions and locutions, to two other nuns at the Abbey.

Seven years later, she was greatly upset when she found out that they had been writing it all down without her knowledge, but she eventually let one of the nuns edit the transcripts into a little book that's still widely read. It's the *Liber specialis gratiæ*, the *Book of Special Graces*, that encourages the use of all the senses to praise God and particularly urges devotion to the Sacred Heart of Jesus. The young nun who transcribed and edited it, interestingly enough, turned out to be St. Gertrude the Great.

St. Gertrude herself (1256-1302), one of the greatest mystics on record, also left a written record of one of her own visions, one of which occurred on the Feast of St. John the Evangelist. She was permitted, in her vision, to rest her head on Jesus's chest, her head just above the wound.

When she heard his Heart beating, she asked St. John if he had heard these beats, too, when he had rested his head on Christ's chest at the Last Supper (Jn 13:23-25) and, if so, why he never said anything about it. St. John replied, she said, that the publication of this supreme symbol of Christ's love for humanity was reserved for a later age in the world, when mankind, having grown cold in their Christian devotions, would

9

need that image to rekindle their love.[6]

For the next three hundred years or so after St. Gertrude's insight, there were a few more reported apparitions of this kind. Just for the record, Julian of Norwich (1342-*c*.1416), the English anchorite, wrote in the private journals of her visions that she saw Christ who "with a kindly countenance looked into his side, and … with his sweet regard drew his creature's understanding into his side by the same wound; and there he revealed a fair and delectable place, large enough for all mankind".

But, like the apparitions to the visionaries at Helfta, this was kept hidden.[7] In the following centuries there were sporadic flickers of devotions to the Heart of Jesus, too, but there wasn't anything like a general movement to develop the idea. The Franciscans, for example, promoted the devotion to the Five Wounds of Christ, and the wound in the Heart predominated in that, but there wasn't any widespread devotional activity that focussed exclusively on the Heart as the primary symbol of Christ's love.

But, starting in the century before Sister Margaret Mary, things started to come into focus more quickly, all over Europe. As it happened, there had been good deal of activity in that direction in the order of the Visitation itself. The Heart of Jesus had already been the object of personal devotion of their founder, St. François de Sales, who had adopted the image of the Heart as the badge of his order. Investigators soon found that other members of the order had reported similar visions: Mère Anne-Marguerite Clément (d. 1661) and Sœur Jeanne-Bénigne Gojos (d. 1692) had both independently claimed to have seen Christ in similar form, but they never said that he asked for a special devotion or feast.[8]

Another nun of the Visitation, Mère l'Huillier, had already devoted a book of meditations to the subject, in about 1655. In fact, there was a generous sprinkling of other books written all over Europe, particularly by Jesuits, at the time—Jesuits later

6. Her visions are recorded in Book 2 of her *Insinuationes* (or *Revelationes* or *Legatus divinæ pietatis*), the only part of that work directly written by her. Sorting out St. Gertrude's literary production has been confusing because some books (like her *Spiritual Exercises*) were actually written by her while others were partially written, dictated, or just inspired by her. Devotion to St. Gertrude was never all that widespread (she was not canonized until 1677), but all of the books attributed to her were particularly popular during the sixteenth-century mystic revival in Spain; because of them she was made patron saint of Tarragon. (Interestingly enough, St. Teresa of Avila evidently never read them.) The *Preces Gertrudianæ* was fairly well known a century later, but it's only a *pastiche* of that time, made up of fragments and quotations from other works. St. François de Sales knew her works, but the evidence and depositions indicate that Margaret Mary didn't; and in any case a pre-existing written record of a phenomenon does not logically mean that the phenomenon may never happen again.

7. Julian's account circulated in England in a few manuscript copies, but her texts weren't published until the Benedictine Serenus Cressy put out his edition of them in 1670. Even then they were not widely known in Europe.

8. Neither knew St. Margaret Mary personally, and their reported visions were not known to her; Sœur Jeanne-Bénigne wrote her visions down only in 1693, three years after St. Margaret Mary died (the manuscript wasn't published until 1846). The Visitation Nuns, like the other orders, don't want people to get the idea that extraordinary events are common or even probable in their ranks: "not suitable", again.

beatified or canonized (St. Francisco Borgia, St. Aloysius Gonzaga, and St. Alphonsus Rodríguez among them[9]) and other saints had begun to write about the private devotions to Christ's Heart that they themselves practiced.

There was also already an Office of the Heart of Jesus, connected to the Office of the Heart of Mary established by St. John Eudes (1601-1680). In fact, the first Feast of the Sacred Heart had already been celebrated in connection with St. John's devotions in 1670, at the Great Seminary at Rennes. Considering all of this, Margaret Mary's local bishop saw the excellence of the idea on its own merits, and so, in 1685—ten full years after the Sister reported Christ's request—the Feast of the Sacred Heart was celebrated at Paray-le-Monial, the little French town in which Sister Margaret Mary's convent stood.

These were all local observances, the kind that can perfectly well be ordered by the local bishop for his own diocese, but, like the sporadic publications about the Sacred Heart, they seemed to imply universality: "Consider," St. John Eudes wrote, "that the adorable Heart of Jesus is the principle and source of his Incarnation, Birth, Circumcision, Presentation in the Temple, and of all of the other mysteries and states of his life, as well as all of his ... sufferings for our salvation ... The Feast of the Most Sacred Heart of Jesus constitutes an immense ocean of feasts, because it commemorates the principle of all of the other feasts celebrated by the Church."[10]

And after the apparition that Sister Margaret Mary saw came to light, all of these scattered facts, all of these centuries of slow development of the devotion to the Sacred Heart of Jesus, began to condense into a steady and powerful stream of Christian custom.

The local commemoration and devotions at Paray-le-Monial soon spread far beyond the boundaries of that diocese. The laity in parish after parish grouped together to make the "Communion of Reparation" on the First Fridays of nine consecutive months—with the prayers recommended in Margaret Mary's report, which had also been thoroughly scrutinized and found free from error before they were permitted. People all over the region gathered to pray, privately, a Litany of the Sacred Heart, and to meditate in a new way on the humanity of Christ and his love for sinful human beings. The devotion showed remarkable spiritual benefits to those who practiced it, but the

---

9. St. Francisco Borgia (1510-1572) was the great-grandson of the horrible Pope Alexander VI and kinsman of Lucrezia and Cesare, the Spanish family of fratricides responsible for spousal poisonings, the spoliation of the Vatican Library, and other atrocities. His name always raises the same embarrassing question; the *Catholic Encyclopedia* describes his ancestry as "unhappy" and lets it go at that. You have to be careful about St. Alphonsus Rodríguez (1532-1617) and Alfonso Rodríguez (1538-1616); both were Spanish Jesuit writers, but they're two different people.

10. Again, there's no evidence that Margaret Mary Alacoque knew anything about these private feasts and devotions; they were not widely publicized, word of them may not have penetrated her convent's walls, and certainly they don't figure in anything that anybody who knew her noticed about her life. A *mystery*, by the way, is one of those teachings that could only be obtained by revelation, not by reason, although mysteries can be defended by reason—that is, the mysteries make sense. Still, the essence of an infinite mystery like the Trinity or the Incarnation can't be understood by finite human reason alone.

idea of its expansion caused vigorous, almost violent controversy within the Church for more than a hundred and sixty years.

Any number of prominent people, including Mary of Modena, Queen of England, took up the devotion and petitioned Rome in the 1690s to extend the Feast to the universal calendar.[11] But these and many other repeated requests to authorize the devotion were deferred, time and again, at every level, on the grounds of novelty; the time was not right, yet, the investigations not yet conclusive, and the historical perspective not yet understood well enough. Other religious orders and other bishops protested the devotion as an innovation loudly and, sometimes, officially. As late as 1786, for instance—more than a hundred years after the reported apparition—the synod of Pistoia in Italy formulated its objections to devotion to the Sacred Heart as part of its official proceedings.

Still, the devotion survived and grew. It never showed any features contrary to the Faith, and the people who practiced it never did so in defiance. It spread steadily and consistently, developing in strictest obedience to the Church's pastoral and magisterial authority—her right to guide and her right to teach. Despite objections, everything seemed to point to the appropriateness, the rightness, of the suggested feast. The idea of intensified reparation for sin grew naturally from the whole point of a contemplative order like the Visitation; if the idea for a special feast day focussing on reparation to Christ's wounded Heart were to come from anywhere within the Church, the Visitation was in exactly the right spirit to offer it. Putting the feast on the day suggested, the Friday after Corpus Christi, would underscore the other commemorations of Passiontide and the Easter season, summing them up in a single object, the human Heart that is the core of Jesus's humanity, the symbolic source of his divine love for mankind.

The investigations continued, but they only showed that all of the elements of the proposed devotion had been present always in revelation, since Old-Testament times; it was just that nobody had ever put them all together that way before. Even the official formulation from the bishops assembled at Pistoia appeared to serve only as an occasion for the Church to answer those objections definitively and lay them to rest forever. And so the chain of events started in that remote French convent in 1675 moved forward.

Rome kept a close and cautious eye on the developments for another century, and then, in 1765, judged the moment right for action. In that year, Clement XIII Rezzonico granted the petition of the bishops of Poland and the Roman Archconfraternity of the Sacred Heart for a Feast. In 1794, Pope Pius VI Braschi formally approved the devotion to the Sacred Heart for the whole Church, but it was not until 1856 that the Feast of the Sacred Heart was listed in the Church's universal calendar. Only in 1889, two hundred and fourteen years after Christ's request was reported by Margaret Mary, was it raised to the rank of a commemoration of the first class. The

---

11. Mary of Modena was the wife of James II, the Stuart king exiled for his faith in 1688; they were living in France at the time, pensioners of his cousin Louis XIV. Because of her personal sanctity, she was proposed for canonization as a saint herself, just after her death.

Litany of the Sacred Heart was not approved until 1899.[12]

Today, there are no fewer than twenty orders, congregations, and institutes devoted to, and named for, the Sacred Heart, and any number of societies, leagues, schools, and universities that focus their work through this special devotion to Christ. There are countless parish churches dedicated in the name of the Sacred Heart, too, and several major shrines in that dedication around the world. Because Margaret Mary Alacoque—a simple nun in an obscure little convent in France—focussed the Church's attention on Christ's humanity and on his love for humanity in the way that she did, it's virtually impossible to understand Catholicism today without knowing at least a little about devotion to the Sacred Heart of Jesus.

But when Sister Margaret Mary died in 1690, five years after the first local celebration of the Feast that she prompted, there was yet another full-scale investigation, this time to test the possibility of formally declaring her a saint. She happened to be a person of particularly great sanctity, which she proved by the fervor of her devotion to the Sacred Heart, by her meekness, her absolute obedience, and her heroic patience through the trials and humiliations to which she was subjected, year after year. And she had led an exemplary life of penance and reparation even in chronic ill health and, through it all, she had shown a calm and irrepressible joy.

Her reported apparitions were ignored by the inquest, as apparitions are always ignored whenever a reported visionary comes up for sainthood—the basis of which is a life of heroic virtue, not any extraordinary spiritual phenomenon. Most saints are canonized without ever seeing an apparition, and a person can see an apparition, even a credit-worthy one, without ever coming close to canonization; the cases of the visionaries Mariette Béco, Maximin Giraud, and Mélanie Mathieu are particularly interesting in this regard. In fact, any extraordinary phenomena stand in the way of canonization; the more spectacular the occurrences, the less willing the Church is to put the person before the Faithful as a model, and the more strenuously the investigators look into the whole matter. Pope Gregory IX dei Segni, who knew St. Francis of Assisi personally and had kissed his stigmata, purposely assigned the case to those cardinals who actively disliked Francis, and stood back. The decision was unanimously in favor of canonization, but that was despite the extraordinary phenomena, not because of them.

For Margaret Mary, this process, too, seemed to take forever. Depositions of those who had known her stretched well into the next century. She was not declared Venerable until 1824; after she passed forty more years of further investigations, she was beatified in 1864. Not until 1920 was she officially enrolled in the calendar of saints. And even then, the focus of her commemoration is her own virtue—on how heroically she lived up to Christ's teachings as embodied in the Church's doctrine—not her apparitions.

---

12. Pius XII emphasized again, in his centenary encyclical letter on the devotion, "the fact that this devotion stems from the principles of Christian doctrine ... clearly demonstrated by the fact that the Apostolic See approved the liturgical feast before it approved the writings of St. Margaret Mary ... paying no special attention to any private revelation, but graciously granting the petitions of the Faithful."

When the Church chooses to give some kind of official approval to a reported apparition, when the Pope visits its site or seems to take it for granted in a reference in a public address, or even when he makes a formal declaration about the matter, nobody asserts that it's a matter of Church doctrine. Nobody says, yes, it's a matter of fact, Our Lord Jesus Christ or the Virgin Mary appeared visibly to such-and-such a person at such-and-such a time. In fact, any declarations connected with apparitions are likely to deal strictly with the public feasts and approved devotions that were prompted by them, not with the matter of the apparition itself. Even if the apparition is mentioned, the most that the Church gives is a negative approval: she says that there's nothing in the account that runs contrary to the Faith, and that, therefore, it's creditable; it's "worthy of belief".

That's why papal documents about devotions that were prompted by private revelations center on the Scriptural and Traditional matter of the celebration—on public revelation, the official teachings of the Church celebrated by the devotions—not on the matter of the private revelation itself. Because the Church doesn't require belief in any apparition (apart from those in the Bible), belief in creditable reports of apparitions is never enjoined on the Faithful, only permitted.

But this permission itself presupposes that it's entirely possible for Christ to present himself to the senses of a human being and speak to him, telling him such things. And that might be a little hard to take, these days. It's easy to dismiss reports of visits from Christ or from Mary as superstition, to tamp them firmly into the mold of science and go back to business as usual. But if you look into the matter a little more deeply, science can never really account for more than a fraction of the facts. At the great shrines that commemorate various apparitions, inexplicable and spontaneous healings—the actual regeneration of flesh and bone—are attested to consistently by qualified doctors. The messages conveyed by purported visionaries, even little children, communicate theological information of astonishing subtlety that gives new focus to some facet of the Church's universal experience since the beginning. And even the children remember those messages *verbatim*, often across years of hostile interrogation, as Moses remembered all of those instructions from God on Sinai (Ex 20:2-31:18).

There's the matter of prophecy, too. As predicted, sometimes, in the visionaries' reports, whole nations have been changed, whole governments have fallen. If all of the evidence is weighed, some parts of it at least will stick in your consciousness. And some of those parts, at least, will prod you to think about prayer and about kindness, about life and religion, as you haven't quite seen these things before.

So visionaries like Margaret Mary or Bernadette or the little shepherds of Fátima just prompt a particular train of thought; they're not prophets adding something to Christianity. Their messages simply make people, popes and parishioners alike, think: and they only make us think about things that Christ already told us. But their reports make us think about these things in a new way, from a new perspective, through a new lens, as it were. Or you might say that a credit-worthy apparition is like the neck of an hourglass, where countless grains of faith and knowledge come together closely all at once to move forward in a steady stream, now purposefully aimed to carry a clear sig-nificance, and then spreading wider again at last.

That's why apparitions and other mystic phenomena matter. They encourage us to refocus our devotion to God and the things of God. And that's why the global effects of the devotions that come out of these reports—the building of great shrines, the mirac-ulous healings, the rise of nations and the fall of states—these effects are credited not to anything that the apparitions said or did, directly, but to the conversions, and the grace, generated by the practice of these approved devotions by thousands and thousands of per-sons who perhaps would not otherwise have turned their minds and hearts to prayer.

But the best thing about apparitions is that everybody has them.

two

the study of the mystics

The study of the mystics,
the keeping company however humbly with their minds,
brings with it as music or poetry does—
but in a far greater degree—a strange exhilaration,
as if we were brought near to some mighty source of Being,
were at last on the verge of the secret that all seek.

— Evelyn Underhill, *Mysticism* (1911)

Maybe not everybody has the flash-of-lightning, voices-and-trumpets kind of apparition, but every practicing Christian has the softer, quieter kinds—the feeling of settlement after you've taken your problem to communion, the sudden and solid knowledge of what to do in your difficult situation, or just the answer to a question offered in prayer.

These experiences are apparitions of a sort, if you define an apparition as the phenomenon of a heavenly being touching the senses, communicating directly with the intellect and the consciousness.[13]

But the word "apparition" is only a noun form of the verb "to appear"—that is, to make oneself seen or heard or, in one sense, understandable. And since talking to God, or to the angels and saints (Tb 12:12, Rv 5:8, 8:3, etc.), is the ordinary business of Christians, getting an understandable response is simply the other half of that very ordinary experience of prayer.

But what about those reports of *extra*ordinary responses from Heaven? There are consistent reports of more spectacular apparitions in which a being that isn't nor-

13. Some moral theologians make a distinction between visions and apparitions; a vision might be defined as seeing a scene or participating mystically in some episode of Christ's life, or Mary's, while the appearance of a single figure, Mary or an angel, for example, might be called an apparition. Many seem to use the words interchangeably. You just have to find each writer's definition of them.

mally within human sight and hearing simply appears to a person but is sensed without any of the verifiable visual stimuli that we normally get when we see material objects.[14]

There are also reports, consistent through the ages, of miraculous healings, heavenly voices and fragrances, and of identifiable states like ecstasy—visible apparitions of Mary or of Christ himself are only one part of a whole panoply of remarkable occurrences that seem to defy the laws of our natural world and point to the existence of a world beyond. How can these possibly fit into the general scheme of things?

We have to defer to experts. It may come as a surprise, but there are people, there always have been people, who devote their lives to the systematic study of apparitions and related spiritual phenomena, and they do so within the context of formalized university study. But the fact that apparitions can be studied systematically is crucial, because it means that apparitions can be approached logically. Of course, they have to be approached logically within the premises of the Faith, but logically nonetheless. And the importance of this approach can be clarified with an analogy to the logical processes of the natural sciences—physics, chemistry, astronomy, and the rest.

SCIENCE AND THEOLOGY

Think of some homegrown soothsayer, someone completely uneducated in science as science is taught in our universities today, who stands up and proclaims a theory of how the material universe is structured and how it works. Ignoring the prevailing theories about atoms and molecules, stars and planets, he just makes up a theory of his own, based on whatever pops into his head. He might win some fiercely loyal followers who like the simplicity of his teachings. Sometimes these people think that a theory like this gives them some kind of special knowledge, that it makes them chosen insiders, a privileged group, a people set apart. Sometimes they're disturbed by evidence of things around them that they don't understand, or they may even feel threatened when they see that the mainstream community takes this evidence in stride as a basic part of the way it understands the universe while they themselves can't grasp it.

So the street-corner theorist and his followers might embrace his ideas with a kind of emotional relief. They don't have to struggle to understand things, as long as they stick with their leader's theory. But the theory itself wouldn't stand questioning by a professional scientist or even, probably, by anybody who'd taken an undergraduate course in physics. That's why soapbox theories about the universe don't get much respect among the mainstream educated population. Their proponents just haven't studied all of the evidence—the actual matter—of the subject, and they haven't reviewed the contributions that recognized experts have made to our understanding. The theories themselves raise more questions than they can possibly answer, and they can't account for all of the evidence in a logically consistent framework of method.

14. That is, nobody else would report that there was a physical body there to cause the reflection of light, the vibrations in the air, that normally trigger sight and hearing in this world. It's important to state, also, that apparitions don't happen in a twilight world of consciousness as dreams do, nor as a modification of a three-dimensional object like a statue or a picture; see below, on dreams and hallucinations.

And people who follow these off-the-cuff theories may even be unaware that there's a community of responsible intellects who study these things professionally. They may not realize that these experts are the intellectual heirs of other professionals, part of a venerable discipline that has systematically clarified our understanding of the subject matter over the centuries.

It's the same in the study of spiritual phenomena. Most of us seem to think that apparitions and the like stand on the fringes of religion, in some vague area of the optional, where the world is divided into the gullible people who jump at any report of a vision and the sensible people who scoff at that kind of stuff no matter what. Either position seems arbitrary, and rather emotional, but most of us seem to *know* very little about apparitions and nothing at all about the logical ways in which they're interpreted.

That's probably why so many self-proclaimed prophets draw such large and enthusiastic audiences whenever they claim even the most outlandish apparitions, or if they propound the most irrational theories to account for them. And this, in turn, is why so many of us find stories about any apparition so distasteful, even those most worthy of belief. But apparitions, when you think about it, are an indispensable part of theology—you can't get far in the Bible without encountering any number of apparitions, and they're usually pivotal to the whole course of revelation. Think of God's appearance in the Burning Bush, the vision of Ezechiel, the Annunciation, or St. John's vision of the whole Heavenly Jerusalem. The Bible itself, if you consider it the inspired word of God, is entirely a transcript of apparitions of one kind or another. Well, then, the apparitions of the Bible, the ways in which God communicates to Man, must constitute a perfectly respectable field of inquiry. And, if they do, then the whole question of apparitions must be a normal part of Christian theology. "Well, what are you astonished at?" the Bl. Lydwine of Schiedam asked in the fifteenth century, when a whole torrent of mystic phenomena poured down upon her and around her. "Isn't it written in the Gospels?"

Yes, it is; which is precisely the problem. We people in the pews don't know much about apparitions because we don't know much about what theology is and how it works.

THE SCIENCE OF THEOLOGY

Theology is the formal study of God and of God's plan for the universe. The Church has always taught that God wants everybody to be with him, after they die, forever (1Tm 2:4). And Christians have always understood that this salvation—being saved from the unending torment of Hell—depends on two things, your faith (what you know and believe about God) and your works (how you behave, how you conduct your thoughts, words, and deeds).[15]

15. Check Gn 2:16-17, 6:5-6; Ex 32:33; Nm 9:13; Jt 11:12; 2Th 1:7-9; 2Tm 2:5; Ja 1:19-27, 2:14-26; 1Pt 1:17; 1Jn 2:4; Lk 6:46-49; Mt 25:31-46, 7:21-27; Rv 2:2, 19; 3:1, 7; 22:12; and so on. Biblical references here are given to clarify doctrines, but the Church doesn't hold those doctrines—profoundly different from those of separated sects—because they're in the Bible; they're in the Bible because the Church has always held them to be true, since long before she wrote and compiled the Bible.

Because faith and works are equally important, Christian theology falls natural-ly into two halves. Matters of faith are handled by *doctrinal* theology, which deals with things that we ought to know, like the nature of God or, to begin with, his existence. Matters of works fall under the heading of *moral* theology, which deals with things that we ought to do (like supporting the poor) and not do (like killing people) if we want to draw closer to God in this life and join him in Heaven after we die. Moral theology is sometimes described as the science of the attainment of God.

Because Christians have always understood that God judges salvation by both faith and works—on what you believe and on what you do, as the Bible says—the Church has always held the two halves of theology in equal esteem. And she has devel-oped both as academic disciplines that operate with the strictest logic. The logic of the-ology is stricter, in fact, than that of disciplines that study the material world, because besides revelation (things that God has explicitly told to humans) logic is about all you have to go on, in theology. You can get a doctorate in either doctrinal theology or in moral theology, in the Church's universities.

But Protestant denominations don't study moral theology. You see, Protestant denominations in this country all derive ultimately from one of two heresies, that of Luther or that of Calvin. Luther taught that "justification"—in common parlance, sal-vation—is by faith alone; his teachings are the source of the idea that you only have to proclaim Jesus Christ as your personal lord and savior to be "saved". This view is called *antinomianism*, which comes from the Greek ἀντι-, meaning against, and νόμος, mean-ing law; it means that adherence to the laws doesn't make any conclusive difference in your salvation. John Calvin, in his *Institutes of the Christian Religion*, taught that "all are not created on equal terms, but some are preordained to eternal life, others to eternal damnation; and, accordingly, as each has been created for one or other of these ends, we say that he has been predestined", and that's that. His view is called *predestinarianism*.

So both of these heresies teach that there's nothing that you can do to make any difference in your salvation. Of course, antinomian and predestinarian denomina-tions usually exhort people to be charitable and not to kill, or they assume that if you love Christ you'll behave, but the point is that they can't logically develop these ideas.[16]

When it comes to cases, when someone asks, "If I'm saved and I know it, what difference does it make if I steal or not?", Luther and Calvin alike would be stumped. Having put things as they did, they were at a loss for a logically convincing answer. So they abandoned the moral half of theology as an integral part of their teachings, although they continued to make purposely vague pronouncements on it in response to

16. Although not all of them do preach these things; sadly, increasing numbers of splinter sects preach killing and being killed or even terrorizing and killing innocent bystanders who are content to leave them in peace. And some Protestant denominations in this country assert unequivocally that Christians are not bound to follow the Ten Commandments—not that a good-hearted Christian will follow them although they are not necessary, but that no Christian need bother about them at all. These antinomians may not positively encourage violation of the Commandments, but logically this position only leaves the ideas that thou canst steal if thou want, or commit adultery if thou feelst like it.

questions arising from the doctrinal theologies that they themselves had invented.

It's this loss of a vigorous moral theology, moral theology properly so called, among Protestant sects that has so seriously impaired our understanding of apparitions in America, because moral theology includes the study of mystic phenomena. One subdivision of moral theology is *spiritual* theology, which deals with the development of a person's spiritual life; spiritual theology is divided into *ascetic* theology, which studies what humans can do to enhance their spiritual lives, and *mystic* theology, which studies how God reaches out to call people to further development in spirit.[17]

Apparitions happen when movement from God and to God, the outreach by both the human and the divine, meet; so apparitions fall into the field of mystic theology, that subsection of moral theology, and they're really only a small part of that field.

In fact, the whole spectrum of mystic phenomena is the stock in trade of mystic theology. Textbooks in the field refer routinely to "visions, levitations, tears of joy, stigmata, odors of sanctity, and the like", all of which are as riveting as the luminous appearance of Christ, Mary, or an angel among us here on Earth today, and all of which form a context in which apparitions themselves look less like bolts from the blue and more like business as usual, as they are in the Bible. And mystic theology also extends to prodigies like bleeding Hosts or healing fluids exuded by the gallon from the relics of certain saints. It also covers *interior* spiritual phenomena, like the ability to read hearts, the ability to distinguish holy persons and holy things without use of the five bodily senses, the phenomenon of being in two places at once, and bodies that remain as fresh as those of living persons through decades in the grave.

All of these, and more, are mystic phenomena. The word "mystic" really only means hidden or veiled from our view; it comes from a Greek word meaning *to close one's eyes*. It has some unfortunate connotations, nowadays, being used loosely to stigmatize anybody who's enthusiastic—as Ronald Knox uses the word in his classic study of religious aberration, *Enthusiasm*[18]—somebody vague and unfocussed, unrealistic in his views, unable or unwilling to live among normal people and mistaking dreams for reality.

But creditable mystics are among the most engaging and cheerful, the most sociable people in the Church's annals. Their writings have no soft sentimentality, no sermonic platitudes about them; they're clear, sharp, and brilliant, flashing unexpected light into the reality of this world. One and all—and in contrast to their contemporary princes and magnates—they look back at us from their portraits and photographs with a piercing and powerfully attractive intensity. They are remarkably practical people, the movers and shakers in this world—people like the lay Carmelite Bl. Mary of the Incarnation, who bossed dockworkers and teamsters to bring her late husband's business

17. Spiritual theology is completed by a third subsection, *pastoral* theology, from the Latin word for shepherd, which studies ways to arouse other people to a fuller possession of God's grace. It's called "the cure of souls", which is why an English pastor is called a curate and a French one *Monsieur le curé*, titles related to the word "curator".

18. Oxford, 1950; it's an indispensable starting point for any study of mystic phenomena, and it's still in print.

out of bankruptcy, or St. Joan of Arc, who bossed whole armies—or St. Catherine of Siena, who bossed pope after pope and made them love her for it.[19] They're the founders and reformers like St. Paul, St. Augustine, St. François de Sales, St. Francis of Assisi, and St. Dominic de Guzmán; they know exactly what they're doing and why they're doing it, and their organizations endure and prosper. "As a matter of fact," De Montmorand (himself a non-believer) wrote in his classic *Psychologie des mystiques*, "good sense seems to be their fundamental quality."

The branch of moral theology that studies what God does with them is really only called hidden because it concentrates on the interior life, the direct and completely private relationship between God and them, or in fact between God and each individual soul within the Church. Maybe "spirituality" would be a better term than "mystic theology", because this study is only a subdivision of the study of the development of the spirit—conversion, submission to God's will, striving to do his will, undertaking penances to make up for it when you don't, and so on—that in general investigates the ways in which a soul can communicate ever more intimately with God.

And since people communicate with God through prayer, prayer is really the main business of mystic theology.

---

19. "Bl." is the abbreviation for "Blessed" ("BLESS-ud", not "blest"), the proper title of a person who's been formally beatified, that is, declared to be with God after a formal canonization process. Such a person stands as a worthy example of Christian virtue and is commemorated in a local or regional feast day, but not with one in the Church's universal calendar. "Ven." is short for "Venerable", a title given to a person at the stage before beatification in the process; it means that the person has practiced Christian virtue to an heroic degree and is worthy of respect and emulation. After receiving the sequential titles of Venerable and Blessed, a person can be advanced, after more investigations and procedures, to full canonization, being enrolled in the Church's universal "canon" or calendar of commemorations and given the title "Saint" (St.).

three

pray a lot

What are you doing! Pray! Pray a lot!

— The Angel of Portugal,
at Fátima (1916)

Prayer is how we here on Earth keep in touch with God and with the angels and saints, the way humans draw closer to God; and closeness to God results, if God wants it to, in a closeness to Heaven that you can feel, hear, see, taste, and even smell. St. Francis of Assisi summed up the function of prayer this way:

> Since happiness is nothing other than the enjoyment of the highest good, and since the highest good is above us, no one can be made happy unless he rise above himself, not by ascent of the body, but of the heart. But we cannot rise above ourselves unless a higher power lift us up. No matter how much our interior progress is ordered, nothing will come of it unless accompanied by divine aid. Divine aid is available to those who seek it from their hearts, humbly and devoutly; and this means to sigh for it in this valley of tears, through fervent prayer. Prayer, then, is the mother and source of the ascent.[20]

Prayer is a movement of the heart that happens whenever a human soul reaches out to God, individually or collectively, formally or spontaneously, to ask him directly for something that we need or want, to offer thanks for things that we've already received, to express regret for the times that we've offended him, or simply to open our souls to him

20. It's important to remember that St. Francis wasn't innovating, here; he just says something that the Church has taught from earliest times. He also says that this reasoning is why Dionysius the Pseudo-Areopagite (*Mystic Theology*), "wishing to instruct us in mystic ecstasy, puts prayer at the outset". On the skills of Christian prayer, see the author's *Rosary: Mysteries, Meditations, and the Telling of the Beads.*

in adoration. The angels hear our prayers, too, and the saints, although of course all we can properly ask them to do is pray with us and for us, as we'd ask any other friends to pray with us and for us.[21] "If the Apostles and martyrs, while still in the body, can pray for others, at a time when they should be solicitous about themselves," asked St. Jerome, "how much more will they do so after their crowns, victories, and triumphs?"[22]

And there are plenty of ways for the angels and saints to let us know that they've heard and helped. Most of these are very quiet answers, again, but some of them are truly extraordinary mystic phenomena. The archangel Raphael appeared to Tobias and his son to help them on account of their prayers (and their other works, incidentally; Tb 12:12-15; cf. Dn 9:21-23). And as for the saints, "who would not be convinced," asked the *Catechism* of the Council of Trent, "by the wonders wrought at their tombs? Diseased eyes, hands, and other members are restored to health … But why multiply proofs… Of this we have a proof in the restoration of life to the dead body that was accidentally let down into the grave of Eliseus, and which, on touching the body of the prophet, was instantly restored to life".[23]

So prayer is a two-way communication. It can take any of an infinite variety of forms. Prayer can be mental or vocal, embodied in formalized devotions like the Rosary or novenas, in liturgies like the Mass—the greatest prayer of all—or in more personal activities. St. Ignatius of Loyola, whose past sins so distressed him during a retreat that he considered the sin of suicide the only way out, just hung on, shouting again and again, "Lord, I will do nothing that offends you!", which must have raised some eyebrows in the next cell. Other Christians report that, at certain times in life, the most effective prayer may mean holding on to the living-room carpet and repeating through clenched teeth, "God will give me what I need!" or standing with arms outstretched, yelling at a cloudy sky, "What is going on?" Or prayer may consist of more temperate activities like quiet meditative prayer or just remembering always the presence of God.

But whatever form it takes, however loud it gets, prayer is always a work, an act, a decision of the will and an action of the intellect—that is, you decide to talk with God (or an angel or a saint), and you do so. Now, just as you picked up the language skills that you need to communicate with the people around you, you probably just picked up the basic skill of prayer without thinking much about it. But just as you can improve

---

21. The difference between an angel and a saint is that an angel is a created spirit that has identity and life but no body; a saint is a human being, created body and soul, who has lived in accordance with God's will so as to pass judgement after death and live forever in God's presence, his soul rejoined to his body, which is now glorified. People do not become angels after death; they are two entirely distinct kinds of being.

22. *Contra Vigilantius* (406), in Migne, *Patrologiæ cursus completus, Series latina*, 221 vol., Paris, 1844-1855, vol. 23, 339-352. Father Jacques-Paul Migne also produced the *Patrologiæ cursus completus, Series græca*, 161 vol., Paris, 1857-1866. These are the starting points for any later scholarly edition of anything that the Fathers of the Church wrote; they're usually referenced simply as *PL* and *PG*, or just as "Migne". You can find the series in any large public or university library, and on microfiche, too.

23. 4Kn 13:21. A part of the body of a canonized saint is called a *first-class* relic; anything that the saint, or Christ, is known to have worn or used, anything intimately connected with his physical presence, is a *second-class* relic (see Mt 9:20-22; 14:34-36); anything touched to a saint's body is a *third-class* relic.

your communication skills on an earthly level, you can work to improve the skill of prayer. In fact, you're pretty much obliged to, in the view of the Church.

THE UNKNOWN SKILLS OF PRAYER

The new *Catechism* stresses that prayer always requires effort, and it recalls that even Moses had to learn how to pray, after God called him.[24] You have to pray, and not just when you have the time, the *Catechism* warns; you make time for the Lord and you pray, with a firm determination not to give up, no matter what trials you may encounter.

And you can't do it casually. "Anyone who has the habit of speaking before God's majesty as though he were speaking to a slave, without being careful to see how he is speaking, but saying whatever comes to his head and whatever he has learned from saying at other times, in my opinion, is not praying. Please, God: may no Christian ever pray in this way … carrying on in this way like brute beasts," said one Doctor of the Church. And another, St. Alphonsus of Liguori (1696-1787), summed it up this way:

> If a subject came into the presence of his sovereign, and, while petition-
> ing some favor, gazed about and occupied himself with irrelevant matters
> so that he scarcely knew what he was saying, would not that sovereign be
> justly offended? For this reason St. Thomas Aquinas teaches that he who
> permits his mind to wander about during prayer cannot be excused from
> sin, because by such conduct he seems to be guilty of contempt of God.[25]

In fact, praying well demands effort in every province of life, not just in prayer itself, because the efficacy of prayer depends on the general moral condition of the one who prays—the Lord is far from the wicked, Proverbs says, but the prayer of the just he hears (15:29). This pattern holds up, logically enough, in the rest of Scripture; if nothing bad is allowed in Heaven, if sin caused Adam and Eve to be expelled from familiar conver-sations with God as he walked in the Garden, then it must be sin that keeps us from see-ing and hearing God on a regular basis, before bodily death as well as after.

This idea permeates the Bible—check Gn 3; 6:9-13, where God picks the blameless Noe to speak to, Jb 1:1-22, Mt 5:8, Rv 21:27, or countless other passages; he reaches out to those who make every effort to avoid sin and to make reparation for it. Every mystic who writes stresses this idea again and again. "The highest bliss," noted Julian of Norwich, "is to possess God in the clarity of endless light, truly seeing him, sweetly feeling him … I saw … that sin was the greatest opposition to this, so much so that as long as we have anything to do with any kind of sin, we shall never clearly see the blessed face of God."

And those who have the most extraordinary kinds of spiritual gifts testify that even the slightest faults keep the communication from coming through clearly. At

24. Part Four of the new *Catechism of the Catholic Church*, Christian Prayer, is recommended as absolute-ly basic background reading.

25. Alphonsus of Liguori, *The Twelve Steps*. See also St. Teresa of Avila, *Interior Castle*, 1:1:7.

Beauraing, Albert Voisin, the only boy in the group, often didn't hear the apparition as the girls did, and he didn't always fall into an ecstasy as profound as theirs. And at Fátima, little Francisco Marto, who as yet knew virtually nothing of his catechism and still indulged in some boyish pranks, said that he saw the angel that had come to the children, and he could see that the angel was talking to the girls, but he couldn't hear him at all. Later, when the two girls Lucia and Jacinta saw and heard the heavenly Lady, Francisco could not; through Lucia, the apparition told the boy to begin praying the Rosary—that great weapon against evil—and he saw her after he had recollected himself and said five or six prayers of a decade. But he still didn't hear her.

To take a less-familiar example, Bl. Anna-Maria Taigi (1769-1837)—a fairly ordinary Roman housewife who was the exact contemporary of Napoléon—saw, as her Decree of Beatification puts it, "for forty-seven years a kind of Sun," a luminous disk hanging always in front of her, in which she "saw things at hand and things far off, foresaw future events, scrutinized the secrets of hearts and the most hidden and most inward impulses," including cabinet meetings in France, political and religious prisoners in China and India, plots to assassinate popes, and anything else she needed to know for her own salvation or that of others (for one biblical precedent, see 4Kn 6:8-12). She was already well advanced on the road of Christian perfection long before the apparition first came to her, but this disk started out obscured by a cloudy film. An interior voice told her, she said, that this obscurity would clear up according to the increase in her own purification, and it did. The more she distanced herself from worldly cares, the more penances she took on voluntarily, the harder she worked at the skill of prayer, the more clearly she saw things as the other world sees them.[26]

Naturally, the Church has always supplied guidelines for growth in this skill. Like the prophets before them, Christ and the Apostles gave us specific instructions on the matter.[27] And ever since, all of the mystics and Doctors who teach the skills of prayer recommend starting there—it's always good to base your prayer on prayers coming from the mouth of the Lord, St. Teresa of Avila used to say.

But, like everything else that the Church expresses, her articulation of the mechanisms, techniques, and results of prayer have crystallized over the centuries, condensing into greater clarity and capturing more of the light. The epistles of the first great Christian mystic, St. Paul, touch just about every point of Christian mysticism, but, as St. Peter observed, "in these epistles there are certain things difficult to understand, that the unlearned and the unstable distort" (2Pt 3:16). The writings of even the earli-

---

26. One of Bl. Anna-Maria's latter-day precedents is St. Frances of Rome (1380-1440), who lived there during the invasions by Ladislaus of Naples, had a similar family, similar housewifely duties, similar gifts like healing, and a similar apparition: an archangel always visible to her who showed her whatever she needed to know. She could see clearly at night by the light of his splendor, which is supposedly why the motorists of Rome adopted her as their patroness. Bl. Anna-Maria herself, by contrast, used to tie up traffic by slipping into ecstasies in the middle of the street if she happened to see a cross or an image of Christ or Mary.

27. Mt 6:5-6, 21:22, 23:14; Lk 19:46; Rm 12:12; 1Cr 7:5; Eph 6:18; Cl 4:2; 1Tm 4:5; 1Pt 4:7; etc.

est Church Fathers and those of the earliest hermit monks are full of good practical advice, too, but our present understanding of prayer started to come together in the Middle Ages, beginning in the twelfth and thirteenth centuries.

It was the time when doctrinal theology started to coalesce into the rigorously logical form preferred by sharp scholastic minds like St. Albert the Great (*c.* 1200-1280) and St. Thomas Aquinas. The Scholastics treated doctrinal theology as an independent intellectual process, trying to grasp some aspect of God by figuring it out. They dominated the universities and produced an immense amount of brilliant doctrinal tracts, the ones that give rational, convincing answers to all of those perennial questions about whether God is everywhere, or whether the names that imply relation to creatures are predicated of God temporally, whether there is an irascible and a concupiscible appetite in the angels, and so on. Their statements are all interesting, but tough; and prayer, as the province of moral theology, doesn't figure very prominently in their studies.

As if to keep things in balance, spirituality—the science of cultivating the interior life through prayer—grew parallel to the more intellectual efforts of the Scholastics, maturing not in the universities but among the regular clergy, the contemplative monks and nuns, and among the laity. This was a time of intense focus on the life and humanity of Christ, a time of growing pious practices like meditative prayers in which the soul contemplated Jesus as a model of perfect faith and behavior, striving with the imagination to grasp Christ's life as the unequalled pattern of perfect submission to the will of God. You can see this focus on the human nature of Christ in the devotional art of the time, those tender representations of the Mother and Child—God made Man—and, by contrast, in those super-realistic crucifixes, the paintings and the illuminations, that depict the torments of Christ with startling detail.

TO GAZE AT THE HUMANITY OF CHRIST

You can see the same emphasis on the humanity of Christ in the books of the time. Those gifted minds who led the growth of spirituality in those days wanted to help everybody, ordinary people, develop the skills of using their senses and their imaginations to bring their own souls into conformity with the soul of Christ, to meditate on his humanity as a way of purposefully, deliberately, climbing the steep path toward full spiritual union with God. At first, in the thirteenth and fourteenth centuries, these books mainly grouped passages from the Gospels about the life and passion of Christ— as the Rosary, which Pius XII Pacelli called "the compendium of the entire Gospel", does, or as St. Bonaventure's great *Tree of Life* does. Sometimes they added commentaries, or they suggested prayers, to get the point across more clearly. A lot of these books, like the thousand-page *Life of Jesus* by the Carthusian monk Ludolph of Saxony or the handy little *Imitation of Christ* by Thomas à Kempis, have been in use ever since.

But as Christians generally grew more adept at the spiritual exercise of prayer, they needed something a little more sophisticated. By the middle of the fifteenth century, books started outlining the forms and mechanisms of meditative prayer in general,

M I S S A L

The Order of Mass in English

Approved for Use in the United States by the Committee on the Liturgy of the National Council of Catholic Bishops

Puzzled by changes in the liturgy? Unsure of exactly what's proper and what isn't? Here, at last, is the answer—an accurate, permanent, and exceptionally beautiful presentation of the approved Order of Mass, handsomely printed in an edition that even children can afford.

Archive-quality paper in durable soft cover

51 pages - ISBN 0-9653660-2-2 - Suggested Retail $4.00 - Bulk discounts available.

PANGÆVS.

Ask for it at this bookstore, or write Pangeus Press, Box 670127, Dallas TX 75367, to order! Include payment and $1.00 shipping and handling per copy.

so that a person could choose any episode of Christ's life, or Mary's, or that of any other saint, and meditate on it profitably. It's hard to pin down the first such meditation manual; discursive prayer has always been a major occupation of monks and nuns, and there have been plenty of little "how-to" manuscripts on meditative prayer ever since the beginning. The first real best seller about how to pray meditatively, though, is probably the *Ladder of Meditation* that Johann Wessel Gansfort wrote in about 1450. It's a difficult method, every bit as complicated as the syllogisms of the Scholastics and every bit as logical, but the laity snapped it up as quickly as monks and nuns did.

Of course, more than anything else the Rosary popularized meditative prayer and sharpened people's skills at prayer; of all forms of meditative prayer, the Rosary is the most profound for the learned, the simplest for the unlettered, and the easiest for anybody. But after the middle of the fifteenth century, more and more books appeared, giving systematic techniques of interior renewal and showing ways to go beyond meditative prayer and train your own soul in the ways of genuine acquired contemplation. That's an intermediate state between meditative prayer and a genuine mystic state in which God reaches back to the person in an extraordinary way, and most people can achieve it. "Ordinary meditative prayer," St. Alphonsus of Liguori said, "usually succeeds after some time in producing that contemplation that is called acquired and that consists of perceiving at a glance truths that we only discovered before by a long discourse"—that is, by long meditative prayer.

Oddly enough, it was the Protestant Reformation that triggered the most vigorous growth in mystic theology. As the heretics started to tear theology in half and throw away the moral part, great mystic saints arose in the Church, asserting, vitalizing, and clarifying the whole business.

In fact, the best way to understand the skill of prayer, and the best way to get a frame of reference on apparitions and other mystic phenomena, is to look at the writings of three of the greatest mystics who ever lived: St. Teresa of Avila, St. Ignatius of Loyola, and St. John of the Cross. All of them were endowed with repeated, almost constant, apparitions and other spectacular spiritual gifts, all of them were born at about the same time and in about the same region of Spain, and each of them described with unequalled clarity some distinct areas of the continuum of mystic experience.

four

a person at prayer

A person at prayer is like a bed of coals:
as long as a single spark remains,
a great fire can be kindled.
But without that spark there can be no fire.

— Hasidic saying

Saint Teresa of Avila, which is pronounced with the accent on the first syllable, *ávila*, was born in that little town in Spain in 1515. Her father's family, named Sanchez, was of Jewish extraction, pious and prominent cloth merchants who had converted during the reconquest of Spain from the Moors.

This was during the reign of Ferdinand and Isabella, a time when Spain was struggling to unite a patchwork of cultures and kingdoms into a single Christian state. To do this, the Catholic Kings (and the word means, here as everywhere else, nothing more than "universal") undertook to expel the last remnants of the Arabic and Jewish elements that had been gradually pushed out of Spain for seven hundred years. The monarchs got, somehow, the privilege of naming their own inquisitors; it was a major papal mistake, and pope after pope objected strenuously, but no pope could abolish a civil office any more than one could abolish the Federal Bureau of Investigation today.

The Spanish Inquisition (the "Holy Office"), now a government department like any other, got corrupt pretty quickly. Politics, race, and religion were so mixed together in those days that nobody could separate them. Jews and Muslims who had converted willingly were suspected of political disloyalty just as much as those who had gone through the forms for business reasons, and half the time the government didn't bother to inquire which was which. The national Holy Office kept pestering the *recién convertidos* anyway, even if the family's conversion was no more recent than three generations before. It got so bad that Teresa's grandfather packed up his family and moved out of his native Toledo to Avila in about 1500.

They survived in this remote little town and even prospered. Alonzo Sanchez de Cepeda, the merchant's son, soon married, but his wife died two years later, leaving him with two children; twenty-three years later, his second wife died, leaving him ten more, one of them named Teresa de Ahumada after her maternal grandmother. Growing up in this big, prosperous family, Teresa was a cheerful and extroverted child, well cared for and not exactly spoiled, but curiously devoid of imagination. Like most children in that time and place, she was familiar with the lives of the saints through the *Golden Legend*, but she didn't take these as more or less abstract patterns of desirable behavior. She took them literally.[28]

Figuring that the quickest and easiest way to win Heaven was martyrdom, she took her brother Rodrigo and set out for the nearest Moorish territory so that they'd be killed instantly in hatred of their Faith and go straight to God. Well, things had settled down somewhat since the *reconquista* was accomplished, and the Moors in those days would probably only have fed them lunch and taken them home, but in any case they only got as far as the city walls when they ran into their uncle, who brought them back to their parents in very short order. But the episode tells you a lot about the kind of person we're dealing with.

Physically, Teresa was of medium height and rather plump. Her black eyes were round and lively, protruding a little from her nondescript face, which was a clear white set off by three little moles, one above and one below her mouth on the left and a third below the center of her small, straight nose. Altogether, she must have been attractive rather than pretty; but the surviving portraits make you see the personality more than the face, and a personality like that doesn't come along very often.

"Profoundly baffling", was how one biographer described it. In the last century they tried to write her off as an hysteric. But hysterics, as the term was then defined, couldn't get much done in a practical way, and Teresa was a supremely practical businessman—as a nun, she reorganized an entire branch of her order before she was through. Today, she's still a case study for psychologists, whose diagnoses range from neuropathy to simple hallucinations. But any of these one-word estimates has to overlook a lot of very complicated evidence. It seems more reasonable, really, to consider her as a highly intelligent person, weak in some respects just like the rest of us, who had a willpower of truly historic proportions and knew how to use it. And who was called by God to attain through prayer a union with the Divine seldom seen outside the pages of Scripture.

28. *Legenda* is another of those Latin words that don't translate very well into English. "Legend" now means an imaginative story that isn't really true, but it didn't take on that derisive meaning until after 1600, when the Protestant Reformation in England relegated this heritage to the level of fairy tales. *Legenda* (from the Latin *legere*, to read) means things to be read, readings; the meaning is closer to "legend" as on a map or coin. Originally, these accounts of saints' lives were read aloud in public, as parts of devotional or educational exercises, or even as homilies, and they're not fabrications. The biographies in the *Golden Legend*, for example, reproduce early-Christian, patristic, and mediæval sources verbatim, and the author, Bl. Jacobus da Voragine—like any good scholar—notes doubtful dates and documents explicitly. But you do have to sort out the mnemonic passages and the moral tales—the *fabulæ*, literally "fables"— that most of these collections add to the beginnings and ends of their documents.

TILLING THE GARDEN OF THE LORD

As a child, Teresa must have enjoyed gardening—she certainly knew a lot about growing things. But she undoubtedly got this at home; at school, she wasn't taught much more than the mastery of cooking, sewing, and other housekeeping skills that became her lifelong habit. There was probably a little religious education thrown in to the curriculum, but she was by no measure a trained theologian. Evidently no heavy-duty books like those of the Scholastics were available to her, but in any case you get the impression that, while their painstaking syllogisms might have appealed to her tidy mind, she wouldn't like reading them very much. Fortunately (or providentially), one of her schoolteachers, the Augustinian nun Doña María Briceño, was a woman of high spiritual ideals who talked a lot about prayer. She awakened Teresa's interest in prayer and, to Teresa's own surprise, thereby got her thinking about a religious vocation.

Now, Teresa had been in bad company, or at least in dangerous company, running around with a cousin of hers who encouraged all kinds of vanity and frippery. Teresa's will was torn between the allurements of fine clothes and parties and the more elevated appeal of the spiritual call. She got so upset about the decision that the stress ruined her health, and she had to leave school. An uncle let her read spiritual books from his own little library, and finally, she said, something that she read in the letters of St. Jerome made her willpower assert itself. She would be a nun, she decided, not because she was so attracted to that life but because it was obviously the safest way to get to where she wanted to be: Heaven. She ran away from home again, this time not to the Moors to be killed for God, but to the Carmelite convent of the Incarnation, to live for him.

When she got there, the convent was home to about two hundred people—servants, relatives, novices, and a few nuns. Life was austere, but the convent followed the "mitigated" rule, which allowed some comforts (like shoes) and some pageantry (like splendid liturgies) that hadn't been allowed by the original Carmelites.[29]

Teresa of Jesus delighted in the life there, at first, but just after her profession she collapsed in illness again. The doctors were at a loss, and, as usual in those days, their remedies nearly killed her; probably the contrast between life at the Incarnation and her ideals of austerity and prayer were at war within her.

It got so bad that the convent released her to her family for care. On the way home, she passed the house of her uncle, the same one who had sent her home after her Moorish adventure. He gave her a book on prayer, the *Third Alphabet Book (Tercer*

---

29. The Carmelites (officially "The Brothers of the Order of the Most Blessed Mother of God and Ever-Virgin Mary of Mount Carmel") trace their origins back to the prophet Elias and the hermits who lived with him, continuously since Old-Testament times, on Mount Carmel in Palestine (3Kn 18:20). St. Berthold organized the monks there in 1155, and in 1452 a parallel order of nuns was founded. Reforms were gradually granted as the order expanded all over the world, but the work of St. Teresa and St. John of the Cross branched the Carmelites into the Old Observance or "Calced" Carmelites (from the Latin *calceus*, shoe), who wear shoes and follow the Mitigated Rule, and the Teresian or "Discalced" Carmelites, who don't wear shoes and follow the Primitive Rule.

Abecedario) by Francisco de Osuna, still considered an excellent introduction to the mystic life. She loved it; it was the first clue she had, she later said, about how to proceed in prayer.

But as her spirit got stronger, her body got worse. Her illness was compounded, again, by the remedies inflicted on her by the local *curandera*. She eventually fell into a coma so deep that they figured she was dead—she woke up four days later with the wax on her eyes, she said, the wax from the vigil candles that Castilians in those days used to close the eyes of the dead. She ended up paralyzed for about three years, but even after she sort of recovered from that her whole body was wracked by illnesses until the end of her life. But that didn't keep her down.

Her energy, like her literal-mindedness, was always a consternation to her superiors in the order, and it was undoubtedly an irritant to her sisters, too. She, of all people, went over their heads to found a separate convent on the "primitive rule" of her order: looking back past the licit and proper mitigations of that rule granted by various popes over the centuries, she sought to establish a way of life more like that led by the original Carmelites. Then she founded another, and another, fourteen more in all (and two others by proxy, as well as fourteen monasteries for men), until reformed houses dotted Spain. And she ran them, too, as well as running interference on their behalf against the Holy Office, Rome, the rest of the Carmelites, and the general populace, who were often up in arms about a new convent in the neighborhood.

Nobody could reasonably have expected this from a virtual invalid, but her spiritual life was beyond anybody's guess. She took on a formidable array of penances, she advanced tremendously in the skill of prayer, and she was given a dazzling array of spiritual gifts, including ecstasies, heavenly voices, and apparitions. She saw Christ, she saw her departed friends being taken up to Heaven, and she physically levitated, from time to time.

But even in her transports, there was never any nonsense about her. When she was assailed by a particularly horrifying pack of devils—which she understood as fully able to thrash her physically—she took her cross in her hand and said, "Come on now, all of you, for, being a servant of the Lord, I want to see what you can do to me." They backed down, and although she saw them again occasionally, she wasn't afraid of them any more. "I paid no more attention to them than to flies," she wrote.[30]

Although she kept these experiences confidential, between herself and her confessor or her spiritual director, word leaked out—it's hard to conceal something like levitating off the floor after communion, even if you hold on to the altar rail as she did. Naturally, this kind of thing piqued the interest of the Holy Office, as well as that of her superiors in the Church and in the order, but she passed their inquests with her combi-

30. Often, saints have recourse to blessed sacramentals, relics, and holy water to disperse demons, but it's evidently enough to make the Sign of the Cross and command them to adore it, or to pronounce the Holy Name, as St. Alphonsus Liguori used to do, because at that Name every knee below the Earth, as well as on it and above it, must bend (Phl 2:10). Heresy, of course, deprecates these measures, which can leave people without much defense against supernatural phenomena usually understood as being ghosts, vampires, and other horrors.

nation of innocent humility and absolute obedience.

Fortunately for us, they made her write down everything that had happened to her. She was immensely resistant to the idea, but, under the compulsion of obedience, she overcame her willpower and wrote the *Book of Her Life* (1565; the first version, done in 1562, is lost) and her *Spiritual Testimonies*, where she describes most of her highly unusual mystic experiences. Naturally, when her sisters found out that she'd finally been compelled to write it all down, they were dying to read it; but the Holy Office held on to the manuscript, thinking it best to keep the extraordinary events private for a while. The Holy Office finally fell in with the suggestion that Teresa write something else for the sisters, something more specifically about prayer. So Teresa put together *The Way of Perfection* (1566), a manual of prayer, and *The Interior Castle* (1577), which is usually regarded as her best synthesis of the mystic path of prayer.

As with St. Jerome himself, you can spend a pleasant evening with St. Teresa whether you like religion or not. Every sentence in her writings calls out to be read aloud. Her style, her unique common-sensical voice, owes a great deal to her own strong personality and something to the heritage of her Sephardic forebears; her books sparkle with phrases that can only have come out of their spoken Ladino into her written Castilian but still have an Old-Testament ring to them.

She obviously wrote exactly as she spoke; her books read like transcripts of a recording. Eyewitnesses said that she wrote fast, too, as fast as a notary taking dictation, and that she never paused or crossed anything out to reword it. Her censors at the Holy Office evidently complained of illegibility, and, as two of her modern editors note, "she doesn't punctuate".[31]

Yet her books came out like snowflakes, symmetrical and graced with an intricate logic, as if they were spontaneously worked out in her head before she put pen to paper—most have perfectly balanced chapters, all of almost exactly the same length.

In fact, she attributed the whole plan of *The Interior Castle* to a vision she saw in a flash one Trinity Sunday, but wherever they came from her books reflect the orderly state of her mind. All of her writings are easily available in good translations, and all of them deserve to be better known. They won her the title of Doctor of the Church;[32]

31. Kieran Kavanaugh, O.C.D., and Otilio Rodriguez, O.C.D., translators of the *Collected Works* published in 1987. She herself said that she wished she could write with a pen in each hand, to get it all out faster.

32. That is, she was officially recognized by the Church as a writer of great learning and sanctity distinguished by her defense, exposition, and preservation of the Church's doctrine, although Doctors' works aren't certified free from error, necessarily. The title *Doctor*, which means "teacher" in Latin, is an encomium, a term of praise, not a certification or commandment to accept everything that they taught. It was first granted by the Council of Chalcedon in 451, but during the centuries since then only about thirty Doctors have been proclaimed, including St. Augustine, St. Thomas Aquinas, St. Albert the Great, St. Bonaventure, and Teresa's friend St. John of the Cross, which indicates the caliber of writer that receives the title. St. Teresa was the first woman to be so honored. Her books mark a watershed in the history of spirituality as the first by a woman mystic that were not, like those of St. Gertrude or St. Catherine of Genoa, dictated by an ecstatic lady to eager *devotées*. They are of an entirely different order and quality from anything previous in that line.

their accounts of a wide range of mystic activity are unsurpassed, and they constitute a most accessible manual of the business of prayer.

THE SPECTRUM OF MYSTIC EXPERIENCE

You can't find an exact hierarchy of prayer in her works, no precisely measured recipes with guaranteed success. She never speculates, and she never lays down absolute rules about mystic experiences. She goes precisely as far as her own experience took her, not an inch farther—reporting personal experience is really all that a mystic can do, anyway. That's why she described four stages of prayer in the *Book of Her Life* but seven in the *Interior Castle*: she had more than a decade between the two, and she kept growing. The mystic path isn't divided into definite degrees like a thermometer; it's more like the colors on a spectrum of visible light—green always stands between blue and yellow, orange between yellow and red, but it's impossible to find clear lines between any two colors.

So, although they all begin at the same low place and end at that same high plane of union with God, different mystics divide the continuum of mystic experience differently. Some distinguish three phases or stages, the *purgative*, in which the soul reaches out to God through ascetic practices; the *illuminative*, in which God reaches back mystically; and the *unitive*, in which the two draw together intimately. St. John Climacus (579-649) crossed that same distance in thirty steps in his seventh-century *Ladder of Divine Ascent*, and in the thirteenth century St. Bonaventure used the number six to organize his *Soul's Journey Into God*. However the mystics organize their accounts, whatever vocabulary they use, the states and phases blend into one another, or they may all exist together.[33]

Mystics don't necessarily move through the whole spectrum of experience in a given order, nor do they all experience all possible mystic phenomena as they go. And there's no definite moment at which you can be assured of passing from whichever stage you might be in to another. God decides where you'll go, and how far, and how fast; again and again, St. Teresa recalls how she's seen God do more for some beginners in prayer in three months, in three days, even, than he did for her in twenty years.[34]

He can encourage a soul with extraordinary experiences if he wants to, but he probably won't; he may let a person work on through a lifetime of the most rigorous penance without any sensory sign of a response, or he may allow the most dazzling extraordinary phenomena to someone, like St. Bernadette or the little visionaries of Pontmain

33. Some may describe a state exactly and discuss it without naming it, while others give it a distinctive label: you'll find terms like "vocal prayer", "recitation", "affective prayer", "active recollection", "active quietude", "acquired contemplation", the "prayer of simplicity" or "of simple regard" or "of the heart", many of which describe the same state or contiguous parts of what other moral theologians define as two successive states. You just have to follow each writer as he defines his own terms.

34. The intensity and splendor of St. Teresa's mystic experiences may make it seem that she was given unparalleled gifts in that way, but that's probably because she wrote about them so clearly and fully. She first experienced ecstasy at age 43, but Ven. Mary of Agreda was given that gift at 18, Teresa's friend St. Pedro of Alcántara at 6, and St. Hildegard, St. Catherine of Siena, and many others by the age of 4.

or Fátima, who never gave penance much thought. So it's not all cut and dried for you.[35]

So, although every Christian is obliged to exert the greatest possible effort toward his own salvation—"for faith without works of justice is not sufficient for salvation," as St. Gregory of Nyssa phrased it in the fourth century—nobody can guarantee levitation or a miraculous healing; no amount of personal struggle toward holiness is going to earn a personal appearance from God, a saint, or an angel. "I understand at last," Julian of Norwich said, "that it's not that I didn't earn these gifts, but that these gifts are so great that nobody could possibly earn them."

Yet while nobody can predict when God will reach back to a soul, people can still see consistent patterns in how he reaches back when he chooses to. Creditable mystics, as a group, describe the same distinct kinds of states and phenomena century after century, from the Bible to the present day, and consistency with this catalogue is a primary way that reported phenomena are judged for genuineness. And through St. Teresa's books, you can learn a lot about exactly what these experiences are like; but more than that you can learn how to advance in the skill of prayer. St. Teresa uniquely brings the inexpressible truths of the spirit home, capturing them in terms of pots and firewood, chickens and donkeys, babies, bottles, mice, and mirrors, making them as solid and comprehensible as any other household items.[36]

The four kinds of prayer outlined in the *Life*, for instance, she phrases in terms of a garden. You can water a garden in four ways, she writes. You can draw the water from a well and haul it to the garden bucket by bucket. Or you can bring the water to the garden by means of a water wheel, turning the wheel and letting the water run down an aqueduct to the garden. (I've drawn water this way, she says; it's less work, and you get more water.) A third way would be to have the garden near a river or a stream; this way, the ground is more fully soaked, and you don't have to water it very often—much less work for you.

Or the garden can just be watered by rain. In this case, the Lord just waters the garden himself, without any work on our part. "And this way is incomparably better than all of the others mentioned," she concludes.

The First Steps on the Mystic Path

The decision to learn more about the skills of prayer, to go to the well in the first place and draw out as much as you can, is crucially important for the wandering soul, not only

---

35. Jb 1:21, 12:13-15, and really all of the other biblical passages about the Lord's withholding rain; Ps 6:4, 12:1, 88:47, etc.; Hc 1:2; Zc 1:12; Jn 3:8, 33; 1Cr 12:11; etc.

36. All of which she knew intimately from experience. She saw to every detail of management, seeing to the altarcloths and flowers, sweeping what needed sweeping, and keeping the convents as tidy as the accounts. She even grieved of sin in terms of slack housekeeping: how miserable the state of those poor rooms within the castle, the soul, of a person in sin, she complained; "among the custodians, the stewards, the chief waiters—what bad management!" In fact, a persistent concern for cleanliness seems characteristic of the great mystics; St. John of the Cross, St. John Vianney, and St. Louis-Marie de Montfort were always scrubbing something, and St. Francis himself used to carry a little broom with him on preaching tours, chiding negligent clergy and then sweeping up himself.

because it marks an important stage in conversion—literally a turning from this world to God—but because so much happens during this phase. This is the activity that teaches so much about the nature of sin, the distance between even a willing soul and God, and the need for penance as well as repentance. The creditable mystics speak with one voice about this elementary stage of prayer: it's agonizing beyond description, it's joyful beyond ordinary experience, and it's very, very hard work.

This first kind of prayer is like hauling water in buckets, St. Teresa says. Beginners in prayer do it this way. They've already freed themselves from the more blatant kinds of mortal sin, and they've decided to try *discursive prayer*, which may be called meditative prayer; it's when you discourse in your mind about some aspect of God, for instance. Meditative prayer can be aided by the vocal prayers of devotions like the Hours or the Rosary, and it's characterized by reasoning, or resolutions, or just mental communion with God and the saints. But beginners tire themselves out trying to focus their attention on prayer.

She did this, herself, for those twenty years. She prayed rigorously, daily, for hours at a time, but, she says with the voice of experience, no matter how hard you work at it you never can get quite enough water to the plants. Finally, though, she was praying before a devotional image of the Man of Sorrows, the Wounded Christ, and she was lifted up to the first step on the road of detachment from this world and closeness to the next. As often happens to an ascetic at this stage of prayer, she received a remarkable and puzzling spiritual gift, the *gift of tears*.

The Gift of Tears

The gift of tears is sometimes called the gift of *compunction*. The tears may be of the body or of the soul, or both, as Jeremia said (13:17), but the gift of tears is not just a fit of depression; it's the result of a genuine and sudden shift in perspective, a pervading attitude of sorrow for sin. These tears are like the tears of a baby just born, as Isaac the Syrian said back in the seventh century, because when you get this gift your soul has come out of the prison of the world and begun at that moment to breathe the wonderful air of Heaven. This breakthrough into the light is a matter of seeing things as God sees them—you see just how far your soul is from God, and how seriously your sins separate you from him. A person gifted with tears also sees how badly people live in this world, how soaked in sin everything really is. St. Teresa may have drawn from her tears one of the most poignant images in her writings:

> Because we have heard and because faith tells us so, we know that we
> have souls. But we seldom consider the precious things that can be found
> in this soul, or Who dwells within it, or its high value... There are many
> souls who are in the outer courtyard ... and don't care at all about enter-
> ing the castle, nor do they know what lies within that most precious
> place... Souls who do not practice prayer are like people with paralyzed
> or crippled bodies; even though they have hands and feet they cannot give

orders to these hands and feet. Thus there are souls so ill and so accustomed to being involved in external matters that there is no remedy ... They are now so used to dealing always with the insects and vermin that are in the wall surrounding the castle that they have become almost like them. And though they have so rich a nature and the power to converse with none other than God, there is no remedy ... if the Lord himself doesn't come to order them to get up ... How disturbed their senses are! ... How miserable the life in which we live! ...[37]

For one who sees sin in all its seriousness, and who sees so many people lost to sin, so many people beyond one's own reach, the pain is simply unbearable. The soul—knowing itself as imperfect as any, knowing that its own prayers alone cannot begin to heal even one of these lost ones, watching countless souls sifted like snowflakes into the flames—the soul stands bewildered, helpless, overwhelmed with sadness, not knowing what to do but cry. "I felt like a person who is bound hand and foot," St. Margaret Mary said, "to whom no freedom was left, either interior or exterior, except tears." It hit St. John of God (1495-1550) so hard during his conversion that they locked him up for a lunatic, at first. Even St. Francis of Assisi, the most cheerful saint imaginable, wept so much in private that he contracted a serious eye disorder from it. He was entirely blind, the last years of his life among us.

Once received, compunction returns again and again during one's life, bringing with it physical or spiritual tears. But compunction brings with it more than just a clear view of how bad sins are. Cassian (*Collationes* XXIV, 9:11) and Pope St. Gregory the Great (*Morales sur Job*) note that compunction also brings an understanding of the need to beg pardon; and as the gift develops, it has more to do with love of God than with terror of punishment.

Love and Tears

In fact, it's important to remember that the whole point of the gift of tears, its governing principle, is the love of God, which is the virtue called *charity*. It's easier to grasp the relationship between the gift and the virtue if you think of love in purely human terms. Think of a person with whom you have a loving relationship—a child, maybe, or a teenager. You can punish the child for disobedience, but if the child doesn't love you the discipline of punishment doesn't do much good. Punishment from someone you don't love just seems like arbitrary cruelty from someone who has no right to tell

---

37. Note that St. Teresa, like all of the other great mystics, points to the "high value" of each human soul and laments again and again one of the greatest psychological problems of our day, low self-esteem; the Church, insisting that humans are by nature good, stands firm against the heretical idea that humans are by nature depraved, or the equally incorrect notion that humans are merely animals whose behavior is prompted only by animal impulses—as St. Teresa herself says in the subsequent sentence, "all our attention is taken up with ... the diamond's setting or the outer wall of the castle; that is, with these bodies of ours." We can't comprehend the beauty of a soul, she said, just as we cannot comprehend God; but he himself says that he created us in his own image and likeness.

you how to behave. Even strictly fair punishment seems intrusive, like downright brutality, because the child just doesn't care whether his actions offend you or not.

In a loving relationship, though, the child will consider your feelings before he acts. He'll be less likely to offend you deliberately because he loves you, and he'll pay more attention to his actions so that he won't offend you inadvertently. That's the discipline of love; it works because it resides within the person, and it isn't just imposed from outside. A loving child takes confidence from the love, too, knowing that, if he's sorry that he offended you, and if he tries to make it up to you and promises to use all his strength never to do it again, you'll forgive him, out of love, and you'll help him learn to act better.

With that kind of discipline he doesn't feel deprived, because the rewards of that love are greater than the pleasures of the offenses—the offenses always exact their price in pain, sooner or later, but the love only brings lasting security and happiness. As he grows in love, he'll just gradually lose the taste for those deceptive pleasures, and he'll draw more and more sustenance from the growing love. And he'll see more clearly the cruel, ungrateful, and vicious nature of his offenses against that love; that is, he'll see it as you see it.

And, beyond that, a loving child also knows that anything he does that hurts himself—lying, cheating, stealing, illicit sex, or the like—hurts you as much as anything deliberately aimed at hurting you possibly could. This kind of thing wounds your love, too, and if you're not the direct object of the offense it's much, much harder to achieve reconciliation; you're just an innocent bystander. What's more, you're an innocent bystander who would rather die than see your loved one hurt himself that way.

In basically the same way, charity governs the relationship between God and humans—St. Augustine's classic *Enchiridion on Faith, Hope, and Love* gives the scriptural and patristic reasoning behind the comparison more fully (so does John Paul II's encyclical *Veritatis Splendor*). The idea of God as vengeful and condemnatory is classed by moral theologians as a failure of charity; nobody who loves God would see his commandments as the whims of a volatile taskmaster, a tyrant exclusively concerned with hellfire and damnation if you don't do whatever he feels like saying. In fact, since God is love, it's sometimes said that the fires of Hell and Purgatory weren't created separately for punishment: they're just the same flames of God's love. That love is understood as permeating the universe, which was created in and because of God's love; there's nowhere you can go to escape it. And just as the Sun gives life and light to those creatures that accept it but burns the worms and slugs that seek to hide from it, the inescapable charity of God illumines the souls who seek it but torments those who reject it, loving the darkness rather than the light.

That's not exactly catechism, but it makes the point; and the great mystics, acutely aware that sin offends God in and of itself, also know that the willful rejection of charity that's involved in sin magnifies the offense. They know that God cries out to see so many of his beloved creatures hurting themselves by rejecting his love, condemning themselves, in fact, to everlasting torment. They realize that Christ preferred to die in torment rather than see us sin, to paraphrase the Apostle. And they know that he did this because his Heart loves mankind so much that it spared nothing, even to exhausting and consuming itself, to testify to them its love, as St. Margaret Mary reported.

This inexpressible heartache that sin inflicts on God is why Christians have always asked for the gift of *compunctionem cordis*, compunction of the heart—the old Roman Missal included a specific standard prayer for the purpose.[38] And that same heartache is what triggers in these mystics an irrepressible grief: how could any pain be greater, asks Julian of Norwich, than to see him who is all my life, all my bliss, and all my joy suffer? There is no pain, she said, that could be suffered that's like the sorrow she felt to see Christ in pain. So compunction is sorrow for sins "because I dread the loss of Heaven and the pains of Hell," as the Act of Contrition puts it, "but most of all, because they offend you, my God, who are all good, and deserving of all my love."

The Gift of Consolation

The puzzling thing about the gift of tears is that—wrenching, agonizing, as it is—it doesn't leave you depressed. On the contrary, St. Teresa says, it leaves you with true humility, which consoles you and acts quietly, gently, and with light. Humility, after all, isn't a denial of your gifts and talents but an exact knowledge of them; it's not some destructive kind of self-deprecation but an exact knowledge of your true worth.

People with the gift of tears (or just with a healthy humility) see things from God's perspective, not from ours any more. And while nobody can move to that viewpoint without suffering the most urgent pain, the pain of tears comforts the soul by letting it see that the pain itself is given by God as a great favor and that the whole exercise of compunction is well worth the results. So the soul gifted with tears grieves for its own offenses and those of others, but at the same time rejoices in the divine mercy with which God meets those offenses: "Happy are you who weep now," as Christ promised, "for you shall laugh" (Lk 6:21; Ps 125:5).

This *consolation* is the puzzle of tears. St. John Climacus was always amazed at how inward joy and gladness mingle with the grief, like honey in a comb—which he took as a proof that this gift, so different from ordinary weeping, is truly a gift from God, "since God secretly brings consolation to those who in their heart of hearts are repentant." And those who receive this gift, one and all, are given to smiling and exclaiming through their tears, "How happy I am! How good God is! What a pity that others don't know this joy! How can people live without this joy!" and to cry out irrepressibly with other expressions of the kind.

They generally maintain this level of joy in daily life, too, as indeed all of the saints do. You wouldn't expect this, remembering the painful chronic health problems that most of them had, but still, they're all remarkably buoyant spirits.[39] The tears of

38. It compares the process of drawing forth tears from our hearts to that of drawing forth water from the rock (Ex 17:2-6), and begs a flood of tears to extinguish the flames of our sins.

39. St. John Climacus stands almost unique among mystics because he evidently didn't think that the joy should show. "If nothing benefits mourning [tears] so much as humility," he wrote, "nothing opposes it

the visionary mystic St. John of the Cross have caused him to be depicted, usually, as a gloomy, prim-lipped ascetic, exclusively given over to horrible penances, but his letters show him to be warm, sweet, deeply loving, and funny—not so funny as St. Teresa or St. Bernadette, maybe, but then so few people are. St. Philip Neri's two favorite volumes were his Bible and a book of jokes; but still, having read the hearts of his penitents, he would often burst into tears that prompted them to confess sins they'd hidden from him (and when they did, he burst into tears of joy).[40]

The people around St. Ignatius of Loyola during the day, his companion Jerónimo Nadal records, were always laughing, but he never got through Mass without crying. And in St. Dominic de Guzmán (1170-1221), as Bl. Jacobus Da Voragine tells it in the *Golden Legend*,

> there was a complete evenness of spirit, except when he was moved by compassion or pity; and because a joyful heart makes for a happy face, he showed this inward composure by his outward gentleness. During the hours of the day, when he was with his brethren and associates, there was nobody more affable, and in perfect modesty and discretion; during the night hours nobody was more constant in vigils and prayers. Thus he gave the day to his neighbor, and his nights to God; and then from his eyes there flowed as it were a fountain of tears.

But all in all, the gift of tears is much more agreeable than a related mystic gift, the one that St. Teresa calls an *impulse*. This is a sudden, unpremeditated remembrance of how far the soul is from God. An impulse is like when you get bad news, she says, or some other sudden shock that makes you forget what you're doing or talking about. But this pain, too, has a purpose, she says: it makes you see that the whole purpose of prayer— union with God—is worth dying for, and worth living for. After an impulse passes, the body is so stressed that it seems disjointed; she found it hard even to hold a pen to write, after her impulses. If impulses were frequent, she says, this life wouldn't last long.

so much as laughter." (He admits elsewhere, though, that he couldn't resist teasing his brethren, so maybe he was all right.) Of course, not even the saints can keep it up all the time—St. Jerome got downright crotchety now and again, and St. Louis-Marie Grignion de Montfort once wrecked a whole café, like Christ cleansing the Temple, because the noise interfered with his Mass. But canonization commissions reportedly look for "evidence of joy", and, in any event, the Church of the saints is not a Church for long faces. Even the ordinary of the Mass reminds us that we "wait in joyful hope for the coming of our Savior, Jesus Christ", and the very word "blessed" (*beatus*, in Latin) means "happy".

40. The mystic gift of reading hearts, of knowing the secret thoughts of others or the state of their souls without communication, is called *cardiognosis*, from the Greek καρδία, heart, and γνῶσις, knowing. It's undoubtedly a gift from God, because the Devil doesn't have access to a person's spiritual faculties, and no human can know the mind of another naturally without communication. Still, the Devil can make a good guess and communicate that, or a proud person can be deluded into thinking that his own conjectures are supernatural revelations. The genuine gift comes to advanced ascetics, evidently; St. John Climacus noted that a perfectly purified person can look at another and see his soul. Cardinal Bona, among others, remarked that this gift is an immense benefit to a spiritual director, just as the gift of diagnosing even hidden ailments of the body would be for a physician.

The Ascent to the Second Level of Prayer

St. Teresa's initial problems with this first kind of prayer came down to a matter of technique, or of skill at praying: she was trying with her will and her emotions, but these always wander. Most people also use their imagination for this stage of prayer, but Teresa had no imagination. "In fact," she said, "my imagination is so dull that I never succeeded even to … represent in my mind—as hard as I tried—the humanity of the Lord." Most of all, she didn't know at that time of her life that while the mind and emotions are wandering, the soul can remain quiet, in a calm contemplation of God that you won't notice if you keep making a constant, noisy effort to pray.

If this happens to you, she says, "don't kill yourself over it." Beginners have to realize that they're starting to cultivate a garden on very barren soil, full of abominable weeds, sown there by their own sins (Jb 31:38-40; Gn 3:17-18). And there will be times, she warns, when you'll wear yourself out lowering that bucket into the well and coming up empty, but you just have to keep at it. People experiencing this dryness need to relax a little, getting away from daily life and reflecting on their past lives, and they need to practice devoting hours and hours to prayer.

Recollection and Continued Awareness of God

But above all, beginners in prayer need to learn how to "recollect" themselves. "Prayer without recollection," said St. Alphonsus of Liguori, "is insulting and offensive to God, and it calls down his wrath on the offender." St. Alphonsus noted that you need three things to get properly recollected: solitude, silence, and the remembrance of the presence of God. "It was these three things," he said, "that the angel of God referred to when, addressing St. Arsenius (354-450), he said, 'Flee, be silent, and rest'. In other words, seek solitude, practice silence, and rest in God by keeping the thought of his presence ever before you."[41]

It sounds like the kind of practice that would be easy for a cloistered contemplative nun but out of the question for anybody with a job and a family, anybody in the real world. Well, the urge to withdraw from the world and pray is why the contemplative orders got started, back when this world was a lot less complicated than it is now, but getting away from it all physically won't help by itself, any more than a vacation on the beach means that you can leave business behind. No matter where you are, and no matter what you're doing, the detachment has to be interior.

And anyway St. Teresa is far too practical to advise physical flight from your duties; you can pray constantly while being about your daily chores, she says. Even in the cloisters, she, like St. Maria Maddelena dei Pazzi (1566-1607) or many another great mystic, got more work done than any four normal people. St. Margaret Mary, who was sometimes set to watching the convent's livestock or assigned bedpan duty in the infir-

41. See that convenient anthology of the saint's massive works on ascetical theology entitled *The Twelve Steps.* On the skills of prayer in general, see the present author's *Rosary: Mysteries, Meditations, and the Telling of the Beads.* The story of St. Arsenius (Arsenio) is recounted in some editions of the *Golden Legend.*

mary, said the same thing. "Not only during prayer, but also at other times," she wrote, "keep yourself in the presence of Our Lord, as a disciple who is before his Master and anxious to learn to do the Master's will perfectly by giving up his own will."

Still, as nuns, St. Margaret Mary and St. Teresa may not have the credibility of someone like St. Elizabeth of Hungary (1207-1231), who managed to live a full ascetic and mystic prayer life, care personally for her family and hundreds of paupers, and serve as Landgravine of Thuringia, all at once. Bl. Anna-Maria Taigi single-handedly took perfectly good care of her often unemployed (and often crabby) husband Domenico, their six children, and the in-laws with whom they shared a two-room basement apartment. And she had to put up with the endless troop of cardinals, debunkers, pilgrims, thrill-seekers, priests, revelers, reporters, theologians, policemen, petitioners, and other tourists who tracked through the place day and night for fifty years.

Anna-Maria was sufficiently detached from all of this, though, to achieve the highest mystic states. She asked direct questions of the Christ she saw before her and got direct answers. She cured hundreds and even thousands of afflictions, like a neighbor child's diphtheria and her own daughter's torn eyeball, at a touch. If her thoughts happened to turn to God during her housework, she would sometimes levitate, broom in hand, off the floor. But as she levitated, she kept on sweeping.[42]

The point is that anybody, in any state of life, can start hauling that bucket to the garden and profit from the exercise—St. Peter had a mother-in-law, St. John Climacus reminds us, but he got the keys to the kingdom anyway (Mr 1:30; Lk 4:38). You just have to start with the basics. In fact, a later mystic, a lay brother of St. Teresa's own order, concentrated on this first way of prayer almost exclusively. Brother Lawrence of the Resurrection (1611-1691) managed to conceal an impressive intellect even from his religious superiors and ended up assigned to more or less permanent kitchen duty, where he calmly did more work than any two other people. He would have preferred spending days and nights in uninterrupted vigils before the Blessed Sacrament, but he recognized that God is everywhere and always available to draw nearer to those who want to find union with him.

"People seek methods of learning to love God," he said. "They hope to arrive at it by I don't know how many different practices; they take much trouble ... Is it not much shorter and more direct to do everything for the love of God? ... There is no *finesse* about it; one only has to do it generously and simply."

> Dazzled on one side by the brilliance of the divine Sun of Justice who dissipates the shadows of the night, and blinded on the other hand by the mud of my misery, I am often almost beside myself. However, my usual practice is to remain in the presence of God with all the humility of a

---

42. One of her baby daughters, evidently under the impression that everybody's mamma levitated, is on record as having called her down by saying, "Mamma, what are you doing? There's no dirt up there." Her husband, by the way, eventually came around, in a way: "God took this excellent servant from me," he said after she died, "because I was not worthy to have her."

useless but faithful servant… At the beginning of my duties I would say to God with filial confidence, "My God, since you are with me and since by your order I must occupy my mind with these external things, I beg you to grant me the grace to remain with you and to keep you company; but so that it may be better done, my Lord, work with me, receive my labors, and possess all my affections." Then, during my work, I continued to speak with him familiarly, to offer him my services and to ask his graces… Thus, rising up after my falls and making a multiplicity of acts of faith and love, I have arrived at a state in which it would be as impossible for me not to think of God as it was difficult for me to accustom myself to it in the beginning.

So, he said, "I turn my little omelette in the pan for love of God."[43]

Now, *continued awareness of the presence of God* is another of the mystic gifts; it's one way that God reaches out to the soul, although usually to a soul prepared by constant ascetic practices, including the constant practice of the presence of God. "If the soul does not fail God," St. Teresa said, "he will never fail, in my opinion, to make his presence clearly known to her." This awareness sustains a soul and, although you'd think that it would occupy the soul completely, St. Teresa notes that, "on the contrary, the soul is much more occupied than ever before with everything pertaining to the service of God."

And although awareness of God's presence in itself consoled Brother Lawrence, he worked at it without expecting or even wanting any discernible reward. In fact, after his noviciate, by the time he had trained himself to be always aware of God's presence, his visions and locutions stopped altogether. And, like St. Bernard, he took their loss as a reliable sign of his closer union with God.

But even Brother Lawrence, his biographer said, sometimes passed his whole prayer time rejecting distractions and falling into them again and again. So did St. Teresa; this is the hard work of rooting out all of those weeds. The only consolation that she found in this dry toil is that the beginning gardener knows that the effort itself pleases the Lord, and that the whole point of the exercise is to please the Lord, not the gardener. You have to be prepared to keep at it, even if this period of dryness lasts your whole life, she said. God will co-operate, but in his own good time. You just have to await his pleasure. For, clearly, she noted, if the well is dry, we can't put water into it. "We are the vessels," as St. Cæsarius of Arles had put it a thousand years before her, "He is the fountain."

More Perfect Penance, More Perfect Prayer

St. Teresa herself, lowering that bucket every day for those twenty-two years, all those

---

43. This ability to pray always and everywhere is sometimes called the "attitude of prayer". It seems to be particularly prevalent in kitchens. Apart from Bl. Anna-Maria Taigi, there are the monks remembered by St. John Climacus, who were on permanent kitchen duty but were always recollected and had the gift of tears (*Ladder of Divine Ascent*, Step 4, "On Obedience"), and St. Joseph of Cupertino, who was eventually relieved of kitchen duties because he dropped so many things while recollected.

hours, day after day, recalled that when she got a drop of water from that well, she thought that God was granting her a favor. In fact, she's of the opinion that this dryness happens precisely because God tests people who claim to want to draw close to him. He lets them know that they have to suffer, to carry the cross and drink the cup, before he lays any great treasures within them.[44]

That's the use of penance in this stage of spiritual growth. Voluntarily giving up things of this world that give pleasure, or even voluntarily taking on things that cause pain (with the guidance of a qualified director), puts distance between us and this world, and they clear the way to closeness with the next.

It may seem utterly illogical: isn't there plenty of pain and suffering in the world as it is, without asking for more? Isn't it enough, understanding that salvation is judged on your faith and on your works, to just know Christ as the Son of God and Savior and to obey the commandments of Christ and his Church? Well, yes; ordinarily. But these are extraordinary mystics, experiencing extraordinary spiritual phenomena. Still, the difference is only a matter of degree, because, in the Church's understanding of the cycle of redemption, atonement for sin is absolutely necessary.

That's why a Christian is encouraged to endure whatever bodily aches or heartaches happen in the natural course of things, offering that pain as retribution for his sins. Beyond that, God may send, or permit, whatever sufferings he wants to, all of which are supposed to be suffered willingly, or at least in resignation to God's will, as Job did. Sometimes God permits exceptionally hard sufferings to those people who, he knows, can bear them profitably (and they don't accept because they enjoy it, either; it hurts, and the great ascetics know it). Or he sends sufferings to knock some sense into people, letting them see the relationships between this world and the next and giving them a chance to atone here on Earth, where it's comparatively easy.

Easy, that is, compared to what it is in Purgatory, where the sufferings are just as unimaginable as the joys of Heaven. This perspective is where the great ascetics find the heroic strength to endure indescribable physical and spiritual torment, and where a lot of Christians, even people you know, find their impressive strength in everyday suffering. And it's why most Christians ask for the grace of being allowed to suffer sufficiently here, or, under the guidance of a confessor or spiritual director, take on extra little penances, disciplines that God accepts but doesn't send.

But there's another strengthening factor in the penance business that shouldn't be overlooked: the unity of all humans, to one degree or another, in the Church, the mystical body of Christ on Earth. This unity is why good people suffer from disease, loss of loved ones, and all kinds of other tragedies that seem unfair; but it's not always exact retribution for specific personal sins. It may be the result of the sins of everybody else. After all, life on Earth was Paradise, before sin, and sin permeates creation, like pollution of the air or water. The world is indeed harassed by the evil lives of men, St. Cæsarius of Arles said; the effect of attacks upon the good is like the stench of a sewer

44. Compare Mt 10:38, 16:24, 20:22-23, 26:39; Mr 8:34, 10:21, 10:38, 14:36; Lk 9:23, 14:27, 22:42.

blown about by the wind: its unbearable stink goes everywhere. No matter where its exact sources are, sin infects the nature that God made good and saw as good.

But this unity has a positive side, because it means that one Christian can voluntarily take on the penances that other people should be doing but aren't. Just as we suffer the consequences of each other's sins, we can atone for each other's sins, too— "the life of each of God's children," Paul VI Montini wrote, "is joined in Christ and through Christ in a wonderful way to the life of all the other Christian brethren in the supernatural unity of the Mystical Body of Christ, as in a single mystical person... Among them, too, is an abundant exchange of all good things."[45] And there's not a saint in the calendar who didn't contribute willingly everything possible to this exchange.

Of course, the great ascetics, the ones who turn into the great mystics if God chooses them, can handle penances on an heroic scale. But the idea is that God is so eager for sinners to repent that, like the father of the prodigal son, he runs out to meet the slightest sacrifice made in atonement (Lk 15:11-32; 15:3-10; etc.). Even these little penances don't come easy, though, St. Teresa says: "we have such stingy hearts that it seems to us we're going to lose the Earth if we desire to neglect the body a little for the sake of the spirit."

The Prayer of Quiet

But once you've gained control of the situation and learned to let your soul remain quiet, you might begin to practice the *prayer of quiet*, which happens when God, for his own reasons, raises the water level—"I mean that the water is closer," she explains, "because grace is more clearly manifest to the soul." It's like when you turn the wheel and the water gushes into the garden with comparatively little work on your part. This is what theologians call *passive prayer*, and it's a spiritual gift, an elementary kind of mystic experience, because God has to reach out to a soul before it happens.

It's important to remember that this outreach by God doesn't free the soul from the requirements of the Law, nor from obedience to the Church, nor from the need to strive on with all its might to achieve Christian perfection. Even Brother Lawrence, as part of the regular clergy, spent hours in regularly scheduled prayer, too, and moral theologians warn that the practice of the presence has to be reinforced by willful prayer, rewound as you'd rewind a relaxed spring. If anything, the old rule about a lot being expected from those to whom much is given applies even more to the chosen mystics.

But passive prayer brings with it enough consolation, with so little effort, that prayer is no longer tiring, even if it lasts a long time. It's at this point that the soul begins to lose its appetite for earthly things ("little wonder!" St. Teresa exclaims) and sees that the delights of Heaven cannot possibly be experienced here below, and that nothing on Earth, not riches, honors, nor fleshly delights, can compare or really satisfy us. "The

---

45. Apostolic constitution *Indulgentiarum doctrina*; see also Jn 17:21; Rm 14:7; 1Cr 12:26-27; 2Cr 1:6; Eph 3:13; Cl 1:24. The word "indulgence" might trigger a mistaken response, but it's only the remission before God of the temporal punishment owed for sins whose guilt has already been forgiven; see the *Catechism of the Catholic Church*, Part Two, Title X.

soul doesn't know whence the satisfaction comes from or how, nor frequently does it know what to do or what to desire or what to ask for," she says. "It seems it has found everything at once and doesn't know what it has found."

The Gift of Discernment of Spirits

Now, the interesting thing about this second stage of prayer—and it's a safe bet that nobody we know has reached it—is that this new awareness of unfamiliar spiritual delights makes a person a prime target for the Devil. He can disguise himself as an angel of light (2Cr 11:14), St. Teresa and the other great mystics warn, and, because *discernment of spirits* is itself a spiritual gift of some magnitude that few mystics get,[46] a person at this stage of prayer probably can't tell the difference. "In fact," St. Teresa cautions, a soul "must have so much experience that it needs to come close to the very summit of prayer to have such discernment."

St. Teresa's great friend and colleague St. John of the Cross described it this way. The Devil can't know the exact nature of these interior and secret spiritual communications, which are between the soul and God, but he can figure out that you're receiving them because your soul is so quiet and peaceful. So he does everything he can to disturb the sensory part of the person, inflicting suffering, fear, horror, and false visions. Creditable visions, Fray Juan says, are caused by a good angel, but false ones by a bad angel, a devil; and God dictates a certain balance of power between the two in their struggle to conquer the soul. A weak soul who doesn't know the relative value of apparitions can be so beguiled and charmed by the beauty of these false visions that it stops hauling that empty bucket and settles into a comfortable and selfish arrangement with the Devil—he'll supply the counterfeit spiritual delights, and the soul will stop working at prayer, so the Devil wins.

So, St. John advises, forcefully reject any and all apparitions. If they're from God, you shouldn't be greedy for these special favors, and if they're from the Devil, you ought to get rid of them as fast and as completely as possible (*cf.* Ac 5:38-39).

But these diabolical distractions seem to fade away by the time a person achieves the third kind of prayer, the one that St. Teresa compared to watering the garden by means of a running river beside it. This is a sort of *sleep of the faculties*, a state in which the "powers" of the soul (the will, the intellect, and the memory) are suspended as the soul enters complete abandonment to the will of God. This is the kind of prayer that the prophets and psalmists meant when they used the same image, the tree flourishing by the river while the rest of the land was desolate.[47]

This is the stage at which great spiritual gifts begin to produce wonders: every month they shall bear fresh fruit, said Ezechiel, for they shall be watered by the flow

46. Discernment of spirits means that the person can recognize the nature of the spirits involved in supposed mystic phenomena, distinguishing devils from angels, saints, or God (1Cr 12:10). St. Ignatius of Loyola gives some rules for the discernment of spirits in the *Spiritual Exercises*.

47. Nm 24:6; Ps 1:3, 35:9, 45:5, 64:10, 79:19-12, 104:41-42; Jb 28:28; Is 48:18; Jr 17:7-8; Ez 47:1-12; Rv 22:1-2; to name a few.

from the Sanctuary. Their fruit shall serve for food, their leaves for medicine (47:21), their leaves for the healing of nations (Rv 22:2).

For the mystic soul itself, the consolations, the sweetness, and the delights of God's nearness are incomparably greater than those of the second stage, coming upon the soul like a "glorious foolishness, a heavenly madness where the true wisdom is learned." The soul doesn't know whether to speak or be silent, to go forward or back; it rejoices in the agony of the complete death of all earthly things and an enjoyment of God. Even St. Teresa got carried away just trying to describe the state—she goes on page after page about these delights, sometimes addressing God, sometimes her reader, before she catches herself. "Pardon me," she writes with an almost visible blush, "for I have been very bold."

It's interesting to note that St. Teresa thought at first that this kind of experience marked a breakthrough into a higher plane of prayer, but by the time she wrote *The Interior Castle* she had recognized it as simply an intensification of the prayer of quiet. And, in fact, in this stage of prayer, the soul is still conscious of the world, still operating with the senses.

The Fourth Level: The Prayer of Union

But in the fourth and highest kind of prayer that she describes in the *Life*, no power remains in the body, and the soul has no way to communicate the joy that it feels. This is the *prayer of union*, in which the will loves more than it understands, she says, and the intellect stands as though in awe. There is neither memory nor thought in this state, and the bodily senses are lost so that the soul can focus on what it's enjoying. This is the state that she compared with copious showers from Heaven that soak in like the rain, blessings that permeate like the dew, like a downpour upon the grass, like a shower on the crops.[48] This state doesn't last very long, she says, but, like a good rain on a garden, it leaves a residue of humility and other virtues in the soul, enough so that the soul discerns the immense good that has come to it. "In my opinion," she concludes, "if this experience is authentic, it is the greatest favor our Lord grants along this spiritual path—at least, among the greatest."

Now, this state of *ecstasy* isn't just slipping off into a kind of a daydream, but a genuine mystic phenomenon: being drawn, gently or powerfully, by God into a sort of spiritual embrace. The word itself is from the Greek ἔκστασις, meaning "put out of place"; it's being pulled by an external agency—God—out of your normal state of existence. It's exactly the opposite of the meditational states achieved by Eastern hermits, too. Ascetic contemplation is thinking about something (God); yogis and other Eastern adepts aim at thinking about nothing, to achieve states in which the mind is simply emp-

48. Dt 32:2; see also Dt 11:10-25; Jb 36:26-31; Ps 64:10-14, 71:6-7; Pr 16:15; Ez 34:26-27; Zc 10:1—there's hardly a page in the Bible that doesn't refer to this kind of copious communication of divine graces as rain, a natural metaphor in a land where rain is a matter of physical life or death, just as grace is a matter of spiritual life or death. See also 3Kn 17; 18; Jr 3:2-3; for why the drought happens, and Jr 14, particularly 14:14-15, which addresses the effects of false prayer at this level. Lv 26:3, by the way, is one of many Bible verses that show that these phenomena fall clearly within the province of moral theology.

tied of all conscious thought. This is purely natural, and it's not involved with union with a personal God, because those religions—notably Hinduism and all of the branches of Buddhism—don't believe in a unique personal God. Anybody can learn to do it, and it can be done without any religious context whatever.[49] These natural trances, therefore, are something that the person himself does; but ecstasy is something that God does to the person. So the natural trances are quiet and empty, but ecstatic states involve the exaltation and the inexpressible joy of unencumbered communication with God.

St. Teresa notes that in ecstasy, as in all spiritual phenomena, there's a greater and a lesser, with all degrees of intensity in between. If the ecstasy of this prayer of union lasts longer and is more intense, she'd call it *rapture* or, as she preferred, *suspension*: "rapture" was, and is, "a word that frightens". Anyway, in suspension, the union lasts longer, and the body shows different symptoms; the senses of the body stop working, and the senses of the soul take over. The soul is so transfixed with joy at the union, she says, that it seems to forget all about the body.[50]

You're left aching in every nerve after suspension, she notes, but the whole phenomenon comes on slowly. *Transport* is like suspension, but it comes on quickly; in transport, the higher part of the soul leaves the body entirely, which is terrifying. "Courage is necessary," she warns, "for the soul to surrender itself into the arms of the Lord to go wherever he may want to bring it." Beyond transport, she defines the *flight of the spirit*, again a quicker and more intense form of the same phenomenon—sometimes a flame shoots high into the air, she says, but it's still just as much fire as the flames that stay lower.

She was most acutely embarrassed by another form of ecstasy with physical repercussions, *levitation*. "Although this experience is delightful," she says, "it is necessary for the soul to be resolute and courageous." She resisted this, when she felt it coming on, but it made her feel as if she'd been fighting with a giant, and it was usually impossible for her to win the battle. "It carried off my soul," she said, "and sometimes the whole body until it was raised from the ground." She once ordered her nuns to hold her down, and she begged the Lord to not give her any more favors that involved outward show, "for I was tired of being considered so important." Still, these favors are up

49. While this natural meditational trance may well be an enviable state of relaxation, it involves the mind, not the soul. The theological term for the state of the soul during these trances, unfortunately, is "stupefaction", but it's not derogatory; it's from the Latin *stupere*, to strike senseless. It's applied regardless of creed, and whether the entranced person puts himself in that state for some religious reason or not.

50. As with St. Margaret Mary and innumerable other saints, this state happens mostly at the moment of receiving the Eucharist (communion) or while in adoration before the Blessed Sacrament. St. Philip Neri often had to rub his head hard with his fist or lean against the altar to keep from collapsing in rapture at the Consecration, and St. Francisco Borgia's contemplation of the Eucharist was so profound that his Masses, like those of Padre Pio, took too long to be offered in public; Da Voragine records the same thing about St. Dominic. There's also the deep recollection of St. Teresa's friend St. Peter of Alcántara, whose outdoor Mass at Pedrosa in Spain was preserved—like the outdoor crowds who came to hear St. Anthony of Padua in Limoges—from even the raindrops of a catastrophic thunderstorm that he may not have noticed. St. Charbel Makhlouf once went so far into suspension as to ignore the lightning that singed his vestments when it struck the altar on which he was celebrating Mass.

to God, as she said, and they kept happening anyway.

"Well, then," she sighed, "it is only right … that we try to delight in these grandeurs our Spouse possesses and that we understand whom we are wedded to and what kind of life we must live." And although she was drawn into a transforming union with God, the exchange of hearts called a mystic marriage, St. Teresa of Avila is best known for another phenomenon, extraordinarily intense but not quite so long lasting, the one that she calls the *wound*.

The Wound of Love

The wound is sometimes called *transverberation*; it echoes the prophecy to Mary at the Presentation (Lk 2:35). St. Teresa describes this as seeming as if an arrow had been thrust into the soul itself, leaving no physical pain, necessarily, but a spiritual pain, a pain so intense that the soul must groan, but so delightful that the soul wishes that it would never pass. She recalled her own famous experience this way in the *Book of Her Life*:

> I saw close to me toward my left side an angel in bodily form. I don't usually see angels in bodily form except on rare occasions … This time, though, the Lord desired that I see the vision in the following way: the angel was not large but small; he was very beautiful, and his face was so aflame that he seemed to be one of those very sublime angels that appear to be all afire. They must belong to those they call the cherubim, for they didn't tell me their names. But I see clearly that in Heaven there is so much difference between some angels and others and between these latter and still others that I wouldn't know how to explain it. I saw in his hands a large golden dart and at the end of the iron tip there appeared to be a little fire. It seemed to me this angel plunged the dart several times into my heart and that it reached deep within me. When he drew it out, I thought that he was carrying off with him the deepest part of me; and he left me all on fire with great love of God. The pain was so great that it made me moan, and the sweetness this greatest pain caused me was so superabundant that there is no desire capable of taking it away; nor is the soul content with less than God. The pain is not bodily but spiritual, although the body doesn't fail to share in some of it, and even a great deal. The loving exchange that takes place between the soul and God is so sweet that I beg him in his goodness to give a taste of this love to anyone who thinks I am lying.

It was parallel to the same Wound of Love inflicted on Christ by Longinus when the Savior's Heart was opened on the Cross. But because of this passage, and for her mystic marriage, St. Teresa has come under fire in these sad latter days from some literal-minded critics who accuse her of all sorts of mischief, including self-induced sexual activity that she naïvely imagined was some great spiritual event. But if you read broadly in mystics' accounts, physical sensations seem coarse and trivial in comparison to what they're talking about (besides, it doesn't happen just to women; Bl. Carlo de Sezze had the same experience). It's just that, in describing the realms of spirit, mystics have only the medium of highly figured language in which the inexpressible is conveyed by symbols—hence references like flaming arrows, golden crowns, sunlight, sweetness, and the whole vocabulary of earthly love. Childlike faith apart, taking these hieroglyphs literally would be to miss their meaning entirely—as indeed taking literally the high poetry of the Bible misses the point. Certainly the Song of Songs is more explicit than anything that the later mystics ever wrote.

In discussing these conventions of language, moral theologians use the example of a person born blind, who can hear descriptions of light but forms only an abstract and incorrect idea of it unless his eyes are miraculously opened; and even then, how would he describe everything he sees to other people born blind? The Ursuline Ven. Mary of the Incarnation, herself a widow with a son, explained the embrace of God by saying that "it wasn't in the manner of human embraces, because nothing that falls within the cognizance of the senses in any way approaches this divine operation; but we have to express ourselves according to our gross way of speaking, because we're composed of matter." That makes it easy to take things too literally. Even St. Francis sometimes misinterpreted some of his prophetic dreams, as he took his locution literally when the crucifix spoke to him about rebuilding the Church and started hauling stones and lumber. St. Bonaventure says, "he had no experience in interpreting divine mysteries, nor did he know how to pass through visible images to grasp the invisible truth beyond."

In any case, Teresa of Avila was nobody's fool, having dealt with all of the usual foolishness (and peccadillos) of novices for many decades as prioress and superior while reforming her order; and although not highly schooled she was so formidably brilliant that her Jesuit director, Baltasar Alvarez, explained the huge stack of tomes on his desk with the remark, "All of those books I have to read to understand Teresa of Jesus." By the time she wrote the passage in question, she was nearly fifty years old, having been an ascetic for decades; she reported no temptations of a sexual nature, although many mystics do, and, as with St. Ignatius and many others, the first mystic encounter almost always gives them a heightened ability to turn from things of the flesh.[51] And in

---

51. The temptations of St. Anthony in the desert are the best known, a favorite subject of major artists. Eventually, ascetic practices give a person control over sexual appetites as well as the others, but some saints, such as St. Rose of Lima (1586-1617) and St. Maria Maddelena dei Pazzi, like St. Teresa, had no such temptations in their lives. St. Margaret Mary's lasted only a few hours, in her entire life. But most of them are like the rest of us in that regard: St. Benedict Joseph Labre and St. Frances of Rome suffered great and persistent temptations against chastity. Those of Ven. Cæsar de Bus are on record as lasting through twenty-five years of strict penance, and those of St. Mary of Egypt for seventeen. St. Alphonsus Rodríguez endured seven years of temptation (starting when he was fifty) before peace came to him, as it came to many others, after another apparition or mystic experience. The *Golden Legend* records that a lust-ridden scholar who bent to kiss the hand of St. Dominic inhaled an unknown heavenly fragrance, after which he was troubled by no more carnal temptations. St. Catherine of Genoa wasn't tempted that way, either, but after holding the newborn Christ one Christmas Eve she wasn't tempted to fall asleep during devotions any more.

any case she's discussing matters of the spirit, not matters of the mind, and still less matters of the emotions.

Yet this is not exclusively a spiritual event. A spiritual experience so overwhelming must leave its mark also on the emotions and on the mind, certainly. In Teresa's case, there's even some *post-mortem* evidence that the body doesn't fail to share in some of this supreme spiritual experience, and even a great deal.

When she died on October 4, 1582, the heavenly fragrance, the scent beyond the perfume of earthly roses, that had emanated from her person intensified, becoming so strong that the doors and windows of her cell had to be opened. Now, she happened to die while visiting one of her convents, the one at Alba de Tormes, and to make sure that the body stayed there instead of being sent back to her own convent, Teresa de Layz—the lady who had endowed that convent—had her buried the day after her death and ordered a huge heap of stones, bricks, and chalk piled on top of it. The grave was in damp ground, and when it collapsed all of the rubble fell in; but the fragrance continued from the grave. And there were so many miracles and wonders reported from the site that the provincial, Fr. Jerome Gracián, gave permission to exhume the body and put it in some more suitable enshrinement.

The grave was opened on July 4 of 1583. By that time, the wood of the smashed coffin was already half rotten and the clothes disintegrated, but the body itself was as fresh as if it had just been buried. It was removed and washed, still exhaling the marvelous fragrance, as it did for the next three years, until it was reburied in Alba de Tormes. In 1588 it was exhumed again, still intact and fragrant, and relics were taken— among them her heart, which can be seen today at Alba de Tormes, still incorrupt in a crystal reliquary.

Many witnesses have testified to seeing on it the scar left when the piercing wound from the angel's arrow healed.[52]

THE ATTITUDE OF THE MYSTIC SOUL

So, in studying mystic matters, an exclusive focus on psychology misses the point entirely. It gets confusing, sometimes, because some psychological conditions incline people to believe that they're having spiritual activity, and a psychologist who excludes the possibility of spiritual activity wouldn't be able to tell the difference. But authentic spiritual activity leaves the psychology good and healthy. The great mystics all know that clin-

---

52. The relics were examined again by doctors in 1872 and in 1914. Both times the flesh was incorrupt and fragrant, although natural conditions had caused other items in the grave to decompose. The stigmatic St. Veronica Giuliani (1660-1727), by the way, drew in 1700 a picture of the Instruments of the Passion that, she said, were imprinted on her heart during a vision, and her sketch was confirmed at her autopsy thirty hours after she died. Long before her, the heart of St. Clare of Montefalco (c. 1275-1308) was found to bear tiny but distinct images of the scourge, the column, and the cord of the Flagellation, the Crown of Thorns, three nails, the lance, the sponge, and a small crucifix, all in fine detail and made out of nerves and tissues; they were imprinted there, she had said, by Christ during an apparition to her. (These hearts are incorrupt, too, and still on display at the Capuchin convent of Città di Castello and the Augustinian convent in Montefalco.) That of Bl. Carlo de Sezze (1613-1670) had a wound, a crucifix, and a hard fleshly nail, perfectly formed and four or five inches long, straight through it.

ical depression, for example, is an entirely different phenomenon from the gift of tears. "Also note," St. Teresa warns, "that a weak constitution is wont to cause these kinds of suffering, especially in the case of tender persons who will weep over every little thing. A thousand times they will be led to think they weep for God, but they will not be doing so."[53]

And so it is with the rest of the mystic phenomena, all of which are matters of spirit, not of mind. Of course, discovery of a psychological disorder that could possibly cause anything that could be mistaken by laymen for a mystic phenomenon is enough to instantly exclude purported mystics from creditability. But the larger point is that psychology and spirituality are two entirely different things—closely related things, but separate things, as separate as mind is from soul. While mind and soul work together (just as body and mind do), and while the symptoms of spiritual activity might be mirrored in the workings of the mind, authentic spiritual activity stands outside of, and cannot be explained by, pure psychology: remember that, as St. John of the Cross pointed out to St. Teresa, the mind can be agitated or wander while the soul can remain quiet in a calm contemplation of God. Judging by the literature on the subjects, evidently most spiritual activity these days is referred to psychological causes either because many of us no longer believe in the existence of our souls or because, preoccupied as we are with the here and now, it's hard to tell the difference or even notice that you have a soul that's distinct from your mind.[54]

But whenever you look into the bright lights of mysticism, the human contribution setting the stage for this kind of spiritual experience mustn't be forgotten: years and years of intense effort to pray better and better; years and years of intense penances undertaken for all the right reasons and in strict obedience to the Church; years of soul-searching, painstaking self-improvement, and heroic accomplishments in virtue; loving acceptance of every kind of trial. This kind of development by itself is enough to put genuine mystics pretty far out of the understanding of us people in the pews. And even with all of this necessary human contribution to salvation, as St. Teresa and the others remind us constantly, extraordinary efforts won't necessarily result in extraordinary spiritual experiences. He grants these favors for his own reasons; his ways aren't our ways, and his thoughts aren't our thoughts, the mystics remind us. So the Spirit lights here and there, as God wills (Jn 3:8). It's difficult enough to study these movements of the Spirit;

---

53. The distinction has always been understood, but it's not easily discerned; see 2Cr 7:10. St. John Climacus, who wrote a whole chapter on the gift of tears in his *Ladder of Divine Ascent* (Step 7, "On Mourning"), notes that "many of the Fathers declare that this problem of tears, especially where it concerns beginners, is a very obscure matter and hard to analyze because tears can come about in various ways. Tears come from nature, from God, from suffering good and bad, from vainglory, from licentiousness, from love, from the remembrance of death, and from numerous other causes." But as to the actual gift, "there is nothing false in these, no sop to self-esteem. Rather do they purify us, lead us on in love of God, wash away our sins, and drain away our passions." See also *The Interior Castle*.

54. In fact, conscious awareness of one's own soul is a mystic gift; it's not automatic. Still, it seems to be considered one of those gifts that you'll get if you ask for it.

nobody can claim to predict them or control them.

Still, St. Teresa and all of the other great mystics are unanimous in saying that—since God's call to prayer is universal—anybody can start working to acquire more skill at prayer, and anybody can profit from that kind of work. But exactly how do you break ground for your garden? You have to get into spiritual shape. You really do have to exercise your soul, just as you would exercise your body. And for spiritual exercises, the classic source is St. Teresa's great contemporary, St. Ignatius of Loyola.

five

take up and read

But when deep reflection had dredged
out of the secret recesses of my soul
all of my misery
and heaped it up in full view of my heart ...
I heard from a nearby house
a voice like that of a boy or girl ...
chanting and repeating over and over,
"Take up and read. Take up and read."

— St. Augustine, *Confessions*, Book 8

Iñigo de Loyola started out as just about the least likely candidate for high mystic gifts. He was a Spanish, or rather a Basque, aristocrat, born in 1491 in the castle of Loyola near the town of Azpeitia in Guipúzcoa, the last of thirteen children.[55] Young Iñigo was a clever and high-spirited youth, not too tall, if you go by the hyper-realistic Spanish portrait statues of him, and handsome enough to get by on his looks. Evidently he did just that—he certainly wasn't much interested in schooling.

He had a lively imagination, though, and he loved to sing all of the songs about his illustrious knightly forebears. From his cradle he heard the legends of his ancestors, and from the time he was about five he heard about the chivalrous exploits of his older brothers in far-off lands like Naples or Hungary or even Panama, where Hernando de Loyola died on a peak in Darien. By the time he was a teen-ager, Iñigo was more than ready to break out of that little rural castle and take on the world at large.

55. Biographical sources give his name in lots of different ways. His family owned the estates of Loyola and Oñaz since the thirteenth century, and they just more or less alternated the surnames of their children between the two. Older sources sometimes call him Iñigo López de Recalde, but that's based on a copyist's error of long ago. His father was Don Beltrán Yañez de Oñaz y Loyola, and his mother was Doña Marina Saenz de Licona y Balda. That would make his real name Don Iñigo Yañez Saenz de Oñaz y Loyola.

He got his chance when he was sixteen. A kinsman of his, who happened to be the high treasurer of Ferdinand and Isabella, took him to the royal court to see what he could make of himself. It wasn't the kind of education that he needed, but Iñigo was a fast learner anyway. With his imagination fed by the romantic novels of the day, he spent his time dancing, duelling, gambling, carrying on passionate love affairs, and getting into all kinds of trouble. By carnival time in his twenty-fourth year, he was prosecuted in police court for nighttime shenanigans that were described as "*enormes*".[56]

But he was only getting started. Soldiering—that was the thing, riding off in shining armor with his squire and companions on deeds of derring-do. The profession of arms, the career of a knight, would let him live the romance of chivalry and offer him an even better chance to cut a dashing figure. So Iñigo joined up in 1521, buckling his swash and riding off to the defense of Pamplona against the King of France.[57]

Everybody else in Pamplona was ready to give up the fight before it started. The French army vastly outnumbered the city garrison, and it really didn't seem worth it. In fact, the city itself gave up and opened its gates to the invaders, but Iñigo, with his incomparable charm and romantic enthusiasm, talked the soldiers of the citadel into an heroic, hopeless defense. The resulting battle was everything that he'd hoped for, the flags, the smoke, the trumpets and drums, but the cannonballs were a different matter. One of them broke through his right shin and tore his left calf. When he fell, the garrison of Pamplona surrendered—the whole thing had been his idea, after all—and the victorious French patched Iñigo up as best they could and sent him back to Loyola on a litter. (He was lucky that they didn't amputate; that would have ended everything right there. You can still see the exact spot where he fell at Pamplona, by the way, marked by an inscribed paving stone.)

He began to recuperate, but his right leg had been set badly, in the confusion of the field, so his doctors took the customary blunt instruments and broke it again.[58] While he was bedridden recovering from the doctors' care, he sank near death with a week-long fever. He was advised to confess; if he wasn't better by midnight, the doctors said, he was a dead man. Iñigo prayed to St. Peter—it was June 28, 1521, the Vigil of

56. Evidently he started a riot when he led a gang to attack the parish clergy. Iñigo was described by the judge at that time as "bold and defiant, cunning, violent, and vindictive," which shows you what a real conversion can do. But the really bizarre thing about the episode is that Iñigo was accompanied in the fracas by his brother and indicted co-conspirator, *Father* Pero Yañez.

57. Iñigo undertook all kinds of knightly feats and vigils, but, strictly speaking, he was an *hidalgo*, ranking a notch above a knight, a *caballero*. Iñigo was never really knighted. It's a fine point of chivalry, but hidalgos are very punctilious about fine points.

58. Of course, there were no anæsthetics or analgesics in the sixteenth century, but Iñigo underwent this operation with no sign of pain, other than a clenched fist. The novels of the time tell you that this was the only sign of pain allowed to a knight, but Iñigo must have been one of very few who had the willpower to pull it off in reality. (In fact, the stereotype of the great mystics as swooning sissies is the first thing to go, when you start to know them—even the young girls are exceptionally tough.) But at this point his vanity was even greater than his fortitude. He asked for another operation that involved sawing off a protruding piece of living bone that spoiled the symmetry of his legs. His legs ended up symmetrical, but he limped for the rest of his life.

the Feast of Sts. Peter and Paul—and vowed to dedicate to him all of his skills as knight and poet, should he recover.

His fever broke exactly at midnight. Within three hours he was on the way to recovery. In a few days, sick of staring at the ceiling, he called for something to read; more romance novels, he wanted. Well, there just weren't any books in the house—the Loyolas were not known for their learning, is how one biographer phrased it. But one of his sisters-in-law had brought back a few devotional tracts after her service as a lady-in-waiting to Queen Isabella. So the servants hauled them in and piled them by his bed, books like the ponderous *Life of Jesus* by Ludolph of Saxony and the great *Golden Legend* by Bl. Jacobus da Voragine.

STUDY, THE FIRST EXERCISE OF THE SOUL

These books had been written to stir up love for Christ, to encourage imitation of the heroic virtue of the saints, and they worked. The lives of the great saints like his first-century namesake Ignatius Theophorus of Antioch (d. *c.* 110), and the life of Christ himself, hit him like summer lightning, flashing in his mind between flights of knightly fancy. He soon noticed a pattern: daydreams about ladies fair and chivalrous conquests left him feeling dry and uneasy, but when he imagined what would happen if he were to rival one saint in fasting or outdo another in pilgrimages, he was left full of joy and peace. After a few days of this, everything that Iñigo had lived for seemed like a complete waste of time. Lives spent in the service of Christ impressed him as lives more heroic than that of any soldier, more replete with pure love than that of any courtier—and aimed not at earthly glory and fame but an undeniable good, the salvation of souls.

His own life could only suffer by comparison, and Iñigo consequently suffered the most intense torment of the spirit, on top of the torment of his legs. He took on as many austerities and penances as his broken body could bear, fasting and praying until at last he received the gift of tears, spending whole nights weeping aloud for his sins. He vowed a pilgrimage to Jerusalem, where he planned to live out his days as a penitent beggar, atoning for his sins until he went at last to meet his maker.

"And so he began to forget the previous thoughts with these holy desires he had," he wrote in his *Autobiography*—writing of himself in the third person—"and they were confirmed by a spiritual experience, in this manner":

> One night while he was awake he saw clearly an image of Our Lady with the holy Child Jesus. From this sight he received for a considerable time very great consolation, and he was left with such loathing for his whole past life and especially for the things of the flesh that it seemed to him that his spirit was rid of all the images that had been painted on it. Thus from that hour until August 1553 when this is written, he never gave the slightest consent to the things of the flesh. For this reason it may be considered the work of God, although he did not dare to claim it nor said more than to affirm the above. But his brother as well as all the rest of

the household came to know from his exterior the change that had been wrought inwardly in his soul.

It was the completion of his conversion, but it was just the beginning of his spiritual growth. As soon as he could get around, he started out on his great pilgrimage of penance, with the best of intentions. His first stop was the great shrine of Mary at the monastery of Montserrat. It was quite a trip, but once he got there he met his first great confessor, Dom Jean Chanones, who gave him a copy of a book written by a former prior of Montserrat, García Jimenes de Cisneros, the *Ejercitatorio de la vida espiritual*—the *Book of Exercises for the Spiritual Life*—to get Iñigo ready for his general confession.

Conscience and the Problem of Scruples

It wasn't easy. It never is. "Inconceivable difficulties arise when persons who during their youth have contracted vicious habits resolve to change their lives, mortify their passions, and break with the world to devote themselves to the service of God," Dom Lorenzo Scupoli wrote in his classic *Spiritual Combat* in 1589, only a few years later. But the anguish itself is a sign of growth and change; "this onslaught," Bona continued, "is not experienced by those who are settled in their way of life, whether in virtue … or in vice."

Iñigo got through his confession, all right, but it took three days, which gives you some idea of his life up to that point. Then he discarded his fine clothing in favor of the regulation sackcloth, but his plans for a great pilgrimage had to be postponed. He couldn't get started for Rome because Adrian of Utrecht, Governor of the Realm, the former tutor to the King-Emperor Charles V, had been elected Pope Adrian VI. Adrian himself went to Rome on foot, walking like a penitent, but the immense train of courtiers escorting him to Rome clogged the roads and booked every available berth. But, what was worse, it included noblemen who would have recognized Iñigo through his penitential sackcloth and ruined his whole adventure.[59] And he couldn't go back toward Barcelona because a plague had broken out there. So he planned to stay for a few days in a pilgrim's hospice, or sometimes in a cave, at a little town called Manresa.

It was at Manresa that he found a copy of the *Imitation of Christ*, and it was there that he started taking notes on the profound psychological and spiritual changes that constituted his conversion experience. His few days at Manresa stretched into ten months, during which he came to see himself as sadly unprepared for the work before him, intellectually as well as spiritually.

He suffered all of the torments of *scruples*. That is, all of the tiny details of his past life plagued his mind, and he didn't know whether they needed to be confessed again or if they'd been covered in his marathon confession at Montserrat. He was new at

59. It was entirely possible. People that he fed at his beggarly table noted his courtly manners, and even when he let his hair and nails grow unrestricted a lady in Barcelona recognized the nobility in his face and the grace in his hands and knew him for a man of gentle birth. One of the losing candidates in this papal election, by the way, was Cardinal Wolsey. William Roper (*Lyfe of Sir Thomas More*) thought that Wolsey's jealousy at Adrian's election provoked him to induce Henry VIII to repudiate his wife, Queen Catherine of Aragon, Charles V's aunt, but Henry had his own ideas and evidently needed no urging.

penance, and he made the mistake of going about it without a spiritual director. With no experienced hand to guide him, he fell into the trap—common to beginners who have seen just how bad sin really is—of torturing himself mentally as well as physically in a wild attempt to atone even for the sins he'd only imagined. On top of all of his other penances, on top of the week-long fasts and night-long prayer vigils on his exquisitely painful knees, he took the *discipline* every night—that little cat-o'-nine-tails used historically by some great souls to inflict actual or, more usually, symbolic mortification on themselves.

It sounds like enough to make anybody hallucinate, although evidently he never did. But, without a qualified spiritual director, he overdid his penances so much that he nearly killed himself accidentally, more than once, and was only saved by chance. That's why anybody who's attracted to ascetic practices needs a really good spiritual director, in addition to a really good confessor. "Who learns a most difficult science without a tutor?" Cardinal John Bona asked in his handbook of prayer, *Guidance to Heaven*.[60]

"Select him for your guide who is a stranger to flattery," he counsels. "So highly gifted indeed ought to be this guide that he may be able to discern the inward motions of all the different spirits, fix landmarks between the virtues and vices, and benefit the morals of all ... Having learned to detect and elude all of the wiles and stratagems of Satan that lead the soul astray, ... [he must] teach and invite it back to God." Of course, this won't be a layman; the spiritual conflicts that have to be fought by a soul on this kind of campaign require the counsel of a priest, and a priest with specialized training besides. And then there's the question of spiritual obedience to the Church.

Every penitent, every mystic, is obliged to follow the Church's rules strictly, and to follow the director's directions to the letter. No credit-worthy mystic experience will contain anything that countervenes the Church's regulations, because God will not countervene the authority that he delegated to the Church in the first place (Mt 16:17-19, 28:18-20; Lk 10:16; Jn 20:23; etc.). Genuine mystic activity ceases instantly when a priest *recalls* the mystic, even though the person's will and bodily senses are suspended during mystic activity. And in fact even the Devil himself is obliged to obey the Church that speaks for Christ (Mr 3:15, for instance, and Phl 2:10). So the mystic's absolute obedience to the Church is a necessary safeguard against those devilish wiles and stratagems. That's why obedience is really the central test of the validity of any purported mystic

60. Bona (1609-1674), a Cistercian monk from Pignerola in Piedmont, was appointed Consultor to the Congregation of the Index (of prohibited books) and to the Holy Office, and at the death of Alexander VII in 1667 everybody thought he'd be elected Pope. He, like other ascetic writers, points out that these exercises might cause hallucinations unless they're undertaken in strict obedience, under the guidance of qualified spiritual directors. And their prescription has to be based on a thorough investigation of person's whole spiritual experience. If you were to take a good, sensible, moral person off the street and induce him to undergo a year of grueling fasts and the like, he'd probably just hallucinate; but if a person has shown steady and exceptional growth in spirit, and if he's taking these disciplines gradually under strict obedience to a qualified spiritual director, the possibilities for mere hallucination are much reduced, if not eliminated altogether. In most circumstances, a lay person interested in taking on spiritual exercises can be guided by a confessor; the sacrament of reconciliation is a good place to start reconciling your life with the ideal life of Christian spirituality. And your confessor is probably the best source of recommendations about finding a spiritual director, if he judges that you need one.

activity, and only a priest, a person consecrated to God's service through the sacrament of Holy Orders administered by a bishop who stands himself in unbroken apostolic succession, can exercise the authority that mystics and demons alike are compelled to obey.

It's also very difficult for a lay person to tell the difference between the results of ascetic practices and the graces of genuine mystic experiences. By definition, God alone can give a soul mystic states and experiences; by their nature, they're things that nobody can achieve by himself. The problem is that a person working hard at the discipline of the ascetic life can achieve states of prayer that most of us will never experience, and—to hear the great saints tell it—these always come as a surprise. They seem far beyond the power of a mere human, and in the Church's experience they're often reinforced by unusual graces. But the graces that God gives an ascetic, if he wants to, only prolong or intensify a state that, basically, the human being has achieved for himself. When a person, by his own efforts, breaks through to even the first of these unfamiliar states, it can seem as if he's already crossed the line between ascetic and mystic, although in reality he's only begun to climb as far as his own efforts can take him. And, again, this makes him a prime target for the temptations of pride and self-satisfaction.

Changing Course

But Iñigo's intentions must have counted for something, anyway. One day, when he was going to a little pilgrimage church about a mile outside of town, he became recollected in his devotions and sat down for a minute at the side of the road, facing the river Cardoner. And there, he wrote in his *Autobiography*, the eyes of his understanding began to be opened. From his account of the event, it seems to parallel what happened to the Apostles (Ac 2:1-36), and to St. Paul in particular (1Cr 11:1-30; *cf.* Jn 6:45).

Not that he saw any vision, he was careful to state, but suddenly he understood many things: spiritual matters, matters of faith, and matters of scholarship, and such a great enlightenment came over him that everything seemed new. It left his understanding so very enlightened, added his amanuensis Luis Gonçalves de Câmara in a marginal note, that he felt as if he were another man with another mind. This great clarification of his understanding, he wrote, "was such that in the whole course of his life, after completing sixty-two years, even if he gathered up all the various helps he may have had from God and all the various things he has known, even adding them all together, he does not think that he got so much as at that one time."

This outstanding illumination, this *eximia ilustración*, as he called it, straightened him out. He gathered himself together and started out at last, in 1523, on his promised pilgrimage to Jerusalem. Again, everything that could possibly go wrong did, but he bore up bravely; the whole idea of the pilgrimage was penance in the first place. Even so, he got more penance than he had bargained for. The account of his trip reads like a dramatized version of the Book of Acts: shipwreck and capture, sickness, absolute poverty, starvation, ridicule, prisons, beatings—everything. And when he got there the Franciscans in charge of the Holy Places told him to go home.

Well, even a future saint has only so much patience, and after seven months of that kind of travel, Don Iñigo Yañez Saenz de Oñaz y Loyola stood up and demanded to know by what right they had thought to interfere with a pilgrim like him.

We have the right from the Pope, they said; pilgrims like you get captured by the Turks, and we have to buy them back, and nobody has that much money. So the Pope sent us a Bull giving us the right to tell pilgrims like you to go home at once, and would you care to see it? [61]

Iñigo, seeing that it was a question of obedience to the Pope, said that he wouldn't dishonor them by demanding documented proof of what they said, and he went home, even though this changed all of the plans he'd made for the rest of his life. And the voyage back was just as bad as the voyage out.

But Christ the Educator never falls in with the winds sweeping through this world, St. Clement of Alexandria noted back in 190, "nor does he suffer his children to be driven like a ship into a wild and unregulated course of life. Rather, … he brings them safely to anchor in the port of Heaven." And by this time Iñigo had changed course. He'd figured out that you can't go at the life of prayer and self-improvement on your own; you have to guide yourself by the wisdom and experience gathered by the great minds and the great souls of the past. So, with his customary determination, he did something he'd never really done in his life. He studied. He educated himself, arguably better than any self-educated man before or since—after two years of intense study at Barcelona, he was ready for the universities of Alcalá, St. Barbara, and Paris. He swallowed his pride and sat with the little *niños* whenever he had to catch up on the fundamentals, but he made progress, and, finally, eleven years later, at the advanced age of forty-three, he took his Master's from the University of Paris.[62]

His years of schooling were also his years of begging, fasting, and other austerities, during which he also earned the humility acquired by laughingstocks everywhere. In fact, the extreme penances taken on by Iñigo and his companions—the kernel of the future Society of Jesus—brought them all kinds of attention, including that of the Holy Office. He was beaten up, harassed, and even thrown into prison for about six weeks, just on suspicion. It was the trip to Jerusalem all over again, year after year.

He and his companions decided at last to try the pilgrimage again, and again they couldn't go—open warfare with the Turks had broken out. So they pledged to wait it out

---

61. A "Bull", by the way, is a certain kind of papal document sealed with a big leaden seal. *Bulla* is the Latin word for the metal blank into which such a seal is pressed; hence the English word for the document itself.

62. During this time, he said, God was treating him "just as a schoolmaster treats a child." But to the end of his life he never stopped regretting the time he lost in his youth, when itinerant teachers were the only educators around; he was determined to make good education available to everybody. "The children of today become the adults of tomorrow," he wrote, "and their good education in life and doctrine will be beneficial to many others." He developed his own theory of Christian education and, by the time he died in 1556, he had opened thirty-three colleges around the globe and had approved six others, the world's first systematic educational organization on that scale. By 1710 there were more than six hundred Jesuit universities and nearly two hundred seminaries.

for a year, and if they still couldn't make it, they promised, they'd go to Rome and offer their services to the Pope, to make whatever use of them he wanted. While they waited, they were ordained; and after this point, Fr. Iñigo's visions came more steadily, refreshing him, encouraging him, and consoling him through the private tears that never left him.

Just outside of Rome a year later, Iñigo was stopped in his tracks by one of these visions. He said that he saw God the Father associating him with Christ; and he heard Christ speak the words, "*Ego vobis Romæ propitius ero*"—in Rome, I will be propitious to you. He was in the habit, like any creditable mystic, of keeping his apparitions entirely to himself, but in this case he made an offhand remark that's absolutely typical of him: "I don't know if we'll be crucified in Rome or not," Iñigo told his companions, "but Christ will be propitious."[63] They arrived in Rome at last and met with the warm approval of Paul III Farnese, who almost seemed to be expecting them. And, in 1541, Ignatius—now using the Latin form of his name—and his companions became the first members of the Society of Jesus.

St. Ignatius now had his hands full, working out the *Constitutions* for the new order,[64] but in that same year, 1541, St. Francisco Borgia, S.J., asked him to turn in a copy of his little handbook of spiritual exercises to the Holy Office. That way, they could get it approved and use it, anywhere at any time, to guide other people in spiritual growth as St. Ignatius had guided them.

THE GENESIS OF THE *SPIRITUAL EXERCISES*

The *Spiritual Exercises* began in the notes that St. Ignatius had begun jotting down back in the cave at Manresa, so many years before. In fact, they grew out of everything that he'd learned since the Battle of Pamplona. The *Golden Legend* of Bl. Jacobus da Voragine left its mark on it, as did Ignatius's own three-hundred-page notebook of his readings from the days of his recovery at Loyola, in which he neatly copied out the words of Christ (in red ink) and those of Our Lady (in blue) from all of the meditational books that he had read.

Having read these great lives and started to meditate on them, he saw the great struggle going on between good and evil, with his own soul as the prize. From these pious readings, he gained the realization that it was only when he finally decided to give

---

63. Not surprisingly, the prospect of asking the Vicar of Christ to confirm this kind of undertaking is so stressful for the founders of the great orders that they're almost always comforted by a vision. Poor little St. Francis of Assisi, on his way to the Vatican to deal not with the easygoing Paul III Farnese but with Innocent III dei Segni—Innocent the Great, Innocent the Terrible, the Supreme Pontiff at whose glance emperors quailed—saw an impossibly tall tree and was lifted up to grasp the top and easily bend it to the ground. He interpreted this, correctly, as a sign that the Holy See would condescend to hear him. And even then Innocent had to have a vision of a palm tree springing up from the ground before him, symbolizing the vigor of Francis's spirituality, before he'd listen. Countless grubby little penitents, in groups or as free agents, pestered the Pope in those days, as they still do. The fact that Innocent could see through all of their heresies and eccentricities and pick the orthodox, if surprising, Francis speaks as well for his perspicacity as for the creditability of his vision.

64. Even after all he'd been through, working out a new way of life for his Society was as hard for him as it would be for anybody else born to wealth and privilege. The phrase "fixed income" appears time and again in the surviving fragment of his spiritual diary.

himself generously to God that he opened himself to all of his extraordinary mystic experiences—his knowledge of the Trinity, of Christ and Mary, and of the Eucharist, and his illumination on the banks of the Cardoner. A detailed description of the workings of his own soul as he embraced this infused knowledge, he thought, would have some value in and of itself, if he could communicate it to other people and give them some method of prompting that same kind of openness to God's graces, the ordinary ones as well as the extraordinary.

The idea behind the exercises was a simple one, an idea already well established in the Church through books like the *Ejercitatorio de la vida espiritual* of García Jimenes de Cisneros. "Just as strolling, walking, and running are bodily exercises," St. Ignatius wrote, "so spiritual exercises are methods of preparing and disposing the soul to free itself of all inordinate attachments, and, after accomplishing this, of seeking and discovering the Divine Will regarding the disposition of one's life, thus ensuring the salvation of the soul." In other words, you can train yourself, as an athlete trains, to pray better; and through his immense trials and tribulations, St. Ignatius had learned better than anybody else just how disciplined that training had to be.

The Training and the Trainer

The exercises stimulate the best progress, St. Ignatius says, if the exercitant "withdraws from all friends and acquaintances, and from all earthly concerns; for example, by moving out of one's place of residence and taking a different house or room where one can live in the greatest possible solitude." This makes a person freer to use his natural faculties to seek what he desires and to order his emotions and affections.

And the book has a strict schedule. It's divided into "weeks", which can really be of any length of time, depending on the person's particular schedule. The first is devoted to contemplation of sin and its consequences; the second to the Kingdom of Christ; the third to the Passion; and the fourth to the risen and glorified Christ.

Of course, this sort of thing is what the contemplative orders are all about, and meditation on the life of Christ is the point of the Rosary and all other kinds of discursive prayer. St. Paul, of course, constantly exhorted his readers to remind themselves of Christ's sufferings, as a way of keeping on track and growing in strength to avoid sin. So did the Fathers of the Church. "Contemplate with awe the Lord being judged," St. Cyril of Jerusalem advised in the fourth century (*Catechesis* 13). "He allowed himself to be led about and carried by soldiers. Pilate sat in judgement, and he who sits at the right hand of the Father stood and was judged. The people whom he had freed from Egypt … kept shouting against him, 'Take him away! Take him away! Crucify him!' … Listen … see and touch."

Ignatius was probably most familiar with this technique through the *Life of Jesus* by Ludolph of Saxony. "If you want to draw fruit from these sayings and deeds of Christ," Ludolph advised, "put aside all other preoccupations; and then, with all the affection of your heart … make yourself present to what the Lord Jesus has said and done, … just as if you were actually there … You should meditate upon them as if they were taking place now, in the present".

But Ignatius focussed this imaginative immediacy as nobody had before. The book of the *Exercises* itself is made up of instructions, meditations, examinations of conscience, and warnings—psychologically and spiritually, these are dangerous waters for a beginner. Through these practices, a person can learn to use his understanding, his sensory impressions, and his imagination to purposefully move his will toward the decision to pursue Christian perfection. It's a way to trigger, to some controlled degree, the same spiritual crises that the great mystics earned through heroic penances and such physical sufferings as they were given to endure.

That's why, although a person can direct himself through the exercises, the book is really written for a director, not for the "exercitant". An experienced director isn't there to pressure exercitants or to impose his own psychology on them, but to simply "permit the Creator to deal directly with his creature". He's there to give points of departure for the exercitant's meditative prayers, and to help him understand what's going on in his soul. That's why the director is supposed to be skilled in the discernment of spirits; the exercises are psychological dynamite, and there's always the danger of exercitants slipping off into purely personal fantasies about the Faith or, having seen clearly the struggle between good and evil, being tempted to pick the evil.

And the *Exercises* really can't be used by itself; even while St. Ignatius was still alive, the Society of Jesus produced manuals or "Directories", some more than eight hundred pages long, to explain exactly what St. Ignatius meant in this little book. If St. Ignatius was a compelling talker (remember the Siege of Pamplona), frankly, he was not much of a writer. The language of the *Exercises*, like that of his seven thousand surviving letters, is truly singular.[65]

St. Ignatius was a Basque, and the Basque language is unlike any other language and baffling to the outsider—there's a joke in Spain that was probably already old when St. Ignatius was a boy, about how the Devil himself studied Basque for seven years and only learned three words. St. Ignatius's Basque must have crashed into his Castilian, somehow, and everything got mixed with his Latin and Italian; everything that he wrote is plain at best and usually downright cumbersome. Even his letters are so full of emendations, strikeouts, and idiosyncratic usages, as well as so many added, and completely unnecessary, subordinate clauses, that you can hardly untangle the sentences.[66] Fortunately, his translators and editors long ago made his books presentable. And the spiritual depths, and heights, that he ends up putting you through make reading them more than worthwhile.

65. Although, unlike Aquinas and some other saints we could name, he had beautiful handwriting. Good penmanship was a polite accomplishment among gentlemen of St. Ignatius's day, and the Loyolas were particular about their sons' polite accomplishments. The problem is that even though you can read the words, it's often hard to make head or tail out of them, or even figure out if they're Spanish or not.

66. One of the first Jesuits, St. Ignatius's nephew Antonio Araoz, wrote that he'd be interested to see how a man who had such difficulty writing prose would manage in poetry. But Iñigo, unlike the other

In fact, his little book, one of the most influential tracts ever produced, formed the spiritual basis of the Society of Jesus, and it went on to provoke an almost universal refreshment of the Church's spirituality. St. Teresa herself consulted members of the new Society frequently, and, although it isn't clear whether they took her specifically through the *Exercises*, they certainly used what they had learned through them to help her achieve her remarkable spiritual heights. It's not too much to say that this booklet turned European civilization to a new course, and it motivated two hundred years of the most glorious art, architecture, and music that the world has ever known.[67] It's still the basis for most retreats given to clerics and lay people, and it's still spiritually explosive.

The Measure of Disconsolation

St. Ignatius understood God as having something special planned for each and every soul and working actively in the world to call that person to that particular kind of service. So he designed his spiritual exercises to help a person answer that call by choosing a state of life—married, single, religious, whatever—amending the state of life he's chosen, or steering through some kind of turning point in his spiritual life. This means making a lot of big decisions, and it means tearing away from the lures of the world, the flesh, and the Devil. Which is even more reason for an experienced director.

The director can tell when a prayer is successful by what St. Ignatius calls "consolations" or "disconsolations", the movements of the soul that make the exercitant feel either peace or trouble, attraction or repulsion. If this doesn't happen, one way or the other, St. Ignatius recommends that the director look into the thing a little more closely and give that exercitant a little more guidance. Successful completion of the exercises—which, like any other exercises, can be done again and again throughout life—introduces you into a total spiritual experience, letting you achieve an interior dialogue with God. They help you perceive God's plan for you, leaving you free to embrace your destiny and participate in that divine plan.

If you're a beginner in prayer, just reading the *Exercises* leaves you winded, like a quick run after years of indolence. Even if you think of yourself as fairly well advanced in spiritual development—especially if you think of yourself that way—St. Ignatius's coaching shows you that you haven't even begun. But the program that he outlines will let you conquer that spiritual flabbiness and get you in shape for the lifelong race along that most difficult path of prayer. And his countryman, St. John of the Cross, outlined what you'll most likely see along the way.

---

hidalgos educated in the royal court, made only one stab at it, the long poem that he'd promised St. Peter. It was lost long before Antonio came on the scene. Or it may have been discarded.

67. The *Exercises* had a profound impact on artists like Gianlorenzo Bernini, the great genius of the Baroque who's responsible for the way St. Peter's looks today (as well as countless other churches, any number of palaces, and the best-known statue of St. Teresa of Avila). Bernini used the *Exercises* throughout his long life as a way to experience the intense emotions of the lives of Christ and the saints, so that he could represent these events movingly in marble, bronze, and paint.

six

the darkness

and the night

What did he say? "You made the darkness and it was night.
In it, all the wild beasts ... go forth ... roaring for prey ...
The Sun rises, ... and they go to lie down in their dens." ...
So, too, when a prayer, like a ray of the Sun, ...
comes forth from your mouth, ... all the savage passions
that destroy our reason slink away and flee to their own lairs,
if only our prayer is diligent,
if only it comes from a watchful soul and sober mind.

— St. John Chrysostom,
On the Incomprehensible Nature of God (386-387)

If St. Teresa of Avila shows the mystic's clarity of mind and hard-headed practicality, if St. Ignatius of Loyola testifies to the immensity of the gulf between worldly life and spiritual life and the immensity of the effort needed to leap it, the life of St. John of the Cross testifies to the power of the human spirit to triumph over all manner of opposition, misfortune, injustice, poverty, and over every kind of torment—economic, physical, and spiritual. He was born Juan de Yepes y Alvarez in the city of Fontiveros in 1542, twenty-seven years after St. Teresa and only about twenty miles northwest of Avila. And, like St. Teresa's, Juan's family were prosperous silk merchants originally from Toledo.

His father Gonzalo, on a business trip to the little town of Medina del Campo in 1529, had met a poor young silkweaver and married her, for some reason. His family disowned him instantly. He moved to her home town, learned to weave, had three sons, and died. His illness had lasted just long enough to deplete the family's resources completely, so his widow Catalina took her three little boys, including the newborn Juan, around to her husband's relatives for help. They threw her out, one and all.

Little Juan ended up back in Medina del Campo in a sort of an orphanage, a catechism school that fed, clothed, and basically educated destitute children. He also picked up a lot of practical knowledge through apprenticeships to local sculptors, painters, carpenters, and tailors,[68] but he must have distinguished himself academically, too, because he was given the post of acolyte at the nearby Augustinian convent. This was followed by a stint at the plague hospital, which allowed him to continue his education at the brand-new Jesuit college in town.

He got an amazing education there. With the Jesuits, and later at the University and the Carmelite college at Salamanca, Juan heard lectures from some of the greatest names in Renaissance humanism.[69] He learned Greek, Latin, philosophy, ethics, astronomy, music, and grammar (universal grammar, the kind that you can use for any language), as well as theology, of course. Just as before, he proved himself outstanding enough to win an appointment, this time as prefect of studies—while he was still a student himself. He knew the *Summa* of St. Thomas Aquinas inside and out (which is quite an accomplishment in itself), and he pretty much knew the Bible by heart. He was ordained in 1567, having become a professed Carmelite in 1564, under the name Fray (Brother) Juan de Santo Matías.

We don't know much about him, personally, except that he was short. This testimony comes from an unimpeachable source; when Juan was brought to her as a second priest for her convent at Valladolid, St. Teresa of Avila glanced up from the flow of her writing and said, "Good. Now we have a priest and a half."[70] By that time, though, Teresa and Juan were already great friends. They had met when he went back to Medina del Campo in September, 1567, to celebrate his first Mass in his home town, and Madre

68. For the rest of his life, he couldn't resist helping at any manual labor that came along, bricklaying, carpentry, gardening, whatever. And, like St. Teresa, he scrubbed and swept the monasteries he ran, and he took care of the altarcloths and flowers. Using his training with the painters, he was one of the few great mystics to draw one of his visions; a little pen-and-ink sketch that he gave to Ann Mary of Jesus, one of the sisters at the Incarnation, survives. It shows Christ crucified from a perspective unprecedented in contemporary art.

69. "Humanism" is a loaded word, nowadays, because it's taken to mean concentration on humans without regard for God. That is not correct: it means the study of the rhetorical traditions of the Greeks and Romans. In other words, humanism is the study of the way that the western human mind works, thinks, and uses language to define and express itself; a well-trained humanist is an intellectual athlete who can run marathons of thought with comparative ease. Humanists have no distinct philosophical tradition, and humanism can flourish in any western religious context; it's not too much to say that no westerner can call himself truly educated without a sound basis in the humanities properly understood. Certainly, every time humanism is encouraged, we have a new Renaissance.

70. In fact, she never stopped teasing him about it. "Little Seneca", she called him, or "holy little Friar John". Of course, diminutives like these are endearments in Castilian, not insults, but she even joked about the cell in which he was imprisoned for assisting her Reform. It was so small, she said, that even he couldn't turn around in it.

Teresa de Jesús happened to be there, too, establishing the second convent of her Reform. He was moved to confide to her his own secret desire to transfer to the Carthusian order, who adopted a deeper life of prayer; she told him that he could get all of that in the Carmelites, and she in turn confided to him her plans for reform. In 1568, he transferred to her reformed branch of the order and took the name Fray Juan de la Cruz, John of the Cross.

But that was only the beginning of the remarkable partnership between these two great visionaries. A little while later, Teresa had been sent back to her first convent, the Incarnation, which had fallen on hard times. Economic problems made them shut down the refectory, so it was every nun for herself. They were busy all day out looking for alms, or in the parlor entertaining friends who brought them food. Oddly enough, when Madre Teresa showed up there, in obedience, to take over, the nuns locked her out. They were afraid that she'd impose the Discalced Reform on them, but she managed somehow to talk her way in and get properly installed as Prioress.

Obviously, she needed exactly the right priest to serve as confessor, somebody wise, prudent, and above all holy, somebody who understood the discipline of the Reform but wouldn't impose it on nuns who had vowed to follow the Old Observance. Obviously, the only choice was Juan de la Cruz.

Their co-operation took them both to new spiritual heights. His guidance as her spiritual director brought her to many new breakthroughs, and her reform brought him all kinds of trials—inquests, humiliating punishments, and, in 1577, imprisonment from his adversaries in the Carmelites of the Old Observance—that he turned to good purpose as penances in preparation for his own mystic experiences.

It's interesting, in view of their personal relationship and the similarity of their subject matter, that St. John's view of the mystic life is really different from St. Teresa's, though. St. John walks through the night, spiritually speaking, while St. Teresa walks in the light; not that she didn't have truly heroic trials along the way, but she walks in the light. With Teresa, everything is as clear as possible, perfectly distinct in the sunshine of God's grace; that's why her highest mystic states of union with God are expressed in visions—things seen and understood with the senses of the body as well as with the senses of the soul. They end up at the same point, but St. John of the Cross views the soul's struggle to unite with God as a long, dark night. He jumps over most of the bright sensory experiences that St. Teresa describes and stands astride whole stormy landscapes of spiritual experiences.

And he stands alone, with consolation from neither God nor Man, which is really a measure of his simplicity as well as his magnanimity. "It is no great thing to despise human comfort when the comfort of God is present," Thomas à Kempis had reflected, "but it is a very great thing, and it is a right thing, for a man to be so strong in spirit that he may bear the lack of them both, and for the love of God … bear the desolation of spirit."

MAKING STRAIGHT THE PATH

The map of St. John's mysticism lies in the poems that he wrote while he was in prison. Their lyric quality has earned him a place as one of the major poets of classical Spain, but some of these delicate verses also form the framework of his longer prose mystic works, which are really commentaries on them. Their high-flown language makes it easier to comprehend the rocky terrain of his prose, prose that opens to view the dark and mountainous regions across which the spirit struggles under the tempestuous skies of unremittant trials.

His major prose works, the *Ascent of Mount Carmel* and the *Dark Night*, are evidently parts of one huge work, and it isn't—they aren't—really finished. The *Ascent* ends abruptly in the middle of a sentence. Some critics suspect that he finished the whole thing but deliberately destroyed some parts of it, thinking it more prudent to keep these mystic things of God hidden, which makes you think. But all of his literary output suffered a lot at the hands of his enemies. When he was imprisoned in 1577, all of his writings were seized and, evidently, destroyed, and after that he didn't have much time to write. Only for about three years, from 1582 until 1585, did he have a chance to put anything on paper. And even then he had to write with one eye on his ecclesiastical superiors and the other on the Holy Office. After that period, even his clandestine writings were suppressed by the Carmelites of the Old Observance, and a great deal of it was lost forever.

When you look at the writings that remain, the tragedy of this loss—amounting to more than half of everything that he wrote—is overwhelming. Those fragments that remain earned St. John the title of Doctor of the Church; and when Pius XI Ratti proclaimed him in that title, he noted that these books are rightly seen as a code and a guide for the faithful soul endeavoring to embrace a more perfect life.[71]

Like St. Teresa, he doesn't speculate on anything; he tells of his own experiences, nothing more. His plan of the devout life is so concrete, in fact, that he drew an actual diagram of it, a climber's guide to the mystical Mount Carmel. And he describes the way to the top with a rigorous logic worthy of any Scholastic. He poses very penetrating questions, and like Aquinas he derives answers that leave no other possibility.

He moves quickly past the childlike initial steps of progress, the gift of tears, and discursive prayer, on the assumption that a soul ought to pass this stage as soon as

---

71. St. John of the Cross draws heavily on the Bible, as do all of the Church's great mystics, starting with the experiences of the great Jewish mystics—David, Solomon, Jeremia, Job, and the other prophets—and St. Paul, and never advancing any concept not in complete harmony with the Gospels. Full citations for his biblical quotations are given in the standard English edition of his works (*The Collected Works of John of the Cross*, translated and edited by Kieran Kavanaugh, O.C.D., and Otilio Rodriguez, O.C.D., Washington, D.C., 1979). Before approaching the *Ascent of Mount Carmel* on your own, it may be helpful to have a look at another, briefer, ascetical tract, the *Morals* by St. Basil of Cæsarea (*c.* 329-379), written about 370. These are seventy-nine "rules" presented with Bible verses that together summarize some of the basic points of the Church's views on redemption, works, and the theological basis for asceticism. In fact, you can find St. Basil's ascetical works together in a single volume, *Saint Basil: Ascetical Works*, translated by Sr. M. Monica Wagner, C.S.C. (Washington, D.C., 1962).

possible, aided by the grace that God always extends to people of good will. Of course, this grace has to come before a person can get any farther along the path of Christian perfection, he notes, and he stands in agreement with St. Teresa that God can and does sometimes dispense with this first stage altogether, bringing the soul past meditative prayer fairly quickly.

He wants to talk about the final arrival at the summit of that mystical Mount Carmel, union with God. This mystic union isn't just the normal presence of God in every soul, the indwelling by which the Creator conserves the being of the creature. Without that union, he reminds us, every creature would cease to exist, but he's talking about a different kind of union, here, the supernatural "union of likeness", the transforming union in which God's will and the soul's will are in absolute uniformity. It's the mystic gift that marks the soul's most intimate union with God (Mt 22:4), and that means changes. "When the soul completely rids itself of what is repugnant and unconformed to the divine will," he explains, "it rests transformed in God through love."

THE TRANSFORMING UNION: EXCHANGING HEARTS IN MYSTIC MARRIAGE

Mystics sometimes use any of several terms for the *transforming union*—*mystic marriage* and *exchange of hearts*, most often—or they use certain terms allegorically. But the transforming union is a fairly definite phenomenon. Among mystic phenomena it has the distinction of being virtually permanent, lasting even in daily occupations, rather than coming and going as ecstasy and the other mystic states do.

The Ursuline nun Ven. Mary of the Incarnation said that "in this state, one can talk on any subject, one can read, write, work, and do what one wills and yet this fundamental occupation always remains, and the soul does not cease being united to God, whose greatness, even, does not distract it." Her son (she was widowed at the age of twenty-two and joined the Ursulines at Tours eleven years later) said that her Jesuit spiritual directors thought it seemed that she had two souls, one of which was united with God as constantly as if she had nothing else to do but contemplate him, while the other was as busy with her conventual duties, her embroidery, and her painting as if she were entirely occupied with them. Not that she had two souls, which is impossible, but that she seemed divided from her own soul, as St. Teresa said of her own experience.

Now, the mystics best known for the mystic marriage are women, St. Catherine of Alexandria (d. 305) and St. Teresa of Avila; but you have to step back from their symbolic language and get a broader view of the phenomenon, theologically. The term "mystic marriage" is more than just symbolic, but then again it's not precisely parallel to the earthly sacrament of Matrimony, either. It's immensely difficult to express, probably beyond human language altogether; but the essential property of Christian Matrimony that all of the mystics seem to be talking about is the union of it: two beings becoming one (Gn 2:21-24). That's why male mystics can talk about their own soul's union with "her" bridegroom, Christ, too, as St. John of the Cross did. The tendency for Romance languages to have feminine words for the soul—*anima, alma, âme,* and so on—might encourage this metaphor for these saints, but using the term "marriage" also conveys a sense of the change of state of life that the soul undergoes, which is also like the change brought about by the sacrament of Matrimony: it's permanent.

The transforming union might also include a permanent intellectual vision of God or of some divine attribute, although St. Teresa, St. John of the Cross, and most other mystic theologians don't include it as a necessary part of the experience. But, then, no mystic experience is necessary, and the concomitant, you might even say the ornamental, phenomena of the mystic marriage have an interest all their own.

The Rings of Mystic Marriage

One of the marks of an earthly marriage is the ring, and occasionally a mystic bears a similar token of betrothal.[72] These aren't earthly rings, and they're not exactly heavenly rings, either. Some of them form out of flesh, like the nails in some stigmatics. The ring on the finger of Célestine Fenouil (b. 1849) of Manosque in France, studied by a Dr. Auvergne and written up by him in the *Annales de Dermatologie* in 1874, was a vivid red line around her finger with little crosses spaced evenly around it, and a heart pierced by three swords set in the top of it like a jewel. It wasn't scratched into her skin, and it wasn't scar tissue or blood clots, but thickened skin; and like other mystic wedding rings it changed appearance depending on who saw it and when.

Célestine's ring appeared redder than usual on Sundays or even shone brightly. The one on the finger of St. Veronica Giuliani, which was also made somehow from her living flesh, was either what she called her Ring of Love, with a white or yellow stone as big as a bean, or her Ring of the Cross—warning her of approaching suffering—with a red stone as big as a pea, either of which was seen periodically by witnesses but disappeared after a while. The ring on the previously normal hand of Marie-Julie Jahenny formed before fourteen witnesses on Friday, February 20, 1874, during one of her stigmatic ecstasies. But one of the best-documented mystic rings is that of St. Catherine dei Ricci (1522-1590), which appeared when she was in her convent in Prato.

She just came to herself after an ecstasy and found a ring on her finger, a ring of gold with a large, brilliant stone in it. She was surprised to see it, and as a nun she didn't want to wear it, but she couldn't get it off. So she kept hiding her hand. She was astonished to find out that other people didn't see it, but that sometimes happens with mystic wedding rings—the one on the finger of Ven. Joan Mary della Croce (1603-1673) could be felt but not seen by anyone taking her hand. But during the depositions for St. Catherine's canonization process some more intriguing testimony came out as the other nuns of the convent testified to what they had normally seen on her hand.[73]

72. For rings as a symbol of acceptance and personal union, see Gn 41:39-42; Es 3:8-10; Lk 15:20-22; references to "seals" in the Bible are often to be understood as indicating rings, too, the usual form for personal seals in antiquity.

73. The details, taken directly from the files of her beatification process, are given in Herbert Thurston, S.J., *The Physical Phenomena of Mysticism* (Chicago, 1952).

One of her sisters in religion said that she had noticed that the flesh on the finger was raised up like a ring, and another said that it was as if a coral ring, hard and red, had somehow been put under the flesh. Sr. Dorothea Vecchi said that she only saw a plain gold ring with a fleshy protrusion where the stone would be. Sr. Serafina Baronici said that it looked like a gold ring with a white stone so brilliant that you could see yourself in it. Sr. Angela Arrighetti said that it dazzled her, once, when Sr. Catherine raised her hands in prayer in the oratory, and Donna Dianora de Salis, a laywoman visiting the convent, reported seeing the dazzling ring two years before the saint died.

And sometimes these mystic rings last beyond death. The one on the finger of St. Catherine of Siena (1347-1380), of gold with four pearls and a diamond of unearthly beauty, was visible only to herself during her lifetime, but that finger was kept as a separate relic. Even today, some innocent visitors to the reliquary ask why the finger is wearing such a splendid golden ring, with four pearls and a diamond.

Like most physical phenomena of mysticism, the symbolic rings of mystic marriage attract a lot of attention. But St. John would really prefer that you look past the physical effects of the transforming union and try to see its essential effect: it transforms the soul's faculties so that they work in a different way (hence the name). This isn't easily described, much less explained, but evidently the soul knows that in the supernatural acts of her spiritual faculties—her will, intellect, and memory—she participates in the life of God, or in those of God's acts that are similar to her own. It's sometimes conveyed in terms of an iron heated in a fire until it's red hot; the iron takes on some of the character of the fire, not losing its own nature but being transformed to give off some of the heat and light that are integral characteristics of the fire. But even that image doesn't quite capture all of what the great mystics mean by the term, which is what you'd expect in discussions of such a high mystic state. "Otherwise," said one moral theologian, "it would no longer be a mystery, but merely a difficult question."

Illumination and Happiness

To shed a little more light on that mystery, St. John uses the metaphor of a window. A ray of sunlight falling on a dirty window can't light up the window and transform it with its own light. But if the dirt and stains are washed away from the window, if the glass is polished, then the sunlight falling on the totally clean and pure glass makes it seem as if the window and the sunlight are one and the same. Of course, the window by nature isn't a sunbeam, but you can still say that the window is the ray of light by participation, if not by nature.

In the same way, a soul that has cleansed itself of all worldly appetites is so open to the flooding light of God's purity (1Cr 2:14) that, if God decides to grant this kind of supernatural gift, the soul enters into intimate union with God and appears to be one with God and to possess everything that God possesses. Its nature has to remain distinct from God's as the window is from sunlight or as the creature is from the Creator, but still the soul participates to some degree or another in this supernatural union.

And this is like the way the saints in Heaven see God, he says: some see him more, and some see him less, because the degree of union depends entirely on how much God wants to give. But all of the saints see him, and all of them are happy in this *beatific vision* according to their capacity.[74] In this earthly life, St. John says, there are those happy souls who have reached this state of perfection and enjoy this blissful peace, and, again, it's enjoyed by each according to his own degree.

But a person who doesn't reach purity to the utmost of his ability never enjoys true peace and satisfaction. Just as a man who digs for mythical buried treasure wears himself out in pursuit of an empty dream, he says, the person who chases after the wind of worldly happiness finds only fatigue. Even if he satisfies those appetites for a time, he's only digging cisterns that leak: he is still faint with thirst, and his soul is empty, as Isaia said (Is 57:20).

And again, the whole point of stepping on to the steep mystic path of asceticism is the attainment of that supreme happiness, full union with God—and again, the language of mysticism resonates to that idea of joy, as *blessed, beatus, beato,* all mean *happy.* But it may seem paradoxical that you begin to achieve this happiness by voluntarily embracing pain, the pain of penance.

The Struggle for Conversion and Cleanliness

The gift of tears that often marks the first moment of God's extraordinary outreach to the ascetic soul is only the beginning. That first touch of the divine urges the soul to exert every possible effort to reach back to God, to answer that call voluntarily and with every bit of strength of heart and will: to present to God a pure soul, one as clean and polished as you can possibly make it.

Fray Juan, like all of the other great mystics, like Christ himself, says that the way to cleanse your soul is to detach yourself from the things of this world. You do this by studying the practice of prayer, as he and St. Teresa outlined, but also by voluntarily giving up things that aren't really necessary—by fasting and abstinence. Anna-Maria Taigi, cleansing her soul to achieve a clearer view of God, had given up all the pleasures of the world, "even the most innocent," Domenico Taigi mentioned during her beatification process in 1852, "but I sometimes said to her, Marianna, let's go to such and such a place, and she met my wishes with a most charming readiness, as, for example, when I wanted to go to see the puppet show. But eventually I noticed that she went in obedience rather than for the pleasure of the thing, and that for her it was a penance. I left her in peace," he said, which is exactly the course of action usually advised for those closest to dedicated ascetics.

74. The detachment from this world so arduously sought by the great ascetics reflects the situation in Heaven, too, because the overwhelming love of God that souls there experience subsumes all other affections. Which is why the Church entertains only by toleration the surprisingly frequent questions about whether people will be able to take their dogs or their cats into Heaven, or statements that if they can't take their pets with them they don't want to go themselves. That, and the fact that, unlike humans, animals—creatures into whom God didn't breathe an immortal soul—die thoroughly when their bodies die, anyway (*cf.* Gn 1:20-25, 2:7).

Those whom God draws up along the mystic path can, under the guidance of a qualified spiritual director, take on additional penances, not just omitting things that give pleasure but doing things that actually hurt (1Cr 9:27). But even the minor suffering caused by the willful moderation of permissible pleasures, the mystics say, has immense value in detaching a person from this world, converting the heart to a focus on God, and even in making reparation for sin.

St. John devoted the whole text of the *Ascent of Mount Carmel* to the soul's struggle to purge itself in preparation for meeting its maker, during this life or after it. It all falls under the heading of ascetic theology. In fact, the necessary *active* purgation of the soul is the whole point of ascetic theology. This outreach to God that the soul can make by its own efforts takes immense willpower, and it isn't easy. Think how hard it is to stay on a diet, or to break a habit for tobacco or coffee; and multiply that to include literally everything in the world. But "the sufferings of the present time are not worthy to be compared with the glory to come that will be revealed in us", as St. Paul (Rm 8:18; 2Cr 4:16-18) and the Church's other mystics avow. "Pay attention to the saying, 'Blessed are the pure of heart, for they shall see God,'" St. Augustine reminded his congregation back in 393. "Whatever we do, whatever good deeds we perform, whatever we strive to accomplish, ... we shall no longer seek any of those things after we have attained to the vision of God. ... Cleanse the medium through which he may be seen" (*Sermon 53, On The Beatitudes*; Cl 3:1-10).

Active purification is integral to the Church's way of life. It's the idea behind the sackcloth and ashes of the Old Testament, and it's the basic concept behind Christ's admonitions about selling all that you have, so that it will be easier for you to get into Heaven than it is for a camel to pass through the eye of a needle. Since Apostolic times, the Church has commanded elementary and minimal ascetic practices, and she sets apart certain seasons for exactly that purpose. Lent, for example, is an annual forty-day time of special fasts and abstinence enjoined on all the Faithful before Good Friday and Easter. Advent, the season before Christmas, is another regular time of preparation, although it has a less severe penitential character than the time before Passiontide. (The exact rules about fasting and abstinence during those seasons can and do change from time to time, because they're only disciplinary, not matters of Faith and Morals.) During these times, or really during the whole year, people are encouraged to make other voluntary sacrifices of natural appetites—that is, not just the taste for food and drink, but the taste for anything of this world, anything that God created, any creature.

Ascetic exercises are the basis of monasticism, too. The great orders of monks and nuns all got their start in the desire to retire from the world and design a way of life that allowed the fullest possible voluntary purification of the soul. In fact, the word "ascetic" itself comes from a Greek word meaning a hermit or a monk, and that Greek word, ἀσκητής, comes in turn from the word for exercise. A monk or a nun is literally an exercitant, someone who undertakes a life of spiritual exercises to purify the soul and draw as close to God as possible in this life. Which is why mystic phenomena are so concentrated in monks and nuns.

But regardless of your station in life, these exercises help you control desires for illicit pleasures by getting you to the point of being able to take the innocent ones or leave them. They're also ways of putting things in their proper perspectives and seeing them at their relative values: a person who has seen, or can otherwise appreciate, the infinite beauty of God, Fray Juan says, sees that all the beauty of creatures compared with it is supreme ugliness; all the grace and elegance of creatures, compared with God's grace, is utter coarseness and crudity.

The Martyrdom of Conversion

All of the credit-worthy mystics revel in the glories of nature as giving glory to the Creator, but the changed viewpoint to which active purgation turns a soul is why so many of them report a real disgust for things in this world that we take as normal. St. Bernadette, for instance, was surprised to find herself revolted at the sight of her little sister's leg, as if the flesh of a child were somehow bestial, in comparison with the beauty she'd seen; once you have seen the Lady, she sighed, you never have any more liking for this Earth. That's why St. Ignatius said that after he saw Mary and Jesus he never gave the slightest consent to sins of the flesh.[75]

Even ordinary human conversation was a real hardship for St. Teresa, as it was for St. John of the Cross; they found it hard to eat or sleep, too, having seen what they'd seen. "Since the soul sees it is bound in such a way that it cannot enjoy God as it would like," she said, "a great abhorrence for the body comes over it. The body seems like a thick wall impeding the enjoyment of what the soul, in its opinion, knows it possesses within itself at that time without the hindrance of its body. Then it sees the great evil that came upon us through the sin of Adam when this freedom was lost." From this standpoint, it's fairly easy to "mortify" your sensory desires—from the Latin *mors*, death, literally killing an appetite.

It's kind of like martyrdom. We're impressed when we see the great piles of martyrs' gnawed bones in Rome or hear the grisly stories of how the world would rise up in opposition to Christians in fierce and bloody ways; but the world still rises up in opposition to Christians, and in little, gentle ways, too, and in some ways that are downright attractive. Mortification is a way of standing up to the world and its temptations, cheerfully—voluntarily—suffering a thousand little deaths every day before the big, final one. Killing the appetites is a way of preferring at least symbolically to die a little rather than offending God a little.

Some of the great ascetics are on record as having so thoroughly killed their

---

75. St. Christina the Astonishing (d. 1224) went farther than any other saint to avoid the intolerable smell of sinful human flesh, even that of people physically clean. She climbed trees and towers, she crawled into ovens (emerging unsinged), and she jumped into rivers. She even levitated out of her coffin to get away from it. Anna-Maria Taigi had a similarly unfortunate olfactory sensation: the stench of sin in the world was a constant added torment to her.

appetites that they didn't even taste anything any more. When somebody accidentally put a flagon of oil in front of St. Bernard (1090-1153), for example, he drank it as if it were water and didn't notice until somebody asked him why he had oil all over his lips. (He must have known there was something a little odd about it, though. He said that he usually recognized water "because when I drink it, it cools my mouth and throat.")

But Fray Juan points out that you don't have to kill every desire. There are voluntary and involuntary appetites, he says, and the involuntary ones "do not so hinder a man as to prevent him from attaining divine union."[76] And he doesn't say that you have to mortify every voluntary appetite, either, just those that are in some way "inordinate". The only point is that, to walk that path to union with God, you have to be in control, to put aside anything in your life that isn't ordered in some way to honor and glorify God, no matter how small it may be: it doesn't matter whether a bird is tied down by a cord or by a thread, he says; it still can't take off (see 2Pt 2:18-20, for example).

The touchstone for the mortification of the appetites is Christ himself, because he lived only to do the will of God. "Have an habitual desire to imitate Christ in all your deeds," Fray Juan says.

> For example, if you are offered the satisfaction of hearing things that
> have no relation to the service and glory of God, do not desire the plea-
> sure or the hearing of these things. When you have the opportunity for
> the gratification of looking at objects that will not help you come any
> closer to God, do not desire that gratification or sight. And if in speak-
> ing there is a similar opportunity, act in the same way. And so on with all
> the senses insofar as you can duly avoid the pleasure. If you cannot
> escape the experience of this satisfaction, it will be sufficient to have no
> desire for it.

Or, as the Psalmist said, "If riches abound, set not your heart upon them" (Ps 61:11).

And because it frees the soul from the familiar material world and takes it out of the day-to-day context of the senses, Fray Juan calls the process of purgation the long, dark night of the soul. "Just as night is nothing but the privation of light, and, conse-quently of all objects visible by means of the light," he explains, "the mortification of the appetites can be called a night for the soul." A man by means of his appetites feeds on

76. Fray Juan wrote his book for nuns; remember that virtually all languages refer to a soul, whether a man's or a woman's, as feminine, just as God is referred to as masculine in Judeo-Christian writing, although God is understood as above gender. The feminine is used for attributes of God, institutions (like the Church), and other abstracts. In the Old Testament, for example, the Divine Wisdom is per-sonified as "she", although everyone has always known that this Wisdom is identical with Jesus Christ, true God and true Man (Pr 8:22; Ws 9:18; 1Cr 1:24). Some languages have a separate neuter case to dis-tinguish subjects of indefinite gender or indefinite human persons—anybody or somebody. But in oth-ers, including English, the neuter happens to have the same forms as the masculine. Throughout this book, neuter references are in the neuter: a venerable rule in educated English that, if anything, gives spe-cial distinction to the feminine. To interpret these ancient and basic conventions of civilized discourse as relating to the genital or hormonal configuration of a fleshly body is ill informed, at best, and at worst sees nothing beyond the animal part of humanity.

worldly things that gratify his senses, he says, and, when these appetites are extinguished, he no longer feeds on the pleasures of these things but lives in a void and darkness.

The Great Silence of God

Abstaining from innocent pleasures for God's sake is uncomfortable, and the optional physical austerities and penances beyond those regularly prescribed by the Church—taken on only under the advice of a qualified spiritual director—can cause real suffering. There's also the pain of being misunderstood, or written off as a case of depression, but this suffering is different, not a psychological disorder but a spiritual condition.

Fray Juan warns that a person in the long, dark night will almost certainly encounter people like Job's comforters (Jb 4:8-11) who will proclaim that all of this is due to melancholia, or depression, or temperament. Such talk, he says, only doubles the trial of the poor soul. But the real pain of the ascetic life is that God will usually remain silent during this process of active purgation. This is what gives disconsolation to the hard, dry work that St. Teresa described, hauling her empty bucket to her barren garden year after year.

This is the desolation that Julian of Norwich described, too: sometimes a man is left to himself, she says, for the profit of his soul, although his sin is not always the cause. She recalled that when this happened to her, she hadn't committed any sin that would merit God's withdrawal from her that way. But she knew, too, that nobody deserves the spiritual joys that she'd had, either, and that God gives both consolations and disconsolations out of the same overarching love. "Therefore," she says, "it is not God's will that when we feel pain we should pursue it in sorrow and mourning for it, but that suddenly we should pass it over, and preserve ourselves in the endless delight that is God."

The Lord loves a cheerful giver, in other words (2Cr 9:7). Or, as Fray Juan put it, "The Christian should keep in mind that the value of his good works, fasts, alms, penances, etc., is not based upon their quantity and quality so much as upon the love of God practiced in them, and that consequently they are deeper in quality the purer and more entire the love of God is by which they are performed".77

A Love Beyond the Human Heart

Maybe it's not noticed so much as it might be, but most of the Old Testament, and all of the New, are about love—about the love of God, about charity. In fact, because Christian morals are based on the relationship of the individual person to God, and because the love of God is the basis of that relationship, the history of Christian morality is really the history of charity and its workings among us. Wherever you start studying moral theology, you come back quickly to one or another facet of charity, the virtue that St. Paul simply calls love.

77. Ja 2:20; Mt 16:25; Lk 9:24; Jn 22:25.

We all know the experience of human love, how eagerly we'll do anything to draw closer to the loved one, how readily we'll suffer any inconvenience or discomfort for his sake. Everybody who has ever loved another person knows how you're happy only when you're together, how you spend your hours apart thinking about how happy you'll be when you're together again. How clearly the image of your lover persists, how you remember every detail of how he looked, of how he sounded, and even what he smelled like the last time you saw him. How any indifferent thing that you see, a car like his, maybe, or a box of his favorite crackers, sets you off into a reverie so that you drive past your destination or wander around the grocery store until past lunchtime.

The great ascetics love God that way. And the infinite superiority of their loved one to any earthly lover means that their love is infinitely more intense. What's more, God himself responds to their love, pulling them away from things of this Earth and to himself. The mystics lose themselves in this love, and the loss of connection to this world is far stronger than the absent-mindedness of a sweetheart's daydream; it overwhelms all possible distractions caused by any created thing. When the mind first begins its charitable union to God, Fray Juan writes, a person will forget to eat or drink, or fail to remember whether or not he performed some task, or whether he saw a particular object or said something. He himself used to rap his knuckles against the wall, when he was in company, to keep from slipping away from the conversation and into a reverie about God. One Trinity Sunday, when he and St. Teresa were talking after Mass, standing, presumably, too far from the walls, both of them were seized by the love of God and levitated. "You can't talk about God to Fray Juan de la Cruz," she fussed, "because he goes into an ecstasy at once and makes other people do the same."[78]

In this light, it's important to remember that, although they may be detached, although they may have seen heavenly beauties that make earthly beauties seem rather more bestial than they do to the rest of us, the great ascetics still appreciate this world. All of them, all of the hundreds of detached souls recorded in the history of the Church, love the beauty of creation—but only because it reminds them of the beauty of the Creator. They are forever falling into reveries at the sight of a sunset, or a landscape, or a flower or bird—St. John Vianney used to burst into tears when the songs of birds reminded him that they were doing what God made them to do while humans, created to love God, weren't (Is 43:20-22). Brother Lawrence of the Resurrection reports that

---

78. Lots of saints have to put up with this kind of distraction. St. Catherine dei Ricci, for one, was so rapturously drawn to God when she entered the convent at age thirteen that she went around as if she were half asleep, inept at choir, manual labor, and even recreation. It was years before her director figured her out; until then, he thought she was just an idiot. His brother friars nicknamed St. Joseph of Cupertino *boccaperta*, open-mouth, because he gaped as if thunderstruck when in his frequent, and unrecognized, ecstasies. Even vocal prayer triggers ecstasy in most mystics; St. Philip Neri had to have a companion alternate lines with him so that he could get through the Office without falling into ecstasy, and St. Ignatius himself was excused from even trying, after a while, because it was taking him all day. The lay Carmelite Bl. Mary of the Incarnation sometimes played her spinet to distract herself and get through the requisite prayers, but she usually fell into ecstasy before she got through a Hail Mary. She was so liable to ecstasy, in fact, that her confessors couldn't give her the usual penances to say.

he was converted at the age of eighteen by the sight of a tree in winter. He'd seen count-less barren trees before, as we all have, but this one touched him with the knowledge that the leaves would return, and flowers and fruit; the sight so impressed him with the prov-idence and power of God that, he declared, it detached him completely from this world and filled him with a great love of God that never diminished or left him, the rest of his life. In short, the glories of nature make the great mystics think of the glory of God and the majesty of his handiwork, which is perfectly in line with charity, loving all things because you love the God who made them.

Still less does this detachment mean that the great ascetics push other people aside. "To offer yourself to God," St. Thérèse of Lisieux explained, "doesn't mean that you lose anything at all of his natural tenderness. It's just the opposite, for this tender-ness deepens as it becomes purified by centering itself on divine things." The mystics' overwhelming love of God makes them all the more eager for the spiritual and moral growth of their loved ones, and it makes their prayers for them all the more urgent. "Make haste to come to me shortly," St. Paul wrote time and again to Timothy and Titus; make every effort, he urged, asking them to give his greetings to other people whom he missed. St. Teresa of Avila wrote to the prioress of the convent to which she had assigned St. John of the Cross as confessor, "You would not believe how lonely his absence makes me feel." And Fray Juan himself was known for presenting people to his brother with the words, "May I introduce you to my brother Francisco, who is the trea-sure I most value in the world." St. Catherine of Siena, mystically enabled to hold the baby Jesus, took advantage of the opportunity to whisper into his tiny ear the names of all those dearest to her.

Naturally, the torrential love of the great mystics flows out to all mankind. St. Francis of Assisi himself, moved with the love of God, embraced and kissed the leper; St. Elizabeth, Queen of Hungary, cuddled filthy beggars and tended them with her own hands, cutting up her royal linen to make clothes, and shrouds, for them. St. Martin of Tours is still best remembered for having split his cloak of office with a nameless beg-gar that winter's day at Amiens.[79] All of them lived to heroic degree Christ's admoni-tion to love one another, remembering that whatever they do for the least of us, they do for him. So it's not that the great mystics reject anybody or hate anybody in the world. It's just that they all love someone in the next world even more.

Because, simply, it is love alone that can reach God in this life, as the anony-mous *Cloud of Unknowing* (c. 1380) sums it up.

The Discipline of Divine Love

The intensity of the love that the great ascetics feel for God is why they so willingly embrace such intense levels of discipline and penance. "A genuine spirit seeks the dis-tasteful in God rather than the delectable," Fray Juan wrote, and it "leans more toward suffering than toward consolation, more toward going without everything for God

---

79. He later saw Christ in a vision wearing that half-cloak, by the way, which makes you think about Gn 18 and Hb 13:2, not to mention Mt 25:31-46.

rather than toward possession." They're happy to forego even their own wills, for the love of God, heroically living the discipline of love.

As in ordinary human relations, the discipline of love works because the discipline resides within you, and it comes out of the love. So it's a healthy discipline, not a cowering fear of cruel and arbitrary punishment. It lets you be yourself, and more than that it lets you grow into a better self—that kind of love insists, almost, that you grow into a better self. It lets you grow into the love, and it lets the love broaden and deepen.

Unlike those who focus their love on another human being, though, the great ascetics never expect any reward for their sacrifices, other than the knowledge that they've done everything humanly possible—or, rather, heroically possible—to make themselves fit for presentation to their God. And so, struggling to cast off any tiny impurity, they push onward, reaching out in love to a God who may remain silent through years of austerities and penance.

But no matter how much a person does through his own efforts, Fray Juan says, he cannot actively purify himself enough to be disposed in the least for the divine union of the perfection of love (as in Jb 22:2-3). Sometimes, though, God reaches out to finish the work of purification, drawing the soul across the line that separates the ascetic theology of the *Ascent* from the mystic theology that Fray Juan expounds in the *Dark Night*.

THE PULL TO PASSIVE PURGATION

At that point, "behold: the fiery Sun appears," Aurelius Prudentius Clemens wrote in his *Morning Hymn* (*c.* 400). "Disgust and shame now fill Man's heart; for in the splendor of the day no man can persevere in sin." This is the transition from active purgation to *passive purgation*, the mystic gift in which God takes over and does all of the work or purification. It can come after a life of the most rigorous penance for someone like St. John of the Cross, or it may happen out of the blue during a normally pious childhood for someone like St. Bernadette. However it comes, it's always a matter of *gratia gratis data*, extraordinary grace freely given.

Maybe the earthly parallel of the telephone is the best way to grasp the way this call from God works. If you call somebody, you can let the phone ring as long as you want to, but unless the other party wants to answer, you're not going to make contact; and even if you pray as hard as you can in thought, word, and deed, taking on all kinds of ascetic practices, God doesn't have to answer at any given moment or in any certain way, with any mystic phenomena. Looking at it from this side, humans can get the call from God, too, and refuse to answer. Most of the great mystics report that they resisted picking up that receiver for as long as they could possibly hold out, because, in humility, they didn't want any special consideration. God couldn't possibly be calling me, they thought.

But in the end they couldn't resist, because humility nourishes the other virtues, including those three theological virtues—not just charity, but faith and hope as well—and when God floods a soul with these infused virtues, that soul wants nothing other than the closest possible union with the divine. Mystic phenomena like apparitions, locutions, and levitation can happen at this point, because they're by nature *concomitant phenomena*, attendant events that may accompany this level of spiritual activity. But the important thing is that nobody at that level wants them.

Choosing Consolation or Love, Effect or Cause

After all, "He who is greedy brings ruin on his own house, but he who despises gifts shall live" (Pr 15:27). Of course, Moses asked to see God, but he didn't know what he was saying—he was blazing a new trail in terms of intimacy with God. St. Thérèse of Lisieux, one of the most influential of the Church's mystics, reported only one apparition (and that was a small one, and doubtful), and never had any very spectacular mystic gifts, but she never wanted any—"to ecstasy," she said, "I prefer the monotony of sacrifice."[80] St. John of the Cross attributed the taste for these experiences to a "spiritual sweet tooth", a matter of unwholesome greed. It makes a person an enemy of Christ, he said.

People who take on all kinds of penances and spiritual exercises in the hope of seeing or hearing from the divine, or people who'd like to claim that they've seen an angel or a saint, Fray Juan tells us, are pretty much ensuring that they never will. They're looking for something that makes them special, something to draw attention to themselves, which is from pride, a vice directly contrary to the virtue of charity that governs the mystic's relationship with God. Maybe they're after the delights without paying the price—"no one would be unwilling to stand on Mt. Tabor and see Christ transfigured," St. Philip Neri wrote, "but how few are willing to go up to Jerusalem and accompany him to Mt. Calvary." Or maybe they think that God owes it to them, which puts a stop to even the possibility, not to mention further personal growth. "I consider it certain," St. Teresa said, "that spiritual persons who think that they deserve these delights of spirit for the many years that they have practiced prayer will not ascend to the summit of the spiritual life," which is in line with Mt 12:39 and 23:12, as well as Cn 2:7, 3:5, and 8:4.

That's because mystic phenomena aren't the point. The point of ascetic practices or simple prayer is salvation, ultimate reunion with God, and phenomena like levitation, visions, and locutions aren't essentially connected with salvation. They're called "concomitant" phenomena (from the Latin *concomitare*, to accompany, to go with) because they're just secondary effects that sometimes accompany real spiritual activity. Most people who end up in Heaven, evidently, get there without any of this, and creditable mystics, one and all, couldn't care less about seeing or hearing here below. As St. Bernard put it, a soul striving toward union "will be far from content that her Bridegroom should manifest himself to her in the common manner, that is, by things that are made, or even in the manner peculiar to a few, namely, dreams and visions."

More than that, the kind of pride that asks for mystic experiences opens a person up to the deceptions of the Devil, who can perfectly well cause any and all kinds of false mystic gifts. Now, because the ordinary sacramental life of the Church is sufficient

80. Which is kind of ironic, because in the ninety-odd years since her death she herself has appeared in more creditable apparitions than any other saint except Mary, St. Francis, and her namesake St. Teresa of Avila, all of whom had long head starts.

to attain ultimate union with God—salvation after death—and because reveling in the spiritual delights of extraordinary phenomena is harmful to a soul, St. John of the Cross laid it down as an absolute rule that visions and locutions must always be rejected.

Don't even stop and think about it, he says: reject them instantly. Those from the Devil only cause dryness, agitation, vanity, or presumption, he says, whether the recipient wants them or not, so rejecting them loses you nothing. But even with those that may come from God, "this rejection is no affront to him, neither will one upon voluntarily dismissing them cease to receive the fruit God wishes to produce through these communications."[81]

The reason, he says, is that if the vision or the feeling of the senses comes from God, it will do its work in the soul at the moment it's perceived. There's no need to deliberate about wanting it or not wanting it. Because God causes these phenomena without any effort or ability on the part of the recipient, he says, God also works his will in the receiving soul passively. Just as fire brought into contact with the flesh will burn the flesh whether you want it to or not, so will these good visions and *sensible* communications—those apparent to the senses—produce their effects in the soul, whether you want them to or not. And, like fire held too close, they're not really all that delightful.

The Pain of the Heavenly Pull

Extraordinary mystic gifts, like the gift of tears, may leave a person calm and happy, but they put people through unspeakable torments of the spirit first. Well, the shepherds at the Nativity feared with a great fear when the angel of the Lord came upon them, and nobody enjoys an impulse. Nobody.

In fact, every credit-worthy visionary on record has said explicitly that he didn't like any of these mystic experiences. A few, like Julian of Norwich, have been beguiled by the idea of their ineffable pleasure at first but very quickly learned better: if I had known what the pain of it was, she said later, I never would have asked for it.[82] The children of Fátima were more curious than frightened at these graces freely given, but even they had to agree to suffer the trials that God would send them. They did so willingly, but like Julian they probably didn't know what they were in for, either.

"I was left very frightened and disturbed," said St. Teresa of Avila of her first vision of Christ, "and didn't want to see that person any more." Like St. Ignatius, she says that she "did nothing but weep." Even after several years of apparitions and locutions, she said, "my hair stood on end, for the voice frightened me." The great honor implied by such direct contact, she said, "is often directly contrary to my desire." She

---

81. "Be assured," St. Margaret Mary said Christ told her, "that I am not by any means offended by all these struggles and the opposition that you make toward me through obedience ... but I will teach you that I am the Master."

82. St. Catherine Labouré said that hearing another nun talk about Mary "gave me so great a desire to see her that I went to bed that night with the thought that I would see my good Mother that very night— it was a desire that I had long cherished." But her other depositions and her life itself show that she wanted this only to bring herself closer to God, not so that she could brag about it or even enjoy it privately.

fought her apparitions and locutions for two solid years, begging God with all her might (and she was mighty) to take them away, whether they were from the Devil or from him; but to no avail.[83] Many visionaries, like St. Catherine dei Ricci and St. Margaret Mary, have begged God to leave them alone, sometimes in those very words—"Leave me alone, Lord," Bl. Anna-Maria Taigi would say, "I have work to do."

And even if they can't resist God's outpouring of mystic phenomena, every visionary on record has also asked that they be allowed at least to keep these things entirely hidden. It's hard to imagine now, but the thousands who followed St. Catherine of Siena didn't know about her visions; they were attracted by her sanctity. In the same way, those who have received some kind of errand from on high, like St. Catherine Labouré or St. Margaret Mary, have tried to get the thing done while remaining anonymous. But of course, if they're required to step forward and say something to the public at large, to convey some distinct message from an apparition, they all submitted their wills to God's completely in this matter, as in everything else. But only after immense struggles and inexpressible agony.

BLINDED BY THE LIGHT

Being pulled across the line from progress through one's own efforts to abandonment to God's overpowering love means that the soul has to move ahead in darkness, unable to rely on its faculties—the will, the intellect, and the memory that have taken it to this point. By all accounts, this is unimaginably frightening.

You might think that this first response from the object of the loved one fills the soul with happiness, but Fray Juan notes that "when this pure light strikes in order to expel all impurity, a person feels so unclean and so wretched that it seems that God is against him and he is against God." Paradoxically, when God responds to the contemplation of a pure soul, it seems to the soul that, after all of its hard work, God must have rejected it; that sudden heavenly light blinds the soul to the immense favor of it all, only making it see the infinite distance between the supernatural perfection of the Creator and the natural nothingness of his creatures.

This night blindness always confuses beginners, who think that ecstasy means joy. The soul can just give up on the whole thing, thinking that there's no point to prayer any more. Fray Juan quotes Lamentations at length to illustrate this point, as when Jeremia, at exactly this point in his spiritual development, complained that God had shut him out with square stones, tightly fitted, and put a cloud in front of the prophet's soul so that his prayers wouldn't bother him any more. And when Jeremia did muster the strength to cry out to God again, it wasn't much; he figured that God wouldn't pay any

---

83. The confessor told her to make the derisive hand sign called "the fig", and St. Teresa records obediently flipping the fig to her apparitions for some time thereafter. It never worked, and she never got used to seeing her visions. At one point, Christ tried to reassure her; "I treat only my friends this way," he said. "No wonder you have so few," she answered.

attention, anyway.[84] But this inactivity is what finally frees the soul from its last tendencies to imperfection. "Usually," Fray John says, "a soul never strays except through its appetites, or its gratifications, or its discursive meditation, or through its knowledge or affections... Once all of these operations ... are impeded, [the soul] is freed from error in them, because it is not only liberated from itself but from its other enemies, the world and the Devil."

In other words, when we people in the pews pray, we get some satisfaction and some reassurance from our senses. The will, the memory, and the intellect all play a part in it, and we know where we are and what we're doing. It's all very comprehensible to us. But when God touches a fledgling mystic, those faculties aren't used in communication with God any more; he communicates directly to the soul. Eventually, the appetite that the person usually has for those reassurances, for the comfortable world of the senses, dies away from lack of use.

That's the level of complete detachment from this world, and it leaves the way clear for the supernatural mode of operation: God is coming into the soul under his own power, and he's not coming in response to anything that the soul does or knows or senses. The problem is that, in this stage of passive purgation, the feeling of being abandoned by God only intensifies, precisely because the soul can't pray in the normal way any more—precisely because of the suspension of its normal faculties. So the soul searches almost desperately for ways to please God and win back his favor. It's not necessary, of course; God has already decided to accept the soul in an extraordinary way. But at least these efforts make the faculties focus entirely on God. And at this point, St. John notes, there's no satisfaction from any other object, anyway; the mystic is loving God with the whole heart, the whole mind, the whole soul, and all his strength (Dt 6:5).

So, at this level of spiritual development, the soul has come through the long, dark night of passive purgation and out at last into the sunlight; at last it can receive the fullness of God's grace, becoming the clean window that's virtually indistinguishable from the sunlight itself. And a person so illuminated is willing to suffer any earthly trials for the love of God.

The Perfection of Penance: The Victim Soul

By making a person aware of the inexpressible difference between the Creator and his creatures, passive purgation makes him acutely aware of his own imperfections (Lk 5:8). St. Ignatius during his apparitions didn't dare look up to Heaven; St. Teresa apologized to Christ for the stink that he had to endure when he approached a creature like herself. St. Margaret Mary, typically, was exquisitely sensitive to the least of her human imperfections when she stood before Christ spiritually, sacramentally in the Eucharist, or visibly:

---

84. This is largely included in the third chapter of Lamentations, the one that begins with how the prophet has been led through the darkness, not in the light, and has been individually singled out by God to be left in the dark like a dead man. Lm 3:49 also suggests that the prophet had received the gift of tears.

My Sovereign Lord continued to favor me with his real and sensible presence, which grace ... he promised would not be taken from me. And truly he never deprived me of it for any fault that I committed. But as his sanctity cannot endure the slightest stain nor the least voluntary imperfection or one caused by negligence, he shows me the smallest fault. And since I am so imperfect and miserable as to commit many ... I own that it is an intolerable torment to me to appear before this sanctity when I have allowed myself to commit some act of infidelity. There is no kind of torture that I would not endure rather than bear the presence of the All-Holy Good when my soul is stained with some fault; no, I would prefer a thousand times to plunge myself into a burning furnace.

This marks another level of penance; it's not just embracing natural suffering in reparation for your imperfections, and it's not just purposefully inflicting discomforts on yourself. These are ascetic penances, but the higher level of mystic penance happens when God sends a great deal of suffering to his chosen soul. They accept; in fact, they ask for it.[85] Through their lives, even more than through their writings, the great ascetics and the great mystics imply unmistakably that one of the most effective ways of praying for the conversion of sinners is to take on the penances that the sinners should be doing for themselves, on top of the ones the saints take on for their own sins.

In a world in which appetites must be satisfied at once, in which we rush to the medicine cabinet to relieve even the slightest pain, it's unthinkable that people might willingly ask for pain. Those who have seen the horror of sin, those who have received the gift of tears, may seem to overreact in their eagerness to suffer, but from their viewpoint the fact that the rest of us can't or don't see things this way is just part of the problem—what blindness, what blindness! they always say.

As with St Margaret Mary, St. Teresa, St. Ignatius, and St. John of the Cross, people who receive the call to a particularly close union with God all go through torturous illnesses and traumas, and none of them ever fully recovers robust health. But the characteristic bad health of all of the great mystics only makes their characteristic joy stand out all the more clearly.

Still, you have to be careful about that. On the one hand, there's biblical precedent for physical suffering as part of purgation and atonement. St. Paul was struck blind, like Tobias before him, as part of his conversion, and he obviously had other afflictions to bear on behalf of those who needed conversion—what is lacking in the sufferings of Christ, I fill up in my flesh for his body, which is the Church, he said (Cl 1:24). But on the other hand the inability to cope with natural health crises, the lack of sufficient maturity to handle physical suffering intellectually or morally, can and does prompt people to regressive behavior—childlike conduct that offers an escape from an

---

85. Not only that, but they sometimes ask for it on behalf of other people, too. "May God bless you and send you many little crosses," St. Louis-Marie Grignion de Montfort used to say, cheerfully.

overwhelming sense of personal inadequacy—that's often mistaken for genuine spiritual growth coming out of a genuine humility.[86]

The difference between ordinary illness, even extreme illness or the illness endured as part of purgation, and illness sent as a gift is most obvious in the mystic phenomenon known as the *victim soul.*

86. The literature on regression is vast, but see for example Josef Breuer and Sigmund Freud, *Studies in Hysteria* (Boston, 1958); Joel Allison, "Adaptive Regression and Intense Religious Experiences," *Journal for the Scientific Study of Religion* (VIII, 1, Spring, 1968); Heinz Hartman, *Essays on Ego Psychology* (New York, 1965); John P. Kildahl, *The Psychology of Speaking in Tongues* (New York, 1972); J. N. Lapsley and J. M. Simpson, "Speaking in Tongues: Infantile Babble or Song of the Self?", *Pastoral Psychology* (September, 1964); K. Runia, "The Forms and Functions of Nonsense Languages," *Linguistics* (1969a, 50); and W. J. Samarin, "Glossolalia as Regressive Speech," *Language and Speech* (London, 1973). Strictly speaking, "glossolalia" should be reserved for the genuine mystic gift of comprehensible speech, of languages learned supernaturally; the spurious counterpart should be called "idioglossia".

seven

the end

of the expiation

You must know that all sickness is an expiation and that,
if God does not consider it finished,
no doctor can interrupt it. ...
[T]he doctor only heals if his intervention
coincides with the end of the expiation
determined by the Savior.

— Paracelsus, *Opus paramirum* (*c.* 1530)

A victim soul is an innocent person who's called to emulate the mission of Christ himself: a person who's asked by God to suffer torments of reparation for the sins of others and accepts (Mr 14:36; Mt 16:24). To those persons, as to Job, God permits a particularly spectacular battery of illnesses, making some point about sin and repentance— for whom the Lord loves, he rebukes, as it is written, and he scourges every son whom he receives (Hb 12:6; Pr 3:12; also 2Cr 1:6).

But, unlike Job, the Church's victim souls don't just have suffering dumped on them, and they're not just left to figure it out for themselves. "For it says," St. Gregory of Nyssa reminded his readers fifteen centuries ago, "'He delivered himself up for us, an offering and a sacrifice.' Through these words we learn ... that the person looking towards that One delivers himself as an offering and a sacrifice and a passover, and will show himself to God as a living sacrifice" (*On Perfection*).

The victim souls on record all acknowledge having been asked if they'll accept suffering on behalf of sinners, and they all agree of their own free will, although the call is hard to resist. Sister Josefa Menéndez, one of the more recent victim souls, was asked by her apparition of Christ if she was willing to suffer, to act as a victim soul, and she recoiled from the questions. The apparition left her quietly, but, having refused the call, she entered a time of spiritual dryness so desolate that she called him back, and he answered; she accepted him at any cost, and she in due course became another in the long list of victim souls.

The matter of need also helps distinguish the victim soul from those who simply contract natural diseases, and from those who have the spiritual strength to accept those diseases as atonement for sin. St. Paul's sufferings, of course, helped get the Church started against all odds; subsequent victim souls seem to arise whenever things just get so horribly bad that we need someone to take on the punishment due for our sins, a scapegoat who can make us understand how far astray we've gone.

In fact, virtually all of the more spectacular graces freely given seem to be given in anticipation of urgent need. The miracles of Exodus prompted Pharaoh to release Israel from bondage; St. Ignatius was converted the same year that Luther was excommunicated, 1521; the prayers triggered by the apparition at Pontmain evidently turned away the destruction the Franco-Prussian War from innocent populations; and the apparitions at Fátima bore warnings about the first World War and the Russian Revolution. Sometimes it's just a matter of too many people compromising revelation, drifting away from the completeness of God's teaching and neglecting his commandments: those Israelites who drifted from the Covenant experienced extraordinary phenomena to get their attention—at Haseroth and Pharan, for instance (Nm 12:1-14:38), where apparitions, locutions, instant illnesses, instant healings, and other extraordinary interventions got them back on track. And recent stigmatics like St. Gemma Galgani seem to be called when formerly faithful nations become a little too secular.

In the same way, victim souls arise when we need someone to remind us of the horror of sin, in terms that a violent age can understand. Bl. Anna-Maria Taigi focussed moral opposition to Napoléon, and in our own days Therese Neumann (1898-1962), the Bavarian stigmatic and victim soul, directly confronted the Gestapo more than once simply by suffering an astonishing array of afflictions. The worse things get for the Church, the more God reaches out, it seems, to intervene and to get people's attention back where it needs to be.

And, at times, he does this by permitting victim souls to endure not just natural but supernatural sufferings, sufferings far beyond those that unaided nature could survive.

Blessed Lydwine of Schiedam

One of the Church's most impressive victim souls, Blessed Lydwine (lyd-VEE-na) of Schiedam, is a great person to remember when you think you've got problems. She was born in that little town just west of Rotterdam in 1380, which makes her more or less contemporary with St. Joan of Arc (1412-1431). Now, history concentrates a lot of attention on the still small voices that came to St. Joan, and rightly so; they echoed across

Europe in the clash of armies and worked to the birth of a nation.

But you don't hear much any more about the far more spectacular mystic phenomena—extraordinary even among mystic events—that turned Europe's attention back to God and the things of God, the mystic events centered on Bl. Lydwine. Her story is extreme, and it's not for the squeamish, but it's the most concentrated account of the sufferings willingly embraced by a victim soul in reparation of her own sins (tiny though they must have been) as well as for the sins of others.

And her story is also exceptionally well documented. Three notable religious writers recorded it: Jan Gerlac Peterssen, whose *Soliloquies* are still in print; Jan Brugman, who was one of the most famous preachers of the day; and Thomas à Kempis, the author to whom the *Imitation of Christ*, the devotional tract that still ranks second only to the Bible in number of sales, was long attributed. Of course, religious writers are always suspected of bias, but in Bl. Lydwine's case there's an immense amount of information from unbiased or even downright hostile witnesses.

The burgomeisters of Schiedam, who wanted to discourage the vast numbers of pilgrims (or tourists, apparently) who came tracking through town to stare at her, ordered a twenty-four-hour watch on her for several months, with explicit instructions to certify, once and for all, that she was a fake—not to determine whether she was a fake, but to certify that she was. They ended up proclaiming officially, on September 12, 1421, that nobody could live through what she endured for so long without direct and extraordinary help from God. Burgundian soldiers, stationed in her house by Philip of Burgundy when he conquered the territory, sent her family away and watched her day and night for many weeks; they too testified to the genuineness of her afflictions and all of the other wonders that attended her. And, because Schiedam stands at the crossroads of the great wars of her time, wars in which St. Joan herself commanded, Bl. Lydwine was inspected in pretty much the same way every time the territory changed hands.

Dukes, counts, and great ladies—every person of note in northern Europe, practically—dropped in to witness Bl. Lydwine's sufferings; some were puzzled, some were fashionably revolted, but they all bore witness to the same details. She was seen by every prominent physician of her day, men who examined her initially as a medical anomaly, seeing her as a supernatural phenomenon only after exhausting all explanations possible to their science (or our own, for that matter). Medical men and clerics sent to inspect her, thugs and ruffians sent to rape her or kill her, came away one and all convinced of her sanctity and testifying to the absolute impossibility of anybody's surviving her afflictions for so long without direct divine intervention.

Denying Herself and Taking Up Her Cross

It all started normally enough, even though Lydwine's parents for some reason gave her that odd and prophetic name, derived from the Flemish word *lyden*, which means "to suffer". Still, she was by all accounts a cheerful and a very pretty little girl, so pretty, in fact, that her parents were counting on an advantageous marriage for her. They both came from families that had once stood fairly high in the social register, although they themselves were having a tough time feeding Lydwine and her eight brothers. They took it one day at a time, hoping for better things ahead, and certainly Lydwine's good looks, with their families' respectability, drew a steady stream of upper-middle-class suitors.

Lydwine herself had other ideas. By the age of seven she had already decided to dedicate her life to the service of God, as a nun, she thought originally. Her parents still pushed for a good marriage, though, until even her remarkable patience wore thin. If you press me further about marriage, she said at the age of fifteen, I'll ask God to take away my looks so that nobody will want to marry me.

Her consequent smallpox didn't kill her, but it left her scarred enough to kill any social career she might otherwise have had. The sickness drained her strength and wasted her flesh, so that her skin, now dry and greenish, stretched tightly across her bones. The stream of suitors dried up, too, almost overnight, and Lydwine herself was left so weak that she hardly ever went outdoors. But, like the other great mystics, she never lost her sense of humor. She was still the life of any party, so popular in Schiedam that her girlfriends invited her to go skating on the frozen canals before she was really recovered—they wouldn't have any fun, they said, unless Lydwine was with them. So she picked herself up from her sickbed that winter morning, a few days before the Feast of the Purification, in the Year of Our Lord 1395, and she went out to skate.

She had hardly strapped on her skates and stood up when another of the girls, going too fast and out of control, knocked her against a piece of ice that broke one of the ribs on her lower right side. Her friends carried her home and laid her on the sickbed that she would not leave for nearly forty years.

Her family called in all of the doctors they could find. Her father Pierre was drawing a miserable salary as town watchman, but many eminent Dutch doctors, some whose names still figure in the literature of medical history, came without charging a fee, drawn either by motives of charity or irresistible curiosity about the whole series of medical puzzles that Lydwine presented. For one thing, her broken rib didn't heal properly; it formed a tumor or hard abcess that wracked the girl with unremitting pain, lying, sitting, or standing. Against her own will—she was never a complainer—she sobbed constantly from the pain, until at last she couldn't stand it any longer. In a sudden convulsion, she threw herself from her bed onto her father's lap as he sat praying at her bedside. As it happened, her tumor struck his knee and burst.

But it burst inward, not outward. She began to vomit pus, filling the basin that they kept at her side, and then filling basin after basin until at last she fainted away, exhausted. Her parents thought that she had died, but she revived. In continuous torment, unable to stay long in any one position and finding relief in none, she moved constantly from place to place in the little house, dragging herself along but finding no rest. Soon she lost even the strength for that movement, but when she settled in her bed the wound in her side, which had never healed, became gangrenous and alive with worms, worms carefully described, weighed, and counted by her physicians. They moved under her skin, feeding on such healthy flesh as she had left until they caused three ulcers, each "as round and big as the bottom of a bowl". Eventually, her whole body seemed to boil with them.

She contracted two of the great plagues that had come back to Europe with the Crusaders. The unmistakable buboes of the Black Death popped up on her shoulders and putrefied, devouring flesh and bone until her right arm was attached only by a single tendon. The "burning illness", an indescribable plague that consumed skin and muscle with an unremitting fire until the bones themselves burst, split her face from her hairline to her nose.[87] She became epileptic; she lost all sight in her right eye, and in fact her left eye bled at the least light. She lost blood through her mouth, ears, and nose, too, so copiously that the doctors wondered how she could lose more blood than her body could possibly hold.[88]

At one point, her lungs and liver decayed, her stomach, swollen on her skeletal frame, burst, and her intestines spilled forth—the doctors, at a complete loss by now, just trimmed the dead parts away and replaced the rest, strapping them in with a big linen pillow as a compress. Whenever her family had to lift her, to change the sheets or to replace the straw that she insisted on using instead, they had to tie her body together with linen to keep it from falling apart entirely.

To Suffer Lovingly

The full catalogue of her diseases and illnesses would fill a book larger than this one, but by now you get the idea.[89] These horrors aren't mentioned here for their shock value, but shock value is why they happen to victim souls; God permits these things, evidently, to shock us into seeing things from his point of view, to open our eyes to the horror of sin. Looking back to the truly monumental sufferings of victim souls like Lydwine— and they are many—we're supposed to learn something about the value of pain, the viewpoint of God, and the way the universe is organized.

Specifically, victim souls are understood as pointing out the need for large-scale conversions, for a general shift of perspective away from sin, a shift from a godless culture to a God-centered culture. Historically, victim souls have appeared at just such times, and, from what they say, you get the impression that if everybody in the populace at large had been doing some small penance, each person taking on moderate voluntary suffering in reparation for sin, all of the pain owed in the divine balance of things would-

87. One of her biographers, J. K. Huysmans (*Saint Lydwine of Schiedam*, London, 1923), posits that she didn't get leprosy, the third great Crusader plague, because the laws of the time would have required her to be shut away, as if dead, with the rest of the lepers, and she could not then have served as an example and a warning as she did. But she got everything else.

88. Even in this, she joked about her afflictions, asking them if they knew where the inexhaustible supply of sap comes from to swell the vines, so black and bare in winter. God even joked back, as it were; when Lydwine contracted two pestilential abscesses, she remarked that three, in recollection of the Trinity, would have been more appropriate. The third developed instantly. The same extraordinary flow of more blood than the entire volume of the body, by the way, is reported of Ven. Serafina di Dio (d. 1699), St. Catherine of Genoa, and many others.

89. She had a bad toothache, too, but it hardly seems worth mentioning, now.

n't have to be concentrated in a single person. In other words, if charity is generally distributed in a nation, fewer people have to have it in heroic proportions, willing to lay down their lives for their friends.

And the mystic context of a genuine victim soul has to be taken into consideration, too. A victim soul isn't just a person who has an unusual agglomeration of diseases, and not even just a person who offers up an unusual amount of suffering as atonement for sins; resignation to the will of God, in those cases, is a matter for ascetic theologians, not a mystic phenomenon. A genuine victim soul is specifically called by God to serve in that way, and the nature of the illnesses makes absolutely clear the line between unusual natural suffering and the victim soul; the diseases of these mystics run to symptoms that are above those of nature, literally supernatural.

Of course, the most amazing thing about Bl. Lydwine's case is that she didn't die when her body fell to pieces and, virtually, rotted from the countless diseases that afflicted her. Her nearly detached arm was still alive, and so was her putrefying flesh. But beyond that her flesh never smelled of the sickroom; instead, the doctors report, her body yielded a fragrance lovelier than anything you can smell on Earth, normally. First it was a spicy-sweet perfume something like cinnamon and cloves, but more exquisite and delicate. After she was given the *stigmata*, receiving the unhealing wounds of Christ's nails in her hands and feet, this faded and was replaced by a smell described as like that of fresh roses, violets, and lilies.

She consistently saw angels, including her guardian angels, who filled her dark little room with blinding light that crowds of onlookers could sometimes see, themselves. She gave evidence of a vast and sophisticated theological knowledge, and, lying immobile on her heap of straw, she knew an immense amount about public events far away, and even more about the inner workings of the hearts of those who came to see her. And no matter how horribly she suffered, she never lost her sense of humor. When at last she died, her body was made whole again, taking on the fresh and beautiful appearance that it had had before she even got smallpox. In fact, she showed the full catalogue of recognized mystic gifts. But these supernatural symptoms were all secondary to the workings of her main vocation: to suffer willingly for the welfare of the Church, and lovingly.

"To suffer lovingly," said St. John Vianney, "is to suffer no longer." And the crucial role of love, both human and divine, is probably why so many recent apparitions have happened to those who love most purely, without condition or reservation: to children.

eight

the voice

of the children

It is the voice
of the children of God.

— St. Augustine,
On Admonition and Grace (427)

There's been a shift in the circumstances of creditable apparitions, in the past century or so. Earlier apparitions tended to come to professed religious—monks, nuns, priests—or to pious people who had taken some kind of private vow that dedicated them to a lifetime of prayer and atonement, like Julian of Norwich or Anna-Maria Taigi. But now the visionaries are children, as mentioned in Mt 11:25 and Lk 10:21; and they're usually untutored but sincere children in remote or at least impoverished places.

Like the seers themselves, recent apparitions have a somewhat different character, too. Earlier apparitions were single, or maybe a few events in sequence. But, since the apparitions to St. Catherine Labouré in 1830—the watershed usually taken as dividing early from recent apparitions—creditable apparitions have been serial, coming one after another and often at intervals specified by the apparition itself. And they're public. Earlier apparitions tended to be private, even if they resulted in public movements of devotion. But now crowds gather around the visionaries at the anticipated or predicted time of the next apparition, and, although the crowds don't expect to share the vision, they expect whatever it says to be reported to them. Or they expect some sign, some unusual or miraculous healing, maybe, or an extraordinary movement in the Sun, the Moon, or the stars.

Recent creditable apparitions have also spoken of the need for conversion from widespread indifference to Christianity, lukewarm devotion, active heresy, or other disorders in the Church, as they have since St. Paul was knocked off his high horse. But in the past, their emphasis has been on converting or encouraging one of the great founders of orders and movements that strengthen or refresh the Church, or on spreading some devotion that the laity themselves can take up as a way of countering the disorder. Other apparitions have encouraged the construction or repair of a shrine as a focus of renewed devotion in that particular region.

Nowadays, shrines are built at the sites of major apparitions, but that's not the major purpose of the visit. People today expect apparitions to contain some kind of message about spiritual matters and their connection with temporal matters, with the course of human history. They expect the message to be universal in scope; and while the visionary is supposed to make some part of it available to the whole world, people also expect that part of what's conveyed is supposed to remain a deep secret. There's a strong continuity in this, that some parts of private revelations are supposed to remain secret. St. Paul said so (2Cr 12:4), and St. Bonaventure notes in his *Life of St. Francis* that he told about his stigmata only under compulsion, although he added that the one who had appeared to him had told him some things that he would never disclose to any man as long as he lived. But these days people conjecture that the "secret" has something to do with the end of the world.

Of course, it's reasonable to assume that no mystic communicates absolutely everything heard during an apparition; some of it must be deeply personal and nobody else's business. And apparitions have often had a kind of Apocalyptic message to them, like the famous case of the vision of St. Dominic in 1217. As it's recorded in the *Golden Legend*, St. Dominic saw in the sky above Rome an angry Christ brandishing three lances, one in retribution for each of the vices predominant at the time (pride, concupiscence, and avarice). He saw Mary approach and intercede for mercy. "I have a faithful servant and valiant warrior," she said, "who will go throughout the world and conquer it for you; and I will give you another servant who will be his rival in zeal and valor." Then she presented a man whom St. Dominic saw clearly. The next day St. Dominic was surprised to see that man in church. He ran to him, embracing him and kissing him, saying, you are my companion; you will walk with me step by step. Let us stand together, and no enemy shall stand against us.

It was St. Francis. Between them, these two founders established two of the greatest orders of the Church, those that turned the tide and renewed the faith of Christendom, and, presumably, held back the hand of God from just retribution. But in the past century or so apparitions have taken on a new urgency, calling not just one or two key people but humanity as a whole to repentance, warning of dire consequences if the prophecy isn't taken to heart and acted upon. And while credit-worthy apparitions of Christ and most saints seem to have diminished, all of the major creditable apparitions of modern times have been appearances of Mary alone.

THE QUEEN OF PROPHETS IN THE ECONOMY OF SALVATION

Mary's pivotal role in the Cycle of Redemption has been a matter of discourse in the Church since the beginning, but the part that she was to play in later apparitions was outlined in detail, prophetically, by St. Louis-Marie Grignion de Montfort, who lived from 1673 to 1716.

France at that time was wracked not only by the heresy of Calvinism but by the much more insidious heresy of Jansenism, a creed that seriously misunderstood the role of grace in the economy of salvation. It was a powerfully attractive cult—its members claimed raptures and convulsions, falling on the floor and speaking in tongues, all with the attitude that they were a particularly holy bunch of people within the Church specially gifted by the Holy Spirit.[90] In fact, Jansenism was so fashionable that it attracted droves of upper-class Frenchmen and even some French bishops.

Louis Grignion de Montfort, evidently, was made to order to fight this heresy and extinguish it. Since his childhood, he was tirelessly devoted to prayer before the Blessed Sacrament, and he never failed to visit the tabernacle at least twice a day, no matter where he was. He almost didn't make it to priesthood, though; he became dangerously ill as a seminarian and was virtually given up for dead, like most nascent mystics, but he recovered and was ordained at the age of twenty-seven.

Louis-Marie devoted himself to preaching to the laity at large, giving retreats and missions across western France. He was so engaging and so persuasive a speaker that whole crowds came back to the Faith with new fervor—even the canal boatmen and stevedores he met during his travels ended up kneeling on the deck praying the Rosary, when he was on board. The whole garrison of La Rochelle, all of those case-hardened soldiers, came marching out after hearing him preach, barefooted and carrying crucifixes, singing hymns through their tears.

His early successes so maddened the heretics that they disrupted his public devotional exercises as well as his Masses, excoriated him in public, laid in wait to bludgeon him, and even slipped poison into his broth, just to silence him. They spread false reports to the bishops—some of whom were Jansenists themselves, in those sad days—and, one after the other, these prelates refused him the right to say Mass in their dioceses. He proceeded, as all saints proceed, in strict obedience to the institutional Church, even when the incumbent seemed personally in error; but then he walked to Rome to

---

90. The best account of this kind of cult is Ronald Knox's classic *Enthusiasm* (Oxford, 1950). See also, for instance, Marc Galanter, "Charismatic Religious Sects and Psychiatry", *American Journal of Psychiatry* (139: 1539-48, 1982), and his *Cults: Faith, Healing, and Coercion* (Oxford, 1989); Felicitas Goodman, *Speaking in Tongues: A Cross-Cultural Study of Glossolalia* (Chicago, 1972); Heinz Hartman, *Essays on Ego Psychology* (New York, 1965); E. Hilgard, *Hypnotic Susceptibility* (New York, 1965); Natalie Isser and Lita Schwartz, "Charismatic Leadership: A Case in Point," *Cultic Studies Journal* (1986 Spring, Summer); G. H. Lang, *The Earlier Years of the Modern Tongues Movement* (Wimborne, England, n.d.); Benjamin B. Warfield, *Counterfeit Miracles* (New York, 1918). The Church is usually silent about charismatic groups because these sects dissolve when the leader leaves and because the syndrome includes the need to project blame for one's perceived failures on another person or an institution that can be seen as the opposition; people mistaking this psychological relief for spiritual activity tend to leave the Church if confronted.

ask Clement XI Albani to clarify things. The Pope appointed him apostolic missionary to France, directly responsible only to the Holy See, and charged him personally with the reconversion of those dioceses.

And so he went on, drawing thousands of people away from the glitter of Jansenism and Calvinism, not by fire and brimstone but by the genuine force of his secret austerities, no less than by his quiet miracles. Total strangers walked in unannounced and on time with meals for him and his co-workers; even in depressed areas people brought him what he needed to make enough soup to feed any number of the poor, dependably, every day. When his parents invited him to bring his friends to dinner while he was preaching in the area, a meal planned for a few somehow expanded to feed the hundreds of paupers Louis-Marie brought with him.[91] He cured the sick, made the blind see, triggered the gift of tears in those who came to jeer at him or stone him, and stirred whole cities to rebuild their ruined churches. And to use them.

He was denounced time and again to civil and ecclesiastical authorities for committing miracles, but his most impressive faculty was his gift of prophecy. Almost offhand, he would sum up the future careers of people in the crowds: you will be the guardian of such-and-such a chapel, he told one young girl; you will be nuns, he told two others, blood sisters for whom that life was the farthest thing from their minds. But they all ended up living exactly as he had said they would. He predicted happy deaths for the converted, and, sadly, foretold miserable deaths for the unrepentant. He predicted the fall of whole cities, weeping over them as Christ wept over Jerusalem—cities that now stand only in ruins.[92]

And the most remarkable prophecy of all is that he predicted the whole course and substance of the apparitions of Mary that began a hundred and fourteen years after his death, in the apparitions to St. Catherine Labouré in 1830.

The Buried Treasure of Prophecy

It was through the Blessed Virgin that Christ came into the world, St. Louis-Marie wrote, and it is through her that he must reign in the world. His devotion to Mary, in fact, is the secret to his success as a missionary, Pius XII noted when he formally canonized

---

91. Similar miracles, patterned after the miraculous distributions by Christ (Mt 14:13-21; 15:32-38), are recorded for St. Dominic (at the church of St. Sixtus in Rome) and many other saints. After Giacomo Benincasa of Siena gave his daughter Catherine permission to give whatever she wanted to the poor, his hogshead of wine just didn't get empty, although the whole household drew wine from it. It tasted better than any other wine in town, too.

92. Generally, though, the gift of prophecy is a matter of seeing the consequences of sin, and of having the gifts of understanding and knowledge to an extraordinary degree; its characteristic expression is saying that if the person, or the nation, continues living that way he, or it, will have to face certain consequences. The part about being able to see what will happen in the future is only a kind of secondary result of that viewpoint. Sometimes, though, people come forward with the uncanny ability to simply predict the future, calling themselves "psychics" or being called "fortune-tellers". Most usually, they have only a talent for picking up clues in conversations and maybe some learned skills in phrasing responses to eager questioners, like the spiritualists around Mary Ann Van Hoof. On the other hand, "one shouldn't marvel that demons could know and predict ... events, also," St. Augustine warned (*The Divination of*

Grignion de Montfort in 1947. He had converted those thousands through the Rosary, through his preaching about Mary, and through his books like the *Secret of Mary*, the *Admirable Secret of the Rosary*, and his *Little Crown of the Blessed Virgin*. When Louis-Marie had died, though, it looked as if his ministry would end with him.

To further the missionary work that he had started, Louis-Marie founded two orders just before his death, the Daughters of Wisdom for women and the Missionaries of the Company of Mary—the Montfort Fathers—for men.[93] In human terms, these organizations must have been classed as utter failures when he died, because they consisted of only four sisters, two priests, and a few brothers, in total. They hung on, somehow, but, just when they reached significant numbers some seventy years later, they were nearly wiped out by the persecutions of the French Revolution.

Those few Montfort fathers that remained, figuring that the little mother house at St.-Laurent-sur-Sèvres would likely be burned or torn down by revolutionaries, gathered up all of their founder's books, and all of his manuscripts that they knew of, and buried them in a wooden chest for safekeeping.[94]

When they returned to the site after the Restoration of the monarchy years later, those few survivors of the calamity were surprised to find the abandoned house still intact. By this time, the process of canonization for Louis-Marie de Montfort had begun, so, remembering the buried chest and the treasures that it contained, they dug it up and sent the contents to Rome.

The cause proceeded slowly, of course, but it got an extra boost in 1842, when a priest was rummaging through the attic at St.-Laurent-sur-Sèvres in search of sermon material. At the bottom of a trunk full of old books, he found a manuscript, its first few pages torn off; and he was astonished at what he read.

"I clearly foresee," its author had written, "that raging beasts will come in fury to tear to pieces with their diabolical teeth this little book and the one the Holy Spirit made use of to write it, or they will cause it at least to lie hidden in the darkness and silence of a chest and so prevent it from seeing the light of day."

That was true enough; but, more than that, the manuscript outlined in detail a future Marian age, a time in which Christ would make himself better known, better loved, and better served, through Mary. "God wishes therefore to reveal Mary, his masterpiece, and make her more known in these latter times," he wrote. Among the reasons that he lists for this are that Mary must shine forth more than ever in mercy, power, and grace: in mercy to bring sinners back to the Church through her intercession, in power to combat the enemies of God who will oppose the Church, and in grace to inspire and

---

Demons, c. 408), "insofar as it's allowed them to know and foretell." It's part of their nature, he notes, because they easily surpass the perception that earthly bodies have.

93. The Legion of Mary follows St. Louis-Marie's spirituality and his vision of the future in *True Devotion*, but it wasn't founded by him; it was established in Dublin in 1921 by Frank Duff.

94. It must have been a large chest. St. Louis-Marie wrote comparatively small books, but he also wrote the rules for his orders and for the lay organizations he founded, a great many letters and sermons, and nearly twenty-four thousand verses of hymns.

support those brave souls who are fighting for the cause of Jesus in this world. And, he said, she must come forth like bannered troops to oppose the Devil and his followers: Satan, knowing that he doesn't have much time left, tries harder and harder to destroy souls day by day. So, as the years roll by, those people who want to serve God find more, and more subtle, traps—snares that are increasingly hard to overcome.

"It is chiefly in reference to these last wicked persecutions of the Devil, daily increasing until the advent of the Antichrist," St. Louis-Marie wrote, "that we should understand the first and well-known prophecy and curse of God": the perpetual enmity that he put between Satan and the Mother of God. This is the root, he says, of the enmity between the children of Satan and the children of Mary—that is, between the friends of this world and all Christians.[95]

He outlined the kind of devotion and service of Jesus through Mary that all faithful Christians ought to embrace, to prepare themselves for this battle; then, he wrote, "then they will clearly see that beautiful Star of the Sea, as much as faith allows... They will experience her motherly kindness and affection for her children. They will love her tenderly and will appreciate how full of compassion she is, and how much they stand in need of her help."

And there's another prophecy in the manuscript, one that has its echoes in all of the saint's written works about the coming Marian age. "Mary must be known and openly revealed by the Holy Spirit so that Jesus may be known, loved, and served through her," he wrote. "This will happen especially toward the end of the world."

Revealing Things to Little Ones

The manuscript was sent immediately to Rome, where it was compared with known examples of Louis-Marie's handwriting and found to be genuine. More than his other writings, it established him as a major author and theologian. It's published now as *True Devotion to the Blessed Virgin*; it's an expansion of his discourse on those facets of the Faith that he discussed in his earlier book, *Love of the Eternal Wisdom*, which calls for spiritual perfection through those same themes of charitable conversion—ardent desire for Christ—continual prayer, mortification of the appetites, and a genuine devotion to the Blessed Virgin Mary.[96]

One feature of recent apparitions that St. Louis-Marie didn't explicitly predict is that they've come to children. In fact, he seems to have envisioned future seers, generally, as adults and specifically as priests. Still, it's interesting that the children of recent apparitions fit his description of visionaries to come.

95. Jn 19:25-27 has always been understood as Jesus's commendation of all of his followers to Mary's motherhood—St. John standing for all—and his charge to Mary to stand as mother to all of his followers. "All who believe in him," St. Augustine explained, "are rightly called children of the Bridegroom (Mt 9:15) [and] she is obviously the mother of us who are his members" (*Holy Virginity*, 6).

96. On the devotion to Christ as the Eternal Wisdom and on the End of Time, see the author's "*In Ivonem Explanationes*: The Meaning and Purpose of S. Ivo alla Sapienza in Rome," *Artibus et Historiæ* (Vienna, 1982) and "Solomon, Apocalypse, and the Names of God: The Meaning of the Chapel of the Most Holy Shroud in Turin", *Storia Architettura* (Rome, 1985).

Their devotion to Mary will come straight from the heart, he says, and it will be completely trustful. They will turn to her "in every need of body and soul with great simplicity, trust, and affection," an affection that's constant and disinterested, the love of a child for his mother. And their devotion will be holy, he writes, showing lively faith, absolute obedience, surpassing purity, and heroic patience, among other virtues; and, while these characteristics are admittedly uncommon in children, it's also true that the little visionaries have been uncommon children.

In fact, St. Louis-Marie predicted the steadfast insistence of future visionaries, too, writing that they will rekindle the flames of divine love, becoming in Mary's hands like sharp arrows (Ps 126:4) to transfix the enemies of his Church. Touching on the theme of repentance, he says that they will bring the sweet fragrance of Jesus to the poor and lowly, but a warning, the "odor of death", to the rich and proud. Attached to nothing, surprised at nothing, troubled at nothing, they will have the eloquence and strength that they need to do their work. Their hearts will not be troubled, nor will they fear anyone, no matter how powerful he may be, he says. And, more important still, they will move without concern in the midst of "priests, ecclesiastics, and clerics", which is highly suggestive, in view of the little seers' steadfastness during grillings by ecclesiastical authorities.

He does not seem to have foreseen that, like St. Teresa of Avila, young seers tend to be rather less imaginative than the norm. In fact, they're usually not excessively bright. When someone asked St. Bernadette why God would pick her for the message, she thought for a minute and said that it must be because he couldn't find anybody stupider. St. Catherine Labouré couldn't figure it out, either; "I have always been so stupid that I do not know how I shall be able to explain myself in Heaven," she said.

Of course, there's the credibility factor: children singled out for extraordinary mystic experiences that include a message for the world would, logically, have to be children that are known to be unable to make up such a thing on their own.[97] Most don't have the basic communication skills that they'd need to convey the message. The apparition of Fátima told Lucia to learn to read and write so that she could handle it.[98] And when the seer of La Salette, Mélanie Mathieu, was taken to the residence of the Archbishop of Lyon to write out her account of the apparition and what she had heard, she worked away at it in silence for a while, but then raised her hand to ask what "infallible" meant. The attendant witnesses said that it depended on the context, and she said, "will come about infallibly". She wrote on for a while, asking only what "defiled" meant. Then, toward the end of her task, she asked, "how do you spell 'Antichrist'?"

But it's worth considering that the messages reported from these recent appari-

---

97. And even for ascetic endeavors, a person with a restless mind and an active imagination is going to have a much harder time achieving even the basic states of contemplative prayer; memories, images, and all kinds of emotions come flooding in to distract a person like that, and by temperament they're not easily going to be satisfied with a state that's as peaceful and serene as a desert. The whole process of detachment from the world must get progressively harder in direct proportion to the liveliness of a person's interest in it.

98. True to form, the Reverend Mother of the school to which she was sent tried to refuse her, saying that she didn't need any simpletons.

tions don't necessarily refer to the Apocalypse. They may be in reference to vast numbers of persons living outside of the Christian ideal or in active rejection of it—vast numbers who, from the Church's perspective, would be living in such a way as to put themselves in clear danger of judgement. Rather than predicting the general Armageddon, rather than warning about the Second Coming as an event in the near future, the messages of the apparitions may simply be reminders that each of us, at death, faces a personal Apocalypse, and they may be prompted by the fact that too few of us give it much thought. In other words, anybody who dies at any time before the sky is rolled back ought, in the Church's view, to be as ready as he possibly can be to meet his maker at the moment of his death.

In fact, the messages center on an offended God, a God provoked by the sin that seems to be pervasive in the culture of so much of the West (or East, for that matter). At La Salette, for instance, the Lady said that her son's hand was so heavy that she could not hold it back much longer; people must not offend the Lord any more, she added at Fátima, because he is already greatly offended. The apparent disintegration of the quality of life on Earth—the wars, pestilence, famine, the breakup of the family— are all attributed to a decline in morals and a general turning away from religion, and they're all referred to the workings of divine justice.[99]

The cure prescribed for all of this divine retribution, in all of the credit-worthy apparitions, consists of conversion, reparation. And, above all, central to all of the messages, central to all of the mystic experiences of all of the credit-worthy visionaries—the little innocents as well as heroic ascetics—is devotion to the Eucharist.

99. The perspective is, though, not so much that God strikes out to punish people but that once we turn our backs on him he just leaves us on our own and doesn't reach out so strongly to restrain the evil among us, as in the Book of Job. He just lets us reap as we sow, you might say. On these topics and their cure, see Leo XIII Pecci's *Lætitiæ sanctæ* (1893) and John Paul II Wojtyla's *Salvifici doloris* (1984).

nine

the body and blood
of Jesus Christ

Eat and drink the Body and Blood of Jesus Christ,
horribly outraged by ungrateful men.
Make reparation for their crimes, and console your God.

— The Angel of Portugal, at Fátima, 1916

All of the great mystics of the past found their highest spiritual elevations while in worship before the Sacrament or at the moment of communion. All of the credit-worthy
apparitions, from earliest times to Margaret Mary to Fátima, urge making communions
of reparation, embracing Christ's Body and consoling him for the outrages inflicted on
him. The miracles associated with apparitions take place in close conjunction with the
Eucharist. Many of those at Lourdes, for example, happen not in connection with the
springs but during the procession of the Eucharist in the Blessing of the Sick at 3:30
every afternoon.[100] In fact, no other mystic phenomenon happens without reference to
the Eucharist; separation from it seems to preclude anything even approximating the
extraordinary spiritual experiences of the great mystics, and indeed no separated sect can
show anything like the miraculous phenomena that have characterized the Church's life
since the beginning.

       That's why it's important to view miracles, apparitions, and all of the other
extraordinary phenomena within the context of the whole of Christianity across the
whole of its history. The life of the Church, the sole heir of the authority of the

---

100. At other sites, like Fátima, where there is no spring, the cures likewise happen in connection with
the Eucharist, which makes you think about what can happen at your local parish church.

Apostles, is a continuum; and it isn't as if the Book of Acts came to a close and everything was all right. The same trials and tribulations assail the Church today as in the days of Herod Agrippa.

And, as God sees the need, those same attacks are countered with the same mystic events that you see in Acts—and all the way back to Genesis. The cases mentioned here are only examples, selected because they give a good idea of things that happen consistently and fairly steadily as the Church moves on from age to age. None of these great mystic events is unprecedented; no aspect of a credit-worthy phenomenon is without its credit-worthy precursor, its Scriptural predecessor.[101]

The only thing that's changed since the death of the last Apostle is that now nothing new is being revealed. Christ taught all there was to teach to the Apostles, and his same teachings are being taught in their fullness by their successors just as they were taught by the Apostles themselves. "'I say unto you that you are Peter, and upon this rock I will build my Church,'" St. Cyprian of Carthage (d. 258) reminded the lukewarm among his flock, "'and the gates of Hell will not overcome it.' From that time … the Church flows on through the changes of times and of successions … This has indeed been established by divine law" (*Letter to the Lapsed*, 250).

So modern mystic phenomena are still normal, if unusual, parts of the Church's life today, just as they were then, just as they have always been. The same distinction applies to them as to revelation itself: belief in ecclesiastical miracles, the ones that happen since the death of the last Apostle, John, in 70 AD isn't required for membership in the Church any more than belief in private revelations given since that date is. But the belief that God can still perform miracles is.

THE CORNERSTONE AND KEYSTONE

The central miracle in the Church's life, continually since the Last Supper, is the Eucharist, the absolute basis of Christian teaching, the cornerstone of the Church's spiritual life. The word "Eucharist" comes from the Greek meaning thanksgiving; the consecrated bread and wine are sometimes also called the Blessed Sacrament. The liturgy in which the Eucharist happens is the Mass, which, in early Christian times, was called the Breaking of the Bread; and the act of partaking of the consecrated bread and wine is called the Lord's Supper or simply communion.

The Eucharist in the Mass has always been the basic act of Christian worship, since the beginning (Jn 6:35, 48, 54-60; 1Cr 10:14-17, 11:27-29; etc.). The new *Catechism of the Catholic Church* (Part Two, Article 3), gives the best recent outline of the Church's teachings on the Sacrament, but naturally there's an immense amount of writing on the Eucharist, beginning in earliest Christian times. Back in the middle of the second century, for instance, the Roman Emperor Antoninus Pius wanted to know the truth about

101. In other words, the spiritual life of the Church—one, holy, and apostolic—is today exactly what it has been since the Annunciation, rooted in the Judaism of the Old Testament; the Bible simply records specific events of biblical days. Separated sects are cut off from this continuum, which can make the biblical examples seem unrelated to their own experience. Lack of space limits the number of biblical citations given here, but St. John of the Cross, St. Teresa, and other mystic theologians give them fully.

Christians—people were urging him to exterminate them, again—so he asked a prominent professor of philosophy, a Syrian Christian named Justinus, to write out an explanation of what Christians did and what they believed.[102] The result is Justinus's *Apologia*, an "apology", in the sense of an explanation. It's by no means the earliest written account of the Mass, but one of the most detailed.

After answering the usual charges of atheism and subversive intent, Justinus outlines Christian doctrine and, to counter the prevalent charges of blood-rites and human sacrifices, relates exactly what happens at Mass—which at that time was secret, available only to baptized Christians who could be trusted with receiving the Body and Blood of Christ.

> We call this food Eucharist; and no one else is permitted to partake of it, except one who believes our teaching to be true and who has been washed in the washing that is for the remission of sins and for regeneration ... For not as common bread nor common drink do we receive these, but since Jesus Christ our savior was made incarnate by the word of God and had both flesh and blood for our salvation, so too, as we have been taught, the food that has been made into the Eucharist by the Eucharistic prayer set down by him, and by the change of which our blood and flesh is nourished, is both the flesh and the blood of that same incarnated Jesus. The Apostles, in those memoirs that they produced, which are called "Gospels", have thus passed on what was enjoined upon them.

The point that still seems to escape so many people, inside and outside the Church, is that, through all of this Christian teaching, the consecrated bread and wine don't *represent* the Body and Blood of Christ, and they don't *symbolize* them: they *are* the Body and Blood of Christ, in which he, the living God, is truly and substantially present, just as you are truly and substantially present in your own body. This simple tenet is the most basic teaching in all of Christianity; without the True Presence, all the rest of Christ's teachings fall into illogic. This may not be immediately apparent, but history shows that it's true: heretics have a way of taking out this foundation-stone of Christianity first, and without it the rest can't be kept from falling away. That's why Christ made it the test of faith when he taught it in the synagogue at Capharnaum (Jn 6:60-70). That's why the Church has always held the consecrated Bread and Wine in such high reverence; that's why so many Christians have died rather than allow the Sacrament to be defiled.

But for a lot of people the True Presence is still a hard saying. Christians take it on faith; there isn't really anything in our experience, other than Christ's words and the prophecies in the Bible, that helps us get a handle on it. But once the fact of the True Presence is grasped, all the rest of Christ's teachings fall into perspective, and it's a radically different perspective from any that denies the Presence: "Our way of thinking is

---

102. This Justinus is known to history, ironically enough, as St. Justin Martyr, having been killed in hatred of the Faith by the prefect Rusticius, during the imperium of Antoninus's successor.

attuned to the Eucharist," St. Irenæus said, "and the Eucharist in turn confirms our way of thinking."[103]

Form and Substance

The way in which Christ changes the bread and wine into his living Body and Blood is impossible to explain, just as any other miracle is impossible to explain; that's why it's called the Mystery of the Faith. But to organize your thinking about it, you might think about the difference between form and substance. Everything in this world has substance, but we can't directly see the substance of anything. We can only see its form. That is, when you look at a cube of iron, you see that it's dark gray, it's cold, it's hard, it's square—you're seeing characteristics of its form, the descriptors that language captures in adjectives. You can only conclude that the thing there is a cube of iron because you can see and feel that there's something there that's gray, cold, hard, and square, and it all adds up to a cube of iron. But you can't directly experience its substance, its essential ironness, with your senses at all. You can only sense its form.

Now, form is subject to change. You can change the form of the iron by heating it until it's red and no longer cold; you can temper it to make it harder or softer, and you can re-shape it. When its form has changed, it's been transformed, from the Latin *trans-* meaning "across" and *forma*, "form". But substantially, it's still identically the same iron. No matter what you do to the iron cube, you can't make it into a block of aluminum or a potato. You can't change the substance of anything.

But Christ can, if you hold the Bible as true. When he changes the bread and wine offered at Mass into his living Body and Blood, just as he said they would change, their forms stay the same, but their substances change. The elements of the Eucharist aren't transformed; they're transubstantiated, from *trans-* and *substantia*, "substance". That's why the appearance, taste, and smell of the Eucharist are usually the appearances, tastes, and smells of bread and wine.

THOSE WHO HAVE SEEN AND BELIEVED

But there are times when the form of the Eucharist changes to keep pace with the changes in the substance of the elements. The oldest phenomenon of this kind on record is the Miraculous Host of Lanciano, in Italy, which happened in about 700.

The town itself takes its name from the centurion—Longinus, in Latin—who thrust the lance into the side of Jesus at the Crucifixion (Jn 19:34). He's said to have

---

103. The Church's teaching is that Jesus is present as long as the appearances of bread and wine last. When the Host is digested, or if a Host is left to decay naturally, then it is no longer Jesus. Christ is within the communicants for about fifteen minutes, then, which is why a period of silent adoration is mandated in the Mass after communion. St. Philip Neri, seeing a woman leaving Mass immediately after reception, sent two altar boys with lighted candles to escort her, as she was at that time an ark of the Savior. And, after all, her behavior both set and followed a bad example; the first person to dash out of Mass that way was Judas (Jn 13:30).

been born in that town, back when the Romans called it Anxanum.[104]

The church at Lanciano in which the miracle occurred was, at that time back in the early eighth century, dedicated to Sts. Legontian and Domitian, and it was in the care of Basilian monks of the Greek Rite—this was long before part of the Greek Rite of the Church split off in schism to form the modern Greek Orthodox church.

Anyway, a Basilian monk was celebrating Mass there one day, troubled mightily by the various heresies that were sweeping through the area one after another. Even some of his brother monks had fallen victim to them; and they all centered on the denial of the True Presence in the Sacrament. He himself prayed constantly for guidance in the matter, but it was a losing battle. He felt himself unable to resist the pressure to conclude that this was simply impossible, that the bread and wine stayed exactly that, bread and wine, nothing more.

Still, for the benefit of his parishioners, he celebrated Mass that day. And as he elevated the Host, he looked at it; his hands began to shake violently. He stood there trembling for a long time, until the parishioners began to wonder what could be wrong. Finally he turned to them—this was at a time when the Mass was celebrated with the priest facing in the same direction as the people—and blessed God. "To confound my disbelief," he said, "God has revealed himself in this Most Blessed Sacrament and made himself visible to our eyes. Come, my brothers and sisters, come and wonder at our God, so close to us. Behold the Flesh and Blood of our most beloved Christ."

And, in fact, in place of the host, the flat disk of unleavened bread, the priest held a disk of flesh, exactly the same size and thickness as the bread had been, and a chalice filled with fresh human blood.

The Host, ironically enough, was later pinned flat on a wooden board with little nails—crucified, almost—so that, when it dried, it wouldn't curl up. The Blood coagulated into five pellets of different sizes that were put into a crystal chalice so that they could be seen. The miracle put an end to the heresies in the area, and veneration of the Blessed Sacrament was restored to its rightful place in the order of things in and around Lanciano.

The Weight of Evidence

But it didn't end there. As part of the investigation, the pellets of blood were weighed. The idea must have been to find out the total weight of the pellets and then the weight of each individual one, just to get an accurate description, but any combination of pellets weighed the same as any other combination. All five together weighed the same as any one of them; any two or three of them weighed the same as any one of them or as all five. The thing is so puzzling that investigators can't help thinking that there must have been some mistake. So the pellets were weighed time and time again. The same

104. His real name is lost; *longinus* simply means a soldier with a long lance, the way "musketeer" means a soldier with a musket. But the lance head belonging to this particular *longinus* was kept as a relic; it's now in one of the little reliquary chapels dug into the great piers of the crossing of St. Peter's, the one with the forty-foot statue of Longinus carved by Gianlorenzo Bernini. You can see the statue in almost any picture of the basilica, just behind and to the right of the main altar, if you're looking from the nave.

phenomenon was observed in 1574, and in 1636 a marble plaque with an inscription was put up commemorating the fact, after which time the phenomenon ceased.[105]

There was a full-blown scientific investigation of the relics in 1970, with electrophoretic tests, protein analyses, zonal precipitation, photomicrographs, electrographs, and everything. The results showed that the flesh of the Miracle of Lanciano is flesh indeed, and the blood is blood indeed; both are truly human; both bloodgroups of the flesh and blood are the same—in fact, they both came from the same person—and the proteins in the blood, even after twelve centuries, were found to be normally fractionated with the same percentage as they are in the serotherapeutic table of fresh, normal human blood. In other words, even after twelve hundred years on display, the pellets of blood show all of the characteristics of fresh human blood, characteristics that our blood would lose within about twenty minutes of being shed.[106]

As to the flesh of the transformed host, it's interesting to note that it's cardiac tissue: heart muscle, suitably enough in a town named for the Lance and for a miracle that occurred when the Sacred Heart was wounded again by heresies. The doctors and anatomists who examined the Host said that, even if the bit of flesh had been sliced from a cadaver heart, only an extremely experienced dissectionist could get a slice of such uniform thickness cutting tangentially to the surface, as the Host of Lanciano is configured.

And, even nailed to its board and exposed for the veneration of the Faithful, and then exposed for centuries in a glass ostensorium that wasn't hermetically sealed, it never corrupted (Ex 16:14-20, 32-36). It has turned a little brown in reflected light, but when light shines through it, it's still rose red, and it didn't decompose as normal cadaver heart tissue would if so exposed. The 1970 investigation found no salt or any other kind of preparation on the Host that would have preserved it; it's a little dry, but, in fact, this slice of myocardium is still fresh. Even if you overlook the fact that nobody in the eighth century could dissect like that, even if you conclude that a clever priest switched real flesh and fresh blood for the usual bread and wine, it's hard to explain away the fact that they don't act like ordinary flesh and blood.

The Breaking of the Bread, and the Blood

There are lots of other similar phenomena centered on the Presence of Christ in the Eucharist. In Ferrara, Italy, for instance, on Easter Sunday, March 28, 1171, when Father Pietro de Verona broke the Host, a stream of blood spurted out from the halves, copi-

---

105. The same kind of weight phenomenon occurred with three pellets as big as hazelnuts, taken from the gall bladder of St. Clare of Montefalco when she died in 1308. Any one of them weighed as much as any two or all three. They can still be seen in a reliquary at the Augustinian convent of Montefalco.

106. The results were published In the *Osservatore Romano*, April 3, 1971. The study was headed by Professor Doctor Odoardo Linoli, professor of anatomy and pathological histology and in chemistry and clinical microscopy as well as head physician of the united hospitals of Arezzo, with Dr. Ruggero Bertelli, professor emeritus of normal human anatomy at the University of Siena. The only unusual thing that they found about the blood was that, interestingly enough, it had very low sodium.

ous and forceful enough to stain the marble vault above the altar.[107] Witnesses, including Father Aimone, Father Bono, and Father Leonardo, as well as the rest of the congregation, all saw the blood and also noticed that the Host itself had turned to flesh. You can see the bloodstained vault today in the same church, Santa Maria del Vado, in the side chapel to which it was transferred in 1500 for easier access by pilgrims.[108]

When Pius IX Ferretti saw the vault in 1857, he remarked that the bright-red drops were like the drops on the corporal at Orvieto. And, in fact, the most famous, and the most consequential, Eucharistic miracle of this kind is the one that happened in Bolsena, a little town just outside of Orvieto and about seventy miles north of Rome, in 1263. But the chain of events leading up to it started long before that and far from Italy, in about 1250 in Liège in present-day Belgium. There was a nun living there, Sister Juliana of Mont-Cornillon, known for her sanctity and devotion. But from the time she was a little girl, she'd been puzzled—annoyed, even—by a persistent apparition. She saw a kind of luminous disk, glowing softly like the Moon, with a black band across it. The apparition wouldn't go away, year after year, and she couldn't make head or tail of it, and she got tired of it.

Like most credit-worthy visionary nuns, she didn't brag about it; in fact, she didn't tell anybody about it for about twenty years. At last, she had another apparition, this one more transitory and more comprehensible. Christ came to her, she said, and explained that the disk represented the Christian year, while the black band represented a major feast that was missing, a feast celebrating Christ in the Blessed Sacrament, to come, logically, after Pentecost.

Juliana tried as best she could to prompt the adoption of just such a feast day, but no visionary can do that alone, no matter how good an idea it is. She told three prominent people in the Church: the bishop of Liège, a Dominican named Hugh who later became Cardinal Legate in the Netherlands, and a distinguished archdeacon in the city, Jacques Pantaleon. But it was only instituted as a local feast confined to the diocese, celebrated for the first time in 1246. That was about it—again, the Church is never in any hurry to institute new feast days, and the observance stayed confined to the diocese of Liège. Juliana herself, like many highly gifted mystics, was elected prioress, steadily hated by her sisters in the order, deposed, exiled, and left to die in 1258, alone, and in obscurity and sickness.

Jacques Pantaleon, though, had lost touch with her by then, having been

107. He broke it during the *fractio panis*, the breaking of the bread that's a normal part of the Mass; Mt 14:19, 26:26; Mk 8:6, 14:22; Lk 9:16, 22:19, 24:35; Jn 6; etc.

108. Another example of a fleshly Host is kept in the Church of the Holy Cross in Augsburg, Germany, this Host having turned to flesh in 1194 after being stolen by an overly pious woman who wanted to reserve the Sacrament in her home; it is truly human flesh, unembalmed yet incorrupt for nearly eight hundred years. Still others are in the Church of the Holy Miracle in Santarem in Portugal (1266); in the Church of St. Quentin, Hasselt, Belgium (1317); St. Jacques in Louvain (1374); and St. Oswald's, Seefeld, Austria (1384). The bleeding fleshly Host of Offida, Italy (see following note), like many others, has vanished over the centuries.

appointed papal legate to Poland and Prussia and later consecrated Bishop of Verdun, just before he was made Patriarch of Jerusalem and shipped overseas in 1255. In 1261 he had to go to Italy to settle some patriarchal business, only to be elected pope— Alexander IV had died some three months earlier, and the election had dragged on inconclusively since.

Reigning as Urban IV, Jacques Pantaleon did what he could to correct the particular heresy raging at the time—Berengarianism, it was called—which, like many another heresy, started by denying the True Presence. It had already affected central Europe, and by 1263 it had touched one priest in particular, an otherwise obscure cleric known only as Peter of Prague.

Peter thought that if he could walk to Rome to pray at the tomb of his namesake, he could resolve his confusion about the Presence. He got as far as Bolsena, where he stayed the night at the rectory of the little church of Santa Christina. The next morning he celebrated Mass there, praying as he always did for sure knowledge of the truth about the True Presence. As he held the Host and pronounced the words of Christ, "This is my body," the Host turned to flesh in his hands and began to bleed profusely.

The blood cascaded onto the corporal, the linen napkin that's spread on the altar to catch the Host should it fall or to absorb any droplets of consecrated wine. Father Peter wrapped the Host in the corporal and left it on the altar as he ran out of the church, but it was bleeding so profusely that blood poured out of the linen onto the marble floor.

Now, Urban IV was living at Orvieto then (he never went to Rome) and that's not far from Bolsena. Father Peter went straight to the Holy Father to tell him what had happened. The Pope sent a bishop back to Orvieto to verify the story and to bring back the Host and the corporal. The bishop found everything exactly as had been reported, including the corporal and the bloodstained altar stones, which you can still see in the church of Santa Christina in Bolsena.[109]

But the pope was so intrigued that he didn't wait for them to get back with their report; he went out to meet them at the Bridge of the Sun, outside of Orvieto. When he saw the bleeding Host, he fell on his knees before it. He went back to the papal palace at Orvieto and showed the Host to the people from the balcony. During the next year he wrote the Bull *Transiturus*, which established the Feast of Corpus Christi, the Feast

109. Among other corporals stained with Eucharistic blood are those preserved from the miracles of Daroca, Spain (1239), in the church of the Colegiata; at the Cathedral of Macerata, Italy (1356); and at Stich, Germany (1970), which were tested and confirmed not only as human blood but blood of a man in the agony of torture—blood chemistry changes with stress. A blood-stained altar cloth accompanies the fleshly Host of Louvain (1374), and an altar-rail cloth stained with blood by a dropped Host on Easter Sunday, March 31, 1331, is kept in the Church of Blanot, France. A stained roofing tile and tablecloth in which a stolen bleeding Host was wrapped in 1280 are preserved in the Sanctuary of St. Augustine, Offida, Italy, and a breviary page stained with blood from a Host in 1330 is kept in the Basilica of St. Rita in Cascia, Italy; it shows the profile of a sorrowing Jesus. It's interesting, too, that those prodigies of flesh and blood examined with modern techniques have, across centuries and continents, the same blood type, AB positive, which is exactly the same as the blood on the Holy Shroud of Turin.

of the Body of Christ, that filled the gap in the calendar pointed out to him years before in the vision of Blessed Juliana of Liège.[110]

The Feast of the Body of Christ

But the new feast needed a new Mass—that is, a special proper for a Mass with Bible readings selected to underscore the point that was to be made, and with antiphons and other transitional verses, set with hymns and accompanied by vespers and other minor liturgical texts and songs. So Urban IV turned to the foremost theologian of the day, Thomas Aquinas, and asked him to write everything that was necessary. The result was not only the Mass of Corpus Christi but the great hymns *O Salutaris Hostia* (*O Saving Victim*) and his *Tantum Ergo*, both of which are still cherished by the Church as great treasures of poetry, music, and spirituality. But more than that, the research that St. Thomas had to do in preparation for this task stood him in good stead when he was asked by St. Louis IX of France to settle a dispute at the University of Paris about the True Presence.[111]

He prayed fervently, and he studied hard. Finally, St. Thomas wrote a treatise on the subject that the University considered definitive and that the Church as a whole later adopted as a theologically sound exposition of the doctrine.

And Thomas himself got a special reward for it. One day at Mass, kneeling before the Sacrament, he saw Christ as an apparition who said to him, "You have written well of the Sacrament of my Body." Struck with ecstasy, St. Thomas levitated and remained suspended off the floor long enough for the phenomenon to be witnessed by everyone present.

THE DEPENDABLE MIRACLE OF THE EUCHARIST

As at Lanciano, the miracle of Bolsena sounded the death-knell of the heresy then current. The Feast of Corpus Christi, too, reinforced the Church's teachings on the True Presence, and there have always been reports of remarkable physical healings associated with devotions centered on the Sacrament, just as the healings in the Gospels happened in close proximity to the Body of Christ.

In fact, going by the record, more creditable miracles happen in the presence of the Eucharist than anywhere else, just as more creditable mystic experiences of any

110. This may seem like working fairly fast, but the Feast of Corpus Christi was not put on the Church's universal calendar until a hundred years later. Not even the personal support of the pope can speed things up that much, when it comes to a major change like a new universal feast. This was, by the way, the first feast day that Luther abolished for his followers.

111. The story is told that St. Louis was working one day in his palace study, years later, when an excited courtier burst in. "Sire!" he yelled, "Come quickly! The Infant Jesus is appearing on the Host in the chapel monstrance!" Louis looked up at him calmly for a moment, as if to say, well, why shouldn't he? and went back to his writing. He later said that he already knew that Christ is present in the Sacrament, and that seeing it wouldn't make any difference to him, which is precisely the reaction that the Church hopes for, when these things happen.

kind happen there. So, the Church asks, why be overly concerned with the one-time appearance of a saint when the reality of Christ is always present in the Sacrament? And why be so impressed with supernatural healings of the body when supernatural healings of the soul are just as remarkable and infinitely more numerous?

Most of the miracles in Christianity seem to be interior, working in the individual soul to get its attention, to turn it—to convert it, if we use the Latin-based word. Not everybody who goes to Lourdes or Fátima or La Salette finds physical healing, but apparently most find spiritual healing, coming away with a new understanding of the place that their suffering has in the world. And only God can reach out to the heart of the sinner, the skeptic, or those who have not been evangelized, turning their hearts to his love. Sometimes this just happens suddenly, quietly, as it did with Bl. Angela of Foligno. She lived a worldly (that is, sinful) life until she was forty, and then all of a sudden she turned her back on it all and became a Third-Order Franciscan. She never told anybody anything about exactly what hit her.

Which is not to say that interior conversions can't be fairly spectacular, just like St. Paul's.

The Revolutionary Conversion of Frances Allen

Ethan Allen had evidently been favorably impressed with Canada when he had invaded it during the War of Independence. He'd been captured near Montreal in 1775, and after the War he decided to send his daughter Frances to the convent school of the Sisters of the Congregation of Notre Dame there. That way, she could take advantage of the excellent education available—education that, at that time, only the Church offered to girls. Frances was eager to go, but once she got there it didn't look like it was going to work out. Her background was against her; Ethan, described by a sympathetic biographer as "a blustering frontier … ignoramus of rough-and-ready humour", was also a self-proclaimed prophet. He wrote a strange little book called *Reason, the Only Oracle of Man; or a Compendious System of Natural Religion, Alternately Adorned with Confutations of a Variety of Doctrines Incompatible with It.*[112]

With this kind of religious upbringing, Frances evidently figured that the nuns were right about everything that they taught except religion. She was a clever enough student, and in fact a pleasant enough person, but she took every opportunity to ridicule the Faith, which never goes over well in a Catholic school. And she singled out the Blessed Sacrament for particular mockery. Finally she became such a disruption that the sisters decided that they had no choice but to expel her. One of the nuns interceded for her, pleading for a little more time, but it was decided to ask Frances to leave.

---

112. Published in 1784. The biographer referred to, M. C. Tyler (*Literary History of the American Revolution*, New York, 1897), really does seem fairly even-handed in his assessment, so you can imagine. Allen did endow the University of Vermont, too, which has to stand to his credit. It's also important to remember that Christianity is a *revealed* religion; *natural* religions, like the one that Allen proposed, are developed by humans in response to nature. Like paganism.

The afternoon of the day that she was to go, Frances was helping the sister arrange some flowers for the altar. On impulse, the sister asked her to go into the oratory and put them on the altar for her; and, also on impulse, she added, "Be sure to adore the Lord while you're in there."

Frances got as far as the altar rail when, she said, her legs became paralyzed, and she was unable to move farther. She must have cried out, because some of the sisters saw her fall to her knees. By the time they got to her, she was pouring out a stream of words of praise and faith. Frances Allen never told anybody what she had seen or heard that afternoon, but when she told her family that she wanted to become a nun, they (understandably) pulled her out of the school and took her home to Vermont. But her vocation persisted, and within about a year she had persuaded her mother, or at least reconciled her to the idea. They went back to Montreal, where Frances entered the nursing order of the Sisters Hospitallers of the Hôtel-Dieu of St. Joseph, becoming the first American nun born in the thirteen colonies. Nobody investigated the event officially—Frances herself never claimed an apparition—but there are countless stories of just this kind of conversion and spiritual healing in the annals of the Church.

In fact, if you define mystic phenomena as God's reaching out to make himself apparent to the human senses, then the Eucharist is the most central and most powerful mystic phenomenon of all, and the only apparition that occurs constantly and predictably.

ten

such light as shines
in the world

I saw light,
but not such light
as shines in the world;
I perceived an odor,
but not like that of plants
or anything of the kind;
... Then I immediately heard a voice,
but from no human lips ...

— Mary's account of the Annunciation,
from the *Revelations*
of St. Bridget of Sweden (*c.* 1343)

The appearance of bread and wine that the Eucharist retains makes it easy to taste and see the goodness of the Lord, but the mechanisms of other appearances of supernatural beings are less easily grasped. How exactly do human beings sense the presence of an apparition? How does the invisible make itself visible?

First, it's important to distinguish apparitions from other times when people see things, or think that they see things, that aren't physically there. In terms of both this world's reality and the other-worldly reality of the spirit, the Church has always understood that there's a definite distinction between creditable apparitions and psychological phenomena like illusions, hallucinations, or dreams. Psychological events come from inside the person himself, but the evidence implies that apparitions have an objective reality of their own.[113]

Now, it can be hard to tell the difference, on your own; many psychological or emotional disorders make people think that their own ideas come from somebody else. But if you look at these things through a more objective lens, it's fairly easy to see the differences in the natures of these phenomena.

ILLUSIONS

An *illusion* is a mis-perception of something completely natural, the altered appearance of something that really exists, but not in that form or in that place. If you put a pencil into a glass of water, for instance, it appears to bend where it enters the water; you know that it doesn't, but the combination of a straight pencil and clear water causes the illusion that it does. Or you might be out on the prairie or in a desert and see a city on the horizon, even though the city is really far too distant to be seen from that spot. Atmospheric conditions just bend the light and give you the illusion that the city is there.

So an illusion is seeing something real but not as it really is; the event itself gives appearances that are somehow altered to imply or suggest that some other event happened. That's why magician's tricks are properly called illusions: the magician manipulates things so that you get a carefully controlled, and wrong, impression of what's happening. But illusions dissolve pretty quickly in the first light of investigation, and it's not that difficult to expose the causes of illusions. Physicists can explain the optical tricks of atmosphere and natural lighting that cause people to see things that aren't there, and some professional illusionists make a good living exposing fraudulent faith healers and the like.[114]

Besides, illusions require material objects with a physical reality; even with the best will in the world, you can't produce an illusion just by wanting it, and you can't make it go away once you see it. Any number of people in the proper position can see it with their bodily eyes, just as they'd see anything else. So illusions are by nature different from apparitions, which have no material substance and are not usually seen by all of the people present.

HALLUCINATIONS

An *hallucination* is the appearance of something that doesn't exist, and it usually happens through the action of some psychoactive substance or extreme emotional stress. Now,

---

113. Of course you'd have to accept that supernatural entities exist, and since that's a matter of faith it can lead to a circular sort of argument. The evidence for their existence consists of apparitions, miracles, and other mystic events that are, by definition, an outreach by one of these supernatural entities into the natural world; but some people dismiss or refuse that evidence, which lets them say that beings causing such evidence don't exist, either. Creditable accounts of levitations, bilocations, regeneration of missing flesh and bone accord with the normal rules of evidence, though, and parallel evidence of any other occurrence would hold up in court.

114. Unfortunately, there are fatal flaws in the reasoning of many professional debunkers that keep their exposures from being really convincing. See below, Part Five.

plenty of purported apparitions happened when the seer was very clearly under immense emotional stress—rigorous penances, long fasting, and the like are inclined to provoke hallucinations sooner or later, if they're kept up too long. That's why the Church has always had strict safeguards in the uses of these disciplinary abstentions. Most creditable mystics, sensible people that they are, assume at first that they're hallucinating. Julian of Norwich did, for instance, but "when the vision had passed," she said, "our Lord Jesus in his mercy would not allow it to perish, but he revealed it all again in my soul, saying these words ... 'Know it well now, it was no hallucination that you saw today'". Which was only more confusing—was it an hallucination telling her that it wasn't an hallucination?

Like dreams, hallucinations of this kind have their uses; they can focus a person's attention on a problem or a course of action. But nobody makes too much of them in a theological way. If a person were to have an hallucination that happened to have some constructive content, that clarified a course of action or an attitude—provided that it didn't tell the person anything contrary to the Gospels—that's fine. The person's work might really amount to something after the experience, and it might add color and vitality to the pageant of the Church's life on Earth. But the hallucination itself doesn't mean much for the whole of Christendom, not directly.

But in substance apparitions are very distinct from hallucinations. Apparitions can happen without particular emotional stress, certainly without drugs or other factors that alter one's consciousness. Apparitions persist; hallucinations fade. Apparitions can't be induced—again, you can't make God do something like that—and they often convey information that the seer didn't have before and could not have had by natural means, which no hallucination can do. And of course psychological events like hallucinations come from within the person, even if he's not aware of it.

Dreams

Apparitions aren't *dreams*, either. Dreams happen when people are asleep, but apparitions happen to people who are wide awake and, often, who aren't thinking about anything supernatural at the time. Dreams and visions are always mentioned as two distinct phenomena, in the Bible, as when Job complained of being frightened by dreams and terrified by visions (7:14), or when Daniel, like some other prophets, was described as having understanding of both visions and dreams (1:17). And dreams are different from prophecy, too: there are prophets, on the one hand, and dreamers of dreams on the other (Dt 13:1,3,5; also Nm 12:6; Jl 3:1; Ac 2:17), and dreams aren't always prophetic (Jr 23:25-27).

Still, divine messages in dreams appear throughout the Bible, sometimes standing at the center of the story, like Pharaoh's dream interpreted by Joseph (Gn 41:8) or Nabuchodnosor's dream that Daniel explained (Dn 2). Sometimes the whole course of revelation pivots on a dream, as when St. Joseph's dream prompted him to take the Child to Egypt to keep him safe during Herod's persecutions (Mt 2:12).

These biblical dreams were evidently prompted by God, which would put that class of dream in a kind of special category as a mystic experience, a sort of apparition that happens to come while the person is asleep. But it's entirely possible—and in some emotional or psychological states it's entirely likely—that a person can have impressively vivid dreams that include God or an angel or saint or devil, an image of some independent entity, that comes to give some message or other.

That's why mystics and moral theologians have always cautioned very strongly against putting any faith in your dreams, particularly those in which it seems that some powerful being tells you to do something. The chances are overwhelming that it's really from your own mind, because dreams do have a lot of wish fulfillment in them. "Often in sleep," St. Augustine noted, "when we are thirsty we dream of drinking, and when we are hungry we dream of eating, and many other such experiences are transferred from the body to the soul by a certain industry of the imagination." It's the same with any other problem or desire that you may have—what you already expect, Sirach says (34:5), the mind depicts. A qualified spiritual director can tell the difference, but you almost certainly can't distinguish it by yourself, because you're so involved in the dream and because you're involved in it all alone. So, basically, the advice that St. John Climacus gave nearly fourteen hundred years ago is still sound: "the one who believes in dreams shows his inexperience, while the one who distrusts every dream is very sensible" (*Ladder of Divine Ascent*, Step 3, "On Exile").[115]

Still, in the purely natural order of things, dreams can often serve as a way for your mind to solve problems and answer questions that you can't quite think about during the day, even religious questions. But these, too, come from inside of you, not from any outside agency, even though you might be surprised that you yourself have the power to work things out.[116] For example, Agusto Odone, an employee of the World Bank, worked out the metabolism of adrenoleukodystrophy (ALD) in a dream after he fell asleep while reading all available scientific literature on the disease—he's the man who won an honorary medical degree for the discovery of "Lorenzo's oil".

But the classic modern example of this is the German chemist Friedrich August Kekulé von Stradonitz (1829-1896). When Kekulé was working, organic chemistry was a complete mess. There had been lots of epochal discoveries that had pretty well destroyed the old way of looking at things, but nobody could integrate them all into a single new theory to replace it. Nobody could figure out how carbon atoms—the basis of all organic compounds—were structured in organic molecules. The central puzzle of this was the structure of benzene; if anybody could figure that out, all other organic molecules would be easy. Well, Kekulé struggled with the benzene problem for nearly

115. St. Gregory the Great (*Dialogues* 4:50) gives six reasons for memorable dreams: a full stomach, an empty one; illusions or your thoughts combined with illusions; actual private revelations or your thoughts combined with actual private revelations. So only one of the six possible causes would result in anything really worthwhile; and that's the rarest of all possible causes.

116. René Descartes assembled the basis of his philosophy in three dreams he had November 9-10, 1619 (*cf. Discours de la méthode*, 1637; *Méditations*, 1641). The ability to put together, while awake, surprisingly accurate solutions from clues imperceptible to the average person is, of course, a skill acquired by many business negotiators, detectives, forensic pathologists, and professional fortune-tellers. But it's also true that the Devil can reveal, God permitting, some truly unknowable facts or even the future.

ten years, as did every other chemist in the world. He got nowhere with it.

Then one day in 1865 he fell asleep on a city bus. In only a few seconds, he dreamed of a colorful swirling snake that took its own tail in its mouth, bending itself into a ring. He woke up with a start, having realized that the benzene molecule was structured as a ring. With this insight, everything else known about organic chemistry at the time fell into place, forming the strong and unified theory that's still the basis of the field today. Kekulé himself is remembered as the father of organic chemistry, and it all happened in that brief dream—a dream he'd been studying for, but a dream nonetheless. He didn't attribute this to the intervention of any supernatural agent, of course. He just knew that, in that state of relaxation, he'd been able to put together everything he'd studied and thought about for a decade.

Naturally, these dreams of discovery can have a religious theme, if you have a religious problem to work out, and they can have imagery just as strange as Kekulé's. But a lot of these pivotal dreams don't seem to even have any visual imagery in them at all. Back in the seventh century, for instance, St. Bede (better known as the Venerable Bede) wrote about a servant named Cædmon who lived in the abbey run by that formidable lady, St. Hilda of Whitby. Cædmon wasn't much of a servant, apparently—he had grown old in service as a cowherd, work assigned to him because he couldn't do anything else.

He didn't fit in socially, either. People people used to take turns, in those days, singing little epics off the tops of their heads of an evening, sitting around the fire, but Cædmon used to run back to the cows before it was his turn to extemporize, because he couldn't do it. Until someone spoke to him by name in a dream. "Cædmon, sing to me," it said. "Sing to me of creation." And Cædmon got up and promptly began to sing in praise of God, St. Bede says. After that, although he could neither read nor write, Cædmon blended Latin literary traditions with Anglo-Saxon ones; he'd listen to the monks reading the lessons from Mass or the Office, go home to bed and ruminate like one of his cows, St. Bede says, and wake up with that story composed in Anglo-Saxon verse.

Dreams, then, can be a way of working out your own problems, and they can carry those brief messages that focus your life on a mission or an attitude. But, useful and inspiring as they may be, dreams are completely different from apparitions in their nature because dreams, by definition, normally come from within you, just as hallucinations do.

So a credit-worthy apparition can't be attributed to psychology, parapsychology, or neurosis. It's distinct from the results of these factors. And, whether you believe in divine intervention or not, something unique happens in an apparition, something that has, to the person who experiences it, an objective and independent reality; something that conveys information that the seer didn't have before, and information moreover that often constitutes a message of some importance for the whole world. Something happens that changes the life of the seer and of many, many people around the world for years after. But what?

SIGHT BEYOND SIGHT

Normally, when we see three-dimensional objects with our three-dimensional eyes or hear them with our ears, their physical bodies reflect light or make the air vibrate into sound waves. When we smell things, our noses inhale microscopic particles that these bodies give off. Well, in some cases, St. Thomas Aquinas reasons in the *Summa*, angels must take on some kind of physical body, because they don't have bodies by nature, and some of them—like the ones who appeared to Abraham, to Lot, and to Tobias—were seen by everybody at large, walking around like humans. His idea about condensing bodies out of air (*Summa Theologica*, Question 51, Article 2) would explain some, but not all, apparitions. Sometimes, as at Fátima or Beauraing, two or three people may see an apparition while even fewer hear it; people standing nearby may see and not hear, or they may sense nothing at all. Apparitions can't be photographed, either, so evidently they don't depend on reflected light for their appearance.

Besides, it's not necessary to actually have functional bodily eyes to see an apparition. Bl. Sibyllina Biscossi, for instance, was blind from the age of twelve, and Ven. John de Saint-Sampson was since he was three, but they saw visions anyway, as did St. Lutgardis, who was blind the last eleven years of her life. And when people are in ecstasy they may see apparitions, but they're oblivious to everything in their physical environment.

They can do this, St. Thomas Aquinas continues, because the soul senses things, too, in a way parallel to the way that the body does. The soul senses the body to which it's united, and through the body's five senses it senses every material body that can be perceived—that is, through your body, your soul knows fully where you are and what you're doing. "And there is yet another kind of ability of the soul," he says, "that regards a still more universal object: namely, not only the sensible body but universally all being."

There exists, then, "an operation of the soul that exceeds the bodily nature [of humans] by so much that it is not even performed by any bodily organ," not only "with regard to things that are joined to it, but with regard to things outside of it."[117] In other words, the soul has its own five senses, the spiritual counterparts of the sight, hearing, smell, taste, and touch of the body. And these can sense everything, even things of the next world. Mystics and visionaries are given the extraordinary grace of being in touch with the senses of their souls, while most of us aren't.

This is why many mystics can distinguish holy things from ordinary things. They can tell consecrated Hosts from plain ones, blessed items like rosaries from their unblessed twins, priests from laymen, relics from bones. They can even sense the presence of hidden holy things, either in an experimental game of hide-and-seek or because those things have been genuinely lost. This is the mystic gift called *hierognosis*, from the

117. *Summa*, 1:75-89. In this he follows St. Augustine who (like everybody else), notes that the Bible attributes vision not only to the body but also to the spirit, and more to the spirit than to the body; otherwise, he says, Scripture would not be right in giving the name "seers" to the prophets who saw the future by spiritual sight.

Greek ιερō, holy, and γνωσι, knowing. And it goes all the way back to biblical days. Consider St. John the Baptizer, who recognized the presence of Christ even when they were both *in utero* (Lk 1:44), or Simeon at the Presentation: the Babe looked like the infant son of a carpenter, but he made himself known truly to Simeon, not through the eyes of the body, but through the eyes of the soul.

Through the soul's sight, mystics see apparitions. Through the soul's hearing, they sense heavenly voices or music. Their spiritual smell is opened to the celestial fragrances so often experienced around apparitions.[118] "Also," St. John of the Cross says, "it happens in regard to taste. They experience very exquisite savors … and concerning touch they feel extreme delight, at times so intense that all the bones and marrow rejoice, flourish, and bathe in it. This delight is usually termed *spiritual unction*, and it is common with spiritual persons." Bl. Angela of Foligno said that this unction softened her limbs; "liquefaction", she called it.

But these spiritual senses usually don't open up the next world because they're united to the body, which is stuck in this world. After the body dies, though, the soul is free to meet her God face to face; and, reunited to the glorified body again at the resurrection, those who make it through the Judgement have beatific vision, the sight of God and of all spirits, as well as of the other glorified bodies in Heaven. Then shall the eyes of the soul be opened, as it were. In that sense, apparitions are a little foretaste of the beatific state, because you can see into Heaven without the interference of the material world. But, having looked at hundreds of apparitions over the centuries, moral theologians distinguish three distinct kinds: corporeal, imaginative, and intellectual.

Corporeal Apparitions

The most common kind of apparition is called a *corporeal* vision, or sometimes an *exterior* vision. A few authorities call it an *ocular* vision, because it's seen with the eyes of the body. This is the kind with an assumed body, a contrived physical presence that reflects light just the way any other physical body does. It's the kind that St. Thomas Aquinas figured was made somehow out of condensed air, somehow.[119] The Angel of Peace who appeared in the clouds of Fátima in the spring of 1916 was probably this kind of apparition, because all of the children saw him in that form. The apparition of St. Michael on the Castel Sant' Angelo, or of Raphael to Tobias and his family, must have been this same kind of apparition, too.

These are the ones that we most usually think of when we think of apparitions. But, according to St. John of the Cross, "the more exterior these corporeal visions are,

---

118. St. Teresa may have had this sense all of her life; certainly she didn't realize that people don't normally smell these heavenly fragrances. When she had to describe that fragrance, she just said, in an offhand manner, well, it smells like relics.

119. St. Augustine, *Enchiridion* 59, figures that it's not very profitable to try to figure out exactly how these things work; "for what's the need to affirm, or deny, or define accurately these subjects and others like them, when we can blamelessly remain entirely ignorant of them?" Not worth worrying about, in other words.

the less profitable they are to the interior and spiritual part of the soul. This is due to the extreme distance and disparity between the corporeal and the spiritual." You can get some spiritual consolation from these visions, he says, but a lot less than when the communications are more spiritual in nature. "Palpable, tangible, and material as they are," he says, "they strongly affect the senses so that in one's judgement they seem worthwhile." But a person receiving these corporeal visions is likely to develop a secret high opinion of himself, "that now he's someone in God's eyes." They distract you from what's really important, he says.[120]

Imaginative Apparitions

Another kind of apparitions is called *imaginative*. That's unfortunate, because it echoes our word *imagination*, and that makes it sound as if the person just fantasized about the apparition and believed himself. But your imagination is your ability to generate pictures of things in your mind; the imaginative sense is an entirely different thing. It's that sense inside you that can receive and comprehend direct communications from some supernatural agency to your soul. So when one of these occurs, you get a clear image of the external entity—God, an angel, a saint, or a devil—in what you might call your mind's eye.

The interesting thing is that the mystics can usually tell the difference among the kinds of apparitions. Julian of Norwich knew that her vision of the Scourging was imaginative, not corporeal, because as the torrent of hot blood ran to where it should have fallen, it disappeared.[121] St. Teresa of Avila said that she never saw a vision with her bodily eyes, and she knew that her first imaginative vision of Christ, on St. Paul's Day, was that kind because she saw his humanity with such wondrous beauty and majesty—nobody could describe this beauty without ruining it, she said. In other words, it was clearly not something that appeared as a solid, three-dimensional body. It was an image that came to her through her imaginative sense.

Intellectual Apparitions

When St. Teresa had her first *intellectual* vision, though, she didn't quite know what to make of it. When she was praying on St. Peter's Day one year, she said, "I saw, or, to

120. It's important to note, though, that corporeal apparitions aren't ghosts; ghosts are different from apparitions, in any case. The idea of a ghost, supposedly the spirit of some (usually) undistinguished person made visible, isn't really compatible with Christian theology. Although the business about Saul and the Witch of Endor (1Kn 28:7-20) shows that God can let a living person see a departed soul if he wants to—as, for instance, to give help or obtain prayers—the story weighs against it (1Kn 28:3), as do Lv 19:31; Dt 18:11-12, etc. It hasn't happened creditably enough since then to be listed as a mystic phenomenon in its own right, and the idea that a soul can be stuck on Earth in a particular place is contrary to the Cycle of Redemption implicit or explicit throughout Scripture and Tradition. Moreover, devils can perfectly well appear corporeally, taking the form of departed loved ones, which is obviously delightful to the viewer but always works toward indifference in religion; it's reported far more often than you might think. Apparitions of angels—literally "messengers"—and departed saints (Mt 17:3, for instance) are obviously different, scripturally as well as ecclesiastically.

121. She classified visions as "bodily", "bodily yet more spiritual", and "spiritual"; the more or less standard terms "corporeal", "imaginative", and "intellectual" came later.

put it better, I felt Christ beside me; I saw nothing with my bodily eyes or with my soul, but it seemed to me that Christ was at my side ... Since I was completely unaware that there could be a vision like this one, it greatly frightened me in the beginning... However, by speaking one word alone to assure me, the Lord left me feeling as I usually did: quiet, favored, and without any fear."

This kind of apparition is a simple intuitive knowledge that you just know, with no help from your bodily senses. She later described this kind of vision as being as if food were put into your stomach without your having eaten it or knowing how it got there. These two kinds of apparition, she says, almost always come together: the imaginative lets you see, with the eyes of your soul, the beauty and glory of Christ's most holy humanity, while the intellectual one lets you understand how God is all-powerful and all-loving. For example, on May 29, 1571, she was at prayer after communion, and she was grieved, she said, because she couldn't concentrate. Turning her distraction into prayer, she complained to God about the weakness of human nature in this regard. Then, she said, "my soul began to enkindle, and it seemed to me I knew clearly in an intellectual apparition that the entire Blessed Trinity was present." She understood how God is three in one, she said, and all three persons spoke to her.

LOCUTIONS: HEARING THE WORD OF THE LORD

Apparitions that are heard rather than seen are called *locutions*, whether they're heard physically through the ears or spiritually through the heart. Sometimes they're called *auricular supernatural words*, but usually just locutions. They're among the most frequently reported mystic phenomena, just as in the Bible (1Kn 3:9-10, for instance), but they seem to proliferate whenever times start to change for the worse. Back in 1901, for instance, when the French government was considering laws to suppress all of the religious orders in the country, one self-proclaimed locutionary who went to Rome to prophesy to the Pope about it had to wait in line—ten other French prophets showed up that day alone to bend the ear of the Cardinal Secretary.[122]

There are two basic kinds of locution, the exterior and the interior. *Exterior* or *auricular* locutions are heard by the bodily hearing. They consist of normal sound waves in the air, but sound waves produced by some supernatural agency. Anybody within earshot could hear them, or part of them (Jn 12:28-30; 2Kn 22:14; Jb 37:1-4; Ps 17:14; Dn 10:6; Ac 2:2). Like corporeal visions, they rank pretty low on the scale of mystic phenomena.

Interior locutions come in two kinds. *Imaginative interior* locutions also consist of words, but they're perceived by the imaginative sense without the use of the ear. Here, too, the term "imaginative" shouldn't be confused with the imagination. The locutions of St. Michael and St. Catherine of Alexandria to St. Joan of Arc, or of the

---

122. As usual, they were all politely heard, but none of them got through to the Pope personally. Their numbers have increased as new modes of transportation have made it easier to get there—Pius IX Ferretti must have been tired of them by 1872, already, when he said that he didn't give much credit to prophecies, "because especially those that have recently appeared do not merit the honor of being read." They still come, though.

crucifix of San Damiano to St. Francis of Assisi, were one or the other of these kinds of locution, because they consisted of words definitely understood—those saints gave direct quotations of what they heard—but there's no way to tell exactly which kind they were because the saints were alone at the time. You can tell imaginative locutions from the auricular kind because they're directed specifically to a person, and (because they're not apprehended with the bodily ears) nobody else around can hear them. At La Salette, for example, the Lady turned to Maximin and spoke to him, but Mélanie, standing at his side, could not hear her; then the Lady spoke some secret to Mélanie that was not audible to Maximin.

Intellectual interior locutions are those that are communicated without words. This, says St. Teresa, is a foretaste of the way communication happens in Heaven, the blessed understanding each other without speaking. Like every other hint of what Heaven's like, an intellectual locution is beautiful beyond description. In fact, any heavenly locution, of any type, is ravishing. St. Ignatius of Loyola described all kinds of locution—*loquelas*, he calls them—as comparable to heavenly harmonies. They were so surpassing lovely, he said, that he sometimes got carried away with the beauty of them and forgot to pay attention to what they were saying.

In fact, looking back over the histories of the creditable mystics of the past, it's clear that these phenomena give us a glimpse into another world, a world normally invisible to us and infinitely superior to our own in power and duration—a world literally supernatural.

eleven

a middle term
between worlds

Sempiternity differs from Time, and from Eternity,
as a middle term existing between them ...
Eternity lacks a beginning and an end;
Sempiternity has a beginning, but no end;
Time has a beginning and an end.

— St. Thomas Aquinas, *Summa Theologica,*
Prima Pars, Quaestio X, articulus V

The Bible often speaks of Heaven and Hell in very elementary imagery, but it would be somewhat simplistic to visualize Heaven and Hell as places like our own world but hidden away from us somehow, literally above the sky or below the Earth. You can't take it literally; like the other great mystics, the human authors of Scripture used figurative language to get their points across. And behind the imagery of the Bible and of Sacred Tradition is a clear understanding that neither "place" is arranged according to our familiar three dimensions of height, width, and depth.

If Heaven and Hell were just like our world, we would be able to see spirits all the time—anything that has height, width, and depth is a three-dimensional object, and it can be apprehended by our senses. But we can't see, touch, hear, or smell angels, saints, and demons, or God himself. Not normally, anyway. So Heaven and Hell stand somehow outside of our dimension, outside of the space that we perceive because it has three dimensions.

And they also stand outside of the *Time* that we perceive. Time structures all of our sensory experience—three-dimensional objects, like moons and planets, and like people and animals, move through Time as they move through space. Time is our fourth dimension. Obviously, Heaven and Hell don't operate according to that dimension, either: they're outside of the reality that we call Time.

Time is defined as the interval between the movements of three-dimensional bodies through three-dimensional space. Before there were such bodies, of course, there wasn't any Time, so Time had a beginning—the evening and morning, the first day, if you believe only in the biblical account of creation, or the Big Bang if you believe only in the scientific account of it. Or both, if you take the Church's view.[123]

Everything that exists in Time comes to an end: plants, animals, and the physical bodies of people all come into being at a given point, live a while, and then die at another given point. And, one way or another, Time itself will come to an end, either because of command of the trumpet of judgement or because of the destruction of the three-dimensional space of the material universe, or both.

But Heaven and Hell are different, because they stand outside of Time. The beings who live in Heaven or Hell are there forever, and they won't die as we will here in the dimension of Time, where all things come to an end, just as Time itself will come to an end one day. The angels, saints, and demons inhabit the dimension that theologians call *Sempiternity*.

Sempiternity is a dimension unto itself where there isn't any change: spirits don't get older, they don't get sick, and they don't die. It can be thought of as what St. Augustine and St. Thomas Aquinas described as a "now ever standing". In Sempiternity, it's always "now"; there's no "before" or "after", because there's no Time there. This dimension is hard to imagine, but, to understand apparitions, you really only have to understand that Sempiternity is the dimension of the angels, saints, and demons, a dimension in which things can come into being at some definite point but will never come to an end.

God himself, in the Judeo-Christian understanding, is the only spirit that stands outside of Sempiternity. God always was and always will be; he's eternal, existing in a dimension that has no beginning and no end: *Eternity*. So, for God, just as for the angels, saints, and demons, there aren't any such things as "before" or "after", "above", "below", "through", "under", or any of the other concepts that we use to describe the positions and movements of three-dimensional things that move through Time. The spiritual realm is one that stands and moves according to its own coordinates, not the "up", "down", "left", "right", not the "now" and "then" that form our familiar frame of

123. Not that the Church officially endorses any particular physicist's account of the origins of the universe, but she has always insisted that there can be no conflict in truth, and both science and theology strive to understand the truth; scientific theories about how the material world came into being can be true, but they have to be compatible with the doctrine about it all, which is also true. But the act of creation requires both a command and a response. We can only understand the command through theology, and we can only describe the physical response through science—it's a matter of two separate kinds of question being studied by two different intellectual disciplines. Still, it's always been very difficult for most of us to make that distinction (which is why Galileo got into so much trouble), and scientific theories, products of the human mind, come and go, but revelation stays intact within the Church from age to age.

reference here in Time.[124]

THE OTHER DIMENSIONS OF MYSTIC EXPERIENCE

Now, stick with this part, because it's important for the understanding of apparitions and all of the other mystic phenomena. When you die, you move instantly out of Time and into Sempiternity. Christ's teaching is that the bodies of the dead will rise again on the Last Day, when Time ends for everybody, united with their corresponding souls and "glorified" as his own was at his Resurrection. St. Paul describes the process (1Cr 15:35-55), noting that these glorified bodies are the real, physical bodies that we have now. St. Thomas Aquinas deduced from Scripture and Tradition, and from the commentaries of the Fathers of the Church, that glorified bodies are like the angels in some ways. For one thing, they're *immortal*, of course. And he shows that they're *immune* or *impassible* (having no disease, decline, or injury, nor any change; Mt 6:20, for instance, or, as St. Augustine commented, they can have no change because every change is a kind of death: the former state has to pass away before the change can take effect).

Aquinas points out that they're also like the angels in that they're *agile* (able to traverse space quickly or instantaneously, and not subject to human limitations on knowledge and wisdom; Jb 2:1-2; Tb 8:3; Zc 1:9-11; Lk 9:30-31; etc.); *subtle* (free from earthly restraints like gravity and solid walls, as in Jg 13:20; Jn 20:19, 26; Ac 1:9; etc.); and, most important for apparitions, they're normally *invisible* to Earth-bound humans but can sometimes be seen, if God wants them to be. We also know that, to us, they appear indescribably beautiful (Jg 13:6; Lk 24:5; Ac 6:15; etc.) and radiant with light beyond any light that shines here in Time and space (Ez 1:13; Dn 10:6; Mt 28:2-3; Mr 9:1-3; Lk 2:8-9; etc.). And their beauty and brightness are enough to astonish humans—those of us who haven't died yet, anyway. They're also possessed of *beatific vision*, which means that they can see God.

Note that this list of characteristics is also how you would describe apparitions. But this is simply what the angels are already like, and what we're all supposed to be like after resurrection, those of us who make the grade and pass judgement, anyway.

The Church teaches that immediately after death, we each face an individual judgement, and then, at the end of Time, there's a general judgement, too. But, looking at it from the standpoint of Sempiternity, the instant your soul is separated from your body, you're outside of Time, and you probably can't perceive the things that happen in Time and in the other three dimensions here on Earth any more. Once you're in Sempiternity, there's no before and no after; so you probably won't recognize any delay between the instant of your death and the instant of your resurrection in a glorified body, although, from the viewpoint of other humans, your body will rest in the grave

---

124. St. Hilary of Poitiers (*The Trinity*, 3) notes that Christ's words about how he is in the Father and the Father is in him (Jn 14:10) are incomprehensible if seen only in the context of Time and space, in which anything containing something else has to be outside of the thing that it contains, and in which it is not possible that something that's inside another thing can also be outside it.

until the general judgement at the end of Time.[125]

That's because Time ends for each of us the moment we die—"Today," said Julian of Norwich as she felt death spreading through her limbs, "today is my Doomsday." And that, in turn, is why the Church doesn't waste a lot of energy fussing about "end-time prophecies" and the like. Nobody can know the moment at which the angel will scroll back the sky, so to speak, ending Time and bringing Heaven and Earth together (Mt 24:36; 25:13; Rv 6:14). So why worry about something that you can't know, when you do know that you'll most definitely die—and probably unexpectedly? For the Church, the idea is for each of us to prepare carefully for the certain day of his own death, which is, for all practical purposes, the Apocalypse.

The nature of Sempiternity and its relationships to us here in Time have always been extremely difficult to express, because all of our thoughts and language are stuck in those four dimensions. We say, for instance, that Christ is seated at the right hand of God, "but," as Julian of Norwich says, "this does not mean that the Son sits on the right-hand side as one man sits beside another in this life, for there is no such sitting, as I see it, in the Trinity; but he sits at his Father's right hand, that is to say right in the highest nobility of the Father's joy." Even St. Augustine had a hard time with describing life out-side of Time. "Those who consider this matter are baffled because of the tough resis-tance that the senses and habit offer," he said. "Who can comprehend this even in a thought, so as to express it in a word? Who can explain this?"

So mystics, like theologians, like the Bible itself, have to resort to symbolic lan-guage when they try to convey what these dimensions outside of Time are like. Historically, this has been difficult because people just didn't understand the physical uni-verse in a way that would even let them find metaphorical ways to express the nature of Sempiternity—attempts to describe the fact that spirits don't take up any space, for instance, degenerated into that old platitude about how many angels can dance on the head of a pin, which misses the point entirely. Now, ironically enough, science fiction has made the idea clear to most Americans. We're used to stories about portals between dimensions, between worlds that are normally invisible and insensible to the other. And we're used to tales of superior beings—stronger, smarter beings with far greater powers than ours—coming through those portals to interact with Earthlings. If you think of that other dimension as Heaven, that's basically the age-old mechanism of apparitions, in a nutshell. And the spiritual truth, you might say, is a lot more interesting than sci-ence fiction.

---

125. In fact—although this isn't part of the Church's official teaching—the instant you die, you will prob-ably find not only yourself resurrected in a glorified body but all of your friends, too, who were alive at the time of your death, because you're outside of Time already. They may enter Sempiternity after you in Time because they die after you in Time, but in Sempiternity there's no before or after. Which is not to say that the resurrection has already taken place (2Tm 2:18), because there's no "already" in the dimen-sion of Sempiternity. It's tough to imagine.

twelve

beyond ordinary
consciousness

The deliciousness of some of these states
seems to be beyond anything known
in ordinary consciousness.

— William James,
The Varieties of Religious Experience,
Lecture XVI (1902)

In mysticism, the cases of mystic activity properly so called, there are two contexts that you have to consider: the spiritual and the physical. The spiritual consists of gifts like the experimental knowledge of God, passive purgation of the senses and of the soul, continued awareness of God's presence, and, at the highest level, total death to oneself, the practice of heroic virtue, joy in persecution, an urgency about the salvation of the souls of others, and relative confirmation in grace—all of the consolations and comforts that the mystics receive in the midst of their sufferings. But it's the physical context that draws the most attention; and the basic physical state of the active mystic is *ecstasy*.

Ecstasy brings with it certain bodily concomitant phenomena; the body shares in some of it, and even a great deal, as St. Teresa said. The physical symptoms of this, the basic starting state for mystic experiences, run with fair consistency in the Church from earliest days—from the days of the Old Testament, for that matter—until the present. Of course, these bodily effects happen in any degree, from the fairly mild to the excruciating, and there are always exceptions; some creditable mystics don't exhibit all of these concomitant phenomena, and a few don't exhibit any of them.

But when God first reaches out to people, usually those who have learned to pray well through their own ascetic efforts, they generally show some of these symptoms in a fairly mild way. This is a symptom of the prayer of quiet, not quite ecstasy; the body doesn't move, and if the eyes stay open they only see the world as if through an even white mist, something like gentle fog or the smoke that comes from incense, the smoky mist moving and pulsating, increasing and decreasing in density with the progress of the prayer itself. Others close their eyes, which feel as if they were being darkened; the eyelids, in this case, don't flutter as they do when people simply close their eyes but stay absolutely still. The respiration falls off, too, and the body feels a slight chill.

When God reaches out more forcefully to one who prays well or even to a little innocent who may receive some special message, the person falls into full ecstasy. Heaven opens up to a person in ecstasy; he becomes aware of reality through the senses of the soul, and the senses of the body just stop working entirely, as St. John of the Cross explained. Many mystics, like St. Frances of Rome and Therese Neumann, could hear their confessors but nobody else. But normally the ecstatic sees and hears nothing around him and can't speak.

There are a few exceptional cases, like St. Catherine of Siena and St. Catherine dei Ricci (1522-1590), who were able to describe what the senses of their souls experienced during their ecstasies, and some of their reports have been written down, from time to time, but that too has its difficulties. St. Maria Maddelena dei Pazzi talked so superhumanly fast, for instance, that as many as six scribes had to be called in to catch everything that she said.

Respiration and even the pulse stop, usually almost entirely, and the body becomes cold, all of which is hard to fake and often gives bystanders the impression that the visionary is dead. Jeanne Abadie thought so when she and Marie Soubirous saw St. Bernadette during the first apparition at Lourdes (Marie threw rocks at her, to find out). The seers feel no pain, either (*insensibility*), and they evidently have *immunity* from injury, as when the candle drifted in St. Bernadette's grasp so that its flame played against her hand without burning her. At Beauraing in 1933, the attendant physicians were downright aggressive in their "tests" on the ecstatic little visionaries, shining flashlights into their fixed eyes, pinching their cheeks, scratching their temples with a pocket knife, and, perhaps remembering what had happened accidentally to St. Bernadette, holding lighted matches to their hands. None of these things roused them; and after the apparition ended, there was no trace on any of the children of bruises, scratches, or burns.[126]

This is another hallmark of genuine mystic experience, real communication with God as distinct from a natural meditational trance; anybody can learn to achieve a state of insensitivity to pains like pinpricks and candle flames, but these things still work their

126. The second time the doctors tried this nonsense, though, the apparition vanished at the first touch of the knife. The visionary said, "Leave me alone. It's because of you that the Blessed Virgin has gone away!" When Albert Voisin, one of the seers at Beauraing, didn't see or hear anything during the only apparition during which he felt discomfort from kneeling on the cobblestones, it was interpreted as indicating that he was not then in ecstasy. The four other children who saw and heard, though, knelt painlessly on the rough stones.

effects on the body, and the physical trauma lingers afterwards. In a true ecstasy, though, they don't leave a mark at all, which can't be faked or achieved by natural means.[127]

THE PAIN OF MYSTIC EXPERIENCE

Still, there can be considerable pain associated with ecstasy, not from external causes but from the nature of true ecstasy itself. Usually, a person in ecstasy can't move; the body can become as heavy as stone and as rigid as wood. Like Job (4:13-14), St. Teresa record-ed feeling painfully disjointed afterwards, but the lay Carmelite Bl. Mary of the Incarnation (1566-1618) was so violently caught up that her bones audibly cracked—sev-eral hundred times, she said, and she didn't expect to live through it. The general of the Discalced Carmelites, Dominic of Jesus-Mary (1559-1630), ended up so bruised that he couldn't move at all afterwards, and he even vomited blood. And in some cases the trau-ma is compounded by the people who try with all their collective strength to move ecsta-tics while they're immobile.[128]

It may seem cruel, or even wholly at odds with the character of love, for God to inflict such abuse on someone singled out for particular charity, but remember that these physical phenomena are simply the attendant material effects of a spiritual action of inexpressible joy, an event during which God draws the soul to him, almost detach-ing it from the body.

St. Teresa compared the way that God draws the soul out of the body to the way that water is gathered up as vapor into a cloud; "in these raptures," she said, "it seems that the soul is not animating the body ... although this happens with the great-est ease and delight ... without any forethought or any help there frequently comes a force so swift and powerful that one sees and feels this cloud ... raise it up and carry it aloft". The physical pain happens as a consequence of this spiritual elevation, but the joy of that ascent is so great that none of the great mystics ever complains about the residual physical effects.

So genuine ecstasy is a partial separation of the soul from the body: a little death, as it were. "It is a greater marvel to see that the soul does not leave the body in this union," says St. Catherine of Siena, "than to see a host of dead bodies resur-rected." It must be indescribably painful and terrifying, even if it is offset by inex-pressible spiritual joy.

---

127. Naturally, the ecstatic immunity to pain is often advantageous. St. Thomas Aquinas, who also let his hand drift into a candle flame when ecstatic, had his leg cauterized painlessly by a doctor while in deep meditation. And the lay Carmelite Bl. Mary of the Incarnation underwent a serious surgical operation without pain or anæsthetic while in ecstasy.

128. Even after their ecstasy, the children of Beauraing could be lifted from the ground only with great, almost violent, force. The same kind of thing is reported periodically in older sources, as when St. Lucy of Syracuse, about to be taken forcibly to a brothel so that she could be violated by all and sundry for refusing to worship idols, became bodily affixed to the spot where she stood "like the pillar of a church". The *Golden Legend* records a report that even oxen were resorted to, with no effect.

Nearer, My God, to Thee

But because the soul doesn't separate entirely from the body, the body sometimes moves upward with the soul. "It is not because the weight is taken from it," St. Catherine of Siena explained, "but because the union with God into which my soul has entered is more perfect than the union between the soul and the body, that the power of the soul lifts up the heavy body from the Earth." This is *levitation*, an ecstatic state in which the mystic simply rises from the ground and stays there for a fairly short period of time, caught up in the contemplation of the divine.[129]

It might not sound exactly biblical, but it is: Ezechiel, Habacuc, and St. Paul all report being raised up between Earth and Heaven.[130] Since the Christian era, this kind of mystic experience almost always happens in connection with the Eucharist, the cornerstone of the New Covenant, which means that it happens in circumstances that virtually exclude deliberate illusion.

When professional illusionists stage an apparent levitation, they do it, usually with low lights, in a theater or in another controlled environment where they have sufficient space and equipment to pull it off. They also have an audience assembled there for the purpose of seeing that illusion, sitting there in expectant attention. But when the levitation of the mystics is reported, it happens to the same person in a variety of settings, often outdoors or in churches in broad daylight, or in illuminated liturgies (or with an attendant brilliance of the aureole). And even in a career like that of St. Teresa or St. Francis, who were known to have such experiences, the phenomenon is rare—it doesn't happen every day.[131]

And it usually comes upon the mystics unexpectedly (although the *Golden Legend* records that St. Mary Magdalen, in her desert hermitage, was elevated by angels every day at each of the seven canonical hours, like clockwork). Those saints who may be able to move freely this way at will never do it for purposes of mere exhibition, nor on command, except in obedience; and they wouldn't think of interrupting the Mass by flying around any more than they would by doing anything else that would be in their own power, like shouting or running in circles. So even if a known mystic is to be in attendance, nobody goes to Mass expecting anything more than the normal liturgy. It's important to remember, too, that most mystics are professed religious, and that cloistered monks and nuns are kept separate from the congregations, hearing Mass from an arm of the oratory closed to the public and, in some oratories, taking communion through a grille or even a special little window. So, even when levitation happens at

---

129. St. Thomas of Villanova (1486-1555) levitated for twelve hours one Ascension Day, which is probably a record.

130. Ez 3:14, 8:3, 11:1; Dn 14:33-39; 2Cr 12. Enoch (Gn 5:22-24) and Elias, of course, were swept up into Heaven (4Kn:2), but they haven't come back down, yet.

131. Judging by the records of mystics who were accidentally discovered alone in their cells ecstatically suspended in the air, or cases like St. Francis's levitations in his hermit's retreat, it would seem that the overwhelming majority of levitations are never witnessed and never reported.

Mass, it's not on public view.

Well, there are exceptions. The sisters of Ven. Mary of Agreda (1602-1665) opened the shutters of the choir so that she could be seen levitating for two or three hours after communion, and while she was on display the crowd at the grille enjoyed making her drift around by blowing on her.[132] She was so embarrassed when she found out about it that she prayed for the external manifestations of her ecstasies to be removed, and they were.

In fact, because it's such an uncontrollable physical phenomenon, so attractive to bystanders, and so trivial (it's nothing more than a physical result of a spiritual gift), levitation is generally the least favorite mystic event of all. Mystics willingly accept the excruciating sufferings of the stigmata before they'll accept levitation, and virtually every mystic in the annals of the Church has begged God to take away this favor. St. Teresa of Avila herself is perhaps the best-known case of the embarrassment of levitation, because she made such efforts to stop it, holding on to the altar rail or ordering her nuns to hold her down. Strategies like these don't always work, though; she once grabbed the mats on the floor and took them up with her. St. Joseph of Cupertino (1603-1663) levitated so forcefully that he even took with him the brothers that he grabbed to steady himself, and when St. Gerard Majella (1726-1755) started to levitate while he was speaking to a prioress through the iron grille of the convent parlor, he took hold of the grille and bent it like wax as he rose into the air.[133]

There doesn't seem to be any standard altitude for levitation, either. St. Joseph of Cupertino (who levitated at will, and so frequently that he's invoked as patron saint of air travel) was seen celebrating Mass with only the very tips of his toes touching the floor from the consecration until after the distribution of the Eucharist, and St. Ignatius of Loyola, St. Margaret Mary, and many others stood (or knelt) only a few inches above the floor during their ecstasies. St. Catherine of Siena levitated for as long as it would take to say the *Miserere* (Ps 50), but only high enough that people could pass their hands under her.

Other ecstatic mystics rise to greater heights. St. John Vianney (1786-1859) ascended once during his homily so that his feet were above the top of the pulpit. Bl. Thomas of Cori (d. 1729) rose up during the distribution of the Eucharist, still holding the ciborium, until he bumped his head gently on the vaults of the church, after which he descended slowly and went on distributing the Hosts as if nothing unusual had happened. According to the testimony of his confessor Brother Leo, St. Francis in retreat

132. Most levitating mystics just hang there in the air—a Dominican lay brother was badly frightened, and understandably so, when he entered the darkened oratory at night and walked into the dangling feet and legs of Bl. John Masías (1585-1645), for instance. But Fray Gerónimo Garzía, of Mexico City, reported that one day, looking for the source of the strong wind that he felt blowing through the oratory, he saw Ven. Antonio Margil (1657-1726) levitating, his arms stretched out as on a cross, whirling around at incredible speed. But that's unusual.

133. A skeptic who took hold of Bl. Dominic of Jesus-Mary, O.C.D., to prove the whole thing an illusion or a fraud, was also taken up with him to a considerable height. The man panicked and let go, sustaining fairly serious injuries in his fall.

on Mount La Verna sometimes levitated five or six feet off the ground, sometimes above the highest trees on the mountain, and sometimes so high that he couldn't be seen any more.

Moving Beyond Space and Time

Like the other physical signs of mystic activity, this kind of exemption from the usual earthly laws of gravity prefigures something of the character of life in Heaven. Departed saints and angels aren't subject to the normal laws of time and space, either— Raphael carried the devil to Egypt in a single night, of course, and angels miraculously transported people from one place to another, like Habacuc and St. Philip (Tb 8:3; Dn 14:33-39; Ps 17:30; Ac 8:39-40; etc.). Moral theologians term this mystic ability to transcend time and space *agility*.

Sometimes these movements are fairly subtle, as when Bl. Passitea Crogi (d. 1615) came through a hike without a speck of mud on her while her companions were all soaked, or when the disabled Sr. Maria della Passione (d. 1912) was whisked quickly and smoothly up the steps to her infirmary after having been carried by her sisters down to the oratory for communion. But ecstatic mystics often move in more impressive ways. St. Athanasius, in his life of St. Anthony of the Desert, recalls how the third-century Egyptian monk Amun was carried across the flooded Lycus river, dry and more quickly than his companion Theodore could swim. The *Golden Legend* relates that a Christian named Macro grabbed the immense stone with which the consul Aurelian had commanded him to be crushed and ran with it for two miles. St. Miguel de los Santos (1591-1625) once ran across a field with such power that eight of his brethren couldn't hold him back, and so fast that nobody could even begin to catch him. St. Peter of Alcántara (1499-1562) sometimes shot out of the narrow door of his cell "like an arrow from a bow".[134]

Some few mystics seem to be able to use this extraordinary ability to move whenever they see the need. It's reported that St. Joseph of Cupertino once flew over to a massive cross that ten men couldn't raise at a shrine and slipped it into place (the documentary evidence for this episode is sketchy, so it isn't taken too seriously, but then he also levitated more than a hundred other times, with his usual shrill cry, his "outburst of love", as he called it, in front of bishops, cardinals, ambassadors, princes, and crowds). St. Maria Maddelena dei Pazzi, on the Feast of the Finding of the True Cross (May 3, 1592), ran into the choir of her oratory, leapt up to a narrow cornice thirty feet above the floor, took up a large crucifix, and brought it down for the veneration of the assembled nuns. And even the sickly Anne-Catherine Emmerich, becoming recollected in her duties as sacristan at Agnetenburg, used to ascend to clean or decorate the cornices and other places that couldn't normally be reached, much as Bl. Anna-Maria Taigi levitated during her housework, but a little more purposefully.

---

134. Lukardis of Oberweimar (d. 1309) was a paralytic who occasionally ran too fast to be caught and too forcefully to be restrained, too, but she once shot straight out of her cell and smack into a stone wall. Her case is still under discussion.

Probably the most famous case of agility, and one of the best documented, is the trip that St. Anthony of Padua (1195-1231) took from Italy to his home town of Lisbon. And, like most mystic phenomena, it occurred in a whole context of miraculous events.

One day, the murdered body of a young nobleman was found in the garden of St. Anthony's father, Don Martino de Bouillon, whose palace was near the cathedral. With no other suspects and no other evidence, the authorities arrested Don Martino, who was more surprised than anybody else, except maybe his son Anthony, who knew instantly about the problem although he was secluded in the friary of Arcella in Padua—in Italy—at that moment. St. Anthony was serving as Provincial, the head of his order in that area, so he could have just gone to Lisbon on his own authority, but out of humility he asked the Father Guardian, the head of that particular friary, for permission anyway. That evening, he started walking to Lisbon.

He showed up in Portugal the next morning. He went straight to the courtroom and protested his father's innocence. The judge, naturally, asked for proof, and Anthony answered that the murdered man himself would give the necessary evidence. By this point in his career, St. Anthony was already known across Europe as a creditable miracle worker, so the court adjourned to the cemetery and ordered the grave opened.

When they had opened the coffin, St. Anthony ordered the victim to state whether Martino was the guilty party. The man sat up, leaning on his left hand and raising his right hand to Heaven, and said, "No." The judges asked who had done it, in that case, but Anthony said that he had come to protect the innocent, not to condemn the guilty.[135] With the case, and the coffin, closed, St. Anthony set out for Padua and arrived quickly back at Arcella, having been gone only two nights and one day.

Here and There at Once

Sometimes, too, great mystics can nullify the rules of time and space by becoming a kind of apparition themselves: that is, while remaining physically at one place, they appear, and act, at some other place far distant. Moral theologians call this *bilocation*, and they figure that the person isn't physically in two places at once, but in one place at once, while a representation of the person, perfectly convincing to the bodily senses of other people, is at the other.[136]

One of the earliest of the Church's bilocating saints is St. Mary Magdalen. According to the *Golden Legend*, she and St. Maximinus, one of the seventy-two (Lk 10:1), went to Marseilles to preach the Gospel fourteen years after the Crucifixion. She was preaching in front of the local pagan temple when she saw the local magistrate's wife coming to offer sacrifice and beg the god for a child. Mary Magdalen later appeared to the lady, evidently inside her house, and reproached her for neglecting the Christian

135. The man in the coffin, who had died under excommunication, asked St. Anthony for absolution before he fell dead again, which the saint gave him.

136. While most physicists maintain that a single physical body can't possibly be in two places at one time, some theorists, notably Leibniz, say that such a thing doesn't violate the laws of physics.

poor. The woman didn't mention the apparition to her husband, but when it happened again and again, he admitted that he'd seen her, too. They weren't converted by the experience alone, but it got them asking questions, which is precisely what apparitions, or bilocations, are supposed to do.

The *Golden Legend* doesn't mention the state of St. Mary Magdalen herself during her bilocation, but it gives more information about the bilocation of St. Front, who was celebrating the Mass at Périgueux and was also seen at the same time in Tarascon at the funeral of Mary Magdalen's sister, St. Martha. After the reading of the Epistle, the *Legend* says, St. Front fell into a deep sleep; Christ appeared to him and reminded him of his promise to attend St. Martha's funeral, and together they went instantly to Tarascon, about a hundred and seventy miles away by air, chanted the entire funeral service with the others there, and laid the body in the tomb.

Meanwhile, at Périgueux, the deacon who was about to chant the Gospel went up to the throne to receive the bishop's blessing. He forcefully roused the bishop (probably fearing that the man had died), but when St. Front came to himself, he told them where he had been and what he had been doing. "As I made ready to bury her," he said, "I left my gold ring and silver gloves with the sacristan; and you recalled me so suddenly that I forgot them. Send messengers there to bring them back!"

The messengers found that everything had happened just as St. Front had said. They brought back the bishop's ring and one glove, but they left the other at Tarascon, as testimony of the miracle.

This might be seen as an act of mercy that Christ performed, to help St. Front keep his promise, but some few saints evidently can bilocate at will. St. Anthony of Padua, for instance, who had unimaginable demands on his time and attention, was preaching to a crowded audience in the cathedral of Montpelier one Easter. Suddenly he remembered that he had been appointed to celebrate Mass at a certain convent oratory at that same time. Of course, he could have found a substitute, but he'd even forgotten to do that. Failure to show up would not only be an act of negligent disobedience; it would be a dreadful disgrace on this, the holiest day of the year.

Like St. Front, he pulled his cowl over his face and drew back in the pulpit, standing motionless for a long time, in full view of the puzzled congregation. At the convent oratory, though, he appeared absolutely normally, celebrated the entire Mass, and left. He came to himself at the cathedral and picked up his sermon where he had left off, "with incomparable eloquence".

Like the bilocation of St. Front—who celebrated an entire funeral liturgy in the few moments between the Epistle and the Gospel—St. Anthony's bilocation at Montpelier must have abridged Time as well as space. His listeners would hardly stand waiting for the hours it would take for a chanted conventual Mass on Easter. (Although the sisters of Bl. Jeanne de la Croix Delanoue, the seventeenth-century Poor Clare, recorded that she picked up her lecture just where she'd been interrupted by falling into ecstasy seven hours before.) But some mystics apparently stay within Time while abolishing space through bilocation. St. Francis was sometimes mystically and visibly present at distant provincial chapters during his lifetime, as when he attended the one at Arles presided over by St. Anthony of Padua. A friar named Monaldus was the first to see him doing this, lifted in midair, his arms extended like the Cross, blessing the friars.

The range of bilocation seems practically unlimited. Padre Pio, to take another Franciscan example, never left his friary at San Giovanni Rotondo after 1918 and was forbidden to correspond or receive personal callers, but he reportedly paid very brief visits to some of his friends frequently through bilocation. A bilocational visit from San Giovanni Rotondo to Florence prompted the first questions about his ability to make such "little trips", but as the years went by any number of independent witnesses, from all over Italy and from as far afield as Hawaii and even Uruguay, reported that the friar had appeared for a few minutes, apparently solid and alive, comforted them, and then disappeared. At exactly these times, his brothers at San Giovanni Rotondo noticed that he would rest his head on his arms, in a deep sleep or trancelike state, for only about five minutes or so.

And in the same way, the ability to move outside of the usual three dimensions of this Earth (four if you count Time) means that, occasionally, solid material bodies don't obstruct an ecstatic. Just as the glorified bodies of the resurrected Faithful are subtle (Jn 20:19), those mystics who can penetrate space and Time can also, necessarily, simply move through solid walls and other objects. If they couldn't, they could hardly appear inside of other buildings far away, or move out of the ones they're in when they start out.

This is called the *compenetration of bodies*—in a way, it's the converse of bilocation: not having one object in two places, but two objects in one place. It, too, is a kind of hint about what life must be like in Sempiternity, where there's no "in" or "out", nor any "over", "under", "around", or "through".

The Light of Truth

Also like angels and the glorified bodies of the resurrected, living mystics often show themselves resplendent, illuminated with the intense supernatural light of the *aureole*. From the Glory of the Lord in Exodus (16:10) and Daniel's vision of the angel with a face like lightning (10:6) to the jewel-like radiance of the enthroned One of Revelations (4:2-3), angels and other apparitions tend to dazzle the mortals who see them (Mt 17:2, 5).

The figure poised in the air above the trees at Fátima, Lucia dos Santos recalled, "looked like a statue made of snow, rendered almost transparent by the rays of the Sun. … transparent as crystal when the Sun shines through it, and of great beauty" (*cf.* Mr 9:2). The great mystics can show the same characteristics; in fact, light, the first-born of creation (Gn 1:3; *cf.* Jn 1:5, 8:12), seems to be an integral part of closeness to the divine or even the substance of which apparitions are made.

But it's a mystic light, visible only with the eyes of the soul; not everybody here on Earth can see it, and those who do see it can't see it all of the time, as it came and went at the Transfiguration (Mt 17:1-8).[137]

For instance, when St. Anthony of Padua first got to that city, he went to confront the tyrant Ezzelino of Treviso, who had inflicted a forty-year reign of terror on the people there—he once executed twelve thousand of them in a single day, having heard that they'd refused to put up with him any more. St. Anthony found him in one of his strongholds near Verona, surrounded by legions of shock troops ready to kill anybody Ezzelino pointed to.

But when the saint described the tyrant's crimes and called for repentance and reform, the man shook with fear, looped a halter around his own neck, and lay prostrate on the floor in front of the friar. His henchmen didn't know what to make of it until after St. Anthony left: I saw a divine splendor radiating from his face, Ezzelino said, and if I had laid hands on him, I know that I would have been carried away to Hell immediately.[138]

This is not a splendor that dazzles, St. Teresa of Avila specifies; it has a soft whiteness giving the most intense delight to the sight, so different from earthly light that it seems like pure running water in comparison to muddy water flowing along the ground. Still, it takes different forms. For example, it appeared as a radiant globe over the head of St. Martin of Tours while he was celebrating Mass. That was obviously not a natural conflagration, but sometimes, as with the Burning Bush and the pillar of fire in the desert, it's evidently hard to tell this mystic illumination from natural fire. When flames were seen floating over the head of St. Ignatius of Loyola as he celebrated Mass, Fr. Nicholas Lannoy ran forward to put them out. He stopped in his tracks when he saw the saint's face, which was transfigured in ecstatic contemplation.[139]

In fact, mystic aureoles seem to transfigure the body, too, which again recalls the nature of the glorified body. St. Louis-Marie Grignion de Montfort, worn out and prematurely old from overwork and penances, appeared so beautiful one day in 1715

137. Benedict XIV Lambertini, who before his elevation to the Throne of Peter was Devil's Advocate, was inclined to attribute luminosity to natural but unknown causes. But natural luminosity is extremely rare, and explanations aren't all that convincing. A certain Dr. Protti of Milan, sent to investigate the luminous woman of Pirano in 1934, said that it was obviously caused by the interplay of ultraviolet rays from the blood and excessive sulfides on her skin—the radiant power of her blood, he said, was three times the norm, so that explained it, as far as he was concerned. Besides, she had only a faint bluish glow, different from the peculiarly soft, white, gentle, yet brilliantly overpowering, painfully beautiful light that only seems to happen to mystics and only at appropriate moments and in a context of other concomitant phenomena.

138. He got a little more agreeable after that, but his one-shot conversion experience didn't last. When St. Anthony died he relapsed; all of the princes of Lombardy united against him, captured him, and left him to die in prison, unrepentant.

139. There's a related mystic phenomenon, rather rarer than visible flames, called *ardors* or *flames of love*. These are burning sensations in the body itself, usually persistent and intense heat around the heart that may spread to other parts of the body, that may become unbearable and even blister the skin or scorch the clothing, again usually around the heart. St. Catherine of Genoa bathed her hands in a large silver vessel of water for relief, heating it so intensely that her maidservant couldn't pick it up. The blood from her last illness scorched her own flesh and heated the vessels in which it was caught. That vomited by Ven. Frances dal Serrone was so hot that it cracked the ceramic bowl it was caught in.

when he began to radiate heavenly light that his parishioners only recognized him by his voice.[140]

The faces of countless other saints, notably Benedict Joseph Labre, Francis de las Posadas, Maria Maddelena dei Pazzi, Peter of Alcántara, Philip Neri, and John of the Cross, became transparent as crystal during their luminous ecstasies, their cheeks a fiery red, which recalls the image of faces like diamond and flint in Ezechiel (3:9). For that matter, St. John of the Cross sometimes had an actual halo, a celestial brightness radiating from his head. Closer to our own times, the Abbé Marie-Dominique Peyramale, parish priest and forbidding naysayer of Lourdes, reported that he saw a bright halo around the head of young Bernadette Soubirous when she came to the altar for communion one day. Both of these saints were completely unaware of their luminosity.[141] But, because these matters of the spirit manifest themselves as physical phenomena, most mystics seem able to feel them with the senses of the body as well as with those of the soul.

The Foretaste of Heaven

Interestingly enough, mystics often talk about spiritual taste as being the first spiritual sense to awaken during ecstasy: taste and see the goodness of the Lord, Psalm 33:8 says, "taste" first, then "see". "It was as sweet as honey in my mouth," Ezechiel said (3:3). This first extraordinary experience of God's presence, which moral theologians term *savors*, sparks the understanding in a supernatural way. The Ven. Louis du Pont says that this kind of *experimental* knowledge—knowing God because you experience him—is as different from knowledge that comes from human learning as tasting a little honey is different from talking about honey.[142]

And evidently, just as with the bodily senses, taste and smell are intimately related. St. Ambrose (*Sermon VI on Psalms*) mentioned that

> The soul of the Just is the bride of the Word. If this soul burns with desire, if she prays without ceasing, if her whole being goes out toward the Word, then she tastes inwardly the odor of his Divinity, which thing

---

140. It was February 2, to be exact, and like most other mystics he didn't miss a beat in his homily. It was an assigned duty taken on in obedience. But it's also reported of Therese Neumann that, when she was taken by ecstasy in the middle of a fit of coughing or laughing, she fell silent and motionless until it passed and then resumed coughing or laughing as if uninterrupted (*cf.* Dn 10:15).

141. Two other saints were seen reading by their own light; St. Francis de las Posadas (d. 1713), whose missal was illuminated with a ray coming from his mouth, and St. Alphonsus of Liguori, whose pious readings before the Blessed Sacrament in a dark church were facilitated by a ray from his forehead.

142. This association of taste and understanding works not just spiritually but on some deep psychological level, too, that we don't often think about. Psalms, particularly, associate the Law with a sweet taste, and our word "savor" is derived from the same root as words like *savoir, saber, sapientia*, and other words relating to knowledge or wisdom. This wisdom is one of the Seven Gifts of the Holy Spirit, infused, to a degree, sacramentally at Confirmation, but given to the great mystics in an extraordinary degree. Once received, it has to be actuated through practice, like any other infused virtue or gift. If you don't use it, you refuse it; and, as with any earthly gift, if you refuse it, you lose it.

often comes to those who are strong of faith. Suddenly the soul's sense of smell is filled with a spiritual grace and, being aware of a sweet breath that tells her of the presence of him whom she seeks, she says, "Behold him whom I seek …"

An indescribably sweet odor, in fact, is one of the mystic phenomena most often reported in the lives of hundreds of saints, in connection with their ecstasies as well as with their apparitions.[143]

The Odor of Sanctity

From Genesis to the Apocalypse, the Bible makes innumerable references to the sweet fragrance of the acceptable sacrifice, the *odor of sanctity* (Gn 8:21; Sir 24:15; Phl 4:18; Rv 5:8). Sometimes the image is used metaphorically or symbolically, as every image in the Bible is used at least occasionally (2Cr 2:15-17, for instance), but a lot of evidence has accumulated steadily from the earliest days of the Church that demands a more literal interpretation. Back in 177, for instance, the surviving Christians of Vienne and Lyons wrote to the churches in Asia Minor, telling them about the persecutions that they'd suffered. Those heroes among them, they said, who went out joyously to their martyrdom carried their chains like bridal ornaments, and they were fragrant with the sweet odor of Christ—the onlookers thought that the victims had been anointed with perfume.

During the persecutions of Diocletian (284-305), when the father of St. Vitus locked his son in a room full of music and call girls to convert him away from Christianity, seven angels appeared to stand guard over the boy, and the whole house was filled with a heavenly perfume. And, more modestly, it was the persistent rose-like fragrance that emanated from a branch of the little holm oak from the Cova at Fátima that convinced Maria Rosa dos Santos that her daughter Lucia was telling the truth.

It wasn't something that she expected, and it wasn't something that could be otherwise explained, but it has countless parallels in the history of mystic theology. The *Golden Legend* records the early Christian report that a sweet perfume emanated from the decapitated body of St. Paul, which so impressed Nero that he locked himself in his closet.[144] St. Helena (255-330) was reportedly led to the site of the True Cross by a prophet named Judas, grandson of Zaccheus, who smelled a delightful aroma of spices when he stood over the spot on Calvary where it had been buried. That's also how the priest Lucian found the remains of St. Stephen. And the neglected grave of St. Bibiana (Vivian) was rediscovered when workmen doing minor repairs to a church in Rome reported the strong smell of roses at that altar.

---

143. Now, of course, the term "odor of sanctity" is most usually used figuratively, to mean that the person died a holy death, resigned to God's will and in full sacramental communion with the Church. It's also used ironically, to indicate a pecksniffian attitude about oneself, so it shouldn't be taken literally unless it's clearly meant that way.

144. He still couldn't get away from what he'd done. St. Paul appeared to him there and reproached him.

The bodies of St. Mary Magdalen, Sts. Gervaise and Protase, St. Alexis (d. 398), and countless others, including of course St. Teresa of Avila, exuded the powerful scent of supernatural roses, too. One of the men who exhumed the incorrupt remains of St. Stanislaus Kostka (1550-1568) two years after his death described "a fragrance, more delicious than that of the sweetest flower ... so delicate, so pure, so exquisite ... [that], instead of only delighting the senses, seemed to penetrate the souls of those present, that one and all felt that it was a perfume not of Earth but of Paradise." It's a scent so penetrating that it can fill a whole neighborhood, and sometimes it's remarkably durable. The body of St. Rita of Cascia (1377-1447) has been fragrant since her death, and not only the bones of St. Dominic but the earth from his grave retained a penetrating celestial odor, as did the hands of those who handled the relics.

But these aren't just the fragrances of heavenly beings or the holy dead; the incorrupt Hosts of more than one Eucharistic miracle gave off that perfume, sometimes for centuries, like the ones stolen in 1730 from the Church of St. Francis in Siena. It's reported around the living persons of holy people like St. Dominic and St. Teresa, too, as well as modern mystics like Therese Neumann. Even the books and clothing of the Ven. Mother Mary of Jesus (d. 1640) still reportedly smell of fresh roses and jasmine.[145]

And, in fact, these odors are one of the things that distinguish true mystic suffering from natural chronic illness, because the lesions of stigmatics and victim souls don't give off the usual sickroom smells. Bl. Lydwine's mother used to gather up the pieces of flesh and bone that fell off her daughter's body and keep them in an earthenware jar, where they still exuded the heavenly perfume that her doctors described as sort of like the smell of cinnamon, but sweeter.[146]

Her wounds also exhaled that same spicy scent at first, which later changed into a flowery perfume that, like the scent of the wounds of most other stigmatics such as St. Gemma Galgani (1878-1903), emanated from her wounds day and night, winter and summer, although they continued to putrefy and resist any kind of medication.

Mystic and Miraculous Cures

What's even more remarkable, really, than the fragrance of mystics or victim souls, or even more remarkable than the fact that they don't die from their diseases, is that they're so often miraculously cured of them. Well, it's remarkable that they're all given diseases in the first place. Yet almost every saint on record since Job has had this kind of physical trial; they don't complain about it, of course, and it's not something that people like to dwell on, but it almost seems that appalling diseases are a prerequisite for exceptional sanctity.

145. The fragrance even spread to a borrowed handkerchief offered to Joan Mary della Croce during an access of tears. She herself had become fragrant on her finger after her mystic marriage, but when she went through the sufferings of a victim soul the indescribable perfume spread to her whole body.

146. The flesh in that jar never decomposed, either, but it attracted so much attention from tourists that Bl. Lydwine told her mother to seal it up and bury it in the cemetery.

The great mystic St. Hildegard of Bingen (1098-1179) put it this way:

> The gift of miracles gives birth to delight and joy... [But although] the soul by its nature tends toward eternal life, ... the body, holding in itself this passing life, is not in accordance with it; for, though they both unite to form Man, yet they are distinct in themselves; they are two. Therefore, when God pours out his Spirit on a person by the light of prophecy, the gift of wisdom, or miracles, he afflicts the body by frequent sufferings, so that the Holy Spirit might dwell in the person. If the flesh be not subdued by pain, it too readily follows the ways of the world, as happened with Samson, Solomon, and others who, inclining to the pleasures of the senses, stopped listening to the inspirations of the Spirit.

Or, as Anne-Catherine Emmerich reported that Christ told her, "Your body is weighed down by pain and sickness so that your soul may labor more actively, for he who is in good health carries his body as a heavy burden."

The unique supernatural origin of mystics' diseases is shown not just by the fragrance or the longevity of their victims, but in the sudden and complete reversal of the diseases themselves. St. Margaret Mary, St. Teresa of Avila, and St. Bernadette are probably the best-known examples, but countless other saints all report having their numerous chronic illnesses taken from them. It feels like taking off a sweater, they say, and their bodies instantly show themselves free of any symptoms, even lesions and the visible ravages of long illness.

But their relief is only temporary. Usually, they go right back to sufferings far beyond the norm in human life; that's their vocation. Miraculous cures of people who invoke the aid of saints or make pilgrimages to the sites of famous apparitions, though, are permanent. These cures aren't really all that well understood by the laity at large or even by the people who go to some effort to assert that they can't happen. So it's as well to get a perspective on just what miraculous cures are and how they're recognized.

The Logic of Miraculous Cures

To start with, there's the question of determining exactly what the disease is in the first place. A lot of the cures reported as miracles in ages past may very well be things that can be handled by routine medicine today, so some critics assert that "miracles" will necessarily decrease as medical sophistication increases, and that they, themselves, foresee an end to the days of so-called "miraculous cures" at places like Lourdes.

But when you think about it, medical sophistication has been increasing for centuries, and there are still miracles. It doesn't make any difference if an American doctor today can routinely cure something that only a miracle could cure six or seven centuries ago, or if some hopeless case cured at Lourdes today is something that will be routinely treatable six hundred years from now. Anything beyond the reach of medical science at the moment is incurable, and miracles occur to cure the incurable—people given up as hopeless cases in that place and time, with the medical care available to them. Besides, medicine will always be imperfect, and new incurable conditions appear every day, such is the disorder of this world. Christ cured leprosy in the Bible; medicine cures it now, but now lupus is cured at Lourdes. And medicine still can't regenerate the flesh and bone lost to these diseases, but the miracles did, and do.

There also seems to be a tendency to scoff at older stories of miracles because doctors in ages past are generally considered to have been fools; and certainly anybody would be foolish to practice medicine today as it was even a hundred years ago. Still, it's interesting that this prejudice seems to extend to foreign doctors today, crossing space as well as time. There seems to be no logical reason to assume that any doctor before the twentieth century was a complete incompetent, any more than there is to assume that all American doctors today are always absolutely and uniquely right. Theories of healing may be different from ours, but the records of many miraculous cures from other times and places do show detailed descriptions of symptoms consistently and astutely observed.

And then there's the nature of the phenomena themselves. Even if you leave some miracles aside, on the assumption that they might have some natural cause that just wasn't understood at that time and place, there are too many really remarkable events that don't go away so easily. Bl. Lydwine of Schiedam would baffle an intensive-care unit as much as she puzzled the black-robed medicos of her own time. Like the cases of other victim souls, hers is so extraordinary that any doctor anywhere would pretty much have to conclude that her worm-eaten, putrefying body, falling to pieces as it was, could not possibly survive in the natural order of things, particularly when she hadn't eaten anything in years. Not to mention the ineffable fragrance of her decaying flesh, the radiating light intense beyond natural fire, her naturally impossible knowledge of things far from her sickbed in Time and space, or the equally well-attested fact that when she died her body returned to its original soundness and beauty. These things aren't in the province of medical science in any age, but they've been a normal, if extraordinary, part of Christianity since—even before the coming of Christ.

Diagnosing the Devil

So it's not all that easy to attribute miracles to mistaken diagnoses. Beyond that, the very nature of cures called miraculous in the Church is often misunderstood.

The only way to prove that an event under consideration is not a genuine mystic event is to prove that God didn't do it; and because that's a negative proposition nobody can prove it directly. You can only prove that something else caused it, something other than God: not that some other cause could result in similar appearances, but that something other than God caused this particular event. That's extremely difficult. So the Church's aim in investigations of reported miraculous cures is more than just excluding any and all natural causes; she seeks beyond that to exclude even the possibility of natural causes that happen to be badly understood at the moment.

In other words, when the best available medical scientists return a report stating that no known natural cause can account for an apparent cure, the Church does not make the leap into the logical fallacy of concluding that, therefore, some supernatural cause is responsible. She says at that point, rather, exactly what the doctors say: that no known natural cause can account for the apparent cure. Then she adds the notation that an *unknown* natural cause may have been responsible; and unless the nature and circumstances of the reported cure are substantially different from any possible natural phenomenon, that's where the matter rests. That's why afflictions like cancer, those that have causes that are not well understood and a fairly high rate of spontaneous remission, are generally excluded from consideration, because there's a chance—however slight—that the remission just happened to occur at that moment.[147]

That's also why people may come away from Lourdes, Fátima, La Salette, or Banneux without the cancer they went there with, but also without much chance that this would be certified as a miracle. Any number of other conditions may not make the grade either, if the cure is simply a matter of quick remission; even if the cure must be supernatural rather than natural, there's always the Devil. It may not be a popular concept, nowadays, but diabolic manipulation of disease makes sense, in the context of moral theology. Adam and Eve, before they introduced sin into the world, had no disease or even any physical pain; their closeness to God excluded that. But with sin came death, and with death, disease; so before humans (as a collective group) can have disease, they have to have some distance between themselves and God. Well, the Devil is about as far from God as you can get; so disease is his province, and God evidently allows him to inflict it on people, even people who aren't at fault, themselves (as in the Book of Job).

In fact, many ostensibly miraculous cures might very well be caused by the Devil, just as a way of keeping people away from the Church. Some separated sects are based almost entirely on the promise of physical healing or even on the presumption of it, and some may even deliver cures that seem medically inexplicable; but before calling them miracles, it's as well to consider what St. Bartholemew did in India. He went to a temple belonging to a cult that was famous for its remarkable healings, but he found that inside the temple's idol was a demon, Astaroth, who pretended to remit illness just by not tormenting the person any more with diseases that he himself had caused. But to the casual observer it was a very attractive phenomenon, and it encouraged thousands of people to worship the demon as a god. When St. Bartholemew took up residence at that temple as a pilgrim, though, all of the inexplicable healings stopped. Eventually, the Apostle exorcised the demon and turned the temple into a church, but the point is that even the inexplicable or sensational remission of disease, in and of itself, doesn't count

147. Strictly speaking, cancer is not a disease but a *syndrome*, from the Greek meaning to run [a course] together, a more or less definite catalogue of symptoms that appear concurrently. A disease is rather a condition caused by a known and identifiable agent and recognized by the particular catalogue of symptoms that the agent produces. Diseases can be cured by effectively attacking that specific cause, but syndromes are incurable because similar collections of symptoms may be produced by any number of different causes; that makes it impossible to attack the specific cause that's generating those symptoms in that patient.

as a miracle, no matter how well timed it is. The Church's creditable miracles are substantially different.

THE BIBLE AS A GUIDE TO MODERN MIRACLES

Miracles aren't just cures beyond medicine but cures beyond nature; not just remission of disease but instant return to full health; not just cessation of symptoms but the actual regeneration of healthy tissue, in minutes or even in seconds.[148] So, to be considered miraculous, a cure has to exclude both natural and diabolic causes; and, just as humans don't regenerate lost organs, it has to be supposed that, while the Devil can just stop tormenting people, he can't do anything as constructive as creating new bone and flesh (Jn 10:21, for instance[149]). That being the case, there's something in Tertullian's insight that it must be true, because it's impossible.

And the cures of the certifiable miracles, those that do seem to occur even today, come in close procession after biblical precedents. "Ezechiel … saw a plain, large and boundless, and a large mound of bones scattered haphazardly upon it," St. Gregory of Nyssa (c. 335-394) noted. "Then, sorting themselves out through the divine power, 'the bones came together each one to his own joint'. Then, they were covered with sinews and flesh and skin … and a life-giving spirit roused all that lay there" (*On the Soul and the Resurrection*, c. 380). There were also the cures effected by washing in the Jordan at the direction of prophets (4Kn 5:14 *ff.*). Or, bridging the Old Covenant and the New, there's the pool of the five porticoes at Jerusalem (Jn 5:1-4), predecessor of the healing springs like those at Mount Gargano, La Salette, or Lourdes.

It's important to remember at this point that the Church never innovates when it comes to doctrine; her mission is to preserve exactly what Christ taught and to make it available to all people everywhere, in all ages, without any additions or deletions. And in this mission, if you go by the Bible, she's uniquely guided by the indwelling Holy Spirit (Mt 28:20; Ac 1:8, etc.), and Christ himself is always physically, sacramentally present in the Eucharist (Jn 6, etc.); so God himself is always present in the Church, giving her life and vitality from day to day and from age to age.

This consistency, this absence of innovation, is reflected in the extraordinary happenings, too. The countless stories of restored limbs and eyes in the Church's annals are not paralleled in separated sects, but they're precisely consistent with the cures that Christ himself worked. And those biblical miracles seem designed for maximum credi-

---

148. Some separated sects do publish testimonials claiming that the substance of a leg, a lung, or another organ was restored through application of that sect's beliefs, but canonical inquiries or, for instance, agencies like the Medical Bureau at Lourdes would not accept such testimony without previous independent documentation of diagnosis from more than one doctor and without subsequent documentation of regeneration.

149. God, the Creator, can produce manna or loaves and fishes (Ex 16:4-15; Mt 14:13-21; *cf.* Gn 1:1*ff.*) and restore lost limbs and organs (Mt 12:9-13; *cf.* Mt 9:1-31), but although the Devil can offer or promise all kinds of things (Gn 3:4-5; Mt 4:8-11), he can't deliver (Mt 4:3), which is why he's called the Deceiver and the Father of Lies; he can't bear good fruit or give you anything fruitful, or even anything that will do you any good. And the Devil certainly can't create anything.

bility, like the case of the man with the withered hand made whole (Mt 12:10-13), or Christ's giving sight to a man born blind—curing temporary accidental or infectious blindness with some superior knowledge might pass for a miracle among the ignorant, but "not from the beginning of the world has it been heard that anyone opened the eyes of a man born blind," as the man himself said (Jn 9:32), and he was in a position to know. Jesus's contemporaries agreed, saying that a man who could do this could cure anything (Jn 11:37).

Certified ecclesiastical miracles, based on Christ's charge to his Church (Mt 10:8), have the same character. New flesh, new bone, empty eye sockets filled with seeing eyes—these things are miracles because they simply do not happen in the natural course of things. Given adequate independent medical documentation, there's no way that misdiagnosis can be involved. When functioning flesh instantly appears where no flesh had been before, or where organs damaged beyond repair suddenly begin to work normally despite the damage, there's no way that the cause of the recovery can be mistaken, because recovery of this kind doesn't otherwise happen. Even when it happens in association with miraculous waters, it happens very obviously in direct response to the presence of Christ (sacramentally in the Eucharist, now, and corporeally in the days of the Gospels, as in Jn 5:1-9; 9:1-12). In fact, two of the earliest cures associated with Lourdes show that the pattern set by Christ has lasted to the present day. And they're good examples of the differences between purely natural spontaneous healings or remissions and cures that stand a good chance of being certified miraculous.

The Case of Louis Bouriette

During the ninth apparition at Lourdes, on February 25, 1858, the Lady had told Bernadette to go and wash in the spring, but there wasn't any spring. The girl dug away at the spot to which the Lady had pointed, and a trickle of water came up through the mud. Bernadette drank some of the muddy water and smeared some of the mud on her face—to the scandal of the onlookers, who thought she'd gone mad.

But there was a stonecutter living at Lourdes, a man named Louis Bouriette, who had worked in the local marble quarries until an explosion sent a stone chip flying into his right eye, piercing the cornea and partially detaching the retina. The eye healed over, but it was still blind, and worse than that it stayed inflamed, itching and burning, year after year for twenty years. One of the local doctors, a physician named Dozous,[150] gave him something for the pain, but because of the mechanical damage to the eye no cure was possible.

After the thirteenth apparition, though, Bouriette started to think about that spring, and he told his six-year-old daughter to go and get some of the mud for him. She brought him a lump of it wrapped in a piece of sackcloth, and Bouriette retired into the darkness of a local stable to apply it. He held the muddy pack against his eye for an

---

150. There were actually three doctors in Lourdes at that time, Dozous, Peyrus, and Lacrampe, but Lacrampe was from a wealthy family and didn't practice medicine regularly.

hour or so and then walked out into the light.

He was overcome with the brightness, as anybody would be after so long in the dark, but he closed his good eye and saw the outlines of people and objects clearly, although through a kind of white veil. He ran to Dozous's office to tell him, but the doctor didn't believe him; Bouriette couldn't read the letters of the test with his right eye. When the doctor tested the left one, though, he found out that Bouriette couldn't read them with his good eye, either—he'd never learned to read at all.[151]

Exasperated, Dozous told the man to leave. But Bouriette kept applying the mud, and his sight kept improving, although the corneal scars and detached retina stayed as they were before. By the time he went to the grotto for another dose, the spring had rinsed itself free of the mud, and he started using the water itself. Although physically his eye stayed as it was, his sight was restored perfectly, and he, experienced stonemason that he was, helped in the construction of the first basin that caught the miraculous waters of Bernadette's spring.[152]

The Case of Justin Bouhouhorts

Bouriette's was the first miraculous cure reported at Lourdes, but by the time he got the basin finished there was another. Justin Bouhouhorts, the son of Jean and Croisine Bouhouhorts, was two years old in 1858, and he had never been well. His legs were underdeveloped, only about as thick as a man's thumb, and about once a month he had convulsions, drawing his tiny knees up almost to his face and losing consciousness. He had no appetite, and he often couldn't keep food down at all. Dr. Dozous's records list diagnoses of rickets, severe colonic catarrh, periodic convulsions with high temperatures and lack of reflexes, and progressive paralysis of the legs, among other things. He wavered between a final diagnosis of tubercular meningitis and poliomyelitis, or both, but the paralysis and deformity of the legs were beyond question. And in any case, he knew, nothing could be done. There just wasn't enough leg left on the boy to ever let him walk. If he lived, he'd never walk or even sit upright.

The women of Lourdes, including Bernadette's mother Louise Soubirous, helped Justin's mother as best they could by giving him endless folk treatments—wrapping him in hot cloths, exercising his deformed legs, and dosing him with herbal teas. Nothing helped in the least. Three days after the doctor last visited the boy, on March

---

151. There was no disability relief in France in those days, so Bouriette, blind and illiterate, got a civil-service job instead. He was a letter carrier with the local post office in Lourdes.

152. Basically the same thing happened to a Madame Biré at Lourdes in 1908. She was almost completely blind in both eyes, only able to see a little shadowy light in her left. Her eyes and optic nerves had atrophied, for some unknown medical reason, and she went to Lourdes in hope of a cure. She didn't use the water because the crowds were too great, but during the Blessing of the Sick that afternoon she uttered a loud cry and fainted just as the Blessed Sacrament passed her. When she came around, she saw the crowds around her. She ran to the Medical Bureau, where an eye doctor examined her. Her sight was normal, although her organs of sight were still in the same atrophied condition as before. Over the following few months, though, they gradually returned to normal, with no interruption in her sight.

4, 1858, the family gathered for the death watch. His face had turned brownish yellow, his breath came in rattling gurgles, and his eyes had turned back in his head. One neighbor sat sewing the little boy's shroud; another tried to console the mother by saying that the child, baptized and without sin, would soon be with the angels, rather than struggling to survive as a hopeless cripple.

Suddenly Croisine Bouhouhorts shrieked. She grabbed the dying boy and ran all the way out of town to the grotto. By the time she got there, nearly the whole town had turned out, attracted by her cries and the shouts of the neighbors who chased her. At the basin, she unwrapped the baby and put him into the water up to his neck. She looked up and repeated the age-old prayer of the exhausted: "Take him, Blessed Virgin," she said, "or give him back to me."

Croisine Bouhouhorts kept interference away for fifteen minutes, snarling like a lioness at anybody who came near her, until even the boy's death rattle fell silent. She had killed the boy, everybody thought, plunging him into ice-cold water like that. But then they heard a thin cry, like that of a newborn infant. Croisine pulled the boy out of the basin, wrapped him up again and took him home.

Little Justin slept the night through, and the next morning drank two big glasses of milk. Croisine stepped out to get some water from a nearby well, and when she came back the boy was sitting up in his bed for the first time since his birth. The next day, he tried to get out of his crib, and the day after that his mother saw that he had succeeded. She found him running around the room like any other two-year-old.

Dr. Dozous summoned Dr. Lacrampe for a consultation. They found new enervation and new muscle, actual functioning flesh that hadn't been there during Dr. Dozous's examination only seventy-two hours before. In the days that followed, there was one cure after another at the spring of Lourdes, some of them fairly spectacular, most of them spiritual—a coming to terms with suffering, a conversion, or a deeper experience of religion. And most of these seem to have been permanent. When Justin Bouhouhorts was seventy-seven years old, he was present at the canonization ceremonies held for St. Bernadette in St. Peter's in 1933.[153]

But if incurable illnesses like his can be cured, the ultimate miraculous cure would be curing death.

THE RESURRECTION AND THE LIFE

When it comes to resurrecting the dead, nobody would deny that diagnostic mistakes are made—remember St. Teresa waking up with the wax on her eyes. But you can't attribute

---

153. Bernadette herself, like many another saint, had the ability to cure. When she was a novice at Nevers, a lady brought her little crippled son to the convent, hoping that Bernadette would heal him with her touch. Mère Imbert, then Superior-General, called Bernadette into the parlor, handed her the child, and said simply, "Take this child into the garden while I'm with this lady." Bernadette, who with her tubercular knee was never very well, couldn't support him, so she put him down immediately. He ran back to his mother, laughing. Her superiors used the same tactic on other occasions, telling her to carry a sick child or just straighten a patient's pillow—cf. Ac 5:15—at which they were immediately cured of whatever ailed them, according to attestations in her beatification process.

all old accounts of resurrection to the ignorance of our ancestors; generally, we're really less well prepared to know death when we see it than they were. We insulate ourselves from death; we expect doctors to pronounce people dead for us, often on the basis of readings that we can't understand from machines that we can't operate, and few of us ever encounter a life-threatening situation or even see a dead body outside of a funeral home. In other times, as today in other places, death was more immediate, and people expected to handle the business of death and dying themselves, just as they had to take care of illnesses and injuries themselves, even in the larger cities. Certainly a life that includes epidemics, wolves in the streets, raids by bandits and marauders, or even large farm animals teaches people the difference between being killed and just having the wind knocked out of you; and this was the norm of life even in Europe until well into the twentieth century.

But even giving the widest possible latitude to the gray area of diagnosis between life and death, and the difficulty even today of defining the moment of clinical death, there's still the phenomenon of reviving the dying on command, which is just about as impressive as resurrection of the dead—particularly because the patients come back restored to full health.[154] Even the thousands of episodes on record of saints instantly bringing back to consciousness people who may have been stunned or comatose are impressive; nobody else could revive them, and they recovered instantly, on command. And, more than that, there are also thousands of cases in which the bodies in question were so mangled that life was impossible by anybody's standards.

This, too, follows the precedent of Christ's own miracles. By the time he arrived to cure the daughter of Jairus, she was already so certainly dead that the crowd "laughed him to scorn" when he said that she was only sleeping (Mr 5:40). And he raised Lazarus from the dead after four days, when the body was already putrefied.[155] Nobody could attribute that to a coma that coincidentally ended the instant the man was called by name.

St. Paul himself was revived after being stoned (Ac 14:18-19; cf. Nm 14:1-11), which isn't often noticed, for some reason. That's particularly impressive because they didn't just throw hand-sized rocks at you, in those cases: they threw you into a pit and smashed you with stones that took two or three people to lift, and then they let you die of shock and compound fractures.

There's also the boy who fell from a high window and was revived by St. Paul (Ac 20:9-12; 26:8), and another who fell out of an upper window in Orbatello, Italy, in September, 1741. The boy was lying so broken on the stone pavement that he was pronounced hopeless by doctors and horrified bystanders alike, but he was made whole and

---

154. Those who might confuse actual resurrection with the so-called "near-death experiences" so popular these days need to consult T. Lempert, M. Bauer, and D. Schmidt, "Syncope and Near-Death Experience", *The Lancet* (344, September 17, 1994, 829-830).

155. Also 4Kn 8:5; Mt 9:18-26, 10:8, 27:52-53; Mk 5:35-43; Lk 7:12-23, 8:49-56; 20:37-40; Jn 11:14-12:19; etc., etc.

revived by the touch of Paul's namesake, St. Paul of the Cross, C.P. Another child four centuries earlier fell from a high balcony onto the stones of Città di Castello but was restored to life and health by Bl. Margaret of Castello (1287-1320). She also brought back to life, whole and healthy, a woodman who had been killed by bears and, evidently, partially eaten.

In the same vein, there's young Neapolion, nephew of Cardinal Stefano of Fossanova, whose fatal fall from his speeding horse interrupted Mass at the church of St. Sixtus in Rome. The presiding priest that day happened to be St. Dominic de Guzmán. He put the body into a locked room and went on celebrating Mass—during which he levitated in ecstasy—and afterwards commanded the boy to rise, which he did, whole and safe. There's also case of the young monk whose body was crushed so flat by the collapse of the stone wall on which he was working that his brothers had to carry the pieces to St. Benedict of Nursia (480-c. 547) in a sack, but St. Benedict brought him back to life in about an hour, without even a bruise.[156]

Stories like these—and there's a surprising number of them—seem perhaps a little less incredible once you've seen Pierre de Rudder's restored bone. And such cases still happen today. Kent Lanahan of Pennsylvania, whose skull was crushed when he was pinned between a car and a utility pole in July of 1949, was lying in the hospital nearly dead, one eye protruding, and running a high fever when a piece of a cassock once used by St. John Neumann (1811-1860) was put near him. That night, he was found sitting up in bed, fully restored to health. Granted, Lanahan wasn't dead at the time, but still, recovery like that has to count as a miracle. It's all the more impressive because he went on to become Pennsylvania's champion weightlifter.[157]

St. Martin of Porres (d. 1639) revived the dead and dying from time to time, too, but he never made much of it, not wanting to be revered as a saint during his earthly life, and as a result reports are sketchy. But his compassion extended even to animals—he used to warn the rats in the monastery when exterminations were planned—and it's recorded that he restored an eighteen-year-old dog to life and vigor after it had been put out of the way because of its decrepitude.[158]

---

156. There are also a lot of cases of suicides by hanging restored to life by saints such as St. Ignatius of Loyola, St. Martin of Tours, and everybody in between, but the details are not always clear. If you hang yourself properly you break your neck and die instantly, but most attempts are bungled, and the person chokes in extended torment, passing into unconsciousness or a coma first. Either way, though, revival on command is impressive enough.

157. This was one of the miracles admitted as evidence in the canonization process of St. John Neumann. It's interesting, too, that restoration to life evidently happens for specific dead tissues as well as for people entirely dead, as with Lanahan's crushed bones and the necrosed broken ends of De Rudder's, and the man with the withered hand in Matthew (12:10-13) as well as the innumerable similar cases cured at the great Marian shrines.

158. A similar miracle is reported of St. Nicholas of Tolentino (1245-1305), but St. Paul of the Cross, C.P. (1694-1775), took things a step farther. Dining with the Goffredi family one evening, he paused as he was about to say the blessing over a roasted chicken, sensing that the bird had been stolen by the man who sold her. "You've done wrong to kill this poor animal," he said, "because she supported with her

All of these cases center on faith, usually the very vehement faith of the surviving loved ones. There's the woman who pressed through the crowd to St. Martin of Tours carrying her dead baby son, who said, "You are the friend of God. Give me back my son!" Then there's the farmer who accosted St. Benedict and yelled, "Give me back my son! Come on! Bring him back to life!" Or the woman who stood in the path of the Abbot Libertinus's horse with her dead baby in her arms and said simply, "You shall not pass until you bring my baby back to life." Which he did, through the intercession of the sainted Abbot Honoratus, by means of his sandal, which Libertinus kept with him as a relic.

People who ask such favors need this kind of determination. Saints who stand close enough to God to get such stupendous answers to their prayers get there through absolute submission to his will, and they resist with all their might any form of questioning his judgement. Pope St. Gregory the Great (*c.* 540-604) tells us about the two sisters of a certain Marcellus of Todi who notified his good friend, Todi's bishop Fortunatus, that Marcellus had died. "You are the successor of the Apostles," they said, "and you cleanse lepers and give sight to the blind. Come with us and bring our brother back to life." Fortunatus wept profusely over his loss, but he told them to go home and not ask such a thing, because "your brother's death occurred by the will of God, which no man may oppose." They had to postpone the funeral for several days because it was Holy Week, but on Easter morning Fortunatus went to the bier and murmured, "Marcellus, Marcellus!"

Marcellus rose up whole and fresh, opened his eyes, and looked at his friend, really a little bewildered. "What are you doing?" he asked.

"What am *I* doing?" Fortunatus answered.

They went on to the celebration of the Eucharist together that Easter morning, and Fortunatus lived to a ripe old age in his renewed life. Evidently, God not only restores human life but maintains it, and sometimes without natural support like food or drink.

DESIRING ONLY THE BREAD OF GOD

Aversion to worldly goods is one thing; like St. Teresa and St. Bernard, most ascetic saints just don't care all that much for fine food any more than they care for fine clothes. But the mystic gift of *inedia* means that they eat virtually nothing, or absolutely nothing, year after year.

Well, that's not strictly accurate. They don't live on nothing. They live on the Eucharist. That consecrated bread, the Body of Christ, is evidently enough to sustain life and even make some mystics plump.

---

eggs the poor woman to whom she belonged. Let's do an act of charity. Open the window." Then he blessed the hen, which sprang back to life, fully feathered, and ran back to her owner. He did it again later, too, in the town of Fianella, and St. Francis di Paola (1416-1507) did the same thing with a cooked fish when at dinner with the King of Naples, although details about the reason for it are sketchy. It must have been edifying at the time.

The *Gospel of Pseudo-Matthew* and the *Protevangelion of James* report that Mary always gave to the poor all of her food because she didn't need it, being sustained by angels who brought her heavenly bread; the scene was engraved as early as the fifth century in a marble plaque at the church of St. Maximin in Provence, and it occurs in Christian art from time to time after that. But it is certainly true that some early Christians, like St. Gerasimus in Palestine (d. 475), lived on nothing but the Eucharist during Lent, and St. Ignatius of Antioch evidently prolonged the fast even longer, all the way to the Colosseum in Rome, where he was to be eaten by lions for being bishop of Antioch. "I have no taste for corruptible food nor for the pleasures of this life," he wrote; "I desire the Bread of God, which is the Flesh of Jesus Christ, who was of the seed of David, and for drink I desire his Blood, which is love incorruptible" (*Letter to the Romans, c.* 110).

The first mystic whose inedia was examined, documented, and recorded extensively was Bl. Alpais (d. 1211). She was a farm girl who was stricken with leprosy, or something very like it, but she was cured during an apparition of the Blessed Virgin. A little later, though, she suddenly became a quadriplegic, and she stopped eating and drinking.

But she took communion regularly. After she went on this way for a while, the Bishop of Sens started an investigation; the commission watched her day and night and confirmed that, in fact, she was eating nothing besides the consecrated Host, and she didn't even take that every day. After that, inedia was recognized as a distinct mystic gift, and moral theologians began studying it systematically.[159]

With most later inedics, though, it's not just a matter of refusing food but of being physically unable to keep it down. After her tumor burst, Bl. Lydwine couldn't keep even water down (although she still passed a stone the size of a small egg). She only took the small wafer of the Eucharist, once a week, for the remaining forty years of her life. St. Catherine of Siena went into torments of vomiting when she ate, under obedience, anything like normal food—just automatically, not by inducing it. She didn't like the condition ("I say it to you," she wrote, "and I say it in the presence of God, that I have tried in every possible way to take food, … and I have prayed constantly and still pray that I may live like others"[160]). Only the Eucharist stayed with her, and it was enough. As to the days when she didn't communicate, she said, the mere presence of Christ within her, or even the sight of a priest who had just celebrated Mass, was enough.

Finally, she asked her confessor why he kept forcing her to eat; if my fasting caused me this kind of distress, she said, you'd order me to stop it. He left her alone, after that, but the inevitable rumors started—it wasn't possible, she was faking it to gain

159. Still, they don't give it much weight, in a mystic sense. St. Catherine of Genoa, an occasional inedic herself, said that her will played no part in it and that it didn't mean much, anyway. A related mystic gift is the ability to go without sleep for years at a time; this is termed, in the language of mystic theology, *insomnia*. Bl. Anna-Maria Taigi, Bl. John de Chiaramonte (d. 1339), St. Catherine of Siena, Bl. Lydwine, St. John of the Cross, and countless other saints went without sleep entirely or slept extremely little, year after year. So did the stigmatic Therese Neumann, one of the best-documented cases.

160. She even wrote to her friends and asked them to send recommended medicines for the condition, although it's hard to figure how she would have taken them.

attention, she eats when nobody sees her, and so on. She ate in public, for a while, so that everybody could see what was going on, and she was virtually never unattended. Her suffering was so bad and so obviously genuine that even her severest critics eventually turned around, and many of them left detailed records about it.

But certainly the best-documented inedic is the Bavarian Therese Neumann (1898-1962). She's best known for her stigmata, which was unusually full in its manifestations and very closely observed by objective clinical people. But hers is also the best-documented case of inedia on record, as well as one of the longest: it began in 1922 and lasted until her death forty years later.

She had already had a lot of mystic experiences, but after 1922 she just lost all desire for food. She took only a small particle of the consecrated Host, with a sip of water, but after 1926 she didn't even take the water. Yet she steadily gained weight. This and her apparent other mystic gifts brought literally millions of pilgrims flocking to her home in Konnersreuth, and, with the civil instability that came before the rise of the Nazis, this started to attract unwelcome attention from the government. So the local archbishop ordered a strict scientific investigation of her mystic gifts, particularly her inedia. Four nurses were appointed to stand watch over her, two per shift, twenty-four hours a day; a non-Catholic Dr. Ewald from the Psychiatric Research Clinic of the University of Erlangen, and a Dr. Seidl from Waldsassen were enlisted, too.

Everything that happened was to be written down; one of the nurses knew shorthand, which made this easier. Therese was never to be left alone, not for a moment, day or night, and her temperature and pulse were checked at regular intervals. Absolutely nothing resembling sustenance was to be brought into the room; she was even bathed with a damp cloth, because a sponge might have carried too much water to her skin. The water used in cleaning her teeth was measured before she rinsed and after, to ensure that nothing was swallowed; all of her bodily discharges were to be kept for measurement and analysis.[161]

During the fifteen days of the observation, Therese showed no desire to eat anything, but the other results are even more surprising. She only took in 45 cubic centimeters of water, to help her swallow the tiny particle of Host, but she discharged 345 cc. Her weight fluctuated during that time, too, starting at 121 pounds and ending up there, but going to a low of only 112 after her Passion sufferings. A week later it was up to 115 and then, five days later, it jumped back up to 121. By 1935—without having taken even a sip of water for five years—she was up to 140; by 1950 she weighed more than 200 pounds, and by 1955 more than 215. "I'll no doubt be as heavy as my grandmother was," she laughed.[162]

---

161. After 1930, though, she didn't have any at all, no urine, no feces, and no menses.

162. Not surprisingly, everybody wanted to get her as a specimen; countless secular doctors and clinics petitioned the family for permission, and they allowed her to be poked and prodded occasionally, but only under obedience to Church authorities. Some researchers tried to go over their heads to the Pope, but Pius XI answered tersely, "*Lässt mir das Kind in Ruhe!*"—leave the kid in peace.

Now, Therese's family eventually drew the line and refused to obey the ordinary's insistence on some of the tests and the conditions under which they were administered, so even the documentation that these doctors and nurses compiled isn't conclusive proof of her mystic experiences. But her robust health without food or drink is all the more remarkable because she bled so profusely on those Fridays when she relived blow by blow the Passion of Christ, enough to completely soak her clothing, her bed linen, and the mattress. Apart from a genuine mystic activity, nobody could explain how she could survive such a loss of blood, much less produce it in the first place.

SWEAT AS DROPS OF BLOOD

Blood, the seal and symbol of the Old Covenant as well as the New, stands at the center of a whole array of physical mystic phenomena, just as the heart does, for obvious symbolic reasons. Like Christ in the Garden (Lk 22:44), a few mystics have evidently experienced *hematidrosis*, sweating blood. This is a particularly rare mystic phenomenon, and it's not easily confirmed because similar effects can be produced by involuntary but completely natural means. Some diseases—very rare diseases—can cause a reddish liquid to be exuded from the pores, but it's not blood; it's perspiration colored by an additional substance created by the infection. Sometimes, too, reddish patches on the skin or even reddish sweats can be induced by hysteria, but no known natural condition produces a genuine flow of blood through the pores without any wound or abrasion. So, because of its rarity and the difficulty of accurate diagnosis, reports of hematidrosis are most usually discounted. Other *blood prodigies* and *cardiac phenomena*, though, are better attested and more clearly supernatural in origin.

For example, the heartbeats of St. Ignatius of Loyola could be heard throughout the church sometimes when he was celebrating Mass. Doctors performing the autopsy on St. Philip Neri understood what the saint had meant when he said that his heart had been extraordinarily filled with God while he was meditating in the catacombs in 1544: his heart had become so enlarged with love that it had broken two of his ribs.[163] They didn't know how he could have lived like that, but he did, and the heart evidently functioned perfectly normally. And like the blood associated with Eucharistic miracles, some saints' blood shows extraordinary properties like perpetual freshness.

Blood taken medically from St. John Vianney—therapeutic bloodletting was a popular remedy for just about everything for two thousand years—was kept in vials, and it's still fresh and liquid. The body of the martyr St. Nazarius (d. *c.* 60) was discovered, still covered with fresh blood, by St. Ambrose in the fourth century. Other relics have been known to bleed when the situation warrants—the thumb of St. John the Baptizer left a trail when it was stolen, centuries after the saint's death. The body of St. Charbel Maklouf (d. 1898) started to perspire blood when it was exhumed four months after his death, a phenomenon that was reported as continuing as late as 1977, so copiously that

163. He had mentioned this because the people who hugged him—he was always hugging people—asked what the swelling on his chest, as big as a man's fist, was.

his clothing used to be changed twice a week. The body of Bl. Mattia Nazzarei of Matelica (d. 1319) began to perspire copiously when it was exhumed in 1536, and it started to exude fresh blood when it was moved during church restorations in 1756. It still does, but not continuously; blood flows before the death of a member of her community or before some major world event like a war.164

The best-known blood prodigy involves the blood of St. Januarius (San Gennaro, in Italian; d. *c.* 300), which is kept in a reliquary in the cathedral of Naples. He'd been bishop of Benevento, killed at Nola during the persecutions of Diocletian; he was beheaded, and his body was taken to Naples for safe entombment. By about the fifth century, appeals for his intercession through the relic had a reputation for averting eruptions of Mount Vesuvius, and by the fifteenth century the vials of his blood were shown regularly to the people twice a year, in May and in September. Sometimes, during the exposition, the caked blood liquifies and regains its freshness, which is taken as a sign that Vesuvius won't erupt before the next exposition, and that things will generally be all right in Naples.165

Of course, his blood wouldn't be available at all if the pagan judge had anything to say about it. The first time he tried to execute St. Januarius, he had him thrown into a furnace. But the bishop walked out unharmed.

THE FIRE HAS NO POWER

When Saint Catherine of Siena was beginning her mystic life, she fell into ecstasy and into the hearth fire at home, at the same moment, but when her sister-in-law found her there some time later and pulled her off the coals, she was entirely unhurt. She didn't feel anything, either, when a candle fell onto her head in church and kept burning, just as St. Bernadette and the seers of Beauraing weren't injured by candle flames.

Of course, accounts of *bodily incombustibility* (parallel to the impassibility of

164. The linen pads kept under her hands and feet to soak up the blood are usually saturated, though. A related and surprisingly widespread phenomenon involves the exudation of sweet-smelling, clear oil or other healing fluid from relics. The body of St. Elizabeth of Hungary, for instance, began to perspire oil copiously the minute her tomb was opened after her canonization, in the presence of several bishops and monarchs, including the scientist-Kaiser Frederick II von Hohenstaufen. That of St. Maria Maddelena dei Pazzi exuded a sweet fluid, most copiously from the knees, for twelve years; analysis couldn't identify exactly what it was or where it came from. The passage in Judges (15:17-19) isn't taken as a biblical precedent for this phenomenon, because the water came from a subsequently perennial spring in a place named Jawbone (Lehi), not from the bone itself, which Samson had thrown away already (15:17).

165. Since the eighteenth century some skeptics have proposed that the blood is really a thixotropic substance (one that starts out thick but liquifies when shaken, like ketchup) that can be compounded from naturally occurring substances in the area. But by 1902 spectroscopic analysis confirmed that it's really blood, and, even if some similar substance could be prepared artificially, that wouldn't logically prove anything about the substance in the vial; it would only show that a similar effect might be produced in more than one way (see Part Five). Artificial compounds don't react precisely the same, anyway, and the prodigy happens even when the vial isn't moved. There are similar prodigies, too, like the blood of Saint Pantaleon (d. 305) in Ravello, Italy; its vial stands untouched in the stonework above the altar, but, as Cardinal John Henry Newman saw, it liquifies on his feast day in July anyway, as it has done for nearly seventeen centuries. So does the blood on St. Januarius's basalt execution block, by the way, which is kept in Pozzuoli—but only on his feast day, when his blood in the vial in Naples liquifies.

angels and glorified bodies) appear in the Bible, notably in the third chapter of Exodus and the third chapter of Daniel, but they're more frequent from early Christian times, when death by burning was an especially popular method of execution, as the most painful death the persecutors could think of. The *Golden Legend* collects lots of early records—St. Christina's spending five days in a fiery furnace, singing with the angels, for instance, St. John the Evangelist's emerging unscathed from a cauldron of boiling oil at Ephesus (which is memorialized in Rome by the little church of San Giovanni in Olio, St. John in Oil), and St. Primus's easily drinking the hot lead poured down his throat by Diocletian's henchmen.[166]

The indestructible Bl. Lydwine of Schiedam proved immune from the effects of fire, too, as when a candle fell from the shelf above her onto the pile of straw on which she lay, reducing it to ashes but not harming her at all. But sometimes incombustibility radiates, you might say, from a mystic to protect even the building he's in. A conflagration destroyed the entire town of Schiedam in 1428 (just as Bl. Lydwine had predicted, by the way—it was in retribution for the town's sins, she said, and she regretted that she was powerless to stop it), but her own house stood undamaged when the smoke cleared. The same thing happened a thousand years before that in Auxerre, when the house where St. Germain (d. *c.* 430) was lying ill survived a fire that levelled the city.

Even the royal palace of France was saved in 1667 through the fast thinking of Jacques-Bénigne Bossuet (1627-1704), Bishop of Meaux, tutor to the young Louis XIV and a moral theologian of some standing. The fire broke out as Bossuet was discussing religion with the great Calvinist general Henri de Turenne, who balked at accepting the True Presence in the Eucharist. The fire was soon far out of control, but Bossuet ran around the fire to the palace oratory, took the ciborium containing the Blessed Sacrament, and actually walked through the conflagration from one end to another, intoning the words of Benediction. As he passed, the flames subsided. Turenne's disbelief did, too, and from that moment until his death in battle he was a fervent and humble convert.

THEY SHALL NOT UNDERGO CORRUPTION

The living bodies of some victim souls like Bl. Lydwine, of course, are the most extraordinarily durable in the whole history of medicine, and they foreshadow yet another mystic phenomenon: *incorruptibility*, the immunity of some mystic's bodies to the natural processes of decay after death.

When Bl. Lydwine finally died, what was left of her body suddenly became as whole and beautiful as it had been when she was fifteen, before she started on her aston-

---

166. St. Francis di Paola used to routinely pick up live coals, and even hand them absentmindedly to other people, as part of his normal housekeeping chores. He'd also walk into live limekilns, brick kilns, and charcoal piles to repair them if they collapsed partially during firings. Of course, this is entirely different from firewalking, which is within the normal order of things and can be learned by anybody who finds some attraction in that kind of thing. It's not just that the bodies of these saints don't burn: as in the biblical precedents, their clothes don't, either, and when they come out there's no smell of smoke or fire about them.

ishing career of suffering—as if to confirm that her illnesses were of purely supernatural origin. The same phenomenon is reported about many other saints, like St. Germaine Cousin of Pibrac (1579-1601), whose physical deformities, her withered right arm and scrofulous neck, were replaced by surpassing beauty after she died in 1601. Or St. Etheldreda, who died about 679; when she was exhumed in some fifty years later in 730, her surgeon Cynefrid noticed that the gaping incision he'd made to lance the swelling under her jaw three days before she died was healed to a fine scar.[167] He could see this clearly because her body, like those of hundreds of other saints or candidates for sainthood, was found intact and free from any trace of decay.

In centuries past, the bodies of hundreds of saints, some as prominent as St. Albert the Great or St. Edward the Confessor and others as obscure as St. Guthlac (c. 674-714) or the English martyr St. John Southworth (1592-1654), who was quartered, have been found this way after months or years in the grave. In these cases, the discovery was usually incidental to moving the body to another site, as with St. Elizabeth of Hungary or St. Teresa of Avila. In more recent times, though, examination of the corpse is a routine part of the canonization process; this is really to establish beyond doubt that the body in the grave really is the body of the candidate, but it also means that incorruptibility is now one of the best-documented mystic phenomena.

The graves of persons whose sanctity has caused formal investigations are opened in the presence of a committee of doctors, Church officials, and any civil authorities (judges, magistrates, policemen, notaries, etc.) whose presence at exhumations is required by civil law. Usually, they find about what would be expected after that time in the grave, but surprisingly often—particularly in the cases of creditable visionaries—they find the body supple, the skin soft and not discolored, the eyes bright and clear, the hair intact, and the joints flexible. This is what happened with Ven. Solanus Casey, O.F.M. Cap. (d. 1957), in Detroit, who was exhumed in 1987. He looked more like a person asleep or unconscious than a corpse, and so have many canonized saints whose bodies were found to have the really mysterious gift of incorruptibility.

But incorruptibility doesn't mean unlimited preservation in the lifelike state. There's usually some discoloration and shrinkage after an extremely long time or after some significant date, like the formal declaration of beatification or canonization. In some cases, the bodies fall into dust and bones after the declaration, immediately taking on the nature of a body dead for that length of time. The bones of Bl. Anna-Maria Taigi, for example, were recently placed in a figure representing her, its face and hands of plastic, when her body lost the incorruption that it had from her death in 1837 until at least 1867, four years after Pius IX introduced the cause of her beatification.

Others take on something of the appearance of a mummy, but they still don't decompose, and unlike natural or artificial mummies they stay soft and supple. Still others may be altered by well-meant interventions like washing, which discolored the face

---

167. The event was recorded in the *Ecclesiastical History of the English Nation* by St. Bede, who got his information directly from the people involved.

of St. Bernadette's incorrupt body in 1909, or by transfer to adverse conditions, as when the body of St. Benedict the Black (1526-1589) was pompously entombed in 1611 by King Philip III of Spain at Santa Maria di Gesù in Sicily; evidently, the new sepulchre caused the remains to dry out, but they still didn't rot.[168]

Now, this may reflect God's special favor for the person and the promise of resurrection (Ps 15:10), but it's important to note that incorruptibility alone isn't counted among the genuine mystic gifts, which don't happen in isolation. Some separated groups of Christians, like the Russian Orthodox Church, take the phenomenon more seriously (remember the consternation caused by the whiff of corruption at the bier of Father Zossima in *The Brothers Karamazov*), but the Church doesn't consider incorruption proof of sanctity. It doesn't count for anything at all in the canonization process.

The Pathology of Corruption

But incorruption is still a fascinating subject, and it does still occur in a lot of cases, maybe in a majority of cases, when the person in question is a creditable visionary. However, by way of preface, this is another of those sections that the delicate may want to skip. First of all, the corruption of the dead human body isn't really so well understood as you might think. It never has been. That's one reason that—short of soaking the whole thing in arsenic—no really effective method of permanent embalmment has been found, and it's why lack of decay doesn't count in canonization investigations.

Usually, there are enough microbes, and enough moisture, inside the body itself to guarantee fairly quick decomposition, no matter what's done to the corpse. Some natural causes can delay this or prevent it indefinitely. People sometimes discover bodies, usually those that have been buried accidentally or hastily, that haven't decayed as one would expect, and nobody can figure out why. Some kinds of soil seem to harbor microbes that themselves prevent putrefaction, but that's neither very common nor very well investigated.[169]

Some factors that prevent corruption are known, though. Cool temperatures delay putrefaction, of course, and extreme dryness can draw the necessary moisture from the tissues quickly enough to kill the microbes or force them into dormancy, which is what happens when bodies are buried in desert sands like those of Egypt—natural mummification. Freeze-drying, removing the moisture while keeping temperatures low, works, too, as does just freezing a body permanently preserves it, as in the Arctic or in the glaciers of the high Alps. Keeping a body from air in a germ-free environment can preserve it, which is why honey was used as an embalming fluid in many northern countries, and why ancient bodies are sometimes found intact in peat bogs.[170]

---

168. In these cases, the face might be covered with a thin mask of wax if the body is kept on public display, as relics that don't come from incorrupt bodies are sometimes encased in wax figures.

169. There's a process called *autolysis*, though, in which the enzymes naturally present within organs like the pancreas, released at death, break down the tissues from within, even without germs.

170. Colonic bacteria can destroy tissues, if not slowed down by dryness, cold, or other factors. But peat moss and honey both happen to have strong, broad-range antibiotic properties, which is why they've

A body buried in certain kinds of wet soil, away from air, can undergo a process called *saponification*, literally "turning into soap". Soap is made by the action of some alkaloid, like lye, on some kind of fat, and in some conditions of burial the soft tissues of the body turn into a hard, yellowish, impure form of natural soap called *adipocere* (from the Latin *adeps*, fat, and *cera*, wax).[171]

Now, these effects are sometimes observed in the bodies of particularly holy people, but statistically it's just about as often as they're found in the bodies of regular people. St. Mary de Sainte-Euphrasie Pelletier (1796-1868), for instance, was found to have become saponified, and there are hundreds of natural mummies in the Capuchin burial vault in Rome, which has always been a kind of tourist attraction. But there's no way to confuse these kinds of preservation with the mystic gift of incorruption. The symptoms are all different.

The Pathology of Incorruption

Whenever anybody, any normal person, dies, *rigor mortis*, literally "the stiffness of death", sets in. It starts two to five hours after death, and by twelve to eighteen hours, the entire body is completely rigid.[172] As putrefaction sets in after about thirty-six hours, the rigor passes and the body becomes limp, but by then it's definitely dead and beginning to decompose.

But the bodies of incorrupt saints or mystics are exactly like those of people sleeping or unconscious, except that they usually go cold. Not always, but usually: the body of St. Benedict Joseph Labre (1748-1783) stayed warm for a long time after his death, and in fact when the body started to slide one hand grasped the bench on which he had been laid, to keep from falling. Naturally, this raised some doubts, but when his surgeon, a doctor named Valenti, opened a vein to see if the saint were really in a coma, only a little blood came out, as with any dead body.[173]

The body of Sor Maria Villani (d. 1670) was so inflamed with ardors that heat and steam issued from her autopsy incision nine hours after her death; her heart was so hot that her doctor couldn't hold it in his hand.[174] In fact, although she was eighty-six years old, dark, and emaciated when she died, her body became fresh, youthful, and sup-

often been used to dress wounds (but don't try that at home), and why seedlings are sown in peat—it kills molds, fungi, and diseases that could kill the plants (that one you can try at home).

171. Naturally saponified bodies are sometimes exhibited as curiosities. One is kept at the Mutter Museum of the College of Physicians and Surgeons of Philadelphia, for instance.

172. Some known causes of death, like running until exhausted after receiving an eventually fatal wound, speed the onset, while others, particularly suffocation by carbon dioxide, can delay the onset of stiffness until perhaps twenty-four hours after death, but every dead body gets *rigor mortis* sooner or later. Except the incorrupt.

173. Still, given the fact that many incorrupt bodies bleed fresh blood copiously years after death, it seems an odd sort of test to make.

174. Some warming can happen from keeping the body in an exceptionally hot place or from sepsis, but not to this degree, and neither cause can heat a living body as hers had been heated.

ple in death. Eighteen days after the burial of St. Catherine of Genoa (1447-1510), directly in the ground with no coffin or wrapping, her body was exhumed when Church officials had second thoughts about preventing a public expression of grief. Her face had been crushed in the hasty burial, but when she was washed and dressed it regained its beauty, and rosiness replaced the pallor in her cheeks.[175]

Even those incorrupt bodies that retain, rather than regain, natural, healthy coloring stay soft to the touch, too, not hard or waxy but just like living flesh. They remain supple, but mummified bodies are stiff, and saponified ones tend to fall apart at the joints. Incorrupt bodies can be freely posed, washed, and dressed, and some of them, like those of St. Pascal Baylon (1540-1592) and St. Teresa of Avila, will stand upright if placed in that position, even while their clothes are being changed. In living people, that's caused by the tonic reflex, which means that your muscles constantly (and imperceptibly) relax or contract to keep you upright as you tend to fall one way or another; in the dead, naturally, this reflex doesn't work any more, so you can't stand a corpse upright, not even during *rigor mortis*, but some incorruptible bodies do manage it.

More remarkably, their eyes remain fresh and bright, and their internal organs don't decay; in the purely normal course of things, the viscera are the first to go. In mummified bodies they're shrivelled and dry, and in saponified bodies they sort of melt together into an indistinct soapy mass, but the viscera of incorrupt bodies remain soft, well formed, and fresh.[176]

Also, bodies preserved by some natural means don't last very long if they're removed from whatever circumstances, known or unknown, caused the natural preservation. But incorrupt bodies can stay in this state for centuries at a time. St. Isidore the Farmer (b. 1070) died in 1130, but his incorrupt body was displayed for ten days the last time it was moved to a new tomb, in 1969. St. Cecilia was martyred in 177, but when her body was exhumed in 1599 it was still incorrupt and, like virtually all other incorrupt bodies of the Church's mystics, it was fragrant with the odor of sanctity.[177] That's another way that incorruption is distinguished from other kinds of preservation: mummies have a distinct and unpleasant odor of death about them, and adipocere stinks, but incorrupt bodies have no odor at all, or they're fresh with the scent of those celestial flowers.

It's interesting, too, that incorruptibility doesn't necessarily extend to the whole body, but sometimes only to a significant organ—the hand of St. Stephen of Hungary (d. 1038), for instance, or the heart of St. Bridget of Sweden, which were found incorrupt among their bones and ashes. Or the tongues of the great preachers St. Anthony of Padua, St. John Nepomucene (*c.* 1350-1393), and Bl. Battista Varani (1458-1527),

175. Her body also bled copiously from a wound in the foot, enough to fill a cup with fresh blood.

176. Reportedly, the viscera of Archbishop Oscar Romero of El Salvador, placed by physicians in plastic bags and buried in a cardboard box at the edge of the jungle, were unearthed accidentally in 1982, two years after his death, and found to be incorrupt, the blood on them still liquid. To date, there has been no report that the tomb containing the rest of his body has been opened.

177. This was also one of the first exhumations supervised by a professional archæologist, Antonio Bosio, the man who systematically investigated the catacombs.

which were soft, red, and flexible as long as four centuries after the rest of their bodies had crumbled to dust.

A similar piece of evidence against some unknown natural cause of preservation is that the body of a holy person frequently remains incorrupt while those of others buried exactly the same way undergo natural decomposition, as was that of St. Andrew Bobola (b. 1591). His body certainly should have decayed, if ever a body should have. He was burned, partially flayed, dragged by horses across country, and hacked with sabers by Kazaks in 1657—while still alive—but his body was still fresh and incorrupt as late as 1827. Even his really appalling wounds still had perfectly fresh blood on them.

Usually, records, witnesses, and *post-mortem* examinations establish that the body was never embalmed or treated in any way. The overwhelming majority of incorruptible bodies belong to religious, and that kind of treatment is contrary to the custom of many religious orders, anyway. In fact, some of the major orders bury, or used to bury, their dead without a coffin of any kind, simply washing the body, dressing it in the usual habit, and sometimes nailing the habit to a plank so that the body could be lowered into the earth. Only a small percentage of those holy bodies reported as incorruptible are shown on investigation to have been treated somehow before burial—about one in a hundred, roughly. Other bodies embalmed by the same process (whatever process was used at that time and place) decompose naturally, and no known embalming can account for the lifelike suppleness; but, even so, nobody makes any claim for a supernatural cause, in those cases.

Many incorrupt bodies also resist the worst possible natural conditions, such as submerged gravesites or wet soil, tropical climates, or even direct attempts at hastening decomposition. When St. Francis Xavier (b. 1506) died in 1552, on a little island within sight of Canton, his Chinese companion and interpreter Antonio de Santa Fe fell in with the "excellent suggestion" that he put quicklime beneath and over the body in the wooden coffin, to speed up decomposition so that the priest's bones could be moved more easily to a permanent grave in the future.

But when the cold, wet earth was removed two and a half months later, the body was found perfect under the corrosive. When they got the remains to Malacca, they found that the grave dug for them in front of the altar was too short, so they took the body from the quicklime, stuffed it into the grave (breaking the neck to make it fit), and filling the grave with mud. The body lay there for five more months, until one of Francis's friends heard about it and had the body exhumed. It was still perfect, once they got the mud off of it, and it ended up in Goa, at the cathedral. It remains there today, incorrupt despite all of the abuse.

St. Paschal Baylon was packed in quicklime, too, even though his body was already incorrupt, fragrant, and exuding healing oil as perspiration on the forehead—the guardian of the friary thought that shiny, clean bones would look nice in his reliquary. Still, after eight months, his body was as fresh and unharmed as that of a living person. The same thing happened, to a degree, with the body of little Ven. Jacinta Marto, one of the seers of Fátima, who died of influenza, pleurisy, bronchial pneumonia, tuberculosis, and runaway infections. Her body was packed in quicklime in a leaden coffin, but when this was opened fifteen years later her head and face were found to be unaffected. Thirty years after her death, when her remains were translated to the basilica at Fátima, the phenomenon was seen to have persisted, although with some discoloration.

Because of the corrosives used in her burial, it's hard to say if Ven. Jacinta was really incorrupt, but the odor of sanctity was reported, and evidently the ravages of her diseases weren't evident on her body. Bl. Lydwine is the most striking example a kind of *post-mortem* healing, of course, but there are others who show some signs of restoration after death. St. Bernadette's tubercular leg was normalized when she died, for instance. But most striking of all are the cases like that of Bl. Crispino da Viterbo (1668-1750).

He died of gangrenous necrosis—that is, his body just started to progressively die and rot. When he died completely, he was supposed to have been buried immediately, but as soon as his body was laid out the lesions disappeared suddenly, and the discoloration went with them. His knees, feet, and hands, which had been contorted and knotted from his diseases, straightened and filled out, like those of a person in full health. His body was completely transformed, from head to toe, while his caretakers watched it happen. His flesh became healthy again, like that of a child, a witness wrote.

These miraculous cures, even if they happen after death, would point to a supernatural origin for the really excruciating afflictions that these saints embraced willingly in reparation for their own sins and the world's. They can give the rest of us some perspective, in that way, on just how bad sin is. And perhaps they can remind us that our sins are the cause of our sufferings, showing us vividly of just how much pain sin inflicts on God, as well as on us. That's why the most interesting wounds that come and go mystically are those that symbolically reproduce the Wounds of Christ: the stigmata.

TOUCHING THE MARKS OF THE NAILS

Most books on mystic theology say that the first of the Church's stigmatics was St. Francis of Assisi, but oddly enough they seem to overlook the great biblical precedent for St. Francis's experience: St. Paul says that he was the first stigmatic, himself. "With Christ I am nailed to the Cross," he says; "I bear the marks of the Lord Jesus in my body," which is about as explicit as you can get (Gl 2:19; 6:17).

The word "stigma" comes from the Greek root meaning a wound made by a pointed instrument, a puncture; *stigmata* means wounded in this way. Now, you might think that, if the Crucifixion is an actual historical event, the wounds of a genuine stigmatic would all be the same, and that they would reproduce exactly the wounds of Christ, the wounds that you would have seen if you'd been there at Golgotha. But mystic theologians, like the stigmatics themselves, take it for granted that the wounds are symbolic.

That's why the wounds vary in intensity and in number. Bl. Alphonsus Orozco (1500-1591) just had little purplish marks on the soles of his feet, which weren't discovered by other people until after his death. Mary Agnes Steiner (d. 1862) of Nocera got red marks and the odor of sanctity, but no bleeding; and blood oozed from the stigmatic wounds of Louise Lateau, but the skin wasn't broken.[178]   Others, like Padre Pio, have full wounds in the hands, feet, and side. Some don't have the marks of the Crown of Thorns—St. Francis didn't—and others have only those wounds. St. Rita of Cascia had only one of them, a thorn puncture in her forehead. Still others have the full array, the nail marks in the hands and feet, the marks of the scourge, the wound in the side, and, in some cases, the bruise and abrasions on the shoulder from carrying the Cross.

The positions of these wounds vary, too. The shoulder wound is on the left or on the right, and the nail wounds are usually in the palms, not the wrists. Like anatomists and physiologists, the mystics themselves have always known that a person can't be crucified on nails through the palms (to support the weight of the body, the nails have to go through the hollow of the wrist, which also severs important nerves and veins), but, again, they remind us that the wounds are symbolic.

Now, wounds are easily enough faked, and there have always been fanatics and mentally unbalanced people who injure themselves in the name of enthusiasm or even delusion. The disciplinary records of the Church across mediæval Europe show many cases of people, people usually in remote rustic areas sparsely supplied with missionaries, who allowed themselves to be crucified from time to time, as still happens in some parts of Latin America that haven't been completely evangelized. Some of them did it because they misunderstood the whole point of Christianity, some of them did it as a voluntary penance, and some of them did it because they thought that they were Jesus.[179] This kind of thing, undoubtedly, put the whole question of reproducing the wounds of Christ in disrepute for a long, long time after St. Paul.

That kind of record also helps explain the unusual nature of St. Francis's stigmatic wounds. His biographer, St. Bonaventure, gives the whole story of this extraordinary phenomenon. In September of 1224, two years before he died, St. Francis went

178. Clinical psychologists have shown that hysterics can produce reddish spots on their bodies by autosuggestion, but none has yet been found who can produce spontaneous hemorrhage. That is, you can convince yourself to get locally inflamed, but without some mechanical intervention like a puncture or a deep abrasion, you can't think yourself into bleeding. The stigmatic Marie-Julie Jahenny was observed by the specialist Dr. Imbert-Goubeyre (who literally wrote the book on the stigmata) to have a cross, a flower, and various inscriptions, including the words O CRUX AVE, "Hail, O Cross", appear on her chest. Similar inscriptions have reportedly been produced by autosuggestion, and they may have been in her case, too, although her stigmata itself was undoubtedly genuine, in the judgement of her local bishop. Even though, ironically enough, she lived in a village named La Fraudais.

179. Or Mary, which makes even less sense. The Church, always taking a dim view of excessive penances, treated these unbalanced cases rather strictly, if humanely, in the days before psychotherapy. In 1222, for instance, the Council of Oxford convened by the saintly Archbishop of Canterbury Stephen Langton (who wrote the Magna Carta), heard disciplinary cases involving a deacon who had abjured Christianity in favor of Judaism, an "hermaphrodite" and his—or her, or whatever—"accomplice", and a man who had perforated his hands, feet, and side. This last case was judged insane and "immured" at Banbury (that is, confined to a cell adjoining the church, as anchorites confined themselves voluntarily, not suffocated with brick and mortar). Another English spurious stigmatic of the time, who refused the sacraments and wouldn't enter a church but insisted on being addressed as Jesus, was handled the same way.

on retreat up to Mount La Verna, where, as he had often done before, he fasted for forty days in honor of St. Michael the Archangel. During these fasts, he would open the Gospels at random to find some passage to meditate on, but this time the book always fell open to one or another account of the Passion. He was already worn out by austerities, but these passages made him burn with an even greater desire to share in Christ's sufferings.

On the Feast of the Exaltation of the Cross, September 14, he saw a six-winged seraph descend. Two of his blazing wings were held above his head, two were extended for flight, and the other two covered his whole body (Is 6:1-13). Between the wings he saw the figure of a man crucified, nailed to a cross. He understood that the vision was intended to tell him what it would be like to be transformed into the likeness of the crucified Christ; and as soon as it disappeared, the marks started to show, but he didn't just get wounds as if nails had been put through his hands and feet. He got the nails.

They were black, shaped exactly like hand-forged nails, but made out of a hornlike substance like tendon or cartilage. The heads of the nails on his palms and on the tops of his feet were round, while the points on the opposite sides were bent down, as if beaten with a hammer. They protruded beyond the skin, on both sides. He wore special underwear to hide the wound in his side, which never healed but bled intermittently, and he concealed the nails as best he could, but people saw them anyway—his brethren were forever trying to trick him out of his tunic, on the pretext of caring for him in his final illness. When he died, people noticed that the nails could be moved in the hands and feet; if they were pressed on one side, they stuck out on the other, just as metal nails would. You could put your finger under the bent points, when the nails were extended like that.

After St. Francis established that the stigmata is a legitimate mystic phenomenon, or re-established it for the first time since St. Paul, there have been hundreds of others. There are still fakes, of course, even more than before St. Francis, but the wounds of a genuine stigmatic are materially different from those that you can make yourself. For one thing, the wounds are often fragrant with the odor of sanctity rather than the smell of fresh wounds. They never smell like infected wounds, either; they're "inaccessible to corruption", as the doctors put it, never getting infected or putrefying even if they're open for years and decades. Genuine stigmatic wounds are "rebellious to medication", resisting any pharmaceutical treatment and often reacting violently to any applied medication. They bleed copiously, too, gushing out apparently arterial blood, even if the wounds are superficial or not even visible. In some cases they run with blood constantly, as with Padre Pio; in other cases intermittently, and in a few only on certain significant dates. They even bleed on dates contrary to the victim's expectation, as the Church has transferred certain feast days to another date without the victim's knowledge.

But there are very, very few cases of fleshly nails like those of St. Francis. St. Gemma Galgani's appeared gradually during her ecstasies; first red marks on her hands and feet that gradually tore open and bled copiously, and then the nails themselves formed out of flesh, hard and dark, just like St. Francis's, but they disappeared after her torments subsided, leaving only whitish marks on her skin. John-Mary Bononi (d. 1670) had the nails more or less permanently, as did the nineteenth-century stigmatic Domenica Lazzari and the twentieth-century Therese Neumann.

The Stigmatic as Victim Soul: Therese Neumann

The fleshly nails in Therese Neumann's hands and feet, unlike those of St. Francis, had square heads. And she didn't just walk around with inert marks on her body; she suffered the entire Passion time and again, dying in torment more than seven hundred times in her life. If extraordinary mystic gifts are given as a countersign to the depravity of the times, then this Bavarian peasant woman was chosen to stand against the horrors of the Third Reich, much as Bl. Lydwine stood, or lay, against the political chaos of her own day.

To all appearances, Therese Neumann was like any other farm girl of the region, completely ordinary; but the depth and range of her spiritual life was anything but. As the First World War drew to a close, she received an extraordinary series of physical afflictions that came and went at significant dates in the Church's calendar—beginning in 1918, interestingly enough, just when the German High Command awarded the Iron Cross, first class, to Corporal Adolf Hitler. These sufferings increased; in hindsight, their intensity can be seen to have grown as Hitler's political strength increased, corresponding generally with pivotal events like the beer-hall *putsch* he staged in Bavaria's capital, but evidently nobody made the connection between the two relatively obscure chains of events in the early years of either career. But as violence, godlessness, and chaos swept over Europe, Therese was to become the best-documented stigmatic in history. Her wounds were seen by millions of pilgrims over four decades; her ecstatic replications of the Passion of Christ were witnessed by lay doctors, photographed, and even filmed. It all came upon her gradually, just as the second World War came.

In the morning of the first Friday of Lent, March 5, 1926, only a week or so after Hitler took over complete control of the National Socialist Party, Therese had a vision of Christ with three Apostles on Mount Olivet. Coming out of a state of semi-consciousness, noticed that her nightgown was stained with blood from a wound just above her heart. She didn't tell anybody about it, not wanting to worry them about a trifle, so she just cleaned the wound and hid the stained cloths. Then the next two Fridays the wound bled again, but despite having visions of the Scourging and the Crowning with Thorns, she didn't make the connection. On the fourth Friday of that Lent, she saw Christ Carrying the Cross and the First Fall, and the wound on the outside of her left hand appeared. The other visions, completing her mystic Stations of the Cross,[180] came to her during Holy Week of that year, as did the wounds in her hands and feet, which went completely through.

---

180. This devotion consists of meditations on episodes in Christ's Passion, which are represented by pictures, sculptures, or simple crosses on the walls of just about every parish church. The history and nature of the devotion are outlined in Chapter 11 of the author's *Why Do Catholics Do That?*. On the skills of meditative prayer in general, see his *Rosary: Mysteries, Meditations, and the Telling of the Beads*.

More than that, she suffered fully the whole Passion, herself, the wounds appearing in sequence, just as in the Gospel accounts. Blood streamed from the wounds of the Scourging and those of carrying the Cross and falling with it; from her hands, feet, and side; and from her eyes. The blood poured out, soaking her bed. Her torments were real—the wounds hurt as much as ordinary traumatic wounds of that kind. At three o'clock in the afternoon of Good Friday, she fell exhausted and, to all appearances, dead. After about an hour, she revived, but she endured the Passion again and again, always on Fridays. By November she received the wounds of the Crown of Thorns, making her stigmata complete.

From that time on, she relived the Passion on the Fridays of Lent and Advent, as well as those within the octaves of those seasons, about twenty-six to twenty-eight times a year, for thirty-six years. During these ecstasies, doctors in attendance cut her with knives or stuck her with needles—doctors always seem eager to do that to ecstatics—but it didn't have any effect in her case, either.

During these reproductions of Christ's Passion, her suffering started in the morning. One by one, in Gospel order, her wounds started to bleed, the blood flowing upward on her feet as she lay in bed, toward the toes, as it would if she were nailed to a vertical cross, and from her lowered hands upward to the elbows.[181] She wept, too, but at the instant of the nailing her tears turned to blood. She lost about a quart and a half of blood, in all, but showed no ill effects afterwards; and, remember, she was eating and drinking exactly nothing during these years.

Even so, after the long and bloody torment, she collapsed with no pulse, no breathing, and no other sign of life. The doctors in attendance said that in any other context she would be declared dead, lying there with no vital signs for so long. But after an hour or so, she stirred again, and after another hour she was up and around. She bandaged her hands and side, and she wore special shoes that kept her considerable weight off the wounds in her feet, so that she could manage her housework and even her farm work.

Her mystic experiences attracted millions of pilgrims, hundreds a day, every day, and as many as fifteen thousand on the Passion Fridays. After her home town of Konnersreuth was liberated, more than half a million American soldiers visited her house. There were so many that the staircases up to, and down from, her room had to be replaced six or seven times, and the house itself started to fall to pieces from the traffic. She put up with all of this in good humor, apparently feeling that part of the purpose of her sufferings was that people should know about them. And certainly she was a focus of faith in Nazi Germany.

But other stigmatics have tried to avoid publicity. When St. Catherine of Siena's stigmata attracted more attention than she was comfortable with, she asked for it

---

181. The same phenomenon is reported of other stigmatics throughout history, as, for instance, Domenica Lazzari (d. 1848).

to be made invisible, and it was. But the thing that impressed her about it was that she didn't die from the pain; that, she said, was the real miracle.[182]

Naturally—or, rather, supernaturally—the stigmata doesn't occur in isolation; it strikes victim souls or other heroic mystics who show an impressive array of the other mystic gifts. Not all ascetics are mystics, and not all mystics are stigmatics, but all stigmatics are mystics. They experience agility, aureoles, bilocation, blood prodigies, bodily incorruptibility, flames of love, hematidrosis, inedia, insomnia, levitation, miraculous cures of their diseases, or the odor of sanctity, in any intensity or combination, in addition to bearing the marks of the Passion. They suffer heroically, not just in their re-enactments of the tortures of their Savior, but in their bodily infirmities too, which, by common medical consent, would kill anybody else.[183] But they receive extraordinary mystic consolations, too. They are mystics because God moves close to them; they feel him working in their souls. And they sense his presence with the eyes of the body as well as those of the soul.

182. Ven. Joan Mary Solimani (d. 1758) also asked for her stigmata to be made invisible, for similar reasons, but the flesh that covered them was so soft that her confessor could easily insert a key into them to the depth of about half an inch.

183. One specialist, Dr. Imbert-Goubeyre, *La stigmatisation et l'extase divine* (Amat, 1894), noted that the life of stigmatics is nothing more than a long series of pains that lead up to the "divine malady" of the stigmata and then constitute an escort for it, continuing with it up to the hour of death. An interesting statistic, though, is that visionaries who experience creditable apparitions of Christ, Mary, or another saint or angel virtually never become stigmatics.

part two

certain apparitions

of Christ

And as he went on his journey,
it came to pass that he drew near to Damascus,
when suddenly a light from Heaven shone round about him;
and falling to the ground he heard a voice saying to him,
"Saul, Saul, why dost thou persecute me? ...
Arise and go into the city,
and it will be told to thee
what thou must do."

Acts 9:3-6

thirteen

Ostia 387

God spoke to me in peace and love.
I looked upon him, and I saw him.
You ask me what I saw?
It was God himself, and I can say no more.

— Bl. Angela of Foligno, *Visions* (*c.* 1290)

In the year 332, a baby girl was born to Christian parents in the African city of Tagaste, about sixty miles outside of Carthage, near modern-day Tunis. Her parents named her Monica, and they saw to it that she was raised strictly, but fairly. They assigned her care to a governess who never let her drink any water between meals, on the grounds that when the girl grew up she'd be wanting wine instead, if she got used to drinking during the day.

Nevertheless, when the girl got old enough to take on some little household duties, she started sipping from the wine whenever they sent her to get some from the cellar, and before long she was drinking it by the cup, all day long. She didn't think much about it until a servant called her a drunkard. Her shame overwhelmed her, and, asserting her substantial willpower, she never gave in to the habit again.

Now, even though her parents were Christians, they arranged an advantageous marriage for her with a pagan named Patricius. He had a violent temper, and he ran around with a fast crowd, but the worst of it was his mother, who lived with the couple; evidently she was the one who taught Patricius all about bad temper. The interesting thing is that Monica didn't give in, and she didn't descend to their level; she eventually converted both of them by her endless prayers on their behalf and by her exceptional patience and generosity toward them. She bore at least three children by Patricius, a daughter Perpetua and two sons, the younger named Navigius and the elder named Augustine.

Augustine inherited his mother's willful gentleness and his father's inclination to dalliance. Monica managed to get him into the catechumenate, though, but he didn't agree to Baptism until he fell seriously ill and found himself near death. But as soon as he got better he decided to put it off, indefinitely. He had plenty of other things to think about; he was a brilliant young man, and Monica and Patricius groomed him for a career as a rhetorician, a teacher of political speaking, a civil servant. So he packed himself off to Carthage to study.

Carthage in those days was the typical university town, or, as he put it, a cauldron seething with shameful loves, and he was in love with love. When he looked back on those days that seemed so free and exciting, he recognized that the only thing that prompted him to jump into that cauldron was an emptiness inside him, a void where God should have been; and, having cut himself off from the love of God and from acceptance of God's love, he kept trying in vain to fill that void with what he thought he loved.

So the young Augustine did what young people have always done, before and since. He paid too much attention to the theater, and to professional sports and other kinds of entertainment—since the emptiness inside him didn't permit him to form real relationships with people, he used entertainment like tinder for his fires, he said, to stimulate, and simulate, feelings that you usually get when you really care for someone else, the joy, sorrow, anger, horror, pathos, and all the rest. His soul, empty and devoid of love, he recalled, was eager to be scratched over by the things that appealed to the senses, just so that it would feel something.

He paid even more attention to women, and not in a very edifying way; he plotted, planned, and fantasized about his affairs even in church, and he ended up taking a mistress, living with a girl outside of marriage.[184] They had a son whom he named Iatan-Baal, which shows you where his religious awareness was at that time, the Baal of the Bible still being worshipped by pagans in that area; eventually, the child's name was changed to the more orthodox Adeodatus, given by God, but that was a long way off.

At that point, so well prepared, he fell in with heretics, the Manicheans. Well, like all heresies, Manicheanism had a few disjointed elements of Christianity in it, but it borrowed bits and pieces from a lot from other religions, too—it was a compound of heresies, you might say, and it put them all together into a single oversimplified view of the universe and Man's place in it. Manicheanism had some characteristics that you still find in separated sects today, such as the idea that Christ isn't really God but just a visible spirit who taught humans the difference between the light and the dark, that Satan really created everything, and that the principal struggle in this world is that between the light of the good and the darkness of evil. The followers of Mani also believed in two classes of souls, the elect and the damned, period, and they had a view of the material world that didn't tally with even casual observation—"they spoke falsehoods, not only of you," Augustine wrote to God in his *Confessions*, "but even of the elements of this

---

184. What was worse, he said, his studies at that time were directed at the practice of the law, a field in which he would become more successful if more crafty.

world, your creation."[185] And to support their view of things, they put out deeply edited versions of the Bible, mixed up with other scriptures.

When Monica found out about the life that her nineteen-year-old son was leading, it nearly killed her. She prayed for him constantly, as she had prayed for his father
and grandmother, with hours of tears. She fasted, too, and she begged prominent
churchmen in the area to try to argue him out of his heresy and his irregular life, particularly a local bishop who had been a Manichean once, himself. "His heart is too stubborn, now," the bishop answered—Augustine, as you might expect, took great pride in
his own sophistication—"but God's time will come." She wanted him to try, anyway, but
the bishop said, go, now: "it cannot be that the child of so many tears could be lost."

But she still couldn't stand to look at him; when he came home to Tagaste, she
wouldn't let him live in her house or even eat at her table. Until she had a prophetic dream.

She saw herself deeply grieved, standing on a wooden ruler, and a brilliant young
man came toward her, asking her why she was crying every day. I weep for my son's perdition, she told him, and he told her to look at where she was, and to realize that her son
was there with her, too. She looked along the ruler and saw Augustine standing there.

Augustine told her that it just meant that she shouldn't worry about his life, but
she was insistent: he didn't say, "where he is, you are, too," but "where you are, there he
is." This gave him pause, but it would be nearly a decade before they figured out exactly what it all meant.

By the time Augustine was twenty-nine, he decided to go to Rome to teach
rhetoric and make a success of himself. Monica was going with him, she said; if he went
to the capital alone, who knew how long his conversion would be delayed. But he tricked
her, getting on the ship while she was spending the night kneeling in the church of St.
Cyprian, praying for his safety and conversion.

But her son's faith in Manicheanism was already eroding, worn away, no doubt,
by the endless stream of her prayers but also by the wheels of his own intellect. One of
the things that had attracted him to the Manicheans was their absolute insistence on
celibacy outside of marriage (inside of marriage, too, for that matter). This was an
immensely attractive ideal for Augustine, as it is to anybody stuck in a promiscuous
lifestyle; he was smart enough to know that his sexual life was inhumane and objectively wrong, and he must have known that the Church is right about these things. But, like
lots of other people in that position, he was also stubborn enough to fight what he knew
to be right with every ounce of his strength. And it bothered him that the Manicheans
couldn't put that mandate into a logically consistent system of morality. They just insisted on it, and on a lot of other rules like those about what you could eat and who could
handle it before you got it, without any unifying precept of faith at the center. Little by
little, he was seeing that Manicheanism as a whole was neither consistent nor logical.

185. This dualism, always a popular feature of heretical sects, gives a person a kind of religion without
requiring any moral endeavor. It let Augustine leave his body wallowing in an evil lifestyle while letting
his spirit think that it was religious—another aspect of the absence of moral theology in separated sects.

So, as the *Confessions* show, step by step he was turning from heresy to God. As a professional debater, he also had to notice that the Manicheans didn't answer any of the basic questions; they only deflected them by appealing to an unreasoning faith or by asserting that the questioner must have one of those damned souls and therefore could never understand anyway. By the time he left Tagaste to take up teaching in Rome, he was completely out of touch with the Manicheans—which was particularly unfortunate, since they were just about the only people he knew in Rome.

He was miserable among them there for a whole year. And then the call came from Milan. They needed a master of rhetoric there, and, after applying for the competition through the highly placed Manicheans in Rome, Augustine went off to Milan, taking his mistress and their son Adeodatus with him. Just after he left, Monica tracked him down, at last, and she set out for Milan, too.

It happened that the bishop of Milan was one of the great Fathers of the Church, St. Ambrose (*c.* 339-397). He set the standard for a whole Rite of the Church, which is still named after him.[186] So Monica, newly come from Rome to his diocese, had a lot to get used to. She asked Ambrose about memorial banquets, liturgy, and fasting, which were observed differently in Rome. His answer ended up as one of the principles of canon law: when I'm in Rome, he said, I do as the Romans do.

Augustine went to hear St. Ambrose every chance he got, out of professional interest, because St. Ambrose was already renowned as one of the best rhetoricians alive. Augustine didn't even listen to the subject matter, at first, just the style and method of presentation. But he noticed that, unlike the Manicheans' wandering around among logical fallacies, Ambrose spoke simply, directly, and clearly, drawing on his immense learning. Augustine started to see that Catholic Christianity could be defended logically while the heresies couldn't.[187]

"This was especially true," he wrote, "when I heard various passages in the Old Testament explained by way of allegory, those same passages that had killed me when I had taken them literally." And he couldn't avoid the realization that the Manichean view of the material world didn't make sense, either; Aristotle and Ptolemy, Plato and Thales—the great scientists of antiquity—consistently accounted for a lot more of what

---

186. He defined Ambrosian Chant, too, drawing its forms from ancient Roman music (which wasn't so ancient, in the fourth century) and laying the foundations for the more familiar Gregorian chant. The voices of Ambrose's sweet-singing church moved Augustine to tears, he said after he converted.

187. Heresies, as the deletion of key points of doctrine, always get into logical binds, which are particularly intrusive if Scripture is taken literally. So heresies have to define faith differently, too, abandoning the *theological* or *confessional* faith of the Church (which is accepting revealed truths on God's word alone) and replacing it with *fiducial* faith, simply trusting in Christ's promises without reference to any particular set of doctrines. Since divine revelation by definition would be more perfect in its scope and consistency than anything that human agents can devise, theological faith means that religion has to make sense to you and encompass perceived reality meaningfully; but heresy tends to define faith as something beyond reason or otherwise incompatible with it, something that doesn't have to make sense. Which is one reason that it's harder to convert a heretic than someone of a completely different creed: if they think that you're not supposed to reason about religion, you can't really discuss anything.

he saw around him. "I didn't see how I could persist in a sect above which I had to place so many philosophers," he said.

So, although he had come to hear Ambrose out of professional interest, he stayed to listen to him as a Christian speaker. He had a million questions, and he wanted a chance to cultivate an acquaintance with this brilliant and educated bishop. But Ambrose was busy heading off the Arians, heretics led by the Emperor Justinian's mother, the lady Justina.[188]

And while Ambrose found time to talk with anybody who came to him with a problem he certainly didn't have time to sit around talking philosophy with a young swell like Augustine. Still, Augustine was so powerfully attracted to what he heard that he used to go and stand quietly in the bishop's study, just looking at him and waiting for a chance to talk, until, afraid of interrupting the steady stream of callers, he just left quietly. But he came back again and again to hear Ambrose preach; and, studying the Epistles with his best friend Alypius, he fell headlong into the struggle between his love of sensual pleasures and the call to holiness.

He was pulled one way and then the other, during these months. He stopped his habit of profanity, and then he started swearing again. He sent Adeodatus and his mother away and got engaged to another girl, but in the meantime he took another mistress. Monica was tormented by his conflict, and she had a lot of dreams and visions about it all, vain and fantastic things, Augustine recalled, the kinds of things generated by the human spirit when it concentrates on a thing like this. But she could tell, by a kind of savor that she couldn't explain in words, the difference between God's revelations and the dreams of her own soul. So she didn't make much of these fantasies.

Then a man he knew from Tagaste, a man named Pontitian, dropped by and told him about St. Anthony of Egypt (Anthony Abbot, 250-356) and his hermits, and about a monastery that had been started along the same lines just outside of Milan. Two other officials, about Augustine's age, he said, and just engaged, had quit their jobs, broken off their betrothals, and joined up.

It was more than Augustine could bear. He ran out of the house and threw himself on the ground in the garden under a fig tree, bursting into tears. And then he heard a voice from above singing gently, *Tolle, lege; tolle, lege*—pick up and read, pick up and read. It sounded like the voice of a child from the house next door, but it was certainly an odd thing for a child to say; and the message was so apt that Augustine took the book of the Epistles from Alypius and opened it. "Let us walk becomingly as in the day," he read, "not in revelry and drunkenness, not in debauchery and wantonness, not

188. Arianism is named for Areios (or Arius), a Greek-speaking African cleric of Alexandria. It asserts that Christ was not true God and true Man as the Church has always taught, but that he was only a creature although as close to God as a creature can get, being endowed with all divine attributes except divinity itself. It makes things easier to grasp, initially, but since it's incompatible with Scripture it raises more questions than it can answer. It would never have achieved a foothold in the later Empire if the armies, then made up of men outside the cultural orbit of Rome, hadn't embraced it. The Council of Nicæa was called in 325 to settle it, which is why the Nicene Creed is such a clear statement of the Trinity.

in strife and jealousy. But put on the Lord Jesus Christ, and as for the flesh take no thought for its lusts" (Rm 13:13-14). This passage pinpoints exactly the struggle that Augustine had been trying to win since his school days, the problem of laying aside the works of darkness and putting on the armor of light, the whole idea that had attracted him to Manicheanism in the first place.

"Instantly," he said, "at the end of this sentence, all the dark shadows of doubt disappeared, as if from a peaceful light streaming into my heart." He ran into the house and told his mother that he was ready to accept Christianity. For God, he recalled in the *Confessions*, had converted me to himself, so that I would seek neither wife nor worldly ambition, standing on that same rule of faith where God had shown me to her so many years before.[189]

When his students left for summer vacation, Augustine retired to a country estate at Cassisiacum, to study the Faith and discuss it with Monica and other Christian friends. By the next Holy Saturday, 387, at the age of thirty-three, Augustine was baptized by St. Ambrose, along with Alypius and Adeodatus.

(The story goes that, at that moment, Ambrose paraphrased Psalm 150:1 to give thanks to God: *Te Deum laudamus*, we praise you, O God, he said. And Augustine answered with another quotation, we confess you to be the Lord. They continued, matching each other quote for quote, until they had composed a magnificent canticle of praise and thanksgiving, named the *Te Deum* after its first two words—as the Our Father and the Hail Mary are named. It's still one of the Church's great hymns, set to new music by every great composer, but heard too seldom, these days.)

With Monica's prayers answered, and with Augustine's life clarified and settled, they set out again for Africa, for home. They got as far as Ostia, the port city of Rome, when Augustine and Monica shared a great vision, apparently of the Trinity, the Godhead. It's not exactly clear what they saw, but he described how they saw it in particularly exalted language that still stands as one of the best descriptions of what apparitions are and how they work, of the differences between the senses of the body and the senses of the soul, and of how mystic experiences affect people:

> Think of a man in whom the tumult of the flesh fell silent, silent the images of Earth, and of the waters, and of the air; silent the heavens; silent for him the very soul itself. Think of this man passing beyond himself by not thinking about himself; silent his dreams and all imagined appearances, and every tongue, and every sign. And everything that comes into being through change becomes wholly silent to him—because if any man can hear, then all these things say to him, "We did not make ourselves, but he who endures forever made us." And after they have said this, think of them falling silent, for they have raised up his ear to him

189. Her unwavering dedication to the cause of her son's conversion is emulated by the international Society of Saint Monica, made up of some ten thousand members around the world whose daily prayers beg the return of inactive Christians to the Church; they're at 215 Falls Avenue, Cuyahoga Falls, Ohio 44221.

who made them. Then imagine God alone speaking, speaking not through such things but speaking himself, so that we hear his Word, not uttered by a tongue of flesh, nor by an angel's voice, "nor by the sound of thunder", nor by a parable, but himself, the one whom we love in everything. Imagine that we could hear him without these things, that we could reach out and in swift thought attain to that Eternal Wisdom that endures beyond all things.

If this could be prolonged, and other visions of a far inferior kind could be withdrawn, and this one alone, ravishing, absorbing, and drawing its beholder into the very depths of joy—sempiternal life would be such as that moment of understanding was. This is the moment we sighed for; and would it not be this: "Enter into the joy of your Lord"? When shall this be? When "we shall all rise again".

After this ecstasy, Monica said that she found no joy in the things of this world, any more. "What can I still do here, and why am I here? I do not know, now that all of my hopes in this world have been accomplished... What am I doing here?" She fell ill, then, and died a few days later. She was buried there—not, as she had once wanted, in Africa according to the customs of Tagaste, but in Ostia according to the custom of the Ostians.[190]

Augustine himself stayed on at Rome for about a year, and in September of 388 he went back to Tagaste. He lived an exemplary life as a layman for three more years, staying on his own property in a sort of quasi-religious community of his friends and associates. But then the people of the diocese saw their bishop Valerius doddering into old age and their unity threatened by the heresy of the Donatists—who chiefly departed from the Church on the grounds that any sacrament is invalid if it's administered by a priest whom they found objectionable, or even one who might have had secret sins on his soul.[191] So they took Augustine, almost by force, to the bishop's seat at near-by Hippo Regius and demanded that he be ordained and set up as Valerius's assistant. He was soon raised to coadjutor, and when Valerius died he was himself appointed Bishop of Hippo.

He turned his attention to the Donatist problem and, just as he had done with the Manicheans, wrote and preached so effectively that he converted everybody back to the Church. His writings, in fact, are now the only source of information about those

190. After 1162, some of her bones were taken to a monastery near Arras in France, a monastery that runs according to the Rule written by her son, and in 1430 other relics were taken to the church dedicated to him in Rome, where they rest in a full sculptural sarcophagus by Isaia di Pisa. St. Augustine's tomb is in the cathedral of Pisa.

191. Well, since nobody's perfect, that obviously doesn't hold up, and the priest isn't the source of the sacrament, anyway, but only its minister; sacraments happen between the recipient and God. Luther's original heresy, of course, was tinged with Donatism, but he took it farther, asserting that the whole of the Church's teachings were debatable because the morals of some of the hierarchy were questionable. So he told everybody to listen to him instead and then—a priest himself, of course—married a nun.

sects. Besides these works, which are still interesting because those heresies still crop up now and again,[192] we have from his pen stacks of books, sermons, and millions of letters (well, hundreds, anyway, those that survive). In the great collection of patristic writings published by Father Jacques-Paul Migne during the nineteenth century, Augustine occupies sixteen folio volumes, each with about twelve hundred double-columned pages. That's the equivalent of more than thirty-eight thousand regular pages, right there.

If you think about the limited years he had as priest and bishop, and all of the things that a priest or a bishop has to do—duties compounded, in his case, by all those heretics—and then you stack up his writings, it's virtually impossible to comprehend that a parochial cleric in so short a time, against such disorders, could possibly produce so much work besides. But he did. Well, there are a few spurious works under his name, but those were sorted out long ago, in part because in the last years of his life, he went back over his immense output and revised it all, realizing that in his younger years he didn't know so much. In fact, he wrote another book, called *Retractions*, to set the record straight about the mistakes in his books to date. And then, having edited that one, too, he wrote a couple more, two books entitled *On the Editing of Books*. Ecclesiastes 12:12, indeed.

---

192. They were Scripture-only sects, for instance, and they either practiced or advocated artificial birth control.

f o u r t e e n

P a l m a   1 2 6 6

Without some manifestation, however imperfect it might be,
of the ineffable mysteries of the divine life in souls,
there would be nothing in the world
except lying and confusion.
Therefore, a soul illumined by light from on high
cannot be silent; love inflames her
to the point of making her overcome all obstacles
so that she can diffuse the fruits of inexpressible peace
that the God of All Consolation produces in her.

— St. Catherine of Genoa, *Dialogues*, 3:2 (*c.* 1551)

Bl. Ramon Lull[193], more than most other mystics, was a late bloomer. That may have been because he faced every possible disadvantage. He was born to wealthy parents, and he was born bright—brilliant, in fact. He was born in the city of Palma on the island of Majorca in 1232 or 1231,[194] just after the end of Moorish domination of the island. Everybody in Majorca was thoroughly tired of religious disputes, and they were all too ready to just forget about religion entirely and enjoy things, for the time being. And Palma was just the place to forget all about religion and enjoy things.

193. His name varies with time and place. In Spanish, it's Ramón Lull, with the accent, but he was not Spanish; he was Catalán, so it's more properly Ramon Llull, nowadays. But you may also find his works listed under the name Lull or Luyl. In Latin, it's Raymundus or Raimundus Lul, or Lullus, or Lullius, which last is why older English editions call him Lully and Spanish ones Lulio. But they're all the same person.

194. Old or ancient dates are hard to establish, sometimes. It's not that there's any doubt about the event or the person, but that calendars generally aren't very good, and it can be hard to tell exactly how that year is supposed to be numbered, if rectified to agree with our modern calendar. It's tricky to pin down the year of Christ's birth, for one thing; Julius Africanus missed it by about three years, Dionysius Exiguus

It was a pretty dissipated place; oriental luxury, power over much of the commerce of the western Mediterranean, immense wealth—all unchecked by Christian (or Islamic) morals. And even as a boy Lull moved in the highest circles of power and fashion, as a page at the Majorcan royal court. In his own words, Ramon Lull was as dissipated as anybody else there. He served as seneschal of the table of the king, a sort of executive butler-courtier, but basically he frittered away his time lying around in the fragrant fountain courtyards of the palace, writing love songs that can only be described as profane to his mistresses (plural), before and during his marriage.[195] He was writing one of those "vulgar" love songs in his room one night in 1266, and he looked to his right and saw Christ crucified, the Cross and the Redeemer hanging in midair. He jumped into bed and pulled the covers over his head.

He got up the next day and thought nothing more about it. At least, it didn't prompt any noticeable change in his behavior. Then about a week later, the same thing happened, at exactly the same hour: in his room, trying to finish that same love song, he looked up again and saw the same apparition. This time, though, it seemed to have a little more life to it, the sufferings depicted in more hideous detail. Again, he jumped into bed and tried to forget about it.

Every time he tried to finish that song, the apparition came to him. Again and again it came, five times in all, always unbidden, always more and more detailed, clearer, showing him at last the full horror of the tortures inflicted on Christ by ungrateful men. No matter what Lull did, he couldn't make the apparition disappear, and he couldn't make any sense out of it all.

by four, when they tried to set the starting point for numbering the years since (even the Magi got no closer than two: Mt 2:16). It tells you a lot about those persistent anxieties about the Millennium. Also, there's no compelling astronomical or cultural reason to put New Year's Day on the first of January, and until recently almost nobody did. Some local calendars turned to new years on Easter, others at the vernal equinox in March. Gervase of Canterbury remarked in the thirteenth century that almost everybody in England set the new year at Christmas, but in fact some localities were already beginning to put it at the Annunciation, which the English generally did until 1752. And from time to time people just switched to some other date for New Year's; they could end up as much as ten years either side of the date in the next town. So some dates have to be labelled *c.* (for the Latin *circa*, meaning "around"), particularly birth dates; nobody kept birth records, so you have to go by baptismal ledgers, and who knows at what age a person was baptized, let alone what year it was. To this day some lists of the popes don't bother to give their birth dates, only those of their reigns, because it doesn't really matter when a pope was born. Death dates are often more certain because people naturally pay more attention to the passing of a distinguished person, but even then it can be impossible to reconcile them with our calendar.

195. "Profane" is from the Latin *pro*, outside, and *fanum*, temple; it means all of those things in earthly life that are separated from religion. "Vulgar" is from *vulgaris*; it means having to do with the real daily life of common people, as distinct from the formal ceremonial life of court and cathedral (which is why the Latin Bible is called the Vulgate; the Church's Bible has always been in the language that anybody off the street could understand—now, with the decline of education, people can't, which is why an author has to define all of these Latin-based words for them). "Infidel" is from *in*, not, and *fides*, faith; strictly speaking, it just means anybody who's not of your particular religion, not a person who rejects religion altogether. That's an *apostate*.

Finally, the fifth time, Lull spent the whole night under those covers trying to figure it all out. Now, the choices that Lull saw in all of this are interesting; evidently the touch of that apparition had already burned his soul. It wasn't that he wanted to cling to his old playboy ways and reject the vivid reminder of Christian teachings; he saw himself between two other propositions entirely. He saw the vision as at least a call from his own conscience—maybe really from Christ himself—to abandon his licentious life and dedicate himself to the service of God, in some way. The other side of it, for him, was not that his past life was so pleasurable, but that it had been so scandalous, so utterly destructive of the rights and decency of others, so thoroughly insidious to divine and human love, that he saw no way that Christ would accept him, even if he did repent and reform.

While he tossed and turned that night, though, the terror of the apparitions faded. And, as his mind grasped the realities that the apparitions recalled to his mind, Ramon remembered the infinite mercy of Christ. Before morning, he had decided to get reconciled with Christ in his Church and devote the rest of his life to converting Muslims.

One problem with the plan, though, was that he had virtually no education, none that counted, anyway. He was glib enough, but even those lascivious lovesongs of his took him a long time to write, even when he wasn't interrupted by heavenly visitors at all hours. He knew that there was simply no way that he could stand up to the learnèd mullahs of Islamic Africa in debate. So that was out.

Then—and this is the really odd part of all of this—he got the idea that what he really ought to do is convert everybody by writing a book. He'd write "the best book in the world", and that would definitely convince everybody of the reality of Christianity. Now, as soon as he had this idea, he was very much amazed, as his mediæval biographer notes.[196] He had no concept whatever of the form of such a book, or its contents, and he didn't know the first thing about writing books, anyway, least of all in Arabic, if he aimed to convert the Saracens. He didn't even know how such a notion could have popped into his head, in the first place. Yet the idea had the ring of rightness about it.

And with Ramon Lull it was always a quick giant step from the particular to the general, which resulted in an epochal realization: nobody in Europe was prepared to write such a book. Lying there that night, he decided to go to the Pope and to all of the secular Christian princes of Europe and convince them to establish special teaching monasteries where missionary monks could gather to learn the languages of infidels and reach them in their own terms, something that hadn't occurred to anybody else in the thirteenth century. With firm resolve to do these three necessary things—dedicate himself to Christ's service, write the best book in the world, and set up monasteries for the study of exotic languages—he went to sleep and forgot all about the whole thing.

Then on the feast of St. Francis he heard a homily about how Francis had given up everything, even the clothes on his back, to follow Christ's example, and that got his

---

196. Nobody knows for sure for sure the name of his biographer, but many scholars figure that the surviving early lives of Lull were written by Carthusian monks living at a monastery called Vauvert, which stood on part of the ground now covered by the Luxembourg gardens in Paris.

interest again. Ramon liquidated his considerable assets that very day, setting up a kind of trust fund for his wife and children, and he left Majorca on a long pilgrimage to the great shrines of Europe, vowing never to return.

He came back to Majorca about two years later.[197] His advisor at that time was the erudite Dominican who had compiled the *Decretals* for Pope Gregory IX, a monk also named Ramon; he talked Lull out of his plan to walk to the university in Paris, and he may have kept him from going back to his original sins. In the end, Lull didn't return to his old job and old habits but, still in his pilgrim's sackcloth, started studying right there in town, disavowing all worldly wealth, just as St. Francis had done.[198] He did get hold of enough of his money, though, to pay for the equipment he needed to learn Arabic: he bought a Saracen slave, and he learned it from him.

But, what's just as impressive as his mystic experiences, he seems to have mastered whole regions of Arabic mathematics, logic, and philosophy in a very short time. He locked himself away for nine years of intense study of languages, theology, grammar, and everything else he needed to know. In fact, he got so intense about it that he exhibited signs of either "mental exaltation" or extreme stress, depending on whom you read. He was so excited about the horizons of learning that were opening up to him that his family thought that he was *non compos mentis* and sued for an administrator to be appointed for his estate. Nobody understood what he was talking about, at that point, but there's no question that he was the first westerner to present Christendom with great works like the logic of Al-Ghazzali. In fact, he was advanced enough in his studies to write a compendium of it in Arabic, which he translated into Latin and then again into Catalán.

This and his other translations from the Arabic alone would have earned him a place as a pivotal figure in western intellectual history, but he also wrote original works in Catalán. The first of these, his immense *Book of Contemplation*, was probably his first stab at writing the best book in the world. He got it finished by 1272, just before his Saracen teacher-slave, for some reason, tried to kill him with a sword. Lull was severely wounded, but he overpowered the man, and the rest of his servants—you get the impression that he still hadn't really grasped the concept of voluntary poverty—wrestled the man to the floor.

At this point, as soon as he had recovered, he went up to a mountain outside of town, to really get away from it all. After about a week up there, alone in prayer and

197. He had gone first to the shrine of Mary at Rocamadour in the Dordogne, although it's sometimes misreported that he went to Rocatallada, the Catalàn name for Montserrat, where St. Ignatius of Loyola went centuries later.

198. In fact, he entered the Franciscan Third Order, an organization parallel to the Franciscan Order that lay people can join. The Dominicans, the Carmelites, and the Augustinians have "Third Orders", too, in addition to those for professed religious men and women. You can be either a Third-Order Regular, in which case you leave the world and lead a religious life in a community under simple vows, or a Third-Order Secular, which means that you stay in the world, in your job and family, and you seek Christian perfection according to the spirit and spirituality of that particular order. You get the benefits of the order's experience and counsel, their ability to channel your gifts to appropriate works of mercy, and the right to be buried in their habit after you die. A lot of prominent historical figures—kings and queens, presidents and prime ministers, scholars, philosophers, and generals—have been Third-Order Seculars.

fasting, he had another kind of vision, sort of like the *eximia ilustración* that St. Ignatius of Loyola had on the banks of the Cardoner three centuries later. For Lull, this was a mystic illumination in which he saw the whole world in relationship to the attributes of God. In that flash of insight, he understood that all human wisdom pales before knowledge of God, and that human reason and human memory had to be used, just as the emotions and the heart, in the soul's ascent to God—also foreshadowing St. Ignatius in the intellectual tenor of his mysticism. More intriguing, he also saw that human science had to be rearranged in accordance with this view, and, evidently, he saw how to do it.

He put this all together into the second version of his best book in the world, his *Ars compendiosa inveniendi veritatem*, "The Brief Art of Finding Truth", which is usually called either the *Ars major* or *Ars generalis*, the "Great Art" or the "General Art"— "art" in its classical meaning of practical intelligence, the ability to put sound decisions into practice. He meant the book as a way of grasping the whole material universe with the mind, and it put him in the ranks of other great innovators like Newton and Einstein. If you understood Lull's system of observation and logic, you got consistent answers to lots of sensible questions about reality: in other words, you got something like science, with real explanations of natural phenomena that were obviously far more valid than those of the professors. And that naturally brought down upon him the heavy wrath of every university in Europe.

Remember, Lull worked during the age of Scholasticism, when that hairsplitting approach to learning had dissolved into almost exclusive concern with the questions about how many angels could dance where. But after this mystic illumination Lull asked what we'd consider the right kind of question: how does a flame burn the hand held at a distance from it? Why is a flame hotter at its peak than at its sides? Since fire heats water slowly, why does water quench fire quickly?

Questions like these, posed by Lull as part of a logical system that ordinary people could use, eventually led to physics as we know it. And he was the first man in the world to figure that every problem in every field could be reduced to a mathematical formula: the first to conceive a "unified field" theory expressed in mathematical equations. He didn't have the math that you need to make this work—calculus wouldn't be invented for four hundred years yet—but he got pretty far with it. So Lull deserves a lot more credit than he gets from the scientific community today, and ironically enough he would never have made these contributions to science if he hadn't had the apparitions.[199]

His enemies in the academic establishment must have realized that his method made their own look foolish, because they fought long and hard to have it condemned,

---

199. Lull, by the way, had no interest whatever in astrology, alchemy, or the occult, even though you're most likely to encounter his name that way, these days. All of the occult works attributed to him were written after his death by enthusiasts who wanted to present their bizarre theories as if they were part of Lull's theory of knowledge, which was still hotly debated as the first (and at the time the only) alternative to the Scholasticism that dominated European universities. They've muddied the waters of Lullan studies forever after, and they've permanently clouded his claim to credit for his real accomplishments.

just as their successors did to Galileo four centuries later.[200] Lull himself was evidently astonished by the power and scope of his system, too, because he went back up to his mountain and prayed about it for four months, just to be sure: could he possibly have come up with something this powerful, this revolutionary? Then he had a visitor.

A young shepherd came up to him on his lonely mountain, he said, a youth of extreme beauty, who told him more things in an hour than he could have heard from an ordinary person in two days. He told Lull about God, angels, and other heavenly things, then knelt weeping before Lull's manuscripts and told him that they would bring great benefit to Christ's Church. Then he blessed Ramon and left. Nobody in the region knew who he could have been; they never saw any such person before or since.

But the visitor encouraged Lull. He went on to write nearly three hundred more books, some explaining his system of thought and others blazing new trails in literature. His poetry pushed Catalán into the ranks of literary languages, the way Dante elevated Italian and Chaucer lifted English. He wrote the first novel in any Romance language, a long moral tale called *Blanquerna* (1283)—which also revived the classical idea of writing about ideal cultures and foreshadowed the work of St. Thomas More (1447-1535) and other utopian writers. He adapted the forms of Arabic literature to Christian needs; his *Book of the Lover and the Beloved*, in fact, derives a lot of its character from Sufi meditational tracts. Full of tenderness and devotion, it rivals Thomas à Kempis's *Imitation of Christ* in popularity over the centuries.[201]

He also saw Islam as nobody else did at that time, and as few see it even now. He said that Islam is not so much a false religion as an incomplete religion, a heresy of Christianity, really, that replaced the tribe-scattered idolatry of Middle-Eastern paganism with the basic ideas like a single, invisible, all-powerful God, an individual afterlife, and accountability for one's actions, but leaving out the rest of Judeo-Christian revelation.[202]

He saw, too, that converting heretics is a lot harder than converting people of an entirely different religion. Given a fragmented doctrinal theology, and no moral theology at all, heretics tend to see differences in creed as mere hairsplitting. You couldn't just preach to them as St. Paul had preached to the Athenians. But the Muslims were the heirs of Greek philosophy and logic, and they had applied these rationalist tools to build a brilliant science. So Lull intellectualized the process, approaching the Muslims through their own traditions of contemplation, their own systems of logic and dialectic,

200. It's important to note that the popes involved in these cases intervened administratively as ultimate heads of the universities; papal infallibility doesn't apply in these or in any cases not directly involving official teachings on matters of faith and morals. The best brief source on how this kind of academic opposition happens is Thomas S. Kuhn's *The Structure of Scientific Revolutions* (Chicago, 1962), which was itself published as part of a Lullan idea, the *International Encyclopedia of Unified Science*.

201. Lull wrote it before *Blanquerna* and later put it into the novel as Chapter 99. Both books are still in print, but, unfortunately, it's hard to find them now.

202. Locke and Carlyle perceived this, too, as did Sir Richard Burton, the British orientalist who learned the languages and culture well enough to translate the *Thousand Nights and a Night* and even to live in disguise as an Arab and make the pilgrimage to Mecca—forbidden to infidels on pain of death. About the only recent observer to arrive at this view is Hilaire Belloc, in *The Great Heresies* (London, 1938).

to build on the fundamentals of Christianity that he saw deep at the core of Islam and help the Muslims see the fullness of Christianity in ways that they couldn't deny.

And he saw that he couldn't do it alone. There were whole nations of Islam, filling Africa, Sicily, and the Levant. The task demanded an army of missionaries, speaking the language and understanding the thinking of their converts (another foreshadowing of the strategies developed by St. Ignatius of Loyola for the Society of Jesus, by the way). So Lull went to Rome from time to time, to convince the Pope to adopt a grand plan of seminaries and universities for missionaries, but Boniface VIII Caetani and Clement V de Got turned him down. By 1298, at the advanced age of 66, he ran up to Paris to get support for his scheme, and had a little better success; then he was off to Cyprus, where he was rejected entirely, and to Genoa, Paris, and Lyons, all over Europe in three years. In most of these places, his call for missionary education was weighted down by his advanced scientific theories, which were still hotly opposed by the Scholastic professors.

It didn't stop him. He ran off to Tunis, preaching Christianity as the full perfection of Mohammedan teachings. To their everlasting credit, the Tunisians didn't kill him but only locked him up for a while and then sent him home. Back he came, and back into prison he went, for six months. After the Muslims sent him packing again, he was back up to Paris and then to the Council of Vienne, where he must have been transported with joy to hear the Council formally adopt his educational plans, in general outline.

Well, a man nearing eighty, hearing his life's work validated by a General Council of the Church, might excuse himself from further efforts. But not Lull. In the two years after the Council, he went back to Majorca, then back to Paris, to Montpellier, to Messina, and in 1316 to Muslim Africa, preaching just as fanatically as ever. This time, though, the unbelievably tolerant Muslims finally had enough. They dragged him outside the city and stoned him.

So now Ramon Lull, former playboy and troubadour, was an undeniable martyr for the Faith. Even then, his enemies wouldn't leave him alone. They went on slinging mud at his character, and his orthodoxy, enough to have his works condemned as heretical, hanging them on the very slight hook of Islamic influence in them. His greatest enemy at the time, the Dominican Inquisitor Nicolas Eymeric, apparently presented evidence only from professors who had no idea what Lull had been talking about or who knew but feared losing their jobs if his superior method caught on. They wangled a bull of condemnation out of Gregory XI de Beaufort in 1376. But Lull had his supporters, too, particularly in Paris, and eventually they made a lot of headway toward acceptance of Lull's immense and revolutionary output. They made the nature of Eymeric's evidence clear, and Martin V Colonna declared the bull of condemnation null in 1417.[203]

203. Note the difference between nullification and reversal. Declaring something null means that, on investigation, it turns out that it was never valid or never existed. Reversing something means saying that it existed but now we're going to contradict it or abolish it. Even so, a papal declaration like this is disciplinary, not doctrinal; it doesn't touch any of the Church's teachings. It only proclaims that the specified work contains material that's, say, error posing as accurate information, information openly contrary to the Church's teachings, or material confusing enough to be perilous to the Faithful at that place and time.

But still the controversy raged, century after century. Paul IV Carafa reinstated the bull of condemnation in the sixteenth century, and Lull was misunderstood and ridiculed by satirists from Rabelais to Jonathan Swift. On the other hand, wave after wave of supporters took his work seriously. Some of the greatest innovators in western science, like Nicolas of Cusa, Giordano Bruno, Jacques Lefèvre, and Gottfried Leibniz, asserted the validity (and in fact the superiority) of his system—and wave after wave they were struck down by the academic establishment.[204]

Philip II of Spain, who liked things consistent to the point of uniformity, collected Lull's works in his great library at the Escorial (which was built by another Lullan, by the way, Philip's architect Juan de Herrera) and hired scholars to edit them and defend his orthodoxy in Rome. Francisco de Osuna filtered and clarified Lull's "science of Love" and, through his own writings, communicated Lull's concepts to St. John of the Cross and St. Teresa of Avila, and from them they spread out to enrich the Church at large.

And there was the fact that the seminaries and monasteries founded in response to his educational program really were producing legions of uniquely qualified missionaries, as well as an immense amount of scholarly work on oriental languages, for the first time in the West, laying the foundation of that branch of linguistics. But no serious vindication of Lull's thought and faith was published until 1750, when the biography by the Majorcan Cistercian Antonio Raymundo Pasqual appeared.

Now, as our own science strives again for a "unified field theory" embracing all sciences in a single system, Lull's thought is getting a lot more attention. His religious contributions are slowly gaining ground, perhaps providentially in our modern world. He's revered as a saint in Majorca, although he hasn't been canonized yet, and the Franciscans honor him as the *Doctor Illuminatus*, the Enlightened Teacher. They've always kept a feast of commemoration for him on July 3, in all of the churches of the order, but it wasn't until 1858 that he was beatified by Pius IX Ferretti.

Lull's mystic experiences were all absolutely private, and even after eight centuries they still stir controversy: nobody else witnessed them, and, while they show the character of genuine apparitions, they're virtually impossible to confirm. But there's no question that they served as a sudden stop on Lull's own road to Damascus. And there's no doubt that he never would have made his immense and permanent contributions to science, literature, and language, as well as to spirituality and missionary policy and so many other fields, without these glimpses of a higher world.

---

204. Lull's followers, like his works, were condemned by uncountable local institutions, civil and academic as well as religious, simply because those in authority had built their careers on a different system but couldn't deny that Lull's made a lot more sense than what they were teaching: a fatal situation for any innovator. Newton and Einstein with their new universes, and Pasteur and Semmelweiss with their microbes, had the same problem (Semmelweiss was locked up in a lunatic asylum for lowering *post-partum* deaths in his hospital from 20 percent to less than 1 percent). Well, for that matter, Socrates, Joan of Arc, and Christ himself ran into the same situation, although the penalties in their cases were more severe.

f i f t e e n

N o r w i c h   1 3 7 3

The modern woman will note with pleasant surprise
that Mary of Nazareth,
while completely devoted to the will of God,
was far from being a timidly submissive woman
or one whose piety was repellent to others;
on the contrary,
she was a woman who did not hesitate to proclaim
that God vindicates the humble and the oppressed,
and removes the powerful people of the world
from their privileged positions.

— Paul VI, *Apostolic Exhortation*
on Devotion to the Blessed Virgin Mary (1974)

In the late Middle Ages, the little city of Norwich was exactly what you'd picture if you were asked to imagine a perfect old English town. It stood on a green rise overlooking the fields and flocks in the valley of the little River Wensum; its city walls, looped around the old castle, were only about four miles in circumference, and the spires of more than forty churches packed inside gave the view of the town a festive and chivalrous air. Its cathedral's towers are still the second-tallest in England—only Salisbury is taller. In fact, Norwich was a holy city, in a way; the large Benedictine monastery that adjoined the cathedral was only the centerpiece of the city's surprisingly active devotional life.

There were also some nuns in Norwich, in those days, but religious life for nuns in fourteenth-century Europe didn't exactly match our picture of it. We tend to imagine huge establishments running on an almost military basis, but those came later. The convents in those days were fewer and smaller. In the whole of England there were only about a hundred and forty convents, and most of these had fewer than ten nuns living in them. And although they ran according to one or another of the great Rules, it was probably hard to tell the difference, just by looking, between the *cenobitic* nuns who lived in community and the *anchoritic* nuns who lived as hermits, although in close proximity to other hermits.

But despite their small numbers, religious women in those days were every bit as influential as the more numerous monks and friars. Some of them, like Bugga and Lioba, acted as missionaries, bringing not only religion but civilization itself into darkest Europe. Later, other religious women took on real teaching roles in the Church, as did Hildegard of Bingen, the two great Catherines (of Genoa and of Siena), the two Mechtildes of Helfta, and St. Gertrude, who seems to be the only female saint to attain the title "the Great".[205]

The teachings of these great ladies also has a distinctively vital character. The works of the great male teachers are always there on the shelf when they're wanted, but the messages of the great ladies live in the hearts of generation after generation of the Faithful. By and large, it's the ladies of the Church who motivate the great devotional practices and push for the institution of great feast days; it's they who bring doctrine and dogma into the daily life of the laity. And, overwhelmingly, it's the women who are called to the most exalted stages of mystic experience. They're the ones, like St. Teresa of Avila, St. Catherine Labouré, or St. Bernadette, who impress a spiritual character on whole cities and regions or who turn whole nations to prayer.

Mother Julian of Norwich is just such a nun. Specifically, she was an *anchorite*, a word that comes from the Greek meaning "to withdraw", by way of the Latin and French. It means a woman (or a man, too, really) who devotes herself to prayer and penance, as St. Anthony of Egypt did. St. John the Baptizer was an anchorite, you might say, living in the wilderness and eating only locusts and honey. Julian didn't withdraw by going out into the countryside, though; she lived in a tiny cell built into the wall of the church of St. Julian in the village of Conisford—the Saxon word for "King's Ford"— on the Wensum outside the walls of Norwich, just across from the Augustinian friary. She retired to this "anchorhold" in the 1360s with a maidservant[206] and probably never

205. It's hard to sort out the mystics of Helfta because they all have the same names. Mechtilde von Hackenborn-Wippra (1240-1298), cousin of the Emperor, is still remembered for her contributions to church music and for her lovely voice; she combined the outward beauty and charm of a fairy-tale princess with the secret, intense mortifications of a great ascetic and exalted spiritual life of a great mystic. Trained since childhood by her blood sister, the Abbess Gertrude von Hackenborn-Wippra (d. 1291), and having been the *protegée* of Mechtilde of Magdeburg (1210-1285), she was in turn the teacher of St. Gertrude the Great (1256-1302), who, while often too ill to attend services, was her second in command of the choir. One or the other of these Mechtildes is the Matelda (Matilda) of Dante's *Purgatorio*; Boccaccio tells how immensely popular Mechtilde of Hackenborn's *Book of Special Graces* was in Florence, where parts of it were used as private devotions, but then Dante's whole configuration of the afterlife owes a lot to the books of Von Magdeburg. Both St. Mechtilde of Hackenborn and St. Gertrude are shown in paintings and statues holding the flaming Sacred Heart, but, outside of Germany and Spain, images of them are virtually nonexistent, and until St. Margaret Mary's time they had less influence than you'd think.

206. Anchorites had them, in those days. Their "cells" were sometimes apartments of more than one room, too, so that they could work and even entertain, and some of them kept a few cows or other live-

left it; she heard Mass and received the Eucharist through a slit in the common wall between her cell and the church. Nobody knows for sure where she was born or what her family was like, or even what her birth name was—evidently she took her anchoritic name from the church. She kept her mystic life a complete secret while she lived, too, but she wrote it all down. And although her manuscript wasn't published until more than two centuries after her death, it's had a major influence in bringing together several strands of theological thought that have always run through both eastern and western Christian mysticism but hadn't been woven into whole cloth before her time.

At some point in her young life she made a triple prayer that shows some exceptional intellectual and spiritual development already. She asked for recollection of the Passion, for bodily sickness, and for three wounds: the wounds of contrition, compassion, and longing for the will of God. She asked for the first two things conditionally but for the three wounds unconditionally, and then she forgot about the first two requests.

She was reminded of them at the beginning of May, 1373, when she fell seriously ill. She described the experience of dying that springtime, too, with a really surprising objectivity. She was conscious through the whole ordeal, and in great pain, wracked with fever; by the end of the week, she felt herself dead from the waist down. Her mother and her other attendants saw that she was near death and called for a priest to give her the Last Rites. Still, she lived, although she got worse, and at about three or four in the morning on May 13, 1373—the date that would take on deeper meaning five hundred and forty-four years later at Fátima—they called for the priest again, to attend her in what had to be her last moments.

He came into the cell with a little acolyte to carry the parish's processional cross. By now she was unable to speak; her eyes were locked in a vacant stare at the ceiling, but the priest put the crucifix at the foot of the bed and told her to look at it. It took all of her strength for her to obey, but she did. And at that moment, the whole room fell into a murky darkness, a supernatural darkness filled with the sensible presence of evil. The crucifix, though, began to glow, as if a ray of broad daylight had fallen on it. She could no longer breathe, and the insensibility of death crept quickly up her body. She knew that she was to die.

But then, suddenly, all of her pain and weakness left her. She felt fine, although she didn't trust the feeling, at first. Then it occurred to her that her illnesses gave her a chance to participate in a physical way in the sufferings of Christ; if she were healed, she wouldn't have that any more. This awareness of compassion—understood literally, in those days, as the Latin *cum*, with, and *passio*, passion, a sharing of someone else's suffering—reminded her of her youthful prayer. In that instant of healing, she regretted the loss of the suffering, and she resolved to use any future discomfort as a reminder of, and a sharing in, the Passion of Christ.

stock to tend. The point was not to imprison themselves, but to live in retirement, concentrating on the things of God, and serving, sometimes, as counselors or just good listeners to the local Faithful.

Then the figure of Jesus on the crucifix seemed to change. It seemed alive, and she saw that his face, brown and handsome, was battered and bruised. And then the wounds from the Crown of Thorns began to bleed. Bright red blood collected under the Crown and then streamed down his face; it welled up at the eyebrows and at the edges of his hair before falling like raindrops, then falling in waves down his face, as if all of the blood vessels in his scalp had been cut. He was pained more than her heart could think of, she recalled; there was so much blood that it would have entirely soaked her bed. Then the bruises and clotting blood darkened, first on one side and then on the other, as his face changed from brown to black-and-blue, then to a greenish blue, and finally to the ashen pallor of death. The blood itself dried, turning into a brown garland that doubled the garland of thorns; his torn flesh dried, too, and curled, hanging on the thorns like cloth hanging in the wind.

Julian felt a cold and dreadful wind around her at this point, too, and then, suddenly, the Holy Face was transfigured into a celestial beauty. She felt her heart shift from anguish at the Passion to a heightened joy, and some spiritual assurance of God's love. While she was in this ecstasy her mother, thinking that she was dead, reached over to close her eyes, but Julian couldn't stand for her vision of Christ to be blocked. And then, fully conscious but still ecstatic, she had the revelations.

One after another they came, some lasting only an instant, yet all impressing themselves vividly on her memory. There were fifteen that day, as she enumerated them later. She saw Christ, of course, and Mary, and in some way the whole Trinity. She understood more than she was seeing; she was taught about the divine Love that is God, about the perfect love that God has for humankind, and about the love that Jesus bore for her personally. The visions lasted all that day, from that pre-dawn vision until about three in the afternoon, the traditional hour of Christ's death on the Cross. The instant they were over, her illness and pain returned, with a loud noise. But this time, she knew that she wouldn't die.

That evening, another priest came by to check on her, and she told him facetiously that, while she was feeling a little better, she had been raving from fever the whole day. When the priest laughed, she went on to tell him what she saw—the crucifix, she said, bled profusely! The priest stopped laughing with her about it and started listening carefully, much to her embarrassment; she knew that she should not have made light of it. "I believed this truly at the time when I saw him," she said, "and it was then my will and intention to do so forever. But like a fool I let it pass from my mind. See what a wretched creature I am! This was a great sin and a great ingratitude, that I was so foolish, because of a little bodily pain I felt, as to abandon so imprudently the strength of all this blessed revelation from our Lord God."

She fell asleep that night, and immediately awoke. Somebody, or something, was trying to choke the life out of her. Her mother and friends wet her temples, and she came to, but then she smelled smoke, a particularly foul stench of smoke, and a great heat. "Blessed be the Lord!" she cried out. "Is everything on fire here?" This visit from the Devil renewed her assent to everything that she'd seen that day, and she lay awake, calm and peaceful, the rest of the night.

It was then that she received the sixteenth and final showing, which lasted until the next morning. She sensed that the Trinity was dwelling within her, in a sort of City of God ruled by Christ. The Devil returned to try disrupting the vision or pulling her away from it, but he had no power over the binding Love of God that had caught her up into itself; and when she came back to this world, she understood what Christ's victory over evil on the Cross meant. Christ himself came to her again, telling her that it was no hallucination; accept and believe it, and hold firmly to it, he said.

That's exactly what she did. For the next twenty-five years at least, she thought about what she'd seen and what she'd been given to understand in her corporeal, intellectual, and spiritual visions, and she wrote it down in a unique manuscript usually called *Revelations* or *Showings*, which is the better title and the one that she used most often herself. The first version, written soon afterwards, is known today as the *Short Text*, and the other, the *Long Text*, was after much contemplation and, evidently, additional infused knowledge.[207]

Just from a literary standpoint, Julian's accomplishment is noteworthy. *Showings* is, as far as anybody knows, the first book ever written in English by a woman, which would be enough to establish it as a landmark in English literature. But even without that historical accident it would still be recognized as a major masterpiece of English literature of the age. There's no record of how she was educated—she herself says that she was ignorant and unschooled [208]—but, in her mastery of style and language, she stands next to her great contemporaries William Langland and Geoffrey Chaucer.

Interestingly enough, *Showings* is mentioned only rarely in English literary histories, and then only in passing. From what the critics write, they seem to be put off by its emphatically Catholic doctrinal content. But the value of that content more than matches the value of *Showings* as a literary masterpiece. Her ability to bring together so many strong but previously separate threads of contemplative theology is one thing, but her personal emphasis on certain points of doctrine are her own unique contribution to Christian understanding.

In those days, the days of the Black Death and hard life generally, people tended to see Christ as the stern ruler of the universe, the judge and weigher of souls. But

207. Like other authors who have been understood as receiving infused knowledge, Julian employs and integrates a good many relatively obscure points of Christian theology that are otherwise written only in texts that she could never have seen or studied, and she reproduces them almost verbatim, at times, which would indicate that she and the other authors are writing about a pre-existing, independent reality to which they had some extraordinary access. But it's important to note that these authors never innovate, and they never claim new revelation from God; only a clearer understanding of something already revealed by Christ and the prophets.

208. She uses the word "lewd", but that's what it meant, back in the fourteenth century. You have to be careful, in general, because monastic life has its own vocabulary; "fornication", for instance, is used to mean "disobedience to one's superiors", which makes a lot of monastic records seem racier than they really are. And when documents speak of "exterminating" a heretic, they mean putting him outside of (*ex-*) the boundaries (*termini*) of the monastery or the district, not rubbing him out.

Julian saw more clearly his overwhelming love, and she saw the whole system of salvation as growth in that love, an opening up to it through which the human person becomes all that it is intended to be. Her most surprising expression of this viewpoint is her metaphor of God as Mother, as well as our Father. "He revealed that in everything," she says, "especially in those sweet words where he says:

> I am he; that is to say, I am he, the power and goodness of fatherhood; I
> am he, the wisdom and the lovingness of motherhood; I am he, the light
> and the grace that is all blessed love; I am he, the Trinity ... Our Father
> wills, our Mother works, our good Lord the Holy Spirit confirms... and
> so Jesus is our true Mother in nature by our first creation, and he is our
> true Mother in grace by his taking our created nature. All the lovely
> works and all the sweet loving offices of beloved motherhood are appro-
> priated to the second person ..."

Naturally—literally naturally—there is something in the nature of fatherhood that is of God's nature, and we're told to call God "Father"; and Jesus himself is male. But Julian found in motherhood a particularly effective symbol of the way in which God cares for humanity. Our precious Mother Jesus, she says, can feed us with himself in the Eucharist just as a mother gives her child to suck of her milk; as the mother lays the child tenderly to her breast, Jesus can lead us into his breast through his sweet open side, and show us a part of the godhead, the joys of Heaven.

As she develops this image of Jesus as Mother, Julian takes an idea expressed by St. Mechtilde von Hackenborn-Wippra, William Flete, St. Catherine of Siena, St. Bridget of Sweden, and many other lesser lights, and she puts it on a uniquely sound theological basis. She compares Christ's loving guidance of our souls to that of a mother who will sometimes let a child stumble, just so that he can learn, for instance.

And for our part, just as a child doesn't despair of his mother's love, nor rely entirely upon himself, she says, we ought to become in our hearts the true children of Christ.

s i x t e e n

L u c c a   1 8 9 9

For people today, more perhaps than ever before,
are inclined to forget,
if they do not indeed openly ridicule,
any detail of life that transcends the natural order:
an attitude of mind that grows daily worse...
and hence were sown the seeds of that mutual hatred
in which nation has risen against nation
and kingdom against kingdom.

— Benedict XV, *Decree of Canonization*
of Blessed Margaret Mary Alacoque (January 6, 1918)

On May 13, 1878—which happened to be thirty-nine years to the day before the first apparition at Fátima—the baby daughter of the pharmacist Enrico Galgani and his wife Aurelia was baptized in the village of Camigliano in Italy. The baby's uncle and her father suggested that they name the girl Gemma, after Dante's wife, but Aurelia wanted a saint's name. Finally the priest stepped in and put an end to the discussion. We may hope that she'll become a gem of Paradise, he said.[209]

The couple moved the baby and her seven brothers and sisters to nearby Lucca about a month later. By the time she was walking, Gemma distinguished herself as the

---

209. Technically, Aurelia was right. Although there was a St. Gemma venerated in the diocese of Sulmona in central Italy since her death on May 12, 1429, she wasn't canonized until 1890. The practice of naming children for canonized saints or for a virtue, incidentally, avoids the problem of children labelled for life with meaningless or frivolous names or names foreign to a Christian mentality (Canon 855), which would not only handicap them socially but show disrespect for the sacrament of Baptism in which they are born again as temples of the Holy Spirit. It's another expression of the Church's insistence on respect for all persons. Still, Aurelia didn't leave it at that; Gemma Maria Humberta Pia, she christened the baby.

best of the lot; the others were boisterous—rowdy, really—but Gemma showed a precocious self-containment, and later a remarkable spirituality. Not that she was in any way weak or ineffectual; she held her own. But she understood her religion as a working frame of reference for everything that she did in daily life, from a very early age.

She was a great help to her mother, cheerfully and easily taking care of her brothers and sisters, helping to keep their spacious house spotless. She seemed to take it for granted, not seeing housework as any kind of a burden; it was part of life, to her, and she accepted it. Because her father was a prosperous pharmacist, son of an even more prominent physician, Gemma went to good schools, where she did well and was popular; she never compromised, but she never lost her temper, although it was sometimes visibly difficult for her to restrain herself. Still, she spoke plainly, sometimes to the point almost of rudeness, but if she said what was on her mind without diplomacy she also said it without guile or duplicity. The only other fault that people could find with her was her bad handwriting.

She also seemed to take extraordinary spiritual phenomena for granted. She was confirmed on May 26, 1885, just after her seventh birthday, and she stayed in the church to hear the next Mass and to pray especially for her mother. While she waited, she heard a voice in her heart, as she called it: "Will you give me Mamma?" Christ asked her. Yes, she replied eagerly, provided that you take me with her.

"No," the voice continued, "give me your mother without reserve. You must wait, for now, with your father. I will take you to Heaven later." In fact, her mother died on September 17, 1886, the Feast of the Stigmata of St. Francis.

Gemma now had even more family responsibilities, but she continued her studies, too, and by 1887 was ready to make her First Communion, which was scheduled for the Feast of the Sacred Heart that year. She asked her father to let her retire to a nearby convent for ten days of spiritual exercises—this from a girl of nine years—and while there she was moved to write him a letter in her childish scrawl, begging his forgiveness for all of her disobediences (evidently he was hard pressed to think of any) and asking him to pray that when Jesus came to dwell in her for the first time he'd find her well disposed for all of the graces that he had prepared for her.

"I don't know how to express what passed between Jesus and me at that moment," she wrote of her First Communion. "He made himself felt, so strongly, in my poor soul. I then understood how the delights of Heaven are not like those of Earth. I felt taken with a desire to make that union with God everlasting. I felt more detached from the world and more disposed to recollection than ever before."

Having tasted the pleasures of Paradise, though, she went back to school and housework. She joined the Holy Childhood Association and the Society for the Propagation of the Faith,[210] participating and supporting them in addition to all of her

---

210. Both organizations were founded by Pauline Jaricot. The Holy Childhood Association, now the Pontifical Association of the Holy Childhood, is the Church's official agency for children's missions. Funds come in from young people all over the world and are distributed to schools, children's homes, and

other duties. She even took on extracurricular activities, like student theater. But one day the Mother Superior of the convent interrupted rehearsal with a request for prayer for a dying man who was obstinately refusing the sacraments. The girls knelt and prayed for him, and when they rose, Gemma whispered with a smile to her teacher, "The grace is granted," and it had been.

By her sixteenth year, Gemma had grown into a girl of remarkable beauty, which, in addition to her grace and charm of manner, attracted a steady parade of suitors—pharmacists, doctors, and at least one smitten soldier who followed her around in the streets, proposing to her all the time. She had already decided to devote herself entirely to Christ, as a nun, she thought, and these young men were nothing more than an embarrassment to her. So she revised her wardrobe radically, wearing a black woollen dress and mantle, winter and summer. She still wore a little bit of jewelry, very tasteful ornaments like the gold cross that her father had given her and the watch from her confirmation sponsor, the Countess Guinigi. Thus arrayed, she went one day to the archbishop's palace to receive the gold medal that she had won for outstanding work in religious studies, but when she came home and saw herself in the mirror, her guardian angel appeared to her and said, "Remember that the precious ornaments that adorn a spouse of a crucified King cannot be other than thorns and a cross."

At these words, she burst into tears and resolved never again to wear anything that had the least bit of vanity about it. From then on her simple wardrobe became absolutely austere, but that still didn't keep the boys off her trail. So one day she suddenly asked an aunt to walk with her to a milliner's. This was a surprise, coming from a girl who showed no interest whatever in fashion, but the real surprise came when they got there. Gemma ordered a huge, floppy-brimmed, black straw hat. Nobody wears such things, the ladies told her, but she was adamant. It was that hat, she said, and she got it. She wore it whenever she set foot outside the house, from then on.

It was just as well that she had turned her heart away from finery by then. One by one, her brothers and sisters fell ill with consumption; the financial drain of so many bills from doctors and funeral directors pushed her father to the brink of bankruptcy. When he died, painfully, of throat cancer in 1897, his creditors burst into the house and carried away the furniture, the books, and everything else. They even rifled the pockets of Gemma's black woollen dress as she stood there, taking the few pennies she had on her.

So Gemma, only nineteen years old, went to Camaiore to stay with her father's sister and her husband, who owned a little store there. She clerked in that store every day after morning Mass, visiting the Blessed Sacrament in the abbey church during her lunch hour and after work. But her poverty didn't keep the boys away, any more than

other child-welfare projects in a hundred and fifty-two countries; today, it is particularly focussed on rescuing children displaced and abandoned in the course of wars, disabled by bombs, arms, land mines, and torture, or exploited sexually (especially those third-world children sold into slavery for prostitution and pornography purveyed to westerners). In this country, it has its headquarters at 1720 Massachusetts Avenue, N.W., Washington, D.C. 20036. The Society for the Propagation of the Faith is at 366 Fifth Avenue, New York 10001; it's responsible to the Congregation for the Evangelization of Peoples.

her severe dress and that ridiculous hat; her beauty, her manner, and her smile won over everybody in the village, no matter what. So, like many another strong-willed mystic before her, Gemma asked for some way to make them lose interest in her. And, as happened so many times in the past, she got what she prayed for.

It began with excruciating pains in her back and head. Then huge tubercular abscesses formed along her spine; her hair fell out, and she was paralyzed, unable to move anything but her arms. Her family had her sent back to Lucca, and they somehow found the money for a doctor, who cauterized the abscesses and locked her in an iron body brace for a year so that her degenerated spine could heal straight.[211] She bore all of this without complaint, except that she felt shy about all of the bother that she was causing. Her aunt and uncle sent money every month from Camaiore, but Gemma didn't buy any comforts for her body.

She bought a soul. Since her school days, she had never gone out of the house without a little money or spare groceries for the poor, who absolutely adored her whether she had anything left for them or not. Now, lying there in her brace and unable to move, she couldn't go out to meet the poor, but one of them came to her, the woman who delivered drinking water to the house. Evidently the surviving members of the Galgani family had spoken ill of this woman because she was prostituting herself, living in sin with a man to whom she wasn't married. Gemma asked to speak with her the next time she came; why send her away, she asked, when Christ received the Magdalen kindly? The woman acknowledged the irregularity of her life to Gemma, but she said that she didn't have any choice because the man paid the rent that she herself couldn't afford.

"I'll pay the rent," Gemma said, "if you leave him, go to confession, and return to the friendship of God." The woman amended her life, and Gemma kept her promise until the day she died.[212]

During the year that Gemma was lying there paralyzed in her brace, her guardian angel was with her sensibly almost daily, as he had been since he reminded her about the jewelry. And she soon had another visitor, too, an earthly friend who brought her a biography of St. Gabriel Possenti della Madre Dolorosa (1838-1862), although Gemma at that point was in neither the mood nor the position to read it. But then someone else came: she was startled to sense the presence of the Devil who promised not just restored health but every pleasure she could imagine. She cast around quickly for some defense, and she remembered the biography that she had kept in her bed. She invoked St. Gabriel Possenti, and the Devil went away instantly. After that, she felt the saint's presence more or less constantly, and not just through imaginative visions. He

211. If it healed at all, which wasn't likely in those days. The connection between the disease of consumption and the tubercle bacillus hadn't been known until Robert Koch discovered it in 1882. By 1887 there were tuberculosis dispensaries in which patients were isolated, but as late as the second World War there was still no specific medicine for it, and the efficacy of the most usual vaccine ("bile-Calmette-Guérin" or "BCG") was still undetermined.

212. It wasn't just mechanical charity at a distance; Gemma also asked everybody in the house to take a little less coffee every morning so that they'd save enough to have a cup waiting for the woman when she came every day, so that they could chat.

came to her shortly after that in a dream, saying simply, "Be good, and I'll come back to you." When she decided to vow to become a nun, he said, "Make the vow with a good heart, but add nothing to it." She agreed, and when she promised herself to Christ as a nun, she didn't specify which order she'd join.

Gemma's spinal tuberculosis got worse, and it started to spread. Her doctor cauterized her spine again and again, but it didn't help. In January of 1899, she was operated on to remove a tumor in her side. She wasn't given any anæsthetic, ostensibly because she was too weak to recover from it; somehow, her doctors thought that she'd be strong enough to recover from the operation. She sank day by day, until she reached the point of death about a month later. She received the Last Rites on February 2, when nobody thought she'd live through the night, but she held on, neither better nor worse, for the rest of the month. Then on February 23 her confessor suggested a novena to ask the intercession of St. Margaret Mary Alacoque, and St. Gabriel della Madre Dolorosa said that he'd pray it along with her.

On the ninth day, the First Friday of March, Gemma received the Eucharist. She heard Christ speak: "The gift that you have received this morning," he said, "shall be followed by others still greater. I will always be with you and act as your father. And she will be your mother," pointing to Our Lady of Sorrows, *la Madre Dolorosa*, who stood at his side. "Paternal help shall never be wanting to those who place themselves in my hands; therefore, you shall lack nothing even though I myself have deprived you of consolation and help in this world."

Her family thought that she was delirious when she called for her black dress and that hat, but eventually they saw that all of her illnesses had left her at that moment.

During this pivotal time in her life, she tried to enter one religious order after another. None of the nuns in the area wanted to refuse a girl like Gemma, but none could get permission from the archbishop to accept her. True, she had been restored to health, but her family did show a tendency toward tubercular infections, and he couldn't ignore the possibility of a relapse. When she finally got two doctors to certify her health so that she could enter another order, they themselves had to refuse because the stone walls of their convent made the place too chill and damp to be safe for her.

But the archbishop instructed her confessor, Father Germano Ruoppolo, C.P., to watch and report carefully on her spiritual life. Fr. Germano commanded her to write everything down, and she did, in a beautiful hand with incredible rapidity, as much as four pages in fifteen minutes. She was fragrant, with that indescribable odor of celestial roses, and her angel was visible to her every day. She only ignored him, Father Germano said, when she was on the way out to receive the Eucharist.

Now up and around again, Gemma resolved to keep the Holy Hour on Thursdays for the rest of her life. She had a lifelong habit of meditative prayer on the Passion, but adopting this particular devotion was appropriate because the practice was encouraged by the apparitions of Christ to St. Margaret Mary. It involves keeping watch for an hour on Thursday evening, keeping Jesus company in the agony of Gethsemani, compensating him in some way for the grief that he suffered through the abandonment of his Apostles, and imploring mercy for sinners. That Holy Thursday, March 30, 1899, Gemma received yet more mystic gifts while she was performing the devotion. Later, under obedience to her confessor, she wrote down what had happened.

> I felt so full of sorrow for my sins that I passed a time of continual mar-
> tyrdom. In the midst of this immense grief, however, one comfort was
> left me: that of tears. I spent the whole hour praying and weeping, and,
> being very tired, I sat down. My sorrow lasted a little while longer, but
> soon I felt my whole being rapt in recollection. Then, all of a sudden, I
> began to lose the use of my senses. I was scarcely able to get up and close
> the door and lock it. Where was I? I found myself before Christ cruci-
> fied. He was bleeding all over. I lowered my eyes immediately at the sight
> and was greatly disturbed. I made the Sign of the Cross, and immediate-
> ly my anguish was succeeded by tranquility of spirit; but I continued to
> feel even a greater sorrow for my sins than before, and I had not the
> courage to look at Jesus. I prostrated myself with my forehead to the
> ground and there remained for several hours. I came to myself and began
> from that moment to have a great horror for sin; this is the greatest grace
> Jesus has given me. The Wounds of Jesus were so deeply impressed on
> my mind that I have never forgotten them.

In June of that year, her Thursday devotions happened to fall on the Vigil of the Feast of the Sacred Heart. She felt the pain of sorrow for her sins more quickly than usual, she said, and then she saw all of her life's sins and all of the pains that Christ had suf-fered because of them. The Blessed Mother stood with her, as did her guardian angel; they supported her as Christ appeared, with all of his Wounds open but flames, not blood, issuing from them.

Gemma felt as though she were dying. Several hours later, Mary kissed her on her forehead and she came around, finding herself kneeling but still with great pain in her hands, feet, and heart. As she got up, she noticed that blood was streaming from those areas. Her angel helped her get into bed, and the next morning she pulled on a pair of gloves to hide her hands. But the pains didn't leave her until three in the after-noon on Friday, the hour of Christ's death on the Cross.

Later, she received the wounds from the Crown of Thorns and of the Scourging, too. For the next two years, every Thursday evening at eight, she would be caught up in ecstasy again, and the wounds would open. Her confessor, her doctor, and the investigators sent by the diocese saw the wounds open gradually before their eyes, tearing so deep that the bone was visible, and they measured the blood that streamed out of them copiously. The Father Provincial of the Passionists noted that she was insensi-ble to noise, except the commands of her confessor, and to pinpricks or burns from a candle flame. She never complained of the pain of the stigmata, the wracking pain of the dislocation of her bones and the cracking of her joints.

Finally, at three o'clock on Friday, the wounds would close, leaving only a small white scar and the pain. Gemma would get up, wash her hands and face, pull her sleeves down over her hands, and run downstairs to take care of the children, laughing with them and playing hide and seek, or to set the table and get dinner.[213]

Finally, in 1903, the twenty-fifth year of her life, Gemma's tuberculosis returned. On April 11, she received the Anointing of the Sick again, and she asked for a crucifix. "Jesus," she said quietly, "I commend to you this poor soul of mine." She kissed the crucifix and died. It was Holy Saturday.

---

213. To get her work done, she had to avert her eyes from the large crucifix in the dining room so that she wouldn't fall into ecstasy contemplating the Passion again. When her confessor dined there, he would call her back if he saw her eyes drift toward it; and at least once she levitated to receive its embrace. Her confessor had ordered her to remain in ecstasy only so long, so during her raptures she had to cry out, "Jesus, go away! I don't want you any more!" when she heard the clock strike. Her surviving family was no help, by the way. Her sister Angela called her a bigot and a hypocrite, sometimes furiously pulling her hair and throwing her around, and her brother hit her from time to time and once blackened her eye when she said something to console him after he complained of being too poor to afford theater tickets.

part three

certain apparitions

of Mary

The Church expresses ...
the many relationships that bind her to Mary
... when she recognizes in the associate of the Redeemer ...
the prophetic fulfillment of her own future,
until the day on which, when she has been purified
of every spot and wrinkle (cf. Eph 5:27),
she will become like a bride
arrayed for her bridegroom (cf. Rv 21:2),
Jesus Christ.

— Paul VI, *Apostolic Exhortation*
on
Devotion to the Blessed Virgin Mary (1974)

seventeen

Neo-Cæsaria 250

His disciples are called "Christians".
These are they who, above every other people on Earth,
have found the truth:
for they acknowledge God: the Creator and Maker of all things,
the only-begotten Son,
and the Holy Spirit.
They worship no other than him.

— Aristides of Athens, *Apology to Antoninus Pius (c.* 140)

In the year 213 at Neo-Cæsaria in Pontus, which used to be a country in Asia Minor, a wealthy and prominent pagan family had a son. They named him Theodorus, Theodore, and, like many another wealthy pagan, he decided on a career in the law. So, when he was twenty, he and his brother Athenodorus started out for Berytus—Beirut—to finish up their studies in the famous law school there. But they went through Cæsaria itself, on the way. While they were there, they happened to hear Origen.

Now, like Theodore, Origen himself had been born to wealthy parents who gave him the best available education. Fortunately, he'd been born in Alexandria-by-Egypt, the splendid city built from the ground up by the Ptolemies, the Macedonian Greek-speaking Pharaohs of Egypt, the heirs of Alexander the Great. It was the city of the great Library, where the experimentation of the West met the speculation of the East, where scholars and philosophers could meet in peace and prosperity to work things out—it's where Hebrew scholars compiled the Old Testament, the Septuagint that Christ used and that his Church has used forever after.[214] It was also the city of the great

214. After the destruction of the Temple in Jerusalem by Titus in 70, those few remaining rabbis who had not embraced Christianity convened at nearby Jamnia to work out a canon of Scripture that would allow them to argue against Christianity; they deleted some prophetic books and rewrote the remainder

197

Museum, an immense scientific research institute dedicated to the Muses, where the Greek sciences had flourished for five hundred years.

There was no place in the world better suited to educate a bright young man. When Origen himself had been about fifteen, he had heard lectures by St. Clement at the catechetical school in Alexandria. At that time, this was the only school in the world where Christians learned the Greek sciences as well as the doctrines of the Church, and they approached all of their subjects at the highest intellectual level. Origen shot to the top of the class and even surpassed his teachers, setting a new intellectual standard for the study of Scripture and Tradition. He was among the first (probably the very first) to approach the Old Testament as a text that could be analyzed and criticized with the same scholarly methods you'd use to extract the fullest meaning from any other text, and he did it at a level that would have done credit to any of the great scholars of the Library in its heyday. The brilliance of his commentaries—no less than their amazing quantity—put Origen in demand as a teacher and lecturer all over the known world, and they made him a conspicuous target for anti-Christian harassment.

But he got it from both sides. Works that profess to interpret the Bible are always scrutinized by the Church; not only their substance, but their implications have to be clear of error, and when works are as abundant and as profound as Origen's, that takes time, and it raises lots of questions about orthodoxy. So Origen moved from Alexandria to Cappadocia, a quieter, less conspicuous corner of the Empire. He settled in Cæsaria and opened a school of his own, through which his philological methods had a tremendous impact; nobody in that region had ever before shown the power of the most rigorous classical Greek logic to extract the fullest understanding of Christian doctrine.

He slipped, eventually, into heresy. His later works are doctrinally incorrect, contradictory to those that he wrote while still within the circle of St. Clement.215 But during those two brief years when he lectured in Cæsaria he was all right; and that happened to be exactly the moment that Theodorus of Neo-Cæsaria happened to pass

to obtain a version with which they could deny Christ's nature as the Messiah. The Old Testament found in Protestant Bibles follows this latter-day version, which made it easier for Luther, Calvin, and other heresiarchs to deny the tenets of Christ's teachings that they wanted to delete. The city of Alexandria, by the way, is called Alexandria "by" Egypt (*Alexandria apud Ægyptos*) rather than "in" Egypt because it was founded as a Greek-speaking colony, the Macedonian capital separate from the rest of the country.

215. The heresy called Origenism denies basic tenets of the Faith like the Incarnation, the general resurrection, everlasting punishment for serious sinners, and the co-equality of the Three Persons of the Trinity. It's uncertain whether Origen himself held all of the opinions of the Origenists—they deny the factual sense of Scriptures, but it would be odd if he, the great textual analyst, would have. In fact, he erred in the other direction, castrating himself because he took Mt 19:12 fundamentally (both of which, the over-literal interpretation of Scripture and the mutilation, are contrary to the Mind of the Church). The extent of his heresy is obscure because, on account of his fame, a lot of forgeries appeared from lesser, and less orthodox, writers, some using his nickname Adamantius (which, ironically, means "unyielding"). Then again he may have just disavowed his own heretical works, when it came to that. But there's no doubt that he slipped into heresy and stayed there willfully; whatever happened with his written works, he was convicted on his own testimony. He was examined by a synod at Alexandria, excommunicated, laicized, and forbidden to teach. His former assistant and very best friend Heraclas didn't rescind the sentences when he became bishop himself, and Origen's personal appeal to Pope St. Fabian was denied.

through town. What the young man heard was not only doctrinally sound but intellectually compelling in its brilliance.

And as Theodore got to know Origen better, he saw that the man's life was as instructive as his words. Christian life, in those days, stood in plain contrast to pagan life, which still ran on the popular principle of doing whatever you wanted, because the gods (if any) weren't going to care. The simplicity of the Church's moral teachings, her insistence on respect for all human beings, slave, free, or indifferent (and specifically her stipulation of personal chastity); her requirement of active good and the absorption of insults, of forgiveness of trespasses—in short, the moral theology of the Church—made it obvious that this was a way of life leading to self-control, cleanliness of mind and spirit, and ultimate happiness. The simple rightness of Christian life was astonishing to everybody who encountered it. Theodore was transfixed.

Eventually he converted, taking the baptismal name Gregory, which comes from a Greek word meaning watchman. He also converted his talents from the study of civil law to the study of divine Law. Origen was immensely grateful to have been sent such a student, and he virtually adopted him as his spiritual and intellectual son. Use your talents for the glory of God, he told his pupil, and borrow from the ancient philosophers whatever can be turned to the service of the Church, as the Jews recast the gold of Egypt into the furnishings of the Temple.

By about 238, Gregory's studies with Origen ended. He took his leave with an oration that still survives, delivered before a huge audience—thanks to Origen, Cæsaria was largely a Christian city by then. And he went home to Neo-Cæsaria to live the life of a hermit, planning to devote all of his time to contemplation of God. Everybody in town was shocked to see what had happened to him. Theodore, who used to be the smartest, liveliest young man-about-Neo-Cæsaria, now dressed simply, austerely, even. He was so quiet and thoughtful, calling himself "Gregory" for some reason and saying that he was going to go live in a cave somewhere. Nobody understood that; if anyplace in the Empire deserved the name "pagan", it was Neo-Cæsaria. There were shows, sports, brothels, and everything else that marks a city as non-Christian.

In fact, there were precisely seventeen Christians in the whole city. Those seventeen were hardly willing to let such a smart and exemplary young man hide himself away in the wilderness somewhere. They decided to make him a priest. More than that, their archbishop decided to make him their bishop. The only obstacle was Gregory himself. He gave them the slip and went off to be a hermit, as he'd planned. But after a lot of prayer and fasting—and thought—he found a genuine vocation to the priesthood. So he went back and made a deal with the archbishop: give me a little time to myself in the desert, to think and to pray and to purify myself, and when I come back, I'll be at your service for whatever use you want to make of me.

Now, one of the sticking points that Gregory had, doctrinally, was the Holy Trinity. It's one of the central mysteries of Christianity, something beyond human comprehension here in Time and space; no purely human understanding can grasp how God can be three Persons, Father, Son, and Holy Spirit, in one being. Gregory understood that the doctrine of the Trinity was a keystone in the Faith, but he also understood that Origen's view of that mystery was already being labelled by some as heretical. Then again, he also knew that, if he was supposed to lead those seventeen Christians in that unrestrained pagan city, he was going to have to teach that principle clearly, accurately, and convincingly.

He fell asleep during his meditations but was awakened suddenly by an old man who stood before him. "Stay calm," the old man said, "I am here to help you."

The man raised his hand and pointed to the side. When his eyes followed, Gregory saw a brilliant light, at the center of which was a marvelously beautiful woman, who told the old man—Evangelist John, she called him—to explain the mystery of the Trinity to Gregory.

The man turned to him again, and in a flash Gregory was given a glimpse out of Time and into Eternity, the bornless, endless dimension of existence inhabited uniquely by God. In that same flash, he was given to understand, as St. Ignatius of Loyola, St. Teresa of Avila, and many other mystics have been given to understand, something of the ineffable nature of God. "And so," the old man said, "there is nothing created in the Trinity, nothing greater and nothing lesser: the Father has never been without the Son, the Son has never been without the Spirit, and the Spirit never without the Father. This same Trinity is one, immutable and forever without change."

Gregory went back to the archbishop and announced himself ready to assume his duties. Against persecutions, against plagues, against all kinds of opposition, he guarded his little flock of seventeen and began preaching. His first public sermon—and imagine the courage it took to stand in the market in a place like Neo-Cæsaria and talk about faith and morals—drew a crowd that was as fascinated by Gregory as Gregory had been by Origen.

He spoke of morals, no doubt, and of salvation; but he also taught the people of his city about the triune nature of God, laying out before them the principles summed up in that sublime Creed, the clear and sonorous statement of the Church's teachings on the Trinity authoritatively pronounced by the Council of Nicæa in 325 and repeated every day at Mass around the world:

> We believe in one God,
> the Father, the Almighty,
> maker of Heaven and Earth,
> of all that is seen and unseen.
> We believe in one Lord, Jesus Christ,
> the only Son of God,
> born of the Father before all ages,
> God from God, Light from Light,
> True God from True God:
> begotten, not made; one in being with the Father.

Through him all things were made…
We believe in the Holy Spirit,
The Lord, the giver of life,
who proceeds from the Father and the Son.
With the Father and the Son, he is adored and glorified.
He has spoken through the prophets…

The next morning nobody could get into the little church, because the sick had flocked there for healing, completely blocking the way. Gregory healed them all. More and more came, and more and more converted. He was given so many miraculous healings, so many extraordinary phenomena, that before long people just called him *Gregorius Thaumaturgus*—Gregory the Wonder-Worker. Within only a few years, stories of his miracles had surpassed the truth and expanded to almost mythic proportions.

But after the miracles faded, the converts stayed on, secure in the Faith to which the wonders had attracted them. Just before he died, Bishop Gregory ordered a census of his diocese, so that they could find out how many pagans there were still to be converted.

There were exactly seventeen.

eighteen

Guadalupe 1531

If I say that God created Heaven, the Earth, and the sea,
no pagan will stand for this as proof,
nor will he believe me.
If I say that Christ raised the dead ...
no pagan will accept that either...
How should I persuade him?

— St. John Chrysostom,
Demonstration Against the Pagans (c. 388)

One night in the year 1509, in the Valley of Mexico, the Princess Papantzin suddenly fell ill and lapsed into a coma. Her brother, the Aztec emperor Moctezuma Xocoyotzin,[216] thought that she was dead and made all the arrangements for a full state funeral. But as soon as his sister was laid in the coffin, attendants heard her screaming, demanding to be let out. When she recovered, she told her brother about a strange and portentous dream that she had had: a bright creature all of light, marked with a black cross, took her to the eastern coast of the empire and told her to look out over the endless sea. Men will come across that water, the creature told her, from a distant land, in huge canoes marked with black crosses, and they will conquer this empire and bring people knowledge of the True God.

216. His name is now spelled in various ways, the familiar "Montezuma"—probably the result of a mishearing of the native pronunciation—being replaced with the modern Mexican "Moctezuma" or the more academic "Motecuhzoma". Cortéz spelled it "Mutezuma", but he was extremely busy. And it's always been extremely difficult for Europeans to catch the sounds of the Aztec language, Nahuatl, in general, which is why the shrine is called "Guadalupe" in the first place. Anyway, no matter how you spell it, they're all the same man.

Moctezuma listened; he was *huei tlatoani*, the "great lord", head of the Aztec religion. As an incarnate god himself, he paid attention to dreams and prophecies, particularly when they came from one so closely connected to himself, and one who had so nearly been entombed alive while conversing with the beyond.

He watched and waited, now always uneasy about the end of his own rule. And in fact, ten years later, reports came in from the east coast of his empire: great canoes, larger than any on Earth, with great white wings emblazoned with black crosses, had appeared suddenly out of the dawn. The people in the canoes were tall, with eyes the color of the sky, and they wore shiny metal shells; they rode strange animals, "deer, as tall as the roof of a house," the messengers said, and they brought thunder in their arms.

Hernando Cortéz and his four hundred fifty Spanish soldiers made quick progress toward the imperial capital, gathering one tribe after another into their train. But when the group first glimpsed the City of Mexico in 1519, they could hardly believe their eyes. In the middle of a series of lakes more than a hundred miles in length, Tenochtitlán rose up in splendor in the high clear air, a city of mansions and temples studded with pyramids of many colors, all covered with flowers in constant bloom that seemed to spill over in to the lake itself. "And some of our soldiers asked whether the things we saw were not in a dream," said Bernal Díaz, one of the Spaniards present that day.

The Spaniards rode to the capital on a causeway five miles long, a road that no other hoof had ever struck—nobody in this city, or indeed in this hemisphere, had ever seen a horse before. And the Spaniards had never seen a city like this before. The fresh lakeside breezes carried the perfumes of marvelous flowers beautiful as if from another planet. More than a thousand people were employed strictly to sweep and wash the streets constantly; a man could walk through this city, one Spaniard reported, without dirtying his feet any more than his hands. The markets offered indescribable riches to the half-million inhabitants of the city: mountains of jewelry, of gold, silver, amber, turquoise, and jade; gorgeous birds and garments made of feathers; rich fabrics; and an overwhelming abundance of food—including unknown delicacies like maize, vanilla, and *chocolatl*. "We were astounded at the number of people and the quantity of merchandise that it contained, and the good order and control that were maintained," wrote Díaz, "for we had never seen such a thing before."

Moctezuma and his court came out personally to meet the other-worldly strangers, offer them hospitality in keeping with their supposed divine status, and arrange a tour of their brilliant capital. With their native guides, they climbed the highest pyramid to get a good panoramic view of the capital. And at the top they found two temples, one dedicated to Huitzilopochtli, the god of war and of the Sun, and the other to Tezcatlipoca, the creator god who served as another god of war, too, and of sorcery and the night sky. Inside the temples, Díaz said, "the stench was more intolerable than that of the slaughter-houses of Castile." Before the idol of Huitzilopochtli there were stone altars stinking and black with coagulated human blood. In the temple of

Tezcatlipoca, they noticed four or five fresh human hearts on the platter before the idol, put there by priests in garments clotted with gore.

This didn't surprise Cortéz; he knew all about the brutal Aztec religion, which pivoted on periodic human sacrifices to the gods of nature. It was human blood, they preached, that maintained life and the powers of nature; it was fresh, beating hearts on the altars of the gods that made the Sun rise every morning, and that made the rains come in time for the crops. Four priests would stretch a victim across an altar, and the high priest plunged a flint knife into his chest, forcefully enough to break through his ribs. The victim's heart, still beating, was pulled quickly from his body, held aloft, and placed before the idol on a censer. The rest of his body was thrown down the steep steps of the pyramid so that the crowd below could eat it.

Even the mother-god of the Aztecs, Tonantzin, had a terrifying aspect, with nothing maternal about her. Representations of her show her head covered with serpents' heads and her body covered with a tangle of snakes. Her main sanctuary—if that's the right word to use for a site of continuous holocaust—had been about six miles north of Tenochtitlán, atop a hill called Tepeyac, but it had fallen into ruin so long before Moctezuma's reign that virtually no sign of the building was visible there.

The best-known Aztec god today is probably Quetzalcoatl, represented by the feathered serpent that figures so prominently in Aztec art and architecture. He was a gentler deity involved in another prophecy of blond, blue-eyed, bearded people coming from the east in giant ships to teach about the True God; but he had been expelled by his nemesis Tezcatlipoca after an epic battle. As he sailed east over the ocean, he promised to come back some day, but until then he could only leave the warlike gods in control. In fact, it was the bloodthirsty Huitzilopochtli from whom the *huei tlatoani* claimed to take imperial authority; his sanctuary in the capital was the holiest, most dreaded spot in the empire. At its dedication in 1487 more than twenty thousand human beings had been killed and eaten.[217]

The Aztecs, of course, were only one tribe (or rather one nation, one group of related tribes) in the area; the rest of Mexico's population consisted of many, many other nations, each with its own culture, language, and religion. When the Aztecs invaded and expanded their empire across the land, they imposed their bloody religion as well as their harsh rule, much to the horror of their conquered subjects. In fact, the only reason that

217. For some reason, even events that you'd think joyous and innocent centered on human sacrifice in the Aztec world. The springtime festival of Xipe Totec ("Our Lord the Flayed One"), celebrating the new vegetation that would cover the Earth, featured skinning victims alive and then wearing their fresh skins like overalls, their hands still dangling, for twenty days, after which the rotting skins were thrown into a ceremonial pit; children were sacrificed every planting season to Tlaloc the rain god to guarantee good crops, and even the feast of new fire, symbolizing rebirth and celebrated in the name of Tezcatlipoca at the end of every fifty-two year calendar cycle, involved kindling a fire in the empty chest of a fresh victim and distributing it throughout the empire. But then, even flowers symbolized spilled blood to the Aztecs, who called the sites of battles "fields of flowers", which gives a sinister implication to the blossoms that embowered old Tenochtitlán. The civilizing god Quetzalcoatl sounds like a stranger to the Aztec pantheon, and in fact he had been taken into the Aztecs' religion when they conquered his inventors, the Toltecs.

Cortéz and his little force had been able to come this far is that most of the subjugated tribes of the Aztec empire were only too happy to overthrow that hideous religion and adopt Christianity's promise of a divine victim sacrificed once and for all. The hope, the light, and the simple human dignity taught by Christians won them over in their thousands. So Cortéz did not approach Tenochtitlán alone. He had some seven thousand native followers who were all too ready to overthrow Moctezuma and all he stood for.

One way or another, Cortéz and his henchmen did manage to overthrow Moctezuma and take on the government of the empire themselves. Either Cortéz was greedy and cruel or he tried to keep the others from being greedy and cruel, but whatever the native peoples thought of him, he certainly wasn't popular among the Spaniards, either, and he had to go back to Spain in 1528. Charles V, King of Spain and Holy Roman Emperor, vested the governor's authority in a commission of five called the First Audience. But Charles also had sense enough to appoint a Bishop of the New World, somebody as a counterweight to the civil authority, somebody who would look out for the people in case the First Audience got greedy or cruel.

He chose a humble friar whom he had met almost by chance some years before on a retreat at the friary of Abrojo. The Franciscan Fray Juan Zumárraga had impressed the King-Emperor with his good sense as well as with his austerely ascetic life, and by his deep and cheerful sympathy. And he had immediately distributed to the poor the huge gift of money that Charles had pressed on him (overriding the friar's refusal). So, in December, 1528, Fray Juan Zumárraga became Bishop Zumárraga, ordinary of a diocese that extended from California to Tierra del Fuego.[218]

This appointment turned out to be an astute move. The new bishop was a brilliant man of heroic kindness, and he deserves to be better known today. He brought with him troops of missionaries, of course, but he also brought the first printing press in the New World, as well as groups of agriculturalists and of craftsmen to bring American farming and manufactures into the sixteenth century. He imported all kinds of fruit trees, oranges, lemons, pears, and peaches, and he introduced crops like chickpeas, melons, onions, radishes, and other foods that have enriched and improved American diets from that day to this. He founded schools all over Mexico, including the College of the Holy Cross in Tlaltelolco, which today is the largest university in the world. And he really did stand firm against the First Audience.

The governing committee figured that the native Americans weren't really all that human, that they didn't have souls, and that it was perfectly all right to exploit them and keep them in their place.[219] Bishop Zumárraga countered with the view that, since

218. "Ordinary", from the Latin *ordinare*, to put in order, means three different things. It can mean "of or like those things that give normal order to a kind of thing", as in ordinary people, ordinary illness. Or it can mean a basic framework that gives structure to something: the ordinary of the Mass is the part that never changes. It can also mean, as here, the bishop or mitered abbot, or other clerical official, who rules a diocese, giving day-to-day order to its worship, education, and so forth.

219. Sadly, this view of newly encountered peoples as not human seems to have been absolutely normal for the first thirty or forty thousand years of civilization on this planet—the natives didn't think that the newcomers were human, either. Christianity seems to be unique in the opposing view, putting everybody

the Mexicans had reason, like anybody else, they could perfectly well receive Baptism, after which they'd stand as full members of Christ's Church; so you'd have to treat them with the respect that's due to every human being as an inalienable right. The First Audience ignored him, attacked his friars, and threatened him with violence himself. The persecution by these men of their own Church, he wrote, "is worse than that of Herod and Diocletian." They kept Zumárraga under virtual house arrest, cutting off any communication with Madrid, so that he couldn't report to the King.

But Zumárraga outfoxed them by smuggling a note to the King-Emperor in a hollowed crucifix. Charles instantly—as instantly as transatlantic communication allowed in those days—fired the First Audience and replaced them with the Second Audience, headed by Bishop Don Sebastián Ramirez y Fuenleal.

But it was too late. The new rulers wouldn't arrive for a whole year, and already the native population, driven to revolt by the First Audience, was threatening a general uprising. All of the missionaries' work, all of the improvements in life, the suppression of those bloodthirsty sacrificial rituals, and indeed the safety of the intermarried Spanish colonists and their children, were at stake. Bishop Zumárraga implored the Blessed Mother to help. And, secretly, the gardener bishop asked her to send him some Castilian roses, unknown to the New World, as a sign that she had heard him.

On the morning of December 9, 1531, Bishop Zumárraga was at work in his residence in Tenochtitlán—now called the City of Mexico—when one of his servants announced a *campesino* who said that he had an urgent message to be given to the Bishop alone. When the man came in, Zumárraga saw a short, wiry, weathered man of about sixty who knelt before him and started speaking in the Aztec language, the Nahuatl that produced such words as Huitzilopochtli, Tenochtitlán, Tonantzin, and the *campesino*'s original name, Cuauhtlatoatzin. The Bishop called for his interpreter, Juan González.

González had come over with Cortéz and had picked up the Aztec language on his travels through the country as a missionary, after the governor's dismissal. Through the interpreter, the bishop heard the man say that his name was Juan Diego, and that he was a Christian. On his way to Mass that morning before dawn—December 9 was then the Feast of the Immaculate Conception—Juan Diego had passed the hill of Tepeyac, when he heard music the like of which he'd never heard before. It was like the songs of birds, he said, but all harmonious, not random like earthly birds, and it filled his soul. He looked up to the summit of Tepeyac and saw a glowing cloud there, illuminated by a sort of a rainbow that shot out of it in all directions. The instant he saw this, the heavenly music stopped, suddenly and completely.

Then he heard a voice, speaking to him softly. "Juan! Juan Diego!" it said. "Juanito! Juan Dieguito!" He climbed up the hill toward the light, and he saw with supernatural clarity the figure of a young Mexican girl, about fourteen years old, he said, marvelously beautiful and dressed in marvelously beautiful clothes. Even the dry plants,

on an equal footing (Mt 28:19-20; Gl 3:28), and historically it's interesting that in the former colonies of Spain, Portugal, and France, the population today consists largely of Native Americans, while in those of countries outside the Church's jurisdiction the natives were virtually exterminated.

the cacti and thorns, of that wasteland spot seemed made of jewels, if they stood within the scope of that light, crystalline like so many emeralds, like colored glass and gold.

Then the girl spoke to him in his own language, the only one that he could understand: *Nopiltzin, campa tiauh?* My dearest little child, where are you going?

My Lady and my child, he answered, using the forms proper from a servant to a mistress, I am going to Tlaltelolco to hear Mass.

"Dearest of my little children," the girl continued, "know that I am the Ever-Virgin Mary, Mother of the True God, he who gives life and maintains it in existence. He created all things; he is in all places; he is Lord of Heaven and Earth. I want a church built here, in which I will show my love, my compassion, my help, and my protection to the people. I am your Mother of Mercy, the mother of all who live together in this land, and of all people, of all who love me, all who cry unto me, all who have confidence in me. I will hear their weepings and their sorrows here, and I will heal and allay their sufferings, their necessities, and their misfortunes. So, to accomplish my intentions, go to the house of the Bishop of Mexico City and tell him that I sent you, and that I want to have a church built here.[220] Tell him everything that you have seen and heard. Be certain, I will be very grateful to you, and I will reward you for doing what I have asked of you. Now that you have heard my words, my little son,[221] go and do everything as best you can."

I agreed, Juan Diego said, and I came here to see you, *Señor.*

The bishop looked at Juan Diego for a long time, and then, through the interpreter, asked him about his home, his work, and his religious knowledge and practices. It all seemed all right, but the part about the Queen of Heaven appearing to him fell into the category of extraordinary mystic phenomena, and the Bishop was not going to rush to judgement. "You must come again, my son," he said kindly, "when I have more time to hear you. In the meantime, I will take careful consideration of your good will and earnest desire, which have made you come to see me."

Juan Diego went north to the hill of Tepeyac again, thinking that he had failed completely. He went up to the summit again and met the Lady, almost as if she had been waiting for him. He apologized for failing, and he asked her to give the mission to somebody more important, somebody consequential, who could get it done. "Listen to me, little son," she said, "and know that I have many messengers to whom I could entrust

220. She used the Nahuatl word *teocalli*, which comes from *teotl* ("god", curiously similar to the Greek word θεός) and *calli*, which means "home". It refers particularly to the temples that the Aztecs built atop their truncated pyramids, or atop hills similarly shaped, like Tepeyac. In fact, her whole speech resonates to the stirrings of awareness, of revelation, almost, among the Aztecs that had been increasing in the century before Cortéz arrived. The dream of Papantzin and the old prophecies about Quetzalcoatl were only parts of this; a hundred or so years before Guadalupe, for instance, the King of Texcoco had built a temple without any idol in it, dedicating it to the Unknown God, he who is present to all things, the creator of all things, he by whom everything lives.

221. The "little" that occurs so often in translations of what the two said to each other renders the suffix *-tzin*, which is a diminutive. Like the Spanish *-ito* it serves as mark of affection and love, but unlike *-ito* it's also a reverential; it's a very delicate mechanism of respect in Nahuatl. The Lady and Juan Diego used it whenever they addressed each other.

the delivery of my message. But it is absolutely necessary that you should be the one to undertake this, and that it be through your mediation that my wish should be accomplished. Go to the bishop again tomorrow. Tell him in my name, and make him understand my disposition fully, that he should build the church for which I ask. Repeat to him that it is I in person, the Ever-Virgin Mary, the Mother of God, who send you."

He agreed again and went home to his lonely supper—his wife, María Lucía, who had converted at the same time as he, had died two years before, and his only living relative was the elderly uncle Juan Bernardino who had raised him but didn't live with him then. The next morning, the bishop's servants were rather brusque with Juan Diego, but after keeping him waiting all day in the freezing courtyard they admitted him into the bishop's presence.

Zumárraga was surprised to see Juan Diego back so soon, but he received him kindly. The man knelt again, but this time the long walk, the cold wait, and his own inadequacies made him burst into tears as he repeated the message. Zumárraga consoled him and asked him to collect himself sufficiently to answer his questions: where did you see her, how long did she stay, what did she look like, and so on. The bishop questioned him and counter-questioned him, but Juan Diego never departed from his story and never contradicted himself. Finally the bishop said that he needed some proof—a sign from Heaven.

Just say what kind of sign you want, *Señor*, and I'll go right now to ask the Lady for it. Zumárraga was probably taken aback by the confidence of that answer, but unlike certain prelates involved in some other apparitions, he gave a wise answer, himself. I'll leave that up to the Lady, he said.

Zumárraga sent two of his own servants to follow Juan Diego, but when he came to Tepeyac he simply disappeared. The men scoured the area, but Juan Diego was nowhere to be found.[222] But Juan Diego had gone back up the hill to ask for the sign, just as he had said. The Lady reassured him and told him to come back the next day for the sign.

That evening, Juan Diego went to visit his uncle and tell him what had been happening, but his exhilaration crashed when he found Juan Bernardino gone. He searched frantically for the old man and finally found him wounded by an arrow, lying face down at the edge of a forest. He'd been shot for being a Christian, a turncoat, by insurrectionists.[223] Juan Diego carried him back to the house and spent the next day

222. A lot of other people have been reported as mystically hidden. A man pursued by enemies took refuge in Bl. Lydwine's room, for example, and when they followed him they couldn't see him standing there.

223. Another version, often published, maintains that the uncle was stricken with the fatal fever that the Aztecs called *cocolixtle*, but residents of the area have always said that he'd been shot in the native reaction to the invaders, and that they had put up a stone cross on the spot where he fell. Since no cross was there, most scholars opted for the fever, but evidently the cross, like everything else in Mexico City, sank into the swampy soil and was lost until it was exposed again by an earthquake at the time of the Revolution.

tending him. By Tuesday, December 12, Juan Bernardino was obviously dying, so Juan Diego ran from the house toward the city to fetch a priest.

As he passed Tepeyac, though, the luminous Lady glided down from the hill-top to intercept him. She asked where he was going; when he told her, she was moved to tears and reproached him sweetly. "Listen, and let my words penetrate your heart, my dear little son. Do not be troubled or burdened with grief. Fear no illness, trouble, worry, or pain."

"Am I not here who am your Mother? Are you not under my shadow and pro-tection? Am I not your fountain of life? Are you not in the folds of my mantle, and in the embrace of my arms? What more do you need?" She paused, and then said, "Do not worry about this illness of your uncle. He will not die of it. As of this moment, he is cured."

Juan Diego was delighted to hear it, and offered to go at once to the bishop with the sign. The Lady told him to go up to the top of the hill and pick carefully all of the flowers that he'd find there, to gather them together, and bring them back to show them to her.

Now, Juan Diego knew that no flowers grew up there; even mesquite had a tough time surviving, and no flowers would be blooming at that time of year. But he went anyway and found the hilltop covered with Castilian roses, fresh with dew and heavy with fragrance. He spread out his *tilma*, the rough poncho-like garment, woven of maguey fiber, that all of the *campesinos* in the Valley of Mexico wore. He filled it with the roses and carried them down to the Lady.

She rearranged the flowers carefully, taking her time and considering the exact position of each and every one of them. Then she tied the bottom fringe of the *tilma*'s front around the back of his neck to keep them in place and said, "My little son, these flowers are the sign that you are to take to the bishop. Tell him, in my name, that he will recognize my will through them and that he must fulfill it. You are my ambassador, entirely worthy of my confidence."

"Do not unfold your *tilma*, nor reveal what it contains, until you are in the bishop's presence. Tell him everything. Explain to him how I sent you to the top of the hill and how you found these flowers growing abundantly, ready to be gathered. Tell him again everything that you have seen and heard, to lead him to comply with my wishes and build here the church for which I have asked."

The bishop's servants received him rudely, at first, but the penetrating fragrance of the roses stopped them. They let him in and ordered him to open his *tilma*, but, in obedience, he refused. When they threatened to manhandle him, he let them peek, but when the servants reached in to take roses out, the flowers melted into the *tilma* to appear like embroidery, or as if they were painted on. They let him in to see the bish-op, who was with Bishop Don Sebastián Ramirez y Fuenleal, then Governor of Mexico, and Juan González, the indispensable interpreter. Juan Diego told them what the Lady had said, and he opened his *tilma* to let the flowers fall.

The bystanders were astounded by the fresh Castilian roses.[224] But there was more. When Zumárraga looked up at Juan Diego, there appeared on the *tilma* a radiant picture of the Mother of God.

In silence, they all knelt, the Bishop, the Governor, and the interpreter. Juan Diego didn't know what to make of it until he looked down and saw the image himself. It was a portrait of the Lady he'd seen at Tepeyac, he said.

The story spread quickly, and the next day the image was carried in procession to the cathedral. At about noon, the Bishop and the Governor went with Juan Diego out to Tepeyac. They decided to build a little oratory immediately, while drawing up plans for a more suitable sanctuary. Juan Diego was delighted that the Lady's wishes were being taken seriously, and when everything was decided he asked permission to go home to his uncle. The Bishop agreed, and he sent along some of his servants; not this time as spies but as a guard of honor.

Juan Diego found his uncle well, as the Lady had said, and as Juan Diego had never doubted. But the unexpected thing was that Juan Bernardino knew all about what had happened. As he was lying on his deathbed, he said, the hut was filled with light as a Lady appeared to him. He felt cured instantly, and the Lady told him all about the miraculous image on his nephew's *tilma*. And she also told him the title under which she wanted to be venerated on the hilltop of Tepeyac: "Call me, and call my image, the Ever-Virgin, Holy Mary of Guadalupe."

At least, that's what the interpreter said that he said. This was surprising to the Spaniards, because Guadalupe is a famous Marian shrine in Extremadura, centered on another miraculous image of the Blessed Mother, a statue that had been given to St. Leander of Seville (*c.* 534-*c.* 600) by Pope St. Gregory the Great, hidden away during the Moorish wars, recovered through an apparition to a herdsman, and finally deposited by Alfonso XI of Castile in 1340 in the monastery of Guadalupe that he built to enshrine it. Columbus had prayed at that shrine before he left on his first voyage, and he had named one of the islands Guadalupe, but everybody was at a loss as to how Juan Bernardino could have known anything about all of this. In fact, nobody could figure out why she would have specified this particular title, of a shrine tied so closely to a kingdom half a world away, when she appeared in the New World.

But the chances are that "Guadalupe" isn't what Juan Bernardino said. Like anybody else native to the area, he would have found it very difficult to say that: Nahuatl doesn't use the sounds of the letters D, G, or R. The converted Aztecs called the Blessed Mother *Santa Malía*, and they didn't use the title "Guadalupe" for the shrine, or for the Lady, until more than a generation later, when they had all learned Spanish. Even today, most of them don't. And because the Lady herself spoke only in Nahuatl, she probably didn't say "Guadalupe", either. But there are Nahuatl words that make more sense.

During the canonical inquiry in the late seventeenth century, one scholar posit-

---

224. The published accounts vary; there may have been other kinds of flower with the roses, but in any event the Castilian roses, previously unknown in the New World, were the ones that bore significance to Zumárraga.

ed that Juan Bernardino had actually said, "Call me, and call my image, the Ever-Virgin, Holy Mary *Tequantlaxopeuh*." That might well be misunderstood as "de Guadalupe" by a native Spaniard who had picked up the language informally, especially if he were a missionary seeking answers about an apparition of Mary. In Nahuatl, that word means "the one who saves us from the Devourer", which would point to her role as the enemy of Satan and of the terrible gods of the area. Other scholars have settled on *tetlcoatlaxopeuh*, which would also sound like "de Guadalupe"; it means "she who crushes the serpent". Now, this would also have a double meaning. It refers to Mary's role in the Redemption (Gn 3:14-15, "The Lord God said to the serpent … I will place enmity between you and the woman, between her seed and yours, and she will crush your head with her heel"; see also Rv 20:2, which identifies the serpent as Satan). And it refers to the defeat of Tonantzin, Quetzalcoatl, and the other serpent-gods of ancient Mexico. Even today, some pilgrims to the huge sanctuary on Tepeyac sing to the Lady *teotl inantzin*—Mother of God—under the title *Santa María de Coatlalupe* or *Te Quatlasupe*, which seem to take a middle ground between the Old World and the New.

Whatever words they used, the pilgrims started coming almost immediately. In the decade following the apparition, some nine million Mexicans were baptized—one missionary, Father Toribio, reported that he and another priest baptized fourteen thousand two hundred people in only five days at Quecholac, and another, Father Peter of Ghent, himself baptized more than a million during his stay.

Today, more than twelve million a year come to the shrine, where the miraculous image is still on view. Like other images not made by hands, among them the Shroud of Turin, it's been studied and analyzed by scientists and art historians for more than a century.[225] And it does show some curious features. For one thing, the costume of the Lady isn't native Aztec costume nor even contemporary European clothing; she is dressed like a first-century Jewish woman. The image seems to increase in size the farther one stands from it, and, like that on the Shroud, the image of Guadalupe is not clear when seen close on; the details only appear clearly when one is standing far away. And, also like the image on the Shroud, the image on the *tilma* isn't painted on the cloth. Even under a microscope, there's no trace of brush strokes. And in any case paint can't be applied meaningfully to the rough, untreated fibers of maguey; the *tilma* itself has the texture of coarse, rather thin burlap. Chemical analysis finds no dye of any description on the fibers; the color is just there, permanently, on (or in) the maguey fibers.

In fact, it's interesting that the maguey hasn't decomposed after all of these years, as it normally would in about twenty years in that swampy area.[226] The thin cotton thread that attaches the two halves of the *tilma* hasn't given way, either, although the

225. The technical term for such an image is *acheiropoeton* (ah-kee-ro-PO-e-ton), which is from the Greek meaning not made by hands.

226. Not to mention the terrible industrial and automobile pollution that now fills the Valley. The swampy terrain, by the way, caused the old basilica of Guadalupe to sink so much that it had to be abandoned; the new church, built in 1976, is designed to withstand the shifts of the ground beneath it.

cloth it holds is far heavier than that thread should be able to bear even if new. And this despite hundreds of years of enthusiastic veneration by millions of pilgrims who have touched, kissed, and even embraced it, and thousands of sick people who have had the image draped over their bodies in hope of a cure.

Even more remarkable, the cloth is still clean, despite hanging for more than a century in a damp, windowless chapel full of burning candles, which not only spew waxy black smoke but also radiate corrosive ultraviolet light. It seems to be impassible, surviving a spill of the nitric acid being used to clean the gold frame in 1791 and an anarchist's bomb, hidden among the flowers at the altar, that went off during Mass on November 14, 1921. It tore up the masonry of the sanctuary, twisting a heavy iron crucifix like wax, and blew out all of the windows. But not one person was injured, not even the priest officiating at the shattered altar. Even the glass over the image wasn't cracked.

And the image seems to hold a lot more information than any manmade image could. Like the image on the Holy Shroud, it can't be successfully photographed, and no artist has been found in five centuries who can reproduce more than the general impression of the image. Computer analysis of the image has also revealed, in the eyes, tiny reflections of the people present when the image appeared: the face of Juan Diego was first seen in the 1920s, while those of Bishop Zumárraga and Juan González were discovered in 1962. They all accord exactly with known portraits of the people (until his portrait was discovered during renovations to the church in 1960, nobody knew what González looked like), and with the Purkenje-Sanson Law of Optic Physiology, which governs the shape and inversion of images reflected in the eye.

The bust of Juan Diego, the largest of the faces in the eye, was discovered independently again in 1951 by a draftsman looking at a photographic enlargement of the face, and again in 1956 by Dr. Rafael Torifa Lavoignet, who then looked at the eyes with an ophthalmoscope. He found that the eyes of the image, unlike those of painted or photographic images, react more like human eyes. They give the impression of hollow, three-dimensional bodies.

No matter how you look at it, the image of Our Lady of Guadalupe is a remarkable phenomenon. But there's another image, not so well known, that also captures the triumph of little Juan Diego and the miraculous conversion of Mexico. In the little church dedicated to Our Lady of Guadalupe in the village of San Lorenzo Río Tenco, just off the highway between Mexico City and Querétaro along the road to Tepotzotlán, the main altar is carved in a highly unusual form. It's held up by a figure of Juan Diego, his arms spread out to support the weight that rests on his shoulders and his bowed head. It's an unusual posture anywhere, and it's unique as part of a Christian altar, but two such figures have been recovered from old Aztec altars. Both represent Quetzalcoatl, holding up the eastern sky from which he had promised to return. Now the old gods are gone indeed, the serpent crushed; and the humble servant of Mary has taken the place of the civilizing god of the Valley of Mexico.

n i n e t e e n

R o m e   1 8 4 2

It is in this state that souls are most filled with lights,
and in it they form a loftier and clearer idea
of the divine mysteries...
though they may never have studied these subjects,
they speak with a facility and freedom,
and at the same time
with a precision, exactitude, and assurance,
that amaze learned theologians.
The reason for this is that ...
in these ineffable concepts
they learn the whole of a science at one stroke.

— Very Rev. John G. Arintero, O.P., S.T.M.,
The Mystical Evolution in the Development
and Vitality of the Church (1948)

Back in 1830, one of the Sisters of Charity of St. Vincent de Paul on the rue de Bac in Paris reported to her confessor—through the anonymity of the confessional grille—that she had seen the Blessed Virgin Mary. He told her, as confessors will, that it was just her imagination and that she should forget about it. But she came back a few months later to report that she had seen the Lady again. This time, the young nun said, the Lady stood on a large white sphere, crushing a large green serpent under her feet.[227] There were rays of light streaming from her outstretched hands, the nun said, which were explained by the Lady as the graces that she showers on those who ask for them.

The nun said that an oval then formed around the Lady, and around it were the words, "O Mary, Conceived Without Sin, Pray for Us Who Have Recourse to Thee."

227. Gn 3:14-15; also Is 27:1; Rv 14. The serpent is usually shown holding in its mouth the fruit of the Tree of the Knowledge of Good and Evil.

The oval turned around to show her its reverse, Mary's monogram with the holy Hearts of Jesus and Mary. The Lady ordered her to have a medal struck after that pattern, she said, and promised that those who wear it, blessed, around their necks, and who confidently say this prayer, will receive great graces and will enjoy the special protection of the Mother of God.

It took a long time, but the medals were eventually made, blessed, and distributed.[228] Almost instantly, there were so many miracles associated with its use—cures as well as conversions—that the medal came to be called the Miraculous Medal. Millions were made and worn throughout the world, and millions still are. Virtually any parish has at least one family who'll tell you of some exceptional favor that they've received in answer to an appeal to Heaven by way of the Medal, and there are plenty of certified miracles, officially investigated and officially published, in which that Medal and that prayer were pivotal. But there aren't many so dramatic as the history of what happened to Alphonse Ratisbonne.[229]

Tobie-Alphonse Ratisbonne was born in 1814 to prominent Alsatian bankers allied by marriage and by business to the Rothschilds, the Goulds, the Worms, and other wealthy families. He was orphaned at an early age, but his uncle took him in and raised him as his own. Alphonse grew up to be a handsome, dashing, charming sort of *bon vivant*, a man of aristocratic tastes in clothes, carriages, and concubines and absolutely no religion. "Neither in my uncle's home nor among my brothers and sisters was there the least attempt to practice Judaism," he wrote. "I was a Jew in name, and that was all. I didn't even believe in God."

He started his education at the Collège Royal in Strasbourg, but he soon transferred to a Protestant school there where, as he said, the sons of the great Protestant houses of Alsace and Germany went to train for the fashionable life in Paris. He learned a lot in that line before sitting for the finals, and when the grades came out he was as

228. Holy medals are among the oldest sacramentals; they've been found in the catacombs, and they were popular long before the cross could be worn in public. The life of this particular nun (canonized as St. Catherine Labouré) is worth reading about, and there are lots of good biographies of her in print. Until just before her death, nobody even suspected that it was she who was favored with the visions that worked such immense changes in the world, and she, never noted for intellectual ability, was content with the most menial and even disgusting jobs around the convent. Her body was found fresh and fragrant when her coffin was opened in 1933, incorrupt after fifty-seven years in the grave. It's now encased in a glass-sided altar on the spot where she saw Mary.

229. This account is compounded from several different books of the late nineteenth and early twentieth centuries, mostly from a letter that Ratisbonne wrote to the Abbé Dufriche-Desgenettes on April 12, 1842, about ten weeks after these events; see for example *Conversion de Marie-Alphonse Ratisbonne* (Paris, 1919); *l'Enfant de Marie* by Théodore de Bussières (Paris, 1842); *Venerable Catherine Labouré* by Rev. Edmond Crapez, C.M. (Emmitsburg, Maryland, 1918); and the *Narrazione storica della prodigiosa apparizione di Maria SSma Immacolata e instantanea conversione alla fede cattolica dell'ebreo Maria Alfonso Ratisbonne, avvenuta in Roma il 20 gennaio 1842, nella chiesa parocchiale di S. Andrea delle Fratte de' PP. Minimi di S. Francesco di Paolo* (Rome, 1892). The translations and even the French transcriptions of the letters and diaries vary somewhat, evidently from having been translated back and forth between languages, but the quotations here give the substance common to them all without adding anything.

surprised as anybody else to find out that he'd earned a bachelor's degree. Then, like his classmates, he moved to Paris, where he studied for a law degree in pretty much the same way. His uncle called him back to Strasbourg, after another equally surprising graduation, to make him a partner in the family firm.

Now, Alphonse never worried much about money. When he got out of a hired carriage, for instance, he'd just hand the driver his wallet and tell him to take out whatever the price was. Then he'd put the wallet back in his pocket without even looking at it, and he'd be on his way. But he treated charitable causes in just the same way—he was the major support of the local Jewish youth organization, the *Société d'encouragement au travail des jeunes Israélites*, the Society for the Encouragement of the Work of Young Jews. In fact, he used to send them his whole entertainment budget, which was considerable.

By the time he was twenty-eight, everything had fallen into Alphonse Ratisbonne's lap: money, education, position—everything but a wife. But the family had decided that he'd marry the daughter of his eldest brother, and his luck certainly held in that regard, too: his niece Flore was lovely, gracious, and smart, although she was as completely irreligious as he was himself. Still, he said, his love for her awakened in him some sense of human dignity that he hadn't felt before; and that feeling only deepened the love. The betrothal was set, and the family packed him off for a good long tour of Italy and the Levant before the wedding.

Before he left, he went to a meeting of prominent rabbis and laymen of the city who were trying to reform Judaism to bring it into conformity with the thought and culture of the time. The point of a *revealed* religion, of course, is to work it the other way, reforming the times to the religion's unalterable teachings, given by God; and Alphonse later recalled that "they said a lot about human custom, about the demands of modern times, of public opinion, and of civilization. But one thing was forgotten: the law of God. I don't know that the name of God was even mentioned, nor that of Moses, nor the Bible." He left feeling more certain than ever that religion wasn't good for much. He certainly didn't hear anything to change his life about, except that the episode reinforced his habit of making the most abusive puns about anything to do with religion, a habit that even his atheistic friends must have found embarrassing, if you go by his own record of some of the things he said.

He still spent the day before departure signing postdated checks for the *Société* so that they could meet their biweekly obligations in his absence. January 15, January 15, he wrote over and over again, so often that he got tired of writing that date. "God knows," he said, "where I'll be on January 15, or whether it might not even be the day of my death!"

His plan was to sail from Marseilles to Naples, then to Malta, and then to Constantinople before returning to Strasbourg for his wedding. As soon as he got to Naples, though, things started to unravel. Two family friends, a Rothschild and a Protestant banker named Coulman, tried to talk him into a side trip to Rome, but he refused. Rome was the center and capital of Christendom, and a man of his temperament didn't see anything there to attract him, not even the chance to make unprecedented numbers of execrable puns at the expense of the Faithful, the priests, and the Pope himself.

But the ship broke down, somehow, just before it was supposed to sail. Stuck in Naples for a month, Alphonse decided on a little more sightseeing. He was bored by then, and frustrated about the delay, and he wandered around Naples poking his head into anything that looked even remotely interesting. He happened into a church one day just as Mass was being celebrated. He leaned for a long time on one of the pillars in the back of the church, listening at first to the words and music, and his thoughts turned gently to his fiancée, his uncle, and his dead parents. On their behalf, the professed atheist lifted his mind to God. And then his thoughts focussed; he specifically asked God for support and guidance in his efforts to help his fellow Jews, a project, he said, that never left his mind.

All at once, he wrote, "the feelings of sadness left me like a black cloud blown away by wind. I felt an inward calm impossible to describe but imbued with a feeling of consolation like the feeling I might experience if I heard a voice say, 'Your prayer has been heard.'" Certainly, from that point on, things happened as if it was being answered, although—as with most answered prayers on record—not in anything like the way he'd hoped, or even in any way that he could see while it was happening.

He took a wrong turn when he went into the ticket office, and instead of heading for Malta he mistakenly bought a ticket for Rome. Well, fine, he thought; I may as well. When he got there, in the middle of that huge city that he had never visited and never wanted to visit, someone called out to him by name. It turned out to be Gustave de Bussières, whom Alphonse had met in elementary school. They had lost touch over the years, and about the only thing Alphonse knew about him at the time was that he had converted from Protestantism to join the Church and that he had a Catholic brother living in Rome, the Baron Théodore de Bussières. The De Bussières were a family possessed of really astonishingly good manners, taking Alphonse in during his visit and showing him around while putting up with the unending stream of verbal abuse that he shot at anything remotely connected with the Church to which they belonged, which is hard to avoid in Rome. But one day Alphonse happened to come down from the Capitoline Hill to pass through the Jewish Ghetto at its foot.

"I had never been so bitter against Christianity as I was after that visit to the Ghetto," he wrote later. "I could not refrain from mockery and blasphemy." He was thoroughly fed up and ready to go. One courtesy call on the De Bussières, he thought, and I'm going to Malta. He had intended to just leave his card there with the servant in the front hall, as people used to do when they knew how to use cards, and be on his way. But the servant on hall duty didn't speak French, so he just pushed Alphonse into the drawing room where the whole De Bussières family was sitting.

Despite the presence of the Baronne and all her children, Alphonse launched into a whole torrent of invective about the cruelty and stupidity of the Church, of

Christianity, and of anything else he could think of. Théodore de Bussières wrote in his diary that day that Alphonse lost all restraint in the matter and, when his hosts tried to temporize, to ask him at least to study the Faith a little before rejecting it so vehemently, he snarled, "A Jew I was born, and a Jew I will die!"

Well, then, De Bussières said, since your mind is made up, at least promise to wear something that I'm going to give you—it's only a little medal. And De Bussières showed him a little Miraculous Medal on a neck ribbon. Alphonse pushed it aside angrily and cracked a few more blasphemous (and humorless) jokes, but De Bussières persisted. Finally Alphonse accepted it, grudgingly and with more really rude jokes, saying that it would make a nice little curio that would show his fiancée just how superstitious Catholics really were. Then De Bussières pressed a little farther. "And promise me that, morning and evening, you'll say the *Memorare*, a very short and very effective prayer written in honor of Our Lady by St. Bernard."[230]

"Enough of this foolishness, please!" Alphonse burst out. He was sorry that he couldn't offer a Hebrew prayer in return, he said, but he didn't know any. At last, though, he agreed to copy out the prayer as long as he could keep M. de Bussières's original and leave him the copy. It would make a better souvenir to show around when he told the story in Strasbourg, he figured.

It was Saturday, January 15, 1842.

Well, something happened as he copied out that prayer the next day. The words got stuck in his mind, somehow, and as he went around touring Rome over the next few days phrases from it echoed in his consciousness. He kept wearing the Medal, as he had promised, and he said the *Memorare* morning and evening, as he had promised, but his insults to the Faith got worse and worse. If you go by the letters and diaries of the De Bussières and his other Roman acquaintances, it got nearly impossible to take him anywhere because of the foulness of his language. On one tour of the city, De Bussières and Ratisbonne ended up at the Gesù, the mother church of the Jesuits, where a French Jesuit, as Jesuits sometimes do, simply ordered him to kneel down and pray. But nothing worked.[231]

It speaks volumes about Théodore de Bussières's patience that he kept entertaining Alphonse Ratisbonne—who after all was only a school chum of his younger brother—but even he got tired of the ill manners, not to mention the unrelieved blasphemy. At last he exploded, albeit quietly, all over his guest. Despite the way you treat everything I say about the Faith, he said, "I am convinced that you will one day be a

---

230. People who make other people promise to pray usually stress how short the prayers are, but the *Memorare* really isn't all that long. It goes like this: "Remember, O most gracious Virgin Mary, that never was it known that anyone who fled to your protection, implored your help, or sought your intercession was left unaided. Inspired with this confidence, I fly unto you, O Virgin of virgins, my Mother. To you I come; before you I stand, sinful and sorrowful. O Mother of the Word Incarnate, despise not my petitions, but graciously hear and answer me. Amen." People used to ascribe it to St. Bernard, but evidently it was already old when he was a boy. Nobody knows for sure who first wrote it.

231. From what his hosts said and wrote, you get the impression that, far from wishing that he'd convert, they were just hoping that he'd shut up.

Christian, because you are basically such a just man that I believe that you will come to the light of truth even though it may mean that the Lord has to visit you by means of his heavenly angel." Well, that's about what it would take, Alphonse snapped back.

He went back to his hotel and packed for his departure from Rome, which had been rescheduled to the next day, January 20. That night, he said, he woke up with a start and saw a curious kind of cross before him, a cross of special shape, he said, without the Body of Christ being attached to it. It stood on a horizontal bar that was interlaced with the points of a large capital M. "I made an attempt to dispel the picture, but was unable to avoid it," he wrote. "Turn as I might from side to side, it was always in front of me. I can't say how long it lasted." Even at this point, Alphonse Ratisbonne hadn't connected the dots from one coincidence to another, linking into a grand and purposeful chain of events his unexpected trip to Rome, his unavoidable delays, the chance encounter with De Bussières, and his unceremonious entry into the family drawing room that fifteenth of January because the servant didn't speak French.

But the next day, January 20, there was yet another coincidence. Just as Alphonse Ratisbonne came out into the bright sunlight from the little café where he'd gone to breakfast, Théodore de Bussières was passing in his carriage. De Bussières invited his friend to drive with him, if he wouldn't mind that he had an errand to do at the little church up the street. Not at all, said Alphonse, and together they drove to the little church of Sant' Andrea delle Fratte.

De Bussières got out, suggesting that Alphonse wait for him in the carriage, but he got out, too, to see the inside of the dark little church. There was a funeral going on inside; a prominent member of the French colony in Rome, the Comte de Laferronays, had died suddenly a day or two before, and De Bussières had come to pay his respects. They had dined together last on January 16 at the Palazzo Borghese, and De Bussières had mentioned Ratisbonne to the Count and asked him to pray for his friend. "Don't worry," the Count had answered; "if you have him saying the *Memorare*, you already have him!" But because Alphonse had never met De Laferronays, he stayed apart from the obsequies and just wandered around looking at the church.

A black dog sprang across his path and disappeared. Then, he said, the church itself disappeared, and he saw nothing. Or, rather, he said, he saw something that words can't convey. As he recalled the incident a short time afterwards,

> Scarcely had I entered the sacred precinct when all at once I felt that I was in the grip of a disturbance impossible to describe. I raised my eyes. I could no longer see anything of the building. All of the light seemed to be concentrated in one of the chapels, and, in the midst of its brilliance, there stood upon the altar, in an attitude like that represented on my Medal, the Virgin Mary, beautiful, glorious, and embodying majesty and kindness all at once. An irresistible force drew me to her. With a motion of her hand, she bade me kneel, and she seemed to say, "It is well." She did not actually speak to me; still, I understood everything.

De Bussières wrote, "My absence had been a matter of no more than ten or twelve minutes at the most… When I returned, I didn't immediately see Ratisbonne, but then I found him on his knees before St. Michael's chapel." This chapel, he added, "as a matter of fact, contained neither painting nor statue of the Blessed Virgin." De Bussières continued, "I went up to him, and I had to touch him three or four times before he realized that I was there. Finally, he turned to me, his face covered with tears. He joined his hands and said in a way that I can't describe, 'Ah! How this man has prayed for me!'", looking toward the catafalque of the Comte de Laferronays.

"When M. de Bussières recalled me to myself," Ratisbonne wrote, "I was in tears and unable to answer his questions." He pulled out the Medal that was hanging on his chest and kissed it again and again. "I did not know where I was," he recalled. "I did not know if I were Alphonse or someone else. I felt so deep a change in me that I believed myself to be another person. I tried to regain consciousness of myself, but I could not." Nor could he speak about what had happened. "I felt within myself something so solemn and so sacred as to require me to ask for a priest."

M. de Bussières took him to one, back at the Gesù. During the ride, Ratisbonne kept kissing his Medal, crying profusely, and sobbing, "How happy I am! How good God is! How great are the graces of happiness! How we should pity those who do not know this happiness!" When they got to the church, De Bussières took him to see Father de Villefort, the Jesuit who had unsuccessfully commanded him to pray, and Father Johann Philipp Roothaan (1785-1853), Superior-General of the Society of Jesus. At first, Alphonse couldn't speak coherently; he just kept grabbing the Medal and sobbing, "I have seen her!" over and over again. At last he came to himself, and he told the fathers what had happened. Roothaan wrote that, although this was the first time he'd seen Ratisbonne,

> I at once recognized in him an emotion that manifested itself in his whole appearance. The Miraculous Medal of France was suspended around his neck. Without showing any enthusiasm, I watched him attentively. He uttered some broken words of gratitude to God for the favor he had received. "Half an hour ago," he said, "I blasphemed the religion of Jesus Christ, and now! Now I understand why I constantly saw the cross last night, a big black cross of peculiar form without the figure of Christ. It was impossible for me to turn my thoughts from it." A few hours later, accidentally looking at the reverse of the Medal, he recognized his cross, by no means so large as the one he saw in his vision, but identical in shape.

Alphonse Ratisbonne begged to be baptized; he didn't know how he could survive without it, he said. He said that he envied the sufferings of the martyrs that he'd seen in mosaics and paintings in Rome, and he begged De Bussières to take him to St. Mary Major, and to St. Peter's, so that he could give thanks to God. In those churches, he showed that he not only understood the True Presence in the Eucharist, but that it seemed to him a horrible obscenity to even approach it while yet unbaptized, still in the state of original sin—concepts completely absent in the teachings of contemporary Judaism, just as the teachings of Judaism, for that matter, were completely absent in Alphonse Ratisbonne.

In fact, over the next day or so, in his interviews with priests and laymen alike, Alphonse Ratisbonne showed a wide and full knowledge of dogmas relating to the Trinity, the Immaculate Conception, the Incarnation, the cycle of redemption, the Eucharist, and the communion of saints. He also knew that the Comte de Laferronays had prayed for him, as he first said just when De Bussières found him at the church. "How did I know it?" he asked. "I can't say, any more than I can explain how I learned all of the other things that I knew then. I had never opened any books dealing with religion; nor had I read a single page from the Bible. All I can say is that when I went into Sant' Andrea delle Fratte, I knew nothing. When I came out, everything was clear to me."

Naturally, word got around, and Alphonse was truly embarrassed by the attention, but he insisted on the reality of the apparition. He was even visited by a brusque military man, a General Chlapouski, who wanted to get to the bottom of the rumors once and for all. "Well, Sir," he blustered, "you've seen the image of the Blessed Virgin. Tell me in what way."

"The image, Sir?" answered Ratisbonne. "Why, I saw her, just as I see you." But he got tired of the crowds. All he wanted to do was pray. He also knew that his family would think that he'd gone mad, and that they might even commit him to an asylum. So he decided to become a Trappist, and live out his days in silence and prayer, away from the prying eyes of the world.

Father de Villefort called in the Father General of the Society of Jesus to consult on the matter, and they both talked Alphonse out of it. The public scrutiny and the humiliation, they said, were part of the cup that he, like any other Christian, had to drink, the cross he had to bear. They read him a passage from Scripture, Sirach 2:1-6, about endurance in the service of God, and Alphonse had to agree that it made sense.

He begged them to baptize him right then and there, but they thought it best to wait. "Why?" he cried. "The Jews who heard the Apostles were baptized on the spot! And you want me to wait after I've 'heard' the Queen of Apostles!" It was a good answer, and they asked him to make a retreat of preparation at the Gesù for a week beginning January 23. On January 31, 1842, Alphonse Ratisbonne was baptized and confirmed at the great Jesuit church.[232] He conducted himself surely and firmly during the whole ceremony of both sacraments, but when he received his first communion, he overflowed with emotion. He burst into sobs of joy and nearly fainted. He had to be carried back to his place.

Since all of these things happened in Rome, and since they attracted so much attention, a court of inquiry was convened immediately. It sat until early June. On the

232. This may seem like rushing it, too, giving Baptism and Confirmation on the same day, but it follows the Church's practice for admitting adults from outside the Church (Canon 7 of Laodicea).

third of that month, Costantino Cardinal Patrizi Nara, Vicar General of the Holy Father, Ordinary Judge of the Court of Rome, handed down the following decision:

> His Eminence, the Very Reverend Vicar of the City, has stated, pronounced, and declared that he fully assents to the truth of the remarkable miracle wrought by the great and good God through the intercession of the Blessed Virgin Mary in the instantaneous and perfect conversion from Judaism of Alphonse Marie Ratisbonne. And because it is honorable to reveal and confess the works of God, His Eminence, for the greater glory of God and the increase of devotion toward His Mother, is pleased to allow this signal miracle to be published.[233]

The conversion of Alphonse Ratisbonne was one of the miracles that hastened the institution of the Feast of the Manifestation of the Immaculate Virgin—the Feast of the Miraculous Medal, as it's usually called—celebrated every year on November 27.[234]

But what about Alphonse himself? About the same time the decree was issued, he entered the Society of Jesus, and in 1847 he was ordained a priest. After about six years, he left the Society of Jesus, with the permission of Pius IX Ferretti, to establish the Congregation of Priests and Ladies of Zion, an organization devoted to the conversion of the Jews. He went to Palestine as part of his work with the Congregation and on their behalf he bought the ruins of Pilate's *prætorium* where Jesus was condemned, and he built convents, orphanages, and churches in and around Jerusalem, and schools, including a school of mechanical arts.

In the course of his missionary work, he was arrested, mocked, and generally abused, but he stayed cheerful, with the candor and innocence of a child. He never talked about the apparition in the little church of Sant' Andrea delle Fratte, and he never gave out all of the details, only the ones that he had to reveal in direct questioning by the court of inquiry. But one day Mère Stouhlen, his co-founder of the Ladies of Zion, asked if she could ask a question—and asked if he would answer it. Surely, he said.

"Do you still see the Blessed Virgin?"

"She is more and more lovely," he answered. And then he sheepishly lowered his head.

233. Note carefully what this document does not say: it does not say that the Virgin Mary appeared to Alphonse Ratisbonne, only that his conversion—accomplished by God through her intercession—was miraculous, based on the facts that it was instantaneous (until that moment he had no history of religious training and was actively hostile to religion) and perfect (after that instant, he had no doubts, and he knew all he needed to know about the Faith without ever having studied any of it). It concentrates on Alphonse and neither asserts nor implies anything about what Mary did or didn't do, except intercede, and they knew that it had to be she from the natural, physical facts of the case, his sole religious activity being his adoption of the *Memorare* and the Medal. And it only allows the miracle to be published; it does not say that belief in it is enjoined upon the Faithful. This is an administrative document, not a doctrinal definition of anything. With any document touching miracles, you have to stick exactly to what is said, and pay the most careful attention to what is not said.

234. The Feast was instituted in 1894, which is extremely quick, gauged by the time it usually takes.

It's interesting that his history so amply documents not just the fact that he knew nothing about religion, but also that he knew absolutely nothing whatever about the ways in which these things happen, about their content or their pattern; yet the experiences that he reported followed exactly what the precedents indicate about a whole range of mystic experiences, from the gift of tears to a corporeal apparition and infused knowledge.[235]

And until the end of his earthly days his story continued to give examples of classic mystic phenomena. On his deathbed in 1884, he rose up in apparent ecstasy for about three minutes, his face shining, and then he gently dropped off to his rest.

235. It's also interesting that Ratisbonne wasn't alone in the pattern and nature of his conversion. The pianist Hermann Cohen, Liszt's star pupil and a friend of Georges Sand (who had an interesting conversion experience herself), was converted in a similar, though not so spectacular, fashion in Paris in 1847. He filled in as conductor at a Benediction service; emotionally and spiritually overwhelmed when he saw the Blessed Sacrament elevated, he started coming to services regularly after that. One day at Mass his conversion was completed, and from then on, his audiences heard powerful preaching rather than piano. Like Ratisbonne, he became a priest and a founder, establishing the Carmelite monastery of St. Simon Stock in Kensington, England, and serving as its first prior. He died in 1871 while serving as a chaplain in Germany during the Franco-Prussian War.

twenty

La Salette 1846

Now there is a pool in Jerusalem ... having five porticoes.
In these were lying a great multitude of the sick,
blind, lame, and those with shrivelled limbs ...
And the first to go down into the pool ...
was cured of whatever infirmity he had.

— John 5:1-4

On Thursday, September 17, 1846, a farmer named Pierre Selme hired an eleven-year-old boy named Maximin Giraud to tend his four cows near the little village of Ablondins in the parish of La Salette-Fallavaux, high above the clouds in the Alpine region of France. This is in the wild and mountainous Department of Isère, in the province that had been called the Dauphiné before the Revolution. It had been a beautiful and prosperous region, verdant with lush mountain pastures, freshened with copious fresh springs that ran into the green valleys to water abundant crops of potatoes, wheat, and grapes. But since the Revolution, since the Napoleonic wars, things had changed. The crops had failed from disease and pestilence, getting worse year after year. Even the springs and brooks had dried up. It was a hard life for the people of La Salette; calves, lambs, and even the children set to watch them were sometimes lost to wolves on the high pastures, pastures that would not now support more than a few cows.

That Thursday, Selme's regular cowherd was too sick to work, so the man hired Maximin for the week. Selme's pasture was six thousand feet up in the mountains, adjoining the meadow where another farmer, Baptiste Pra, kept his cows. So as it happened Maximin worked that day within sight of another cowherd, Mélanie Mathieu, although they didn't speak. Before dawn the next day they happened to start out from the village to the pastures at the same time, and they went out together again on the day after, Saturday, September 19, 1846.

Mélanie, fourteen, and Maximin had never met before that Friday. They were both from the same town of Corps, which only had about a thousand people in it, but their lives up to that day hadn't given them much time to run around with other children. Maximin was the son of a wheelwright, a man who drank most of the little he earned. The boy's mother had died, and his stepmother hadn't taken well to the boy. Basically, he spent his time running around in the streets getting into all kinds of mischief, except when his father took him along to the taverns.

Mélanie was one of eight children. Her father was a woodcutter whose work kept him away from home for long periods, and her mother, described as "wild", used to take her baby daughter to the local *cafés* to beg, or just turn her out into the streets of the village to ask for alms. Mélanie herself was silent and withdrawn, apathetic about learning, and unresponsive in the local school. Like Maximin, she had never learned to read, write, or know any significant part of her catechism. Neither of the children spoke French; their remote homeland is only about forty miles from the Italian frontier, and they spoke only a nameless border dialect. But Mélanie was dependable as a cowherd, and she had been working for some time tending the few cows belonging to Baptiste Pra when Pierre Selme was persuaded to take a chance on Maximin.[236]

At noon that Saturday, the children heard the bells of the village church and took the cows out of the pasture to a spring called the Fountain of the Beasts. They ate their bread and cheese and took a short nap on the grass. About an hour later they woke up and chased after the cows, by now strayed around in the meadows to graze. At about three-thirty, with the Sun already dipping below the peaks, the children gathered the cows together to head back to Ablondins. Mélanie looked down into the ravine and saw a globe of brilliant light, brighter than the Sun, gently vibrating.

She called out to Maximin, who also saw the globe. Its light grew brighter still, and the children were about to run away when they saw that it was opening. Inside, they saw, very clearly, a luminous Lady seated on a rock with her feet resting in the dry bed of a little brook that ran only in the rainy season or after the yearly thaw. She was holding her face in her hands and crying. Slowly and gracefully, she stood up, crossed her arms on her breast, and bowed her head slightly.

The Lady was wearing the ordinary costume of a peasant of the region, except glorified, somehow—her clothing seemed all of light. Her dress was shining white and gold, like her apron and shawl; and like her slippers the shawl was ornamented with roses. There were roses around her crown, too, which was the only unusual feature of her dress, apart from the golden chain that seemed to weigh down on her shoulders and another that held a crucifix around her neck, a crucifix with the Instruments of the Passion on its arms.

Mélanie dropped her staff in amazement; pick it up, Maximin said: if she does

---

236. The names given in the accounts vary widely. Pra's name is sometimes spelled Prast, which would be pronounced the same way. Names weren't often written down, at that time and place, because people weren't highly literate and because the towns are so small that most people knew each other anyway, and so isolated that it didn't matter if they didn't. Mélanie's surname is sometimes given as Calvat.

anything to us, I'll give her a good crack with mine. The Lady spoke to them, in French. They couldn't understand her very well, but they knew that she told them to come closer, not to be afraid, because she was going to tell them something of great importance.

They came within arm's reach of her, walking into the globe of light. Mélanie saw her in great detail, but Maximin couldn't see her face clearly; he saw only her forehead and her chin. But both heard her when she spoke. "If my people will not obey," the Lady said, "I will have to release my Son's arm. It is already so heavy that I can no longer restrain it. How long have I suffered because of you! I have had to pray unceasingly so that my Son will not abandon you. But you do not take the least notice of it. No matter how well you pray in the future, no matter how well you act, you will never be able to make up for what I have endured for your sake."

She reminded them of the commandment to rest on Sundays, which was neglected in the region at that time. "The carters cannot swear without using my Son's Name," she continued. "These two things are what make the weight of my Son's arm so heavy. It will be your own fault if the harvest fails. I warned you last year with the failure of the potato crop, but you paid no attention. Instead, when you found that the potatoes were rotten, all you did was swear; you abused my Son's Name. As a result, they continue to rot, and by Christmas there will be none left."

At this point, Mélanie turned to Maximin to ask what in the world "earth apples" were—the Lady had used the French *pommes de terre* rather than the local word for potato. "Ah, my children," the Lady said, "you do not understand French, do you? Well, I will speak to you more clearly." She repeated her message again in the local *patois*, and then went on in French.

"If you have grain, it will do no good to sow it. Wild animals will devour most of what you plant, and the rest will fall to dust as you flail it. A great famine is coming, but before that happens the children under the age of seven will tremble and die in their parents' arms. The adults will pay for their sins with their hunger. The grapes will rot, and the walnuts will spoil."

Having thus reminded them, and through them the community, of revelations like Gn 4:11-12, Lv 26:14-45, and Jb 29:1-6, the Lady turned to Maximin and said something that Mélanie couldn't hear, although she saw that the Lady was speaking. The Lady spoke privately to Mélanie, and then she addressed them both again in the local dialect. "If sinners will convert themselves, the very rocks will turn into piles of wheat, and the potato crops will be found to have sown themselves. Do you pray as you should, my children?"

The children admitted that they didn't, and the Lady, sadly, reminded them how important it is to pray morning and evening; say at least an Our Father and a Hail Mary, if you say nothing else, but if you can, you should pray more.

Then she broadened the subject to include the rest of the people in the region. "There are no more than a few older women who go to Mass in the summer," she said. "The rest work every Sunday. In winter, they go to Mass, because they don't know what else to do with themselves, but their behavior there is so bad that it is only a mockery of religion. And during Lent they all go to the butcher shops, like dogs. Have you ever seen rotted wheat, my children?"

They denied it, but the Lady reminded Maximin, in detail and with direct quotations, that he had, when he had gone with his father to a farm in another district. "Ah, yes," he said, "Now I remember, but I had forgotten."

In French, then, the Lady said, "Now, my children, you are to make this known to all my people." She turned and crossed the little brook, and without turning back to the children she said, "My children, will you not tell all my people what I have told you?" She moved to higher ground, walking six inches above the ground without moving the grass and without bending forward to get up the steep slope.

The children followed her to the ridge, where she looked up to Heaven, rose about five feet into the air, and stayed there for a moment. She and her globe of light glowed more brilliantly; then she ascended out of sight. Maximin grabbed at one of the roses on her slipper as she went, but it faded away in his fingers.

Other creditable visionaries never assert that they've seen Mary—only a Lady—but the interesting thing is that the seers of La Salette had no idea who this apparition was supposed to be. "It must have been God," Mélanie said, "or the Blessed Virgin my father talks about, or some great saint."

"If I had thought of that, I would have asked her to take us away with her," Maximin said.

The cowherds took the cows back to the village and had their supper in the houses of their respective employers. That evening, Mélanie was milking the cows in the barn when Maximin came over. "Did you see the Lady?" he asked Madame Pra. "A Lady all afire passing this way through the sky?" Mélanie came in from the barn, and the questions began.

After they told the Pra family what had happened, the farmers sat in stunned silence. Then Baptiste Pra's mother, old enough to remember the happy discipline of the days before the Revolution, spoke up. "You hear what the Blessed Virgin said? I guess you're going to work tomorrow after that!" She was the first to assert that it was Mary who had appeared, and the first to suggest that people observe the Sabbath in response to the message.

The children did as the Lady had told them and repeated the Lady's message to the rest of the villagers when they were asked. People streamed up to the rock on which the Lady had sat, on the bank of the dry stream bed, following the mayor, the town councillors, the police sergeant, and various priests and prelates who each in turn dragged the children up the steep mountain to the site to hear their story.

On one of these trips, someone wanted to break off a piece of the rock as a souvenir. He noticed that the dry spring had come to life, steadily pouring out clear water. They bottled some of it and took it back to a chronically ill woman in the village. She started a novena to the Blessed Mother, drinking a little of the water each day. On the ninth day, she was completely cured. Soon, more than twenty cures were reported from prayers and spring water, and La Salette is still a pilgrimage center where extraordinary healings—spiritual and physical—still happen.

But the greatest miracle of La Salette was the general conversion that spread across the whole region. It wasn't so much rabid fervor centered on the miracles, but a real turning of people's daily lives back into the habits of decency and self-respect. More and more people started lining up for confession; more and more started crowding into the little churches of Corps, Ablondins, and La Salette, as well as the larger ones in Grenoble and other cities in the region. Sundays became tranquil again, and feast days, degenerated into occasions for drunkenness and debauchery, became real festivals once more, with families having a good time together again.

And although the rocks didn't literally turn into piles of wheat, they did so metaphorically. The harvests were more than abundant, in following years. As the Lady had promised, the potatoes really did sow themselves, turning up in the fields without having been planted there.

The only people who didn't end up happy about the whole affair were Mélanie and Maximin themselves. They never got along very well, arguing about everything under the Sun, except their vision. On that, they always agreed absolutely, when interviewed separately or together, all of their lives. Naturally, there was an attempt to educate the children, and it was more or less expected that they'd enter religious life, but it didn't work.

Maximin never really reformed. Even after the apparition, he kept up his career as the village rapscallion. When the bishop came to interview him, the boy danced around him in circles, telling his story, and then ran ahead of the prelate into La Salette. While the bishop was trying to talk to the priest, the church bells kept ringing in an oddly muffled way. The parish bell-ringer investigated, pulling at the rope to clear away whatever was hitting it, but it still didn't ring clear. He climbed the tower to find Maximin straddling the bell, hitting it with rocks and his heels. When the bell started to swing, the boy had hung on, his body muffling the sound.

He was given the chance to prepare for the priesthood, but he had no vocation for it. He could never concentrate on his studies and never found a career that he could perform, and evidently he took to drink, just as his father had done. He was an honest and virtuous man who never changed his story about the apparition, but his life was such a disappointment that many people started to have some doubts on the occurrence.[237] He died, in full communion with the Church, at the age of forty.

Mélanie's story is even less edifying. She was sent to school, first at the nearby village of Corenc and later with the Sisters of Providence in Corps. It was extremely difficult to keep the children out of the public eye. Mélanie was even subject to unauthorized interrogations while boarding at convent schools. She went eventually to

---

237. Not that the personal behavior of a visionary makes any difference, but in Maximin's case it was compounded by a serious misunderstanding with St. John Vianney, the Curé (pastor) of the little town of Ars in France. See below, Part Five.

Darlington in England, about as far away from La Salette as she could get, and became a Carmelite postulant, but she didn't make the grade. She transferred to another convent in Marseilles, but she had no more vocation to the religious life than Maximin did. Well, she seems to have thought that she did, but nobody else agreed with her. She never came to terms with the self-effacement and obscurity that are integral parts of religious life, and she never embraced obedience.

She wandered up and down Europe, attracting a lot of the attention that she felt she deserved. She poured out a continuous torrent of abuse against any prelate who didn't treat her like a celebrity. She settled at Castellamare, near Naples, and in 1879 she published her secret, or what she said was her secret, in a book of her own that somehow got the *imprimatur* from the local bishop but was condemned by Rome—it also consisted largely of personal vituperations against clerics.[238]

Her contact with Heaven may have entrusted her with secret prophecies, but it evidently didn't turn her from expressing them by means of the minor vandalisms of childhood. Certainly, she scratched out the word "Paris" whenever she came across it in a book or on a map. And on her desk at the little convent school of Corenc, which she left shortly after the apparition, she carved the words *Prussians 1870*.

---

238. It was still commended to the clergy, presumably as an example of what to watch out for in a purported visionary.

t w e n t y - o n e

Lourdes 1858

I considered the words of ... St. Luke ...
"And all of the people sought to touch him,
for power went out from him and healed them all."
Therefore the Most Holy Sacrament ...
can heal the sick in soul and in body even now.

— Spontaneously cured priest,
quoted by Thomas à Kempis,
Chronicle of Mount Saint Agnes (*c.* 1465)

On January 18, 1862, the Bishop of Tarbes released the final conclusions of his ecclesi-astical commission on the apparitions at Lourdes, a parish in his diocese.[239] "We judge that Mary, the Immaculate Mother of God, did truly appear to Bernadette Soubirous on the eleventh of February, 1858, and on subsequent days, to the number of eighteen times in all," it read in part, "in the grotto of Massabielle, near the town of Lourdes; that this apparition bears every mark of truth, and that the Faithful are justified in believing it as certain. We humbly submit our judgement to the judgement of the Sovereign Pontiff, who is charged with the government of the universal Church... We authorize in our diocese the veneration of Our Lady of the Grotto of Lourdes... We propose to build a sanctuary on the site of the Grotto ..."

But although the great shrine at Lourdes is what it is, and where it is, because of a creditable apparition of Mary, almost all of the public prayers offered there are

---

239. The best account of the events at Lourdes easily available in English is *The Song of Bernadette* (New York, 1942) by Franz Werfel, one of the more than eighty thousand refugees who were sheltered, fed, and protected at Lourdes during World War II. The film version (directed by Henry King, 1943) follows the book accurately and in great detail; much of the dialogue is taken directly from depositions made in the official investigation. The standard biography of St. Bernadette, a remarkable person who undoubtedly would have been canonized without any apparitions, is François Trochu's *Saint Bernadette Soubirous 1844-1879* (London, 1957, reprinted Rockford, Illinois, 1985).

addressed to Christ, just as in any other liturgy of the Church. Only a few of them address Mary directly and, like any other prayer to any other saint, they only ask Our Lady of Lourdes to pray for us.

And of course, although Mary is venerated under the title Our Lady of Lourdes, the people of any locality can adopt her as their patroness and venerate her under an appropriate name—they only need the permission of the local ordinary (the bishop or mitered abbot who has ordinary jurisdiction over the diocese). That's why there's the cathedral of Our Lady of Paris, or the shrine of Our Lady of Loreto, and countless obscure parish churches around the world with similar local titles.

The really interesting thing about the Shrine is that only about one-tenth of the public prayers regularly offered at Lourdes mention cures of the body. In fact, out of the two million or so pilgrims who come to Lourdes every year, only about one in a hundred comes seeking a cure for some physical ailment. The rest are seeking a spiritual cure—a conversion, perhaps, a return to religion, or the gift of oneself to God in acceptance of his will. The answers to these prayers of the spirit are the hidden miracles of Lourdes, and they must constitute the majority; fewer than a hundred cures of the body have been certified as miracles there, to date. And, like most of the other cures of body and soul reported at the Shrine, they generally occur during the Blessing of the Sick that's administered every afternoon.

Like all of the other liturgies at Lourdes, this one is nothing unique; any parish priest can, and does, bless the sick of his parish as need arises. But this particular ceremony takes a special form. At about four o'clock every day, the baths at Lourdes are closed down, and the pilgrims, troubled in body or in spirit, gather in the large square in front of the Rosary Church. The Blessed Sacrament is carried out in procession, with a priest carrying a consecrated Host in a monstrance under a canopy. And, as the priest blesses the pilgrims with the Host, he and they pray verses from the Gospels:

> Jesus, Son of David, have mercy on us!
> Master, save us, we perish!
> Lord, he whom you love is sick!
> Lord, that I may see!
> Lord, that I may hear!
> Lord, that I may walk!
> Lord, speak but the word, and your servant will be healed!
> Lord, if you will, you can make me whole!
> You are the Christ, the Son of the Living God!
> Lord, your will be done, on Earth as it is in Heaven![240]

So the procession of the Sacrament at Lourdes is a constant continuation of Christ's own passage through the crowds in the Holy Land, when he drew pilgrims to be cured

240. Those would be Mt 8:2, 8; 9:27; 20:30, 33; Lk 8:24; Jn 11:3, etc.

from as far away as Syria.[241] It's also an echo of the essential act of Christian worship, the Mass, when Christ comes again and again in the Sacrament to meet his people physically and offer his healing. Certainly, every parish has the Blessed Sacrament available always and everywhere, and Lourdes claims no other source for the physical and spiritual cures that happen at the Shrine: the miracles of Lourdes can be paralleled at your local parish church, and in a surprising number of cases, they are.

But wherever miraculous cures take place, and regardless of whether they're physical or spiritual, they make sense only in a view of the universe that sees the place of suffering in the Great Scheme of Things. From the Church's viewpoint, it's not part of Christianity to ask, if there is a God, what's he doing about all of the suffering in the world? As that viewpoint is expressed in the Bible, God doesn't cause all of this misery. Sin does. God made the world and saw that it was good, but death and corruption entered with sin. By disobedience, Adam and Eve made our lives imperfect, and by sinning again and again, pushing ourselves willfully farther and farther from God, we keep it that way. There can't be a break or accident in the realm of divine love, but we humans have exiled ourselves from that realm by sin. In other words, our bodies, like our souls, get badly battered by this world, but it's our fault that this happens.

Spiritual or physical miracles can be seen as one way that God reminds us that this isn't the way he wants things to be. They can be thought of as a spark of contact that breaks through the barrier of sin and reminds us that security, health, strength— happiness itself—reside in a close relationship with God and a willing embracing of his will, living in the divine order of things. That's the reason that Christ gave for performing his physical miracles while he walked among us: to show that he has not only the power to overcome the effects of sin but the power to forgive sin, the cause of all of this suffering (Mt 9:1-7). He did them to get people thinking about their relationships with God, and to show them that what he, and he alone, said about that relationship is true (Mt 4:23, 7:29, for instance, and Jn 3:1-15); and he wasn't happy about it when people didn't get the point.[242]

But then it's easy to get stuck in our own time and place, thinking that Christianity is something pressed between the pages of the Bible, something that hap-

241. As in Mt 5:23-25; 8:16-17; 9:1, 18, 20, 27-31; and similar passages in the other synoptic Gospels, as well as Jn 6:1-2; etc. It's important to remember that this procession of the Blessed Sacrament is not a representation of Christ's healing journeys, nor a memorial of them, but, as the Church teaches, the living, physical presence of Jesus of Nazareth in procession among his faithful who seek healing.

242. Mt 11:20-24. The sin of heresy, willful denial of some or all of Christ's truths, or even persistence in adherence to an heretical creed in good faith, as many sincere people honestly seeking Christ are persuaded to do, particularly keep people away from genuine mystic phenomena. "Miracles are beyond the power of nature," St. Alphonsus of Liguori explained. "They can happen only by the power of God, to whom all nature is subject. Accordingly, if a religion has real miracles to show in confirmation of her doctrine, that religion must be divine, for it is impossible for God to sanction and promote a false religion by the performance of genuine miracles." Can other sects and religions, he asks, point to a single miracle wrought in favor of their religious tenets? "They have no doubt made efforts in the past to deceive the people by trickery and the seemingly miraculous," he said, "but the deception was soon discovered." And, indeed, creditable miraculous cures are of an entirely unique nature not experienced outside the Church; see below, Chapter 29.

pened long ago and far away, when God was closer to Man, and people were as different, somehow, as their way of life was different from ours. Our modern world is past
all of that, we often assume. At the mention of reported cures, most of us might be
inclined to stand with that exasperated soldier sent to control the crowds at Lourdes in
1858, the one who shouted, "to think that this kind of nonsense can happen in the nineteenth century!" But even Bl. Raymond of Capua, the biographer of St. Catherine of
Siena, said how strange it was that miracles like hers would happen "in our times"—in
his case, the fourteenth century.

People are people, and Christianity hasn't changed since it was revealed to us,
not within the Church, anyway. There have always been debunkers and scoffers, from
the Pharisees who carped about Christ's working miracles because he did them on the
Sabbath. But three cases in particular serve as good examples of what happens at
Lourdes because they occurred recently enough to be photographed, as well as diagnosed and supervised by an established board of doctors that most of us would trust,
and confirmed by *post-mortem* examination.[243]

One of the most famous Lourdes cures didn't take place at Lourdes at all, but
at a shrine dedicated to Mary under the title Our Lady of Lourdes, in Belgium.

THE CASE OF PIERRE DE RUDDER

In 1867, two men had just finished cutting down a tree on the estate of the Viscount du
Bus de Gisignies, near the little Belgian town of Jabbeke. Pierre de Rudder, one of the
farm workers, offered to help them clear it away, taking an axe and chopping down a
bush that was in the way of the trunk. The other two men shifted the trunk at that
moment, and it came down on De Rudder, crushing the lower part of his left leg in a
severe compound fracture.

The Viscount sent instantly to nearby Oudenbourg for the local physician, Dr.
Affenear. The doctor set the leg and immobilized it in a starched bandage, but the pain
was unbearable—remember, this was before very many painkillers, except opium and
morphine, were readily available; Felix Hoffman, the chemist who first made aspirin
readily available, wasn't even born until the year after De Rudder's accident. De Rudder,
after a few weeks of suffering, implored the doctor to take the bandage off.

Affenear was appalled at what he saw. The compound fracture hadn't healed
correctly at all. It was still open, and horribly infected. The bones hadn't even begun to
knit; their blackened and jagged ends could be seen, completely necrotic, once the pus
had been rinsed away—this was also long before the advent of antibiotics or even anti-
septics. The bone fragments in the wound had to be removed, which left more than an

243. These and many other cases are related in surprisingly few sources in English, notably E. Le Bec,
Medical Proofs of the Miraculous: A Clinical Study (London, n.d.), Don Sharkey, *After Bernadette: The
Story of Modern Lourdes* (Milwaukee, 1945), and some few others that give generally fewer details.
Sharkey's accounts of these and other cures, assembled from newspapers, interviews, medical and legal
records, and pamphlets no longer available, constitute the standard English-language history of the
notable cures at Lourdes, and most subsequent publications, like the present account, are largely based
on his work. Both it and Le Bec's book are unfortunately long out of print and unavailable.

inch between the main parts of the bones. Three more doctors agreed with Affenear that the leg had to come off; but De Rudder refused the amputation. He washed the wound two or three times a day, but it never healed, and the infection never went away.

Because De Rudder obviously couldn't work any more, the Viscount pensioned him off at eight francs a week and let him continue to live in his little house, rent free. Four or five years after the accident, De Rudder started asking for enough money to make a pilgrimage to the shrine of Our Lady of Lourdes at Oostacker, two miles from Ghent. At that time the shrine was just a decorated corner in the garden of the Marquise de Calonne et Courtebourne, open to the public on Sunday afternoons, so while the Viscount said that he'd continue to pay all of De Rudder's medical bills, he wasn't going to pay good money for any nonsense like that. But then in July of 1874 the Viscount died and was succeeded in the title by his son.

The new Viscount had a softer heart than his father, evidently, and in December of 1874 he called in another doctor, a Dr. Van Hoestenberghe from Stahille. Van Hoestenberghe recorded that there was no bone connection between the upper part of De Rudder's leg and the lower; they were separated by more than an inch where the fragments had been extracted, and the wound hadn't even begun to heal. If he could get past the pain of it, De Rudder could double his leg over, or turn it so that his toes pointed backward.

As late as 1875, yet another doctor, Dr. Verriest of Bruges, saw De Rudder and urged him to have the leg amputated. De Rudder still refused, and all of the doctors, Verriest, Van Hoestenberghe, and Affenear, shrugged and left him to suffer as he wished. There was nothing else that they could do.

By now De Rudder's family was in serious and hopeless poverty, so on April 5 of that year he went up to see the new Viscount again. The young man's fiancée happened to be at the castle, and she was curious to see what the trouble was. De Rudder obligingly took off the linen bandages, soaked with pus and blood, revealing not only the raw wound and the dead broken ends of the bones but an unendurable stench. Evidently, seeing the wound in this condition so long after the accident was too much for the Viscount, too, and he arranged for De Rudder to go to Oostacker on the seventh.

By 1875 the little garden shrine at Oostacker had established a reputation for prodigies of spiritual and even physical healing, if not certifiable miracles; it had become so popular that a large, gothic-style church was being built on the site, and at that moment plans were being made to lay the cornerstone on May 22. But on April 7, 1875, the shrine was still just an artificial grotto with a statue of Our Lady of Lourdes in it and a fountain under it, to represent the River Gave.

Some of De Rudder's neighbors dropped in that morning to talk about the trip, which was pretty exciting for people of their condition at that time and place. They saw him dress the wound, or even helped him dress it, and they all looked at it with abiding interest. He even folded his leg over for them, and let them twist it around. Then De Rudder, his wife, and two friends went by train to Ghent, where they got on a bus for the trip to Oostacker. The bus driver, seeing the leg swinging free, joked about it—look, he laughed, here's a man who's losing his leg! He stopped laughing when he saw blood and discharge all over the floor of his bus, but he did carry Pierre from the bus to the ground at the shrine.

De Rudder hobbled over to the shrine and began to pray. He begged Mary, under the title of Our Lady of Lourdes, to intercede for him, but he wasn't asking for a cure. He asked for some kind of a job, a way to support his family. Lost in prayer, recollected, he didn't realize at first that he was walking around without his crutches; but at last it dawned on him that he was kneeling in front of the shrine.244

He ran out to catch the bus again—the bus driver with the crude sense of humor eventually converted, after seeing this. After this, De Rudder attracted all kinds of attention from researchers, freethinkers, and other skeptics. But the cure was so complete, and so astonishing, that any number of people converted: not just doctors and other investigators but people in Jabbeke, even the new Viscount. Dr. Van Hoestenberghe eventually converted, too, and even wrote to Lourdes about it in testimony to the miracle.

De Rudder went back to work as a woodcutter until he died twenty-three years later. Van Hoestenberghe asked the family for permission to exhume the body and remove the legs for examination. Because of the extraordinary nature of the cure, they agreed. The doctor found that the two sections of bone in the injured leg, pock-marked and eroded from years of infection, were joined by an entirely new piece of healthy white bone more than an inch long, perfectly formed, joining the two severed sections precisely.

(Sometimes, people who would rather not believe in miraculous cures ask why, if people are really cured by Heaven, why aren't they entirely cured? Why are there still scars on the flesh, and why are there still scars on the bones? Well, the obvious answer is that these cures are intended as signs; and if you lose any and all signs of the condition, you can't very well be shown in testimony of a cure. Christ himself, risen and glorified, still bears the marks of the Crucifixion, so that people will know that it is he, even though such a tangible proof shouldn't be necessary; Jn 20:24-29.)

The bones themselves were on display for some years, and the doctor's photographs, as well as all of De Rudder's medical records, have been published more than once. Yet this isn't the only regenerative miracle associated with Lourdes.

The Case of Gabriel Gargam

In 1901, for instance, Gabriel Gargam arrived at Lourdes itself, having been paralyzed from the waist down in a train accident some time before.245 He was a postal clerk work-

244. Through the centuries, there are countless similar cases of hopelessly ill people cured while praying for people even worse off, notably that of Mountaha Daher of Bekassin, Lebanon, a fifty-year-old woman disfigured since birth by a serious skeletal deformity that hunched her back and distorted her shoulders and chest. While she was praying at the tomb of St. Charbel Maklouf for needy relatives, her deformities were corrected (cf. Lk 13:10-13). Evidently, she isn't the only such case cured through prayers at his tomb at the monastery of St. Maroun in Annaya.

245. Paralysis, by the way, is usually excluded from consideration when it comes to miraculous cures, because it's a symptom that can be caused by hysteria, as Benedict XIV pointed out. Of course, hysteria

ing in the mail coach at the rear of the Paris Express. The train unexpectedly stopped in the middle of the night at a bend in the track, and a second train came speeding along the track, its engineer unable to see the first train's lights. It crashed into the stalled coach, killing one of the clerks, battering Gargam and throwing him forcefully into the snowy countryside.

He lay there all night until he was found the next morning. Once he got proper medical care, his broken bones healed in good order, but he had severe internal injuries that didn't. He was paralyzed from the waist down, and he had to be fed through a tube—only once a day, because he couldn't stand the pain of more than one feeding.

During the next year, Gargam's case was in and out of court time and again, so the legal records detail the man's horrific suffering. He was never in stable condition. One of the hospital attendants saw that the man's feet had turned completely black; the skin came off at a touch, releasing decomposed matter and pus. The infection and paralysis spread, and before long he lost his voice, too. But his parents never gave up hope. He himself hadn't seen the inside of a church in years, but Gargam's mother was devout, praying constantly for a spiritual cure for her son. And his father prayed, too, having had a kind of conversion experience after his son's accident.

Evidently because he wanted to get away from the doctors, who kept insisting on operations, Gargam went along with the idea of joining the national pilgrimage to Lourdes. In preparation for the trip, he went to confession and received communion, as best he could in his condition, but he later said he didn't feel much different about it all.

The train trip was extremely difficult for Gargam, immobile on his stretcher with his feeding tube inserted. He turned willfully from the crucifix that his mother showed him when they got to Lourdes, and he went to the grotto for communion in his perfunctory manner. But the minute he took the little particle of Host this time, he felt an intense desire to pray, and his faith returned instantly. He surrendered his life to God through Our Lady with all his heart. Later that day, during the Eucharistic procession and Blessing of the Sick, though, he went pale and passed out, his whole body turning so cold that bystanders thought he had died.

As the procession with the Blessed Sacrament passed by, he came to himself and tried to sit up on his stretcher. "Help me!" he cried. "I can walk! I feel that I can!" His attendants wrestled him back onto the stretcher, but his mother pointed out that the man hadn't been able to say a word in nearly two years, so they helped him to his feet. He walked a few steps, following the Sacrament in procession, until his people led him back to his stretcher. Then they took him to the Medical Bureau. There were sixty doctors there that day, and a lot of reporters, but the crowd was so exhilarated by the apparent cure that they couldn't examine him that day. Gargam had to be taken back to the hospital.

is itself a disease, but, "when it is a question of hysteria," he wrote, "it will not do to make the miracle consist in the disappearance of the crises, but in the cessation of the morbid state that has produced them."

Once he was there, he called for dinner. He refused his feeding tube and ate the regular meal, the first solid food he'd had since day of his accident.[246] The next day, he walked by himself to the Medical Bureau, where they found scars from his gangrene but otherwise healthy flesh—except that his leg muscles were gone. The head of the Bureau, a Dr. Boissarie, said that they had to certify that, from a medical viewpoint, the man couldn't walk, not without leg muscles. But he did.

After that, Gargam put on weight and got all of his strength back. Nobody disputed that such a hopeless case, reversed so completely and so instantaneously, could be anything other than a miracle. Even the railroad company accepted the reality of the situation. It immediately discontinued Gargam's lifetime pension.

But another organization, required to indemnify a permanent invalid, seems to have been really rather confused by a cure at Lourdes.

THE CASE OF JACK TRAYNOR

Jack Traynor was pensioned off by the British War Ministry in 1915 for wounds suffered in World War I. He'd been unconscious for five weeks after being hit in the head with shrapnel at Antwerp in 1914, shot later in the leg in Egypt, and sprayed with machine-gun fire in the Dardanelles.

He still carried a bullet lodged in his collarbone, and he was left with his legs paralyzed partially and his right arm paralyzed completely, atrophied and skeletal. None of the repeated operations he had could reattach his muscles or reverse his paralysis. Also, the operation for the shrapnel in his skull left a hole an inch wide, through which his brain could be seen. The doctors covered it with a silver plate, but the trauma left him epileptic; he had as many as three seizures a day. By 1923, he was a complete invalid.

Now, Traynor was the son of an Irish Catholic mother, and, although she had died when he was very young, she had instilled in him a lasting devotion to the Blessed Mother. So when he heard that the local diocese of Liverpool was organizing a pilgrimage to Lourdes, he decided to go. His doctor said that the trip would be fatal. Traynor looked so bad that even one of the organizing priests tried again to talk him out of it. But his wife knew how much Jack wanted the trip, so she pawned some of her jewelry and sold some of their furniture to pay for the ticket.

The story got around, so there was a crowd of reporters and photographers at the station to cover his departure. There were so many onlookers that he couldn't get to the first train and had to wait for the next. Even then people were so alarmed at his appearance that they tried to talk him out of it. I'm going, he said, if I have to ride in the coal tender.

Three times along the way the pilgrimage organizers tried to get him off the train and into a local hospital. He reached Lourdes on July 22, 1923, more dead than alive, and was taken to the hospital there.[247] Two Protestant girls who worked there as

246. He had soup, oysters, a chicken wing, and a bunch of grapes.

247. Maybe "hospice" is a better word; people are sheltered there, but not treated. It's just a place for the sick to eat and sleep while they're at the shrine.

volunteers recognized him from the newspapers and took him under their wings, but his epileptic seizures and hemorrhages were so bad that a woman there took it upon herself to write to Traynor's wife. He'll undoubtedly die, she wrote, but not to worry—they'd bury him at Lourdes.

But his determination didn't waver. He bathed in the *piscines*, the pools that hold the spring water, a total of nine times, although the attendants didn't always want to take him through. It wasn't so much that they thought he'd die from being put into the cold water but that they thought he'd die in his wheelchair before they got him there. He had a seizure on the way, once, and when he came to himself the attendants turned the chair around to take him back to the hospital. But Traynor grabbed the wheel with his good hand with every ounce of his strength and wouldn't let go until they promised to take him.

Finally, on June 25, 1923, his legs became agitated while he was in the water, and he tried to stand on his own two feet, but the attendants kept him down. They wheeled him over to the plaza for the Blessing of the Sick. As the priest carrying the Blessed Sacrament passed, blessing him, his right arm, "which had been dead since 1915," he said, "became violently agitated. I burst its bandages and blessed myself—for the first time in years." He started to stand up, which should have told people that something marvelous had happened, but the attendants thought that he was hysterical and injected him with a sedative. They took him back to the hospital; once there, he explained that he knew that he could walk, and he took seven steps to prove it. Evidently they weren't impressed; they gave him another shot and put him to bed. They even put special attendants to stand guard over him all night, to make sure he didn't injure himself by doing anything rash.

He was awake most of the night, he said, after the injections wore off. Early the next morning, he dozed off for a few seconds, and then knelt on the floor to finish the Rosary he was saying. Then he dashed out the door, pushed the guards aside (he was wasted down to a hundred and twelve pounds by then, but he had the element of surprise on his side), and ran barefoot across the gravel to the Grotto, so fast that the attendants running after him couldn't catch him. He knelt on the bare ground to thank the Virgin. By the time the attendants got there, they realized what had happened, but the interesting thing is that Traynor didn't. He couldn't figure out why he was attracting a crowd. He didn't seem to remember how sick he'd been for all those years.

He went to the washroom at the hospital, got dressed, and went back to the ward. A visiting priest asked if anybody wanted to serve Mass, and Traynor volunteered. The priest didn't know him, and didn't think that anything was unusual. After serving, Traynor went to breakfast, drawing another astonished crowd. "I wish they'd leave me alone," he said. When people breathlessly asked him if he were all right, he answered simply, "Yes, I'm quite well, thank you, and I hope you feel well, too." He didn't understand why the people burst into tears, after he said that.

Finally, on the way home, Archbishop Frederick William Keating of Liverpool came to Traynor's compartment and asked him, "John, do you realize how ill you have been and that you've suddenly been cured by the Blessed Virgin?"

"Suddenly," Traynor recalled later, "everything came back to me." He telegraphed his wife, but all he said was "Am better". She was glad to hear it, having been deeply upset by that volunteer letter about how they were going to bury him at Lourdes. By the time Traynor got back to Liverpool, everybody in town had heard all about the cure—it was in the papers—but oddly enough Mrs. Traynor hadn't. Her friends had kept her in the dark, thinking that the surprise would be nice.

Once again, there was a huge crowd at the station, so thick that Mrs. Traynor couldn't get through. Even the mention of her name didn't help; the station manager said that seventy or eighty women had already been allowed on the platform on the strength of the same claim. The archbishop came out of the train first and asked the crowd to restrain themselves when they saw Traynor, and then to leave him in privacy. They promised to behave, but they stampeded when he walked out of the train. The police had to escort him out.

His restored arm showed new nerves and muscles, although his right forearm was a little thinner than his undamaged left one, and the hole in his skull had closed instantly with new bone. With his strength and health restored, Traynor went into the hauling business, hefting two-hundred-pound sacks of coal all day long.

His stubbornness had paid off. It was almost incredible in a man in his condition. But it was nothing compared to the stubbornness of the British War Office. They had officially declared him incurable and 100-percent disabled, and, miracle or no miracle, they repeatedly refused to cancel his pension.

twenty-two

Pontmain 1871

I feel confident that God's justice,
which is punishing us at this moment,
will yet be appeased by this tender Mother ...
I also think that the Prussians are only doing their job.

— St. Bernadette Soubirous,
Letters (November-December, 1870)

From the fall of the Roman Empire until the turn of the twentieth century, there was no German state comparable in size to France or Italy, as there is today. "The Germanies" were grouped into a Holy Roman Empire, a patchwork of a few hundred tiny states, each with its own government and its own history. Some were storybook kingdoms or vest-pocket principalities; others were just independent cities encapsulated in their mediæval walls. Nine of them were ruled by electors, little monarchs who had the right to vote for the Kaiser—the old German word for Cæsar, or emperor—a title that went back to Charlemagne in the ninth century.

But in the seventeenth century a poor, cold, sandy little state in the very northernmost part of the Empire began a program of expansion. The electors of Prussia couldn't grow crops very well, so they grew armies; they turned their dominions into the Sparta of the North, a society run on military lines. They took over first one neighbor and then another, adding more and more territory to their holdings, and by the turn of the eighteenth century the Elector had forced the Emperor to raise him to the rank of King. By the time of King Frederick the Great, who reigned during the American Revolution, the center of power in the Empire had pretty well shifted from the imperial capital of Vienna to the Prussian capital, Berlin. And the Prussian kings went on expanding their realms and influence, while the Habsburg emperors were powerless to stop the endless little internal wars that tore their empire.

The Holy Roman Empire fell apart entirely, in fact, when the Kaiser Franz II had to abdicate during the Napoleonic Wars of the early nineteenth century. Franz took the title of Emperor of Austria, but he no longer ruled the German states themselves. They contracted various confederations and customs-unions that came and went with the passing years and never really meant anything anyway. The way was clear for a new imperial order, and when King Wilhelm I came to the throne of Prussia in 1861 he decided to take advantage of the situation.

The first thing he did was appoint Otto von Bismarck as his chancellor, and together they planned the final unification of all German-speaking states into a single country, to be governed by themselves. They began building up their armies, and in 1864 took Holstein from Denmark, just to see if their new military machine worked. It did; so in 1866 they shuffled their diplomatic cards and provoked a war against Austria and her allies—a war remembered as the Seven Weeks' War because they won it so quickly. The various treaties that followed the armistice put Prussia firmly in control of Germany, and they prompted France to decide that a war with this new and more powerful German federation was inevitable.

France began to arm immediately, and by the late summer of 1870 the Franco-Prussian War had begun. By December 27 the Prussians had invested Paris; shortly after that they occupied the capital and burned the palace of the Tuileries, the residence of Napoléon III, that extended across the Place de la Concorde at the western end of the Louvre's gardens. They swept across the countryside west of Paris, too, through Normandy and into Brittany, their Twentieth Division's General Karl von Schmidt pushing on toward the French defensive line that stretched from Mayenne to the city of Laval.

At about five o'clock in the evening of January 17, 1871, twelve-year-old Eugène Barbadette came out of his father's barn in the little town of Pontmain, just inside the French defensive line. He looked up from the snowy street to the starry sky, and he saw a Lady, a smiling Lady of great beauty, standing in the air above and between the two great stone chimneys of Jean and Augustine Guidecoq's house just across the way. She wore a smock of dark blue that cascaded straight down to her blue slippers, and a black veil fell from behind her crown to her elbows, framing her lovely face. The crown itself was unusual; it was a simple flaring diadem of gold, with a red line around it in the middle. On her breast there was a little red Latin cross, about as big as one's finger. For a quarter of an hour Eugène stood in the doorway of the barn staring at the Lady, until his father and ten-year-old brother came out.

"Joseph!" said Eugène to his little brother. "Look over there! Above the house! What do you see?" Joseph described the Lady exactly as his brother saw her, and both boys stood transfixed as they called to their father. The man himself didn't see anything, so he told the boys to go back to their work, smashing the tough stems of the *ajonc* bushes that had to be broken down into fodder for the horses.

But after a few minutes their father asked them to go and look again, to see if the vision was still there. She was, smiling just as before. Then go and get your mother, he said; maybe she can see something. When she came out of the house, little Joseph was clapping his hands and crying out, "How beautiful she is! How beautiful she is!" Victoria Barbadette hit him on the arm and told him to be quiet; he was attracting attention. She had never known the boys to lie, though, so she suggested that it might be the Blessed Mother. Say five Our Fathers and five Hail Marys, she said.

By then some of the other children of Pontmain had come out into the street, drawn by Joseph's exclamations. Nobody had told them what the attraction was, but they all described the Lady exactly as the Barbadette boys had done—but none of the adults saw anything. Madame Barbadette went back into the house for her glasses.[248]

The Barbadettes told their sons to come in for supper. The boys obeyed instantly, but they wouldn't turn their backs on the vision that held their attention. Once inside the house, they wouldn't sit down. They slurped up their soup while standing and then ran out.

The apparition was exactly the same as before, standing there patiently waiting for them. The vision had gone on for a whole hour; it was now nearly six o'clock, so Madame Barbadette told the boys to go and get the nuns. "The nuns are better than you are," she said; "if you see, they will see." But not even the Sisters of the Order of *Adoratrices de la Justice de Dieu* saw her. "I beg you, dear Sister," Victoria Barbadette said to Sœur Vitaline, "don't say anything about this. The children are out of their minds."

But Sœur Vitaline had never known the Barbadette boys to lie, either. So she went to a neighboring house and asked the little girls, Françoise Richer, eleven, and Jeanne-Marie Lebosse, nine, to come with her. Both saw the Lady and described her exactly as the boys had done. Sœur Marie-Edouard had joined the group by then, and, hearing what the girls said, she went to get more children. She fetched little Eugène Friteau, and, while she was there, she went to the house next door and got Father Guerin.

More and more of the five hundred villagers had gathered there by then, and Augustine Boitin, twenty-five months old, reached out toward the apparition and cried out happily, "The Jesus! The Jesus!" No matter how they turned the baby, no matter what they tried to distract her with, she turned joyously to the vision and stretched out her arms. These six children, Eugène and Joseph Barbadette, Françoise Richer, Jeanne-Marie Lebosse, Eugène Friteau, and little Augustine Boitin, were the only children to see the apparition.

At this moment, a wide oval formed around the Lady, with four candles on it, two at the level of her shoulders and two at the height of her knees, just like the decorations that their Father Guerin had arranged at the high altar of their little church. In fact, he had made the whole church into a shrine of the Immaculate Conception. He'd painted the ceiling blue with gold stars, and on the wall behind the statue of Mary Immaculate he had painted a blue oval and attached four candle brackets, two on each side of the statue.

248. Later, someone suggested looking through a black silk handkerchief, as was customary in those days for looking at eclipses, but it didn't work. They tried opera glasses, too, but with no luck.

Under the direction of the priest, they decided to pray. If the visitor were from Heaven, they figured, prayer would please her. If she were an agent of the Devil, prayer would drive her away. The whole village knelt and started the Rosary. As they prayed, the Lady ascended and got larger, becoming twice as large as Sœur Vitaline. The blue oval around her got bigger, too, and the stars of the sky came together in pairs beneath her feet and seemed to gather on her dress, like ants covering an anthill, the children said. Soon, she would be completely golden.

As the villagers finished the Rosary, Sœur Marie-Edouard began the *Magnificat*, and everybody joined in. A white scroll formed beneath the Lady's feet, about a meter and a half wide and twelve meters long, stretching from one chimney to the other. Unlike the prophetic scrolls of the Old Testament (Ez 2:9; Zc 5:1-4; or Dn 5:5-30) that carried messages of wrath and destruction, this one was to bring a message appropriate to the loving nature of the New Covenant and to the intercessory role of Mary in the economy of salvation. Slowly, as if written by an invisible hand, the letter M appeared on the left side of the scroll, in brilliant gold. One by one, the letters were called out by the children.

But before they got very far, another villager, Joseph Babin, ran excitedly into the crowd. "You can only pray!" he shouted. "The Prussians are at Laval!"

Nobody moved. "They could be at the entrance to the village," one woman said, "and we wouldn't be afraid."

They kept singing the *Magnificat* as the children spelled out the message. They never hesitated as the letters appeared to them, never contradicted each other: MAIS PRIEZ MES ENFANTS—But pray, my children, they said.

By now it was about 7:30—nobody knows for sure because the clock in the church tower, next to the Guidecoq house, had frozen in the intense cold. Some chairs were brought for the adults, and someone opened the barn door so that the crowd could stand out of the wind and still see the site of the apparition. The priest suggested that they sing the Litany,[249] and more letters appeared, one by one: DIEU VOUS EXAUCERA EN PEU DE TEMPS—God will hear you in a little while. The Lady smiled, and even laughed, as the villagers got this part of the message.

They sang more hymns in honor of Mary, and still more letters formed. As the villagers began singing the *Salve Regina*, the children spelled out MON FILS, My Son; and, having read this to the crowd, they shouted, "It is indeed the Blessed Virgin!" But the rest of the message bothered Sœur Vitaline. MON FILS SE LAISSE … it said.

249. A litany is an approved communal prayer consisting of opening and closing prayers that embrace a list of praises or petitions addressed to Christ or to Mary or another saint; these are intoned by a priest or another prayer leader, and each is answered by the assembled faithful with the appropriate response: "Have mercy on us" or "We beseech thee, hear us" for those addressed to Christ, and "Pray for us" in those addressed to Mary or another saint, for instance. The approved Litanies are the Litany of the Sacred Heart, the Litany of the Most Holy Name of Jesus, the Litany of the Blessed Virgin (often called the Litany of Loreto from the city in which it began), the Litany of St. Joseph, and the Litany of the Saints; the Litany for the Faithful Departed is approved but only for private use. All of them have been translated into every living language, and they've often been set to music over the centuries.

That doesn't make sense, she said; look carefully—doesn't it say, *Mon Fils se lasse*, My Son worries?

"No, Sister," the children said. "There is an 'i'. But wait; it isn't finished." They spelled out the rest of the sentence: MON FILS SE LAISSE TOUCHER. "My Son allows himself to be touched." As if to emphasize this sentence, a golden line underscored it.

The crowd fell silent, now, and the children kept repeating the whole message: "But pray, my children. God will hear you in a little while. My Son allows himself to be touched."

Father Guerin suggested that they sing another hymn to the Blessed Virgin, and Sœur Marie-Edouard began the canticle to Our Lady of Hope, written only a few years earlier by the Archconfraternity of Our Lady of Hope in Saint-Brieuc. At this song, the Lady smiled and raised her outspread arms to the height of her shoulders and moved her fingers in time to the music, smiling sweetly. When this hymn was finished, the inscription vanished, as if, the children said, a roller the color of the sky rolled quickly across it, wiping it out.

As the crowd sang again, a hymn of penitence and reparation to Jesus, the Lady suddenly became sad. The children saw a large red crucifix, hanging in the air about a foot in front of the Lady. She lowered her hands to take it and put it forward, as if presenting it to the village, as they sang:

> My sweet Jesus, at this time,
> Forgive our repentant hearts;
> No longer will we offend
> Your supreme goodness, O sweet Jesus!

And at the top of the cross, in the position at which Pilate had placed the superscription Jesus of Nazareth, King of the Jews, the children saw a little scroll with the words *Jesus Christ*. As the villagers sang the *Parce, Domine*, a star rose from under the Lady's feet, moving to the left, and lit the candle at knee height. It continued to the candle above, at shoulder height, crossed to the right, and lit the other two candles. Then it ascended to above the top of the oval and stayed there.

At about 8:30, as the people sang the *Ave, Maris Stella*, the crucifix disappeared, and the Lady lowered her hands again to the position usually seen in pictures of the Immaculate Conception. On each of her shoulders, two white Latin crosses appeared, each about one-third the size of the red crucifix. She smiled again, at this point. Father Guerin began the usual evening prayers, and the children saw a white veil rise slowly from under the Lady's feet to cover her up to her throat.

Soon her face was covered, too, and only her crown was visible to them. The oval and its four candles remained, but they too disappeared when the crown went. It was about 8:45. "It is over," the children said.

While the children of Pontmain were conveying the message to their elders,

General Von Schmidt received unexpected orders to abandon his campaign in the region and withdraw. He didn't understand why the order had been given, and he regretted not being allowed to break the Mayenne Line—it was unheard of for the Prussian High Command to call back a victorious army that wasn't even facing serious opposition. But Pontmain would not be overrun with German soldiers; western France would remain unoccupied. Ten days later an armistice was signed, ending the war. This is the "great miracle" of Pontmain.

But those few words of the Lady—Our Lady of Hope of Pontmain, as she's called in the missals of the region—contain a message that she has often conveyed elsewhere. And it's interesting to note that the apparition happened in response to a flood of prayers, all across France, for the end of the war. France has always been particularly devoted to Mary; it is the land that honored her with a whole necklace of gothic cathedrals, and in fact the earliest reported apparition of Mary occurred in the year 50, at Le Puy in what's now the Department of Haute-Loire.

Time and again her intercession was credited with saving the French nation, and the Franco-Prussian War was understood as just such an emergency. On January 11, 1871, Bishop Louis Pie of Poitiers had published once again the "National Vow" to build a basilica of the Sacred Heart on the heights of Martyrs' Hill—Montmartre—in Paris, a vow that had been taken in response to the requests made by the apparitions to St. Margaret Mary in the 1670s. In fact, that National Vow had originally been solemnly proclaimed in Laval itself, at the sanctuary of Avenières, on January 20, but neglected until two centuries later.

On the day of the apparition at Pontmain, January 17, 1871, of course, the Prussian army was no more than a mile from Laval. And in Paris, Father Amodru of the Chapel of the Immaculate Heart of Mary had begun a month of solemn prayers to implore Mary's intercession for the end of the war. On that day, too, and at five-thirty in the evening, the Archconfraternity of Our Lady of Hope in Saint-Brieuc—the group that had written the hymn that had so delighted the Lady—had solemnly presented their vow to Mary, begging for an end to the war.

Naturally, the pious people of France were grateful that their prayers for peace and for an end to the invasion had been answered in such an extraordinary fashion, as the confraternities, devotions, and even churches and monuments dedicated to Our Lady of Hope of Pontmain testify. But little by little, the fuller meaning of every detail of the apparition dawned in people's minds.

That simple message, "But pray, my children. God will deliver you in a little while. My Son allows himself to be touched," the only words delivered at Pontmain, sum up the maternal kindness of Mary, extending far beyond the troubles of that time and place. Her sadness when the people sang of penitence, and her presentation of her suffering Son on the Cross, are understood as an encouragement of penance and reparation; the lingering crown as a hint, or maybe a prophecy, of the queenly honors paid to Mary, particularly since Pius XII, in his encyclical *Ad Cæli Reginam*, instituted the

Feast of the Queenship of Mary, celebrated universally on August 22 every year.[250]

The two little white crosses borne on her shoulders may seem mysterious, until it's remembered that the apparition stood so that her shoulders were aligned to the east and to the west. After the message of Fátima fifty-three years later, the message of the conversion of Russia, the image made sense: the two halves of Christianity, the Eastern and the Western, united in Mary after a millennium of schism. Working on this assumption, and reaching out to separated Christians in the Soviet Union, the Blue Army redeemed the holiest icon of Russia, the miraculous picture of Our Lady of Kazan, and presented it to the Russian people.[251]

It rested for a while at Fátima, and the priests and prelates of the Church and of the Russian Orthodox Church met, conferred, and announced that, as both denominations have substantially the same liturgical and spiritual theology, "We have found in this domain," they said, "only differences of a secondary nature."

Of course, the reunion of Russian Christians to the Church may still be a long way off, but events like the crumbling of the Soviet Union, the restoration of the Russian Orthodox Church, and the stirrings of the inborn religious feelings among the ruins of the former Soviet bloc are all hopeful signs—signs, it may well be, foretold long ago above the rooftops of the simple little village of Pontmain.

---

250. It may also have been, like the rest of the message, a sign of the persistence of the Church's temporal organization. In 1870, when the French were compelled to withdraw their troops from Italy to fight the Prussian invaders, Italian troops flooded into the Papal States, seizing them as part of the unification of Italy. Without adequate forces to prevent their being taken prisoner, the popes became voluntary "prisoners" in the Vatican, not setting foot outside the Leonine walls until after the Lateran Treaty of 1929 (signed on the Feast of Our Lady of Lourdes, by the way) settled the issue. And, while the new Kingdom of Italy took over the administration and revenues of the Papal States, it refused to assume their debts, putting the Holy See into a desperate financial situation that further threatened the continuity of the Pope's universal administration of the Church.

251. The icon, the "Black Virgin" of Kazan, is more central to Russian Orthodox life than any image of Mary is in the West. It's customary to bless marriages through a copy of the icon and to give one to every newlywed couple when they start a new home, which is why every home in Russia had one, before the Revolution. It was the center of the family's prayer life; boys leaving for military service were blessed before this image, and so were sick children. The original was taken from Kazan to Moscow in 1612—no city could claim to be the center of Russia without it—and to St. Petersburg in 1710, where it was ultimately enshrined in the Kazan Cathedral on the Nevsky Prospekt, built for the purpose by Paul I in 1801. The Soviets confiscated it in 1917 and sold it, partly for the hard cash (its encasement was encrusted with about three million dollars' worth of jewels) and partly to get it out of the country. Then they turned the Cathedral into the Museum of the History of Religion and Atheism, with exhibits that stressed the advantages of the latter. But now it's been converted back to its original purpose, and regular liturgies are celebrated there. The Blue Army of Our Lady of Fatima was founded in 1947 by Monsignor Harold V. Colgan of St. Mary's Parish in Plainfield, New Jersey, who sought to fulfill the conditions for world peace offered by Our Lady of Fátima. "We in this parish will be a Blue Army of Our Lady against the Red Army of atheism," he said. It grew from that parish and is now an immense international association; Padre Pio said that Russia would be converted when there was a member of the Blue Army for every Communist, and, judging by the numbers, he was about right. Its American address is World Apostolate of Fatima, Box 976, Washington, New Jersey 07882, and it probably has a chapter in your locality.

twenty-three

Fátima 1917

In your distress,
when all these things shall have come upon you,
you shall finally return to the Lord, your God,
and heed his voice.
Because the Lord, your God, is a merciful God,
he will not abandon and destroy you,
nor forget the Covenant
that under oath he made with your fathers.

— Deuteronomy 4:30-31

In 1915, eight-year-old Lucia dos Santos was tending her family's sheep on the mountain called Cabeço outside the village of Fátima in Portugal. She and her companions, Maria Justino, Maria Rosa Matias, and Teresa Matias, ate lunch and then started to pray *o terço*—"the third", five of the fifteen Mysteries of the Rosary, which had been the custom in Portugal since long before anybody could remember. They happened to look down across the treetops of the valley below and saw a sort of a cloud, an isolated transparent shape filled with light, hovering motionless above the swaying treetops. When they finished their prayers, the figure disappeared. It looked like a person wrapped in a sheet, they said when they told her parents about it. Their parents dismissed the report as nonsense, and their siblings used it as an irresistible way to make fun of their sisters.

But later that same year, Lucia saw the same figure in the same place; and then again a third time.

In the spring of 1916, Lucia was out tending the sheep again at the same spot, this time with her cousins Jacinta Marto, aged 6, and Francisco Marto, 8. A misty drizzle began to fall, driven by a steady wind, and the children took shelter in a sort of roofless grotto on the mountainside. By midday, the Sun had come out on a beautiful, calm springtime day, but the children took their lunches back up to the sheltered spot to eat and to pray the Rosary. They were playing a simple game of pebbles when a sudden wind shook the trees hard enough to make them look up to see what had happened.

That same luminous figure had appeared over the valley. It glided slowly above the tops of the trees toward them. As it came closer, the little cousins saw that it had the definite form of an inexpressibly beautiful young man of about fourteen years of age, brilliant with light like a sunbeam striking a crystal glass full of pure water.

He moved to within a few feet of the children. "Do not be afraid!" he said. "I am the Angel of Peace. Pray with me."[252] He bent down until his forehead touched the ground; the girls did the same, immediately, but Francisco didn't hear the Angel's voice; he only saw the apparition. The Angel began to pray:

> My God, I believe, I adore, I hope, and I love you. I ask your pardon for
> those who do not believe, do not adore, do not hope, and do not love you.

He repeated the prayer three times, then rose to his feet. "Pray thus," he told them. "The Hearts of Jesus and Mary are attentive to the voice of your supplications." Then he simply disappeared.

"The Angel left us feeling exhausted, helpless, overpowered, and we remained lost to everything for hours," Lucia recalled years afterwards. The children never spoke about it, except among themselves, and then only with the greatest reluctance. But a few months later, in the middle of summer, the three were playing another game by the well behind the Dos Santos' house. All of a sudden, the Angel was there with them, and this time he seemed a little impatient. "What are you doing?" he demanded. "Pray! Pray a lot! The Most Holy Hearts of Jesus and Mary have designs of mercy on you. Offer prayers and sacrifices constantly to the Most High."

Lucia asked how they were to make sacrifices, and the Angel said, "Make of everything that you can a sacrifice, and offer it to God as an act of reparation for the sins by which he is offended, and in supplication for the conversion of sinners. You will thus draw down peace on your country. I am its angel guardian, the Angel of Portugal. Above all, accept and bear with submission the suffering that the Lord will send to you."

The girls, stunned by the experience, didn't really come to themselves until much later in the day. Francisco pestered them with questions about what had been said, but they couldn't bring themselves to talk about it until the next day. Who is "the Most High", he wanted to know; what does it mean to say that the Hearts of Jesus and Mary are attentive to the voice of our supplications? Lucia, the only one of the three who had gone through catechism classes, didn't know.

252. The children didn't mention the Angel, apart from the early report of seeing him hovering silently above the distant trees, even during the interrogations after the apparitions of the Lady. When she was asked about this years later, Lucia said that they didn't mention him because nobody had asked them about him. For her own part, she said, the priest to whom she mentioned him at the time of the apparitions told her not to talk about the matter again, and, obediently, she didn't. Only when the bishop told her to write everything down did she give the account of the Angel, under obedience, again.

From that time on, the children found it hard to enjoy games, any more, and they couldn't find any interest in dancing, or in singing, or even in talking. But, Francisco said, the Angel is so much more than all of that; let's just think about him. So the three spent hours on their knees, their heads to the ground, meditating on the beauty of that Angel and repeating over and over again the prayer that he had taught them.

The children made every little sacrifice that they could think of. They went without lunch, they drank less water than they wanted, they gave up treats in favor of foods that they really didn't like at all, and they put up in patience with noise, heat, and other little discomforts.

The Angel came to them again in the fall of 1916, getting their attention with a brilliant flash of light while they were praying as he had instructed them. But this time they weren't so dazzled by his splendor. He was carrying a Host from which drops of blood fell into the chalice that he held below it, and these caught and held their attention, being far more beautiful than the Angel himself. He left Host and chalice suspended in the air and prostrated himself before them; then, three times, he said:

> Most Holy Trinity, Father, Son, and Holy Spirit, I offer you the Most
> Precious Body, Blood, Soul, and Divinity of Jesus Christ, present in all
> the tabernacles of the world, in reparation for the outrages, sacrileges,
> and indifference by which he himself is offended. And through the infi-
> nite merits of his Most Sacred Heart, and the Immaculate Heart of Mary,
> I beg of you the conversion of poor sinners.[253]

He rose and took the chalice and Host again; he placed the Host on Lucia's tongue and gave Jacinta and Francisco the contents of the chalice. "Take and drink the Body and Blood of Jesus Christ, horribly outraged by ungrateful men." he said. "Make reparation for their crimes, and console your God."

It took the children some time to come out of the ecstasy; in fact, for the next few days, they went about their business caught in a rapturous contemplation of God, filled with a peace and a joy that they could neither express nor understand. Lucia answered Francisco's questions about what had happened; he hadn't yet been instructed in the nature and meaning of the Eucharist. "Oh," he said. "Now I understand. I did feel that God was inside of me, but I didn't know how."

---

253. The word "conversion" may be used casually to mean leaving a separated sect and officially joining the Church, but within the Church conversion is not seen as involving a single declaration of faith or even Baptism alone; still less does it mean joining up for a lifetime of lukewarm participation. It's a turning from sin; and St. Bernadette characterized sinners as people who love evil. So conversion is a lifelong process of embracing Christ's doctrine in its fullness and purity and living it—the basic business of every Christian. Even St. Peter, already Christ's vicar and Prince of Apostles, had to convert his heart after denying Christ three times, the new *Catechism* reminds us (§1420-§1498, etc.), repent with tears, and be accepted again. Conversion means making your religion real, a matter of lasting contrition—being sufficiently sorry for your past sins that you resolve not to live that way any more, fighting as hard as you can, with the help of God's grace, to submit your own will to Christ's will every day, embracing all of his precepts and commandments with none of the additions and subtractions of heresy.

At about noon on May 13, 1917, there were two brilliant flashes of light, like the one they had seen before the Angel appeared. Still, they didn't make the connection, herding their sheep homeward as quickly as possible to avoid any bad weather. Then they saw the Lady, standing above a little holm-oak tree, radiating indescribable brilliance. "Do not be afraid," she said; "I will not harm you." She was a lady all of light, more beautiful even than the Angel, they said, and for a while the three children knelt looking at her ecstatically. Finally, Lucia asked where the Lady was from.

"*Eu sou do Céu*," she said in the silken tones of Portuguese: I am from Heaven. Lucia asked what the Lady wanted of her, and the Lady asked them to come to that spot on the thirteenth of the following five months, until October. They conversed for a while, and the Lady promised them that they would go to Heaven, although Francisco would have to say many Rosaries. And in reparation for their sins and the sins of others, she asked them to accept whatever sufferings God would send them. When they agreed, she said, "Then you will have much to suffer. But the grace of God will be your comfort." She opened her folded hands, then, and released a flood of light that penetrated into the very hearts of the children.

They returned as requested, despite interference from their families and even from the police, the agents of an officially atheistic government that didn't want crowds of people flocking to religious events of any kind, least of all apparitions. And crowds of people came, too, a few at first, then a few hundred, and at last more than seventy thousand came to the little holm-oak tree to see and hear what they might. And the Lady came, as she had promised. She spoke to them of conversion, of reparation, and of devotion to the Sacred Heart of Jesus and to her own Immaculate Heart.

She told them that certain chronically ill persons would be cured, but that "it is necessary that they amend their lives and ask pardon for their sins." She told them to pray the Rosary every day, to bring peace to the world and an end to the war; and she asked them to add a prayer of reparation after each decade:

> O my Jesus, forgive us; save us from the fires of Hell. Please take all souls
> to Heaven, especially those most in need.[254]

She asked them to take on voluntary penances in reparation for the sins of others, penances that other people should have been doing but weren't. "Pray, pray very much," she said, "and make sacrifices for sinners, for many souls go to Hell because they have no one to sacrifice and pray for them."

But most intriguing of all, the Lady gave them a secret. The secret of Fátima, for some reason, has attracted so much attention that people seem to forget that every creditable apparition has included some private message that was not to be revealed. St. Francis, for example, did his best to keep his stigmata hidden and was afraid to mention

---

254. This prayer is often distorted in the literature about Fátima. The original Portuguese is *O meu Jesus, perdoai-nos e livrai nos do fogo do inferno; levai as alminhas todas para o Céu, principalmente aquelas que mais precisarem.*

any part of his private revelations. He put the question, in a general way, to some of the friars: if a man should have a vision, should he mention the fact to anybody? One of them, Brother Illuminato, knew that Francis was talking about himself; he recognized that the saint was still a little bit astonished. You should realize, he said, that sometimes divine secrets are revealed not for yourself but for others; you may be blamed if you conceal what you've heard. So St. Francis told them what had happened, but he still reserved part of it. The one who had appeared to him, he said, had told him things that he would never disclose to anybody as long as he lived.[255]

But Lucia was instructed to reveal the secret, and she did as she had been told. She wrote it down, under obedience, in memoirs in the 1930s after the other seers had already died, Francisco on April 4, 1919, Jacinta on February 20, 1920.

The "secret" is usually divided into three parts. The first part has to do with the vision of Hell that the Lady showed the children on July 13, 1917.[256] It was enough to scare them to death, Lucia said, if the Lady hadn't already told them that they were going to Heaven. Every penance and mortification was as nothing in Jacinta's eyes, said Lucia years later, if it could only prevent souls from going there.

In the second part of the secret, also given to the children on July 13, 1917, the Lady referred to that vision of Hell and told them what the vision meant.

> You have seen Hell, where the souls of the poor sinners go. To save them, God wishes to establish in the world devotion to my Immaculate Heart. If what I say to you is done, many souls will be saved, and there will be peace. The war is going to end, but if people do not cease offending God, a worse one will break out during the pontificate of Pius XI. When you see a night illumined by an unknown light, know that this is the great sign given to you by God that he is about to punish the world for its crimes, by means of war, famine, and persecutions of the Church and of the Holy Father.[257]

255. The friars, including St. Francis, didn't go on their own opinions to figure it out. They structured their discourse carefully on scriptural passages like Tb 12:7; Mt 25:25; and 2Cr 12:4.

256. Like everything else that happens during a mystical event that proves to be creditable, this vision is precedented throughout the history of the Church, from Revelations to the cases related by Pope St. Gregory the Great (*Dialogues* 4:40); naturally, the details vary, but a good look at Hell is evidently an effective way to get people back on the right track. After it happened to St. Teresa of Avila, everything, all acts of abstinence and penance, seemed easy to her, she said (*Book of Her Life* 32:1-5).

257. This is a double prophecy; at the time of the apparitions, Benedict XV della Chiesa was Pope. He was not to die until January 22, 1922, to be succeeded by Achille Ratti, who took the name Pius XI, as the Lady had predicted. His pontificate ended with his death on February 10, 1939, seven months before Hitler invaded Poland (September 1, 1939), but long after he had invaded the Rhineland (March, 1936), which was the first act of German aggression in the Second World War, and taken Austria (March 11, 1938). Also, many historians date the War from the Japanese invasion of Manchuria in September, 1931; the Japanese took Beijing in July, 1937. In fact, Pius XI's pontificate didn't end until after Mussolini invaded Ethiopia (October, 1935) and the Spanish Civil War had broken out (July, 1936). The "unknown light"

To prevent this, I shall come to ask for the consecration of Russia to my Immaculate Heart and the Communion of Reparation on the First Saturdays. If my requests are heeded, Russia will be converted, and there will be peace; if not, she will spread her errors throughout the world, causing wars and persecutions of the Church.[258] The good will be martyred; the Holy Father will have much to suffer; various nations will be annihilated. At last,[259] my Immaculate Heart will triumph. The Holy Father will consecrate Russia to me, and she will be converted, and a period of peace will be granted to the world.[260]

The third part of the secret is still secret. Lucia, who became a nun, wrote that part down a little after Christmas, 1944, when the official biography of her cousin Jacinta was to be expanded and re-published. The biography had been written originally in connection with Jacinta's beatification process, and Bishop José Alves Correia da Silva asked Lucia to remember everything that she could about Jacinta so that the expanded edition could be as complete and as accurate as possible.[261]

So, acting under obedience, Lucia wrote more of her recollections about her little cousin. But to do so, she would have to give a little more information about exactly what the Lady said to them; otherwise, her cousin's life wouldn't be seen accurately in its full context. This involved writing down the first two parts of the "secret", and she wrote down the rest of it, too, the part that was not to be revealed immediately. She

is generally understood as the extraordinary blood-red *aurora borealis* seen all over Europe during the night of January 25 to January 26, 1938—the Feast of St. Paul, the feast that commemorates his being struck by a heavenly light calling forcefully for his conversion.

258. Socialism, Communism, and other political systems to redistribute wealth are understood as incompatible by their nature with Christianity, being predicated on the violation of the inalienable rights that make people human. As early as 1846, Pius IX Ferretti condemned them, as did Leo XIII Pecci in two encyclical letters, *Quod Apostolici* (1878) and *Rerum novarum* (1891); Pius XI Ratti in *Quadragesimo Anno* (1931) and *Divini Redemptoris* (1937); and all subsequent popes. Such systems, intrusive into private and family matters, can't function unless they make people abandon traditional Christian morality. And because the Church has always taught that all people have an inalienable right to keep the fruits of their labors, and insists that attempts to forcibly redistribute wealth are inherently unjust—no one can coerce charity—leftist governments have always been vigorously or even violently antagonistic to her. An almost prophetic popular treatment of the social problems involved is *El Liberalismo es Pecado* (*Liberalism is a Sin*), written in 1886 by Fr. Felix Sarda y Salvany (tr. Condé B. Pallen, Ph.D., LL.D., 1899) and still in print.

259. *Por fim*, in the original Portuguese, which is the normal expression for "at last" or "finally". It's sometimes translated as "in the end," but there's no reason to hang a whole Apocalypse on that term.

260. In some faulty accounts, the call is to consecrate "the world", but the original text says specifically Russia. The vision of Hell and the statements by the apparition all happened during the same apparition on July 13, 1917; to divide the text into three secrets, some writers make an arbitrary split between the vision and the discourse, others between the first and second paragraphs of the discourse. Sister Lucia's own written account of the apparitions (*Fátima in Lucia's Own Words*, Fátima, 1976) supports the first strategy, but in fact the division of the material delivered on that date into three parts is really somewhat arbitrary.

261. Jacinta and Francisco have only recently been declared Venerable.

sealed it with wax in an envelope, but she didn't want to entrust it to anybody except a bishop. So the Most Reverend Manuel Ferreira da Silva, Bishop of Gurza, took it from her hands on June 17, 1944, and delivered it to Bishop Correira da Silva. Neither read it; Ferreira simply delivered it, and Correia concluded that if God wanted it to be revealed to him he would have made that explicit, and he didn't want to interfere.

Because Sister Lucia particularly wanted Pius XII to read the secret, the bishop tried to send it to the Holy Office in Rome, but they declined to receive it. So, on December 8, 1945, he put the sealed envelope into another larger envelope on which he had written, "This envelope with its contents shall be given to His Eminence Cardinal Don Manuel, Patriarch of Lisbon, after my death". Then he closed the second envelope with his own seal and put it in his safe. Sister Lucia made him promise to read the secret to the world on her death or in 1960, whichever came first. When she was asked why it had to be 1960, she just said, "because the Blessed Virgin wants it so."

In 1957 the Holy Office asked, all of a sudden, that the envelope be sent there without delay. Bishop Correia da Silva asked his auxiliary bishop to take it to the Apostolic Nuncio in Lisbon, but the auxiliary asked him to first read it himself and make a photostat of it. Correia da Silva refused, but he looked at the paper through the envelope, holding it against the light. He said that he saw a text about twenty lines long, about the same length as the quotation from the Lady above. The envelope arrived in Rome on April 16, 1957, and Pius XII immediately put it into a little box in his own office labelled *Secretum Sancti Officii*, the Secret of the Holy Office.[262]

But he died in 1958 without having read it himself. His successor, John XXIII Roncalli, was surprisingly, even pointedly, cool about devotion to Our Lady of Fátima, although he was the first person to read Lucia's note. He had the envelope delivered to him in August, 1959, at Castelgandolfo and read it a few days later in the company of his confessor and the Portuguese translator for the Secretariat of State. He also let Cardinal Ottaviani, Prefect of the Holy Office, read it, but then it was announced in early 1960 that the secret would not be revealed—in fact, that it would probably never be revealed. Although the Church recognizes the apparitions at Fátima, the news release said, it doesn't want to take the responsibility for guaranteeing the truth of the words that the three shepherds say that the Virgin Mary spoke to them. In other words, the Church declined, quite properly, to officially publish a private revelation, which might then be taken for Gospel by some. John XXIII simply put the envelope into the drawer of his desk, and there it stayed until he died.

Still, his successor Paul VI Montini called for the envelope soon after his elevation, and, although he read it, he didn't publish it, either. Paul's successor John Paul I

---

262. Terms might be a problem here, too. "Secret" in this case is derived from the Latin *secretum*, which means hidden, by way of the Italian *segreto*, which means set apart, as in the related word "segregated"; it's also related to the word "secretary", someone to whom "secrets", private business matters, are entrusted. The Holy Office, of course, is better known as the Inquisition, but that term, too, raises groundless suspicions. It's also interesting that Eugenio Pacelli, the future Pius XII, was consecrated as a bishop in Rome on May 13, 1917, the day of the first apparition at Fátima.

Luciani had actually visited Fátima in 1977, long before he was elected, and curiously enough, Sister Lucia asked specifically to meet him. They spoke at length privately, some say about the secret. But it's unlikely that he read it, after he became Pope.

In turn, his successor, John Paul II Wojtyla, didn't read the secret immediately on his accession to the Throne of Peter. But then on May 13, 1981, the sixty-fourth anniversary of the first Marian apparition at Fátima, John Paul II was shot by an assassin in St. Peter's Square. "Why did you not die?" asked the assassin when the Holy Father visited him in prison later. His aim was true, he said, and the bullet lethal: "Why did you not die?"

"One hand fired the bullet," the pope replied, "another guided it." There was no question that he meant the hand of Mary: he sent the bullet removed during surgery to be set in the crown of the statue of Our Lady at Fátima, where it remains today.[263]

While still in the hospital, the pope called for the secret, and for all of the documents in the Vatican Archives relating to the apparitions of Fátima, and he read them all with the closest attention. When he was released, the pope mentioned to an associate that he'd become convinced that the only way to save the world from war and atheism is the conversion of Russia, precisely as the message of Fátima had specified. And he set to work in exactly that direction.

He built a little oratory on the eastern edge of Poland, a building opening toward Russia, to house a copy of the Fátima statue of Mary—staking a claim, as it were, on the eastern empire. Exactly a year after the assassination attempt, he made a thanksgiving journey to the Portuguese shrine, and on the tenth anniversary of the event he was to return to Fátima to publicly proclaim an "Act of Entrustment", consigning the reconstruction of Christian Europe to Mary's motherly care. But most important, on the Feast of the Annunciation, March 25, 1984, he consecrated Russia to the Immaculate Heart of Mary, in collegial cooperation with all of the bishops of the world, fulfilling for the first time one of the requests made by the apparition.[264]

And think about what's happened since. There have certainly been a lot of wondrous things wrought among us, suddenly, since John Paul II fulfilled the final request of Our Lady of Fátima. And while it's never valid to reason that "this happened after that, therefore this happened because of that" (the fallacy called *post hoc ergo propter hoc*), they seem to have happened exactly as she said they would.

Less than a year after the consecration, Mikhail Gorbachev—one of the very few baptized Soviet leaders—became President of the officially atheistic Soviet Union.[265] In 1988, he met with the Patriarch and five Metropolitans of the Russian

263. Of course, John Paul II has always been devoted to Our Lady of Fátima. When he was a cardinal, he had taken a petition to Rome to ask the consecration of Russia in conformance with the specification of Fátima, and the escutcheon that he adopted on assuming the papacy includes Mary's monogram.

264. Previous consecrations—by Pius XII in 1942 and 1952 and by Paul VI in 1964 and 1967—had not filled this criterion, being celebrated by the Holy Father alone.

265. President Boris Yeltsin, too, is a baptized Christian. Although Russian Orthodoxy stands separated from the Church, baptisms are valid if conferred by someone who performs the ritual—using the water

Orthodox Church to enlist their support of his reforms. The next year, Gorbachev met John Paul II himself at the Vatican, and in 1990 diplomatic relations between the Soviet Union and the Vatican were established. By the end of the year Russia officially declared freedom of religion, recognizing that no society can prosper or even endure without a sound basis in faith and morals.

One by one, the captive republics of the Union slipped out of the rusty shackles of Communism. On October 13, 1991, Soviet state television actually broadcast live the Pope's pilgrimage to Fátima, and on November 7 of that year they acceded to popular demand and broadcast a tape of it—instead of showing the usual parade through Red Square commemorating the Bolshevik Revolution on that date. (The only parade there that day was a procession, led by Russian Orthodox clergy, mourning the victims of Communism.) On December 8—the Feast of the Immaculate Conception— President Yeltsin of Russia announced the formation of a commonwealth. On Christmas Day, Mikhail Gorbachev resigned as head of the Soviet Union, and the next day the red hammer-and-sickle flag over the Kremlin was lowered for the last time.[266]

There doesn't seem to be any precedent in world history for a world power admitting its faults like this—there have been reversals of policy every day, but nothing like this. The Soviet Union was not simply ceasing to tyrannize its own people and those of other nations, but actually dissolving itself entirely. This seems really to have been a process of conversion, of people changing their minds about the way to live, abandoning an oppressive, hateful, and cruel government in search of a new respect for those inalienable rights that make us human, and searching also to remember the ways in which they used to reach out to their God.

So the whole chain of events in eastern Europe had a definitely religious character to it. Gorbachev himself, in a 1992 letter to the Italian newspaper *La Stampa*, said that everything that had happened in that part of the world in those years would not have been possible without the leading moral and political roles played in the liberation of the region by "Pope Wojtyla", as he called him.[267]

and saying the few prescribed words—with the intention of doing what Christians do, and Baptism can only be conferred once. All baptized persons, therefore, are to at least some degree members of the Church, although full and formal reception usually involves a rite to supply what may have been deficient in the administration of the sacrament. On a larger scale, there are some hopeful signs of progress toward the reunion of the Orthodox sects, the Greek, Ukrainian, and others as well as the Russian.

266. As with most other politico-mystic phenomena, the role of John Paul II in the fall of the Soviet Union seems less incredible when you consider parallel cases in the past. Napoléon, for instance, attributed the fall of his empire to his enmity with Pius VII Chiaramonti—I should have kept the Pope close by my side, he said on St. Helena; I would have suffered no opposition from the Faithful. Standing outside the Church, he couldn't gain the confidence of Poland or Spain, both countries crucial to his strategies, and by abusing the Church and imprisoning the Pope he lost his subjects' faith in his marriages, his son's legitimacy, and his own coronation, the foundation of his empire. In fact, as Mussolini phrased it, "every time a state has opposed religion, the state has lost."

267. Gorbachev unwittingly echoed the usage of the moribund atheistic government of Revolutionary France, whose officials called Pius VI Braschi *Citoyen Pape* when they held him prisoner at Valence.

Of course, John Paul II didn't act alone. It's the Church, the Pope answered, that has done this, not me. And it didn't happen overnight, although all of the political headlines came thick and fast in only a very short time. Year by year since 1917, the simple message of Fátima—conversion and reparation—has spread across the globe, turning the lives of countless people to prayer and, perhaps, opening their souls to a view of the seriousness of sin, or to an understanding of its reality, of how it corrupts our everyday lives and pollutes the political and economic climate of this world.

Certainly people from every nation under Heaven heard the message of Fátima and took up the habit of saying the reparation prayers while waiting in line or in traffic, using every possible moment to beg forgiveness for their own sins and the sins of others. Many had grouped together into associations, sodalities, and fraternities to act in concert, to keep up perpetual Rosaries or the devotion of the First Saturdays.[268] Together, they number millions of members around the world, all praying and making sacrifices for the Lady's intentions, repairing the damage of sin and righting the balance as best they can.

Certainly, too, the conversion of millions of people around the world, all of them turning their attention to God and trying to correct the effects of wrongdoing, is an immense benefit to the quality of life on Earth, just in and of itself; and millions of people thinking in a radically different way about life and justice must have an effect on whole political systems, sooner or later. Yet all of these vast changes in the soul and the world stem from those few astonishing phrases, so characteristic of creditable Marian apparitions, a few of the simplest words, reported by illiterate children, that can break open a marvelous new view of the universe.

Console your God. Sacrifice everything that you can, and offer it to God as an act of reparation for the sins by which he is offended, and in supplication for the conversion of sinners.

For thus, the Angel said, you will draw down peace on your country.

268. The Lady had said that she would come to ask for this devotion, and, in 1925, Lucia said that she appeared again to her at the convent and outlined the details, promising to assist at the hour of death with all graces necessary for salvation everyone who, on the first Saturdays of five consecutive months, receives the sacrament of Reconciliation, receives the Eucharist, recites part of her Rosary, and keeps her company for a quarter of an hour meditating on its Mysteries with the intention of offering reparation to the Mother of God. Like the devotional practices centered on the Sacred Heart of Jesus, and all other approved devotions, the features of this one resonate to the Church's constant customs; for instance, Saturday has always been, liturgically and devotionally, dedicated to Mary. More information on this and most other devotions is given in the author's *Rosary: Mysteries, Meditations, and the Telling of the Beads*.

twenty-four

Beauraing and Banneux

1932-1933

If they will not believe you,
nor heed the message of the first sign,
they should believe the message of the second.

— Exodus 4:8

Since La Salette, the economic and political consequences of sin or even of indifference have been a constant theme in the messages of creditable apparitions of Mary. All of them make the same point: your indifference, your outrages and ingratitude to God, are the direct causes of the disorders in your individual lives and of your economic and political problems. Convert your hearts to God and make reparation for your sins, before it's too late.

At La Salette the consequences were local; the fields and gardens of the region didn't produce, and the orchards in the area didn't bear. Yet as one apparition followed another, the consequences were described in broader and broader terms. By the time of Fátima, the warnings had extended to blanket the whole world. This repeats on a larger scale the patterns of revelation in each of the apparitions individually. Apparitions of Mary aren't like the thunderous apparition of the Father to Ezechiel or of the Son to St. Paul, for instance. They progress gently, gradually letting the chosen visionary get used to the experience and giving a cosmic message in comprehensible pieces that grow progressively more intense and weightier in their import, until at last the whole message is transmitted.

In this view, the message of Fátima was given in time to avoid World War II entirely, if it had been heeded by everyone who heard it. But evidently conversions were too few; not enough people heeded the call to repentance and amended their lives. So, by the 1930s, worldwide economic failure and simmering hostilities affected everybody on the planet, and as the war approached more and more signs and wonders were given. Two of the most important, moreover, happened in exactly the zone that was to be most devastated by the two world conflicts of the twentieth century.

Beauraing is a little town near Namur in Belgium, about thirty-five miles southeast of Brussels. In 1932, it had about two thousand or twenty-five hundred people, and its only remarkable feature was that the road to Rochefort passed under the railroad line at that point. Near the railroad viaduct, there was a village school, run by the Sisters of Christian Doctrine of Nancy, who had put in a little flower garden and a replica of the Lourdes grotto.

At six-thirty in the evening of November 29, 1932, Albert Voisin (11) and his sister Fernande (15) went to the school to pick up their sister Gilberte, who, as a girl of thirteen, wasn't allowed to walk home alone. They were with two other girls, Andrée Degeimbre (14) and her sister Gilberte (13). Albert rang the bell and turned toward the viaduct while he waited to go in. "Look at the statue in the garden!" he cried. "It's walking around above the bridge!" The girls figured that he'd seen the lights of a car, but when they looked, they saw the figure, too.

The Sister Superior delivered Gilberte Voisin to the door but laughed at what the excited children were saying, and closed the door. The children ran to the fence and saw the apparition still there. They lowered their eyes and ran home as fast as they could.

But when the children returned to pick up Gilberte the next day, they saw the apparition not once but four times, at the fence when they went to ring the bell, above a holly bush when they rang, on the viaduct again as they left, and above a neighbor's house when they got home. Their parents wanted to stop the nonsense, so they took their children back to the school that evening. Sure enough, the Lady showed herself again, but this time, the children said, she didn't look like the statue any more.

They saw her again and again, thirty-three times in all. She identified herself, by nodding in answer to the question, as the Immaculate Virgin, and she said that she wanted them to be "really good". Actually, she said very little, but she answered the children's questions: when they should come again, whether a chapel should be built on the site, and the like. When they came to the site as directed, the children began by saying the Rosary, standing; when the Lady appeared to them, they sank at once to their knees, with their hands still at the same level as when they had been standing. Soon their faces "became beautiful", in the phrase of one deposition, and they kept repeating the prayers in unison as long as the ecstasy lasted.

Word of the apparitions spread very rapidly and attracted huge crowds, among them as many as sixty physicians at a time, all of whom poked, prodded, and otherwise examined the children before, during, and after their ecstasies. Officials separated the children immediately afterwards, to ensure that they wouldn't have a chance to compare notes before interrogation. They put floodlights on the hawthorn bush above which the

Lady was said to appear, but she outshone them; she conveyed her brief messages to the children, among them specific secrets for each of them, and then she disappeared. Her last words to them, on January 3, 1933, were, "Do you love me? Then for my sake, practice self-denial."

Then, during the night of January 15, 1933, in the little Belgian village of Banneux (about thirty miles south of Liège and near the border with Germany), eleven-year-old Mariette Béco was watching out the window for the return of her brother Julien. The night was completely dark and extremely cold, with snow on the ground and in the trees blown around by a fierce wind. Suddenly Mariette saw a radiant lady in the little garden between her house and the road, standing still on a little mound of earth.

Mariette thought that it was the reflection from the lamp, so she took it into the other room and closed the door. But when she went back to the window, the Lady was still there, all in brilliant white, with a blue girdle. Mariette's mother ridiculed the idea and didn't see anything, herself, but the girl said some decades of the Rosary. And the Lady beckoned to her, smiling, but Mariette's mother locked the door to keep her inside on such a night. When the girl looked again, the Lady was gone.

Now, Mariette Béco was really the least likely of any visionary since La Salette. Her own bishop described her later as seeming to be the farthest from God of any child in the village, and her teachers reported that she was "savage" in her dealings with them and other students. She had very little in the way of schooling, in fact, and she didn't go to catechism classes or even to Mass. She had never made her first communion, either. She had only one thing to recommend her, as far as anybody could tell: she was an emotionally and psychologically normal child who kept to her conscience and was completely trustworthy; she stuck fiercely to her own viewpoint, but she never lied.

And the Lady's call couldn't be denied. On January 18, Mariette went out to the little mound of earth and knelt down to pray. It was well below freezing, but she didn't feel the cold; she answered dreamily to her parents' urgent calls to come in, but she didn't move for about half an hour. Then the Lady led her about a hundred yards away to a little spring at the edge of the forest. "Put your hands in the water," she said. And when the girl did so, the Lady said, "This spring is reserved for me." Then she said *au revoir* to the girl and disappeared.

Owing to the climate, and probably to Mariette's reputation as a difficult personality, only about twenty people came to the site to see what was going on. But the Lady came again and again, that winter, eight times in all. She identified herself as the Virgin of the Poor, and she asked again and again for prayer. She said that she had come to relieve suffering, and that the spring was set aside so that the sick of all nations could be cured—someone else had to explain to Mariette what "all nations" meant, because she evidently didn't understand that there were places in the world other than Banneux.

The Lady also asked for a little oratory at the site of the spring, and when Mariette conveyed the pastor's request for a sign, she asked the girl to trust her. At last, on March 2, she took her leave of the girl and—most unusual for a Marian apparition—

placed her hands on Mariette's head. Mariette collapsed on the cold ground, and her father carried her into the house. The girl wept unconsolably, covering her face with her hands, for hours afterwards; the Lady will not return again, she said.

There were the usual canonical inquiries into the reported apparitions at both Beauraing and Banneux, and both were approved by the local bishops, Banneux in 1942 and Beauraing in 1943. The refreshment of devotion welling out from these two shrines is extraordinary; about half a million pilgrims come to the shrine that was built at Beauraing and about a quarter million to the shrine by the spring at Banneux every year since. There have been thousands of reported cures, physical as well as spiritual, recorded at each site; two at Beauraing have been declared miraculous. Today, some five hundred churches and shrines have been dedicated to Our Lady of the Poor of Banneux alone, from Sweden to the Transvaal and from Colombia to the Ivory Coast, by way of Indonesia, Mozambique, and Reunion Island.

Perhaps most remarkable, though, was the change in Mariette herself. Her difficult personality seems to have been changed by the whole experience. Like the good children of Beauraing, she grew up and married, living quietly and happily in the everyday anonymity from which they all came.

twenty-five

Ephesus 1955

*See, I come to you;
it is to you that I turn ...
cities shall be repeopled,
and ruins rebuilt. ...*

— Ezechiel 36:9-10

George B. Quatman, of Lima, Ohio, was the man who gave America its first functional direct-dial telephone communication between cities. He was constantly inventing new improvements to the telephones; he held nearly two hundred telecommunications patents. In 1954, he and his wife visited Jerusalem, in honor of the Marian Year. While they were there they heard of the tomb of St. John and other holy places at Ephesus, some seven hundred miles to the northwest, in Turkey, and they decided to go up there when they came back to the region the following year. But to understand what happened to them when they got there, we have to step back to the little village of Flamske in Germany. And in fact we have to step back to 1774, when Catherine Emmerich was born in that little village.

Catherine, the daughter of poor peasants, was sent out as a servant to a local farmer when she was twelve. At eighteen she was apprenticed to a dressmaker, but she had always wanted to be a nun. At twenty she returned home and started trying to enter a convent. Now, it happened that the convents in that region of Westphalia were poor; they simply couldn't take in a girl without a dowry, an endowment of money or property to support her. They preferred not to accept novices who couldn't read or write, and Catherine could do neither. But she had a friend who also wanted to be admitted to a nearby Augustinian convent, and this girl's parents refused to give permission unless the nuns took Catherine, too. So, on her friend's coattails, Catherine Emmerich became a nun in 1802, at the age of twenty-nine.

The poor nuns must have thought they'd made a major mistake. Catherine—or Anne-Catherine, as she was now known—worked hard and patiently, but her health was never good. And she had visions. In addition to her own pains and illnesses, she experienced the sufferings of Christ crowned with thorns. In 1807 she began to have pains corresponding to some of his other wounds, and the pains in her feet often prevented her walking. Spiritually as well as physically, she was a problem.

By 1811, the convents of Westphalia were suppressed by the new-minted King of Westphalia, Napoléon's brother Jérôme. The nuns who had families to support them left, but Anne-Catherine, an old servant, and a refugee priest had nothing to do but stay in the abandoned building. Taking care of Sister Anne-Catherine became too much for these two to handle, and she was taken in by a poor widow in the village. It was here, bedridden in a miserable little room, that she received the full stigmata, as well as the mystic gift of inedia: never a girl of hearty appetite, she soon stopped eating altogether.

The village doctor insisted on examining her to put a stop to the nonsense but, despite himself, was convinced of the truth of the phenomena and filed an official report about them. This attracted a good deal of public attention, including an official examination by the vicar-general of the diocese and, more important, a visit from the poet Clemens Brentano.

In Brentano, Anne-Catherine found her public voice—a voice she never wanted-ed. But at the command of her bishop she opened up to Brentano, and he began to write down all of the visions that came so constantly to the invalid nun. From their first encounter in 1818 until her death in 1824 Brentano recorded everything she told him. His transcripts of her visions read like an account given by somebody watching a long, detailed color film and describing it to somebody else who can't see the screen. Anne-Catherine saw landscapes, houses, people, and animals, and more than that she understood precisely who they were and what they were doing. The seamstress in her took particular note of the clothes, the rugs, and the draperies, but she also noted the buildings, roads, and geographical features. She felt physically whatever the saints, or Christ, felt in her vision: the heat, the cold, the distress, everything.[269] All in all, she dictated to Brentano a truly stunning account of the day-to-day lives of Christ, Mary, and their family and friends.

Unfortunately, Anne-Catherine told of her visions in little bits, never in chronological order or with any narrative flow, and Brentano did re-arrange a lot of the details. He also may have embellished or refined the language a little; she certainly spoke to him in her Westphalian dialect, which he translated into standard German as he wrote it down. And, some suspect, he may have "corrected" the accounts here and there, thinking that he knew better than she. Brentano himself noted in his preface that these accounts "solemnly reject the slightest claim to bear the character of historical truth. All

---

269. This is called *mystic sensitivity*; other ecstatics experience this, too, reacting physiologically as if they were present in body at the event that they see mystically.

that they wish to do," he said, "is to associate themselves with the countless representations of the Passion by artists and pious writers, and to be regarded merely as a pious nun's Lenten meditations imperfectly comprehended and narrated and also very clumsily set down." (Amen.) Anne-Catherine herself, he added, "never attached to her visions anything more than human and defective value, and therefore yielded to an inner admonition to communicate them only in obedience to the repeated commands of her spiritual directors and after a hard struggle with herself."

Because they really were so clumsily set down, Brentano's transcripts were formally excluded from consideration during her canonization proceedings, but they were published after his death in nine volumes between 1851 and 1855. And, of course, private revelations are never taken by the Church as settling any historical or archæological questions. But countless details of Anne-Catherine's tales—not just locations but descriptions of buildings and artifacts and even of extinct languages—have been confirmed by scholars since her time, although they were unknown in her day or contradicted by the best academic information available. In fact, a good many things that Anne-Catherine saw in her visions actually led archæologists to discover precisely what she had described in the least likely places.

One of the things that she described was the house in which the Virgin Mary lived after the Crucifixion and Ascension. There was an informal group of stories, handed out since the Middle Ages to the pilgrims who came to the Holy City, that Mary stayed on in Jerusalem until her death and Assumption, but Anne-Catherine Emmerich put her house firmly in Ephesus. And to understand why that makes sense, we need to have another look at early Christianity, beginning with the Bible.

At the Crucifixion, Christ commended Mary to the care of St. John, and St. John to Mary (Jn 19:25-27). St. John went to Ephesus, which was an immense seaport city in those days, built almost entirely of the excellent local marble. It was a fiercely religious city, centered on the great Temple of Diana, one of the Seven Wonders of the World, one of the largest stone buildings ever constructed.[270] The city's economy was based as much on pilgrims to this shrine as it was on commerce from the harbor. This profit motive, more than any religious convictions, made Ephesus a hard city to convert, both for St. John and for St. Paul, who had to write a whole epistle to the Ephesian Christians, just to keep them from relapsing into pagan life.

Well, according to the *Golden Legend*, St. John destroyed the great Temple of Diana with a single prayer, when it came to the trial. The Ephesian Christians used its stones in the middle of the third century to build two churches, one dedicated to St. John

---

270. The Artemisium, so called from its dedication to Diana-Artemis, was about four hundred and twenty-five feet long and two hundred and fifty-five feet wide, with columns about sixty feet tall, according to Pliny the Elder, who was in a position to know. Built by the architect Chersiphron, it was gorgeously decorated ("Successive empires, the Persian, the Macedonian, and the Roman, had … enriched its splendour," Gibbon said). It was burned down by a man called Hierostratos or Herostratus, who said that he did it to make his own name immortal. He happened to set the torch to it, by the way, on the night of July 21, 356 BC, the exact time that Alexander the Great was being born in far-off Macedon.

and another dedicated to Mary.[271]

Anne-Catherine Emmerich said that Mary's house was on a little hill about three and a half hours' walk southeast of town, but in the early nineteenth century none of this was visibly apparent. The old harbor had silted up, stranding proud Ephesus many miles inland, and then the Ostrogoths came through and tore everything into very little pieces indeed. The leftovers, wrote one observer in the 1950s, were not "soaring reminders like those of Rome or Athens but more like three square miles of marble garbage dump." The surrounding area was an uncultivated wilderness.

Then, in 1881, a French admirer of Sister Anne-Catherine's actually went into the wilds around Ephesus and found hills, streams, ruins, and even ancient trees precisely as the nun had described them. Oddly enough, nobody made much of the fact. There was only sporadic action over the decades, often disrupted by revolutions and world wars, to acquire and properly excavate the site. Finally, on September 24, 1931, ownership of the House of Mary (the *Panaya Kapulu*, as the natives call it) was confirmed in the name of Father Joseph Euzet, C.M., but he could scarcely make a start at building the place into something like a shrine again.

And then, at long last, Mr. Quatman of Lima, Ohio, came to Ephesus. He and his wife had read Brentano's account of Sister Anne-Catherine's visions, and they decided to see the place for themselves. Captivated by the stunning natural beauty of the sites, the Quatmans were also disgusted by the neglect and by the filthy shantytowns spread all over the marble fragments of the great Church of St. John and the Marian basilica. And they were saddened by the plight of the House of Mary itself—excavated, in part, and in part rebuilt, but desperate for repairs.

The Quatmans took one last look at the desolation in the gathering dusk. As the light died, George saw Mary in the heavens over the valley of Ephesus, and a panoramic vision of the hilltop beautifully restored to its ancient splendor, with the Church of St. John surrounded by lighted walks and gardens, the great Cathedral of St. Mary—site of the Council—also reborn, and, finally, her own house on its hilltop south of town, restored and beautifully maintained, with her own simple Way of the Cross laid out once more around it. He understood the vision instantly, and heart and hand cannot be separated in a person as practical as Mr. Quatman.

Within a few days, he had written to the Bishop of Smyrna outlining a complete campaign of restoration for those monuments. The minute he got home, he founded the American Society of Ephesus, headquartered in Lima and modestly

---

271. It was here, in the Church of St. Mary, that the Council of Ephesus met in the year 431. The Council was called to deal with the confusion caused by some heretics at the time who denied that Mary was the mother of God, because, they claimed, the baby Jesus was only human until his divine nature joined his human body later—that he was not a complete person, not his complete self, from the very moment of his conception. The Council stated officially that, since Christ is God and Mary is the Mother of Christ, she is properly called Mother of God. This Council (*cap. xxvi, Synodical Epistle*) incidentally affirmed that St. John and Mary had lived there. And they reaffirmed the Church's unbroken understanding that people are, too, complete human beings, body and soul, from the moment of conception.

described as having been formed by "some American businessmen, realizing the need for financial assistance of the sacred historical places of Ephesus".

Today, Ephesus is the most popular tourist attraction, or really pilgrim attraction, in Turkey. Through the Society, a new airport, a new harbor, and modern hotels have appeared, along with more and more archæologists who are constantly increasing the store of knowledge about this ancient city, so crucially important for the history of the region and of Christianity itself.

Through all of their work on Ephesus, neither Quatman nor his wife reported anything to anybody about the vision. They weren't the kind of people who like a lot of publicity, and they may have reasoned that the suspicion that clings to any report of an apparition might have hindered the businesslike accomplishment of their aims. But the word got where it needed to be anyway, somehow. In 1956, Quatman's son, Judge Joseph B. Quatman, had an audience with Pius XII during a visit to Rome. The pope gave warm approbation to the Society's work, and he spoke to the judge fondly, and in some detail, about the apparition.

part four

certain apparitions of other saints and angels

... the Law and the prophets are full of marvels similar
to those recorded of Jesus ...
And I shall refer not only to his miracles, but,
as is proper,
also to those of Jesus's apostles.
For they could not have prevailed upon those who heard their doctrines
to abandon the usages of their own people and accept their instructions,
even at the danger of death,
without the help of miracles and wonders ...

Origen, *Contra Celsum*, 1:46 (*c.* 248)

twenty-six

St. Michael

Mount Gargano, 390

Our bodies are so corrupt that they are referred to
by the Holy Spirit as bodies of sin,
conceived and nourished in sin,
and capable of any kind of sin.
They are subject to a thousand ills,
deteriorating from day to day and harboring
only disease, vermin, and corruption.

— St. Louis-Marie Grignion de Montfort,
True Devotion to the Blessed Virgin (1842)

It's often said, by people given to casual language, that after a person dies and goes to God, he's an angel, that the soul of a deceased good person "gets his wings". But people who end up with God are saints, not angels; people are created body and soul and, as the Church teaches, the Faithful departed will end up with their souls rejoined to their bodies, now glorified. Human nature is human nature, and God never changes it.

Angels, on the other hand, are created spirits without bodies; they're intelligent and they have free will, but they're an entirely different species of being from humans. In fact, over time, speculative theologians have distinguished nine separate species or "orders" of angel, each as different from the others as any species of earthly creature differs from any other. These distinctions are no part of the Church's doctrine, only a scholarly convenience, but in ascending order they're Angels, Archangels, Virtues, Powers, Principalities, Dominations, Thrones, Cherubim, and Seraphim.[272] Unlike us,

272. Their names either recall their particular functions with respect to others—Dominations command lower orders (Zc 2:4), Virtues execute miracles (the word means "power" or "ability"), Powers oppose the

267

bound to our bodies and bound in Time, the purely spiritual angels exist in that dimension of Sempiternity, where they endlessly praise God. One is assigned to each of us, from the first moment of conception, "to light, to guard, to rule, and guide", as the old prayer puts it, and a particular angel is given to each nation, too, as a guardian to watch over it and keep it on track. And from time to time one or more of them is sent to convey some message to Earth-bound humans. In fact, that's where they get their name: "angel" comes from the Greek word for messenger. That's why artists give them wings, too, as a visual symbol of their ability to move between Heaven and Earth.273

The Bible describes these celestial messengers as having formidable power and intellect, and overwhelming splendor. Those who appear in the Old Testament are described as looking like men of chrysolite, like burnished bronze, with faces like lightning and voices like the rushing of waters, like the roar of a multitude, a loud voice, as when a lion roars. Their splendor terrified the prophets who saw them (and the fact that Mary replied calmly to Gabriel's annunciation speaks volumes about her purity—she, preserved from original sin as well as actual sin, saw them routinely since birth just as Adam and Eve saw God before the Fall, and they didn't frighten her).

And, going by Scripture, there must be an immense number of angels. But the Bible mentions only three by name: the archangels Gabriel, Raphael, and Michael.274 Nobody knows their real names, of course, but writers and thinkers on these matters assigned them these significant Hebrew names, just for reference. The -el part always refers to God, as in Beth-el, the home of God (Gn 28:19).275 This syllable shows up in a lot of Hebrew names for humans, too, like El-ijah and Emmanu-El.

The other part of these angels' names refers to the particular message that the archangel was dispatched with. Gabriel, the name of the one who came to announce the births of John the Baptizer and of Christ himself (Lk 1:19, 26), means "Man of God" or "Hero of God". Raphael means "God heals"; it's the name given to the

---

forces of evil, etc.—or come from unknown sources, like the words "Seraphim" and "Cherubim" (CARE-oo-bim). These "cherubs", by the way, are sometimes shown as cheerful little wingèd babies, but that's a recent development that got its start when Renaissance artists Christianized the "little loves" (amorini) of classical art. These mischievous babies are decorative, and they represent angelic joy and delight pretty well, but the Cherubim of the Bible are the forbidding guardians that God sent to the gates of Paradise (Gn 3:24), the terrifying apparitions that Ezechiel saw (1:5-13) supporting the very throne of God itself (also Ps 17:8-11; 2Kgs 22:11).

273. They can get their gowns on over their wings, of course, because they live in Sempiternity, where there's no over, under, through, up, down, before, or after: it's outside of space and Time, which is also why their wings can be shown coming through the gowns without benefit of a hole in the cloth. Anyway, that's just an artistic convention; those angels in the Bible who have clothes have no wings, and the wingèd ones have no clothes.

274. Well, Lucifer, too (Is 14:12), which means "bearer of light". After his fall from grace he's also just called Satan (1Pa 21:1), which means "adversary", but he's beside the point here. Those good angels named in the Bible are called St. Michael, St. Raphael, and St. Gabriel, but that's not because they're like human saints by nature; "saint" is from the Latin sanctus, meaning "holy".

275. Beth-lehem, by the way, means "home of the Bread", a prefiguration of the Presence of Christ in the Eucharist.

archangel who took the younger Tobias on his journey and gave him the means to cure both the physical blindness of the elder Tobias and the spiritual disorders caused by the demon Azazel in the house of Raguel—the names of many demons end in -*el*, too (Tb 3:25. So does Raguel's, for that matter).276

And the name Michael means "Who is like God?" That's because he is the commander of the heavenly hosts, the one who threw Satan into the pit for his pride (Rv 12:7-9) when Satan thought that he was like God, himself. That's why he's most often shown in art standing triumphant, ready to impale upon his lance a fallen demon that's sometimes shown in the form of a hideous dragon. As leader of Heaven's legions, Michael was understood as the guardian angel of Israel, which is why he was the one who opened Gabriel's way to the prophet Daniel (another -*el* name) when it was blocked by the bad angel of Persia (Dn 12:1; 10:13; evidently nations who choose to oppose God's will are aided by fallen angels, as a holy nation is guarded by a good one).

The Talmud says that Michael was the one who smote the armies of Sennacherib,277 and in Jewish lore it's Michael who comes forth to defend the Faithful individually against any other demons, too. He's credited with protecting the three men in the fiery furnace (Dn 3:49-50) and with endlessly thwarting the campaigns of the female demon Lilith (Is 34:14), who takes particular advantage of women in the throes of childbirth and tries to strangle their newborn infants.

And just as he's sent with his hosts to defend the Faithful and thrash demons, he's also dispatched to punish the earthly enemies of God. He's supposed to have been the angel of the Passover, and in 590 he seems to have fulfilled this office again, when the Tiber flooded and left piles of dead serpents (and a dead dragon, too, by some accounts) that rotted and filled the air with pestilence. The plague took Pope Pelagius II and spread to exact a terrible toll on the population of the city.

The survivors unanimously elected Pope St. Gregory the Great as pontiff—against his will, according to the *Golden Legend*; he had himself smuggled out of the city in a barrel and hid in a cave, but the search party saw a column of light over his hiding place, with angels going up and down it, so they took him back and elevated him. He ordered litanies and processions to beg God for an end to the scourge, and at last the new pope and the assembled crowds saw Michael standing atop the castle that guards the entrance to the Vatican, wiping his bloody sword and putting it in its sheath, as a sign of the end of the expiation.

In fact, the plague ended then just as quickly as it had begun, and from that apparition the castle was named the Castle of the Holy Angel, Castel Sant' Angelo.278

276. A fourth archangel, Uriel, is referred to in the Talmud (Num R II:10); his name means "Light of God". Raphael himself said that there were seven like himself altogether (Tb 12:15; Rv 4:5).

277. Ex R 18:5; *cf*. 4Kgs 18:13-19:36; 2Chr 32:1-22; Is 36:1, 37:17-37. Michael also defended Israel verbally as counsel for the defense before God, opposing the demon Samael (in the Talmud, Ex R 18:5, again) and other prosecutors (Est R 7:12, Joma 77a).

278. At the top of the castle, standing against the sky on the spot where he appeared, there's still a statue of St. Michael, sheathing his sword. The bridge across the Tiber is decorated with Bernini's statues of

But two of the best-known apparitions of St. Michael run to a different pattern. They both involve bulls, possibly because the four archangels of Jewish thought—Raphael, Gabriel, and Uriel as well as Michael—are sometimes identified with the four great angels who hold up the firmament of God's throne in Ezechiel. These four had the faces of a man, a lion, an ox, and an eagle, which signify the four fixed signs of the Zodiac, the four "pillars" of the night sky: the man is the constellation Aquarius, the lion is Leo; we now call the eagle Scorpio, and the ox is Taurus.

This arrangement, in turn, corresponds generally to the description of the four archangels in the Talmud, where each is said to be stationed at one of the four cardinal points of the compass.[279] The only difficulty with this is that Ezechiel's angels are described like the cherubim that were put over the Ark of the Covenant (Ex 25), and Cherubim are a different kind of creature from the Archangels.

Anyway, back in the year 390, a man named Garganus lost his bull as his herd was grazing on the slopes of Mount Gargano, which is in Apulia, forming the spur on the boot of Italy. No matter where he looked, no matter how many of his servants and townspeople turned out to help, Garganus could not find that bull. By the time they found it in a cave at the top of the mountain, Garganus was furious. He put an arrow to his bow and shot at it.

But the arrow turned in its flight and struck Garganus himself. The people went down to consult the bishop in the nearby town of Sipontum, who suggested a three-day fast and public prayers to beg God for an explanation of this phenomenon. At the end of the third day, an angel ablaze with heavenly light appeared to the bishop and said, "It was by my will that this man was struck. I am Michael, the archangel, and I have chosen to dwell on Earth at that spot and keep it for myself. This sign was to show that I watch over that place and guard it."

The people of Sipontum went back up to the cave atop Mount Garganus and prayed, making their peace with the angel. It's just as well that they did, because by the year 491 the people of Naples (which was still the pagan city of Neapolis) came out after the Christians of Sipontum with their armies. They had taken Beneventum, only fifty miles away, so the bishop—St. Laurentius, at that time—asked for three days of truce,

angels carrying the Instruments of the Passion, and it's called the Ponte Sant' Angelo because it leads to the Castle. The Castle itself, by the way, is converted from the massive ruins of the mausoleum of Hadrian; it's the masonry core that was once surrounded by an artificial mountain of earth planted with cypresses and other suitable funerary plants.

279. Num R 2:10. Oxen also figure in the story of Elias (3Kgs 19:19-21), when he was comforted by an angel, possibly Michael. These four astronomical signs are "fixed" because the Sun appears to be travelling through their sectors of the sky in the middle of a definite season, and the weather is steady and fairly predictable (the Sun's in Leo in the middle of summer, for instance). These four signs, holding up the firmament of God's throne, show that Ezechiel is describing the celestial firmament of the sky, as in Jb 22:14. Those creatures are also a prefiguration of Matthew, Mark, Luke, and John, which is why the Evangelists are symbolized by those same creatures. The "wheels within wheels", while we're at it, are just another cosmological symbol, an image of the stars and planets beneath the sky apparently whirling around the Earth.

during which time the people fasted again and asked St. Michael for help. And again, on the third night, he appeared to the bishop and told him to send the troops against the enemy the next morning.

As soon as the armies met, black clouds gathered at the peak of Mount Gargano, lightning flashed from them continuously, and the skies as well as the mountain itself trembled with thunderous tremors. Those of the enemy that weren't killed converted, the *Golden Legend* says, quoting the old *Tripartite History*.

After the mountain and the battle had calmed, the people went up again to the top of the mountain to thank St. Michael for his intercession. They wanted to build a church on the site of the cave, but they weren't sure that St. Michael wanted that. So St. Laurentius sent an inquiry to the pope, St. Felix III, who advised consulting the archangel himself; if he made his will known, somehow, St. Felix said, then they should do as he wanted. St. Laurentius ordered another three days of prayer and fasting. On the third day, which happened to be September 29, 491, the Feast of St. Michael, the archangel appeared to him again. "There is no need for you to build a church there," he said, "for I myself have already built and dedicated it." He told the bishop to take the people up the mountain by means of a certain forgotten path, and that at its head they would find a piece of marble with a man's footprints pressed into it. They found not only the marble but a whole crypt church let into the mountainside, with three altars, one of which was covered with a red mantle.[280] There was a spring there, too, running out from this cave, with sweet water that worked miraculous cures among the Faithful who drank some after communion.

And, in fact, there was a similarly miraculous spring—as well as a piece of that red altar cloth and some of the marble on which the archangel's footprints were impressed—at another shrine, more famous today, that commemorates another apparition of St. Michael. This is the abbey of Mont Saint-Michel, Mount St. Michael-in-Peril-of-the-Sea, off the coast of France.

Mont St.-Michel was also built because a bull, which was stolen in this case and hidden in a cave atop a rocky coastline mountain, was found under the archangel's guidance in an apparition to the local bishop, St. Aubert (d. 725). When the bishop found the animal but didn't know how to go about building a church on the peak of that steep granite rock, St. Michael told him to build the walls along the lines traced by the bull's hoofprints. The only problem was that two immense rocks stood on the site, far too heavy to move; but St. Michael took care of that, too. He appeared to a layman and endowed him with enough strength to toss them aside.

280. The Feast of St. Michael on September 29 used to be called Michaelmas, or the Feast of the Dedication of St. Michael, but not because of the church not built by hands that was found on Mount Gargano. In the year 530, Pope Boniface II, elevated to his office exactly a week before, dedicated a church under that title in the old Circus of Rome, site of many martyrdoms, in commemoration of Michael's function as *psychopomp*, leader of the faithful souls into Paradise. Michaelmas, celebrated near the Autumnal Equinox, was one of the four great feasts that stand at the corners of the calendar year, too, with Christmas at about the Winter Solstice, Easter determined by the Vernal Equinox, and the Nativity of St. John the Baptizer around the time of the Summer Solstice.

To dedicate the new sanctuary, St. Aubert sent to Mount Gargano and received the bit of the mantle and the piece of marble. And when they wondered how a chapter of clerics could manage to live atop that rock, St. Michael instructed them to chip away at the granite at a given spot, which opened the copious spring that supplied the abbey with fresh water for centuries. The monks there, high in their stronghold, held out against all invaders and troublemakers year after year—in fact, it was difficult to get there even if you were an innocent pilgrim. Mont St.-Michel is an isolated rock that stands nearly a mile from the mainland, and it was usually surrounded by the sea, with treacherous currents swirling around it. It still has the most dangerous tides in Europe—the turbulent waters rise at about six feet a second, sweeping away everything in their path. Only at low tide did the water pull back to allow travel between it and the mainland, sort of like the parting of the Red Sea.

There's a causeway there, now, so some of the charm has gone out of Mount St.-Michael-in-Peril-of-the-Sea. Mount Gargano isn't what it used to be, either. With its grotto and healing spring it was once something like Lourdes is now, but devotion to St. Michael has just dropped off, in the past few centuries, which is too bad. The cult of the angels adds a distinctive supernatural dimension, something singularly lofty and noble to our daily existence. Of course, human saints open our eyes to the immense potential of humankind, and they let us see that there's a hero in each of us; but devotion to an archangel lets us approach an entirely different, and higher, order of creature, someone splendid and glorious, incomprehensible in power and intellect and yet interested in our welfare, who can communicate and even appear to us Earth-bound people.

And St. Michael is the perfect archangel for each of us to think about because, in the unofficial angelology of Christianity, he's going to appear to each of us, one day—he's the one who escorts the souls of the Faithful departed into Paradise, holding high the banner that God's legions follow. "May they not fall into darkness," reads the Offertory of the old Requiem Mass in the *Missale Romanum*, "but may the standard-bearer, holy Michael, lead them into the light".[281]

That's why St. Jude recalls that Michael disputed with Satan about the dead Moses (Jd 9), and why there are, or used to be, so many oratories dedicated to him at or near cemeteries throughout Christendom; it's not by chance that the funeral church of the Czars in Moscow is dedicated to him. What's more, it's up to St. Michael to weigh the souls of the Faithful departed and separate the sheep from the goats, which is why you often see St. Michael standing at the center of scenes of the Last Judgement, his sword of vengeance in one hand and the scales of justice in the other, dispatching souls one way or the other, as their works require them to go.

281. He can do this for each of the thousands who die every minute, of course, because he, like the departed souls, lives outside of Time in Sempiternity, where there's no before or after. Leo XIII Pecci, by the way, recommended saying this prayer after Mass: St. Michael Archangel, defend us in battle; be our defense against the wickedness and snares of the Devil. May God rebuke him, we humbly pray; and do you, O Prince of the Heavenly Host, by the power of God, thrust into Hell Satan and the other evil spirits who prowl about the world for the ruin of souls. Amen.

twenty-seven

St. Anthony of Padua
Segovia, 1455

Give therefore your hearts and your souls
to seek the Lord your God.
And arise, and build a sanctuary to the Lord God ...

— 1 Paralipomenon 22:19

One of the standard statues in every parish church shows a good-looking young man in a brown habit holding a book on which the Christ Child sits. It's possible today that people aren't even sure who this young Franciscan is, but since his canonization in 1232, he's been one of the most beloved, and most lovable, saints in the whole history of the Church. In fact, he was particularly lovable from the very day he was born, which happened to be August 15, 1195, the Feast of the Assumption.

This saint was born Fernando de Bouillon in a palace in Lisbon close to the cathedral. His father, Martino de Bouillon, traced his ancestry to Godfrey de Bouillon, the first Frankish King of Jerusalem during the Crusades. His mother's family had ruled the kingdom of Asturias from some forgotten past until the Saracens invaded in the eighth century.

Their son Fernando was an exceptional child, no matter how you looked at him. Rich, noble, intelligent, and remarkably handsome, he was also sweet natured, cheerful, and immensely popular. He was deeply religious, too, and particularly devoted to the Blessed Virgin. Even when he was an infant, all they had to do was show him a picture or a statue of Mary to stop his crying at once. He'd grow up to be a good prince, everybody thought, using his wealth and position responsibly for the good of the greatest possible numbers of people.

But one day when the boy was praying in the cathedral, before the Blessed Sacrament reserved at the altar of Our Lady, a demon appeared before him. Never one to be distracted from his prayers, he overcame his shock and traced the Sign of the Cross on the marble step on which he knelt, and the apparition vanished.[282]

That was the pivot of his life. He was only fifteen at the time, but he went to the nearby Augustinian monastery of St. Vincent and asked to be received. He loved the life there, but the Augustinians weren't cloistered all that strictly, and Fernando's friends weren't exactly clear on what religious life meant, either. They came out to see him, dozens of them, at all hours, and they never seemed to take the hint. It was enough to try the patience of a saint. Fernando put up with it for two years, but at last he begged his prior to send him someplace farther away where his friends couldn't find him.

They sent him to the motherhouse of the Augustinians, the Abbey of Santa Cruz about a hundred miles away. Now, as it happened, this was one of Europe's major centers of learning at the time, and Fernando almost immediately showed astonishing, almost miraculous, intellectual powers. He had already virtually memorized all available classical literature by the time he got to Santa Cruz, but now he absorbed theology, history, and the Fathers of the Church with no apparent effort.

Like St. John of the Cross four hundred years later, he knew the Bible by heart, and like St. John he learned it in record time. But it was more than just a photographic memory, apparently; he remembered everything that he read or heard, and he could recall it instantly, but he could also synthesize it all, putting it all together fluently, eloquently, to make something new that was greater than the sum of its parts. Yet he took on all of those hours of study in addition to the regular duties of a novice. He was so punctual in his duties that the casual observer—even his superiors—wouldn't immediately notice that he was taking on anything extra.

There were other signs of extraordinary sanctity, too: the raving lunatic in the abbey's hospital instantly and permanently cured by Fernando's cloak spread over him, for instance. One day, he was confined to bed with illness, himself, stuck in the infirmary far from the oratory, but when he heard the elevation bell (rung at that point in the Mass when the priest lifts up the Body of Christ at the altar) he leapt up and prostrated himself in the direction of the altar. Everyone there looked up with him to see that the walls between him and the oratory had opened up, somehow, so that the Mass could be followed from where he was.

But something was nagging him. He saw so much need out in the world, not just thousands of Christians who needed a revival of their faith but millions of people outside the Church entirely—like the Muslims, always on the minds of Iberian Christians. Like all saints at a certain point in their spiritual development, he was eager for martyrdom, but he saw that this particular crown was virtually impossible as long as he stayed inside the enclosure. And he also saw a little Franciscan friary, just outside the walls of Santa Cruz.

282. The cross is still shown at the cathedral, indelibly marked in the marble.

The Franciscans at that time were an entirely new idea in the Church, and the other orders weren't all that eager to have their best and brightest drained off to fill its ranks.[283] Still, Fernando kept asking to be transferred, and he kept making sense, so finally they let him take off the white Augustinian habit and put on the simple brown habit of the Franciscans. He also took off his old name and called himself Anthony, after St. Anthony Abbot, the patron of the little friary at Santa Cruz.[284]

The Franciscans sent him to Morocco as a missionary, just as he'd wanted, but as soon as he got there he contracted some kind of desert fever that nearly killed him. He lay there for four months, evidently without even seeing a Moor, until his superiors called him and his companions back. But on the way from Morocco to Portugal, they got blown off course. A storm—which must have been really pretty severe, when you think about it, and awfully well directed—blew their ship all the way to Sicily. They walked from their landing at Taormina all the way to Messina, where they were taken in at the local friary.[285] Well, the friars there were getting ready to attend the fourth general chapter of the order, in Assisi, which would be presided over by Francis himself. Anthony and his companions went along, too.

He was evidently so moved by seeing St. Francis that he volunteered to be transferred to Assisi permanently, and St. Francis approved eagerly. But then Anthony did something fairly strange, even for an advanced ascetic: having renounced his fortune, his family, and his country, he renounced himself, in a way. He didn't let anybody know how brilliant he was, or how educated. Not by any sign, not by anything he said, not by an expression on his face, not in any way whatsoever. He appeared so perfectly ordinary that the masters of novices didn't want to take him at all. Finally, they put him in the kitchen and assigned him to sweeping up the whole place (which he did excellently, by the way; like all of the great mystics, he liked things scrupulously clean). But he was so self-effacing that nobody gave him any thought at all, until the Provincial of Bologna needed a priest for a hospice in the mountainous countryside in Tuscany and couldn't find one. Anthony, sweeping his way past the Provincial, happened to catch his eye. "You," the Provincial said, "are you a priest?"

283. Usually, transfer from one order to another, for professed religious, requires the approval of the Pope, and it doesn't happen all that often.

284. St. Anthony Abbot, or of Egypt, or of the Desert, was a Copt who took to the Egyptian desert as a hermit and became one of the founders of western monasticism; his sensational temptations are often depicted in art. He's sometimes overshadowed by his latter-day namesake, St. Anthony of Padua, or even engulfed entirely; at one Spanish shrine, they had to put up a statue of St. Anthony Abbot next to the one of St. Anthony of Padua, to make the distinction, and change the name to the Shrine of the Saint Anthonys. Or Saints Anthony. *Los Santos Antonios.*

285. While he was there, St. Anthony planted a lemon tree in the friary garden, which was still flourishing late in the last century and may still be flourishing, for that matter, like the orange tree that St. Dominic planted at Santa Sabina in Rome. The vine that sprouted from the dry stick that the prioress made St. Rita of Cascia water every day as a test of obedience still flourishes, too, at the convent of Santa Maria Maddalena. Its abundant fruit is distributed to churchmen of high rank, and its leaves are powdered and given to the sick all over the world.

Anthony said that he was, so the Provincial took him; not excessively bright, maybe, but better than no priest at all, he thought. Anthony spent the next few years living in a cave near the hospice, deep in penance and in virtual silence; his lay brethren there didn't give him much thought, either. But then he had to be in Forlì for the ordination of a lot of priests, where that same Provincial was supposed to give the customary address to the candidates on the excellence of their priestly life. Well, for some reason, the Provincial didn't want to do it. He deferred first of all to the Benedictines who were there, but they said that they weren't prepared. So he turned to Anthony—it's hard to think of a reason other than divine inspiration—and told him to do it, right now.

Anthony said something about how he was better suited to work in the kitchen, but under obedience he took his place in front of the assembly and started in. It was the first time he had ever spoken in public, much less preached, but everything that he had learned came back to him, and he was inspired, too, in the usual sense of the word. His immense learning, his eloquence, his logic, and the princely charm of manner that he'd so successfully hidden until then all came pouring out. The local Provincial immediately appointed him a preacher in his province, and St. Francis himself extended that mission, giving Anthony permission to preach everywhere.

But they didn't know him, yet. They sent him to study at Vercelli, as if he needed it. He raced through everything that they had to offer, and within a year or so they sent him to Bologna, not as a student but as a teacher, and then to Toulouse and Montpelier. Interestingly enough, he lectured easily in Italian and French, although nobody could figure out exactly when or how he had learned those languages.

(It was probably just his intellect; miraculously infused languages are casually reported in the lives of other saints, too, but, like St. Francis Xavier struggling to learn a little Tamil "miraculously" while everybody else was asleep, they burned a lot of midnight oil. It's reported, if vaguely, that St. Anthony addressed the Pope and Curia, and each man heard the saint in his own native language; this would be about the only time since St. Paul (1Cr 14:18) that the gift of tongues has happened in the Church. The modern phenomenon is the opposite of the biblical events, not a mystic gift at all but a psychological condition prompted by emotional strain, usually an overwhelming feeling of inadequacy or failure. It isn't spontaneous but learned; the pattern can be described linguistically and traced to the charismatic leader who taught it, if only by example, to the speaker. As regressive behavior, it's somewhat anti-social, a "bridge-burning act" that signals allegiance to the sect and rejection of mainstream society. It occurs among separated and even non-Christian sects, but in terms of numbers most frequently among the disordered who believe themselves to be from another planet or dimension, which also sets them apart as superior to those who do not speak thus.[286])

286. See for example T. Flournoy, *Des Indes à la planète Mars: étude sur un cas de somnambulisme avec glossolalie* (Geneva, 1900; C. T. K. Chari's introduction and notes to the 1963 reissue of Daniel B. Dermilye's 1900 translation are particularly enlightening); F. Goodman, "Phonetic Analysis of Glossolalia in Four Cultural Settings", *Journal for the Scientific Study of Religion* (VIII, 2, Fall, 1969); V. H. Hine, "Bridge Burners: Commitment and Participation in a Religious Movement", *Sociological Analysis* (1970, 31); J. Laffal, *Pathological and Normal Language* (New York, 1965); J. N. Lapsley and J. M. Simpson, "Speaking

St. Anthony of Padua, Segovia, 1455

Anthony had pretty much the same effect on his students as he'd had on the audience at Forlì, so, eventually, he was relieved of his duties and sent out to the largest possible audience, the world at large. His preaching drew thousands and tens of thousands, wherever he went in Europe, but it was the miracles that really attracted attention. His mere presence calmed strife in the cities he visited—and cities at that time were almost always in full-blown civil war—and it's reported that thieves restored stolen property, enemies reconciled, and life generally improved. He casually predicted the future lives of passers-by who stopped to hear him, and even the lives of their children yet unborn. People brought him their sick to be healed and even their dead to be restored to life, all of which he did cheerfully. In fact, people just approached him with any little problem, demanding miracles from him just as you'd ask members of the family to get you a snack, while they're up.[287]

But the experience that he's most remembered for was more private, much quieter, and, in its way, a lot more spectacular. Stories about it circulated for years, and it was reported by his biographers without too many particulars until the seventeenth century, when the Carmelite Père Bonaventure de St.-Amable found the original report recorded in the *Annals de Limousin*, the local governmental archive of the Limousin region of west-central France.

Anthony was staying at the house of the Lord of Châteauneuf in the region and, when the household retired, he went to his room to pray all night as usual. Well, the master of the house was awakened by a lot of bright light pouring out from under the door to Anthony's room and through the cracks in the wood—thirteenth-century castles weren't renowned for coziness. All the candles in the house couldn't have made such a bright and such a clear light, so he got up to see if the house were on fire. But he didn't smell smoke: he smelled an exquisite and rosy fragrance purer and sweeter than that of any earthly roses. And he heard a pure music that didn't sound like the music

in Tongues: Token of Group Acceptance and Divine Approval", *Pastoral Psychology* (May, 1964); R. P. Lieberman *et al.*, "Reducing Delusional Speech in Chronic Paranoid Schizophrenics", *Journal of Applied Behavioral Analysis* (6:567-64, 1973); L. C. May, "A Survey of Glossolalia and Related Phenomena in Non-Christian Religions", *American Anthropologist* (58, 1956); K. Runia, "Glossolalia as Learned Behavior", *Canadian Journal of Theology* (15); and N. P. Spanos, *et. al.*, "Glossolalia as Learned Behavior: An Experimental Demonstration", *Journal of Abnormal Psychology* (95, 1986). Speaking genuine languages without study, of course, is one of the more familiar signs of diabolic possession; see the *Rituale Romanum*, Poulain, Garrigou-Lagrange, etc.; but, again, there has been no recent case of genuine languages spoken without study. On the other hand, one might expect that there are groups who define their religious practices with other forms of infantile regression; and indeed there are today and there have always been groups, for instance, that practice "Christian nudity", shedding their clothes periodically in their services or permanently as a style of life.

287. That's probably why today he's the patron of lost objects; there's not much in any recorded biography to account for the practice, except that he has always responded in good humor to even the smallest requests. To this day, men, women, and children who lose things just call on him (sometimes with the least-formal prayer in common use: "Tony, Tony, turn around; something's lost and must be found," which he probably gets a smile out of) and they say a little prayer for his intentions or feed the poor through a charitable donation, favor for favor.

produced by instruments, but that just sort of happened, without the workings of any material body.

He peeked in through a crack in the door and saw Anthony kneeling before a table on which an open book rested. The Christ Child, looking about nine months old and radiant with light, was sitting on the book so that Anthony couldn't turn the pages. The two played silently amid the bright perfumed music until the Child leaned to whisper in the friar's ear. Then both of them looked toward the door, smiling. The master of Châteauneuf, stunned by the sight, pulled himself back to bed, but he knew that the two had seen him.

The next morning, the *Annals* say, the Lord of Châteauneuf said simply, "Father, what did Our Lord say to you?" Anthony answered, "He said that your house will flourish and enjoy great prosperity as long as it remains faithful to the Church; but it will be overwhelmed with misfortune and die out when it converts to heresy." As it turned out, that's exactly what happened. The family died out in poverty after they became Calvinists.

Anyway, that's why St. Anthony is shown all over Christendom with his book and the Child. But after his missionary trip all over France, his superiors sent him to Padua, a wild place in those days, with rival political camps fighting pitched battles in the streets, robbers, brigands, and everything. Anthony pacified the place, and, although he apparently minced no words with them—or probably *because* he spoke plainly—they absolutely loved him. He was allowed to stay there, preaching and teaching until the springtime of 1231; then he wanted to retire, even though he was only thirty-six. His austere lifestyle had worn him out, and he must have had the idea that his work was nearly done.

So he did something that only a son of St. Francis would think of. He went out into the woods around Padua and found an immense walnut tree, and he made a treehouse. He spent whole days and nights in it, fasting and praying, until he came down one day to die. His companions tried to get him into Padua—he'd wanted to die in the city—but he passed on before they got him there, dying in the chaplain's rooms at the convent of the Poor Clares of Arcella.

The loving familiarity with which St. Anthony's followers approached him for miracles is probably why from after his death until about the time of the Protestant Reformation, apparitions of St. Anthony of Padua were reported more frequently than those of any other saint, except Mary. He was particularly likely to appear whenever people neglected their religious duties, and he appeared in a unique manner, also absolutely typical of Franciscan mentality. Not in a blaze of glory, not gliding down out of the sky, he was just there, a simple friar at prayer, who spoke familiarly, even jocularly, to the people who saw him, just as he had always done.

This is how it happened in the little Spanish town of Navas de Zarzuela just outside of Segovia in the summer of 1455.[288]

288. The deposition about the event is posted on the wall of the church there, but it's not widely known outside of Spain. Evidently the only other English-language account of the episode is in William A. Christian's *Apparitions in Late Medieval and Renaissance Spain* (Princeton, 1981).

Little Juan González went in to the village church one morning and saw a friar who called him over and said, "Tell the people of this town to build a church at the wayside shrine on the road to Segovia where it crosses the Monte de Sancho." The friar also told him to establish a brotherhood to take care of the church, and then he simply disappeared.

The boy got the standard treatment for young visionaries. He told the sexton, who came by at that moment, and the sexton told him to keep quiet or he'd whip him. Juan told his parents, who told him to stop lying. A few days later, the friar appeared to the boy as he was getting ready to ring the church bells and asked if he had done as ordered. "I do not know what you ordered," the boy answered. The friar repeated his request, and Juan said, "Well, I told it to my friend and my father, and he threatened to beat me, and they said I should keep quiet." The friar said, "Tell the people of this town to believe what you say," and disappeared again.

Juan was disturbed by the meeting, and his father Luis pressed him to find out what was wrong. The boy told him, and Luis said the same thing as before: stop lying or I'll beat you.

A few days after that, the boy was out in the pasture looking for a burro when he saw the friar again. He ran away as fast as he could, but when the friar called him he was compelled to stop. "Why didn't you do what I ordered?" he asked. Juan explained, and the friar said, "Pay attention. I order that you tell the people of this town to build me a church and set up a brotherhood so that all will join to build my church." Juan turned to run away again, but the friar called out to him. "Tell the people of this town that I am San Antonio, and that it is my will that they build me a church where I have indicated and establish a brotherhood."

Now, this time, maybe because of the weight of the name, Luis González believed his son, or at least took him seriously. He consulted with the artisans of the town, and during the meeting they heard the funeral knell from the village church. Luis knelt down, in front of all the artisans, a notary, and the town officials, and begged Saint Anthony to beg Christ to restore the dead woman to life, much as he had done in Lisbon and elsewhere.

They left for the church, and as soon as they entered the woman, the wife of Antonio Fernández de Mazarías, looked up and praised St. Anthony for having restored her to life. That was enough for Luis; he thanked the saint, too, and told the assembled townspeople what his son had told him.

The church was built, on the spot that the friar had indicated, and rebuilt in the sixteenth century. It's still an active center of the little town's spiritual life. The town itself, by the way, changed its name from Navas de Zarzuela to Navas de San Antonio, after that.

part five

be clear when you judge

That you might be justified when you speak
and clear when you judge

Psalm 50:4

twenty-eight

sciences

with certain rules

All of these sciences have certain and infallible rules,
like rays of light shining down upon our mind
from the eternal law. And thus our mind,
illumined and flooded by such brilliance,
unless it be blind, can be led through itself
to contemplate that Eternal Light.

— St. Bonaventure, *The Soul's Journey Into God* (1259)

When you look at the world's religions, you can see that they fall into certain categories according to a few distinct types. Some religions, like Hinduism or the native religions of North America, Africa, and the Pacific Islands, were developed over a long period of time, as people watched the workings of nature. These are classified as *natural* or *developed* religions, and they continue to evolve and change, with some of their gods fading into obscurity, other gods added, and sometimes whole new religions worked into them as people with other natural religions move into, or across, their territory.

Some other religions get their start from a single teacher, like Buddhism or Confucianism, or the Chinese doctrine founded by Lao Tzu. The Roman state religion established by King Numa was also this kind of religion, and evidently so was the worship centered on Quetzalcoatl. Over time, though, these can blend with other religions, too, or other teachers add to the original body of teachings or change it to keep up with the times, or they write their own ideas down under the name of that original teacher. Since these religions are often based entirely on a single book, these changes cloud the original teacher's ideas, and, as time goes on, it becomes impossible to tell exactly what those teachings were, in the first place.

But a few religions are classified as *revealed* religions. Judaism is one, the first, historically; it claims to have been designed in the mind of God as a whole and revealed through the prophets little by little over the centuries. Obviously, this is different from religions based on the teachings of one leader, because all of the prophets were talking about the same things, the same precepts always standing in the same relationships to each other. Jesus of Nazareth was not a single teacher establishing a new creed, either, but, in the Church's view, the ultimate prophet, God himself incarnate, who came to perfect the revelation that he had given bit by bit for all of those years to the prophets of Israel.

Now, because a revealed religion claims to be given by God, its teachings can't logically be added to or subtracted from by any human agency. In other words, you can't profess to believe that your God gave you a religion and at the same time say that you can change parts of it or tear parts out. The attitude that humans can improve on God's design (or reject the parts that we don't want to be bothered with) is the essence of heresy—the very word comes from a Greek word meaning "to pick and choose". By its very nature, by the way in which it came to be and the way it works day to day, and by its harmony with the rest of creation, a revealed religion is a unit, indivisible: it's not a theological cafeteria in which you can pick and choose. Logically, if God designed it and gave it to you, you have to take the whole thing or leave it.

R EVELATION, P UBLIC AND P RIVATE

Christ's teachings were completed after the Ascension by the Holy Spirit, and they were fully present on Earth by the time the last Apostle died (St. John, in 70 AD; Jn 16:12-15). If you understand Christ as God, then he's not going to leave his work unfinished here or teach us anything inconsistent or contradictory, or just incorrect, that has to be changed later. He himself said that his teachings should be delivered, intact, to all nations until the end of Time and that his Church would be *indefectible* (Jn 14:16, 16:12-15; Ac 13:1-12; Hb 1:1-2; 1Tm 6:14; 2Tm 1:6-14; Ti 2:13; etc.), guarded by the Holy Spirit from allowing any additions or subtractions to the fullness of his revelation and that of the prophets.[289]

So, in the Church today, you have an unchanged body of teachings, called the "Deposit of Revelation" or the "Deposit of Faith", that came from Christ, directly or through the prophets and the Apostles. That deposit has never changed; it's the sub-

---

289. Of course, one of the ways that heretical leaders mislead people away is to claim that the Church has added and subtracted, but the documentary evidence shows that it never happened; even news reports about how the Pope holds to the Church's position (no matter how unpopular that standpoint is at the moment) weigh against this misrepresentation. The Church alone maintains Sacred Tradition, Christ's teachings that have never been written down; the New Testament consists of information that exists in Tradition and was written down by the Church under the inspiration of the Holy Spirit, so the Church is the only organization from which you can get the New Testament intact. In fact, it's the only place you can find the original Old Testament, the one that Christ knew and quoted; the Jews changed it when the Temple was destroyed, at the death of the last Apostle, when they switched to observances based in synagogues instead. Protestant sects, of course, adopted this heavily revised version.

stance of the Faith, and acceptance of this body of teachings is what defines a person as a Christian.[290] Just as she has never subtracted any of it, the Church has never added anything to it, either: "The Christian dispensation," Vatican II repeated, "as the new and definitive covenant, will never pass away, and we now await no further new public revelation before the glorious manifestation of Our Lord Jesus Christ."[291] In fact, that's exactly what this kind of revelation is called: *public* revelation, because Christ said that it was to be given to all nations (Mt 24:14, 28:19; Mr 11:17, 13:10; Lk 24:47).

But there's also an entirely different kind of revelation, a phenomenon called *private* revelation. This is not part of the substance of public revelation, but rather a sort of reminder of some part of it, given by God, sometimes by way of an angel or a saint, to an individual person. This can be a simple and fairly routine matter like the answer to a prayer, or it may be by way of an extraordinary event like an apparition or a locution, or even through a miraculous healing. The important thing to remember about private revelation or any other personal extraordinary phenomenon is that, as far as the Church is concerned, it's not essential to the Faith. But because these phenomena are so attractive, it's always been hard for the Church to make this point. "If you have any sense at all," begged Lactantius early in the fourth century, "if you have any sense at all, learn that we don't believe in Christ, we don't believe that he is God, because he worked miracles but because we have seen that in him all of the things that were announced to us beforehand by the predictions of the prophets were fulfilled!"[292]

290. But of course it's not supposed to be accepted without question; the Church understands that genuine faith questions constantly, wanting to learn more about the Deposit of Revelation and the way it works in the world. Difficulty in comprehending the answers often happens because of communication problems, discrepancies in intellectual capacity, and the like, none of which can incur blame. But basically everybody can understand, and usually the best way around the difficulty is to just assume that you don't understand the matter sufficiently yet—it's certainly not helpful to assume that the fault is with Christianity. Fighting off the truth is culpable; true faith has nothing to fear from the truth, whether that truth is about a spiritual or a material matter—all of creation is understood as the product of God's mind, too, and part of that same overarching truth. But human understanding about the observable universe changes. Scientific theories come and go, and none can ever be definitive, which is why the Church doesn't endorse any as matters of faith; they're all human constructions, by nature outside the Deposit of Revelation. (The case of Galileo was based not on disagreement but on scandal.) Still, the existence of moral theology, unique in the Church, means that Christianity is intimately united with the daily actuality of human life in ways that reflect both human and divine reality and aren't going to change. So questioning is fine, but doubt (thinking that some or all of Christianity might not be true) is inappropriate, because a Christian by definition accepts the Deposit of Revelation, and reason accords with its truth.

291. *Dogmatic Constitution on Divine Revelation*, 1:4 (November 18, 1965). It's also true, though, that human understanding of that fixed body of revelation gets clearer as time goes on, and as it's applied to novel situations; so the Church can articulate it more clearly and extend its provisions to an ever-widening area of human life. It's also true that revelation is living and responsive, the action of the Holy Spirit in and through the Church. So you may find Christianity permeating a part of life where you hadn't noticed it before, but that doesn't mean that something's been added.

292. This distinction is even harder to make if you use latter-day versions of the Bible like the King James or others that use the Jamnian Canon of the Old Testament, which was heavily edited and purposefully re-translated after the destruction of the Temple so that it could be used to argue against Christ's fulfillment of the prophecies.

KEEPING TO THE STRAIGHT AND NARROW

Of course, Christ's miracles and those other extraordinary phenomena recorded in the Bible are indispensable matters of faith, as part of public revelation; but the others aren't. The Faithful are completely free to believe or not believe in any of those later ones that are officially declared worthy of belief. Remember that apparitions and other mystic phenomena fall under the heading of moral theology, not doctrinal theology: they cannot alter, contradict, add to, or subtract from public revelation—the doctrine preserved and taught by the Church—or even imply such change. And since they don't touch the substance of public revelation, any Christian is free to get along without them. The only thing that private revelations can do, at best, is just nudge you back to the truth of public revelation or of some facet of it, drawing your attention to some essential point of that doctrine and the way in which you apply it in your life.

But no matter how inessential apparitions and locutions and miracles are, the most simplistic and irrational claims can draw a great deal of attention and even the fiercest loyalty among the Faithful, and usually most fervently among those whose faith is weakest or whose religious education is not yet complete (Mt 12:38-39, 16:1-4; Mr 8:11-12; Lk 11:16-29; Jn 2:18, 6:30; 1Cr 1:22; and, above all, Jn 20:29).

There are some places where people think that you must have secondary mystic phenomena to be holy. Everybody expects that attitude in southern Italy or South America, but it's easy to forget that there are whole socio-economic classes in Europe and in this country who think that way, too. Some of these are people who won't necessarily go to church or who won't exert themselves to learn all that they might about the basic catechism of Christianity but who will flock in droves to a reported apparition or the tent meetings of a faith healer. Others hinge their whole idea of Christianity on the expectation of a single phenomenon, like miraculous healing, or even on something that would stand outside the normal catalogue of Christian mystic gifts, such as idioglossia or immunity from toxins.[293]

Obviously, this kind of thing leads people away from a clearer understanding of the Faith, if only because it encourages them to concentrate on empty promises—empty because you can't demand real mystic phenomena of God—and to concentrate, in fact, on promises of things that aren't even part of Christian doctrine.

---

293. Cults centered on survival of some kind of toxin usually start when somebody takes Mr 16:18 literally, and out of context. No Christian can presume exceptional treatment under the laws of nature and of nature's God, of course. The enemies of St. Louis-Marie Grignion de Montfort slipped some poison into his broth, to stop his massive conversions; he was warned before he'd taken more than a little of it, but it was enough to leave him weakened for the rest of his life. About the only case of miraculous immunity on record is that of St. Anthony of Padua, who had been invited to dinner by heretics—Cathari who believed Satan was lord of this world (which they saw as the only Hell), that they alone had true spiritual Baptism, that human spirits were reincarnated as animals, and so on. They wanted to poison him because of his massive conversions, too, but he knew of their plot and proclaimed it. When they dared him to eat the poisoned food anyway as a test of faith, he blessed it and ate it without harm, although their request was the sin of tempting God. After which those present at the miracle converted, too.

Looking at it from the other side, the spectacle of people flocking to the face of Mary on a screen door, or of hopeful crowds clamoring around a messianic faith healer, can make a lot of otherwise faithful people turn in embarrassment from genuine mystic phenomena that do have clear precedents in the Bible and in Sacred Tradition, phenomena that really can clarify understanding and strengthen faith. False mystic phenomena are divisive, tearing hostile minorities off from parishes and dioceses, and, because they're usually unedifying, they bring the whole Church into disrepute, turning away potential converts—to say nothing of the lukewarm.

But even if the phenomena are genuine, the last thing a bishop wants is for the Faithful to be distracted by something that isn't essential to the Faith or, as Benedict XIV phrased it, something that isn't necessary for the attainment of sanctity nor for salvation. "One act done in charity is more precious in God's sight," St. John of the Cross reminds us, "than all the visions and communications possible—since they imply neither merit nor demerit—and many who have not received these experiences are incomparably more advanced than others who have had many" (*Ascent of Mount Carmel*, 2:19).

So the Church has to take steps to guard against false mystic phenomena and to make their true nature known to the public, and to advise carefully on those that show themselves creditable. That's why, if a reported mystic phenomenon attracts an unseemly amount of attention before it can be fully investigated, the bishop may remind the Faithful of the unanimous advice of every creditable mystic and every moral theologian: mystic phenomena of any kind should be rejected, if they happen to you, and none is essential, which goes for spectators as well as for visionaries. If the phenomenon is from God, they remind us, then God has some purpose in mind for the occurrence; and if God wills it, then it will come to be recognized even if everybody, out of common sense and caution, holds back until that purpose is clear. And the bishop might also point out that it can take a long time to rule out natural or diabolic causes, too.

The Church is uniquely equipped to do this. Only the Church has a vigorous and logical moral theology—only the Church has moral theology at all. She's also the only religion to have a regular juridical process to evaluate these reports. So only the Church can speak authoritatively on apparitions and other mystic phenomena. Because these phenomena are inessential, because false ones have the power to distract the Faithful, and because all such reports are so disruptive, the whole aim of the Church's investigative process is to find any—any—good reason to discredit the report and keep the Faithful on the ordinary path: regular, day-to-day sacramental and spiritual life within the Church. This often confuses sympathetic onlookers. "I cannot understand why the authorities seek to put obstacles in the way of the free publication of this fact," Monsieur Vène, one of the scientists who analyzed the water at Lourdes in 1858, wrote to Dr. Dozous. "Possibly obstacles are necessary for its manifestation." But then he hit on precisely the reason for taking plenty of time and trying to disprove any extraordinary report. "This at least may be said," he concluded: "if the finger of God is there, all the efforts of mankind will prove powerless" (*cf.* Ac 5:38-39).

Approval, Not Assent

Private revelations never receive any assent from the Church. Even the Church's official approval just says that these extraordinary events contain nothing contrary to the Faith; that they are probable, not that they're undoubted; that they're "worthy of belief", not that they must be believed. And this approval is pronounced on a purely human authority, not on the authoritative teaching of the Church. That's why private revelations are never used as oracles: they're never used to decide any questions about history, science, philosophy, or anything else, least of all theology.[294] Each of us is free to hold a different opinion or to entertain doubts, provided that we rely on good solid reasons—reasons based in sound theology—and particularly if the contrary viewpoint is supported by unimpeachable documents. As for those that have not been officially approved, or certainly those that have been officially condemned, the best counsel is still that same advice from St. John of the Cross: reject them.

Even so, reported extraordinary phenomena draw crowds, and they have to be investigated and evaluated. It's impossible to cover all of the subtleties of this evaluation process in a single book. One of the basic works on the subject, Benedict XIV Lambertini's *Doctrinam de servorum Dei beatificatione et beatorum canonizatione*, runs to half a dozen folio volumes,[295] and there have been many, many other authoritative works written since his day, and long before—even St. Paul had to start outlining the process, when the Corinthians felt themselves extraordinarily privileged by God. Within only a couple of generations, the process had developed logical procedures, rules of evidence, and juridical mechanisms parallel to those used to try civil and criminal cases.

"It's too long a story to set forth here," St. Augustine said. But, he added, "I think that it will occur readily to anybody who thinks about it even moderately." And in fact the process of judgement is basically good common sense, operating through the same rules of logic that govern any other systematic process of human thought, and it centers on factors like the nature of the reported phenomenon itself; the nature of the evidence for it, including the character of the people involved; and the logic with which the evidence is weighed.

294. Although Ven. Mary of Agreda cheerfully answered all of the political and personal questions put to her by the intellectually challenged Philip IV of Spain. He'd write them down one side of a sheet of paper, and she'd write her answers in the other column. The advice that she gave in these double letters, six hundred and fifty-four of them over twenty years, isn't very acute or even very interesting, although it undoubtedly came as a revelation to Philip IV. But the material reported in private revelations is never used or even even cited in theological books, except of course those specialized works on mystic theology that discuss private revelations; the line between private and public revelation is absolute.

295. He wrote it while he was still serving as "Devil's Advocate" in the canonization process—the person charged with trying as hard as the Devil's own lawyer would to keep a candidate from being declared a saint. Because really the whole canonization process is aimed at doing just that, there's no particular office to fill that function any more; everybody involved in the canonization process actively searches for any reason whatsoever to disqualify the candidate.

THE MECHANISMS OF JUDGEMENT

Investigation of any reported mystic phenomenon is reserved to the local ordinary—the bishop who has ordinary jurisdiction over the diocese in which the event occurred (see for example the 1983 *Code of Canon Law*, Canons 752-756). Although the Pope can override the decision of the local ordinary (with sufficient reason), he's not likely to, and he isn't obliged to pass judgement on reported apparitions or any other mystic gifts, any more than the other bishops are. The bishop's silence on things going on in the diocese is important in these cases: it tells you, in no uncertain terms, that the thing isn't worth notice, so you can go on about your business. Even if he makes an announcement about it, what he doesn't say is just as important as what he does say. But whether complete or partial, the bishop's silence, like his declaration that there's nothing happening that's worthy of belief, ought to be taken as definitive.

But if the phenomenon seems to have some religious value or some clearly supernatural source, or if it just persists although obviously fraudulent and worthless, the bishop can assemble a commission of inquiry and begin the regular juridical procedure for investigating and judging the extraordinary phenomena that fall within the scope of that study. There are logical guidelines about ruling out natural but unknown causes, although this might not be immediately apparent because there are always people outside the Church who propose thoroughly illogical procedures that get disproportionate attention in the news media. You often hear professional magicians and other self-appointed debunkers carping about how "The Church" doesn't let them touch miraculous images, for instance, "because they don't really want to know the truth", or "they get a lot of money from it," which is wrong on both counts.

For one thing, because the judgement rests with each bishop, you can't fairly talk about how "The Church" handles it; judgement on these matters is not centralized in Rome. And although there's probably no phone call any bishop looks forward to less than the one about a levitating housewife or a weeping statue, the bishops do investigate apparently noteworthy phenomena thoroughly—after all, a genuine mystic phenomenon has some value in renewing faith, and it would be the will of God, the One and Absolute Truth with whom the Church co-operates in absolute obedience.

The closing of the site is never to obstruct investigation; it's either (like silence) to show that investigation isn't necessary for something of that caliber, or it's to secure the site so that an investigation can be made in good order. Naturally, the crowds have to be kept a reasonable distance away from the phenomenon, to avoid purposeful or accidental tampering or destruction of evidence, just as the police have to close a site so that detectives can work with unimpaired evidence. And the bishop has the added responsibility of preventing sacrilege against something that may really turn out to be a special favor from God. Beyond that, a bishop has to be very conservative about the qualifications of the experts consulted.

A reputed miracle or apparition is first of all a theological phenomenon, so accredited theologians have to be consulted, not just moral theologians but doctrinal ones, too. They can usually tell right off the bat whether the report has anything noteworthy in it; they're experts. But it's a physical phenomenon, too, and so the investigation also demands participants with certified credentials in other fields: medicine, psychology, forensic pathology, physics, chemistry, law (civil, criminal, and canon), and any number of other disciplines, even to geology and astronomy and meteorology, sometimes.[296]

Usually, the most vocal debunkers have neither kind of qualification. Like the policemen who pestered St. Bernadette and the bureaucrats who terrified the children of Fátima, they're not trained theologians, and they're often not accredited scientists, either. In investigating mystic phenomena, just as in civil procedures, the experts consulted have to be professionals who are degreed and respected, not merely entertainers who can figure out a mechanical way to cause the appearances of the event.

The Logic of Proof

Again, the primary principle in thinking about any mystic phenomenon, or any report of one, is that you can take it or leave it; you're free to believe or disbelieve, no matter what. But you're not necessarily free to attack; in fairness you'd have to look at the matter logically, as the Church does, and also to evaluate logically the pronouncements of those who always stand ready to debunk any and all reports, even reports of events judged creditable.

In fact, the major problem that clouds understanding of mystic phenomena these days is simply that so few people know how to think. Most of us aren't taught logic in grade school, any more, which makes us figure that everything's a matter of opinion or feeling; that makes it extraordinarily difficult for competent professionals to communicate their perfectly valid procedures and findings to us. It sets us up as easy marks for all kinds of irrationality when we look at a reported mystic event (or even when we vote or serve on juries, which is really frightening). And although most debunkers clamor for logic and science in the investigation of mystic phenomena, most of their arguments fall into one or another of the fallacies that logic and science prohibit. You don't have to be a scientist yourself to sort it all out. Logical fallacies are basically apparent to common sense, if you think about them: but *think!*, as Dt 10:14 phrases it so well. Take your time and think.[297]

Primarily, the fallacies in many debunkers' work center on the logical impossibility of trying to prove a negative proposition: nobody can prove that something did

---

296. Medical doctors aren't expected to say, yes, that's ecstasy, but they can testify that it's not hysteria or delusion. A good overview of the substantial differences between the physical and psychological symptoms of mystic phenomena and those of morbid phenomena like hysteria, with references to standard medical publications on the subject, is given in Garrigou-Lagrange, 5:57.

297. Older logic textbooks, the kind that used to be used in grade schools before the First World War, are particularly useful these days, and even the children's educational games of a century ago are powerful tools for clarifying adult thinking. Lewis Carroll's *Game of Logic* is still in print, as is his *Symbolic Logic*. If you want to dive into the mainstream of logic as applied to mystic phenomena, find a copy of Ioannes di Napoli's three-volume *Manuale Philosophiæ ad Usum Seminariorum*, Casali, 1961.

not happen. The best that you can do is to prove that something else happened that excludes the event that you want to disprove. For example, the proposition that Person A did not steal something is a negative proposition, and you can't prove it directly; you can only prove that Person B stole it, which means, logically, that Person A didn't. An alibi does the same thing: it doesn't prove that the accused didn't do it, but only that he couldn't have; it demonstrates only that something else happened that makes the accusation impossible.

Debunkers often charge off in the wrong direction, trying to prove that a mystic event didn't happen. Nobody can do that. But they can't even prove that something else happened that excludes the possibility of a genuine mystic event. To understand why they can't, you have to think about the three separate factors that have to be considered in any investigation: the cause of the event, the event itself, and the event's appearances. You already know all about these and about their logical relationships, but you might not automatically apply what you know to accounts of mystic phenomena and debunkers' attempts to disprove them. For instance, if a professional illusionist can duplicate the physical appearances of an allegedly miraculous event—the way that the Pharaoh's magicians did (Ex 7:8-13)—it doesn't logically prove anything about the event itself, because two separate events that result from two different causes can have the same appearances.

Cause, Event, and Appearances

In fact, professional illusionists are in business to shuffle these factors, designing ways of making different events, with different causes, have exactly the same appearances. That's why they're called "illusionists": their business is to generate illusions, as illusions are understood by mystic theologians and everybody else.

When illusionists appear to saw a person in half, for instance, they make it look like actual dismemberment, but it isn't. The events are different, and so are the causes; only the appearances are the same. The stage trick doesn't prove that a person could not possibly be sawn in half for real; still less would it prove that some specific unfortunate person who actually was sawn in half really wasn't, but that it just looked like it. You wouldn't look down at the two halves of a person who had fallen into a sawmill and say, well, I saw a magician do this once, and it wasn't real, so this isn't real, either.

And when the illusionist's assistant leaps out of the box whole and smiling, it doesn't prove that the assistant was actually sawn in half and restored to wholeness; and it doesn't logically prove that a person who really was sawn in half couldn't be restored to wholeness miraculously—that would be a different event with a different cause, even if it had basically the same appearances. The only two things that the magician's illusion proves are that there are more than one way to produce the appearance of sawing a person in half, and that not all of those ways require you to actually saw a person in half.

Similarly, you might rig a system of tubes and tanks to drip water on a statue and make it appear as if the statue is weeping. But you can't logically conclude from this that all apparently weeping statues have tubes and tanks rigged up. There might be another natural, but not obvious, cause for the same appearance, like a leaky pipe in the ceiling above the statue. But beyond that, neither event would prove that no statue ever weeps because God wants it to; both show only that there are more than one way to make a statue appear to weep. By the same token, if a disease disappears by purely natural means or is cured by doctors, that does not mean that no case of that disease has ever been cured by the direct and extraordinary intervention of God; it just means that there are more than one cause that can produce the same event—the cure—and that they'd all end up producing the same appearances.

So you can't offer appearances as proof that a certain event, and only that certain event, occurred, and certainly not as proof that the certain event was caused by this particular cause and no other. That line of reasoning is invalid in any investigation: homicide, particle physics, biology, theology, anything.

THE TWOFOLD LIGHT: REASON AND FAITH

Besides, if you can't control the actual cause of an event, you can't reproduce the event, even if you can come up with something like the same appearances; and the cause of an actual mystic event is, by definition, God, who is not within the debunker's control. The only way to prove that no mystic event can ever occur is to prove that God does not exist, and that's not possible—not because faith fears logic (it doesn't), but because logic can't prove a negative proposition about anything.

That's why many debunkers fall into other logical fallacies. Many announce that apparently miraculous events occur because of unknown but purely natural causes that religious people are just too ignorant to know about, but what they don't know is that the Church takes those into account, and that she extends her investigation to exclude even the possibility of such hidden but natural causes.

That is, if psychological, medical, physical, or biological science says that no known natural cause can account for an event, the Church automatically adds the hurdle of unknown but natural causes, and then the investigation goes on to exclude even the possibility of such a cause. That is, the finding can't be negative; it has to be positive and substantial. In reportedly miraculous cures, this hinges on the substance of the event itself, things that happen in ways that just don't occur in the natural order of things. If it's only a matter of something not previously heard of, something unusual, or something unusually quick, that doesn't merit a diagnosis of genuine mystic activity. That's why things like incorruptibility are never given any real weight in these investigations. On the other hand, it's also why some weight still has to be given to events like the *post-mortem* restoration of the bodies of Bl. Lydwine or Sor Maria Villani, to the regenerated flesh of Gabriel Gargam or the unrestored but functioning eyes of Madame Biré. Investigations of other mystic phenomena weigh similar factors impossible in the natural order: infused knowledge, for instance, as with Alphonse Ratisbonne.

Now, at this point, the investigative abilities of many debunkers break down entirely; these are clearly theological matters, and few debunkers know much about theology. Many resort to scoffing, ridicule, and the *argumentum ad hominem*—pointing to the person who says something rather than to what he says, which is why you often hear them making fun of the Faithful and insulting the clergy. This leads them quickly to another kind of invalid reasoning: *petitio principii*, the circular argument or "begging the question": claiming that the report must be false because this or that person believes it, and such a person must be a fool, because only a fool would believe that kind of report. Or claiming that people who believe these things are fools, so therefore whatever they believe is not true, because fools believe things that are not true. It comes in lots of variations, and it's not often stated so bluntly, but if you boil down what they say, that's the misshapen little crystal of reasoning left at the bottom of the pot.

So, to make these kinds of point, many debunkers introduce all kinds of irrelevancies. One went so far as to label the healings at Lourdes obviously fraudulent because so many tawdry souvenirs are sold in the city outside the shrine precinct; that settled the matter, for him. Another, who had at least made a cursory examination of the documents, said that the cure of Vittorio Micheli at Lourdes on May 24, 1963, was blatantly fraudulent. Why? Not because his medical records showed the instantaneous regeneration of his left hip joint and the immediate disappearance of the huge tumor that had destroyed it, but because the records of his previous stay at an Italian military hospital assert that he had to wait thirty-six days for an X-ray and forty-three days for a biopsy, and that his doctors left him lying in a ward for ten months without any treatment except pain killers. Obviously, said the debunker, these records are just the clumsiest of forgeries, foisted on hopelessly superstitious fools by a grasping Church, a pathetic attempt to establish that the man had had no previous medical treatment, just too outrageous to be believed for an instant.

Well, it seems more reasonable to conclude that they just record what life's like in foreign military hospitals, and show you how good health care is in this country. And of course previous neglect (or even previous treatment) says nothing about the cause of a cure under different conditions: faulty logic, again.

Resistance, Voluntary and Involuntary

One particularly vocal and persistent core of debunkers, faced with the logical necessity of disproving the existence of God and the logical impossibility of doing so, simply deny the evidence for mystic phenomena, purposefully misreporting what happened or taking the processes of *ad-hominem* arguments and ridicule a few steps further. The ironic twist to this denial, of course, is that nobody's insisting that they believe in these things, in the first place. But it's interesting to look at the ways in which some of them try to suppress their own recognition of what they see, and to think about why they do it.

As, for example, with the French novelist Emile Zola (1840-1902). Now, Zola was a political activist; he used his novels to expose and criticize anything that he thought was wrong in French society. To write freely without fear of libel (or duels), he blurred the line between fact and fiction; real personages resembled his characters too closely for comfort, and he fought his cases in the courts as well as in the press—his literary exposure of the Dreyfus Affair brought down the government of France. So when he published a novel entitled *Lourdes* in 1894, some people read it then, and some still read it now, thinking that it's a factual account. But it isn't.

Zola's mind was made up when he started out, but everything that he saw at Lourdes—medical records, doctors, and even some spontaneous cures—ran counter to his assumptions. Still, he wasn't there to find out what was really going on; he had come to put a stop to it. And, most of all, he had a reputation to uphold. He had built his unprecedented literary career by painting France as a broad and dark panorama of greed, lust, gluttony, of all that's bestial and cruel in humanity. So rather than just report what he saw and change the names, he took stories of actual cures and distorted them into hideous tales of delusion and superstition, of abuse and foolish hope.

For instance, Zola knew that Marie Lemarchand, whose face was eaten away by lupus, washed in the spring and experienced an instant, complete, and permanent cure, her face entirely restored; but he presented her case as the story of the fictional Elise Rouquet, who suffered on with only some small, slow improvement. His character La Grivotte died on the train home, her tubercular lungs collapsed and her faith cruelly betrayed, but the real woman on whom this character was based, Marie Lebranchu, lived a long time after her instantaneous cure and never relapsed. She said that Zola tried to pay her off and get her out of the public eye, offering her a substantial amount of money and trying to move her and her husband to a small country place that he had bought for them in an obscure part of Belgium, but her husband threw him out.

Not Even if One Returned from the Dead

This kind of deliberate misrepresentation of the truth, what you'd ordinarily call "lying", is a particularly nasty kind of debunking. But Zola also fell into another kind, one that's often subtler and often found among more highly educated people: not admitting the reality of evidence before one's eyes.

Excluding any possible unknown natural cause still leaves an immense number of cases unexplained and inexplicable, endlessly fascinating; but it's nearly as interesting to investigate people's reactions as it is to look at the unexplained cases themselves. Most people are willing to learn, to expand their horizons of the possible, or they're complacent in their own views and don't bother to look beyond them. But others are grimly determined to slice off anything that doesn't fit their expectations. There they stand; they can admit no other view. Some people reject news of space exploration this way; some maintain that the Earth is flat. Others steadfastly refuse any evidence that God might work extraordinarily in this world.

These seem almost to protest too much, to be denying something that they themselves, by their own view, would really have to admit as true. Some just turn a blind eye to the evidence. One debunker was heard recently to object that, among all of the crutches hanging in gratitude at Lourdes, he didn't see a wooden leg; that would be a miracle, if someone were to grow a new leg, but nothing like that ever happens at these places, he said, and therefore all reputed cures at all Marian shrines are fraudulent. Well, blanket accusations of fraud always indicate that the person's attacking people rather than events—*ad-hominem* arguments that allege malicious intent, again—but the fact is that things like that do happen. The medical records of Pierre de Rudder or Kent Lanahan are available for study, if anyone's interested.

A questioner who didn't want to attribute these inexplicable cases to miracles might go on searching for an unknown but natural cause; that might incidentally prove that the case in question wasn't a miracle, but it might directly result in an improved medical technique, and the Church would be the first to applaud the invention.[298] A person could even drop the whole matter as being of no interest; but one ought anyway to look at the evidence first. Yet some debunkers don't, and they make no bones about their refusal: If I'd see all the crowds at Lourdes cured at the same instant, Zola said before he left, I still wouldn't believe it. It's the same attitude you find in Lk 16:31.

The Psychology of Exclusion

Other debunkers, particularly those who are also trained and qualified scientists, don't exclude evidence deliberately; it's just that miracles don't fit within their accepted boundaries of possibility, so they honestly can't see them. This inability to see what you don't expect to be possible is a normal part of human psychology, and it's been investigated in a fascinating series of experiments that began in 1949 with the work of J. S. Bruner and Leo Postman.[299] In their classic study, Bruner and Postman asked people to identify playing cards that were flashed before them for a fraction of a second. Naturally, the subjects expected that the deck would include red hearts and diamonds and black spades and clubs. But this deck included cards like a red six of spades and a black four of hearts.

The experiment was intended simply to measure how long these violations of expectation would delay recognition of the cards. But Bruner and Postman were surprised to find out that virtually none of the people even saw that there was anything different about the cards. Regardless of what the card actually was, people automatically

298. Of course, because latter-day miracles aren't part of doctrine, and because the Church's evaluations of these matters are made on purely human judgement—never pronounced as infallible doctrine—these judgements can be reversed in light of new evidence either way. But on the other hand, again, reproduction of the appearances of an event doesn't prove that both events were the same, nor that they were both brought about by the same cause; and a disease cured spontaneously or by improved medicine can still be cured miraculously. In other words, if a scientist figures out some way to provoke regeneration of tissue, the Church would honor his contribution to the reduction of human suffering; but that technique, previously unknown, wouldn't prove that God can't do that himself, if he wants to, and it would have no bearing on the case of the half-eaten woodsman restored to intact health by Bl. Margaret of Castello in the thirteenth century.

299. J. S. Bruner and Leo Postman, "On the Perception of Incongruity: A Paradigm", *Journal of Personality*, vol. XVIII (1949), 206-223.

saw something that fit their expectations, and they called out wrong identifications quickly and surely. They'd mis-perceive the color or the shape, automatically making extraordinary cases fit their presumptions about what's possible and what's not.

When the subjects were allowed to look at the cards for longer periods of time, most still couldn't see anything unexpected about them. Some of those who kept looking admitted to seeing something odd, like a black border around the red pips, but they still just could not see what was before them. Others just pushed aside the whole experience and said that the objects before them were not cards at all. Period.

Bruner and Postman noted that "it is either a very sick organism [or] an overly motivated one … which will not give up an expectancy in the face of a contradictory environment. It would be our contention, nonetheless, that for as long as possible and by whatever means available, the organism will ward off the perception of the unexpected, those things which do not fit his prevailing set".[300] In other words, if you don't expect to see something, you physically can't see it. If you don't want to see it, if something deep inside you resists having to adjust your perspective, it's even harder. Even if you'd consciously like to see it, you'll have to struggle against your ingrained presuppositions.

The Quality of Fear

This same psychological mechanism is undoubtedly at work, one way or the other, in a lot of people who look at mystic phenomena. But the really interesting aspect of this reaction is that witnessing an unexpected possibility causes so much fear. Some of the people who looked long and hard at Bruner and Postman's odd cards squirmed; they became agitated and uncomfortable when the evidence before them pushed its way through their expectations and challenged their rigid framework of the possible. They still warded off their perception of the unexpected, but some, when pressed, got irritated, sounding almost personally threatened: "Oh, I don't know what it is!" they said. "Take it away!"

Similarly, some people who look at mystic experiences feel threatened, too; some go through a personal crisis, refusing to acknowledge the evidence and defending to the last possible moment the parameters into which their professional training has fitted their thinking and their perceptions. Some doctors, of course, are violently distressed by things like Pierre de Rudder's bone or Justin Bouhouhorts's recovery. But other doctors are convinced—and sometimes converted—by certifiable miraculous healings. This was an old familiar occurrence long before Bl. Lydwine's time, and more recently Dr. Van Hoestenberghe, who treated Pierre de Rudder, and the Protestant nurses who treated Jack Traynor at Lourdes converted because of what happened to their patients.[301]

300. See also F. S. C. Northrup, *The Logic of the Sciences and the Humanities* (New York, 1959), 269, who, following the terminology of Vilfredo Pareto, notes that "a sentimental theory is retained by its believer without objective evidence and when obvious inconsistencies in it appear." The implications of this and similar studies for the history of academic disciplines are discussed in Thomas S. Kuhn, *The Structure of Scientific Revolutions* (Chicago, 1962), 62-65.

301. The nurses' families followed suit. So did their Anglican minister, and lots of others in Liverpool.

Certainly one of the best-documented cases is that of Dr. Alexis Carrel (1873-1944). He was one of those rare people who see what's in front of them, whether it runs contrary to their expectations or not, which is probably why he was such an inventive doctor. He won not only the Nobel Prize for Physiology and Medicine (1912) but lasting fame for Carrel's Method, a treatment that made transfusions safe and, ultimately, made organ transplant possible. He also invented ways to culture organ tissue *in vitro*, and he's still remembered for Carrel's Mixture, which holds grafts in place on an ulcerated surface, and the Carrel-Dakin Treatment, which has saved thousands of patients from amputation.

But his professors at the University of Lyon weren't so open to evidence as he was. Carrel admitted—he didn't assert, he just admitted when somebody asked him—that one of his patients, a little girl with a tubercular right hip, was completely and instantaneously cured at Lourdes. He didn't make any claims about the cause of the cure, and he didn't jump on any bandwagon; he just answered, well, she was incurable the other day, before she went there, and she's fine now, which would have to fall under the heading of miraculous, wouldn't it. Other doctors confirmed the cure, but the professors in the school's administration shook with anger and told Carrel point-blank that if he entertained such notions the University had no place for him. They severed all connections between him and the University, and they slammed the door behind him.

So Carrel emigrated to the United States, joined the Rockefeller Institute for Medical Research, and became probably the most distinguished medical man in history to convert because of a miracle.

Dr. Carrel's equanimity in accepting what he knew to be true, even without claiming any divine cause for it, points up the fact that all of these attempts to keep mystic matters at arm's length, or to fend off the results of sensible investigation of them, spring from fear, the fear of the truth. Those who genuinely believe that what they're hearing or seeing isn't worth considering don't bother trying to stamp it out. People never skip nervously around the evidence about anything unless they know that it's genuine but haven't the courage to grab it; on the other hand, they never rise up in fury until they see beyond doubt that they must abandon a position that they now know to be wrong.

Either way, people only panic when the cold blade of certainty slides into their hearts, when they know without doubt that this evidence is real, and that they themselves have been entirely wrong. It's the humiliation of seeing their most cherished notions collapse before the truth that makes them fight so hard and shout so loud. People derive much, perhaps most, of their self-image from the pride that they take in their own views and opinions; professionals establish their standing in the world on the basis of what they teach and espouse. Evidence that overwhelms those views cuts the ground from beneath their feet, threatening their whole identity with an abyss of stark terror.

To save face, to save what they see as their very selves, they put up a frantic resistance; and since they can neither ignore the evidence nor explain it away, they can only resort to tantrums. They beat the air and strike vainly at the reality that they see but cannot admit. Some may lash out at the evidence as at a personal attack; some may simply be angry for no longer having things their own way; but all are frightened. This fear of being wrong, and more than that of being shown to be wrong, is the same with anything else—medicine, astronomy, history, anything, not just mystic theology.

This fear moves in many directions. It kept Zola from simply telling the truth about Lourdes, and on the other hand it keeps people flocking to proven quacks. It's why cults keep going for as long as they do, and it's why scientists of the old school harassed Galileo, and then again Pasteur and Semmelweiss. Even open-minded professionals like Carrel suffer from this fear: the fear of repercussions is why some doctors who are themselves miraculously cured at Lourdes or another shrine dare not let their real names be published. They cannot afford to be ostracized as Carrel was.

This same fear, taking a wider scope, is why so many people go to their deathbeds fighting the advent of religion, or die obstinately hating the Church herself. It's why others refuse to abandon the allure of spectacular pseudo-mystical performances for what St. Thérèse of Lisieux called the monotony of sacrifice, or even for the normal life of their religion. Many others weep and wail for a time and then reshape their lives to accommodate what they understand to be true. Only a few have the self-assurance of Dr. Carrel or of St. Thomas himself, to admit it immediately (Jn 20:24-29); only a few can, as they did, frankly value accuracy above their own opinions.

And, in any case, refusing to study the records of mystic events, refusing to stop and think or to adjust the boundaries of the possible, at least, before denouncing the miraculous—or before accepting it—has to be taken as a sign of bad faith, no pun intended.[302] It takes both science and theology to approach mystic phenomena, the science to study the appearances and the events, and the theology to talk about the Cause.

"These exceptional phenomena, when superficially examined, are like a stained-glass window seen from without; from the exterior, their meaning and import cannot be grasped," Reginald Garrigou-Lagrange, O.P., wrote (*The Three Ages of the Interior Life*, 2:607). "But, when examined more attentively in the twofold light of right reason and faith, they resemble a stained-glass window seen from within under its true light; then all their beauty can be appreciated."

The Character of the Witness

It's important to remember that creditable mystic phenomena seldom occur in isolation; it's not just that a girl like Bernadette, one bright sunny day, mentions seeing a beautiful lady, and everybody's surprised. Immediately after her experience, more than seventy others in Lourdes and in the whole region around it claimed all kinds of mystic phe-

302. Frauds outside the Church are outside her jurisdiction, as are non-Catholic delusional cases; and if the Church can't subject these people to scrutiny, she can't logically denounce them. A sort of middle case is composed of those charismatic leaders who claim some kind of extraordinary spiritual powers while also claiming allegiance to the Church; for pastoral reasons, they can't be corrected without endangering the faith of their followers.

nomena—the streets and fields were full of prophets shrieking about repentance and chattering with Jesus or St. Michael. As soon as word got out about Maximin's experience, dozens of other people in the area reported apparitions, too; it was Bedlam, around La Salette. Many credit-worthy mystic phenomena—most, these days—don't stand out against a placid background of steady devotion but rather emerge, strong and intact, from a seething brew of spiritual turmoil.

Unless the more sensational news outlets broadcast them, you don't hear about these hundreds of reported mystics, nor about those that are reported in your own diocese every year, because each is investigated as deeply as it needs to be and handled, usually quietly, before it fades quickly into well-deserved oblivion. Only very, very rarely, once in a century or so, does a report survive all of the procedures that winnow out the chaff; but imagine how much work it is to sort through all of that chaff.

These false reports generate an immense amount of evidence that, with the many distinct possible scenarios into which it all might fit, give a bishop and his commission a great deal of work to do before they say anything about a purported mystic phenomenon, one way or the other. That's why investigations usually start with consideration of the person himself, the source or the focus of that evidence, and it's why those investigations have to be handled with fairly scrupulous procedures.

Why Rules of Inquiry are Necessary

The Church understands that the more spectacular secondary phenomena can be outward signs of an extraordinary interior state, but there's no necessary correspondence between the two—you can be an heroically virtuous cloistered nun like St. Thérèse of Lisieux and not show any such signs, or you can be a little savage like Mélanie Mathieu and talk familiarly with Mary. So, in sizing up the alleged seer, even cardiognosis wouldn't be of any help.[303] It takes very specialized knowledge and skills, and not every priest, not every layman, and not even every saint has them. That's why canonical inquiries run according to certain rules, too, and it's why you're probably better off if you listen to them and not to personal opinions informally arrived at, no matter who arrives at them.

For instance, when little Maximin Giraud was found to have secrets imparted to him by the apparition at La Salette, three local politicians concluded that the privileged information must relate to the political future of France, and they figured that it all centered on the Comte de Richemont, who claimed to be the Lost Dauphin, Louis XVII. But no matter what they did, bribery, threats of death, all kinds of chicanery, they couldn't pry the secrets from the children. So they decided to take Maximin to the pastor, the *curé*, of the church of St. John in the little town of Ars, who's known today as St. John Vianney.

---

303. In any case, cardiognosis is just another gift and doesn't indicate sanctity, anyway. Germana Cele had it, and so do most other possessed people. And of course, like the lay Carmelite Bl. Mary of the Incarnation who saw through Nicole of Rheims, even genuine mystics are always under investigation themselves, and nobody gives their opinions on these things any real weight. Nicole of Rheims could have denounced Bl. Mary of the Incarnation right back, and it would have been one purported mystic's word against another's.

The Curé d'Ars was one of those people whom everybody thinks is a saint during his lifetime. People from all over the region asked him about distant events as routinely as you would turn on a radio to get the news, and he was never wrong about what happened to far-away strangers (in fact, he often volunteered the information, with whole names and details, before the person asked, starting the conversation in the middle). He spoke in the future tense the way most people use the preterit, predicting the subsequent course of events as casually as you might recall things long since accomplished. And he was one of the earliest enthusiasts about La Salette.

So they took Maximin to see him. Maximin went along, he said later, for the ride; he'd never been that far before. They arrived at Ars on September 24, 1850, and the men took him straight to the church. They started off on the wrong foot, lying to St. John's vicar about why they were there; Maximin wanted to talk to the Curé d'Ars about his vocation, they said. The Curé de Corps, the boy's home town, knows him better, the vicar said; talk to him, not us. The men persisted, and even sounded the vicar out about his opinion of the apparitions. More than that, they argued with him when he was reserved about the whole business.

Maximin was never the most congenial child in the world, and by then he was bored with the whole thing. When the vicar asked him if he had invented the whole story, he gave his stock answer and said, "Well, if you want, say that I've told a lie and that I didn't see anything!" Then he turned and walked away. But, after a further interchange described as "acrid", the boy somehow got to see the Curé d'Ars.

Maximin said later that it was hard to understand the Curé because he had very few teeth left, and evidently the Curé didn't understand Maximin's dialect very well, either. He asked the boy if he had lied; yes, Maximin said, referring to his career as the town scamp. One misunderstanding followed another, and although the details of the interview weren't then made public, people noticed the next day that the Curé d'Ars stopped blessing medals of Our Lady of La Salette and handing out pictures of her in that title.

He was terribly disappointed by his interview with the boy. For the next eight years he was tormented because he couldn't reconcile his knowledge of the facts with what he thought Maximin had told him—not with the kind of person the boy was, but with what he thought that the boy had told him. Finally, ten months before he died, the Curé resolved his doubts and frequently referred to his personal belief in the apparitions. Finally the local bishop—the only competent authority in these cases—made his official pronouncement on the creditability of the apparitions of La Salette. If the Curé had waited, he could have saved himself both the torments and the enthusiasm alike.

For both of these decisions, the private and the public, the disappointing careers of the seers after the apparitions made no difference. It seldom really does, because nobody deserves extraordinary mystic gifts, any more than anybody needs them for salvation. As Benedict XIV put it, extraordinary mystic phenomena that really come from God are classed as *gratiæ gratis datæ*, graces freely given. Not earned.

Questioning the Mystic, Not the Mysticism

The unearned quality of mystic phenomena is what makes it especially tough for renowned mystics to get canonized. Canonization means officially setting certain people before the Faithful as models of Christian life; the whole point of the process is to point out that ordinary people, enfranchised in the ordinary sacramental life of the Church, can and do exercise the Christian virtues to an heroic degree. Mystic phenomena are free acts of God, not anything that the mystic himself does; you can't set a person up as an example because of something that somebody else did to him, and usually against his will.[304]

Besides, these events are extraordinary, and they're not the point or goal of Christianity. They may actually come from natural or diabolic causes, and of course they tend to attract more attention than the quiet acts of habitual heroic virtue that candidates for sainthood (or even for salvation) customarily perform. That's why, from the beginning, the housewife sent to the lions, the businessman who takes to the streets as a charitable mendicant, or the exemplary nun that nobody gave a second thought, particularly, have been overwhelmingly more viable candidates for sainthood than the mystic.[305]

So it's highly unlikely that Padre Pio, for instance, is going to be canonized any time soon—most people know him principally by his confirmed stigmata, his bilocations, his healings, and the like, all secondary phenomena, none of which can be taken as certain signs of sanctity. To determine his sanctity, you have to clear away all of that and approach the man himself, which is all the more difficult as the secondary phenomena become more spectacular and more intense.

Even the little innocents like St. Bernadette or Sister Lucia dos Santos have absolutely no red carpet to canonization. If anything, they have to be even more heroically virtuous than anybody else, because the rules of their orders, like those of the Church in general, strive to keep people from giving undue attention to secondary, inessential things like mystic phenomena and keep them focussed on the firm and quiet substance of the Faith. Far from being the darlings of their orders, far from being the favorite children of their Church, mystics are generally seen as extraordinary cases that have to be governed with particular care so that good order can be maintained. And since heroic virtue includes absolute humility, their elevation to the altar has to happen against their absolute determination not to be singled out for any attention whatsoever.

On the other hand, extraordinary mystic phenomena are fairly ordinary for the saints, even those from whom you wouldn't expect them; since the Apostles, there have been thousands of canonized mystics, or rather saints who had creditable mystic experiences. But they, too, were all subject to the same intense scrutiny that any modern-day

---

304. The Bible, of course, testifies that, just as a saintly person isn't necessarily a mystic, a mystic isn't necessarily a saintly person—the Samaritan woman, for one, was a public sinner, yet her whole country met Christ through her after her conversation with him (Jn 4:5-30).

305. Canonization involves an even more massive body of specialized law and even more exacting juridical processes than the evaluation of a reported mystic phenomenon. Some of the trials span decades and centuries. And while there's a vast scholarly literature on some aspects of the many individual procedures,

mystic will get.

So, no matter what station in life the purported mystic fills, canonical commissions normally begin their investigations of reported mystic phenomena by clearing those reports away and looking directly at the person or persons involved. Their first questions are the basic ones—*Quis, quid, ubi, quibus auxiliis, cur, quomodo, quando?* (who, what, where, by what means, what for, how, when?, as St. Thomas Aquinas summed them up centuries ago in his *Summa*, 1-2:7:3). Today, they're likely to be more specific. What are the person's natural qualities? Does this person have a record of claiming any revelations or making any predictions before this? What is the person's degree of education? What is the character of the person's testimony; how was it gathered, and how has it been handled? This includes the related questions of whether the person has been perfectly honest and open with confessors and directors, and whether he's shown a distinct fear of being deceived. They also ask what virtues this person possessed before the alleged event, and what virtues he has after it. They ask if the person has suffered any noteworthy trials before this event—sickness, loss of a loved one, or lack of success?

And investigators ask particularly about the person's reactions to the alleged event, and their questions focus on the particular virtue of humility and its contrary vice, pride. Has this person shown a real lack of desire for mystic experiences, or even a genuine dislike of these extraordinary events, a real aversion to them; or is this person proud to claim divine selection? It's these last questions, probably, that exclude more reported mystic phenomena than any of the others; but even they can't be taken in isolation.

The Question of Natural Qualities

Investigators look closely into such things as whether the person is known as sincere, level-headed, and of sound judgement. Is the person truthful? St. Bernadette's sound common sense and her shy demeanor stood in significant contrast to the antics of the man who danced around the grotto crowned with grass and flowers, yelling, "Repent! Repent!" The boys at Pontmain, the children at Beauraing, and the seers of Fátima all gained credibility from the fact that nobody who knew them had ever known them to lie. The same question of general conduct made it harder for Mariette Béco at Banneux to be taken seriously, just as it did for Mélanie and Maximin.

Investigators also know that some people have livelier imaginations than others. Some who have particularly vivid imaginations also suffer from one or another unfortunate kind of emotional or psychological disorder that keeps them from distinguishing their imagined world from the real world. They may imagine that Christ, or Mary, or an angel, comes to them to discuss things, or to give them some important message that can save the world; and they may sincerely believe what they imagine. Others

there is no full or accurate account of the whole process in the popular press. Pope John Paul II's apostolic constitution *Divinus Perfectionis Magister* (1983) established the process as it now stands, but it's not widely available, and its implications aren't likely to be clear to the lay reader.

may start out as deliberate fakers but end up believing their own fraud.[306]

It's usually pretty easy to distinguish these cases from cases of genuine mystic experience because they're substantially different—nothing within the scope of known mystic phenomena happens, and the specific psychological and emotional disorders that provoke this kind of behavior are routinely diagnosed and treated; the patient himself is confused, but to a professional there's no mystery about these things. Genuine mystics and visionaries, on the other hand, test out to be psychologically and emotionally normal, which makes sense, because above all they have to be creditable.

The Question of the Record

There's also the related question as to whether this person has claimed any revelations or made any predictions before this. A history of this kind of behavior, coming before a claim of an apparition or locution, naturally undercuts the chances of credibility—it's hard to imagine that a report of a genuine mystic event would begin with a statement like, "No, honestly, this time, it's real." But, then again, some brilliant mystic careers began gradually. St. Teresa of Avila was first allowed to see Christ's hand, and only after she got over being stunned by its beauty was she allowed to see more of him. Even the Marian apparitions of Fátima started with an angel, silent and distant in the clouds.

One distinction is that creditable mystics tend to keep these things to themselves; they don't have a record of running off and telling everybody about them, not until the mystic experience itself commands or urges them to do so. There are exceptions, like, again, the savage little Mariette Béco or the voluble Ven. Mary of Agreda, but mystics generally have the reputation of unusual reserve. They're normally cheerful, but even-tempered, not given to emotional extremes one way or the other; they're stable, and they're quiet or even a little withdrawn. Many of them show an interest in devotions that's a little higher than what you'd expect for people in that station in life, but nothing out of the normal range, and then again many don't show any particular interest in religion at all; they're not religious fanatics, at any rate. The people around the mystics are virtually always surprised that this person, of all people—this tongue-tied child, this shy schoolgirl who can't recite her catechism, this most reticent abbess, this quiet little mouse—has reported a creditable mystic experience.

The Question of Education

The person's degree of education enters into it, too, because, as St. Luke notes, it's the fact that these people are unlearned that makes their utterances marvelous (Lk 10:21; Ac 4:13). Reports from recent creditable apparitions have this same marvelous quality to them; the children who report these things could not possibly come up with that kind of message on their own, in the purely natural order of things. In fact, they often don't

---

306. This can happen, evidently, because the decision to initiate a mystic fraud constitutes rejection of God and consent to the Devil. Certainly a good many false mystics, such as Mary Ann van Hoof, show symptoms of full-blown possession, such as episodes of superhuman strength and bellowing, or particularly unattractive convulsions.

understand the meanings of the terms or know how to spell them.

St. Bernadette didn't, when she reported that the Lady had identified herself by saying, "I am the Immaculate Conception." The official definition of that doctrine had only just occurred, and it wasn't widely known, not yet part of the catechism classes that the girl had attended (and that she had flunked, anyway). And the phrasing of the identification was unusual enough to puzzle even theologians when they first heard it; they understood that Mary is the *product* of the Immaculate Conception, but they wouldn't have expected her to say "I *am* the Immaculate Conception". But the sentence rang true when they thought about it, studied the doctrine more deeply, and went back through the documents since the Fathers. It was just as St. Margaret Mary's pronouncements about devotion to the Sacred Heart had resonated to more than a thousand years of theological thought—well, right back to the Bible—synthesizing a vast and complicated body of theological knowledge to which Margaret Mary Alacoque herself had no access.

THE CHARACTER OF THE TESTIMONY

That's why it's important to know exactly what the messages of recent creditable apparitions have been, *verbatim*. Investigators have to get an exact and unaltered written account of the event and the text of whatever message may have been given, and they listen carefully for variations whenever the subject repeats it. Fakers, like the deluded, contradict themselves, embroider, and wander from the point, but credit-worthy mystics don't have any problem providing this accurate record. As St. Teresa of Avila points out, genuine mystic events bring certitude: these words remain in the memory for a very long time, she said, and some are never forgotten. As the Church has seen time and time again, if mystics are given a message to convey, they can repeat even fairly long texts exactly, without change, through repeated grillings and over many years, even if they're not excessively bright, and even if it's in a language that they don't themselves speak.

So the rhetorical quality of any purported message is an important piece of evidence in itself. The messages of creditable mystic phenomena are always beautifully written, and usually extremely brief—often only a few words. The language is elegant in its simplicity, yet it's loaded with universal implications; and none of those implications runs contrary to doctrine. Creditable messages consist of "brief but energetic and lofty sentences," as Fr. Arintero puts it; "these words," St. Teresa said, "bear with them such majesty that, even though one does not call to mind who it is that speaks them, they make one tremble." Some few little phrases can penetrate straight to the heart: "Console your God," for instance, or that last brief sentence of Pontmain, *Mon fils se laisse toucher*. And, as with Scripture itself, the force and beauty of the texts can survive translation. That's immensely difficult for any mortal author to achieve, which is why the Church composes her suggested prayers with such great care, and why those written even by canonized saints are subjected to such microscopic scrutiny before they're approved for use by the Faithful. They have to be that good.

When it's a matter of delusion, though, the language of a reported apparition can't be quite so elevated, because it's the product of a disordered mind. Frauds some-times produce nothing overtly contrary to the Faith; like any other counterfeiters, they try to make their accounts passable, at least. But they virtually never know enough about theology to come up with anything really striking or even accurate. Like many nominal Christians today, they seem to see religion as a matter of feelings and sentiment, not as anything substantial and effective. So the messages from those faulty reports that have attracted immense crowds in the past century or so have been couched in the most banal language imaginable, the kind of thing you might expect from a printed greeting card on a vaguely religious theme, in some famous recent cases.

And false mystics tend to be verbose, issuing an endless flow of revelations and predictions to all and sundry. After all, they're in business to get attention, and the more they say, the more attention they get. This constant flow of repetitive prophecies pattered out in low-brow language appeals to crowds of people who haven't thought very deeply about their religion, maybe, but the quality of the language in which they're conveyed points unmistakably to the seer himself as the author. The quality of the language is one of the rare factors that can exclude the events from serious consideration all by itself.

That's why the delusional and the fakes come and go so quickly; they just don't have anything substantial to say. The homegrown visionary or free-lance stigmatist can't begin to present a convincing case to a bishop's investigation, any more than the soap-box physicist can challenge the Theory of Relativity. And it's extremely unlikely that any-thing they say would stand up to logical evaluation, within the context of Sacred Tradition and the Bible.

Given an accurate text of what the reported visionary said, investigators also look for anything contrary to the Gospels, which makes sense: God can't contradict himself. They look for statements contrary to Sacred Tradition, too, of course; there's no contradiction between anything in Tradition and anything in Scripture, but Tradition is fuller and more vitally dynamic, answering the changing current of particular situa-tions with unchanging doctrine. False mystic events, whether produced by fraud or by delusion, claim to clarify the Faith in incorrect or improper ways; and, without excep-tion, they try to add to Christ's teachings or preach exemptions from them, or they pur-port to correct something that Christ said.

Even if investigators find some parts of the report contrary to faith or morals, they have to find out if those parts are integral to the message itself. That's yet another tricky factor that has to be considered: even people who receive creditable mystic phe-nomena, like witnesses at any other kind of trial, may get things wrong. They're only human. Still—also as with witnesses at a trial—the ways in which they get things wrong can be described and classified, so that things can be sorted out without compromising the validity of the mystic phenomena themselves.

Simple error on the part of a mystic is most noticeable in the matter of predic-tions of future events. Of course, those prompted by the Devil—the Father of Lies—aren't reliable; some of Magdalen of the Cross's predictions were questionable, and some were just wrong, but just enough of them came true to keep people guessing. A lot of genuine prophecies are conditional, too; if the conditions change, the predicted sequence of events changes, too, which is what happened for St. Vincent Ferrer (1350-1419). He was told by a vision that the end of the world would come in his lifetime unless people amended their lives, but by working thousands of dazzling miracles that prompted thousands of conversions across Christendom, he evidently averted it.307

Or the mystic might put an *inaccurate construction* on what's said. When St. Joan of Arc was in prison, she asked her locutionary saints if she was going to be burned; they said things like, "trust in Our Lord", "he will aid you", "you will receive support", and "you will be delivered by a great victory". She, understandably moved by wishful thinking, figured that it meant no, she wouldn't be burned. But then the voices told her not to fear on account of her martyrdom; it will bring you at last into Paradise, they said. That gives an entirely different meaning to the previous locutions, without changing a letter of them.308

Also, the *inadequacy of human thought* can cloud a report by a creditable mystic about a genuine locution or message of an apparition, as happened with Abraham and the Apostles after him (Gn 15:7-13; Mt 17:1-4; Jn 21:20-23); they might just misunderstand what was said or done, or laugh it off as Sara did (Gn 18:9-15). More often, it seems, they're simply overwhelmed by the wonder of it all; St. Teresa of Avila compared the lapse in memory of details to what happens to a person entering a treasury-room full of wonderful things: "Although I was in that room for a while," she said, "there was so much there to see that I soon forgot it all; none of those pieces has remained in my memory ... nor would I know how to explain the workmanship of any of them" (*Interior Castle* 6:4), which happens to a lot of people in museums, these days.

But her last point shows that the report itself might suffer from the *inadequacy of human language* to describe things beyond space and time. The *loquelas* of St. Ignatius of Loyola or the harmonious bird-songs that Juan Diego heard could hardly be conveyed in earthly languages, and even locutions that start in ordinary grammar sometimes get carried away in a kind of linguistic ecstasy—the voice of Bl. Clelia Barbieri (b. 1847), for example, which has been heard in the convents she founded, sometimes changes into celestial music beautiful beyond description. But if the communication is conveyed entirely without words, it may be impossible to translate it into language, and the substance of a valid prediction may be obscured by the recipient's inability to express

307. One biographer said that St. Vincent Ferrer saved the world as Jona saved Nineveh, but he himself knew the prediction to be conditional, which was why he went to the trouble of converting people. He spoke only of the "great probability" of the end if the Great Schism weren't healed and people converted.

308. Her saints Michael and Catherine may have used this technique to conceal information without lying, so that she wouldn't worry unduly, as Raphael did. When Tobias asked him who he was, and of what tribe (Tb 5:18), the archangel said, "I am Azarias, son of the great Ananias", which satisfied the old man. But in Hebrew that sentence also means "I am assistance from God, brought forth of God's great grace," which was true. The mortals didn't figure out what was actually meant until the whole adventure was over.

it all. "They understand them literally, according to their apparent meaning," St. John of the Cross noted, "for, as I have said, the chief purpose of God in sending visions is to express and communicate the Spirit that is hidden within them, and that is very hard to understand. This is much more abundant than the letter, more extraordinary, and surpassing the limits of letters."

St. Mechtilde von Hackenborn-Wippra evidently got stuck in this literalist error, at least once. She reported that Jesus said of her *protegée* St. Gertrude that "the patience (*patientia*) in her that pleases me derives its name from peace (*pax*) and knowledge (*scientia*)," which makes a pun—*pax-scientia* sounds like *patientia*. This kind of word-play is a very common memory aid in mediæval literature; every single saint's name that Bl. Jacobus da Voragine mentions in the *Golden Legend* has two or three different "derivations" of this kind, just so that you can remember what each saint is famous for. But St. Mechtilde sounds as if she took this literally, thinking that it was the real derivation of the Latin word.[309]

Looking at it the other way, sometimes the inadequacy of human language is compounded by the stylistic conventions of the day, which can render written testimony difficult or inaccessible. The works of St. Maria Maddelena dei Pazzi are presented in a highly allegorical, repetitious, and truly baroque style, and their convoluted symbolism impeded serious study of the substance of her mystic experiences until the 1960s, some three hundred years after her canonization. It also happens that the visionary might misunderstand symbolic content, or might not know that historical and archæological statements are often given symbolically or partially or approximately.

Well, the stigmata, for instance, varies, with the wounds being in the palms according to the usual depictions in Christian art, or in the wrists, which is more accurate archæologically, and nobody knows for sure the exact pattern of the wounds from the Crown of Thorns; but no such variation in and of itself proves that a case of stigmata is false. On the other hand, some detailed visions are so puzzling in this regard that they've been a bone of contention in the centuries since they were written down.

Ven. Mary of Agreda's great work, *The City of God (Ciudad de Dios)* was a great favorite of Ven. Solanus Casey, O.F.M. Cap., who read its ponderous volumes again and again over a forty-year period and was associated with an Agredan Society established to spread the word about this work. What a revelation! he exclaimed; what a treasure! Others have found it trivial and tedious (which isn't hard to understand; it took even Solanus eight years to get through it the first time), and a lot of prominent churchmen and theologians have lobbied tirelessly for its condemnation on those grounds.

To some extent, this is a matter of taste—these endless meditations-*cum*-locutions of pious ladies like Ven. Mary of Agreda tend to the saccharine. It's not even always clear at first whether these accounts are intended by their authors to pass as records of visions or only of their own meditations, nor whether they're intended as historical facts or aids to the readers' own meditative prayers. But some purported vision-

309. In fairness, though, it ought to be noted that a woman so ill educated as to take it literally wouldn't be able to come up with the theologically subtle things that St. Mechtilde did.

aries do present accounts of almost cinematic detail and expect them to be taken at face value. It's the historical pretensions that put most scholars off of this kind of sentimental meditation. Ven. Mary of Agreda asserts the minutest details about costume and every other aspect of daily life, and she claims to know precisely that the Blessed Virgin lived twenty-one years, four months, and nineteen days after the Crucifixion. But other visionaries like Anne-Catherine Emmerich who wrote similar long accounts of Mary's life, or Christ's, or other saints', have been just as particular about it all but disagreed with her about every detail.

All of this narrative sort of swarms around the substance of the mystic event without really touching it. Not much of it can ever be proved or disproved, in this life, so there's no point in arguing about the substance of it, and even its symbolic value seems slim or vague. Logically, it's irrelevant, and theologically it's *incompetent*, too, in the literal sense, as this kind of testimony would be in civil or criminal court; it literally doesn't count. It doesn't run toward the question under consideration. On the other hand, there's no question about Ven. Mary of Agreda's heroic virtue nor about her real union with God, and some critics who have plowed through these mountains of prose have come up with a gem, every once in a while. But the fertile minds of these ladies—evidently men don't write works in this form—can be credited with most of them outright, without imputing or ruling out any real private revelation along the way.

In addition to the clutter of more or less irrelevant detail surrounding real infused knowledge, there's the related problem of *mingling of human thought with the message*. Most mystics can keep their own thoughts and insights separate from the substance of their visions and locutions, as Julian of Norwich and St. Vincent Ferrer did: "I have formed an opinion and a belief of great probability in my own mind," St. Vincent said of a certain insight about the Antichrist, "but without sufficient certainty to preach it." So he didn't.

But some mystics aren't equipped to make that distinction, intellectually. St. Hildegard of Bingen was illiterate, but she could write perfectly well what she saw in her visions and could read the necessary Latin books just by looking at the pages, like Therese Neumann and a surprising number of other mystics. Yet—also like Neumann—she subconsciously put in a lot of theological facts that she had picked up from sermons and from her talks with theologians and scholars in addition to the things that came through in her visions; and they both got some of those things a little bit wrong, sometimes, or at least made questionable theological points. This doesn't mean that their other mystic experiences aren't genuine; they could be genuine stigmatics, inedics, and visionaries who innocently added extraneous material apart from those genuine mystic events. It just means that you have to look at each thing separately.

There may also be *mistakes made by secretaries and transcribers*, too. Sometimes they just misunderstand, as Juan González must have misunderstood as "Guadalupe" whatever it was that Tio Bernardino actually said.[310] Sometimes they embellish or inter-

---

310. This is less likely with over-sympathetic translations, as long as the original text is still available.

polate what they hear from creditable visionaries, even if they don't mean to; sometimes they automatically correct the grammar. Sometimes they add little marginal notes, or remarks clearly labelled as coming from their own observations, which are useful, like the little scholia that Luis Gonçalves de Câmara jotted down as he was transcribing what St. Ignatius of Loyola told him. But sometimes they think that they'll improve the literary quality of what they're transcribing by rearranging episodes, clarifying a connection to a Bible passage, standardizing the references and names, or polishing the language, as Clemens Brentano did for—or to—the dictations of Anne-Catherine Emmerich.

This kind of adulteration pretty much excludes the accounts from serious consideration, even though the mystic experience itself may have been perfectly genuine. We'll never know the true extent of the supernatural elements in Anne-Catherine Emmerich's experience, because of what Brentano did to the account. But often, in this kind of case, a lot of this damage can be corrected by scholarly study of the texts; a good editor can tell one voice from another, and scholars have even more incisive ways to separate the wheat from the chaff. Of course, it's best not to have to do this in the first place. Texts that have been reconstructed this way aren't really the best kind of evidence, any more. So judgement of these errors is a matter of degree; it's a matter of the whole context of extraordinary phenomena that seem to be happening. The context of the person's whole spiritual life, in fact.

The Mystics and the Mistakes

In evaluating these kinds of human error, the conduct of the mystic is of paramount importance; a person's reaction when confronted with his personal failures is some of the strongest possible testimony about his virtues. When one of her predictions fell through, St. Catherine Labouré said simply, "Well, I have been mistaken. I thought that I was telling you correctly. I am very glad that the truth should be known." But many people were put off permanently by Maximin's pungent answers and Mélanie's vituperation, which have a lot to do with why the apparitions and the healing spring at La Salette are not so well known as those of Lourdes.

It's also very damaging to find that the purported mystic has contradicted himself in his testimony and in relations with confessors or spiritual directors. By their nature, mystic phenomena are extraordinary, so they might contain apparent contradictions that resolve themselves when the full story is known, and the reluctance of creditable mystics to chatter about these things means that they might appear to conceal things from legitimate questioners. They also may not be in a position, intellectually or educationally, to figure out what's important and what isn't, or to gauge what the questioners already know about these things. But while the truth may come out gradually, it comes out consistently; it pushes its way through the opposition of the authorities, through the morass of any psychotic or diabolic clutter that springs up around it, through the resistance of the mystic himself, and through identifiable human clumsiness in handling it. But the creditable mystics never lie about it.

They also show themselves, one way or another, to be sensibly afraid of deceit. They don't jump to conclusions; they don't run into the marketplace yelling about how they've seen the Virgin Mary or Christ or an angel. Those who, like St. Teresa of Avila, have regular confessors or directors, know that they're supposed to resist these things, and they do; if the events persist, they ask themselves if this is of their own minds, or of the Devil. But even the little innocents don't seem to assert that yes, we saw Mary, period. They speak of "the Lady", which could mean any female who conducts herself like one. St. Bernadette had to ask who the Lady was; so did the seers of Fátima. Even St. Catherine Labouré, who concluded very reasonably that the apparition she saw was the Mother of Christ, went through severe doubts about it, doubts as acute as those that any other sensible person would have in like circumstance. In any case, when they do speak of their experiences, mystics speak with great restraint or with conscious care.

By contrast, many fraudulent or deluded visionaries have been exposed by the character and the tone of what they say, as well as by its content and contradictions. "Lift the lid of the latrine," Richard Rolle de Hampole wrote in his *Fire of Love* in about 1340, "and nothing but stink flies out. Wicked words fly out of the hearts of the wicked."

But even if the investigators find absolutely nothing contrary to the Bible or even implying anything contrary, that doesn't exclude diabolic influence (all Scripture is of God, but then again the Devil quotes Scripture for his own purposes). And even a report that contains nothing contrary to faith can still be offensive to morals. Some would-be visionaries report Christ appearing to them without any clothes, for example, which may make sense in the context of celestial purity—everybody returned to the prelapsarian innocence of Adam and Eve—but it certainly counts as an offense against chastity, here on Earth.

The Personal Context: Virtues Before and After

As St. John of the Cross reminded us, mystic phenomena do their work on a soul, even if they last only an instant; and their work consists, in part, in drawing the visionary to greater virtue. So investigators are careful to gather evidence about the virtues that the reputed mystic had before the event, and then they compare them with those that he has after it.

For instance, there's the question of penance. Ascetic practices often accompany or precede genuine mystic activity, but penance isn't virtue; and the urge to take on more austerities can come from a genuine impulse, or it can come from temptation, which comes more or less noticeably from the Devil. Sometimes it happens in the usual manner, just by being quietly tempting, promising a reputation for holiness in the purely natural order of things. The urge to avoid penance is a problem, too; it can come through the encouragement that the person feels in the exercise of the false mystic gifts—particularly if that person is in a group that sets itself apart by claiming these gifts, like the Jansenists who gathered at Port-Royal around Madame de Guyon.

This group, which included Blaise Pascal and other notables, were among the quietists who have popped up periodically in the Church since their first appearance in the thirteenth century (or really since Corinth). They're the textbook examples of people who take the psychological feeling of spiritual gifts as the basis of their religion. Like Luther and plenty of other heretics ("Every good work, perfectly performed, is a venial sin," he said in his Proposition 32), quietists usually assert that they should suppress all of their acts—turning from alms and devotions like the Rosary, and refusing the regular sacramental life of the Church to one degree or another. At the very least, people who fall into this kind of spurious mysticism think themselves exempt from the normal ascetic and even sacramental life of the Church. They lie in wait for God to work miracles in them; hence the term *Quietism*. They feel themselves free from the supervision of legitimate authorities, pastors, confessors, religious superiors, and bishops alike; they aren't subject to these superiors, they claim, because they understand the Holy Spirit better than common people, better than those who aren't "anointed" or some such term.

Well, they say, look at this: we have special mystic gifts, and you don't. The Jansenists writhed on the floor, barked like dogs, and spoke in gibberish as proof of their sanctity, which naturally convinced themselves and attracted an equally enthusiastic following. You still find this kind of thing, today, and in fact it's growing, but not all quietists are so vigorous. They can be very slick and very subtle; Madame de Guyon's books use the vocabulary of mystic theology throughout, but they use it nonsensically. Unfortunately, they're still in print, still posing as accurate treatises on mystic phenomena.

The Crucial Criterion: Obedience

Like every other spurious mystic on record—like every other quietist on record—the self-anointed at Port Royal steadfastly refused the call to obedience. But obedience is the central test of the mystic, in many ways. For one thing, a confessor or any priest can order an ecstatic out of the ecstasy or call the levitator down.[311] This is referred to as the *recall*, but when you think about it, it's God who obeys.

God is the cause of the phenomenon, and the mystic himself can't hear anything with his bodily ears, anyway, if caught up in ecstasy. But he always follows the commands of a priest, in these cases. The understanding is that, even though God decides to reach out and lift a soul in ecstasy, he will not countervene the authority of his Church when he does so. The Church has her authority directly from Christ, so if Christ were to countervene that authority it would mean that he was contradicting himself. It would also amount to new revelation, and no creditable mystic reports any revelations that even imply any new revelation.

Whether willful fraud or pathological delusion provokes the counterfeit, false mystics won't obey; even if the Devil's at the back of it, causing, say, levitation or a simulated stigmata, he won't obey, either, unless as part of his plan to make it all look real.

---

311. This is different from what happens between a hypnotist and his subject. Genuine ecstasy is an outreach by God, so it can't be induced by any human agency, and the priest, who can be a complete stranger, can come in long after the ecstasy has begun and still command that the mystic phenomenon stop.

But if creditable mystics have one thing in common, one characteristic invariable no matter how varied their extraordinary experiences may be, it's obedience, even while in the middle of the most vehement mystic activity.

But obedience takes other forms, too, all of which are just as definitive. For instance, the orders of nuns, monks, and friars have clear rules about spiritual life, to which all members are bound; the lazy, the weak, and the indifferent are called to work their way up to that standard, and the spiritually excitable or the extraordinarily gifted are called to toe that line, too. The thing that the superiors look out for isn't just departure from that rule—everybody's spiritual life takes discipline and formation—but rather the person's efforts to make up for shortcomings and pull back excess, neither of which is suitable. The farther you are from that line, one way or the other, the more vigorously the superiors have to try to get you back to it.

That's why the people in charge of nuns like St. Margaret Mary or friars like St. Joseph of Cupertino usually press them a little harder than they'd press somebody who departed less from that defined norm; but then, they'd step up the discipline on anybody who departed from the norm the other way, too, showing too little progress as these show too much, in terms of the rule.

Either way, a person who disregarded the whole disciplinary structure of the order would obviously have no real vocation, no genuine call from God to be a member of that order, and he'd either be refused reception or expelled. Every genuine mystic can perfectly well obey; God would not work against himself by calling a person to that life and then making it impossible for him to meet its obligations. Still, people are only human, and genuine phenomena can be taken as a pretext for disobedience, as with Mélanie, or an order can expel an obedient mystic like Juliana of Mont-Cornillon.

But even mystic activity among the laity obeys lawful commands of legitimate authority. For example, Marie Lataste (1822-1847) started life as a fairly obnoxious little girl in Dax, France. She knew housekeeping and just enough about her Faith to make her first communion, although it took her until she was twelve to learn that. But at the instant of receiving the Eucharist, she felt clearly the True Presence; about a year after that, she saw a bright light at the elevation of the Sacrament, and it got brighter as her love of God and her other virtues increased.

She suffered extraordinary interior trials and temptations, but she followed her confessor's instructions to the letter, and she had extraordinary consolations. She saw Christ on the altar during Mass in late 1839 and again on Epiphany of 1840, and virtually every time she went to Mass after that. Christ explained to her all of the truths of the Faith, in terms she could understand, verbal statements, visions, or parables. Angels and the Blessed Virgin completed her education, which exceeded what was offered by the local seminary of Dax.

Marie's personality matured and blossomed during this time; her vices disappeared, her virtues grew, and those around her felt an abiding sense of joy, just from her presence, although she never went out of her way to impress them. The surprising thing was that she wasn't surprised at all of this; evidently she thought that's the way religion works.[312]

She never mentioned any of it except to her confessor, a priest named Farbos. His reaction was precisely what would be hoped for in these cases but is so rarely met: he didn't make a fuss about it, either. Apparently he judged that she had her prayers answered in an unusual, but not impossible, way; she was making admirable strides in virtue, and she wasn't making a disturbance about it, so he never mentioned it to anybody else, although evidently he gave her consistently good advice.

In 1840, though, M. Farbos was replaced by another priest, M. l'abbé Pierre Darbins, and he took more notice of it. He imposed increasingly tough tests of obedience on Marie, and when she passed them all he asked for help from the director of the seminary. They called her to further acts of obedience, including writing down everything that had happened to her; and although her infused knowledge was far greater than their naturally acquired theological expertise, she obeyed them like a stick in their hands. Later, she said, Christ instructed her to join the Society of the Sacred Heart, which had just been founded in Paris and was otherwise unknown to them. Here, too, she was notable for her obscurity and above all for her absolute obedience; she got fairly low-ranking jobs in the infirmary and kitchen, and she served as porteress, as St. Catherine Labouré had, but her spiritual light still shone through. "Sœur Lataste does everything as everybody else does," one of her sisters explained, "yet nobody else does anything as she does."[313]

The Question of Humility

Obedience indicates authenticity in mystic phenomena because it springs from the virtue of humility, and humility isn't widely understood, these days. Humility isn't anything like debasing yourself; on the contrary, the virtue of humility is the gift of having a precise knowledge of yourself, your strengths as well as your failings. It's not denying any of your gifts but knowing them precisely so that you can use them to the fullest, and to good purpose. Humility is knowing exactly who you are, and exactly where you stand in the great scheme of things. That's why creditable mystics tend to be so common-sensical, and why they can get so much work done; you can't go around founding or reform-

---

312. And in a way she was right; her life encapsulates the pattern of Christian life, starting out as a little savage and drawing closer to God through the sacraments as you go, maturing, exercising greater virtues, and ending up as a light on a lampstand when you'd really rather hide under the bushel. It's just that in her case the moderation of her temperament, the increase of joy, and the intimate closeness to God happened faster and with more sensory communication than the norm. St. Gregory the Great (*Dialogues* 4:18), by the way, relates an almost exactly similar case, that of a girl named Musa, the sister of a man he calls Probus.

313. Her story isn't so well known today, precisely because of one of those problems with the record. Under obedience, she wrote down everything that had happened to her, but the editor sought to expand and explain it by transcribing into her narrative no fewer than thirty-two passages taken directly from the *Summa* of St. Thomas Aquinas, and he took it upon himself to improve her language, move things around, and otherwise render her writings useless. Her manuscript, evidently, has been lost.

ing religious orders, for example, if you think that you're above it all, or even if you just think too much of yourself. Nor, on the other hand, if you don't know that you can.

Humility can come only from God, just as pride comes only from the Adversary, and humility is generally considered the first and principal sign by which the value of purported mystic phenomena is judged. Even the evaluation of the texts of the records resonate to humility; no genuine mystic event can override or countervene any of Christ's teachings, and creditable mystics wouldn't think of posing as divine messengers with more authority than Christ, or even claim to speak for him. That's really about the barest minimum of humility a person can have, not setting himself above Christ or on a par with him; yet the overwhelming majority of self-declared mystics trip over that very low threshhold.

You see the workings of humility in creditable mystics not just in their obedience, but in the whole tenor of their lives. St. Bernadette and the children of Fátima were horrified that people should point them out, press money into their hands, offer them clothing or other presents, or ask them to dinner, let alone ask them to bless rosaries and medals—or people. "Why?" eight-year-old Lucia dos Santos asked as she handed back a rosary. "I'm not a priest."

It's why so many of them have a vocation to religious life. As friars, monks, or nuns, they're expected to live in obscurity just like everybody else. St. Catherine Labouré hid herself so successfully that, for the last half-century of her life, nobody had any idea that this cleaner of bedpans was the one who had introduced one of the most popular sacramentals in history, all through the anonymity of the confessional grille.

On a more intimate level, humility is what stands behind a mystic's plea that any extraordinary graces be kept secret, if not withheld altogether. They know that people tend to forget to look past these spectacular graces to the God who gives them and keep staring at the person through whom he displays them: they know that these events have no connection whatever with the sanctity of the instrument on which they're played. "Lord," St. Teresa of Avila said in regard to her levitation, "Lord, for a thing of so little consequence, do not allow so vile a creature as I am to be mistaken for a holy woman."

So, like the quality of the report itself, humility before and after the reported event outweighs almost all other considerations. The minute you see a self-proclaimed visionary giving an interview to the press, more than willing to call in news cameras and appear on television; the minute you see self-proclaimed mystics asserting that they've seen Mary and that they have an urgent message that can save the world; the minute you see someone even permitting himself to be interviewed on such a matter; certainly as soon as you see a reported visionary routinely blessing people, "curing" pilgrims, or even receiving pilgrims at all—you can safely assume that the person is a fraud or, if you want to be particularly charitable, that the person is deluded, genuinely believing that what he said he saw was real.

Of course, a genuine mystic experience is a separate event from the mystic's reaction to it; but the genuine ones do generally stimulate the virtues in a recipient. No virtue known to moral theology would be compatible with a lack of humility. The virtues active in a genuinely gifted soul produce a very different kind of personality, indeed.

The Question of Pride

The vice that stands directly opposed to the virtue of humility is pride, and pride also works in predictable ways in spurious mystics.

Because extraordinary gifts aren't necessary for salvation, and because they do attract a lot of attention, asking God for them specifically is usually an indication of pride; you don't want God, and you don't even want to live humbly—you want to be singled out for extraordinary favors.

Of course, some of the great missionary saints, like St. Francis Xavier and St. Vincent Ferrer, are on record as having asked privately for extraordinary help to convert thousands and tens of thousands, and a lot of saints obtain miracles by invoking God on the spot, as Moses did before Pharaoh. This is never to call attention to themselves, but to God, to let bystanders see that it's God working the miracle through that person. Often, too, they were specifically told to do as they did. Some few, like St. Anthony of Padua and St. Francis di Paola, seem to have taken such gifts for granted, working miracles as casually as St. Joseph of Cupertino would fly or St. John Vianney would speak of future events offhand as if they'd already happened; but that's humility, too, a sure knowledge of the gifts God gave you, and an exact estimation of their extent.

But asking for visible signs from above generally falls under the heading of "tempting God". God is above temptation, of course, but the word is used in this phrase in an archaic specialized sense, meaning to put to the test, as it does in the old translation of the Lord's prayer, "lead us not into temptation". God wouldn't lead us into temptation, in our sense of the word, but he does put us to the test; the point is that we're not allowed to test God. So having asked for any mystic gift is generally considered fairly weighty evidence that the person isn't really all that credit-worthy.[314]

In its more intense forms, pride seems to be the source of more reported mystic phenomena than anything else. Frauds in any field of endeavor always think that they can fool everybody else, even the experts; and that's pride, in a nutshell. The unbearable need for attention can trip people across the line between reality and delusion, too, and while that's not exactly the same kind of pride, it's still a disorder of self-esteem that ends up at the same place. That's why fraudulent or disordered attempts to give the appearance of mystic phenomena always end up making the person seem ridiculous (although, it must be said, that may not make much difference to their followers), provoking only contempt or compassion, depending on the ultimate cause of it all.

---

314. Ex 17:2-7; Dt 6:16; Is 7:10-12; Mt 4:1-11, 12:38-39, 16:1-4; Mk 8:11-12; Lk 4:12, 11:16-29; 1Cr 1:22, etc. One exception to this is St. Catherine Labouré, who was seized with a strong desire to see Mary, and prayed for that favor. But this came after she had received other mystic gifts like apparitions of St. Vincent de Paul (1581-1660); and she made her prayer in childlike simplicity, not for the fame of it but just as a way of drawing closer to the Mother of God.

Even besides pride, the aberrations of false mystic phenomena point to one or another specific personal fault that the Church has seen countless times, every day, every year, since Pentecost. These are usually diagnosed quickly, and the afflicted person is given whatever care he needs, if he'll accept it. And these faults don't always come from some vice inside the person; false mystics can be, and in fact usually are, just ordinary people trying to do the best that they can but failing to manage such trials as life sends them.

The Question of Trials and Tribulations

The severity of the alleged mystic's hardships, particularly, has to be measured against the strength of the virtues that he possessed to handle them with; creditable mystics are well able to handle anything that life throws at them, rabid opposition like the hatred directed against St. Louis-Marie Grignion de Montfort, physical sufferings as crushing as those of St. Thérèse of Lisieux, or even afflictions that pass human comprehension, like Bl. Lydwine's.

One particular difficulty with this personal stage of the investigation is that a person's will can be weakened, and the imagination exaggerated, by practices like long vigils, fasts, and exhausting work among the poor, and truly great ascetics are drawn to precisely that kind of activity. Moreover, chronic or severe illness can change a person's perceptions, too, and scarcely any creditable mystic escapes that kind of trial. In these cases, the investigation takes on another level of discernment. The genuineness of the person's vocation to the ascetic life has to be determined—does this self-proclaimed ascetic wear sackcloth and shout at street corners, or does he comport himself as St. Gemma Galgani did when she pulled her sleeves down over her stigmata and went down to fix dinner? Is this a well-conducted, quiet person who obeys an accredited spiritual director? How does the person react to the suffering—by whining or bragging about it, or with a more mature fortitude? And even after this judgement the reported mystic experience has to be weighed against the possibility of hallucination.

Moral theologians and psychologists agree that stress can make people dream unusual dreams or even hallucinate, and that if the stress becomes more than the person can bear it can provoke attempts at escape: multiple personalities, paranoiac episodes, or simply regressive behavior—or spurious mystic events. Even comparatively mild cases incline a person to look for feelings of consolation or release in religion rather than for its strength and fortification, for a way to escape responsibility for fighting the good fight in the world rather than the spiritual and moral discipline that makes that fight possible. So investigators ask about the person's recent life, looking for episodes like the loss of a loved one; the trials that push some people to claim spurious mystic phenomena are basically the same as those that prompt people to follow these reports devotedly, and they're all clearly known to moral theologians and psychologists alike.

Many people unable to handle these daily tribulations grope frantically for support or for some confirmation of the idea that they're right and that the whole world is wrong. Others may seek for some distinction, which helps them believe that they don't fit in because they're special, not because they can't handle the trials of ordinary life. Sometimes it's just a matter of wanting somebody to pay attention; sometimes it's an attempt to break out of the normal selflessness of the noviciate; and sometimes it means moving into that alternative reality beyond the reach of friends and family, away from all of the responsibilities that adult life brings with it. Sometimes it's done subconsciously, resulting in delusion; sometimes it's done on purpose, resulting in fraud. And sometimes the two blend into one another, over time, as the fraud starts to believe in himself.

Whatever form these psychological and emotional trials take, such people will be diagnosed and, it's hoped, treated by purely natural health-care processes and reconciled to the Church through normal pastoral care. But they're not mistaken for mystics.

THE MYSTIC CONTEXT

After the person or persons involved are found to be worth listening to, and after the character of the testimony is established, you have to distinguish whether the event itself would be of natural origin or if it was caused by some supernatural agency. You work this out, of course, by looking at the exact nature of the phenomenon, and then at the relationship of that phenomenon to the recognized historical catalogue of genuine mystic activity.

The Nature of the Supernatural

A real mystic experience is something that, try as you might, you can't do yourself. You can work at it with every fiber of your being, you can strain every nerve, in an effort to see your guardian angel or Mary or God, and absolutely nothing will happen. You can try to levitate all you want to, but you won't. Not even an inch, and not even for a moment. These things are simply beyond human power to produce.

Naturally, that's an important part of what makes it possible to distinguish real mystic phenomena from the fake or even from delusion. If investigators find that the appearances could be produced by a natural cause—not that they were, necessarily, but that they could be—they're not going to call it a mystic phenomenon. They'd wait, and they'd watch; historically, some courses of mystic activity start small, and virtually none come as bolts from the blue. Even those at Banneux and Beauraing were quiet, just extraordinary enough to call attention to themselves, not enough to frighten or astound. So an unusual but possibly natural phenomenon might be nothing more than it seems, or it might be the overture to something not possible in the natural order of things.

What makes it hard to draw that line, sometimes, is that natural powers are neither so meek nor so predictable as we'd like to think; people seem to have within them strengths far beyond what we think people have. As recently as 1884, for instance, a priest who was also a doctor was called in to manage a convent at which nuns could leap over the enclosure wall at a single bound. To the average witness, this kind of thing is simply impossible in the natural order of things; but it isn't, really. Abnormal strength like this isn't taken as a sign of mystic activity nor of diabolic possession, because it can

317

happen hysterically, when the subjects find some subconscious way of tapping physical strengths that they wouldn't suspect they had. This was exactly what happened in this case, so the doctor cured the nuns by purely natural means—things like steady and varied manual labor.

Going by the Book

Comparison of reported events with the catalogue of unusual but natural events, then, is one important way to separate the truly mystic from the purely human; and comparing the superhuman to the catalogue of creditable mystic events of the past reveals a lot about the case in question, too.

The Church understands that God does not dabble in nonsense, and that mystic phenomena happen so that they can be understood, so that they can get our attention and focus us in an edifying direction, just as Christ used his miracles in the Gospels. So the chances are overwhelming that he's not going to do something so out of line that we wouldn't be able to relate it to previous events, all the way back to the days of the Old Testament. If you know your Bible well enough—if you have a complete and accurate translation of it—and if you accept it as outlining the ways in which Judeo-Christian revelation works, then you should have a fair ability to distinguish reports that are worth investigating from those that are worth instant dismissal.

Christ's regeneration of absent flesh and organs, Habacuc's agility, St. Paul's stigmata, Ezechiel's levitation, Tobias's encounter with the angel (or Jacob's), and all the rest set the pattern; and, as Herbert Thurston, S.J., noted in his classic *Physical Phenomena of Mysticism* (1952), we may fairly assume that the same principle holds good in post-biblical times. After all, Christ is the same yesterday, today, and tomorrow.

That's why familiarity with the basic catalogue of mystic phenomena can go a long way toward clarifying the situation; this book itself is a comprehensive catalogue of mystic phenomena (or at least it was intended to be), so if a reported phenomenon isn't discussed here, it's most likely not worth considering. The kinds of phenomenon listed here, what you might call the ordinary extraordinary phenomena, have a long and perfectly consistent history in the Church and in Judaism before the Church; magic images on rose petals or food items have no such history, not as part of any creditable mystic phenomenon. Beyond that, there are other things, like having a rosary turn to a different color, that have never happened anywhere near a creditable apparition but are virtually the trademark of fraudulent and delusional cases.

And those considerations, in turn, constitute one reason that the Church can instantly dismiss certain kinds of report. Sometimes she might have to disapprove a magic picture of Christ in the pattern of a tree trunk only very gently, or just by silence. You don't want to split people into two camps over something so obviously silly, and the people most likely to flock to such a thing are precisely those most likely to object that the bishop didn't even bother to investigate—they're the ones least likely to realize that he didn't have to. But, in any case, when something not very edifying and obviously outside the normal range of extraordinary phenomena does happen, the Church can instantly say, no, this is not the kind of thing that happens in mystic life.

It gets a little more difficult when the things that happen are fairly close to known creditable events; genuine mystic phenomena aren't all precisely the same. As the creditable cases show, apparitions can add a new emphasis here or a new insight there, the stigmata can take a certain variety of forms, levitation and agility can be manifested in several ways, and there may even be a factor that seems diabolically perverse. And, given Benedict XIV's principle that you don't attribute any extraordinary phenomenon to a divine cause as long as any natural or diabolical explanation is possible, even a single unusual factor can bear a lot of weight. But everything has to be considered carefully, and nothing is evaluated in isolation unless it's substantially improper.

Take the stigmatic Palma Matarelli (1825-1888) of Oria near Brindisi as an example. Dr. Imbert-Goubeyre saw her four times lying on her sickbed "burning" under her chemise, after which she had injuries like those caused by boiling liquids. Of course, ardors do happen with creditable mystics, as with St. Philip Neri, who glowed visibly with flames of love. He kept his windows open and never wore a coat, even in winter, because the heat of the ardors was so intense. Brother Lawrence of the Resurrection had the same thing just as severely, as did many other saints—when St. Teresa of Avila was ill, her body was so hot that the sisters who nursed her couldn't touch her. Sor Maria Villani drank as much as three and a half gallons of water a day to quench her thirst, and it sounded like water dropped on hot sheet iron.

Generally, this phenomenon isn't given much weight by mystic theologians; it might be caused by some rare unknown ailment, and its symbolic value, rather vaguely recalling the flames of love issuing from the Sacred Heart of Jesus, seems limited. But Palma d'Oria's ardors discredited her completely. Cloths left in contact with her skin during these episodes were not just scorched, but scorched in patterns and images of inflamed hearts, nails, swords, and the like; the blood ran from her stigmata-like wounds in flamelike patterns, forming similar images on her clothes. Now, this sort of thing is obviously not in the natural order of things, and it would be virtually impossible to fake. But more significantly, the substance of the phenomena was all wrong in the context of the historical catalogue of similar phenomena.

No creditable apparition, stigmata, or other mystic phenomenon on record has ever been associated even remotely with this kind of magic image, and it's a safe bet that none ever will be. They were just over the edge, as far as credit-worthy phenomena go. That alone was enough to cut through the rest of her purportedly mystic gifts, and it was the wedge that made her confess the whole thing. So, in 1877, Pius IX Ferretti told a journalist point-blank that Palma's phenomena were the work of the Devil, and that he had the documents to prove it, and that was that for Palma.

It's harder to come to that decision when only one factor is wrong. For example, nearly all creditable stigmatics also have the odor of sanctity, too, but the single stigmatic wound on St. Rita of Cascia smelled so supernaturally foul that she had to live isolated from her sister nuns for fifteen years. Her life exhibited heroic virtue and sanctity beyond question, stigmata or no stigmata, and when she died the sweet odor of sanctity filled her cell; but, still, that stench seemed rather similar to the tricks that the Devil plays when he possesses people or wants to mislead the Faithful by faking supernatural events.[315]

So St. Rita's stench raised a lot of doubts. But it was clearly supernatural, and it was the only feature of her experience that approached that somewhat indistinct border between the genuinely divine and the diabolically counterfeit, an area in which only informed common sense—or good taste, almost—can readily distinguish between the two realms. You can have a fully creditable mystic in whose case only one feature is questionable, or a fake exposed by only one questionable feature; even if the source of the superhuman events is infernal, it can either show no redeeming features whatever, or it can counterfeit genuine mystic phenomena so closely that it all seems to fit perfectly all right—at first.

315. St. Gregory the Great (*Dialogues* 4:38-39) mentions that the stench is just another of Hell's horrors, as Job implies (24:20) and Genesis affirms (19:24), as when the smoke of burning sulphur punished Sodom and Gomorrah.

twenty-nine

disguised

as an angel of light

My son, you must deeply distrust
the beautiful and lofty thoughts and lovely undertakings
that the evil spirit, disguised as an angel of light,
often inspires in the most zealous and spiritual souls
to bring about their downfall by his wiles and deceits.

— St. Louis-Marie Grignion de Montfort,
Love of the Eternal Wisdom,
Eleventh Maxim, Voice of the Eternal Wisdom

Miracles, apparitions, and locutions are by definition attractive phenomena that, even if they come from God, only draw people's attention back to God and to his teachings. The more people there are who really need to have their attention turned, the more things that appear to be miraculous there are. The trick is that for every genuine mystic phenomenon that God sends to turn people toward him, the Devil sends dozens to turn people in the opposite direction. A good many of the deluded seers around Lourdes, La Salette, and other sites showed plenty of symptoms of obsession or even of possession. Maybe it was part of a hellish attempt to cloud over the message of the creditable apparition, or maybe it was all permitted as a way of showing how disordered people's spiritual lives were there and then. Or both.

And while moral theologians understand that the Devil can fake virtually all of the physical and sensory symptoms of real mystic activity, there doesn't seem to be a single case on record in which he does so without the person's consent. Usually the Adversary gets that consent in the ordinary way: some particularly susceptible person gets to thinking that spurious mystic phenomena would be a good way to gain financial security or win a reputation for holiness. In these cases, the fakery itself constitutes not just consent but a kind of indirect request for the Devil's help.

In other cases, the faker asks outright for diabolic help, a call that's never refused; and still other cases show that the Devil is always over-generous, overwhelming his petitioners with immensely more interference than they bargained for. If the Devil really is prowling the Earth like a ravening lion (1Pt 5:8), then any call to him, even jokingly or passively, must be enough, and there you are.

THE PARADOX OF CONSPICUOUS HOLINESS

In many cases of indirect requests for diabolic aid (most of them, in fact), the spiritual corruption is virtually invisible. The case of Nicole of Rheims in the seventeenth century is typical. She was outwardly pious and active in her community; she organized prayer meetings and processions and generally ran a large group of devoted followers. People turned to her for advice and spiritual counsel, and she gave it willingly. She even had the ability, sometimes, to make predictions that actually came true. She was a well-known and popular figure in the parish and in the diocese. Only Madame Acarie, better known to history as the lay Carmelite Bl. Mary of the Incarnation, perceived that Nicole's outstanding acts of piety were the products of pride, stimulated by the Devil, but naturally nobody listened to her: as a purported mystic herself, she was under investigation and not an admissible witness.316

The simple acceptance of celebrity, or even of a conspicuous place in parish life, provoked by the claim of conspicuous sanctity or extraordinary gifts, ought to be enough to raise serious reservations about any purported mystic. But many people find it harder to hold back when a faker can apparently read hearts, call up apparitions or bleed on demand, or even levitate. All of these things can be, and are, faked by demonic agencies; so the person's motives, no less than his reaction to the attention that these things draw, is a good indicator of the cause behind those appearances. "Since no human can relate or perform these things, certain persons think it proper to serve the demons," St. Augustine wrote, back in about 408 (*The Divination of Demons*). "They're prompted especially by the vice of curiosity, by their desire for a false happiness, and for an earthly and temporal success."

Of course, even here a distinction has to be made. With purported visionaries like Maximin and Mélanie, the hunger for fame does cloud the Church's view of the reported phenomenon, and it will always delay approval. But, although they enjoyed the attention after they got it, they didn't claim an apparition to get the attention. That shows that a person can have a genuine mystic experience but not be able to handle it very well, which is another reason for studying the person's moral status before and after the event.

It's also noteworthy that this was just about the only reproach that could be brought against the seers of La Salette. They never contradicted themselves on what

316. There are two notable women named Mary of the Incarnation; one is an Ursuline who has been declared Venerable, and the other, this one, is a beatified lay Carmelite.

happened that day. All of Mélanie's questionable behavior, the pursuit of audiences, the clamoring for admiration from the clergy, the torrent of individual prophecies and predictions that she wrote and distributed, all of these things were directly traceable to that one fault, the predictable craving that a neglected child has for simple attention.

Counterfeits from the Father of Lies

But sometimes the temptations get a little more explicit and lot more interesting, as well as getting a lot harder to distinguish from genuine mystic activity. Repeating his rule about instantly rejecting any and all apparent mystic phenomena for precisely this reason, Saint John of the Cross says that the Devil

> is adept at suggesting to the individual a secret self-satisfaction that becomes truly obvious at times. He often purveys objects to the senses, affording to the sense of sight images of saints and most beautiful lights, and to the hearing dissembled words, and to the sense of smell, fragrant odors; and he puts sweetness in one's mouth and delight to the sense of touch. He does all of this so that by enticing persons through these sensory objects he may induce them to many evils... Through the desire of accepting them one opens the door to the Devil. The Devil can then deceive one by other communications expertly feigned and disguised as genuine. In the words of the Apostle, he can transform himself into an angel of light.

There are standard ways to tell the difference between the divine and the diabolic in supernatural experiences, but it isn't always easy to do it. Magdalen of the Cross, for instance, kept experts guessing for decades. She was born in Córdova in 1487, so she was roughly the contemporary of St. Teresa of Avila. She must have been noted for her piety from the time she was little; by the age of five she had creditably supernatural visions, seeing various saints from time to time. Now, everybody thought that she was obviously going to be a nun, but nobody noticed the effect that these apparitions had on her. They didn't make her want to be a saint herself. They made her want everybody to know that she was a saint already.

By the time she was thirteen, her spiritual gluttony for apparitions, and for the attention that they got her, had pretty well cemented her in vanity and pride. So, at that point, the source of her apparitions revealed himself. The Devil stood before her and said, in essence, if you want, I'll see that you get a reputation for sanctity that will last at least thirty years—that way, you'll get all of the attention and worldly glory that you could possibly desire.

Magdalen agreed, and Satan came to her again and again to tell her what to do and how to do it. She instantly regretted her agreement because his appearance was so unspeakably hideous that she could hardly stand it. But she was a great success in her career; she served three times as Abbess of her convent. He also gave her all kinds of physical phenomena mimicking genuine mystic events so closely that even the professionals hesitated in declaring them false. She made predictions that came true, usually; she fell into apparent ecstasies, she levitated, everything. She faked inedia, too, having food smuggled in to her every day for eleven years. And she inflicted herself with stigmatic wounds. She didn't let them heal, opening them again and again for thirty-eight years.

Naturally she attracted swarms of curiosity seekers and sincere pilgrims, as well as cardinals, prelates, and investigators from the Holy Office. From what they could see, the physical phenomena were definitely supernatural, beyond the powers of humans to fake (except for the stigmata and the inedia), and the whole exhibition toed the line very, very closely, never really stepping over into the realm of what you might call unusual extraordinary phenomena. But investigations continued.

Then, in 1543, the inevitable happened. Magdalen of the Cross fell ill and nearly died. In front of all of the pilgrims who had gathered at her deathbed, she blurted out everything all at once. Even Reconciliation didn't shake the Devil off her back; she couldn't break her own will of the desire for what he offered. Because the victim has to consent in some way to diabolic aid in faking these things, and because demons are vastly more powerful than we are, the victim's will is suppressed so that it's extremely difficult for him to rally enough strength to reject the demons, even with sacramental help. After all, to be effective, sacraments have to be received by a person properly disposed to receive them; and anybody who consents to sin isn't properly disposed to receive sacraments.[317]

Magdalen also had to go through exorcism, but finally she recovered, physically and spiritually (as far as anybody could tell). She ended her life confined to another convent of her order, out of the public eye and out of harm's way. She had no more extraordinary phenomena, and she was never again taken for a person of anything more than ordinary sanctity. Which is precisely as it should be. As Benedict XIV pointed out, no extraordinary phenomenon is taken as evidence of the sanctity of the person involved.

That's why people like St. Teresa—so close to Magdalen of the Cross in time and space—are so rigorously investigated, and it's one good reason that the Church doesn't put much stock in reported mystic phenomena of any kind until the investiga-

317. Heresy, or even persistence in a separated sect, evidently constitutes sufficient consent. Recently, Yair Bar-El, head of the Kfar Shaul Psychiatric Hospital in Jerusalem, has defined a "Jerusalem Syndrome" in which pilgrims to the Holy City suddenly begin to believe that they're Jesus, Mary, God, Satan, or some other supernatural being, or at least to worry that they might be. Many dress in bedsheets, preach or sing in the streets, and go looking for locusts and wild honey. The syndrome doesn't run like a psychosis—most attacks happen at the Holy Sepulchre, Christianity's holiest spot, and once the patient is taken away from the city it passes entirely (usually; it persists with some cases, like David Koresh). It sounds like a kind of possession; demons seem particularly numerous at the perimeter of holy sites (St. Bernadette reported hearing a constant tumult of demonic voices at Lourdes shouting obscenities and ordering the apparition to leave, but the Lady silenced them with a glance; cf. Mt 8:29, 17:18; Lk 4:9; etc.). The function of pertinacity in heresy, or refusal to accept Christian doctrine in its entirety, as that kind of agreement (Mt 12:30) is shown by the fact that virtually all of the victims of Jerusalem Syndrome are Protestants or members of another separated sect; Roman Catholics virtually never experience it, and those few who do are mild cases, cured as soon as they leave.

tion is concluded, or even afterwards. And that's why letters from bishops use phrases like "supernatural and divine"—because things can be supernatural and diabolical, too.

Possession, Obsession, and the Human Soul

Taken as a whole, the phenomena of outright diabolic *possession* are substantially different from diabolic imitation of creditable mystic phenomena. Possession is an ugly thing, not just unedifying but downright obscene, at times, or at least foul. Well-documented accounts of possession aren't easily found, not because they don't exist but because the Church considers these messy phenomena as essentially private matters, seriously embarrassing not only to the unfortunate subject of the possession but to the whole Christian community in which he lives. But a case study of diabolic possession helps draw the line between divine mystic phenomena and the toils of the Devil.

The first distinction has to be between possession, which happens inside the person, and obsession, which happens from outside. In *obsession* (from the Latin *ob-*, at or toward, and *sessio*, a sitting or siege—in other words, a besieging), the person is tormented somehow. This happens to people who are trying heroically to detach themselves from things of this world and turn to God; evidently, when the Devil figures out that ordinary temptations aren't enough, he turns to more vigorous measures.[318]

Sometimes they're merely annoying, as when the chair of St. Margaret Mary used to be pulled suddenly out from under her. But sometimes things get a lot rougher. Countless other saints, like St. Nicholas of Tolentino (1245-1305), St. Theodore of Alexandria (fifth century), St. Louis Marie Grignion de Montfort, and St. Paul before them (2Cr 12:7), were beaten by devils frequently. And, reportedly, Padre Pio was, too, and seriously injured. His bloodstained pillow is still shown at his cell at San Stefano Rotondo. The torments and temptations of St. Anthony of Egypt are epic, and St. Teresa broke her arm when she was thrown down the stair by demonic hands, at the age of sixty-two.[319]

On the other hand, in *possession* (from the Latin *possessio*, which means—well, possession), the Devil works from within the person, seeming to replace the person's soul, in a way, or rather to push it into a corner of the person's being and fill the rest of him. One or more demons inhabit the body, seeing through the person's eyes, hearing

318. Obsession may explain some cases of the phenomenon usually called a *poltergeist*, a term derived from Germanic words and meaning a "noisy ghost". These cases seem to center on older children who have some problem adjusting to adolescence, a situation that evidently makes them easy targets for demonic obsession.

319. The doctor didn't make his rounds to that convent until three months later, so you can imagine what she went through. St. Margaret Mary and St. Maria Maddelena dei Pazzi weren't seriously hurt, probably, because they weren't caught unaware, and they took proper defenses, which may be why the devils had to resort to slapstick. St. Anthony just dismissed the devils in the desert by remarking that they must be very weak, to come in such numbers against one little old man. St.Frances of Rome, among others, used the same defense, but generally holy water, the Sign of the Cross, or the Name of Jesus is enough, which is one of the reasons that separated brethren, who don't have these sacramental defenses available, suffer most from these spiritual assaults, and why the habit of daily prayer is necessary for growth in spiritual strength and avoidance of evil.

through his ears, and so on. Now, although pious persons can be obsessed, and in fact the more pious the person the more violent the attack, most mystic theologians agree that possession can't happen unless the person somehow consents to the Devil.[320]

That doesn't say much about who's a target and who isn't, because everybody consents to the Devil, giving in to little temptations all day long, and big ones every now and again. The problem is that, because some kind of consent is necessary, it's extremely difficult to make the demons let the person go—you asked for it, you might say.

It can also be surprisingly hard to tell the difference between certain signs of possession and purely natural, but highly unusual, nervous or psychological disorders. That's why the diagnosis of possession isn't given out in haste. Even St. Philip Neri, who had unusually strong powers over demons and saw them when the situation required, was extremely reluctant to attribute disorders to possession. Churchmen are always advised to call in a medical doctor, someone who knows all about convulsions, psychoses, and other medical conditions that might make anybody else think that something supernatural was happening. So physical symptoms, even things like roaring (within reasonable possibilities) aren't counted as symptoms of possession, in and of themselves.

Sometimes even the most surprising physical symptoms are only the signs of physical disorders; sometimes, though, possession and disease run their course together, so physical symptoms, like any other sign, have to be considered in the full context of the event before possession is diagnosed.

The Case of Germana Cele

The exact nature of possession is clear from a fairly typical and well-documented case that happened in 1906 in Natal, at a mission called St. Michael's about twenty miles from Umzinto.[321] Clara Germana Cele had been a student in the mission school since the age of four, and photographs of her at the age of sixteen show a tall, attractive young lady, shy and reserved in her starched blouse and neat skirt. Her teachers credited her with a fine singing voice and some talent at needlework and knitting.

Germana had been baptized as an infant and grew up in full sacramental communion with the Church, but both of her parents adhered to the old natural religion. They weren't exactly the best caregivers in the world, either. They had violent tempers, and their swearing and cursing—real cursing, calling down all kinds of malevolence on their children—were legendary in the region. In fact, the whole *kraal* in which the girl lived was full of fighting and worse. When Germana was only six or seven, she said one

320. Remember that free will is one of the things that makes us human; the Church teaches that the things to which we consent make a definitive difference in salvation or perdition, and that everybody since Adam has been created with the ability to decide to love God or to reject him, and to act accordingly or not.

321. Only a few of the details of this lengthy case are presented here, condensed into a list of symptoms rather than given as a chronological history. The account of this possession was published in 1927, under the *imprimatur* of the Bishop of Detroit, the headquarters in the United States of the missionary society involved. See also the Congregation for the Doctrine of the Faith's letter, *Christian Faith and Demonology*, July 10, 1975.

day, an old sorceress of her tribe had initiated her into vice or, as we'd say today, sexually abused her, and told her to do the same to other little girls. Her character, her confessor noted, "lacked calmness", and after a while she started refusing the sacraments.

Then on July 5, 1906, Germana gave her confessor, in public, a slip of paper promising her to the service of the Devil. Nobody knows how she got the idea to write this, and it makes even less sense to give it to the priest, but she did. Then at night, especially, she started to have episodes of insanity, almost, flailing around uncontrollably and screaming that she was lost, that she'd made an unworthy communion, and that Satan was calling her. "Always receive worthily," she said, when self-possessed, to the First Communicants of the village, "lest you suffer my fate! Because of an unworthy reception of Holy Communion, I am in this condition!"

Her torments went on intermittently, with Germana fighting violently to get free of her attendants and hang herself. On August 20, one of the nuns, Sister Julia Moehrle, found the girl raving, tearing her dress, and shaking the bed fiercely. Germana gnashed her teeth, howled like a dog, and grunted like a pig, finally calling for Father Erasmus Hoerner, C.M.M.: "I must go to Confession," she said. "I will tell everything. But be quick, or Satan will kill me. He has power over me. I have no blessed articles left. I threw away all of the medals that you gave me!"

Sister Julia gave the girl some holy medals and sprinkled her with holy water. "O, Sister," she cried, "you burn me." The noise of her ravings seemed clearly superhuman, like the roar of armies battling, sometimes close and sometimes at a distance, but always loud. The priest asked her who she was. She answered in her native Zulu, "It is I."

"Are you Germana?" the priest asked.

"No, I am not," a voice from within the girl answered. Her body was convulsed with barking, grunting, howling, and raving, but Father Erasmus demanded again to know the identity of the voice. "I am Satan," it answered. "We were driven from Heaven to Hell, although our sins are not so great as those of many men."

Thinking that the girl was suffering from delirium or insanity, the missionaries followed standard procedure and called in four doctors. Two of them happened to be Protestant and two Catholic, but none found anything physically or psychologically wrong with her. They witnessed what happened to her after that, as did four priests, all of the nuns of the mission and several others called in from surrounding missions, the local bishop, and more than a hundred and fifty villagers.

Whenever she was able to speak in her own voice during the following weeks, Germana begged the village people, all of whom came to see her, for prayers. She cried pitiably for help, saying that she was lost, that she could only despair, and reproaching herself for having invoked the Devil in the first place. "You deceived me!" she cried. "You promised me beautiful days and now you are so cruel to me!"

Of course, all of Germana's symptoms until this point might be written off as natural, if unusual, affectations by an adolescent starved for attention. Even her uncanny ability to project the sounds of warring legions might be written off as surprising but attributable to some unknown talent. But when Germana was in the grip of that demon, she told people about secret sins that they had kept back in Confession; and to one little girl she thundered, "You are all right now, but do you think you will remain so? Just wait; we will get you." Throughout her possession, she urged everyone she met not to go to Confession at all. Holy water always burned her,[322] and she could distinguish it on sight from ordinary water or even water from Lourdes.

She identified relics or pictures of Jesus or Mary that were brought into the room, even those in people's pockets, and roared that they should be taken away; when a relic of the True Cross was placed on her forehead, she groaned that it pressed her down. Her head, neck, or chest expanded as if they were being filled with gas far beyond any pathological symptoms, and her face paled to an ashen gray or turned blue, but the Sign of the Cross relieved these symptoms as quickly as they came.

Or her body stretched, her arms and legs cracking as if they were breaking, until she was nearly nine feet tall; her strength increased proportionally, and she used it to thrash the nuns in attendance.[323] During her attacks, the nuns struggled for hours on end to hold her down. When one of the priests, his patience exhausted, tried to keep her in line by bending her fingers back, she simply flipped him head over heels.

An indescribably foul stench permeated the mission dormitory in which Germana was staying. The room was sometimes filled with fire all of a sudden, or her bed was engulfed in flames. Holy water put them out, but ordinary water didn't; and after one of these episodes, the wood of the bed was scorched but all of the linen and the girl's clothing were untouched. The building itself was rattled by forceful pounding on the doors and walls, sometimes all night; sounds of galloping horses, or of someone stamping around in iron shoes on the tin roof were heard, day and night.

In fact, Father Erasmus recalled, the noise was beyond endurance. "It sounded as if a vast number of wild beasts ... were joining in a hellish concert; a pandemonium of bellowing, roaring, barking, ... whistling, beating of tom-toms, whining, moaning, ... cursing, scolding in such wild and terrible tones as no human voice can imitate." This racket echoed throughout the whole region, about three miles in every direction from the mission, constantly. No outsider would come anywhere near the place.

There was suddenly a plague of frogs and huge toads, which was peculiarly apt; not only did it recall Revelations 16:13, but Zulu women in those days were terrified of frogs and would go to any lengths to avoid them—they believed that touching one brought sterility, bad luck in marriage, and other calamities.

The missionaries took her to Mass that next Sunday, where she grimaced,

322. While the trauma of these burns is visible on the flesh of the victim, the pain is felt by the devil inside; the flesh shows no marks afterwards.

323. This kind of bodily elongation is said to have happened, also, to some creditable mystics, but only very, very rarely, one or two cases in eight hundred years or so. It's not given any weight in investigations because of what moral theologians call its "morbidity" and its "lack of purpose". It's hard to see what edifying moral message it could convey.

growled, and shouted contradictions to whatever the priest said unless he commanded her to confess the truth. In his homily, Father Erasmus exhorted the villagers to keep Sunday holy and to come to Mass on time, but Germana interrupted him: "Don't do it," she roared; "come after the Elevation [of the Host], talk and laugh in church, and run away before the Mass is ended. Oh, your sermon is too long! When are you going to stop?" She barked and growled continually during the Creed and bellowed like an ox.

Then, during the Offertory, she rose from her place and floated, about five feet above the pews, into the sanctuary. She came down behind the altar boys, laughing and joking; she returned when the priest ordered her back to her place, but she turned her back on the altar and said, "Adore me!" She refused to kneel before the Blessed Sacrament, even when the priest ordered her to do so. "We cannot kneel; we cannot pay homage to God. I cannot adore him. Do as I did, and pledge yourself to Satan."

Father Erasmus asked the bishop's permission to perform an exorcism on the girl, which was granted. When he began, her arms were stiff and unbendable, her whole body so rigid that she leaned against her chair like a tree trunk. Eight girls her own age held her down, but she and they levitated, with the chair; later, she suddenly grabbed Sister Anacleta powerfully by the throat, and the chair again rose into the air, taking Germana and the nun with it. All of the attendants fought to pull them down and release the stranglehold. She levitated again and again, challenging the clerics to do the same. Sister Anacleta held on to Germana's waist, but when the priest reached the phrase in the exorcism ritual addressing the Devil as the Serpent, Germana started to snap and snarl at the nun. Father Erasmus interrupted the exorcism to warn the nun, but she said, "Then let him bite. I won't let go any more. I will not be conquered by the Devil."

At this, Germana's neck stretched like rubber from her rigid body until she could bite the nun on the arm—a bite that penetrated the sleeve of the habit and left yellow blisters, as from a serious burn, in the pattern of the girl's teeth, as well as a puncture wound in the center as from a sharp tongue. Germana at other times would slink along the floor like a snake, her clothes distorting themselves to follow her serpentine curves. She managed to escape from the straight jacket into which the doctors put her so that she wouldn't injure herself, and from the manacles put on to keep her from injuring others. She would frequently leap to the top of the partition, or just walk up the wall as you would walk across a floor, to dance on the roof beam or to kick at holy pictures hanging in the room.[324]

At times, it seemed that more than one demon was possessing the girl, because more than one voice could be heard from her, arguing and cursing each other simulta-

324. During her episodes of possession, the girl showed mocking contempt for images of Christ but a real hatred of pictures of Mary. "That is she," she would roar, "Yes, that is the woman whom we hate, of whom God said in Paradise, 'I will set enmity between you and the woman'... Ah, this woman Mary crushed my head when she conceived and gave birth to the Son of Man, Jesus." She also admitted that the sin of the fallen angels was their refusal to worship Jesus, the second person of the Trinity, because he freely took on human nature, a nature inferior to their own; this is a point of speculative theology that isn't discussed all that much, and the missionaries attested that they hadn't taught it to the girl.

neously. Even more interesting is the fact that those voices coming from Germana could speak long and appropriate sentences in languages that the girl herself didn't know. The Rite of Exorcism, in those days, was always performed in Latin, as the Mass was, but Germana couldn't have learned enough Latin to make the responses that she did. She didn't just recite the responsorial parts of the ritual (which would have been impressive enough in itself); she twisted the language, made horrible puns, and perverted the prayers, all with perfect grammar and vocabulary.

She, or whatever was inside her, conversed in Latin with the priests and answered their questions. If the priest made a grammatical error, she caught it and mocked him for it, in sing-song. She listed the sins of the nuns in French or even Polish, the native language of only one of the nuns, who never spoke anything but German to the other nuns and Zulu to the villagers.[325] At one point, Germana even started singing a German song by August Kotzebue—*Es kann ja nicht immer so bleiben*, ironically enough—and composed extra verses to it that were so well written and so funny that the sisters had to laugh, despite their struggle to hold the girl down.

On September 13, it seemed that the exorcism had worked. Germana fell silent, lying there as if she were dead. The priest understood that the demon could be shamming, so he repeated the whole ritual, just to be sure, after she came around, but she was all right. Still, in 1907 she told the priest that the same devil had come back to her and told her that he would possess her again, so they had to go through the whole thing once more. After the third exorcism, Germana stayed on the straight and narrow. She led an uneventful life for six years afterwards, dying of quick consumption in 1913.

Her case, with its unremittingly foul character and lack of an edifying purpose in any of its features, was clearly attributable only to demonic influence. In this case, the Devil made no attempt whatever to counterfeit any part of a genuine mystic experience—even the levitation was a blatant mockery.

Other cases of purported mystic activity are just as easily distinguished from the genuine article, though, when they're caused entirely by human counterfeiters who go at it with no more diabolic aid than anybody else has.

---

325. She didn't speak Polish to them because she wasn't supposed to know it, herself; it was illegal to teach or speak that language in those parts of Poland that had been taken by Prussia in the eighteenth century. Since the partition of Poland among Prussia, Russia, and Austria then, there was no Polish state until an independent Poland was mandated as one of Woodrow Wilson's Fourteen Points. The Polish language and Polish culture survived only by going underground for those two hundred years.

t h i r t y

n o   a t t e n t i o n

s h o u l d   b e   p a i d

In my opinion no attention should be paid
to these latter two kinds of person ...
Tell them to pay no attention to such experiences,
that these locutions are not essential to the service of God ...
This counsel should be given
so as not to aggravate the melancholy,
for if they tell her that the locution is due to melancholy,
there will be no end to the matter;
she will swear that she sees and hears,
for it seems to her that she does.

— St. Teresa of Avila, *The Interior Castle*, 6:3:2

Something that appears to be a mystic phenomenon has either a natural or a supernatural cause. The supernatural phenomena have to come from either God or the Devil, and it's not always easy to tell which one it is, at first. The natural ones have to come from human beings, who are either fraudulent or delusional. That is, they either know perfectly well that they're faking, or they really believe that what's going on is real.

But because the activity in both fraud and delusion comes directly out of the person himself, the Church's assumption seems to be that time will tell. Even in the purely natural order of things, fakery tends to gain size and speed as it rolls along, and fakers have to start out with the assumption that they're smarter than everybody else: a combination of factors that guarantees loss of control sooner or later—the fall cometh after the pride, you might say.

Deluded persons, by definition, find it hard to act consistently, and if a known psychological disorder is indicated the case would be largely in the hands of medical professionals, with whatever pastoral spiritual care is customary. Either way, this is part of why investigations seem to take forever. Time itself is an important investigative tool, and most reports just fade away if the fraudulent or deluded "seer" doesn't get the attention he craves.

But even when supernatural forces, celestial or infernal, can be ruled out, it's often very hard to tell the difference between purely human fraud and purely human delusion. That's a matter of motive, and motive is what's called an inferential fact; you can't look into a person's mind and heart—well, not without cardiognosis, you can't—and you can't believe testimony about motive. Motive has to be established by the facts surrounding the case; it's a fact, but it has to be inferred.

That's why investigators look into the question of who benefits from the reported experience, and how. If the purported mystic accepts money, food, lands and houses, horses and carriages or their industrial-age equivalents, that's a pretty fair indicator of where his heart lies. Many a fraud has hit on the idea of an apparition to bail out the foundering farm, or of prophecy or faith-healing to secure a comfortable living. More than one deluded visionary has thought quite frankly that the donations pouring in from the gullible were a gift of God.

But genuine mystic activity is, by definition, a pull by God away from this world. Spiritual gifts aren't given for the recipient's benefit, but for the benefit of others, and they always bring with them the severe worldly trials of being a channel for the extraordinary activity of God—of standing against this world, not of standing over it. It's hard to think of a creditable mystic who started out rich and died that way; none who starts out poor dies rich.

So the simple love of money is the root of a lot of evil, when it comes to spiritual counterfeiters. But there are related motives, too, that carry their own internal complications. Some fraudulent mystics feel themselves empowered, in a perverse sort of way, if they can promise secondary phenomena the way Simon Magus did (Ac 8:9-23). They had been failures, as the world rates failure, and now they have followers who press money on them; they have congregations of their own who beg them, tear-stained, for healing or for the spiritual elevation of special gifts; and they sell the promises.

This most powerful appeal, the lure of being ranked as somebody special, infects the fraud's followers, too; they can count themselves the anointed, the enlightened, or the otherwise gifted, setting themselves apart from a bewildering world. The problem is that they set themselves apart from the strength and comfort of religion, too, which is just about the only way that they could learn to overcome their own shortcomings and fight the good fight that they want so fervently to win.

The isolation from the mainstream that fraudulent mystic phenomena seem to promise is why these events can generate such persistent and loyal followers, even when the substance of the phenomena is the most tawdry or absurd material imaginable.

THE CASE OF MARY ANN VAN HOOF

Mary Ann (Mrs. Fred) Van Hoof, a farm wife born in Philadelphia in 1909, lived with her husband and seven children outside the small Wisconsin town of Necedah (nuh-SEE-duh). On November 12, 1949, she said, the Virgin Mary came to her in her bedroom and promised to come again. For several years after that, Mrs. Van Hoof described successive visions, locutions, and prophecies, and she proclaimed all kinds of messages to the growing and rabidly loyal following she attracted to the "Sacred Site" in her yard.

> I was pretty tired as I had gotten up in the early morning to look at the temperature, at one o'clock it was 33 degrees. Gosh, I'd been kept up late the night before with company. Heck, I thought to myself, it would freeze, and went to bed. I tried to sleep, but could not. I could hear Pilgrims praying, holding a night Vigil. I got up at 2:45 a.m., the temperature was 32°, just freezing. I grabbed some laundry, sacks, jars and started to cover the peppers and tomatoes. Suddenly around four, Ray spoke to me and I told him what I was doing, so he went and got some rolls of paper. This helped greatly as the tomatoes never froze. I went to bed around 5 a.m. Fred had just gotten up and I was rather tired and restless. After Mass I had a few tomato plants left and knew mother and my brothers would be up. I'd better plant them before the gang gets here... At 12 noon, I went out to the Sacred Spot ... I did not see Our Lady, only a sort of a haze. All the leaves on the Trees seemed to have turned to silver and gold intermittently as the breeze blew the leaves, I could feel Her Heavenly Presence... She told me I was thinking of cutting my hair short and She told me to leave it just as it was... She sure surprised me about my hair, yes I sure had planned on cutting it and getting a permanent as my hair is long and unmanageable. But since She said this I have accepted it.

Transcripts of what Mrs. Van Hoof said, or of what she said the Blessed Virgin said, all show precisely the same grammatical errors—double negatives, plural subjects with singular verbs, "leave" and "lay" replacing "let" and "lie", and so on—and the same vocabulary, talking of "Cops" and "Big Shots". In other words, the apparitions spoke in Mrs. Van Hoof's own voice, exactly; and all of the utterances that she ascribed to Mary jump from subject to subject, in no particular order:

> You are afraid, My Child ... Eat a twig of this bush ... dig right there in the ground, you'll find a rock ... Pray, pray... My Child, Prayer, much, much more prayer... Prayer must come from the Heart... Those of not the Catholic Faith, those that's just Christians, remember your Lord in your way... So those of you, that is, the most of you here, are devoted and very sincere people. There is some here, and I'll repeat it, are just

curious. But all of you must remember My warnings of Fatima, Lipa and LaSalette... The almighty dollar is your God. Forget the almighty dollar! ... Remember God ... He is mighty powerful... Don't neglect your children, leave them run wild... Reach me your Crucifix. Yes, the one in your right hand... With this Crucifix I want you to at least once a week ... place thy left hand over heart and say these words: 'Holy, Holy, Holy, Lord God of Hosts. The earth is full of Thy Glory!' With thy right hand make the Sign of the Cross ...

And so it went, month after month of pious platitudes and childish devotional instructions interspersed with detailed accounts of other landmark events in her life, of taking car trips to Mauston to buy new linoleum, ordering an arbor for the "Sacred Site" from the Sears catalogue, and trying on "the seal skin coat that Joe Markoe had given me, it had belonged to his mother who had died in late spring." Mrs. Van Hoof produced an endless stream of prophecies, year after year, all in the same voice and at the same level of intellectual attainment.

Now, this is fairly standard for reported mystic phenomena; this is about the level of sophistication that you'd find in the average case of delusion or fraud. That level, naturally, makes it unnecessary to look further into the person's educational background, which is obvious; it makes it pointless to sift through the piles of banalities in search of a genuine message from Heaven.

Even so, several crucial factors surfaced fairly early in the game. For one thing, the Van Hoofs had an unfortunate, not to say shady, past. Mrs. Van Hoof's parents had come to America from Transylvania, where they had learned spiritualism from Gypsies; her mother, Elizabeth Bieber, had earned a living by running a "spirit cabin" in Kenosha, Wisconsin. In fact, from 1945 to 1948, Mrs. Bieber was Vice President of the Kenosha Assembly of Spiritualists; she was to be a constant presence at the "Sacred Site", and spiritualists across the country rushed to affirm that their "controls" had verified that it was, indeed, the Virgin Mary who was appearing there.

Mary Ann herself was an accomplished professional spirit medium, familiar with all of the tricks of that trade. As a child, she had worked as her mother's assistant at *séances*, and she had gone to the Spiritualists' camp at Wonewac. Her relationship to the Church is obscure, at best; records indicate that she had been baptized as an infant, but she evidently never went to church. When Fred van Hoof married her in 1934, her knowledge of the Faith was so poor that she was required to take the lessons normally required of converts before she could receive the sacrament of Matrimony. Fred himself had been a pious man before the wedding, but he basically abandoned his Faith afterwards—much to the distress of his family, whom Mary Ann usually referred to as "them damn Catholic farmers."

Evidently her inability to get along with his family prompted her to uproot Fred and their children, sell their Wisconsin farm, and move to Texas. From there, they fled to Missouri to escape creditors; Fred's brother came to the rescue with the offer of a job in his own creamery business. They settled down to a fairly ordinary life, for a time, but a hard one; there was little extra money and less diversion, although Mary Ann recalled later seeing two movies in particular: *Joan of Arc*, directed in 1948 by Victor Fleming, and *The Song of Bernadette* in 1944, a story that, she said, "I accepted as fact".326

Some time later—and without Fred's knowledge—Mary Ann took their slim savings and made a down payment on a derelict farm. Why she did this, nobody knows; some local witnesses, recalling her cryptic comments about her plans to pay off the mortgage, suspect that she already had the whole scheme in mind.

In any case, Fred went along with the idea and set up a small cattle operation on the bleak little farm. It wasn't successful, and their lives out there can't have been happy. A visitor to their simple farmhouse (there was no indoor plumbing) described it in 1949 as filthy from top to bottom and remarked that the children hadn't been bathed in months. And by then the Van Hoofs' financial desperation was as extreme as their squalor. "All of that [cattle] feed," Mary Ann groaned, "and no way to pay for it." It was then, on November 12, that she reported the first visit from above; and it was then that the family's fortunes improved dramatically.

With the dozens of pilgrims that Mrs. Van Hoof attracted to her desolate little farm, "cakes, candy, bread and fruit arrived, also meat", she noted. Also money—a lot of money.327 In return, she gave them reports of vision after vision, in increasing numbers and increasingly rapid succession. She included the standard images of Christianity (the Sacred Heart, chalices and Hosts, crucifixes) and long speeches consisting of repeated excerpts from the Mass, standard prayers, or the messages of La Salette or Fátima, all reported as the very words of the Blessed Mother of God, but nothing new, nothing but the most familiar parts of those sources, and few of them accurately quoted. She had started going to Mass regularly a short time before, but now she abandoned the pews and took to kneeling at the front of the church before a statue of Mary, where she knelt the entire time Mass was being celebrated.

The local ordinary, Bishop John Patrick Treacy, looked at her behavior, her family history, and the quality of her pronouncements, and he had no illusions about the matter. He announced that her activities would "bring dishonor to the traditional devotion to the Mother of God". But neither his official pronouncement nor that of Samuel Cardinal Stritch was quite so newsworthy as crowds of expectant pilgrims. So, while the bishops were ignored, even *Life* magazine sent reporters to the Van Hoof farm. Soon

---

326. She evidently followed the story of the films only very dimly, perceiving, for instance, that St. Bernadette was told to eat the weeds at Lourdes and dig for the spring, but never grasping the significance or consequences of those acts. Sensing that these two things had happened at a creditable apparition, she mimicked them herself and then never mentioned or repeated them. She also denied knowing anything about Fátima, but witnesses placed her at a showing of *The Miracle of Our Lady of Fatima* (1952).

327. After her followers started bringing her those constant tributes of money and food, Mary Ann got fat, tipping the scales at more than two hundred pounds. Her faithful followers accepted this "edema condition due to extreme suffering" as another of her "trials" and became even more solicitous, feeding her more and more to make up for her "inedia". Eventually she took to a wheelchair and let other people push her around.

the numbers increased beyond even Mary Ann's wildest dreams: estimates vary between ten thousand and a hundred thousand, but the crowds on hand for the predicted apparition on August 15, 1950, were certainly the biggest that Necedah had ever seen.

Suddenly the destitute and illiterate woman found herself in control of thousands and tens of thousands of people, vast crowds who hung on her every word and obeyed her every command. If she had indeed planned a series of daylight *séances*, the scheme had worked, and on a grand scale. But soon after her initial success, two crucial things happened to Mary Ann Van Hoof that changed the whole tenor of events at Necedah: the power of it all evidently went to her head, and she met Henry H. Swan.

The Power of the Prophet

At first, Mary Ann Van Hoof had seemed shy, hesitating to put herself forward as a prophetess, not quite believing she'd be believed. But as the crowds grew she began to exhibit quite a flair for showmanship, a real *panache* like that of the more flamboyant spiritualists. And as her self-confidence increased, so did her disobedience.

From the beginning, she and her cohort of insiders had refused to obey the authorities, at first planning ways to "get around" whatever Bishop Treacy directed and later standing in open defiance—ultimately denouncing the Church completely and setting up an alternative hierarchy of her own. Treacy had ordered the priests of his diocese not to celebrate Mass on the property, and they obeyed; but these things always attract fraudulent "priests", or deluded people who claim to be priests, and naturally there was always a flock of "nuns" there, too. About a hundred men dressed as priests were usually on hand, kneeling before Mary Ann and asking for her blessing.[328]

She took full advantage of their presence to make it seem that the Church was not only behind her but beneath her, that Catholics everywhere were obliged in faith to believe every word she said and to submit to her in obedience, as if she herself were more than a priest, more, in fact, than any bishop.

Her practice of freely "blessing" rosaries and other religious items held out by pilgrims would have been enough to disqualify her from serious consideration, all by itself; but Mrs. Van Hoof didn't stop there. The more efforts the Church made to shut down the "shrine", the more loudly she shouted about the hierarchy's ignorance and disobedience of the Virgin's commands, and the more extravagant her apparently mystic gifts became. A few years in to her career as a famous visionary, she began to vomit repeatedly and adopt lengthy fasts, apparently giving up solid food entirely yet gaining weight. Or, rather, she said that she began to vomit constantly; hers is the only testimony in the matter.

By 1951, bishops all across the country had issued statements reminding their Faithful that the events at Necedah had been condemned and forbidden by the local

---

328. Priests have to be *incardinated*, which means that they have to "belong" to a bishop and exercise their office only in his diocese; there are no free-lance priests in the Church, and even a visiting priest has to have permission to celebrate Mass in a diocese other than the one to which he's assigned, or to visit it in the first place. So no mystic phenomenon can attract a crowd of priests.

ordinary, Bishop Treacy, and that those who encouraged others to go there would be liable to ecclesiastical sanctions, which might include formal excommunication. Mrs. Van Hoof countered by starting to exhibit something like the stigmata, with convulsions imitating phases of the Passion. This passes the bounds of precedent; creditable Marian visionaries like St. Bernadette or the children of Pontmain or La Salette don't become stigmatics, as a rule. But it's hard to tell exactly what was supposed to be going on during these episodes because no independent witness ever saw them.

Her attendants kept all but a few initiates, those "close to the Cause", from witnessing the phenomenon, and the mimeographed sheets that fed details to her followers are often incomprehensible, having the same illiterate tone as her other pronouncements. At best they reproduce the vague and evasive pattern of answers from a skilled spirit medium in a trance. The only feature that they all have in common is a strident, at times almost violent, anti-clerical tone; and, evidently, after December, 1951, priests were excluded from witnessing her "sufferings".[329]

That exclusion naturally raised more grave suspicions, but the inedia and stigmata were easily proved spurious. The inquiry committee, which learned a lot simply by showing up earlier than scheduled, at first saw food being brought in to Mrs. Van Hoof through the back door. Then, on April 4, 1952, she finally obeyed the bishop's command to go to Marquette University Hospital in Milwaukee for observation during Holy Week. The report was never made public, of course, but one of the priests on the bishop's committee of inquiry, Claude Heithaus, later gave a lecture on the matter during which he said that her blood tests on admission showed normal levels of salts, which indicated that she had, in fact, been eating solid food despite her claim to inedia. When she insisted on a liquid diet in the hospital, she lost weight, and her blood salts dropped. With her head, hands, and arms bandaged and all sharp objects kept from her, no wounds ever appeared. The staff secretly set her clock back a little each day, but she went into her "passion" whenever it said noon, regardless of the real time.[330]

Taken together, these and similar factors made it apparent that the events claimed by Mrs. Van Hoof grew from a purposefully fraudulent, and really clumsy, design of her own, and they made it unequivocally clear that nothing superhuman, nothing inexplicable, nothing even very interesting was happening at Necedah. By this point, even the *Osservatore Romano* had published a warning against the surprisingly obvious

---

329. Many of the references to priests are indistinct in the documents that Mrs. Van Hoof and her associates generated, and even those that give names in full are questionable. After the "shrine" was officially condemned, it was run by "Old Roman" or "Old Catholic" priests, but those schismatic denominations eventually denounced Mrs. Van Hoof's activities, too. After that, it was reportedly run by impostors, among them—it has been reliably reported from public records—convicted frauds, child molesters, and other felons, but at any rate by characters who took roles as required; one "archbishop" of the Byzantine Rite ministering at the site was recognized by diocesan officials as having posed there previously as a Capuchin priest. Today, with the business of Necedah long since condemned, no genuine priest is associated with the "shrine".

330. The apparitions at Fátima, by contrast, happened at solar noon regardless of local time, which differed from it by more than an hour.

falsehood of the phenomena, and the press, beginning perhaps to tire of the banality of it all, was paying rather more attention to the bishops. But for all of this, Mary Ann Van Hoof had an answer. I'm a free American citizen, she said: This is my own property, and I'll do as I wish.

In fact, it was the issue of national politics that Van Hoof played to best advantage; it was politics that kept crowds coming despite the unanimous clarifications, warnings, and condemnations of the institutional Church; and it was politics that gave her reports a strange and persistent life independent of any religious connotations.

The Role of Henry H. Swan

One of the people attracted to Mary Ann was Henry H. Swan, then chairman of the Chamber of Commerce in tiny Necedah. Almost immediately, he took charge of things like parking arrangements at the farm, and it was he who determined who would see Mrs. Van Hoof, and when. In a surprisingly short time, he abandoned his car dealership, his wife, and his eight children to devote himself tirelessly to "the Cause".

Now, most reputed apparitions that draw a lot of public attention are associated with one or more reporters—sometimes a single insider like Swan, sometimes a knot of professional journalists, but in any case somebody to systematize the seer's pronouncements within a consistent frame of reference (pro or con, but never indifferent). To present a convincing picture, to discredit the event, or to simply formulate press releases, they have to suppress or emphasize embarrassing trivialities or elevate the banalities into something newsworthy. Because these reporters edit events purposefully, the things that you read in the papers about them are very different in extent and in content from the reports that bishop's investigators compile. These journalists, debunkers, and mouthpieces all have to find an angle, a theme that they channel to their own purposes.[331]

In Mary Ann Van Hoof's case, there had always been a strong current of what you might call conspiracy theories, if not nascent paranoia. During one of her earliest apparitions, she said, the Virgin gave her explicit instructions for her personal safety against the scheming forces of evil, at first only vaguely formulated:

331. Even professionally impartial journalists shape their accounts purposefully, because their job is to report events that are out of the ordinary, purported apparitions or traffic accidents, in publishable form; so they have an aim that's different from that of fully investigating the events as they happened. Official investigators gather all available information so that qualified people can decide; journalists have to choose a few features to make up an interesting story that fits a standard journalistic formula. Their job simply doesn't include judging the doctrinal soundness of an apparition, any more than it includes judging whether a political rally is held for the right or the wrong reason. The crowd, not the reason for it or the substance of the message it hears, is what makes news in either case, so a rally for a preposterous report gets as much coverage as an assembly for a creditable one, at first—more, if it draws bigger and more eccentric crowds. Just by their nature, journalistic accounts of purported mystic phenomena are neither adequate nor reliable, not even those from the Catholic press. There's also the problem that the people who write the stories are not the people who write the headlines, and the two compositions often say contradictory things. Beyond that, very few journalists understand fully—well, it must be said: very few journalists understand adequately how the Church works, how she evaluates these things, and precisely what weight they have or don't have in the great scheme of things.

> Do not travel alone at any time. You must go to a trusted person. At no
> time eat with strangers, only if you know the people. Have your spouse
> with you when being questioned and if becoming thirsty, do not drink
> any water unless coming directly from the well and be sure to wash glass
> or pitcher. Have spouse do this, otherwise don't drink no matter how
> parched or dry you may get. Have as your Doctor, only your family
> Doctor. Do not let any other Doctor or other person put needle of any
> kind into you. Do not sign any papers.

Then, one by one, she discovered more plots against her; the conspiracies grew stronger
and more universal, as well as more political. Believing that the Church was plotting to
discredit her, she reported messages from the Blessed Virgin that released her from obedience, such as being told "to tell my Spiritual Director that he must do as She asked".
She began to claim that she was threatened repeatedly by a shadowy figure who told her
to stop her "hysteric allusions" and eventually broke into her house, knocked her down,
kicked her, and tried to strangle her with a cord or something (although her husband
wasn't awakened by any ruckus, and she didn't tell him about it afterwards; it would be
too much for him, she said). "Was it ... an enemy of God - "RED" - was it a fanatic?"
she asked. Nobody else ever saw him, but later this same figure, "our Friend", as they
called him, was supposed to have put a bomb in her kitchen that she discovered by sensing it.[332]

And, according to Mrs. Van Hoof, the Blessed Virgin asked repeatedly for
prayers on behalf of "your Catholic Senator"—Joseph R. McCarthy, a resident of nearby Appleton, then recently elected senator from Wisconsin and already discovering
Communist plots under every desk in Washington. It was a time when many Americans
believed their government infiltrated by enemy agents, the age of blacklisting, the most
frightening decade of the Cold War; and throughout the revelations, McCarthy appears
as a kind of lone crusader assailed by the forces of evil, single-handedly holding back
the tide of godlessness or Communism (one and the same thing, in her book) until he
suffered a kind of martyrdom at the hands of his political enemies. Eventually, Mary
Ann began to sound a clarion call about Communism:

> Wake up America! The Enemy of God is creeping all over America. Yes,
> you believe it can't happen here... Our Constitution is being destroyed
> and the UN has taken its place. We Americans won't have much of a
> chance, we have sold ourselves out to the UN... in Vision I saw a very
> brutal looking fellow and he was the head of the Conspiracy of our water
> fronts and air fields, both the East and West Coasts.
>
> The Vision was of New York harbor where some ships were burning and
> exploding. Then it showed an Air Field ... a train wreck. Over all this

332. It was described as a "dud"; it may not have contained any explosives at all, but what it was supposed to be made of isn't clear. Whether anybody ever actually saw it is also unclear.

appeared a table and many hands as though it were a meeting but no faces were shown ... Deception. You are being deceived. Government ...

"Then," she said, "I was told that the cleansing of the Youth, cleaning of all theaters, books, dances must be done at once!" From her earliest pronouncements, it seems that at first Mrs. Van Hoof was attracting attention by calling upon the vague fears that her community shared about world events—events that, as might be expected of a woman of her condition and background, she found threatening but didn't fully understand.

Other political factions, of course, have tried to exploit even creditable apparitions for their own purposes, as the partisans of Comte de Richemont tried to certify their aspirations with words from La Salette, or indeed as Franco's regime in Spain tried to take advantage of Fátima. But very quickly after Swan's assumption of authority, the revelations from Necedah took on a bizarre, and much more sinister, character. Revelations about home permanents and new dresses gave way to cosmic rays and Russian submarines, accounts of fish dinners to exposés of selective breeding for professional sports (on an industrial scale). Soon, Mary Ann's visionary pronouncements consisted almost entirely of news of huge international conspiracies, blended with only the slightest and most banal religious material, or with material that was flatly incorrect—her elaborate descriptions of "devils" who were supposed to be the departed agents of the Great Plot confuses the nature of lost human souls and that of fallen angels, for instance.

But, more interesting than that, it becomes progressively difficult to distinguish Swan's own writings from Mary Ann's utterances. Soon the apparition started speaking with his diction, not Mrs. Van Hoof's, and the pious banalities degenerated into diatribes against fluoridation, Prince Philip, and the American Medical Association—vituperation filled with the rudest kinds of racial insults, far too crude, and far too uncharitable, to have anything like a heavenly origin.[333] After a point, they didn't bother attributing the diatribes to the apparition at all.

The bishop's committee, showing up once again at the Van Hoof farmstead ahead of schedule, interrupted a rehearsal in which Mary Ann was being coached by Swan with exactly what he wanted said; her testimony, they reported, was not nearly so fluent as usual, that day. Over time, the pattern of their pronouncements showed beyond doubt that Swan seized on Mary Ann's loose threads of conspiracy fears and embroidered them onto the whole cloth of his own political views, imposing on them the definitive pattern in which they were presented to the public. And it was he, not Mrs. Van Hoof, who most securely tied her revelations to a larger web of evil plots.

For Swan, the entire structure of society was spun out by the "Learned Elders" of the "Great Plot". Lawyers, bankers, politicians, doctors, industrialists—anybody enfranchised in the power structure, anybody in urban America who knew how things work or even had a successful professional career, was a tool of Satan pulling secret and

---

333. Mrs. Van Hoof projected Mary, herself a Jew, as the author of an interminable torrent of tirades against "the Yids". As one of the priests involved in the investigation noted to the author, Mrs. Van Hoof was "not a very polished character."

incomprehensible strings in a worldwide conspiracy, stopping at nothing to achieve the scheme of world domination through one world government. "All of our martyred Presidents starting with Abraham Lincoln have been killed because they stood in the way of the Great Plot," Swan wrote. Fiorello La Guardia died "after he had been injected with a heart attack"; so did Senator Pat McCarran (author of the anti-Communist Internal Security Act of 1950), Supreme Court Justice Frank Murphy, and Wendell Willkie. Others were injected with "the cancer germ"; Warren G. Harding was simply poisoned after he discovered the Plot, and the war correspondent Ernie Pyle was shot. Thousands of persons of lesser importance were, too, Swan claimed, and more would be soon.

> You are like the sheep who enjoy the ride to the slaughterhouse... Also if someone only has some gum to pass, you can placidly chew your cud and enjoy the scenery as you ride to the concentration camp. There are several already made for your accommodation in our Country. They also have torture chambers that they can use to exact confessions from you when you fall into disagreement with the powers that be... These places were ordered built by Franklin Delano Roosevelt, an arch devil in human form whom we elected to the Presidency of the United States. In this project, he was urged on by Eleanor, Countess of Hyde Park and always consort and protector of Communists, Left Wingers, One Worlders... She has been mentioned in Revelations on several occasions.[334]

Ultimately, the "one-world" theory itself came to roost at Necedah, as did those of Mrs. Van Hoof's revelations that survive now as bits of underground folklore about God and country—the story of the Marian visions of George Washington, for instance. As Mrs. Van Hoof saw it, he was visited by the Blessed Virgin, who told him about the Revolution, the Civil War, and the World Wars, and he converted to Catholicism on his deathbed.

Today, even after all religious content has dropped away from Necedah, some families still abandon jobs and homes and move to the area, drawn by an unreasoning fear of everyday reality into a life of munitions hoarded in concrete bunkers, of sniper attacks, and of allegiance to a dark morass of doomsday conspiracies. It all stands in telling contrast to shrines like Lourdes and Fátima that, having weathered all kinds of opposition from civil government and the strictest investigation of the Church, still radiate hope and healing to millions. And it's a sobering example of how severely even the most blatant fake mystic phenomena can damage those most susceptible.

THE PROFILE OF CREDULITY

Just as creditable mystics share a genuine and lasting humility, and just as they show growth in virtues after their mystic experience, there's a certain kind of personality pro-

---

334. He means Mrs. Van Hoof's "revelations", not the book of the Bible. Evidently Swan never quoted the Bible in his pronouncements.

file that characterizes spurious mystics, too. In many, perhaps most, cases, the deluded visionary or self-proclaimed mystic—or the person most likely to be exploited by them—is not just a person who turns to religion when suffering illness or disappointment, but rather one who cannot comprehend that adversity, one who fears attack by forces beyond control or who feels powerless to meet the crises of normal adult life.

Women who have recently, unexpectedly, lost a child constitute a particularly high percentage of people reporting mystic phenomena, as do those who are devastated or bewildered by a child's serious illness or even his conduct. Women having marital problems, men suffering incomprehensible setbacks or stagnation in their careers, abused or neglected children, are all much more likely to crave some alternative reality that's more supportive and more consoling, as well as more comprehensible and more subject to the person's own control. So are people who suffer some life-altering accident or illness, or those who thought that they had a religious vocation but find out that what seemed to be a call from God was only the workings of pride.

Sometimes these feelings can be triggered in a person of average or high intelligence by some sudden crisis along these lines, but sometimes it's something harder to define, some quiet desperation bred in a frustrating inability to form normal relationships, to build a career, or to hold a job. It may be the result of growing up with the feeling of doing everything wrong, of never understanding what everyone else was doing and talking about, or of never feeling accomplished or special in some way. Or it may just grow from an inability to understand news from the outside world, which seems to affect a surprisingly large segment of America's churchgoing public.

Most Americans understand the selection process that shapes media coverage of world events. People in the mainstream know that international news organizations monitor world events constantly but package only those comparatively few dramatic stories that they consider marketable. Most realize that local outlets tend to choose the most sensational of these to deliver in concentrated form to the public—disasters always sell the most papers. News of emergency and catastrophe, therefore, tends to be concentrated in newspapers and electronic media, but people usually understand that seismologists would affirm that earthquakes have always happened more or less regularly, and that economists, astronomers, and historians would point out that famines, meteor showers, crime, and disease have been with us always.

But some Americans seem to see nothing except the bad news. Frightened, to some degree or another, by disaster after disaster reported in the news media every day, they may come to believe that things are falling to pieces around us as never before in human history. Some leaders exploit this as a way to pull those people together out of the general population. Swan, for instance, took the process of concentrating bad news even farther: he collated and published headlines about natural disasters, and he asserted that "these plane crashes, train wrecks, cargo ships and tankers burning, great fires and explosions could not all happen just from natural causes."

To which the only reasonable response is, well, yes they can; they always do.

But people in the small towns of the Midwest in the early 1950s had never had this much news before. Even feature films like those Mrs. Van Hoof saw took two or three years to reach the theaters in those towns, if the towns had theaters, and the newsreels that came with them were never up to date. This was the dawn of television, which, combined for the first time with radio networks and wireless news services, poured unprecedented amounts of information instantly into even the remotest corners of the country.

And the media's concentration of this information was particularly overwhelming to a population who had not yet formed a very clear idea of how the world works in its splendor and diversity, and who had not yet found their feet again after the Armageddon of the Second World War. They could not yet grasp the meaning of the Soviet takeovers or the secret networks of concentration camps exterminating millions labelled undesirable by their governments; they did not understand the threat of a Cold War of ideologies. They could not know when, or whether, atomic bombs would be launched from the distant headquarters of some godless tyrant. Theirs was a culture that not only produced Joseph McCarthy but chose him to serve as its Senator.[335]

Even so, it's alarming to reflect that people in rural Wisconsin—people who knew Mary Ann Van Hoof, her irregular past, and her spiritualist history—would have done anything but laugh at her report. But it's still more disturbing to remember that there's always a segment of the population, in the cities as well as in the country, who are too badly educated, too limited in intelligence, or too emotionally unstable to grasp fully even the normal workings of modern societies. Their prevalent drive is not the ambition to master the basic skills of competence in that world but fear, the fear of losing control of their lives. And their numbers seem to be growing.

Whenever the news seems both incomprehensible and overwhelming, it can provoke a crisis in these people; some are all too ready to conclude that all of this bad news can only be signs of the Last Days (Mt 24; Mr 13; Lk 17, 21), while others see the plot of an international conspiracy of Grand Masters. And some from both camps find sudden deliverance from the morass when they find themselves possessed of what they can only interpret as extraordinary spiritual gifts.

Many of these disenfranchised people today find themselves in the position of the early Christian heretical Messalians. Those "fourth-century charismatics", the Congregation for the Doctrine of the Faith notes, "identified the grace of the Holy Spirit with the psychological experience of his presence in the soul... Contemplative Christian prayer always leads to love of neighbor, to action, and to the acceptance of trials, and precisely because of this it draws one more closely to God."[336] But groups that

---

335. A recent study (Etienne G. Krug *et al.*, "Suicide After Natural Disasters", *New England Journal of Medicine* 1998:338:373-378) quantified the emotional and psychological effects of disastrous events, showing that suicide rates increase markedly in affected areas in the first few years after floods, hurricanes, and most of all—by more than 60 percent—after earthquakes. The interior disorder and depression caused by the actual experience of such disasters may or may not be provoked by concentrated news of such events, but it's hard to see how a constant barrage of such information would do people much good.

336. *Letter to the Bishops of the Catholic Church on Some Aspects of Christian Meditation*, October 15 (the Feast of St. Teresa of Avila), 1989.

focus on spurious spiritual events, particularly on private revelations, don't do what religion does, putting individual experience into a universal context. Rather, they cut the world down to personal perception, often restricting members' view of the world severely and suppressing acknowledgement of any evidence contrary to an inflexibly simplistic scheme of things. In other words, they do what cults do.

Spurious Mystic Phenomena and the Development of Cults

A *cult* is not necessarily a religious organization at all; the term is well used to refer to any organization structured in a certain way psychologically, attracting people with similar personality profiles. It's a group whose members recognize, even if they don't admit, that they share a common problem or group of problems beyond their own power to remedy. Acceptance by the cult requires, almost always, what might be called a "bridge-burning act", some public behavior that clearly breaks allegiance to the mainstream culture and shows acceptance of the cult's terms, often making it impossible for the member to return to the mainstream.

But because cults aren't necessarily religious organizations, bridge-burning acts take on any number of forms. Street gangs might require a serious crime as initiation for a new member; and Alcoholics Anonymous and related organizations like Narcotics Anonymous require a public declaration of one's problem. And both of these substance-abuse organizations can be defined as cults in this way, because of the way they're structured psychologically—which makes the point that not all cults are bad. The differences are that in these therapeutic groups the problem is faced head-on and named; that gaining control of the problem, rather than indulging it, is the criterion for members' continued good standing; and that the whole point of the exercise is becoming able to swim easily in the tide of the mainstream, not to escape it.

But many less constructive cults adopt a religious complexion because religion, outside the Church, is understood as a matter of purely private interpretation; only the Church offers an unchanging body of doctrine interpreted consistently through responsive, living Sacred Tradition. Cultists can define any reality they want, as long as it's not of this world. Moreover, cultists join specifically because they can't or won't deal with the problems of this world, and because a shift of focus to the next world relieves them of responsibility at a stroke. Cults offer relief by dividing the world into an "us" and a "them"; anyone who's not with us is against us, and the source of our problems besides. Cults simplify the question of what the problem is, or of who the enemy is—that is, they offer a clear target for blame for the members' individual failures—and they define who can be trusted to understand, usually on a single criterion.

When such groups coalesce around a zealous leader or a spurious mystic event within the Church, they incline to disobedience, since even the bishop's prudence can be interpreted as resistance.[337] And, because they've come together on the basis of not

---

337. See A. Deutsch, "Tenacity of Attachment to a Cult Leader: A Psychiatric Perspective", *American Journal of Psychiatry* (137: 1569-73, 1980); L. Festinger, *et al.*, *When Prophecy Fails* (Minneapolis, 1956), etc.

understanding the way the world works, they tend also to evolve conspiracy theories that set the rest of the world against them, a few chosen few initiates—who, in turn, think themselves extraordinarily gifted by the Holy Spirit in ways that the rest of the world is too spiritually deprived, too evil, or too stupid to understand. Having ascribed the perceived chaos of external troubles to a simple and comprehensible cause, they prescribe a simple, often ritualistic, remedy. These remedies may not be bad in themselves; some gentle little cults—almost every parish has one—prescribe increased frequency of approved devotions, and some just encourage Bible study or group prayer.

But while these may have an intrinsic value, the cult can't work to solve the problem that drew the people together in the first place. By drawing such a sharp line between themselves and the mainstream, members automatically make themselves ineffective as agents of change—religiously as well as politically—and in any case they join the group because they can't or don't understand the causes at work in the world.

Still, destructive cults can relieve a good deal of their members' anxiety, giving them the support and acceptance, the feeling of belonging and even of privilege and distinction, that they cannot achieve in the mainstream culture. They can't prepare their members for integration into that mainstream, though. And, being defined as a group by that particular inability, they can worsen the problem over the long term, congratulating their members for indulging their problems—construing those problems as spiritual gifts, in fact. Or, in some cases, a person fitting this profile finds the use of those spurious gifts an effective way to assert himself over the trials inflicted by his perceived enemies.

THE PREDICTABLE PROPHETS

It's clear that Henry H. Swan was a simple man frightened by the tides of history, and in fact frightened by the world around him. Current events in the Cold-War climate of the time, the overhanging threat of nuclear disaster, and the rabid anti-Communist witch-hunts of his onetime neighbor, Senator McCarthy, were evidently enough to make him see his entire world as one intricate web of incomprehensible plots. This kind of hollow desperation and this overriding fear are, still and always, the mark of the person most susceptible to the lure of an alternative reality, of simple answers from above entrusted only to the initiate.

But when the question of the stresses suffered by the purported mystic is asked about Mary Ann Van Hoof, the answer is particularly interesting. When she was faced with insoluble financial troubles, she might have been expected to fall back on her mother's old trade; all fraudulent mystics use whatever skills and other resources they have available. But even if she did plan the whole thing to bring in all of those cakes and meat and mortgage payments, she might have been expected to set up an operation involving a crystal ball and Tarot cards. Something more, some other factor, pushed her to take up the profession of the spurious mystic; and in fact her background is as typical of those who perform false mystic events as it is of those who accept them enthusiastically.

345

Of course, every fake has to start out with the idea that he's superior enough to outwit his dupes, and Mary Ann's hatred of "them damn Catholics" probably led her to think that they'd be easily enough fooled. That may have prompted her to choose the Church as her target rather than the population at large as another spiritualist might have done; that attitude often does. She was undoubtedly impressed by the films that she'd seen about these events, which were evidently her only source of information about them. But her thinking was never very clear on anything, and she may have been drawn to the idea of Marian apparitions by forces that she neither recognized nor controlled.

For instance, there's the reassuring maternal aspect of Marian devotions in general.' One of the first things that Mary Ann reported from her apparition was sympathy about her childhood, which had been characterized by fear of her abusive father and his frequent beatings prompted by no good reason at all. "She said I was a very unhappy child, always abused, misunderstood. She said: 'You took punishment for others to protect them. You received no love which you longed for in your home…'"

And, evidently, her adult life was no more secure. She gave evasive and contradictory answers about her early career. Working far from home as a teenager, she said, she married a man by whom she had a child; three months after the wedding, she found out either that he was married already or that he'd been married before, and she left him. Or maybe she hadn't married him at all. She couldn't remember where the marriage was supposed to have taken place, and no license ever turned up; no divorce decree was produced, and evidently nobody knows what became of the baby. One of her Chosen Ones published an account claiming that the baby was refused Baptism, which broke Mary Ann's heart and made her vow never to go near them damn Catholics again, but that doesn't make much sense. Well, the refusal of Baptism doesn't, anyway.

In any case, the vague and contradictory accounts of the previous marriage show it to be either an extremely traumatic episode or a delusion in its own right. She evidently wasn't at all happy in her marriage to Van Hoof, either; goading him into one escapade of failure after another doesn't argue much for marital bliss. There may also be evidence for sexual dysfunction or childhood sexual abuse in her growing horror of needles, submarines, the "Great Serpent", and other standard symbols, as in the fact that "Stinking Fred" was one of the archplotting "devils" assigned to torment her.[338]

She admitted time and again, in the flow of her discourse, that she felt unequal to what she saw as her duties as wife and mother. Her eldest son had "gotten into trouble" just before the first reported apparition, and she herself had (or claimed to have) heart trouble, or at least stress-induced angina. The squalor in which the family lived before 1949 is mute testimony to her inability to provide even the most basic cleanliness

338. Even before Fred Van Hoof died, there was some question about Mary Ann's relationship with Swan. After he abandoned his wife and children in her favor, the two were reportedly caught *in flagrante* by one of Mary Ann's daughters. Of course, there are always scurrilous tales about the morality of creditable mystics, but not from their families; and certainly Mary Ann's life was never regular. After Fred's death, she "married" one of the Chosen Ones, Ray Hirt, twenty years her junior, in a mystic ceremony of her own devising presided over, she said, by St. Joseph himself. It was repeated twice for witnesses more corporeally present, but there was evidently never an actual paper license about it.

and order in their lives. She never learned to manage things very well, either; even after the crowds came, her husband's farm was, she says, in serious financial trouble chronically. And apparently nothing that she did or said ever redeemed her in the eyes of her husband's family.

Mary Ann Bieber Van Hoof was evidently a little girl tragically abused, one way or another; a woman unloved, a failure in more than one marriage, if in fact she had more than one; an uneducated woman utterly unable to cope, emotionally or intellectually, with the daily responsibilities of an unhappy home life that she herself had structured; a woman who undoubtedly felt isolated and reproached by her in-laws—her Catholic in-laws. Her visions gave her power, power over her family and power over a growing battalion of unquestioning followers. By the end of her life in 1984 she dictated their diet; their dress; their hours of sleep and work, and even the thermostat settings in their homes, as if by mandate from Heaven. She told the "shriners" of her cult when to rise at night and pray for her; she commanded them to kneel before her and inform on the disobedience of their friends, and they did. No one could make a doctor's appointment, no one could go shopping, without the express permission of Mary Ann Van Hoof; no one could enter, no one could leave, the region within a five-mile radius around her house. Of course, she's an extreme case of the type; but she's still the classic example of the spurious mystic, of the cult leader of the twentieth century.

THE RESIDUE OF FALSEHOOD

Given the fact that nothing in the Necedah experience was even remotely similar to anything that happens in a creditable mystic experience, there was never any question of there having been a genuine apparition or locution that was muddled or falsified later. The whole history of the episode, every word recorded, every medical test, every bit of testimony, shows beyond any doubt that the vaudeville of Necedah was a burlesque purposefully shaped from unredeemed falsehood. The only extraordinary thing about it is that so many people were willing to believe it.

These believers may have included Mary Ann Van Hoof herself, after a certain point; like many another fraudulent mystic before her and since, she may have passed from fraud to delusion. This seems to have happened as early as 1952 when she went into the hospital to have her inedia and stigmata examined; before that time, she evidently wouldn't have thought she'd get past that test.[339] Then again, it may have been that she thought herself sufficiently brilliant to fool the doctors, too, by then.

She may also have opened the door to diabolic help, although nothing inexplic-

339. Her conduct during the reported miracles indicates that she knew that nothing supernatural was happening. Those reported events, by the way, all had a similar tone and the same lack of apparent purpose: white rosaries were said to turn gold or blue, blue statues white; the Sun was reported to spin (as it did as part of the Great Miracle of Fátima), although Mrs. Van Hoof herself never saw any of this and, apparently, never predicted it. On more than one occasion, followers ran into her house to call her so that she could see the rosaries changing, but she never stirred. On seeing the pilgrims' faces fall when she said that she didn't see the solar phenomenon, she added quickly, "Well, I don't need that to be shown," which cheered them. No documented cures happened at Necedah.

able was ever seen by the crowds or by the investigating committee. Private witnesses tell of her superhuman strength, at times, but then she was never a weakling; others tell of her speaking in a resonant and bellowing voice, but then those who knew her before all of this noted that she was somewhat given to bellowing even then. One of her own "priests", a man who went by the title "Archbishop and Metropolitan of North America, American National Catholic Church, Roman Catholic Ultrajectine" (whatever that means), interrupted Mary Ann during one of her prophetic trances and asked the Blessed Mother speaking through her, in the Name of Jesus, to recite the Divine Praises.[340] Mary Ann refused. You are not here to test me, she said; you are here to be obedient.

Frequently, commanding a possessed person to praise God, or commanding the devil who's speaking through a possessed person to do it, is used as a test to find out the cause of the appearance of mystic activity (1Jn 4:3). Of course, this man was least qualified of all possible people to administer a test in this case, and the result may mean that whatever possessed her at the time didn't want to be known, or it may only mean that Mary Ann had no idea what the Divine Praises were, which is more likely. The only thing it means for certain is that she expected her followers to obey without question.

In fact, within a year or so of the first report, Mrs. Van Hoof's "Chosen Ones" had coalesced into a tightly united group. Anyone who understood the bishop's condemnation or even disbelieved Mrs. Van Hoof, anyone not faithful to "the Cause", was ostracized on a charge of "disunity". Swan marshalled the Chosen Ones into an organization, For My God and My Country, Inc., through which he promulgated his own political views.

As to knowing the tree by its fruits, not much can be said in favor of Necedah. The "Thirty-Mile" prophecy that asserts that everything in America beyond a thirty-mile radius from the "Sacred Site" will be destroyed by the coming world conflict persists. But it's been expanded to include forecasts of a twelve-hundred-year-old savior, "Joe"—probably not McCarthy, although you wonder—who will come in a spaceship to sweep the "shriners" away from the "Chastisement", taking them through a hole in the Antarctic ice to a land where apples grow big as grapefruit and bananas achieve two feet in length, after which they'll return to repopulate a purged Earth and establish the True Church. The story of latter-day Necedah is a story of black boxes and alfalfa-filled herbal sachets sold at eighty dollars apiece and touted as miraculously effective against everything from hurricanes to poisons in food—"shriners" naturally worry a lot about

340. That's a prayer composed in the eighteenth century for retired sailors to repeat as a way of making up for the things that they'd said as sailors before they retired. It goes, "Blessed be God. Blessed be his Holy Name. Blessed be Jesus Christ, True God and True Man. Blessed be the Name of Jesus. Blessed be his Most Sacred Heart. Blessed be his Most Precious Blood. Blessed be Jesus in the Most Holy Sacrament of the Altar. Blessed be the Holy Spirit, the Paraclete. Blessed be the Great Mother of God, Mary, most holy. Blessed be her holy and Immaculate Conception. Blessed be her glorious Assumption. Blessed be the Name of Mary, virgin and mother. Blessed be St. Joseph, her most chaste spouse. Blessed be God in his angels and in his saints. May the Heart of Jesus, in the Most Blessed Sacrament of the altar, be loved, adored, and praised, with grateful affection, at every moment, in every tabernacle of the world, even to the end of Time."

poison in their food.

It is indeed sobering to think that this kind of thing could attract and hold followers in America, but every day brings news of yet another such phenomenon, and Necedah has plenty of close historic precedents.[341] But the latter-day examples pass far beyond mere eccentricity, far beyond a benign inability to cope with mainstream views of the world and how it works. Increasingly, these groups exact a grim toll in human suffering, and in fact in human life. At Necedah, the "Cause's" Seven Sorrows of Our Sorrowful Mother Infants Home has been the scene of too many close calls, too many mutilations in botched surgeries, too many infant deaths. At least two people have been shot and killed in standoffs with the police or sniper incidents as survivalist groups entrench themselves around Necedah—within the thirty-mile radius, of course—and wait for the Last Days.

Ironically, Henry H. Swan himself testified to the Church's own record of unanimity and prudent, orderly procedure in these matters: "If you go to a priest for advice on anything other than those things which are strictly a matter of faith and morals," he said, "you can be sure that his advice is going to coincide with that which he knows would agree with the ideas of his superiors"—which, of course, is exactly as it should be, the priests deferring to the properly constituted authorities. Exactly as the alleged visionary and his followers are supposed to do.

341. As early as 1869 Cyrus Reed Teed of Moravia, New York, claimed a vision of "the Mother of the World", on the basis of which he changed his name to Koresh, founded his own religion ("Koreshanity"), and gathered four thousand followers in the wilds of Florida at a "New Jerusalem" called Estero, on the premise that the world is a hollow sphere, the distinctive feature being that Koresh claimed that that we're already living inside of it. His death in 1908 was evidently not taken by his followers as disproving his claim of immortality; the group lingered on until 1961, when the remaining four members deeded the site of the original settlement to the state of Florida. Today, it's operated as the Koreshan State Historic Park, with a campground and a nature trail. Koresh's book, *Cellular Cosmogony or the Earth a Concave Sphere* (1922), is still available in reprint.

thirty-one

that they may testify

And he said, "Then, Father, I beseech thee
to send him to my father's house ...
that he may testify to them,
lest they too come into this place of torments...
If someone from the dead goes to them, they will repent!"
But he said to him, "If they do not hearken
to Moses and the prophets, they will not believe,
even if someone rises from the dead."

— Luke 16:27-31

If angels and saints are perfectly happy in the presence of God, why should they come out of that more perfect union with the divine to appear on this Earth? Why should God himself appear among us? What's the point having people glow, or float in the air, or be miraculously healed of what ails them? If these phenomena don't indicate sanctity, and if they don't set the mystic up as an oracle, what good are they? And, as St. John of the Cross asked, if there's so much danger of misinterpretation, and so much danger of spiritual hindrance in the pride and other distractions that they can cause, why does God perform these extraordinary communications?

Well, that takes a little perspective. In the Church's view, God is the ultimate and principal reality of the universe, the only being that does not depend on some other reality for existence. God, therefore, determines the arrangement and nature of every material thing in the universe. He created the world good, and he created humans good (check Gn 1:31, etc.). Humans—Adam and Eve—saw God, and walked and talked with him familiarly; and because of their closeness with God, they knew no sickness or death.

But God also gave humans free will; and Adam and Eve freely chose to disobey that one simple commandment about not eating the fruit of that particular tree. It may seem arbitrary or symbolic, but if it symbolizes anything it's that the power to decide what's right and what's wrong doesn't belong to humankind but to God alone. That's why the tree in question was called the Tree of the Knowledge of Good and Evil. Because he made humans good by nature, we can distinguish good from bad, and God himself reveals more of that distinction than we could make by ourselves—by commanding, as the Father commanded Adam and Eve or as Christ commanded his followers, and by explaining, as the Spirit teaches through the Church.

But ultimately that knowledge belongs to God. Eating the fruit of that forbidden tree was an act of pride; Adam and Eve figured that they knew better than God, and that they could decide right and wrong, no matter what God said. So taking the fruit of that particular tree was the first, the original, sin.

And sin wracked Creation out of order. Disease, pain, suffering, crime, and the rest of the decay in our lives are the result of sin—the works of God are well ordered, as St. Paul put it (Rm 13:1); he orders all things wisely (Ws 7:30, 8:1), but the world is corrupt because of our works (Gn 6:11-13; Rm 5:12). And since God withdraws from everything corrupt, we can't see him, the angels, and the saints any more. When Adam sinned, we lost all of those gifts above nature—the supernatural gifts—that God had given him.

That's why sin prevents us from seeing the supernatural as casually as Adam and Eve did, before the Fall. Mystic phenomena remind us what life was supposed to be like, and what it would be like now, if we could see past the damage wrought by sin. If we were all perfect Christians, these extraordinary phenomena wouldn't happen, or rather, they wouldn't be extraordinary. They'd happen as a matter of course. We'd see, hear, smell, taste, and touch God as naturally as Adam and Eve did. Mystic phenomena are understood as reminders for all of the Faithful, the fervent as well as the lukewarm. That's why those in the Bible were done for a purpose outside the recipient—not for me did this voice come, but for you (Jn 12:30).[342] But if we can't experience life as it was before sin, God still wants us to avoid sin and overcome it, so that everybody can come back to him, after death and judgement, and enjoy his company familiarly again, as Adam and Eve did before there was sin in the first place.

So he reached out extraordinarily to get humankind back on course. He sent visible angels to Abraham and spoke to Moses; he led his people by pillars of fire, and he shaped history to his own mystic plan. It was through mystic experiences that God told Noe to build the ark and told Abraham to leave his country and his kinfolk. It was through mystic phenomena that he took Israel out of Egypt and forged it into a nation; it was thus that he called Gedeon to rally Israel against Madian, and it was thus that he asked Mary to bear the Savior and warned St. Joseph to flee the Massacre of the Innocents. Time and again in the history of revelation, everything has depended upon how God has reached out extraordinarily to a single person and on how that person has answered.

342. Which is another reason that private mystic phenomena aren't taken as signs of personal sanctity (Sr 37:21; Jn 4:5-30).

That's why the Father worked miracles through the prophets and why Christ worked his own miracles, to get our attention so that we would listen to what he was saying, so that we could answer, too (Jn 3:1-21). And, presumably, that's why he does them now. The healings at Lourdes or Fátima are a way to direct faith, an extraordinary—an urgent—way to say, do this; this is the True Faith (Jn 2:5). Those extraordinary mystic phenomena bring people into the Church in the fullness of her doctrine, which seems like a good reason that healings at the sites of apparitions have centered on the Eucharist—the key target of heresy—and yet another good reason that recent healing apparitions have all been of Mary; separated sects one and all deny the role of the saints, and most particularly of Mary, in the economy of salvation. In that sense, mystic phenomena are another way to emphasize Mary's own command: Whatever he has told you, do (Jn 2:5). And those miracles that the Church takes as evidence in canonization proceedings are indicators in the same way: they're construed as a way for God to say, yes, this person is with me, and I hear his prayers in a special way; he has run a good race and fought a good fight—go thou and do likewise.

So mystic phenomena can happen to correct our course—God reaches out constantly with little actual graces to anyone who tries to walk with him, as a parent steadies a toddler to keep him from falling, but sometimes he has to knock us off our high horses, as he did Paul and Heliodorus (Ac 9; 2Mc 3). Sometimes the correction is in the nature of an eye-catching reminder: St. Teresa levitates or Eliseus makes an iron axe-head float; healthy flesh is re-created at the Pool of the Five Porticoes or at the *piscines* of Lourdes; Daniel reads the handwriting on the wall, or the Blessed Virgin is allowed to inscribe a word to the wise on a scroll in the sky. The repetition of all of these kinds of phenomenon, age after age, reminds us of God's endless patience with us, his infinite generosity and his overwhelming love.

On the other side of the coin, they show us the seriousness of sin. The passionate phenomena, the supernatural illnesses, the desolation of spiritual dryness, and—more vividly than any other image—the stigmata, remind us forcefully of the suffering of Christ on the Cross, of the terrible damage that sin inflicts, of the depth of offenses against the Creator. Even the joyous ones like the celestial perfumes and the ecstasies show us what we're missing; the incorruption and the healings show us something of what life was like before sin, and others, like agility and aureoles, show us something of what life will be like in Heaven. The fact that even heroically virtuous people don't normally have these experiences shows us just how far down the ladder we are and how far we have to go.

So mystic phenomena are insistent glimpses into a reality that many of us would rather ignore, for whatever reason. Yet that reality is the fullness of what God has reached out to explain to us. If you don't accept that revelation as true, or if you accept only bits and pieces of it, then these things are fantastic or even frightening—which is really only a natural part of the way in which they challenge that resistance to the fullness of revelation.

But within their full context, mystic phenomena aren't extraordinary parts of

Christianity, but ordinary parts of Christianity experienced to an extraordinary degree. Prayers may not always be answered with a miraculous cure, but prayers are always answered. Not everybody who surrenders licit pleasures in reparation for sins will be able to do more work than ever before and get along without food or sleep entirely, but even the slightest acts of abstinence make it easier to go placidly amidst the noise and haste, and they make temptations gradually weaker as they make resistance gradually stronger. Not everybody who strives to understand sin and its consequences will know the consolation of tears, but those who fast, for instance, or who strictly simplify their lives in reparation for sin will find a buoyant and sustaining joy, and will find their wills brought more closely into accord with their God's.

And while nobody can earn a locution or a flight of ecstasy, nor even predict them, the gentler mystic phenomena are everywhere. Certainly anyone who approaches Christ in the Eucharist—anyone who maintains the whole moral and sacramental life that reception of this miracle requires—can know the delights of this reliable visible appearance of Christ.

> *And there are many other things that Jesus does;*
> *but if every one of these should be written,*
> *not even the world itself, I think,*
> *could hold the books*
> *that would have to be written.*
> *Amen.*

John 21:25
(paraphrased)

further reading

Two standard compilations in the field of mystic theology are R. P. Aug. Poulain, S.J., *Des grâces d'oraison* (Paris, 1901), which deals with theological aspects of mysticism, and Herbert Thurston, S.J., *The Physical Phenomena of Mysticism* (Chicago, 1952), which focusses on concomitant phenomena. Neither is easily available now. *Devotion to the Sacred Heart: The Doctrine and Its History* by J. V. Bainvel, S.J., translated by E. Leahy (London, 1924) gives a full account of the investigations of the apparitions to St. Margaret Mary and of the ways in which they were evaluated; it isn't easily found these days, either.

Most of the primary sources cited in this book (those written by the ascetics and mystics themselves) are still in print. Many are available from the Missionary Society of St. Paul the Apostle, Ramsey, New Jersey, or from religious-book stores everywhere.

The works of St. Teresa of Avila and St. John of the Cross are absolutely essential reading for anyone interested in mystic phenomena; it's also a very good idea to find a director, through your local parish, who gives the exercises of St. Ignatius. The author's *Rosary: Mysteries, Meditations, and the Telling of the Beads* (Dallas, 1997), a work on ascetic theology, is strongly recommended as a companion to this book, the other half of the story told here. The other following books are good background reading.

Arintero, John G., O.P. *The Mystical Evolution in the Development and Vitality of the Church* (St. Louis, 1949; Rockford, Illinois, 1978). This is one of the best and most easily available books on mystic theology. It's a challenging read, and it will raise a lot of questions in your mind, but it will answer them, too.

Barbet, Pierre, M.D. *A Doctor at Calvary: The Passion of Our Lord Jesus Christ as Described by a Surgeon* (New York, 1963). This account of precisely what happened to Christ's body during his Passion is based on Barbet's work with cadavers. It's not a mystical work, but it gives you a very vivid idea of what the great ascetics contemplate, and what the great mystics see. Not for the squeamish.

De Sales, François. *Introduction to the Devout Life* (tr. and ed. John K. Ryan, Rockford, Illinois, 1966).

Dos Santos, Lucia. *Fátima in Lucia's Own Words* (Fátima, 1976).

Garrigou-Lagrange, R., O.P. *The Three Ages of the Interior Life* (St. Louis, 1947; Rockford, Illinois, 1989). An easily available and very thorough handbook, in two huge volumes, of the ascetic life, touching also on mystic phenomena. This is the best available reading for beginners; beautiful in its clarity and simplicity and overwhelming in its scope. Strongly recommended. Required.

Grignion de Montfort, Louis-Marie. *Love of the Eternal Wisdom* (tr. A. Somers, S.M.M., New York, 1960). All of his books are available in English from the Montfort Fathers of Bay Shore, New York 11706.

Jacobus da Voragine. *Golden Legend.* There are countless editions of this, condensed, unabridged, or supplemented. One of the most reliable is New York, 1941.

John of the Cross. *Collected Works* (tr. Kieran Kavanaugh, O.C.D., and Otilio Rodriguez, O.C.D.). Institute of Carmelite Studies, Washington, D.C., 1979.

Jone, Heribert. *Moral Theology* (Rockford, Illinois, 1961). This book is condensed, just giving the conclusions about questions about everything from amputation or auctions to wax in altar candles or whipping as punishment; so it's not very deep on explanation, but it's systematic enough for you to see the sense of it. Start with the index: you'll be browsing for hours.

Knox, Ronald. *Enthusiasm: A Chapter in the History of Religion with Special Reference to the Seventeenth and Eighteenth Centuries* (Oxford, 1950). This is indisputably one of the best modern books on religious aberration. It's indispensable for anybody wanting to sort through the perpetual flurry of reports of Jesus on tortillas and Madonnas in window-glass, or indeed for anyone whose friends or relatives are attracted to questionable activities under the guise of religion.

Liguori, Alphonsus. *The Twelve Steps* (adapted by Rev. Paul Leeick and Cornelius J. Warren, C.S.S.R., Rockford, Illinois, 1986).

Teresa of Avila. *Collected Works* (tr. Kieran Kavanaugh, O.C.D., and Otilio Rodriguez, O.C.D., Institute of Carmelite Studies, Washington, D.C., 1987).

Thomas Aquinas. *Summa Theologica.* There are several editions of this in every language, and thousands of books containing parts of it. The standard English edition is by priests in the English Dominican Province (London, 1911; Westminster, Maryland, 1981). Evidently there was no general editor, because a lot of fairly important words mean different things depending on which section you happen to be reading at the moment. It doesn't have an index to speak of, either. The standard Latin edition, which is brilliantly indexed, was produced by Joseph Cardinal Pecci in 1886, at the instance of his brother Leo XIII, who mandated that the *Summa* be at the center of priestly education in all of the Church's seminaries. Every Catholic family should have a copy of the *Summa*, and every non-Catholic family needs one.

glossary

ADIPOCERE *see* SAPONIFICATION.

AGILITY The ability to traverse space and time instantaneously; also, the ability to traverse space with supernatural force or alacrity.

ANCHORITIC Having to do with professed religious who live separately, as hermits.

APPARITION The appearance of a being that is not normally visible to human sight. Moral theologians distinguish three categories of these events. Apparitions may be *corporeal* (also *exterior* or *ocular*; those that show an apparent bodily solidity and are perceived by the eyes of the body). They may be *imaginative* (those that are perceived with the eyes of the soul, without the aid of bodily sight, while the mystic is asleep or awake; they cannot be dismissed at will). Imaginative apparitions fall into three subclasses; they may be *symbolic* (Jacob's Ladder, Gn 28:10-22), *personal* (St. Margaret Mary's experience of the Sacred Heart), or *dramatic* (Mystic Marriage of St. Catherine).

　　　　Apparitions can also be *intellectual*; these, as St. John of the Cross explained, are so called because "all that is intelligible to the intellect, the spiritual eye of the soul, causes spiritual vision, just as all that is physically visible to the material eye causes bodily vision." The intellectual apparition is a simple intuitive knowledge acquired without any natural means like study and with no help from the bodily senses. St. Teresa of Avila described it as being as if the food were already placed in the stomach without our eating it or knowing how it got there. As with an imaginative vision, the mystic can be asleep or awake, but an intellectual apparition can last hours or days. Only God can produce an intellectual apparition, because only God has access to the human intellect, but an overactive imagination or the Devil can cause events that seem to the recipient to be a real apparition of any of these kinds.

　　　　All apparitions are specific in the sense that only those intended to experience them can do so. Because all genuine apparitions are outreaches by God, none can be induced or summoned at the will of the recipient, and very few can be predicted.

　　　　An apparition that includes more than one figure, or that recreates an historical or future event, symbolically or realistically (as in the Book of Revelations), is sometimes called a *vision*.

ARDORS The mystic phenomenon of bodily heat that far exceeds the norm; also called *flames of love*, it suggests comparison with the flames of charity, the burning love that God bears for humankind. Ardors take the form of simple but preternaturally high body temperatures, sometimes enough to scorch the clothing, and glowing redness; they are sometimes confined to a particular part of the body such as the chest or the face, and they are sometimes accompanied by other mystic phenomena like the aureole or by natural symptoms like a nearly unquenchable thirst. They do not injure the body. Ardors are not ranked very high in the catalogue of mystic gifts.

ASCETIC Having to do with that branch of theology that studies the ways in which the individual soul can reach out to God through its own will and power; ascetic theology studies prayer, penance, conversion, and the other mechanisms of such an outreach.

AUREOLE The radiance that issues from the body of a mystic, or from a significant part of the body, as perhaps the head, forehead, stigmatic wound, etc.

AWARENESS OF THE PRESENCE OF GOD (CONTINUED) The state of being constantly aware of God's presence in the universe and in the soul. It can be achieved through the "practice of the presence of God", an exercise in which the ascetic seeks intellectual if not physical solitude, practices silence, and rests in God by keeping the thought of his presence ever before him. Some saints, notably St. Louis-Marie Grignion de Montfort, recommend wearing a blessed medal or cross on a chain around the neck as a constant reminder of God's presence and an aid to acquiring this state.

BEATIFIC VISION The complete and immediate sight of God as he truly is, enjoyed by the blessed souls in Heaven. This supreme and everlasting joy is reserved for those who have no sin and no mark of sin (Mt 5:8, Rv 21:27). Some mystics are given apparitions that give a foretaste of this vision to them on Earth, but the intensity and purity of these experiences depend on the mystic's own freedom from sin and its effects; it is never complete because no human is without sin. Mary, because of her sinlessness, evidently enjoyed full beatific vision during her earthly life.

BILOCATION The ability to be in two places at one time, at least apparently; it's similar to the agility enjoyed by spiritual beings who exist outside the bounds of space and Time, in Sempiternity. One of the two appearances of the mystic is probably a corporeal apparition, a phenomenon that can be imitated by diabolically induced illusions.

BLOOD PRODIGIES *see under* CARDIAC PHENOMENA.

CARDIAC PHENOMENA Those mystic events associated with the physical heart of a mystic, symbolically referring to charity, God's overwhelming love of humankind. They include heartbeats audible to crowds or distant bystanders, immense enlargement of the heart, cardiac ardors, images and imprints of religious symbols or actual stigmatic nails found through the heart during autopsy, etc. *Blood prodigies* include phenomena such as preternaturally hot blood (a form of ardors), copious bleeding during mystic states or the stigmata, blood issuing as sweat (hematidrosis), bleeding Hosts, blood flowing from images, liquefaction of ancient but incorrupt blood, anomalies in the physical weight of such blood, transformation of wine during transubstantiation, etc.

CARDIOGNOSIS The ability to "read hearts", to see the state of the souls of others.

CENOBITIC Having to do with professed religious who live in community.

CHARITY The love of God.

CLERGY The deacons, priests, and bishops of the catholic Church, ordained to their offices sacramentally in unbroken succession from the Apostles. Clergy in the hierarchy of parishes and dioceses are called *secular* clergy; those living under one or another of the great Rules of the orders are called *regular* clergy, from the Latin *regula*, meaning rule. *See also* RELIGIOUS.

COMPENETRATION OF BODIES The ability to pass through solid objects such as walls; *see also* BILOCATION, SUBTILITY.

COMPUNCTION *see* TEARS

CONCOMITANT *see* PHENOMENA, CONCOMITANT.

CONFESSOR The priest who administers the sacrament of Reconciliation. Persons called to lives of unusual asceticism usually have a particular confessor who guides spiritual growth; such persons submit absolutely to the confessor's directions in prayer, penance, and religion in general, neither falling short of his requirements nor exceeding them. Others more advanced may ask for a spiritual director (a qualified theologian, always a priest) who can direct their efforts at a higher and more comprehensive level. Qualified spiritual directors are rare in the extreme, and, for the overwhelming majority of Christians, the guidance offered by priests in Reconciliation is sufficient.

CONSOLATION Any of those pleasurable or reassuring spiritual actions supplied by God to a mystic who might otherwise be overwhelmed by a supernormally clear knowledge of the goodness and perfection of God and the horror of sin. Consolation is different from *comfort*, which is a reinforcement of the will to difficult or unpleasant virtuous acts, such as beneficence or resistance of temptation, and which often comes with disconcerting force (Ps 22:4; Pr 13:24, 23:13; 29:15, 3:12; Jn 12:27-29).

CONTINUED AWARENESS OF THE PRESENCE OF GOD *see under* AWARENESS.

CULT A cult is not simply a small religion, nor is it a religion with which one happens to disagree; it is organizationally different from a religion, and therefore a cult can easily be distinguished from a religion by means of its structure, whether you agree with its program or not. A cult is any organization, often but not necessarily based on a religious pretext, that separates susceptible people from the mainstream of life, usually on the basis of an emotional or psychological weakness, feelings of personal inadequacy, or a personal crisis that they themselves feel powerless to correct.

Cults require a "bridge-burning" act that publicly and irrevocably shows one's rejection of society and proves loyalty to the cult; this can be something like acts of infantile regression in cases of Quietism (*see also* IDIOGLOSSIA), criminal acts in the case of gangs, or a public declaration of the problem in cases like addiction-recovery groups. Cults can be beneficial to their members, but only if confrontation and management of the definitive problem stand at the center of their program (*see also* comfort, *under* CONSOLATION). More often, cults prevent people from contacting those mainstream agencies that can help them with their problem, and in fact work to intensify the problem by requiring the person to exhibit greater acts of that weakness or disorder.

CURES (MIRACULOUS) A reversal of symptoms of disease, the regeneration of healthy flesh where none was before, or the restoration of function to a damaged organ, with or without physical restoration of the organ's structure. Spontaneous or unusually rapid remission of disease, no matter how well timed, is not generally investigated as miraculous unless it's accompanied by unquestionably supernatural phenomena.

DIRECTOR, SPIRITUAL *see under* CONFESSOR.

DISCERNMENT OF SPIRITS The ability to see, or sense, spirits and to determine their nature by their effects.

DISCIPLINE The institutional regulations of the Church; any distinct field of study having an established academic structure; also, the small whip sometimes used for symbolic acts of penance.

DREAM A series of images generated in the human mind during sleep or caused by God or by an angel or saint at God's direction. It is virtually impossible for the dreamer to tell the difference unaided, but certifiably supernatural dreams are so rare that all dreams may safely be assumed to be the products of the dreamer's own mind.

ECCLESIAL, ECCLESIASTICAL Having to do with the Church as an earthly institution.

ECSTASY The state of being pulled by God out of one's normal state of existence, closer to him, in prayer of union. During genuine ecstasy, the bodily senses cease to function ("suspension of the faculties"), and the soul very nearly leaves the body as in death. Concomitant physical phenomena such as levitation, immobility, or aureoles may accompany ecstasy, but not always or even usually. Ecstasy of significantly greater intensity and longer duration is often called *rapture* or, more usually, *suspension*. Suspension that happens more quickly is called *transport*; transport that is virtually instantaneous and of an unimaginable intensity is called the *flight of the spirit*.

EFFICIENCY The supernatural ability to accomplish the tasks of daily life to an extraordinary degree, sometimes occurring with inedia, insomnia, and other mystic gifts.

ETERNITY *see under* TIME.

EXCHANGE OF HEARTS *see* MYSTIC MARRIAGE.

FLAMES OF LOVE *see* ARDORS.

FLIGHT OF THE SPIRIT *see* ECSTASY.

GLOSSOLALIA The infused knowledge of a human language, or the phenomenon in which listeners who share no mutually intelligible language hear a single discourse as if it were spoken in whatever language they themselves speak. Glossolalia, a particularly uncommon mystic gift, always produces utterances that can be understood in reference to a known human language; its spurious counterpart, properly called *idioglossia*, claims to consist of utterances in ancient, heavenly, secret, or otherwise inaccessible languages.

HALLUCINATION The appearance of something that is not objectively real; a sensory disturbance caused by the seer's mind, sometimes induced by stress, chemical agents, etc.

HEARTS *see* CARDIAC PHENOMENA, MYSTIC MARRIAGE, SACRED HEART.

HEMATIDROSIS *see* CARDIAC PHENOMENA.

HERESY The willful deletion or alteration of any of Christ's teachings. Heresy, like informed but persistent adherence to a separated sect founded in heresy, constitutes a rejection of Christ and consent to the Devil's influence.

HIEROGNOSIS The ability to sense the sanctity or lack of sanctity in persons and objects.

HUMILITY An exact knowledge of one's self, gifts, shortcomings, and precise rank in the order of the universe.

IDIOGLOSSIA The production of unintelligible utterances under the pretense of speaking unknown languages, languages not studied, or languages from beyond Earth; it is a form of infantile regression, a symptom of psychological or emotional disorder, and it often accompanies Quietism. *See also* GLOSSOLALIA.

ILLNESS, MYSTIC Supernatural afflictions visited upon most creditable mystics. These are normally so unusual (or unprecedented in the annals of medicine), so rebellious to medication, and so severe as to be unquestionably of supernatural origin, particularly when the victim survives conditions that would certainly kill any patient without supernatural aid. Some cases, though, are not easily distinguished from natural illnesses except for the fact that they occur in a context of other concomitant phenomena.

ILLUMINATIVE The second stage often distinguished in spiritual life, in which God reaches back to a soul that has approached him through purgative ascetic practices.

ILLUSION The faulty or misleading appearance of an objectively real object or event, caused by natural disturbances of light or by purposeful mechanical contrivance.

IMMOBILITY The physical fixation of a mystic's body to the spot on which he stands or kneels.

IMMORTALITY Immunity from death.

IMMUNITY Effective resistance to some destructive force. *See also* IMPASSIBILITY.

IMPASSIBILITY Immunity from disease and change.

IMPECCABILITY Immunity from sin, a condition enjoyed in Heaven by the saints and on Earth only by Christ himself. (Mary did not sin, but she was not inherently immune from sin during her earthly life; her will, although free, was—and is—in perfect accord with God's.) Impeccability is different from both *indefectibility* and *infallibility*.

IMPULSE The sudden and involuntary remembrance of the true extent and horror of sin, and of the consequent distance of the human soul from God.

INCOMBUSTIBILITY Immunity from consumption from fire.

INCORRUPTIBILITY (BODILY) Immunity from decay after death. It can be caused by any number of unusual but purely natural factors, and it does not, in itself, carry any particular importance in mystic theology.

INDEFECTIBILITY Immunity from error, a term usually reserved to reference to the Church alone, which enjoys Christ's guarantee of freedom from error until the end of Time; it is different from both *impeccability* and *infallibility*.

INEDIA The ability to live without material food, other than the Bread of the Blessed Sacrament, for extended periods of time.

INFALLIBILITY Immunity from error in teaching; it means most usually that the Pope, when teaching some precept of faith or morals officially as the Vicar of Christ, is safeguarded by the Holy Spirit as Christ promised and will not depart from Christ's teachings; it is different from both *impeccability* and *indefectibility*.

INSOMNIA The ability to live without sleep for long periods of time and with no adverse affects on the general health.

INVISIBILITY The quality of being inaccessible to earthly eyes.

KNOWLEDGE The awareness and retention of facts relating to existence. *Experimental* knowledge is that gained by natural or supernatural experience; *infused* knowledge is imparted by God directly, circumventing the normal paths of study. Genuine infused knowledge never contains anything contrary to the Deposit of Faith nor anything in addition to it, nor does it report any new revelation. Infused knowledge is not prophecy but simply an increase in the recipient's comprehension of the Deposit of Faith.

LEVITATION The elevation of a mystic's body. It can be faked by illusionists or imitated by diabolic forces.

LOCUTION The occasion of hearing an angel, a saint, God, or a devil. *Exterior* or *auricular* locutions are perceived with the bodily ears; *interior* locutions are heard with the spiritual ears, and they are divided into two sub-classes. *Interior imaginative* locutions consist of distinct words. *Interior intellectual* locutions do not consist of words but reportedly parallel the ways in which spiritual beings communicate with each other; they cannot be produced by the Devil, but any kind of locution can be faked by the Devil or by one's imagination.

MORTIFICATION Any ascetic exercise by which one gains control of, or extinguishes, any physical or emotional appetite.

MUMMIFICATION Preservation of a corpse by desiccation.

MYSTIC Having to do with that subdivision of moral theology that examines the ways in which God reaches out to individual human souls.

MYSTIC MARRIAGE The intimate union of the mystic soul with God, also called the *exchange of hearts*, the *transforming union*, or the *union of likeness*. It is termed "marriage" only symbolically and can occur between God and any human soul, regardless of bodily gender.

OBEDIENCE Submission of the will to a lawfully constituted superior authority.

OBSESSION The phenomenon of physical vexation by diabolic forces, which sometimes takes the form of pranks and sometimes imitates the form of genuine mystic phenomena; *see also* POSSESSION.

ODOR OF SANCTITY The supernaturally sweet smell, sometimes compared to that of spices or lilies but most usually described as like that of scented roses, that may accompany genuine mystic activity.

PENANCE Any ascetic exercise, such as intensified prayer, deprivation of some permissible but pleasurable object or activity, or the actual infliction of suffering upon oneself, undertaken in reparation for sin. Penances, usually only token acts, are required as part of the process of the sacrament of Reconciliation (Confession), and are mandated during certain seasons of the year, chiefly Lent and Advent. No unusual penance should be taken on without the express consent of a confessor or spiritual director.

PHENOMENA, CONCOMITANT Those physical and emotional events that accompany genuine mystic phenomena. They can be faked by frauds or deluded people, or imitated by diabolic forces who wish to give the appearance of genuine mystic phenomena.

PHENOMENA, MYSTIC Spiritual events that characterize an extraordinary outreach by God to an individual soul; they are often accompanied by concomitant phenomena.

POSSESSION The takeover of a human body by one or more devils who enter it and virtually replace the soul, squeezing it into a corner of the person's being, as it were. It cannot happen without the person's consent, but adherence to an heretical sect, pertinacious separation from the Church, a weak or casual sacramental life, or even jocular participation in supposedly Satanic rites evidently constitute such consent.

PRAYER The outreach of an individual soul to God or to another spiritual being. Its purposes are usually classified as petition, thanksgiving, reparation, and adoration. In terms of petition, direct prayer to God petitions him for favors and graces for oneself or others, while prayers to angels and saints petition them only for their prayers in support of one's intentions—asking their intercession, their prayers to God (to whom they stand in closer proximity), as you might ask your Earth-bound friends to pray for your intentions. Christian prayer also maintains the distinction of offering honor (in Latin, *dulia*) to an angel or a saint and adoration (*latria*) to God alone.

Prayer takes several forms, being either active or passive. *Active* prayer, which is human effort to communicate with God, the angels, or the saints, is either liturgical or private. *Liturgical* active prayer consists of the public acts of worship celebrated in the Church, chiefly the Mass. *Private* active prayer may be in the form of *vocal* prayer, which is simply speaking to God, an angel, or a saint thoughtfully, using one's own words or approved texts; *meditative* prayer on some aspect of God or on some episode in the life of Christ, the angels, or the saints, which is most often performed by means of the Rosary; or *contemplative* prayer, which is contemplation of God or one of his aspects, such as his goodness. *Passive* prayer is prayer in which God acts toward a human person; broadly speaking, this would include any and all answers to active prayer, but the term *prayer of quiet* is used to distinguish the state of the human soul that occurs when God reaches back with extraordinary force and generosity to the person who prays. The soul, in these cases, stands silent and wordless. The *prayer of union* constitutes a more forceful extraordinary outreach, in which the person at prayer stands in awe, without memory or thought, and in which the bodily senses are lost so that the soul can focus on the object of its enjoyment, God himself; *see also* PHENOMENA, MYSTIC.

PRODIGIES (BLOOD) *see under* CARDIAC PHENOMENA.

PURGATION The purification of a soul. *Active* purgation is that which occurs through one's own ascetic practices; it is studied by ascetic theology. *Passive* purgation occurs when God reaches out to a soul and purifies it himself; it is studied by mystic theology.

PURGATIVE Of or like purgation. The purgative stage is the first of the three stages often distinguished in spiritual life, followed by the illuminative and the unitive.

QUIETISM The heresy that teaches, in whatever form and under whatever name, that a person should cease activity and wait for God's working in the soul. Quietism usually attracts persons who are susceptible because a lack of maturity that makes it difficult or impossible for them to handle the crises of normal life. Quietist cults virtually always claim or exhibit spurious mystic gifts that are no part of recognized mystic phenomena (such as convulsions or idioglossia). Because they constitute a rejection of the sacraments and, like any other heresy, a rejection of at least some of Christ's other teachings, adherence to a quietist sect constitutes effective consent to the Devil, so, in rarer cases, quietists can exhibit counterfeit mystic phenomena such as levitation or the ability to foretell future events, which are brought about by diabolic causes.

RAPTURE (SUSPENSION) *see* ECSTASY.

RECALL The order, given by a priest to a purported mystic, to cease any or all mystic activity. The command may be given mentally or orally, but it is always obeyed instantly in cases of genuine mystic phenomena. On the other hand, demonic possession mimicking genuine mystic phenomena may also cease at command, if the devils involved want to carry their imposture that far; but in general devils, like frauds, the deluded, and quietists, virtually never obey readily.

RECOLLECTION The state of gathering one's thoughts for prayer, turning inward and away from the world and its distractions. Recollection can reach a deep, trance-like state in which the person at prayer seems oblivious to his earthly surroundings, but achieving it is an ascetic practice, not a mystic gift.

RELIGIOUS Persons such as monks, nuns, and friars, living in religious community under temporary or permanent (solemn) vows but not necessarily receiving the sacrament of Ordination, are referred to, on the whole, as *religious*. *See also* CLERGY.

REVEALED Shown by deliberate action. Revealed religions are those that, like Judaism, Christianity, and Islam, claim to have been conveyed or exhibited by a divine being to humans; they contrast with *natural* (or *developed*) religions in which doctrine develops over time as people observe and try to explain natural phenomena, and with those religions that claim to have been initiated by a single human teacher. In Christianity, revelation is classified as either public or private. *Public* revelation includes the "Deposit of Revelation" given to the prophets of the Old Testament, perfected by Christ, and articulated by the Apostles and their successors, the bishops of the Church; it is not subject to change or deletion by any human agency (such alteration is the essence of heresy). Acceptance of public revelation in its entirety and living according to its tenets is, basically, what defines a person as Christian. *Private* revelation consists of all communications from God that occur since the deposit of revelation was closed, at the death of St. John, the Apostle who survived the longest; it includes answers to prayer, creditable apparitions and locutions, and other recognized mystic phenomena. No creditable private revelation can contradict or override public revelation; acceptance of even those private revelations declared creditable is not required of Christians, only permitted.

SACRED HEART The human heart of Jesus of Nazareth, now present in his glorified body in Heaven. As the symbolic seat of love, it is the object of specialized devotions, patterns and cycles of vocal and meditative prayer through which his humanity, his physical sufferings during the Passion, and his overwhelming love for humankind may be thoughtfully regarded, and through which reparation for sin may be made.

SAPONIFICATION A natural process whereby a corpse, stored in any of a variety of favorable conditions, turns to a soaplike substance called *adipocere*.

SAVORS The mystic consolation of an inexpressibly sweet taste in the mouth.

SCRUPLES Excessive worry about one's own sins, or a failure of confidence in the efficacy of Reconciliation.

SEMPITERNITY *see under* TIME.

SENSIBLE Accessible to the senses of the body.

SENSITIVITY (MYSTIC) The experience of bodily reactions to a vision, in which a mystic witnessing an event in the life of Christ, for example, feels the heat, cold, pain, etc., that would be experienced by a person physically present at the event.

SLEEP OF THE FACULTIES The suspension of bodily senses during mystic events.

SPIRITUAL DIRECTOR *see under* CONFESSOR.

STIGMATA The physical but symbolic reproduction of the wounds that Christ suffered during the Passion. It exhibits characteristics beyond the nature of natural wounds, such as the odor of sanctity or resistance to infection and medication. It may be partial or invisible, and it may occur only during ecstasy or remain more or less permanently.

STRENGTH Supernatural levels of physical force and abilities sometimes occurring as a phenomenon concomitant to mystic events. It can be mimicked by diabolic forces, but most usually surprising feats of strength are simply the result of unsuspected natural abilities with nothing supernatural about them.

STUPEFACTION The suspension of the senses that can be induced by purely natural mediative practices. It is different from the insensibility that accompanies suspension of the faculties, principally in that it does not usually include insensibility to pain.

SUBTILITY (*also rarely* SUBTLETY) Immunity from the effects of gravity, solid bodies, and other earthly constraints on movement.

SUSPENSION *see* ECSTASY.

TEARS (GIFT OF) The spiritual and emotional reaction to the pervading sorrow for sin that accompanies spiritual awareness and knowledge, often won by heroic ascetic practices. The tears may be spiritual or bodily, or both, but the gift differs from purely psychological fits of depression in that it usually brings with it consolation. It is often the first discernible mystic gift, differing in substance and in quality from the tears of penitence that characterize advancement in ascetic practice.

TIME The interval between two occurrences. With height, depth, and width, Time is one of the four dimensions that structure earthly existence and experience. In Christian cosmology, Time had a beginning, at the creation of the material universe to which it is inextricably tied (Gn 1), and it will have an end when that universe ceases to exist (Rv 6:12-14, 21:1-4, 22-27). God alone is of *Eternity*, a dimension of being freed from any constraints of space or Time, having, like him, no beginning and no end. Heaven and Hell exist in an intermediate dimension called *Sempiternity*, which had a beginning but will have no end; this is the dimension of angels, saints, and human souls.

    Sempiternity is free from the norms and restraints of height, depth, and width, and, in some way not yet clear, free from the laws of physics that govern the movements of three-dimensional bodies through space and Time (*see also* BILOCATION, COMPENETRATION). Because our bodily senses work only within the framework structured by the four dimensions of bodily mass and Time, humans cannot normally see beings who live in Sempiternity or Eternity. When they make themselves accessible to our Earth-bound senses, the event is called an apparition, a locution, savors, or the odor of sanctity, depending on which bodily sense is affected. Levitation and tactile sensations such as the extreme delight that St. John of the Cross called a rejoicing of all the bones and marrow and Bl. Angela of Foligno termed "liquefaction" may also occur, as may equally intense pains such as feeling wracked out of joint.

TRANSFORMING UNION *see* MYSTIC MARRIAGE.

TRANSPORT *see* ECSTASY.

TRANSVERBERATION *see* WOUND OF LOVE.

UNCTION (SPIRITUAL) The consolations consisting of apparitions, locutions, the odor of sanctity, savors, and what St. John of the Cross termed the rejoicing of the bones and marrow, some or all of which may accompany mystic experiences.

UNION (TRANSFORMING UNION, UNION OF LIKENESS) *see* MYSTIC MARRIAGE.

UNITIVE Of or like union. The unitive stage is the third stage of prayer often distinguished in ascetic and mystic theology as following the purgative and the illuminative.

VISION *see* APPARITION.

WOUND OF LOVE The piercing of the spiritual heart by the love of God (Lk 2:35), accompanied by intensified sorrow for one's own sins and the sins of others; sometimes called *transverberation*. Also, any of the injuries inflicted on Christ at the Passion, customarily enumerated as five: the hands, the feet, and the heart.

index

Saints, persons declared Venerable or Blessed, popes, and monarchs are referenced here by first name. Other persons are listed by surname. Apostles, Evangelists, and prophets are listed by name for their personal acts, but the books of the Bible that bear their names are listed under "Bible". Wherever possible, the dates of birth and death are listed, and identifiers, such as title, office, or the place of the apparition with which the person was involved, are placed in parentheses.

Written works are cited both by author (listed together at the end of that person's main entry) and by title (titles translated in many variant ways are listed by both the original title in the original language and its most usual English equivalent). Encyclicals are listed by the most usual title, which is normally the first word or words of the Latin text.

Spellings of proper names and the titles of the books of the Bible follow those in the *New American Catholic Edition of the Holy Bible, Confraternity version*, Benziger Brothers, New York, 1961. The titles of books of the Bible are abbreviated by any numeral that the title includes followed by the initial letter of the title and the next distinguishing consonant in the title; if no consonants distinguish two books, the numerals and initial letters are followed by the first distinguishing vowel.

Subheadings are indicated by **bold type**.

Deo gratias